100 GRAPHIC DESIGN
SOLUTIONS

INTERACTIVE DESIGN FOR SCREEN

FLAMANT

INTERACTIVE DESIGN FOR SCREEN

100 GRAPHIC DESIGN SOLUTIONS

Flamant is a brand of:
Hoaki Books, S.L.
C/ Ausiàs March 128.
08013 Barcelona, Spain
Phone: 0034 93 595 22 83
info@hoakibooks.es

Sponsored by Design 360°
– Concept and Design Magazine
Edited and produced by
Sandu Publishing Co., Ltd.
Book design, concepts & art direction by
Sandu Publishing Co., Ltd.
info@sandupublishing.com

Publisher: Sandu Publishing Co., Ltd.
Executive Editor: Wang Naidan
English preface revised by: Tom Corkett
Design Director: Wang Shaoqiang
Designers: Liu Xian, Wu Yanting
Sales Managers: Niu Guanghui (China), Winnie Feng (International)

Concept of trasition pages (p009, p135): Inventos Digitais
Cover Design: Claudia Martínez Alonso, Liu Xian

ISBN: 978-84-17084-05-9
D.L.: B 25037-2018

Printed in China

CONTENTS

PREFACE

By Artur Konariev
Founder and product designer, Wadoo Agency

Nowadays, as the world constantly changes and hurriedly evolves, we might summarize firms' priorities as follows:

1. How can we generate new sources of income?
2. How can we enhance recognition of our brand?
3. How can we increase our interactions with customers?

Designers have the potential to solve any business-related problem through creating better user experiences (UX) and user interfaces (UI). They just need to keep one simple thing in mind: "lovely" design alone will never work out.

To achieve the goals mentioned above, designers have to answer these core questions: Why? (Why have I made it? Why is it not working right now?); How? (How do I improve it?); What would happen if ...? And after each step of design and development, they then have to ask another question: What has changed? Has the UX been further developed or not? Have I made any measurable progress? These are the fundamental questions that each designer should think about.

Just as the right melody can touch the depth of your heart, a well-designed UX may hugely improve a product. A good UX means that a digital product is easy to use and intuitive. Do not force users to think: this is the advice of Steve Krug in his book *Don't Make Me Think!* When customers use a product, its designer must want them to have the best ever experience, and one that will keep them using the item as well as make them recommend it to friends and colleagues. Starting to interact with users and receive feedback gives designers an opportunity to further improve the product. This type of consultation is important if designers wish to achieve a good work flow. If you are making a product, keep focusing on its UX as you improve it, because neither testing nor programming will tell you as much as users can.

It's virtually the same story when it comes to UI. It might be difficult to admit that people still judge a book by its cover, but a well created design can sell a product even when it has not yet been developed. An essential feature of a good UI is a harmony with the main brand style that features in all the firm's products. Before they begin designing or redesigning a

Web application, designers need to be sure that they are working in tune with the company's current style and not overriding it. No matter what the device is, design consistency increases reliability and loyalty towards the brand or company, and it prevents users from getting confused.

And this is why it is really important to take UX and UI into consideration from the very beginning of planning a digital project. At my agency, Wadoo, we focus on creating UX and UI that are simultaneously visually attractive and easy to use. If we're developing a product from start to finish, these are some of the steps that we follow:

- Understanding the client's business and the client's actual needs;
- Understanding the client's customers' needs;
- Aligning the client's business goals with the client's customers' needs;
- Defining the direction;
- Producing paper sketches and brainstorming layout and functionality;
- Creating live prototypes that users are able to interact with and collecting feedback;
- Making adjustments and improvements to the prototype, interactions and flows once data have been collected and analysed;
- Working on the finalized structure in Sketch to polish it;
- Documenting everything (workflows, interactions, animations, style guidelines, design implementation specifics) and getting ready for development;
- Beginning the development process;
- Supporting the development process until the final launch of the product.

If you are new to the digital design world, do not be afraid. If you evolve, everything will go smoothly. Competition in the sector may be fierce, but you'll definitely find customers as the world keeps developing and as more and more startups open each day. So don't give up, and make sure you live and learn! If you do not have time to draw for eight hours a day or just decide to give this field a try as you continue in another job or in your studies, learn how to manage your time properly. You are always surrounded with advertisements and brands. My advice is to open your eyes, concentrate and analyse what comes into view. Make it a habit when you are travelling, having lunch or just taking a walk. Try brainstorming, and think about how you would make this logo, flyer, banner or whatever better. What kind of mistakes (for example, in terms of spaces, fonts or colours) have you found in the designs that you've seen? Is everything harmonized? How could you improve it?

I have a good story about a graphic designer—let's call him John—who saw a finance company's promotional leaflet on the way back home from the office. He did not like it that much, which drove him to create his own version of it. He even sent the company his version, along with a letter explaining how he could improve it. You may not believe me, but he soon received a reply from the head of the company, who was really impressed with the letter and John's decision to redesign the leaflet. After a couple of weeks, John was hired as a designer and improved the finance company's visual branding. As a result, the company won new clients and increased its revenue. There are lots of good things happening in our world every day—even more than you can imagine.

The editorial team have done a great job of compiling within this book the best solutions related to user experience and user interface for a range of formats, including mobile, Web and desktop applications and digital products. Learn, investigate and be inspired by the best of the best to surpass them one day. If you are a seasoned designer, try not to remain at a standstill. Become the one who will be followed by others. And if you're just starting out, make the entire world remember your name.

APPLICATION

The Darwin Challenge

App Store

Creative Direction
Dari Israelstam (Universal Favourite)

Design
Bonnie Nguyen (Universal Favourite)

App Engineering
Work in Progress

Branding Agency
Principals

Behavioural Economics
The Behavioural Architects

Illustration
Janine Rewell

Copywriting
John Kerswell (White Label Words)

The Darwin Challenge app was initiated by Chris Darwin, Charles Darwin's great-great-grandson, with the aim of raising awareness, educating and ultimately facilitating behavioural change of people to eat less meat. App users are able to log their successful meat-free days to see the benefits for themselves, others and the planet in 10 heavily-researched metrics—with health, animal welfare and environmental sustainability being key triggers in getting people to eat less meat.

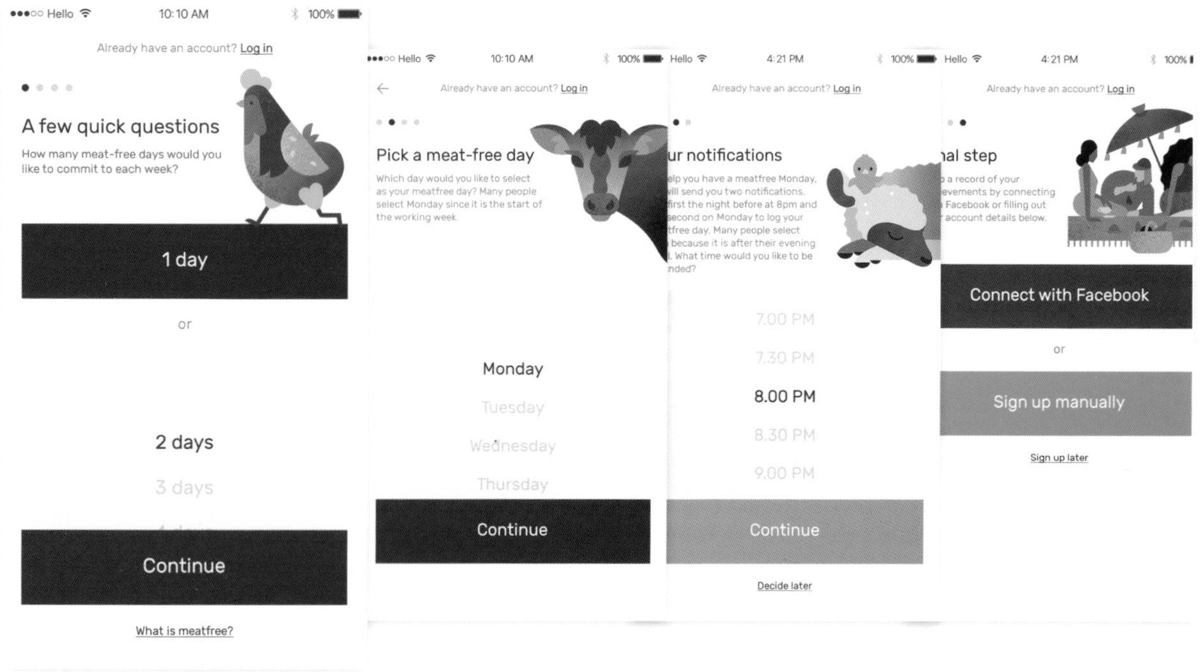

Hello
10:10 AM
100%
Already have an account? Log in
A few quick questions
How many meat-free days would you like to commit to each week?
1 day
or
2 days
3 days
Continue
What is meatfree?
Pick a meat-free day
Which day would you like to select as your meatfree day? Many people select Monday since it is the start of the working week.
Monday
Tuesday
Wednesday
Thursday
Continue
4:21 PM
7.00 PM
7.30 PM
8.00 PM
8.30 PM
9.00 PM
Continue
Decide later
Connect with Facebook
or
Sign up manually
Sign up later

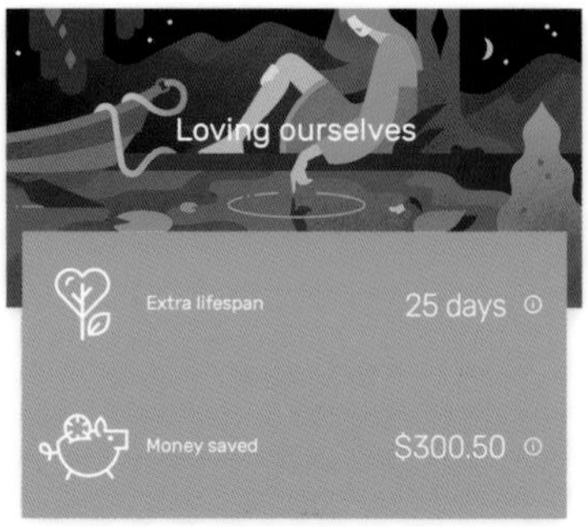

Loving ourselves
Extra lifespan
25 days
Money saved
$300.50

Loving others
Hungry people fed
24
Cows still mooing
5
Chickens still clucking
72
Fish still splashing
21

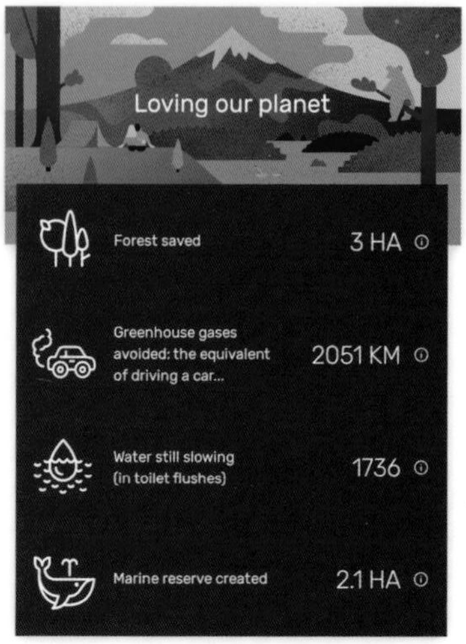

Loving our planet
Forest saved
3 HA
Greenhouse gases avoided: the equivalent of driving a car...
2051 KM
Water still slowing (in toilet flushes)
1736
Marine reserve created
2.1 HA

Central to the app experience is a beautiful in-app scene that changes from barren to plentiful, the more meat free days the app user logs, the more rewarding positive actions.The app balances appealing to a core target of females aged 25-40, as well as the old generation of influential leaders (think Al Gore, Paul McCartney). A feminine-skewed design aesthetic is matched with solid graphic elements, a geometr illustration style and split-complementa colour palette with a distinct call-to-action colour.

Hello
10:18 AM
Achievements
Just me
Everyone
My total meatfree days so far
03
Achievements
Hello
10:18 AM
Achievements
Just me
Everyone
My total meatfree days so far
08
Achievements
Hello
10:18 AM
100%
Achievements
Just me
Everyone
My total meatfree days so far
52
LOG A MEATLESS DAY
Achievements

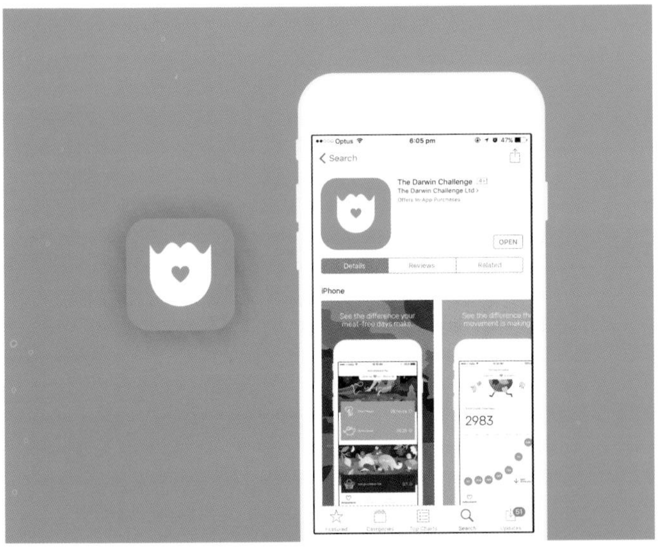

Optus
6:05 pm
Search
The Darwin Challenge
OPEN
Details
Reviews
Related
iPhone
2983

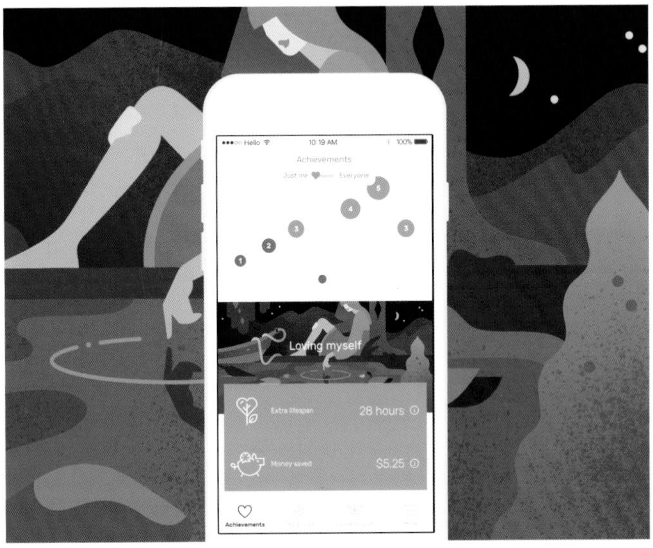

Hello
10:19 AM
Achievements
Loving myself
28 hours
$5.25
Achievements

Hello
10:21 AM
My groups
Tofu Tuesdays
Design & Architecture
26th
2nd
380
6
Invite a friend
1 Theodore Raymo...
02
1
2 You
85
3
3 Chloe Lee
72
0
4 Grant Ward
69
0
My groups

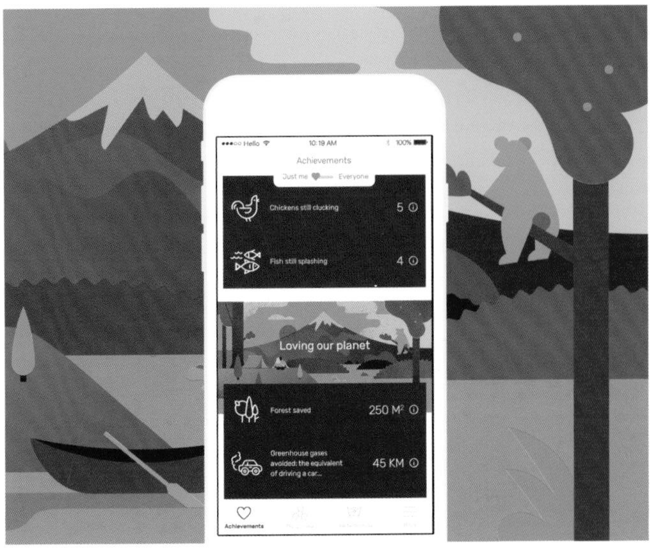

Hello
10:19 AM
Achievements
Chickens still clucking
5
Fish still splashing
4
Loving our planet
Forest saved
250 M²
Greenhouse gases avoided: the equivalent of driving a car...
45 KM
Achievements

Taskhunters

Design Agency
mono.

Illustration
Giulia Zoavo

Client
Taskhunters

App Store

Taskhunters app is a virtual community where people could entrust the tasks to university students. At the same time, students can earn by doing small jobs for people in the neighbourhood.

mono. carried out the redesign of the app. They simplified the user flow, and designed a more eye-catching interface. Nice illustrations were used to introduce the features of the app and clarify the tasks. Both the client and the job taker have their own interfaces with all the profile information that can give security and confidence.

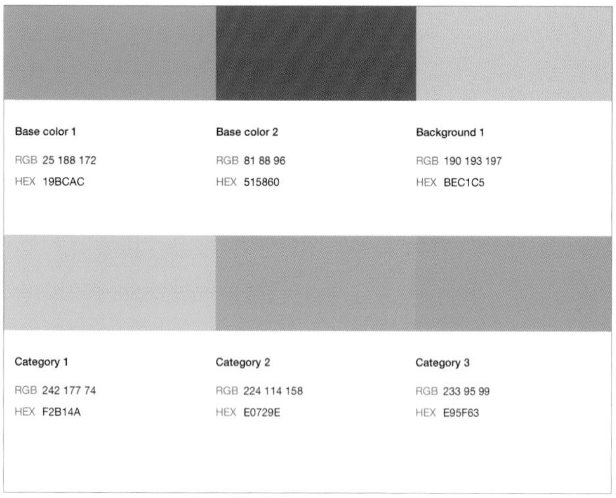

Base color 1
RGB 25 188 172
HEX 19BCAC
Base color 2
RGB 81 88 96
HEX 515860
Background 1
RGB 190 193 197
HEX BEC1C5
Category 1
RGB 242 177 74
HEX F2B14A
Category 2
RGB 224 114 158
HEX E0729E
Category 3
RGB 233 95 99
HEX E95F63

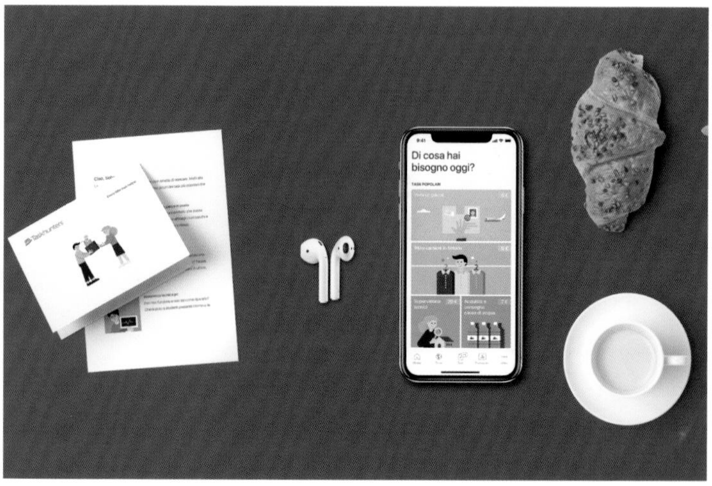

Di cosa hai bisogno oggi?

9:41
Benvenuto
Questa è la community in cui puoi affidare i tuoi task alle persone di fiducia intorno a te e svolgere i piccoli lavori per gli altri.
Salta intro

Slide

9:41
Cos'è un Task?
Sono le faccende e gli impegni quotidiani, che puoi far svolgere ad altre persone se ti mancano i mezzi o il tempo.
Salta intro

Slide

9:41
Tutto pronto!
Crea il tuo profilo, verificalo e comincia subito a utilizzare Taskhunters, recupera il tuo tempo o comincia a guadagnare.
Inizia subito

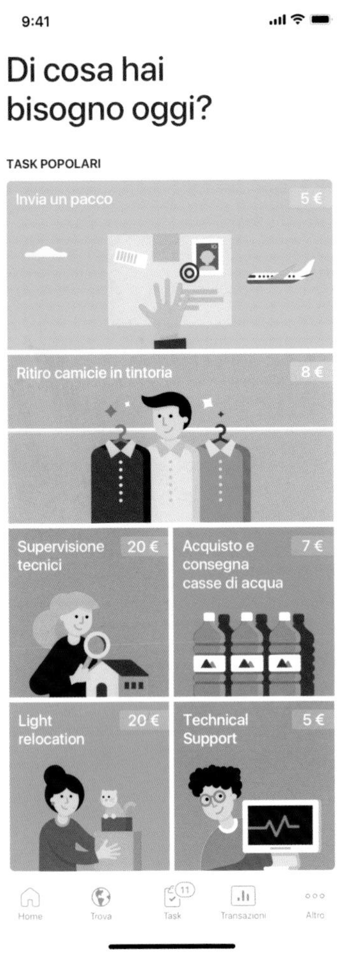
9:41
Di cosa hai bisogno oggi?
TASK POPOLARI
Invia un pacco
5 €
Ritiro camicie in tintoria
8 €
Supervisione tecnici
20 €
Acquisto e consegna casse di acqua
7 €
Light relocation
20 €
Technical Support
5 €
Home
Trova
Task
Transazioni
Altro

Slide

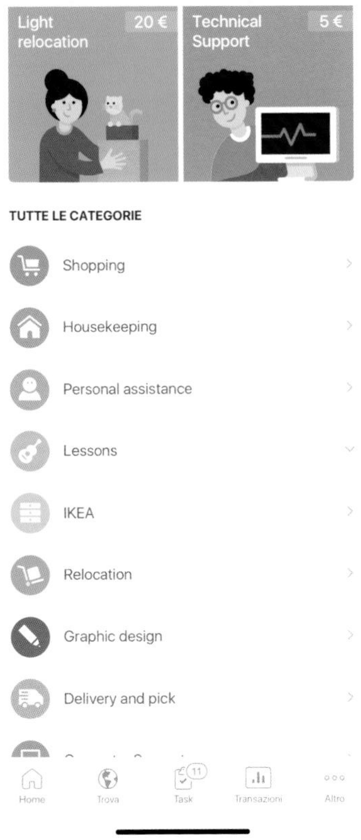
Light relocation
20 €
Technical Support
5 €
TUTTE LE CATEGORIE
Shopping
Housekeeping
Personal assistance
Lessons
IKEA
Relocation
Graphic design
Delivery and pick
Home
Trova
Task
Transazioni
Altro

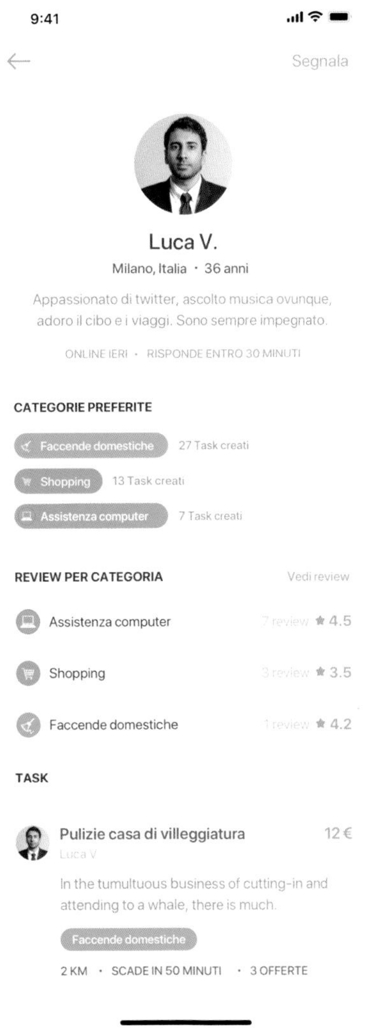
9:41
Segnala
Luca V.
Milano, Italia • 36 anni
Appassionato di twitter, ascolto musica ovunque, adoro il cibo e i viaggi. Sono sempre impegnato.
ONLINE IERI • RISPONDE ENTRO 30 MINUTI
CATEGORIE PREFERITE
Faccende domestiche
27 Task creati
Shopping
13 Task creati
Assistenza computer
7 Task creati
REVIEW PER CATEGORIA
Vedi review
Assistenza computer
7 review
★ 4.5
Shopping
3 review
★ 3.5
Faccende domestiche
1 review
★ 4.2
TASK
Pulizie casa di villeggiatura
12 €
Luca V.
In the tumultuous business of cutting-in and attending to a whale, there is much.
Faccende domestiche
2 KM • SCADE IN 50 MINUTI • 3 OFFERTE

9:41
Lista
Trova task
Filtra
Pulizie casa di villeggiatura
12 €
Mario Rossi
Assistenza personale
2 KM • SCADE IN 50 MINUTI
New York
Trova
Task
Transazioni
Profilo
Altro

9:41
Segnala
Sebastiano G.
★ 4.0
22 anni • Milano
Università Bocconi
Giurisprudenza finanziaria
Vedi +2
Appassionato di legge, ascolto musica ovunque, adoro il cibo e i viaggi. Sono sempre impegnato.
ONLINE 2 ORE FA • RISPONDE ENTRO 10 MINUTI
VERIFICHE STUDENTE
Numero di cellulare
E-mail universitaria
Account Facebook
SKILL
Skill uno, Skill due, Skill tre, Skill quattro
LINGUE PARLATE
Italiano, Inglese, Spagnolo
REVIEW PER CATEGORIA
Vedi review
11 Task totali
Assistenza computer
7 review
★ 4.5
Shopping
3 review
★ 3.5
Faccende domestiche
1 review
★ 4.2

9:41
Pulizie casa di...
Segnala
DETTAGLI
• CONTATTA
Faccende domestiche
Pulizie casa di villeggiatura
In the tumultuous business of cutting-in and attending to a whale, there is much running backwards and forwards among the crew. Now hands are wanted here, and then again hands.
Stato
Aperto
Compenso
25 €
Tua proposta
27 €
Scade il
1 giugno 2016 alle 00:45
Creato da
Luca V.
Luogo
2 Km da te

Bowwow

Design
Annie Hall

Photography
Salt Lake City Humane Society

Behance

Bowwow is an app designed for the "Opt-to-Adopt" campaign for the Utah Humane Society. The app functions as a dog-version of the famous app, Tinder, where future/existing pet owners can find their paw-fect companion in the area based on location, breed, size, age, and compatibility to other animals or small children. Once matched, the owner is able to set up a playdate at the local animal shelter. The goal is to link up compatible pets with qualified owners and educate future pet owners to opt-to-adopt.

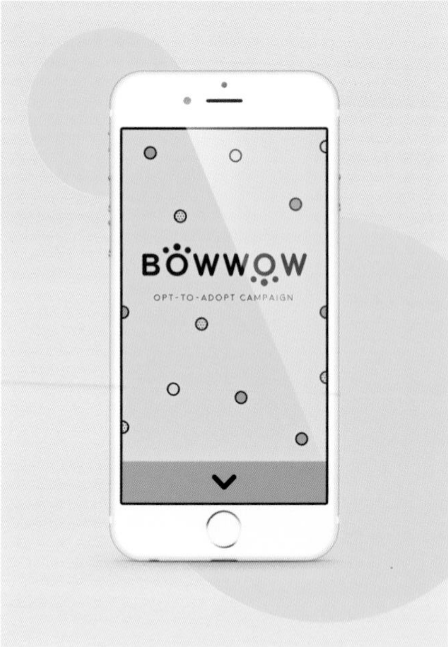
BOWWOW
OPT-TO-ADOPT CAMPAIGN

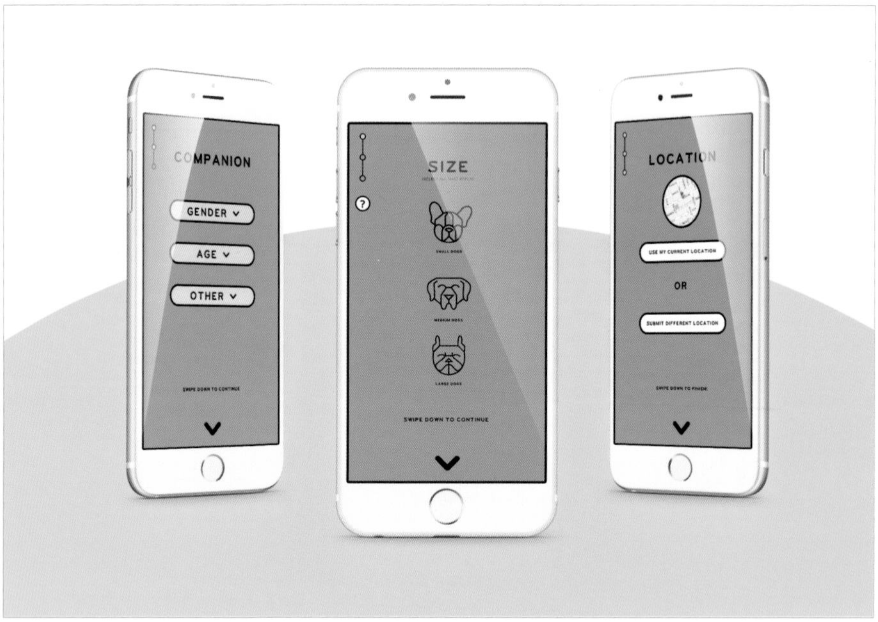
COMPANION
GENDER
AGE
OTHER
SIZE
LOCATION
OR

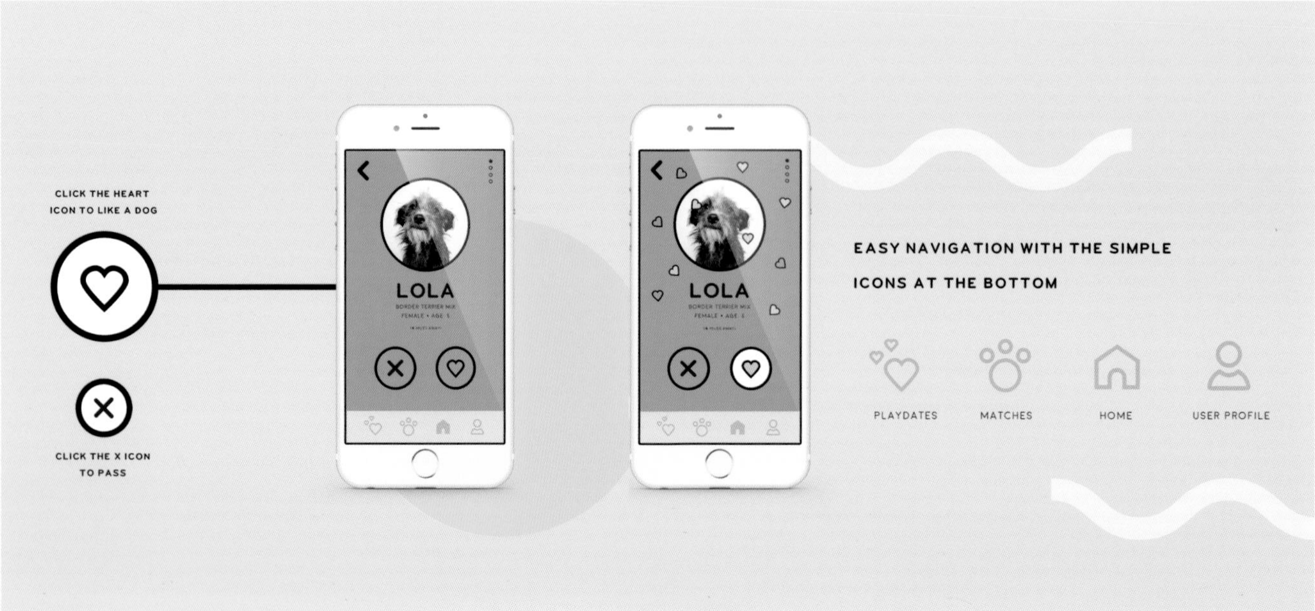
CLICK THE HEART ICON TO LIKE A DOG
CLICK THE X ICON TO PASS
LOLA
LOLA
EASY NAVIGATION WITH THE SIMPLE ICONS AT THE BOTTOM
PLAYDATES
MATCHES
HOME
USER PROFILE

LOLA
ABOUT ME:
ALTHOUGH MY HISTORY IS A MYSTERY, I DO KNOW THAT I LOVE LONG WALKS TO THE DOG PARK AND DOG TREATS (ESPECIALLY BACON FLAVORED). I HAVE LOTS OF SPUNK AND CAN BE GREEDY WITH MY FOOD, SO I MAY REQUIRE A LITTLE MORE TRAINING THAN I ALREADY HAVE
LOLA
MY QUALITIES:
PEOPLE FRIENDLY
HOUSE TRAINING
PET FRIENDLY
ABOUT THE BREED:
BORDER TERRIER
ALTHOUGH HE'S NOT FLASHY IN APPEARANCE AS SOME OF HIS TERRIER RELATIVES, THE BORDER TERRIER IS STILL LIVING LIFE WITH GREAT GUSTO, WHETHER OUT AND ABOUT WITH PEOPLE OR DIGGING A HOLE IN A FLOWERBED.
HEIGHT:
UNSPECIFIED IN BREED
WEIGHT:
11.5-15.5 POUNDS
LIFE SPAN:
12-14 YEARS
PERFECT FOR:
APARTMENT SPACES
AFFECTION
CHILDREN

When creating the app, the designer wanted the look and feel to be fun and easy to use for a multitude of people. So she incorporated a similar interface to that of Tinder—If you swipe left you get a new profile, and if you swipe right it's a match, etc. By using this idea, most people had the knowledge of the basics to the app, making it easy to use. For the branding, she wanted to make the aesthetic playful and fun throughout the experience, such as by incorporating the dog's photo, captured by Utah Human Society, that shows the unique characteristics of a poppy. The designer also created a branding system that was heavy on fun pastel colours, thick bold lines, and the occasional dog pun every now and then.

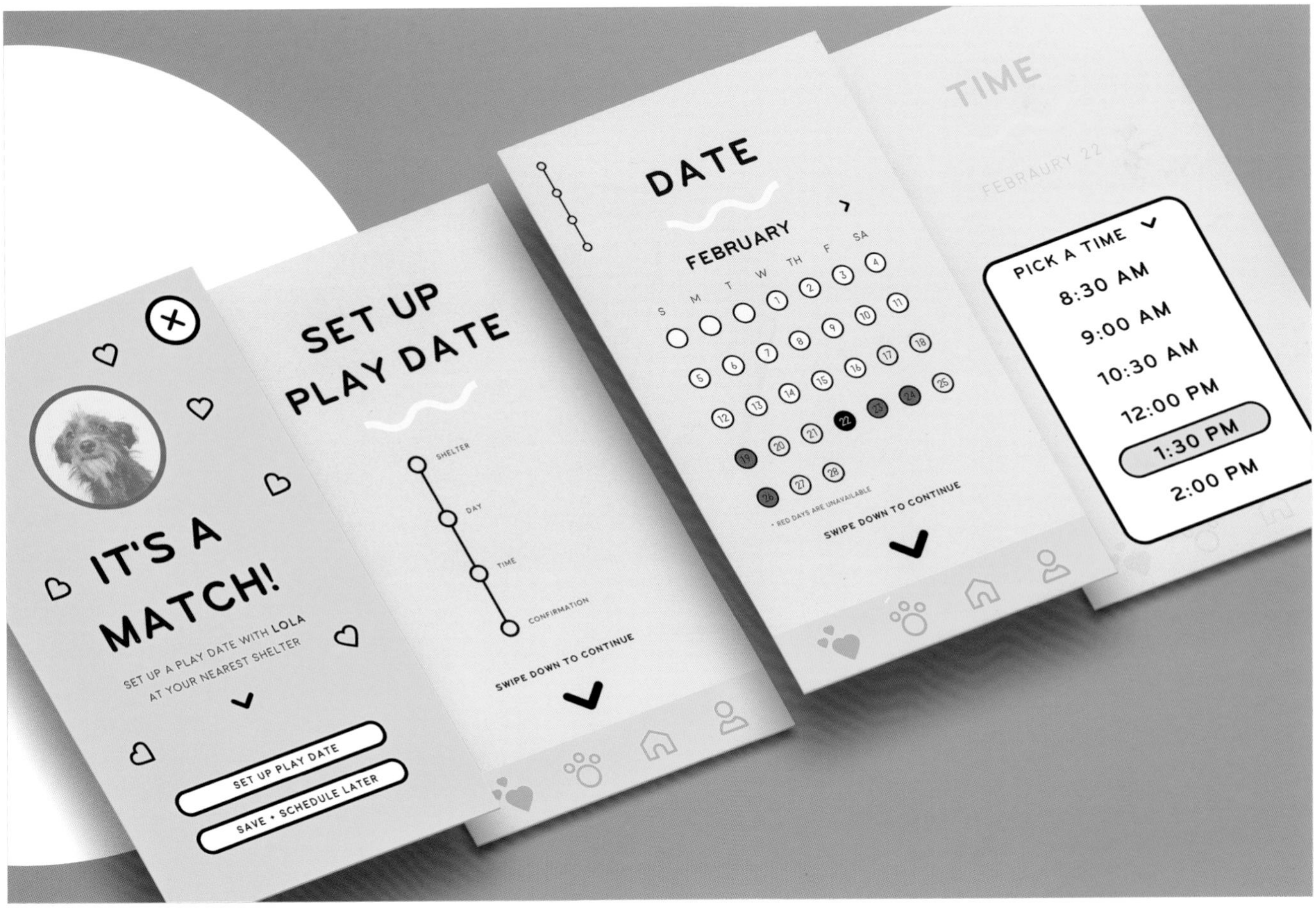
IT'S A MATCH!
SET UP A PLAY DATE WITH LOLA AT YOUR NEAREST SHELTER
SET UP PLAY DATE
SAVE • SCHEDULE LATER
SET UP PLAY DATE
SHELTER
DAY
TIME
CONFIRMATION
SWIPE DOWN TO CONTINUE
DATE
FEBRUARY
S M T W TH F SA
RED DAYS ARE UNAVAILABLE
SWIPE DOWN TO CONTINUE
TIME
FEBRAURY 22
PICK A TIME
8:30 AM
9:00 AM
10:30 AM
12:00 PM
1:30 PM
2:00 PM

PureMind

Design
Yana Syrevich

Client
Grinasys Corp

App Store

PureMind is a complex approach to mindfulness, including goal-based meditation courses, 5-minute singles, relaxing sounds and scientific-based advice on how to meditate.

01
SF Pro Display
Bold
TITLE FONT

02
SF Pro Display
Medium
MAIN FONT

03
SF Pro Text
Bold
SUBTITLE FONT

01
Blue
Anxiety

TIME PRESSURE
4 MIN
#B9E3ED

02
Green
Self-esteem

BAD EATING HABITS
4 MIN
#C5EBDF

03
Rose
Relationship

CONNECTING WITH NATURE
4 MIN
#FCD4D4

04
Orange
Productivity

SPORT RECOVERY
4 MIN
#FEDCA7

05
Violet
Sleep

WALKING IN THE CITY
4 MIN
#B5D3F0

Relationship
Build strong and healthy relationship with all those who matter, deal with past hurts and love fully. Color-themed program is here to support your meditation practice.
Start
Self-Esteem
The program is aimed at self-acceptance, developing loving relationships with yourself and quitting the inner critic. Color theme is designed for a deeper dive into the meditation experience.
Start
Anxiety
Ease anxiety, get more resilient to stress and restore your inner peace. This program has great soothing and relaxing effect, and is supported by specially selected color theme.
Start

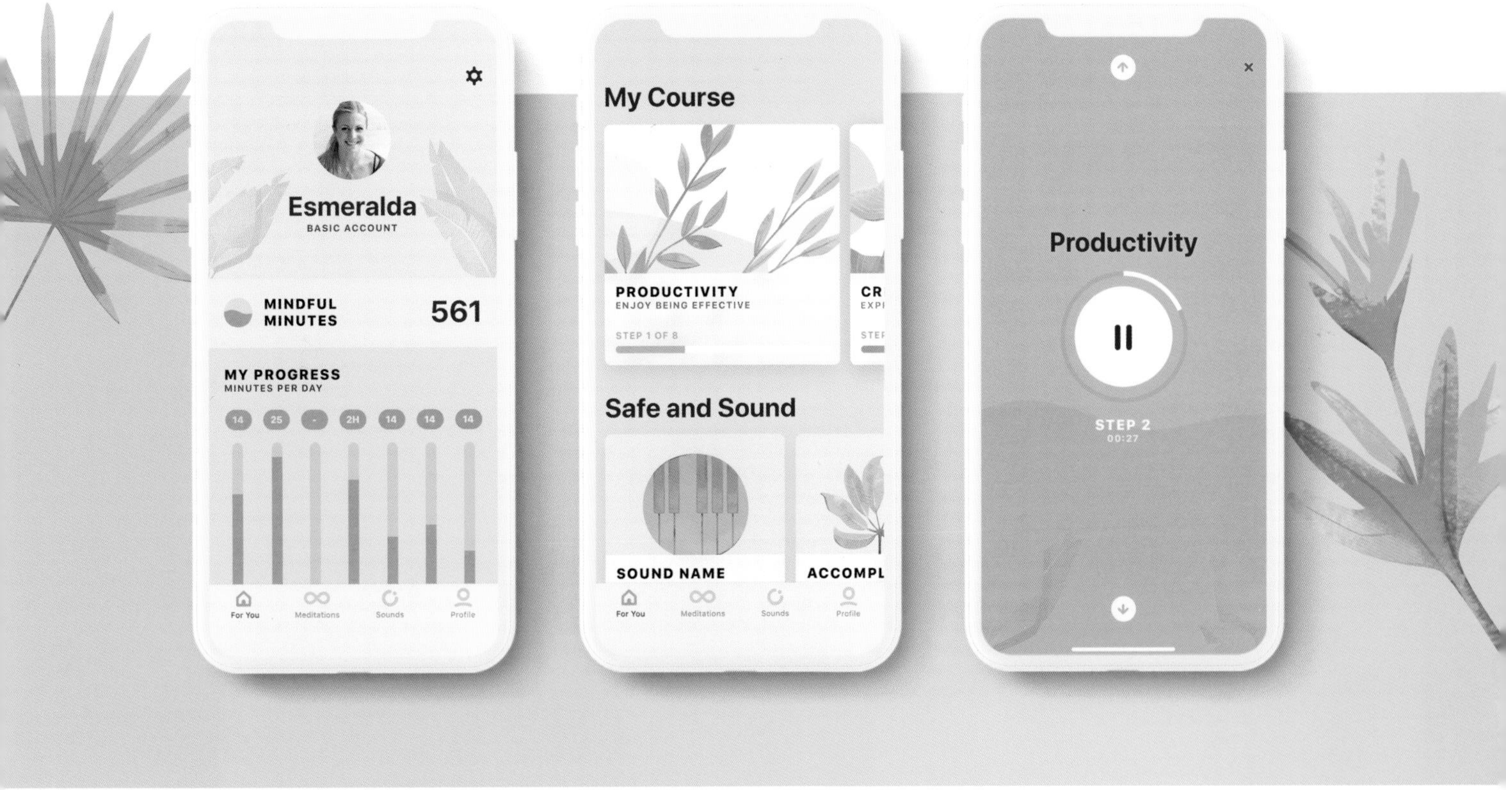

Esmeralda
BASIC ACCOUNT
MINDFUL MINUTES
561
MY PROGRESS
MINUTES PER DAY
14
25
-
2H
14
14
14
For You
Meditations
Sounds
Profile
My Course
PRODUCTIVITY
ENJOY BEING EFFECTIVE
STEP 1 OF 8
Safe and Sound
SOUND NAME
For You
Meditations
Sounds
Profile
Productivity
STEP 2
00:27

ANXIETY
TURN DOWN THE STRESS VOLUME
STEP 1 OF 8
MANAGING STRESS
BREATHE AWAY YOUR TENSION
STEP 1 OF 8
HAPPINESS
GROW YOUR OWN HAPPINESS
STEP 1 OF 8
WEIGHT LOSS
SHAPE YOUR IDENTITY & BODY
STEP 1 OF 8
SELF-LOVE
UNLEASH YOUR INNER CONFIDENCE
STEP 1 OF 8
RELATIONSHIP
DEEPEN RELATIONSHIP BONDS
STEP 1 OF 8

BVG Transit App

Design
Taehee Kim, Yejin Choi

Behance

BVG app is used for transportation service in Berlin. It provides real-time traffic information for U-Bahn, S-Bahn, tram and bus running in Berlin. Users can also buy the tickets on the app. The purpose of the service is to provide transport information and a simple way to buy tickets. Taehee and Yejin redesigned the app for more intuitive usability on UI screen. They reduced overall complexity and focused more on contents in order to optimize the UI design.

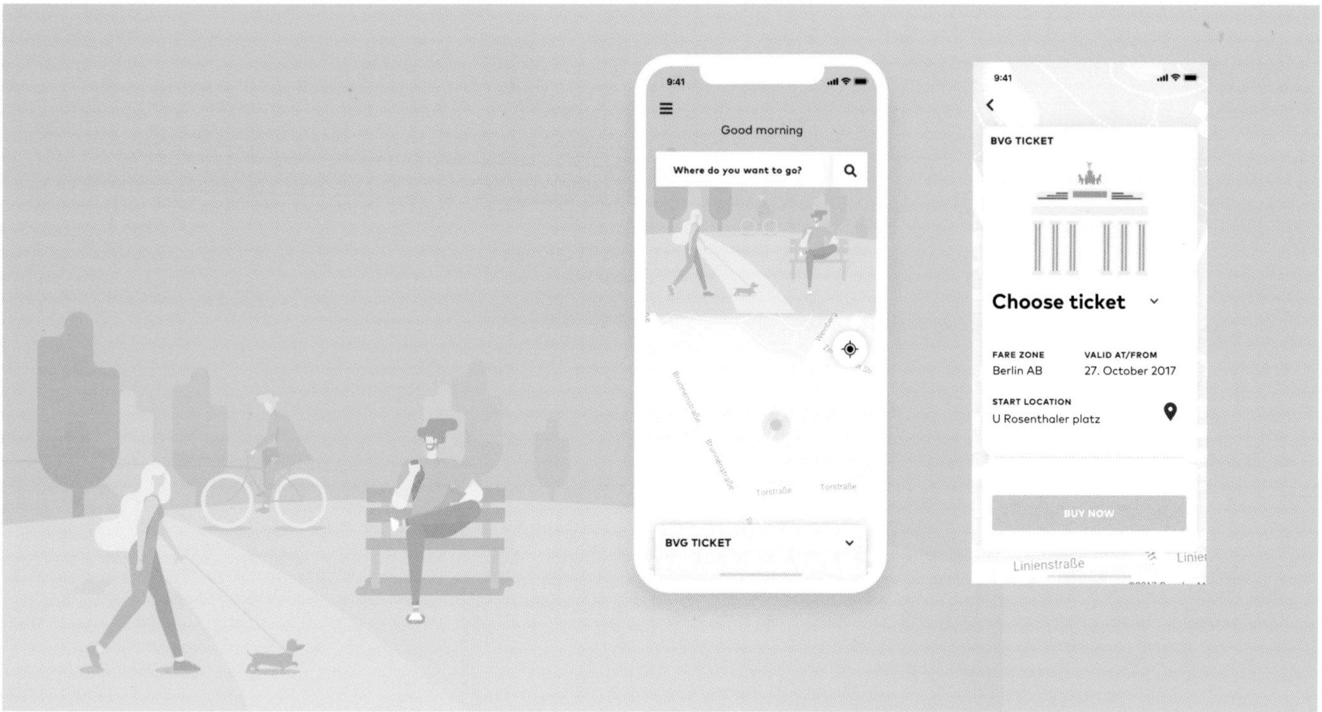
9:41
Good morning
Where do you want to go?
BVG TICKET
9:41
BVG TICKET
Choose ticket
FARE ZONE
Berlin AB
VALID AT/FROM
27. October 2017
START LOCATION
U Rosenthaler platz
BUY NOW
Linienstraße

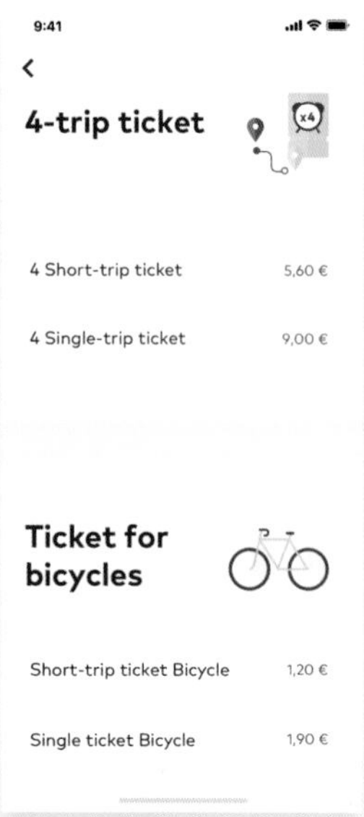
9:41
4-trip ticket
4 Short-trip ticket 5,60 €
4 Single-trip ticket 9,00 €
Ticket for bicycles
Short-trip ticket Bicycle 1,20 €
Single ticket Bicycle 1,90 €

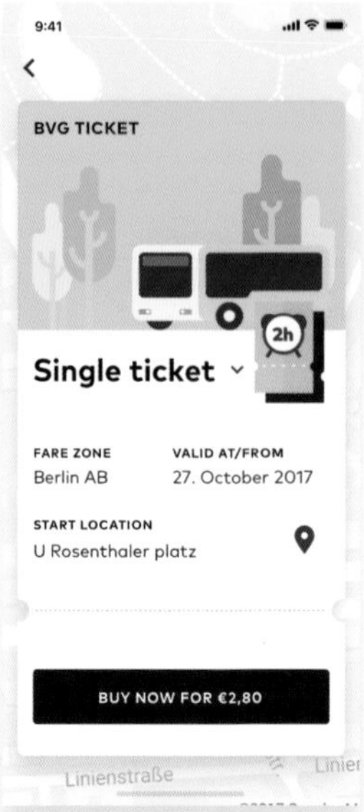
9:41
BVG TICKET
Single ticket
FARE ZONE
Berlin AB
VALID AT/FROM
27. October 2017
START LOCATION
U Rosenthaler platz
BUY NOW FOR €2,80
Linienstraße

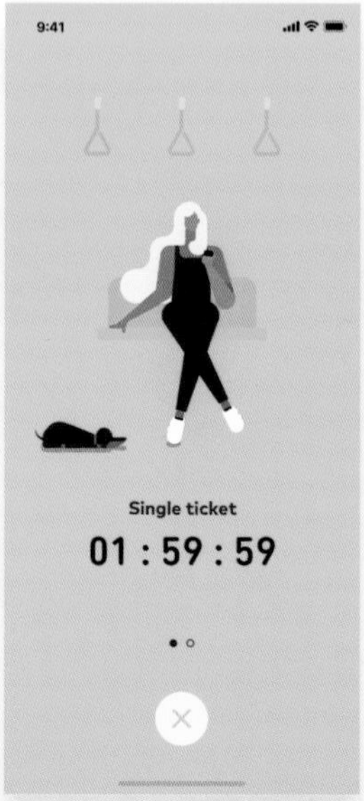
9:41
Single ticket
01 : 59 : 59

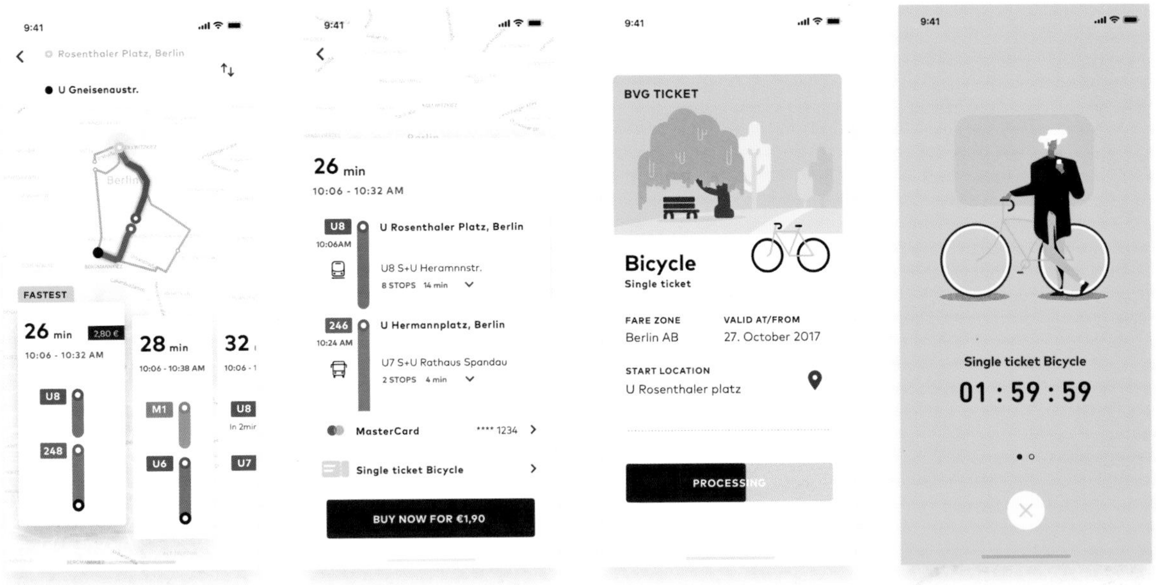
9:41
Rosenthaler Platz, Berlin
U Gneisenaustr.
FASTEST
26 min
2,80 €
10:06 - 10:32 AM
U8
248
28 min
10:06 - 10:38 AM
M1
U6
32
U8
U7
26 min
10:06 - 10:32 AM
U8
10:06AM
U Rosenthaler Platz, Berlin
U8 S+U Heramnnstr.
8 STOPS 14 min
246
10:24 AM
U Hermannplatz, Berlin
U7 S+U Rathaus Spandau
2 STOPS 4 min
MasterCard
**** 1234
Single ticket Bicycle
BUY NOW FOR €1,90
BVG TICKET
Bicycle
Single ticket
FARE ZONE
Berlin AB
VALID AT/FROM
27. October 2017
START LOCATION
U Rosenthaler platz
PROCESSING
Single ticket Bicycle
01 : 59 : 59

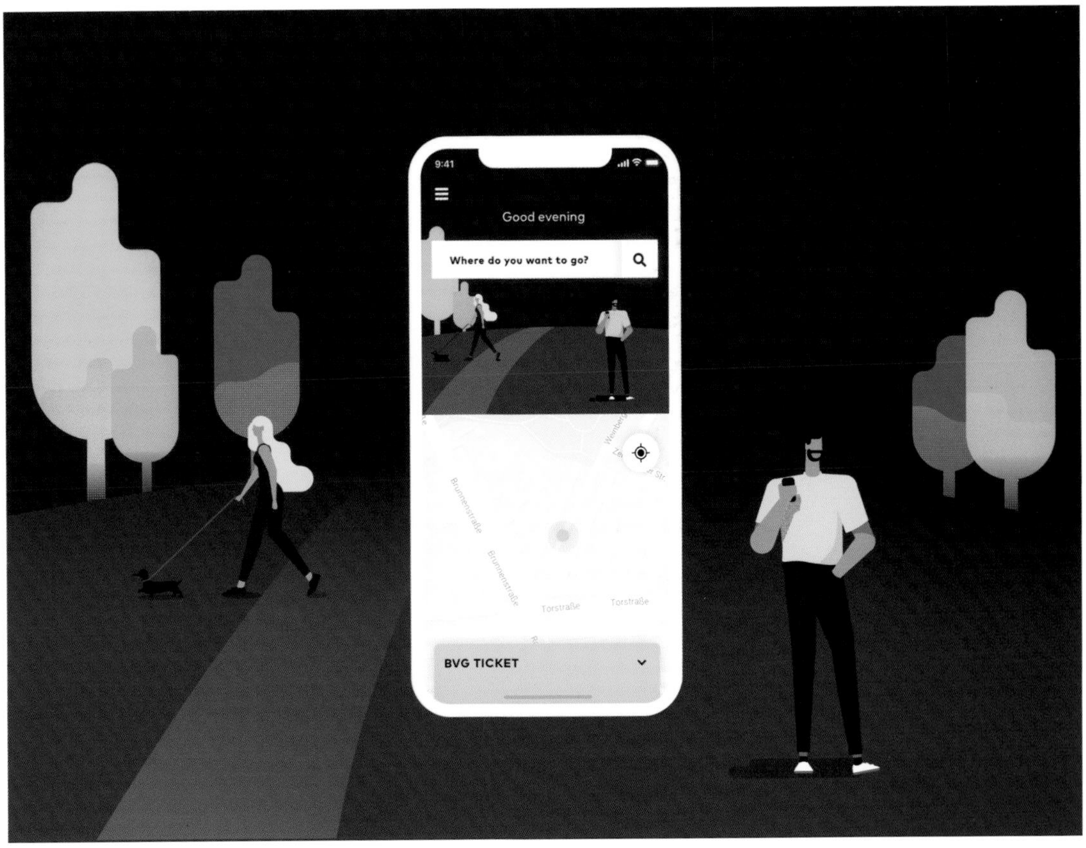
9:41
Good evening
Where do you want to go?
Torstraße
BVG TICKET

myStudio

Design
Kevin Oehmichen

Behance

myStudio app is designed to bring a better experience for exercisers in the gym. With the app, exercisers could scan the QR codes on the fitness equipment and thus keep track of their training statistics, such as body weight, reps and sets in the workout. Besides, it could also offer other useful functions, such as directing users to the fitness equipment through AR technology, and showing tips to improve their workout.

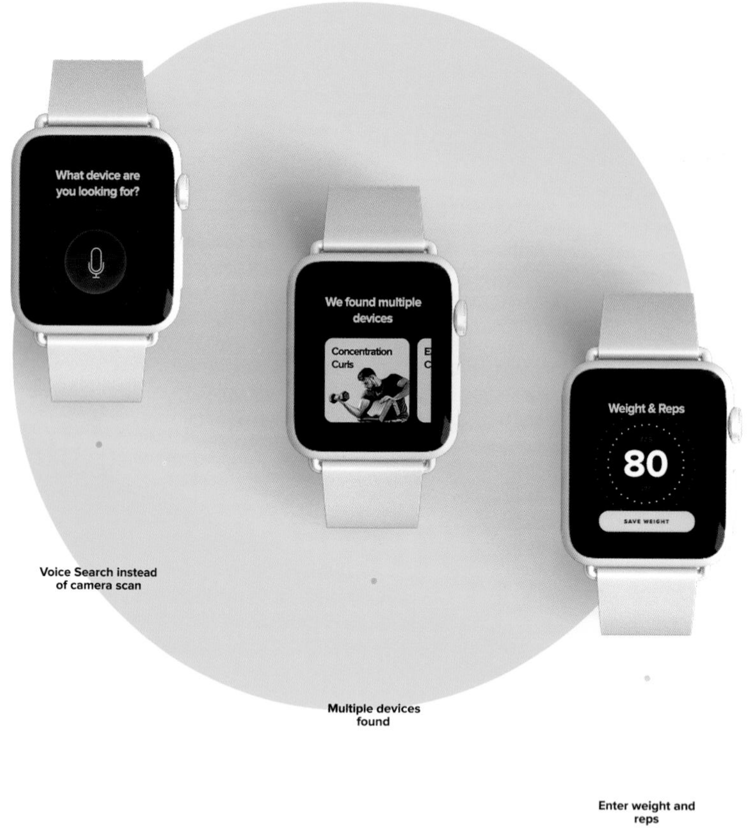
What device are you looking for?
We found multiple devices
Concentration Curls
Weight & Reps
80
SAVE WEIGHT
Voice Search instead of camera scan
Multiple devices found
Enter weight and reps

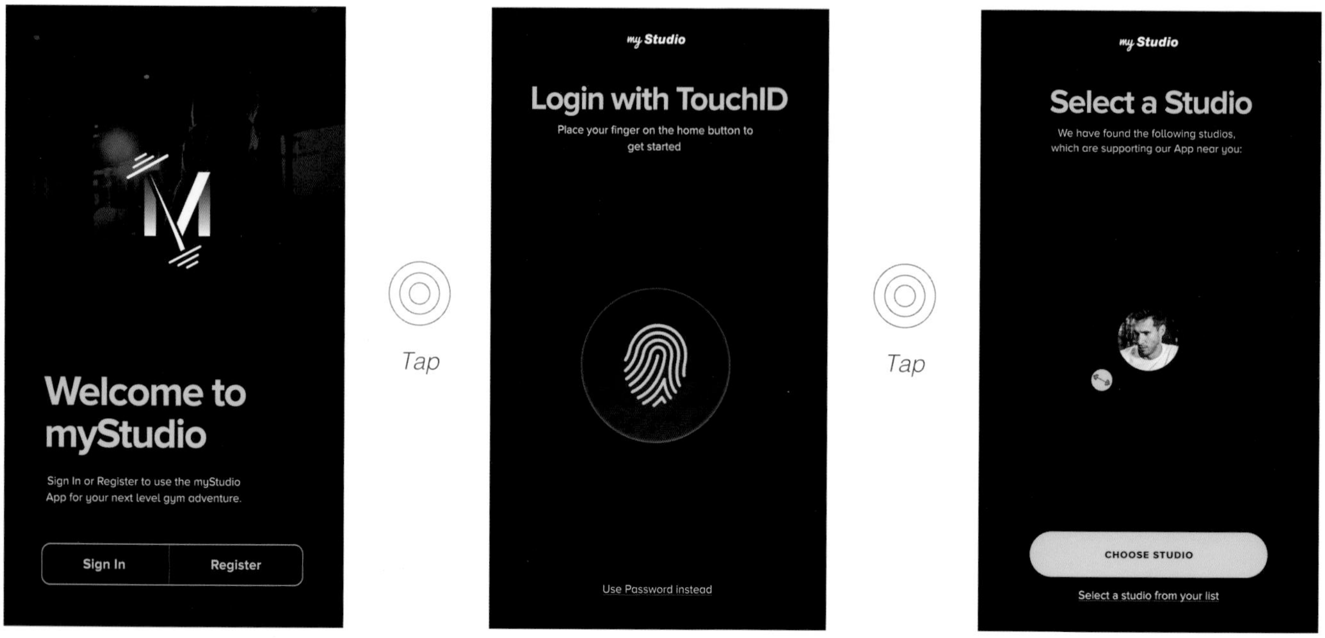
Welcome to myStudio
Sign In or Register to use the myStudio App for your next level gym adventure.
Sign In
Register
Tap
myStudio
Login with TouchID
Place your finger on the home button to get started
Use Password instead
Tap
myStudio
Select a Studio
We have found the following studios, which are supporting our App near you:
CHOOSE STUDIO
Select a studio from your list

my Studio
SCAN THIS DEVICE

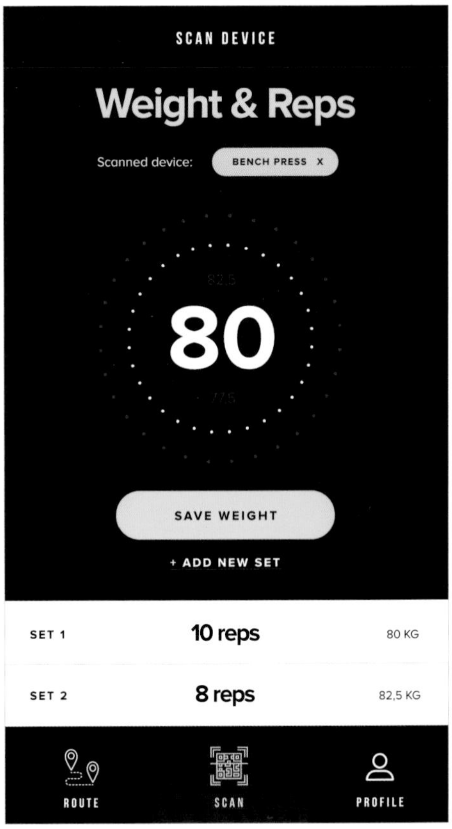
SCAN DEVICE
Weight & Reps
Scanned device:
BENCH PRESS X
80
SAVE WEIGHT
+ ADD NEW SET
SET 1
10 reps
80 KG
SET 2
8 reps
82,5 KG
ROUTE
SCAN
PROFILE

To fit the app's purpose and target users, the designer decided to use dark colour scheme, combined with yellow as highlight colour, which creates an overall bold, strong and powerful look and feel.

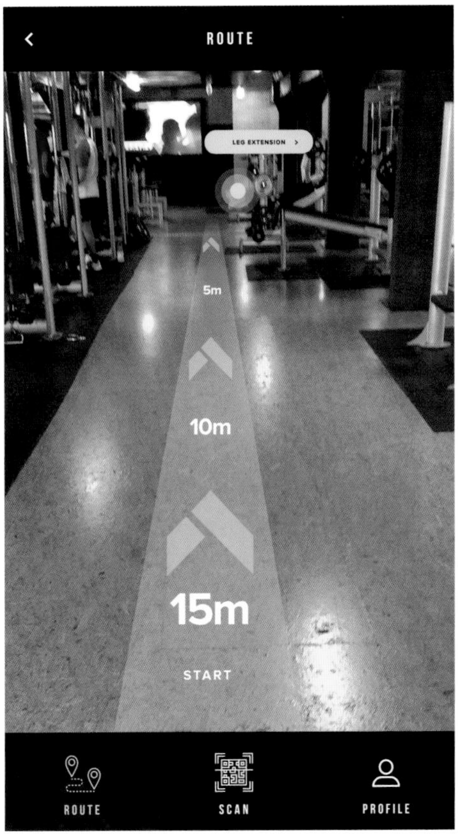
ROUTE
5m
10m
15m
START
ROUTE
SCAN
PROFILE

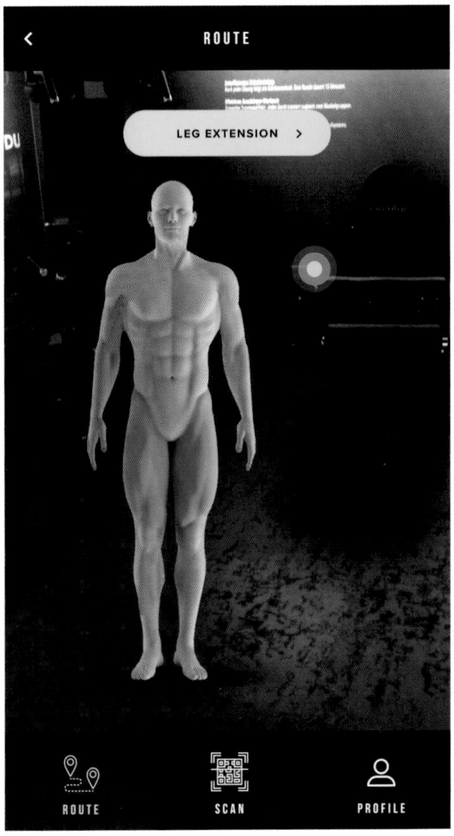
ROUTE
LEG EXTENSION
ROUTE
SCAN
PROFILE

Hopper

Hopper

Design
Isabel Sá, Liliana Ferreira

Behance

Hopper is where travelling meets gaming directly. Using the real world as a map, gamers and adventurers travel specific city courses to earn rewards, participate in challenges, while learn the city's history and culture. Users navigate pre-determined paths, and unlock landmarks, real-life coupons, challenges and other rewards. The presented interface is the "Historian's pack", a map set in Porto, Portugal, chosen in order to conduct effective user testing.

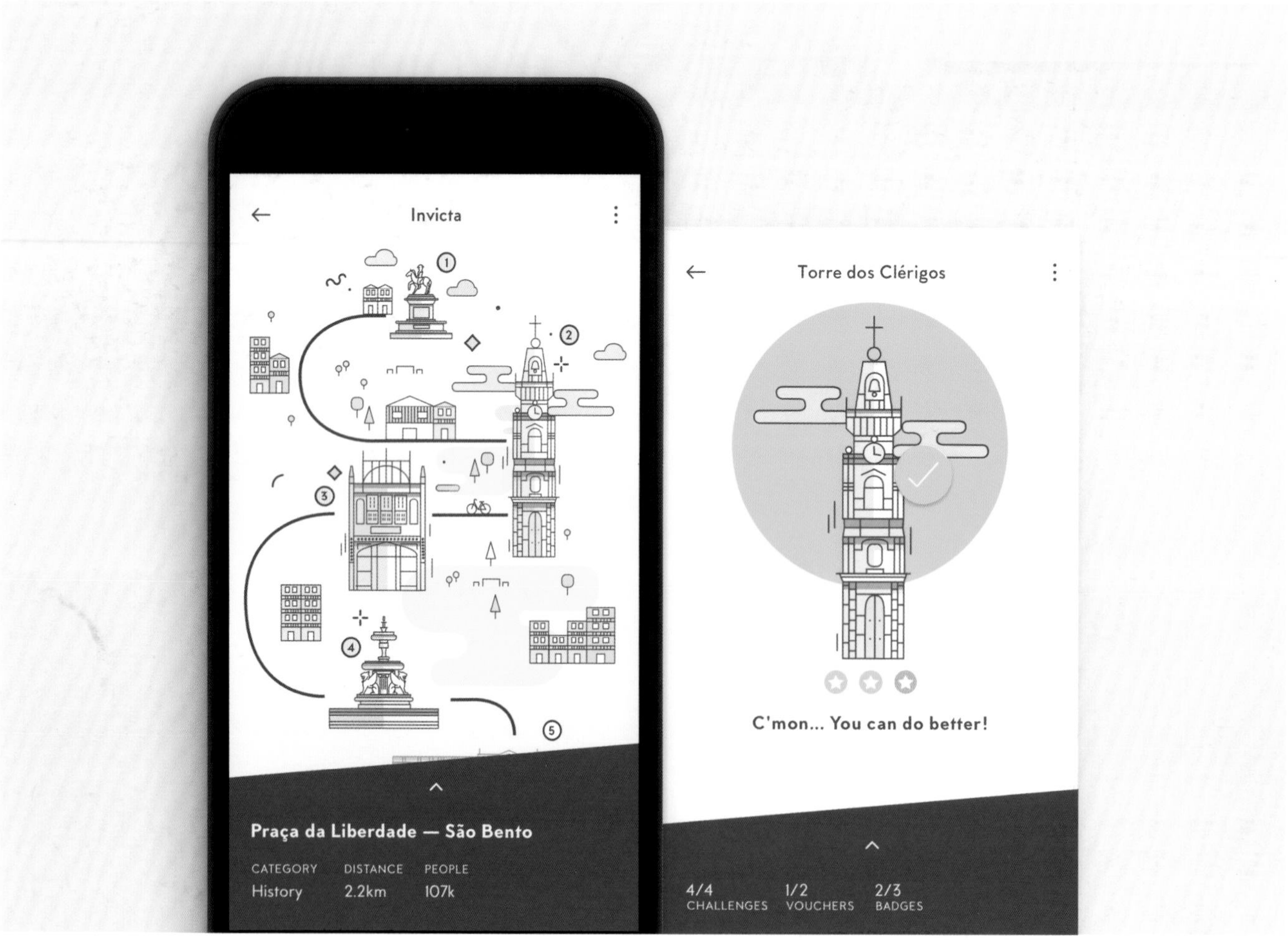
Invicta
Praça da Liberdade — São Bento
CATEGORY History
DISTANCE 2.2km
PEOPLE 107k
Torre dos Clérigos
C'mon... You can do better!
4/4 CHALLENGES
1/2 VOUCHERS
2/3 BADGES

SKIP
Stay connected!
Share your achievements with your friends on Facebook and Instagram!
Is this it?!

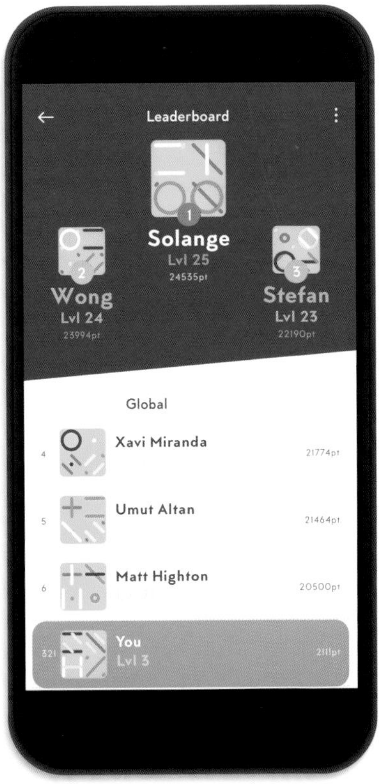
Leaderboard
Solange
Lvl 25
24535pt
Wong
Lvl 24
23994pt
Stefan
Lvl 23
22190pt
Global
4 Xavi Miranda 21774pt
5 Umut Altan 21464pt
6 Matt Highton 20500pt
321 You Lvl 3 2111pt

Torre dos Clérigos
Are you secure of your abilities?
0/4 CHALLENGES
0/2 VOUCHERS
0/3 BADGES
Let's go!
DESCRIPTION
Between the church and the tower lies a building that once served as a hospital for poor members of the clergy. The complex was constructed between 1732 and 1763 for the Irmandade dos Clérigos Pobres de Nossa Senhora da Misericórdia, São Pedro ad Víncula e São Filipe de Nery, a priestly brotherhood more commonly known as the Confraria dos Clérigos. The creator of this monumental building was the Italian architect Nicolau Nasoni, who knew how to overcome the unfavourable READ MORE

Map
NOW PLAYING
Torre dos Clérigos
0/5 CHALLENGES
0/2 VOUCHERS
0/3 BADGES

YOU'VE JUST UNLOCKED
Out of this world
For earning your first voucher.
+450pt
SHARE ON FACEBOOK
That's great

Eatoo

Design
Stephen Tjoa

Behance

Eatoo is a social networking and restaurant searching app that allows users to create social meal plan and connect with each other based on topic of interest. To start with, users can set up their own profiles, meal plans and invite friends to join their plans. They can also browse through and join others' plans based on common interest. The app offers an easy solution for urban dwellers to enlarge social circle.

Eating Together *provides an effective time for* ***having conversation.***

Having Conversation *will be more effective when they have same* ***interest.***

Create Brand that show ***Dynamic*** *and* ***Expressive*** *Value of Urban Lifestyle, also* ***Togetherness***

Concept of visual logo was created and inspired by visual of plate, round eating table, connectivity, and agenda.

ICON SET

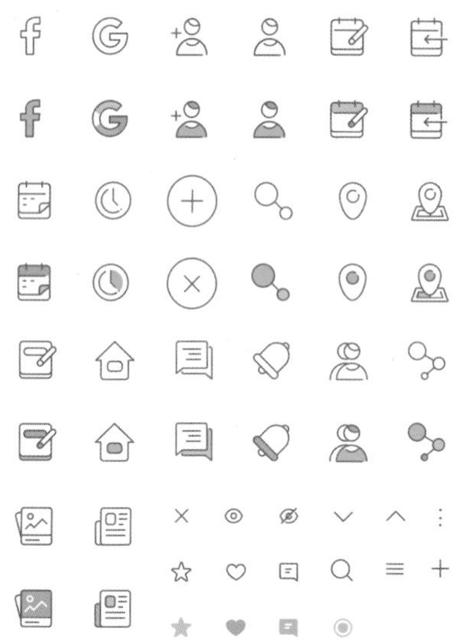

12:30
Organize
Organize your meal plan with friends and family in the easiest way with one click.
NEXT

12:30
Places
Give references of trending resto and cafe in Jakarta with quick booking feature.
NEXT

12:30
Social
Expand your social circle based on your topic of interest with ask to join plan feature.
Get Started
Already a member? Sign in

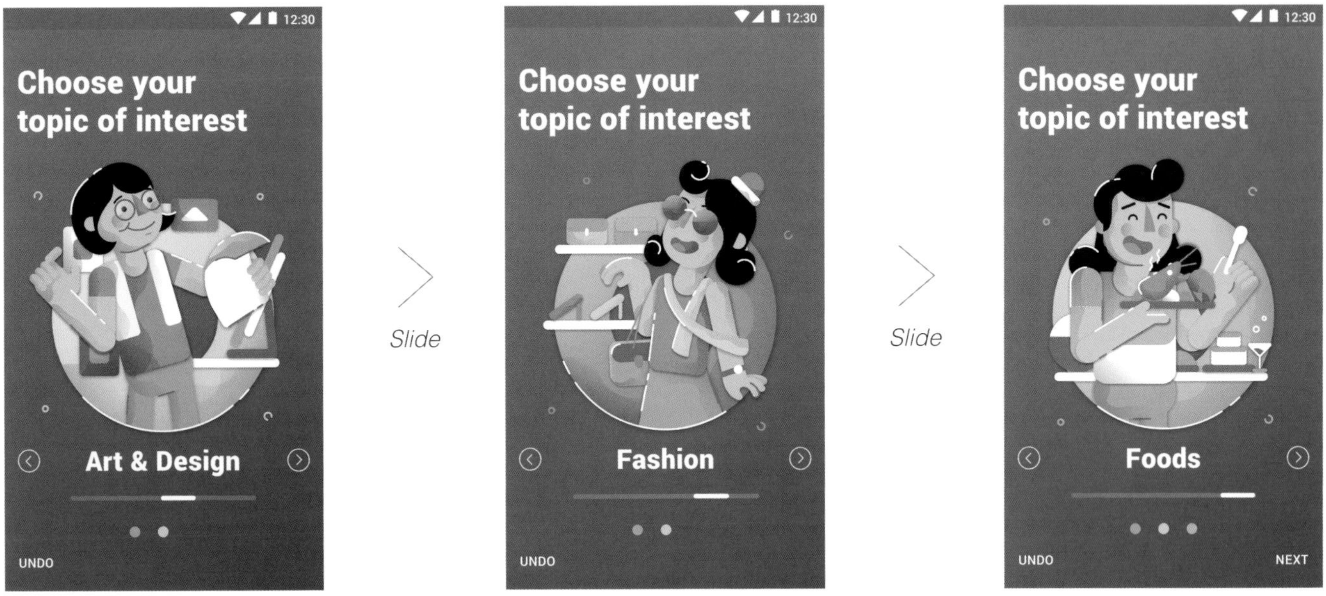
12:30
Choose your topic of interest
Art & Design
UNDO
Slide
12:30
Choose your topic of interest
Fashion
UNDO
Slide
12:30
Choose your topic of interest
Foods
UNDO
NEXT

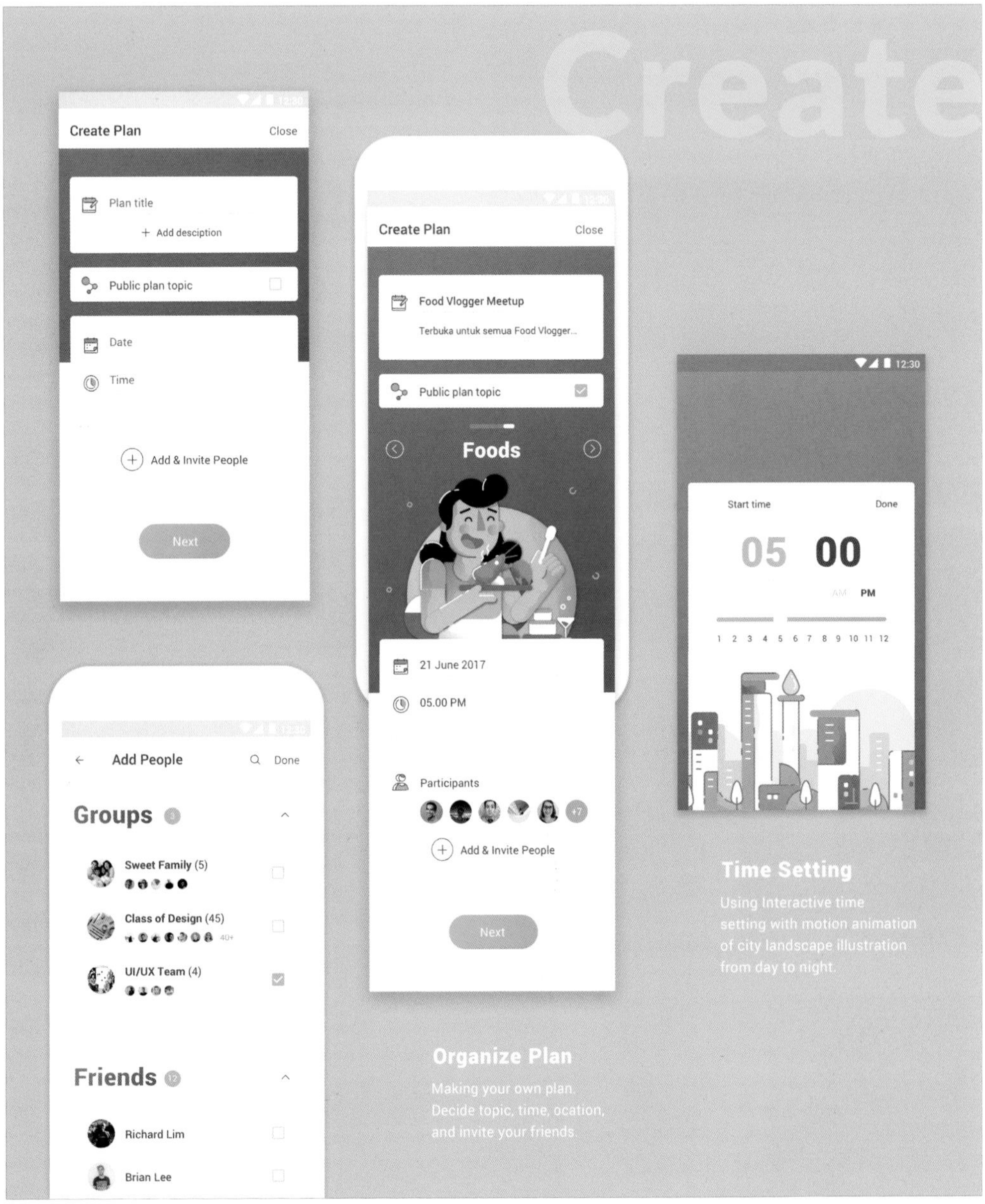
Create
Create Plan
Close
Plan title
+ Add desciption
Public plan topic
Date
Time
Add & Invite People
Next
Create Plan
Close
Food Vlogger Meetup
Terbuka untuk semua Food Vlogger...
Public plan topic
Foods
21 June 2017
05.00 PM
Participants
Add & Invite People
Next
12:30
Start time
Done
05 00
AM PM
1 2 3 4 5 6 7 8 9 10 11 12
Time Setting
Using Interactive time setting with motion animation of city landscape illustration from day to night.
Add People
Done
Groups
Sweet Family (5)
Class of Design (45)
UI/UX Team (4)
Friends
Richard Lim
Brian Lee
Organize Plan
Making your own plan. Decide topic, time, ocation, and invite your friends.

In terms of design solution, the designer applied Card Design System to separate each information layout, keeping a clean and modern style. Joyful illustrations were created to represent categories of interest with a unique way and add more liveliness to the app.

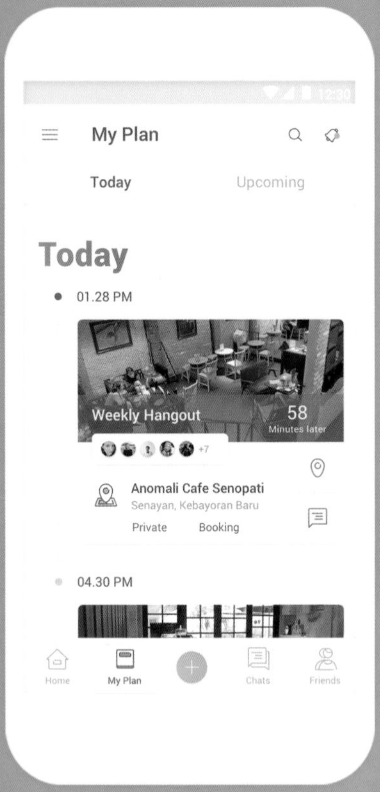

12:30
My Plan
Today
Upcoming
Today
01.28 PM
Weekly Hangout
58
Minutes later
+7
Anomali Cafe Senopati
Senayan, Kebayoran Baru
Private
Booking
04.30 PM
Home
My Plan
Chats
Friends

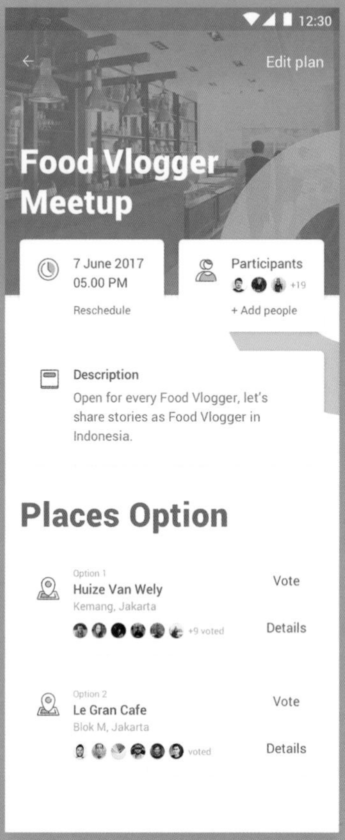

12:30
Edit plan
Food Vlogger Meetup
7 June 2017
05.00 PM
Reschedule
Participants
+19
+ Add people
Description
Open for every Food Vlogger, let's share stories as Food Vlogger in Indonesia.
Places Option
Option 1
Huize Van Wely
Kemang, Jakarta
+9 voted
Vote
Details
Option 2
Le Gran Cafe
Blok M, Jakarta
voted
Vote
Details

MY PLAN

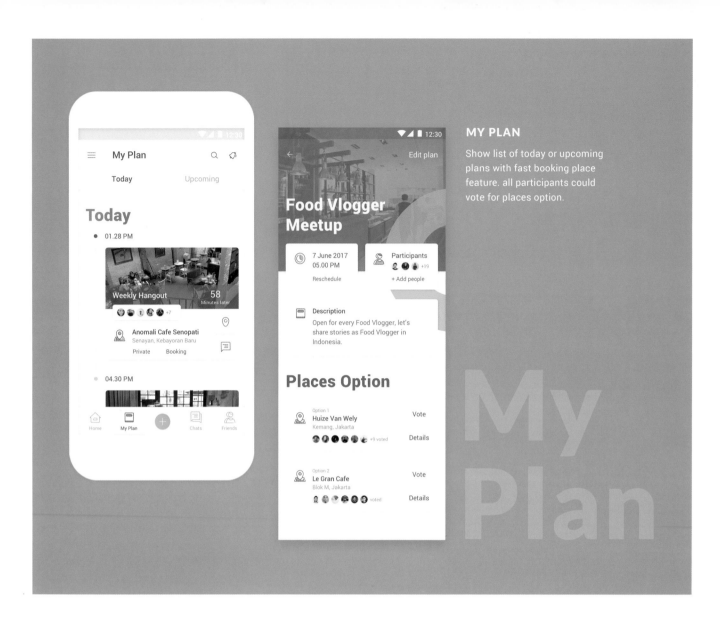

Show list of today or upcoming plans with fast booking place feature. all participants could vote for places option.

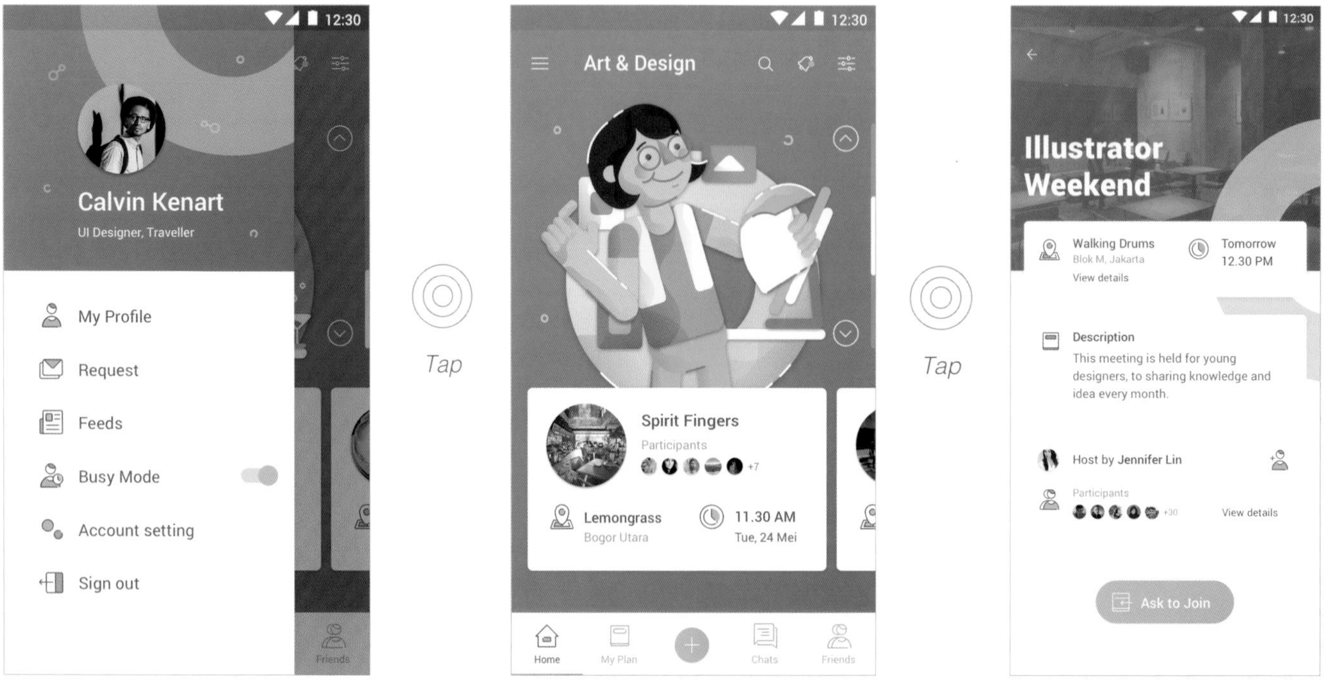

12:30
Calvin Kenart
UI Designer, Traveller
My Profile
Request
Feeds
Busy Mode
Account setting
Sign out
Friends
Tap
12:30
Art & Design
Spirit Fingers
Participants
+7
Lemongrass
Bogor Utara
11.30 AM
Tue, 24 Mei
Home
My Plan
Chats
Friends
Tap
12:30
Illustrator Weekend
Walking Drums
Blok M, Jakarta
View details
Tomorrow
12.30 PM
Description
This meeting is held for young designers, to sharing knowledge and idea every month.
Host by Jennifer Lin
Participants
+30
View details
Ask to Join

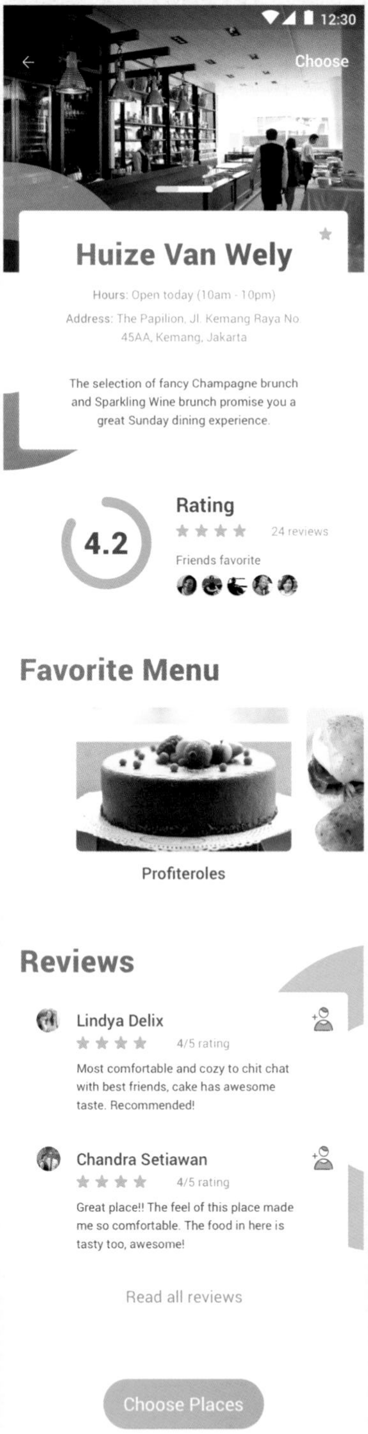
12:30
Choose
Huize Van Wely
Hours: Open today (10am - 10pm)
Address: The Papilion, Jl. Kemang Raya No. 45AA, Kemang, Jakarta
The selection of fancy Champagne brunch and Sparkling Wine brunch promise you a great Sunday dining experience.
4.2
Rating
24 reviews
Friends favorite
Favorite Menu
Profiteroles
Reviews
Lindya Delix
4/5 rating
Most comfortable and cozy to chit chat with best friends, cake has awesome taste. Recommended!
Chandra Setiawan
4/5 rating
Great place!! The feel of this place made me so comfortable. The food in here is tasty too, awesome!
Read all reviews
Choose Places

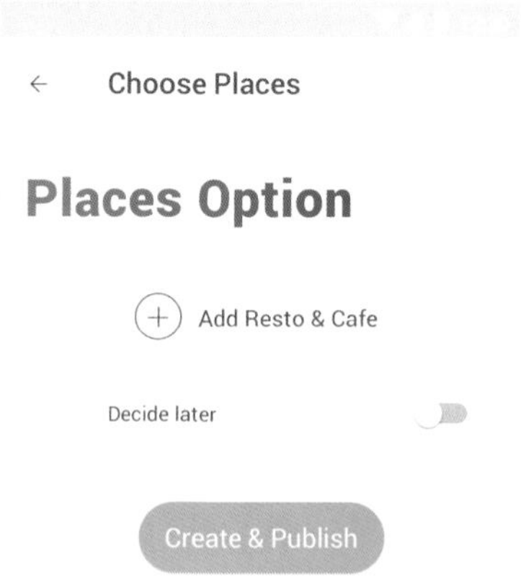
Choose Places
Places Option
Add Resto & Cafe
Decide later
Create & Publish

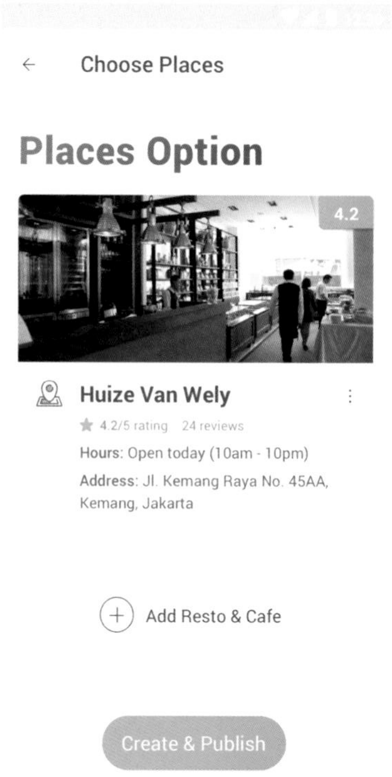
Choose Places
Places Option
4.2
Huize Van Wely
4.2/5 rating 24 reviews
Hours: Open today (10am - 10pm)
Address: Jl. Kemang Raya No. 45AA, Kemang, Jakarta
Add Resto & Cafe
Create & Publish

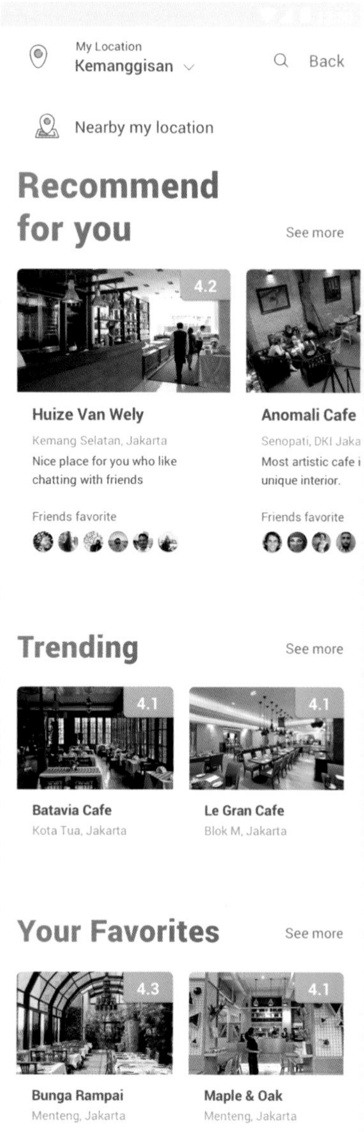
My Location
Kemanggisan
Back
Nearby my location
Recommend for you
See more
4.2
Huize Van Wely
Kemang Selatan, Jakarta
Nice place for you who like chatting with friends
Friends favorite
Anomali Cafe
Senopati, DKI Jaka
Most artistic cafe i unique interior.
Friends favorite
Trending
See more
4.1
Batavia Cafe
Kota Tua, Jakarta
4.1
Le Gran Cafe
Blok M, Jakarta
Your Favorites
See more
4.3
Bunga Rampai
Menteng, Jakarta
4.1
Maple & Oak
Menteng, Jakarta

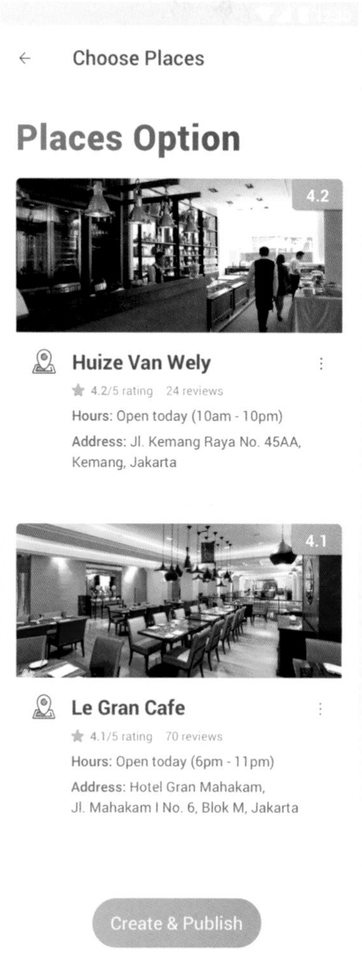
Choose Places
Places Option
4.2
Huize Van Wely
4.2/5 rating 24 reviews
Hours: Open today (10am - 10pm)
Address: Jl. Kemang Raya No. 45AA, Kemang, Jakarta
4.1
Le Gran Cafe
4.1/5 rating 70 reviews
Hours: Open today (6pm - 11pm)
Address: Hotel Gran Mahakam, Jl. Mahakam I No. 6, Blok M, Jakarta
Create & Publish

FitWave

Design
Olha Uzhykova

App Store

FitWave is a time tracker that helps people work out at the optimal level. The user doesn't need to count on himself or think about right rhythm while he is doing his exercise. The user can build his custom rhythm and FitWave will assist him in creating a great workout session according to his fitness level.

FONT

Gotham Pro
ABCDEFGHIJKLMNOPQRSTUVWXYZ
abcdefghijklmnopqrstuvwxyz
1234567890

San Francisco
ABCDEFGHIJKLMNOPQRSTUVWXYZ
abcdefghijklmnopqrstuvwxyz
1234567890

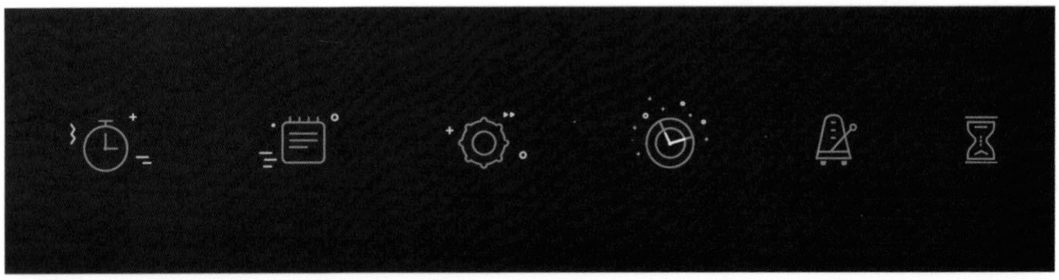

Welcome to FitWave :)
Skip
Next
Awesome rhythm timer
Next
Flexible timer settings
Next
Manage timers
Start

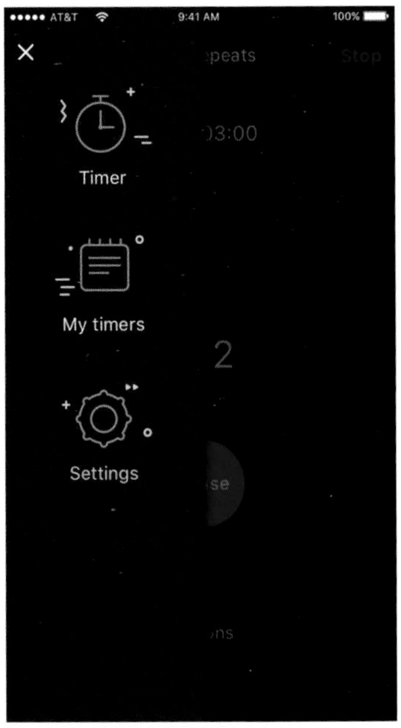
●●●●● AT&T
9:41 AM
100%
Timer
My timers
Settings

Tap

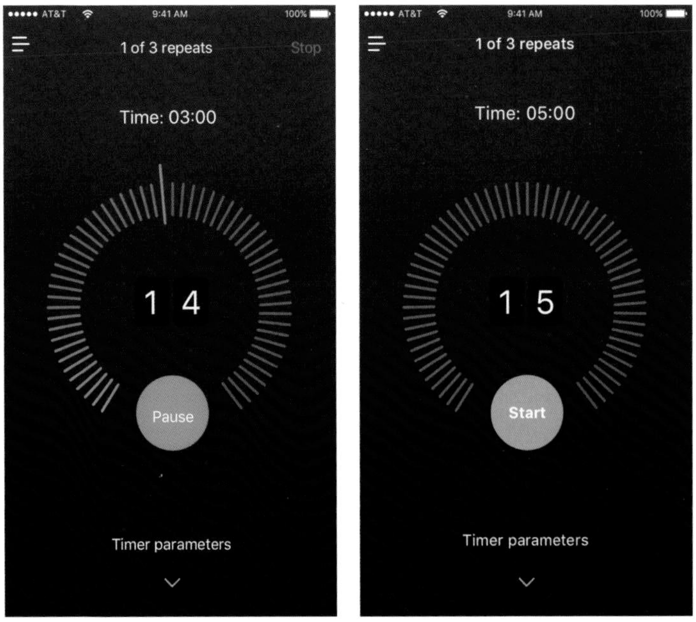
●●●●● AT&T
9:41 AM
100%
1 of 3 repeats
Stop
Time: 03:00
1 4
Pause
Timer parameters
●●●●● AT&T
9:41 AM
100%
1 of 3 repeats
Time: 05:00
1 5
Start
Timer parameters

Designer Olha Uzhykova shares her design and implementation process: "I have worked on this project from idea stage to user testing and ongoing support mode. The work began with user interviews and analyzing feedback received. The goal of the project was to launch Minimum Viable Product to see if the right direction had been chosen. So when functionality of the app was confirmed, I began with wireframes and simple prototype which had been shown to target audience. After analyzing feedback and flow improvements I started the UI part. The final design was selected based on feedback from potential users and design trends at that time of launch."

1 of 3 repeats
Stop
Time: 03:00
Non-stop
Countdown
My timers
Delay
2 sec
Number of Exercises
2
Rhythm
3
Time
15 min
Rest
2 min
Repeats
3
Apply
●●●●● AT&T
9:41 AM
100%
Add timer
Save
Timer 1
Non-Stop
Countdown
Delay
2 sec
Number of Exercises
2
Rhythm
3
Time
15 min
Rest
2 min
Repeats
3
Start now
1 of 3 repeats
Stop
Time: 03:00
Non-stop
Countdown
My timers
Delay
2 sec
Rhythm
4
Apply

Helf

Design
Amelia Rams

Supervisor
PhD Michał Kracik

Mockups
Pablo Coronel, www.ui8.net

Behance

The subject of this work was a project of blood collecting service which suits patients' needs. The main goal is to provide as much information as possible to the patient before the procedure (preparation), improve communication between medical staff and patients, speed up the procedure and make it more friendly. Project is the part of Master's degree in Academy of Fine Arts in Kraków, Poland.

helf.
Zarejestruj się
Zaloguj się
helf.
imię
nazwisko
pesel
Potwierdź
helf.
e-mail
hasło
potwierdź hasło
Potwierdź

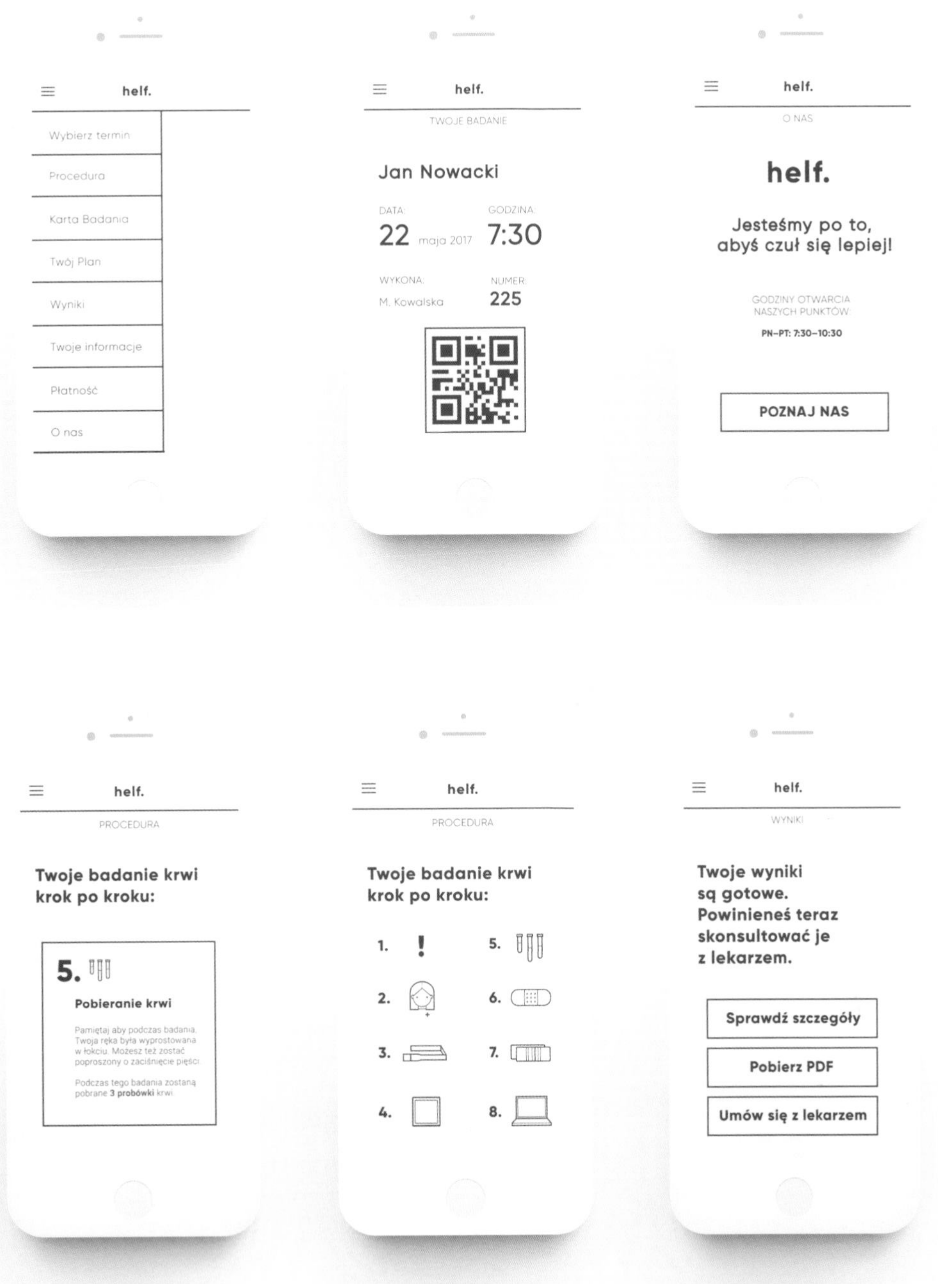
helf.
Wybierz termin
Procedura
Karta Badania
Twój Plan
Wyniki
Twoje informacje
Płatność
O nas
helf.
TWOJE BADANIE
Jan Nowacki
DATA:
GODZINA:
22 maja 2017 7:30
WYKONA:
NUMER:
M. Kowalska
225
helf.
O NAS
helf.
Jesteśmy po to, abyś czuł się lepiej!
GODZINY OTWARCIA NASZYCH PUNKTÓW:
PN–PT: 7:30–10:30
POZNAJ NAS
helf.
PROCEDURA
Twoje badanie krwi krok po kroku:
5.
Pobieranie krwi
helf.
PROCEDURA
Twoje badanie krwi krok po kroku:
1.
2.
3.
4.
5.
6.
7.
8.
helf.
WYNIKI
Twoje wyniki są gotowe. Powinieneś teraz skonsultować je z lekarzem.
Sprawdź szczegóły
Pobierz PDF
Umów się z lekarzem

The main goal in design was to create clear and simple interface, which is understandable for all patients to help them go through the whole procedure in nice way. The designer decided to use neutral colours associated with the medical industry. White colour is associated with purity, navy blue stands for professionalism and trust. This simple layout is supplemented with icons, which gives friendly characteristics.

helf.
Jakie jest Twoje samopoczucie w związku z pobieraniem krwi?
Dalej

Slices

Design
Kirill Emelyanov

Behance

Slices app helps users to create stylish covers, banners or announcements for social networks in just few taps on their smart phones. It could become indispensable for bloggers, SMM managers or small business owners. It is simple to use—creating a new masterpiece with the settings of canvas or with the addition of elements (images, text, stickers…). Users can play with layers, changing their order or applying effects to them.

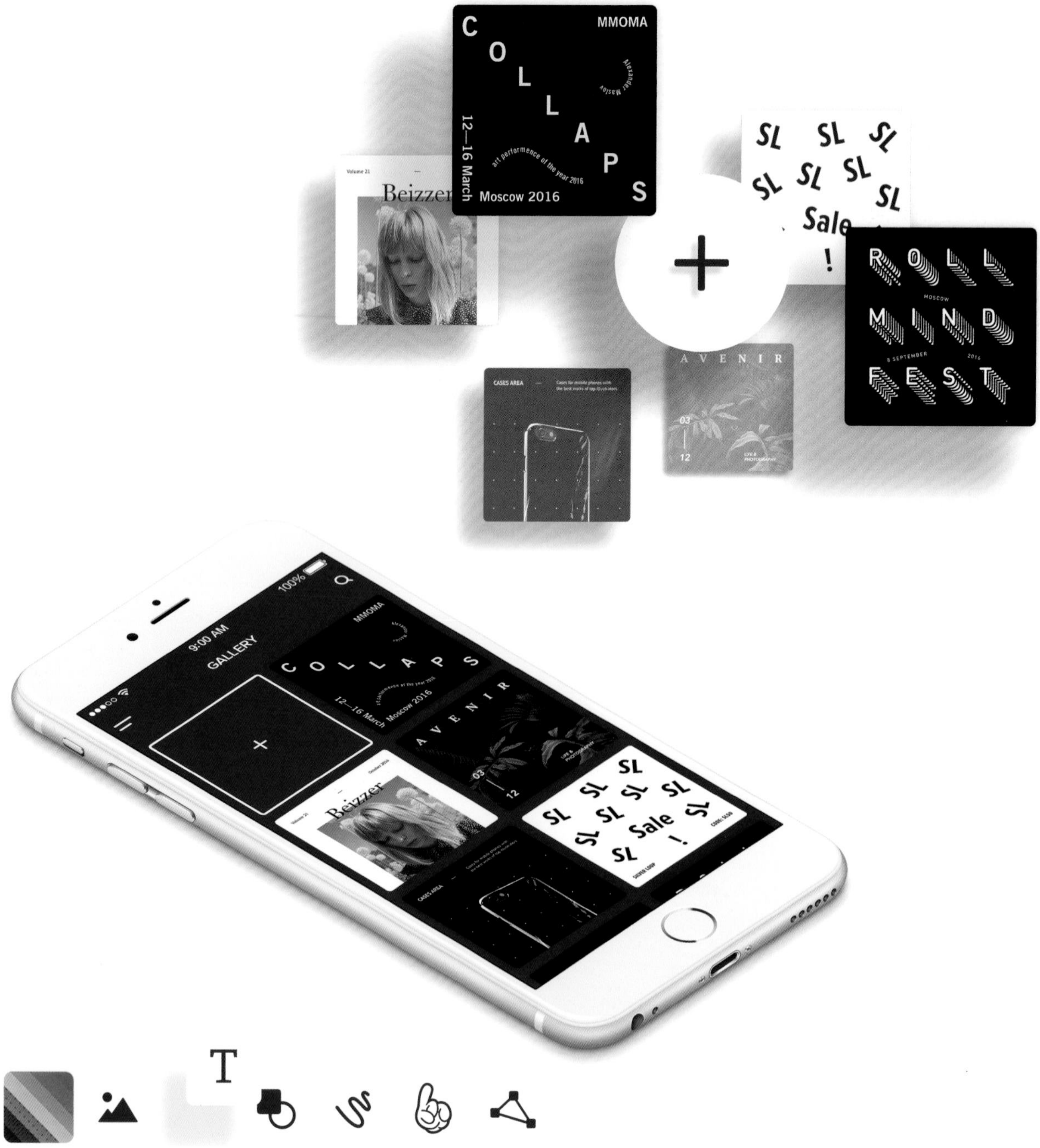

MMOMA
COLLAPS
12—16 March
Moscow 2016
art performence of the year 2016
Beizzer
SL SL SL SL SL SL SL
Sale
!
ROLL MIND FEST
AVENIR
CASES AREA
9:00 AM
100%
GALLERY
T

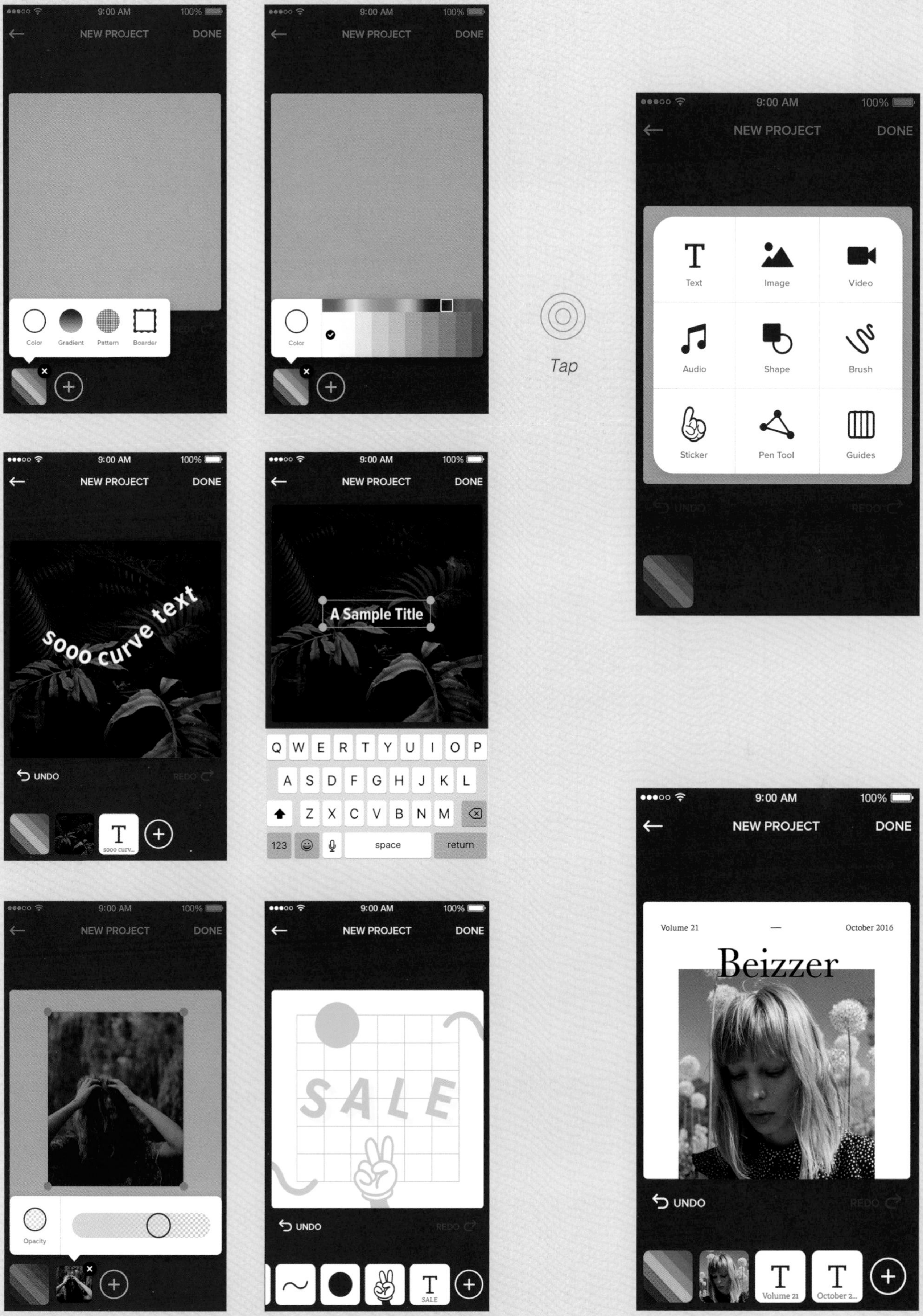
9:00 AM
100%
NEW PROJECT
DONE
Color
Gradient
Pattern
Boarder
Tap
Text
Image
Video
Audio
Shape
Brush
Sticker
Pen Tool
Guides
UNDO
REDO
sooo curve text
A Sample Title
Q W E R T Y U I O P
A S D F G H J K L
Z X C V B N M
123
space
return
Opacity
SALE
Volume 21
October 2016
Beizzer

Newvo

Design
Belén Fernández-Santos Ruiz

Behance

Newvo is an app for learning and memorizing new vocabulary. It offers simple solution for users who wish to improve the languages they are studying. With Newvo, users could translate and save the word, and set a reminder to notify themselves to study regularly.

#3200FF
ultramarine
#140A40
middle red purple
#FFFFFF
white
Primary &
Secondary colors
#FF005A
folly
#0EE8CD
bright turquoise

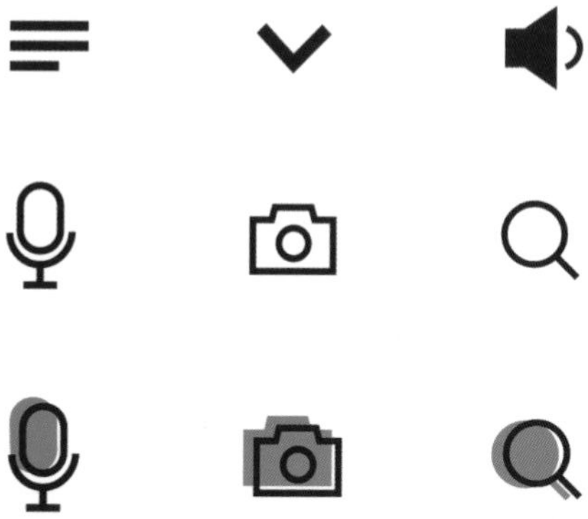

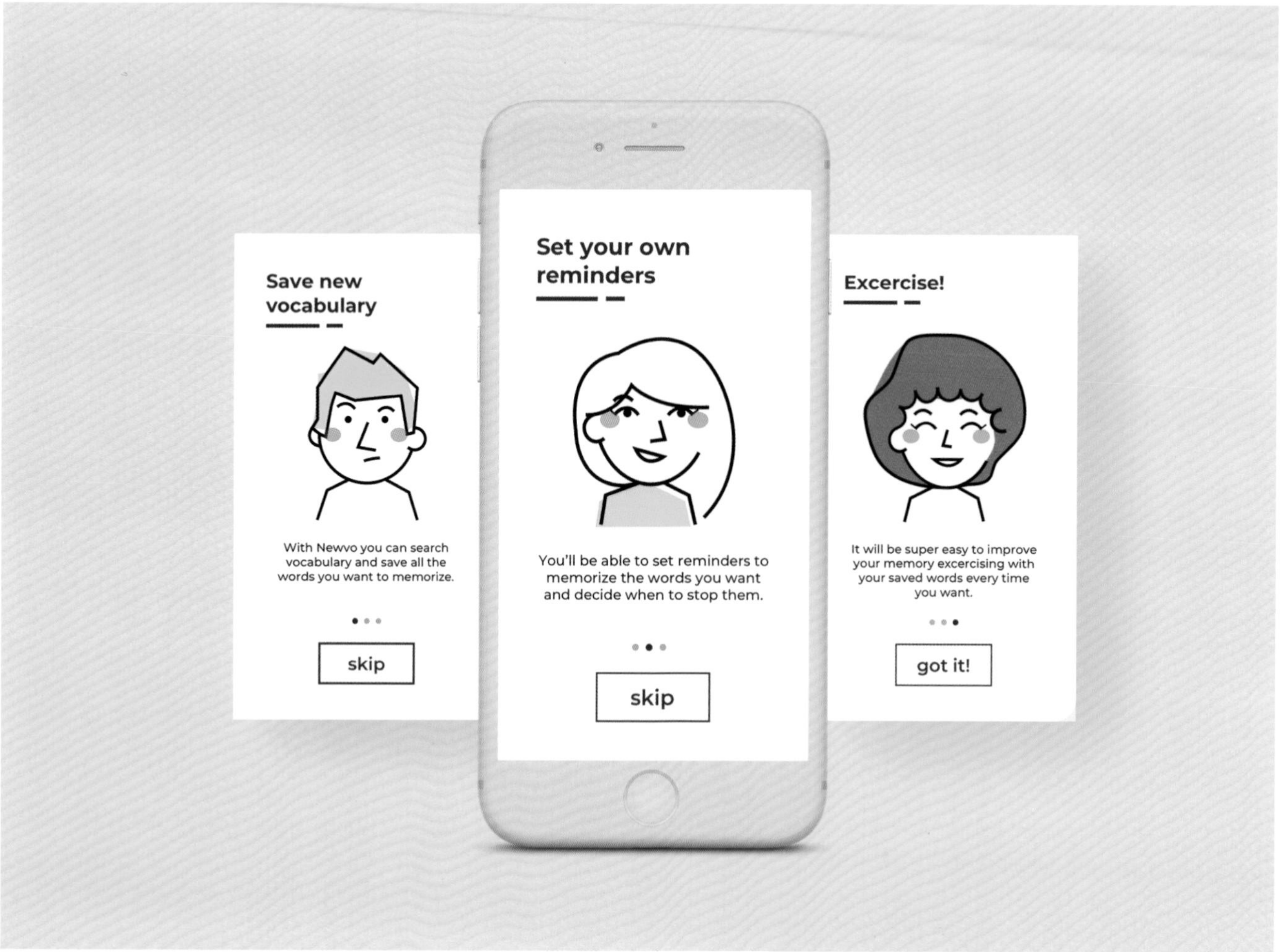
Save new vocabulary
With Newvo you can search vocabulary and save all the words you want to memorize.
skip
Set your own reminders
You'll be able to set reminders to memorize the words you want and decide when to stop them.
skip
Excercise!
It will be super easy to improve your memory excercising with your saved words every time you want.
got it!

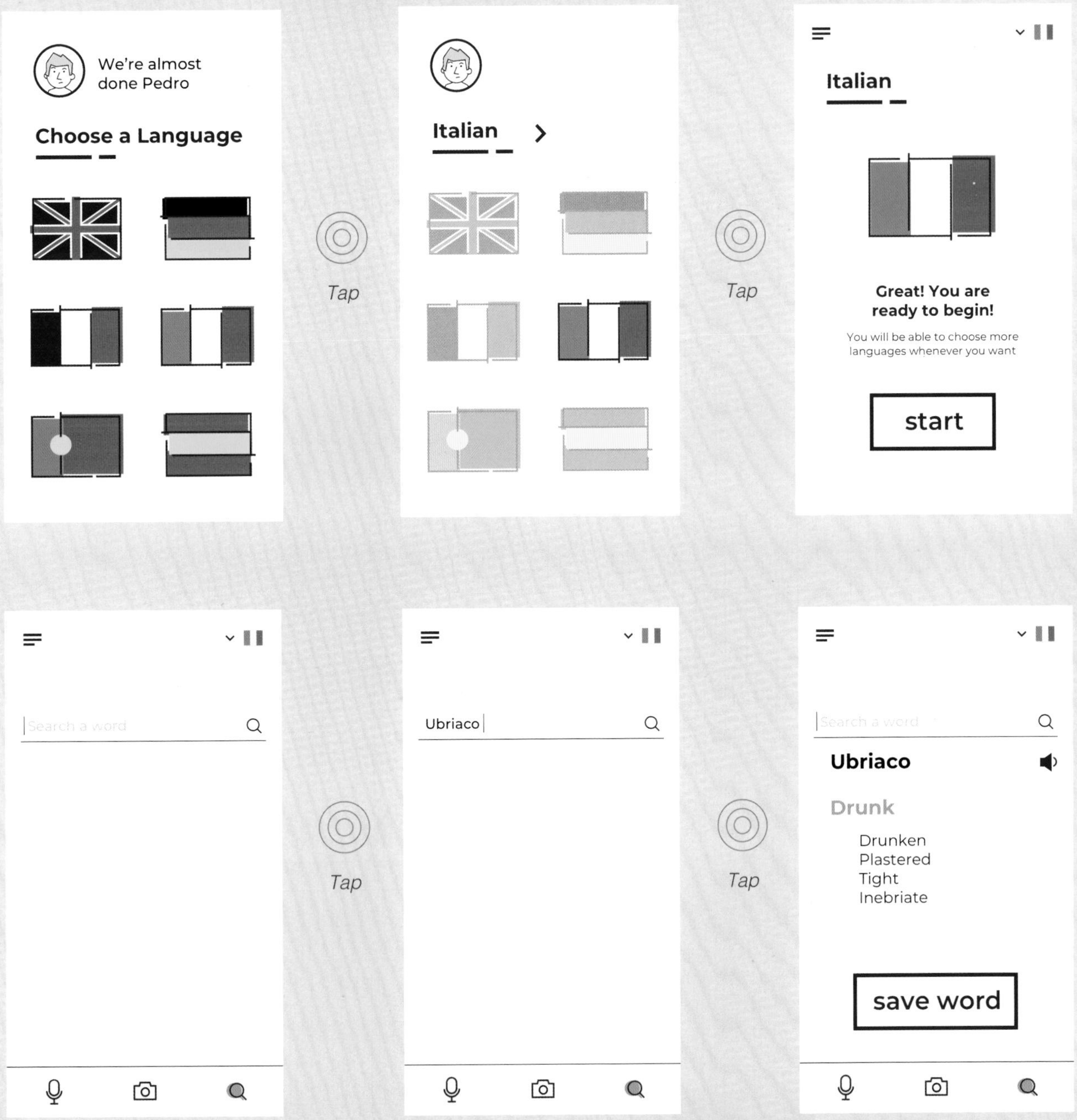
We're almost done Pedro
Choose a Language
Tap
Italian
Tap
Italian
Great! You are ready to begin!
You will be able to choose more languages whenever you want
start
Search a word
Tap
Ubriaco
Tap
Search a word
Ubriaco
Drunk
Drunken
Plastered
Tight
Inebriate
save word

The base of the project is the concept of simplicity, using just a few colours and a sans serif font. The aim of this layout is to make the user experience as agile and intuitive as possible. Blue and white are the main colours, looking for the easiest interaction. Illustration also adds a point of energy and usability.

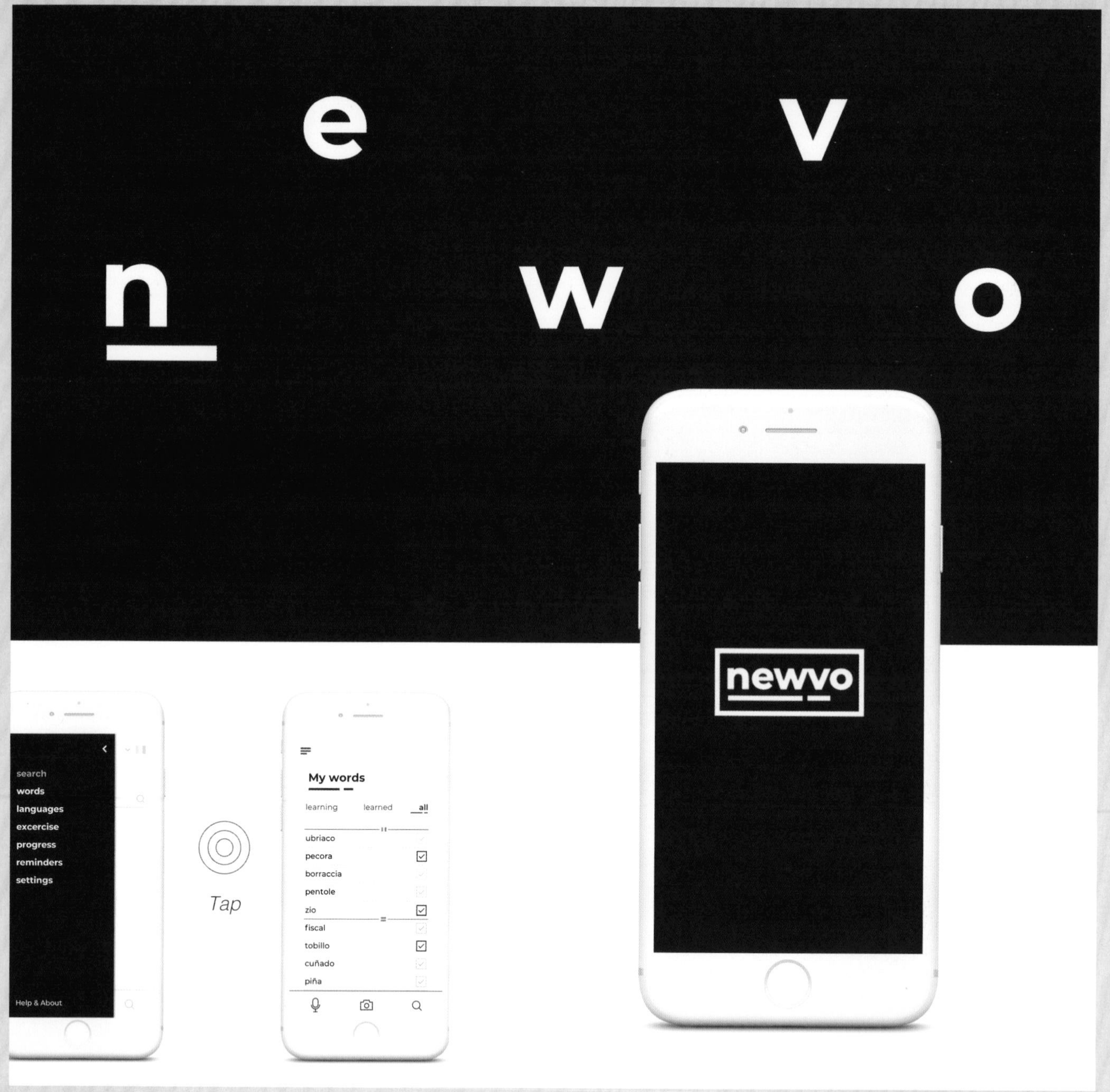
n
e
w
v
o
newvo
search
words
languages
excercise
progress
reminders
settings
Help & About
Tap
My words
learning
learned
all
ubriaco
pecora
borraccia
pentole
zio
fiscal
tobillo
cuñado
piña

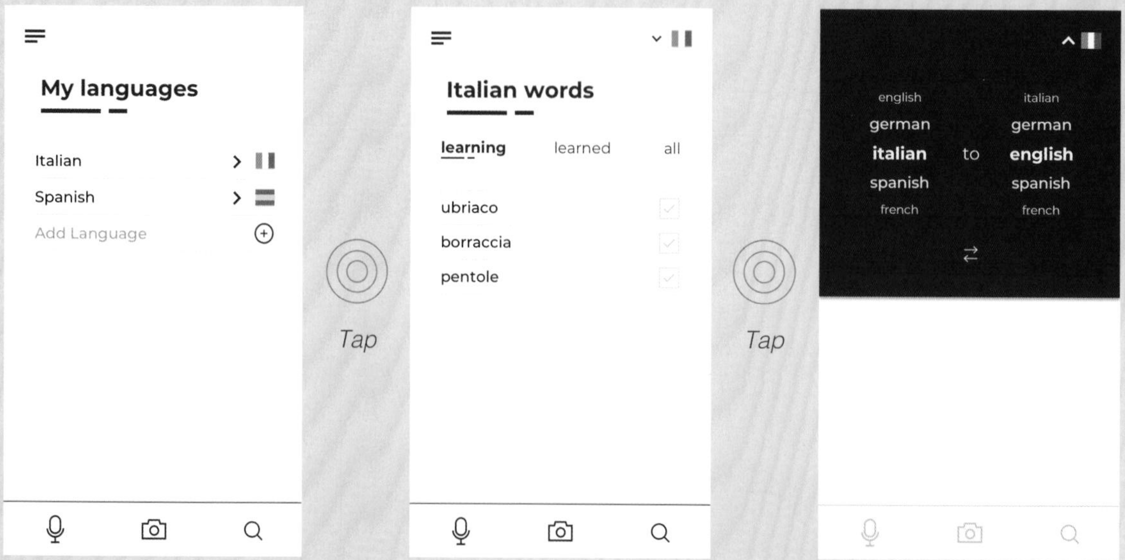
My languages
Italian
Spanish
Add Language
Tap
Italian words
learning
learned
all
ubriaco
borraccia
pentole
Tap
english
german
italian
spanish
french
to
italian
german
english
spanish
french

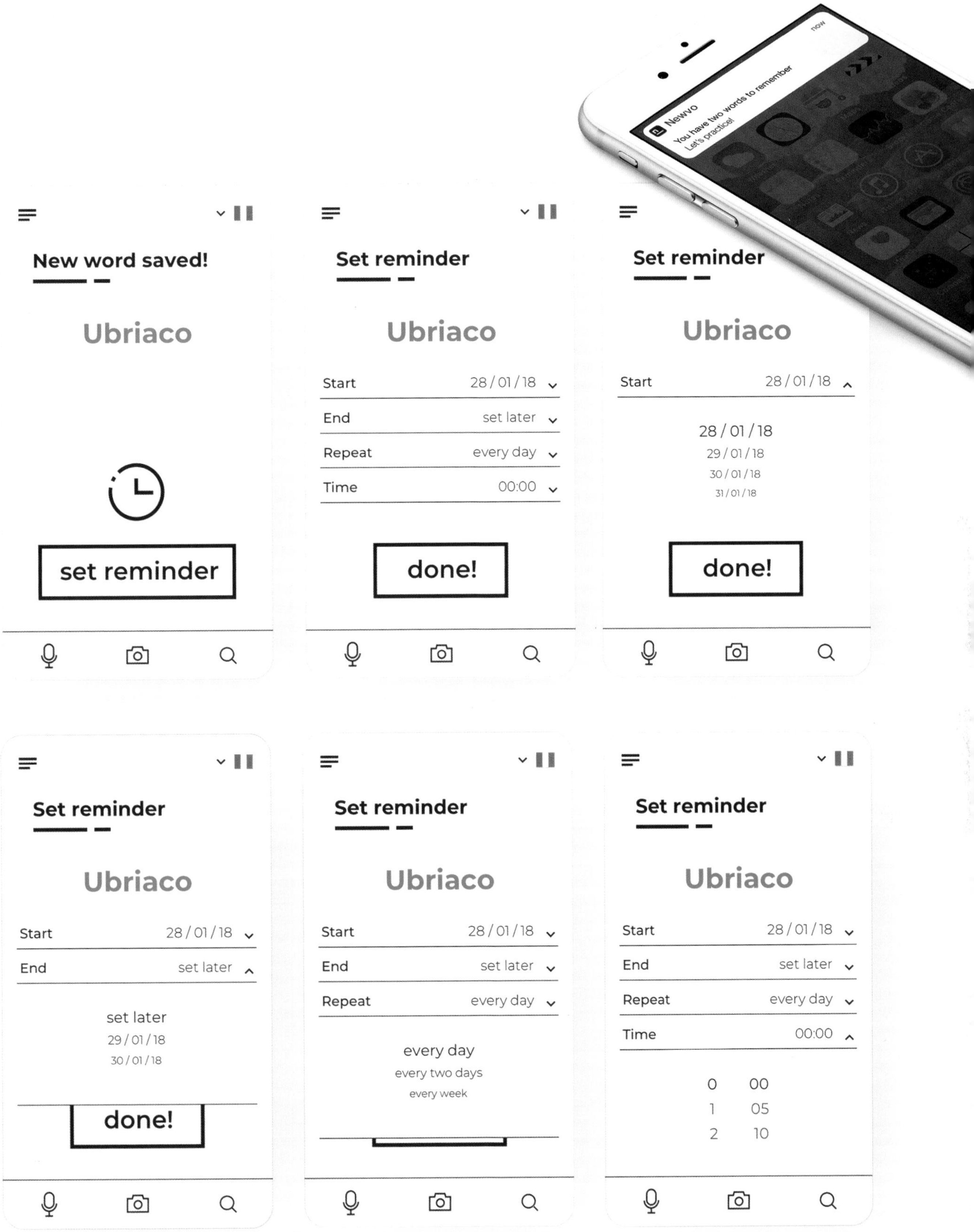
Newvo
You have two words to remember
Let's practice!
now
New word saved!
Ubriaco
set reminder
Set reminder
Ubriaco
Start 28 / 01 / 18
End set later
Repeat every day
Time 00:00
done!
Set reminder
Ubriaco
Start 28 / 01 / 18
28 / 01 / 18
29 / 01 / 18
30 / 01 / 18
31 / 01 / 18
done!
Set reminder
Ubriaco
Start 28 / 01 / 18
End set later
set later
29 / 01 / 18
30 / 01 / 18
done!
Set reminder
Ubriaco
Start 28 / 01 / 18
End set later
Repeat every day
every day
every two days
every week
Set reminder
Ubriaco
Start 28 / 01 / 18
End set later
Repeat every day
Time 00:00
0 00
1 05
2 10

Praha 3

Art Direction and Design
Jakub Carda

Development
COMTESYS s.r.o.

Client
Sprava Zbytkoveho Majetku MC Praha 3 a.s.

App Store

Prague is the capital and largest city in the Czech Republic and the 14th largest city in the European Union. Praha 3 is the official app of the City District of Prague 3. The district has an area of 650 hectares and lies east of the city center. The district has more than 80,000 residents who are the main target group of the mobile app, which provides useful information, such as district news, events updates, and helpful contacts (relevant departments, SOS).

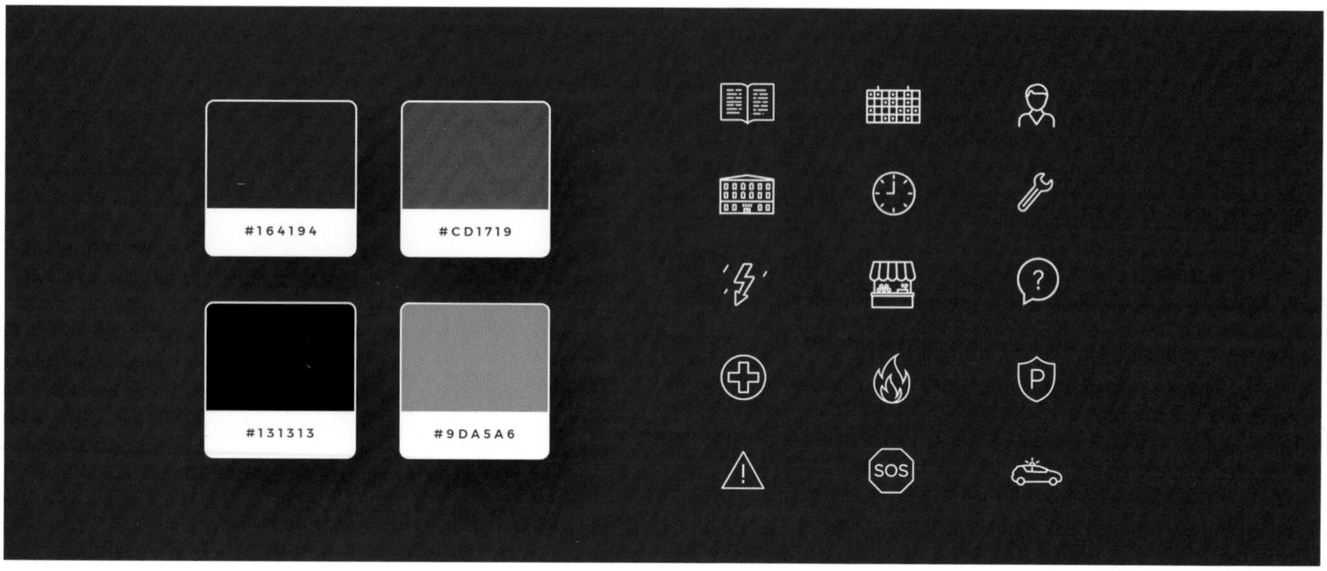
#164194
#CD1719
#131313
#9DA5A6
SOS

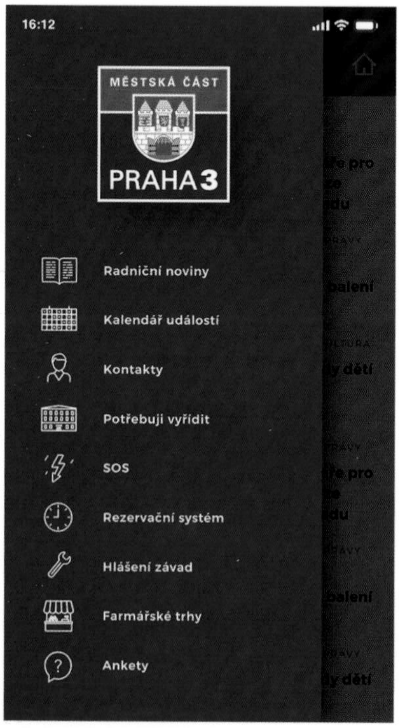
16:12
MĚSTSKÁ ČÁST
PRAHA3
Radniční noviny
Kalendář událostí
Kontakty
Potřebuji vyřídit
SOS
Rezervační systém
Hlášení závad
Farmářské trhy
Ankety

Tap

16:12
KALENDÁŘ UDÁLOSTÍ
Literáti z naší čtvrti - velmi prozaický večer Terezy Semotamové a Ivany Myškové - KC Vozovna
6.11.2017, 18:00 – 6.11.2017, 19:30
AKCE POŘÁDANÉ MČ
+ PŘIDAT DO KALENDÁŘE
Ivana Myšková je rodačka z Roudnice nad Labem. Vystudovala tvůrčí psaní a mediální komunikaci na Literární akademii v Praze. V letech 2007-2013 působila na stanici Vltava ČRO 3, kde přispívala do pořadu Mozaika a vytvářela i delší literární komponované pořady. V letech 2015-2016 pracovala pro projekt Praha město literatury. V současnosti spolupracuje s časopisem Hobulet, je

The colour scheme is based on the city district's brand manual. Main font was selected Montserrat for headlines, menus, buttons and short text. Secondary font is Abhaya Libre for paragraphs. The designer used two icon styles—linear for menu buttons and filled for not active elements.

16:12
MČ PRAHA 3
Radniční noviny
Kalendář událostí
Kontakty
Potřebuji vyřídit
SOS
Rezervační systém
Hlášení závad
Farmářské trhy
Ankety
RADNIČNÍ NOVINY
19.10.2017 | ÚŘEDNÍ DESKA
Na radnici se konaly semináře pro žadatele o dotace, žádosti lze podávat až do konce listopadu
19.10.2017 | ÚŘEDNÍ DESKA

Tap

16:12
KALENDÁŘ UDÁLOSTÍ
Ombudsman pro seniory - Informační centrum Praha 3 - Vinohrady
Dílna se Sofií: Adventní věnce - KC Vozovna
Den pro pěstounské rodiny - Nová Trojka
Jednání Rady městské části Praha 3
Fidži - země přátelských kanibalů (přednáška) - Informační centrum Praha 3 - Vinohrady
Laktační poradna - Nová Trojka

16:12
PŘEHLED ODDĚLENÍ
VYHLEDAT KONTAKT
Odbor bytů a nebytových prostor
Odbor dopravy
Odbor ekonomický
Odbor informatiky
Odbor kancelář úřadu
Odbor kontroly
Odbor kultury
Odbor majetku
Odbor občansko správní

Tap

Na radnici se konaly semináře pro žadatele o dotace, žádosti lze podávat až do konce listopadu
14.10.2017 | ÚŘEDNÍ DESKA
Oba semináře se konaly v 17:00, v sále zastupitelstva MČ Praha 3, Havlíčkovo náměstí 9. Účastnilo se jich kolem 50 zájemců.

16:12
SOS KONTAKTY
Záchranná služba 155
Hasiči 150
Policie ČR 158
Městská policie 156
Tísňová linka 112

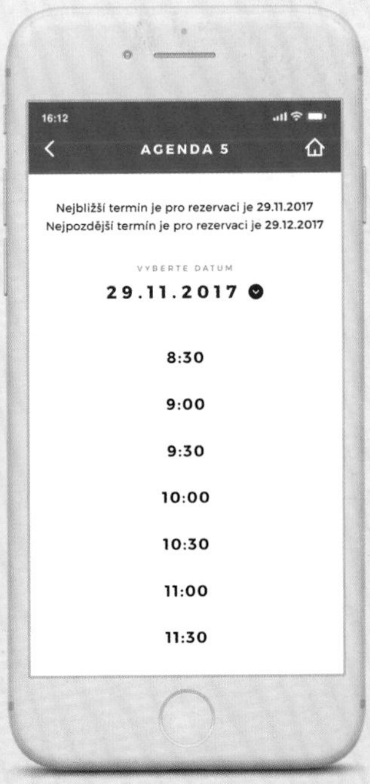

16:12
AGENDA 5
Nejbližší termín je pro rezervaci je 29.11.2017
Nejpozdější termín je pro rezervaci je 29.12.2017
VYBERTE DATUM
29.11.2017
8:30
9:00
9:30
10:00
10:30
11:00
11:30

Fitness App

Design
Huy Phan

Behance

The project is the designer's entry for a fitness app design challenge. This was the first time he challenged himself to design a whole app with hand drawn illustrations. The idea behind is like regular health apps that motivate people to do more exercise and track user's daily activities such as walking, running, number of steps, floors climbed, etc. Users could also participate in fitness challenges and track the record. The designer wanted the app to target general users, so he kept the app as clean as possible, easy to scan and use.

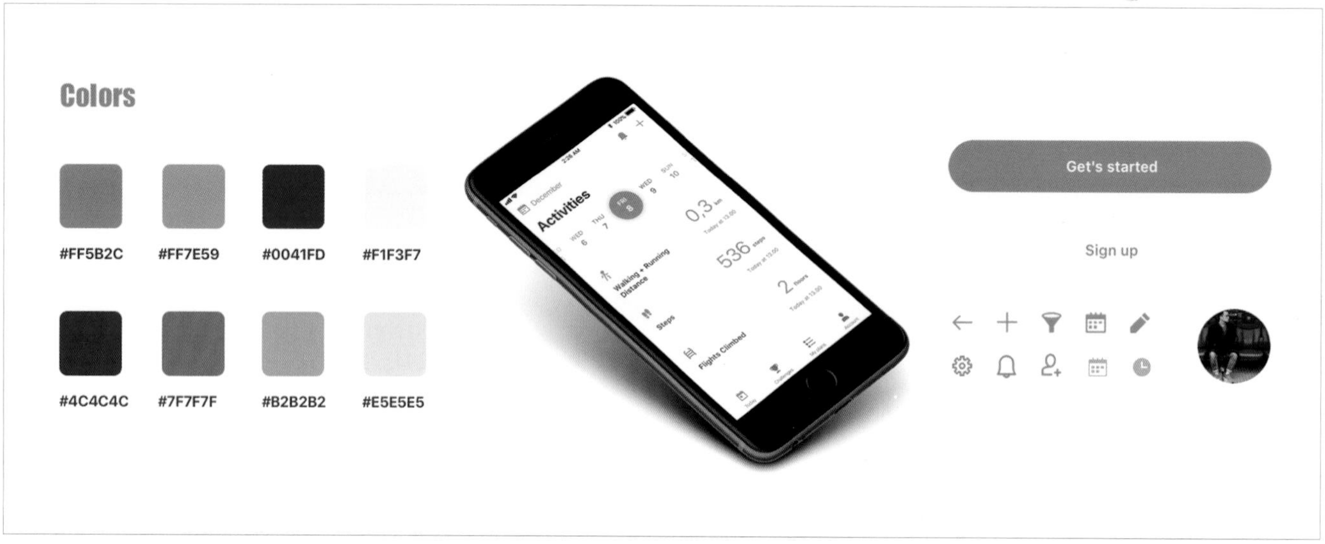

Colors
#FF5B2C
#FF7E59
#0041FD
#F1F3F7
#4C4C4C
#7F7F7F
#B2B2B2
#E5E5E5
Activities
Walking + Running Distance
0,3
536
2
Steps
Flights Climbed
Get's started
Sign up

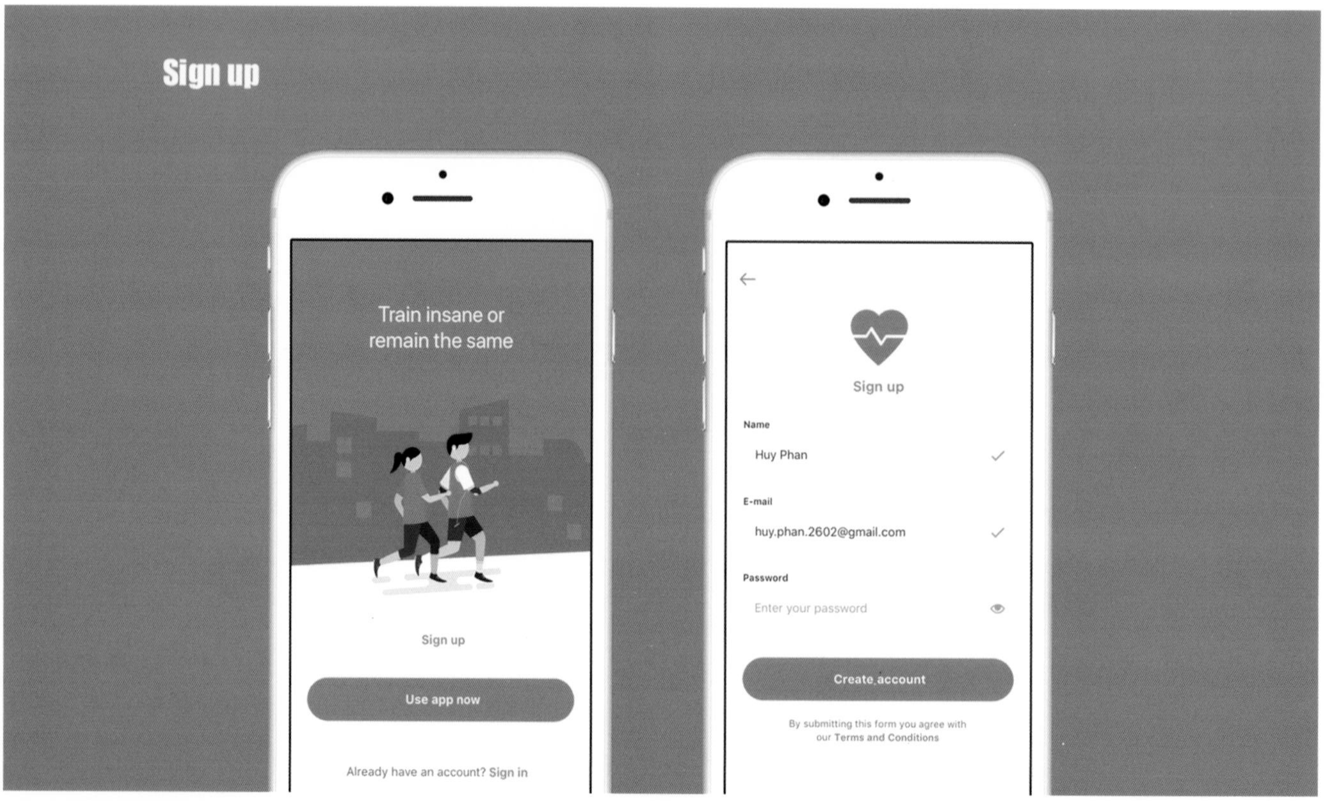

Sign up
Train insane or remain the same
Sign up
Use app now
Already have an account? Sign in
Sign up
Name
Huy Phan
E-mail
huy.phan.2602@gmail.com
Password
Enter your password
Create account
By submitting this form you agree with our Terms and Conditions

Onboardings

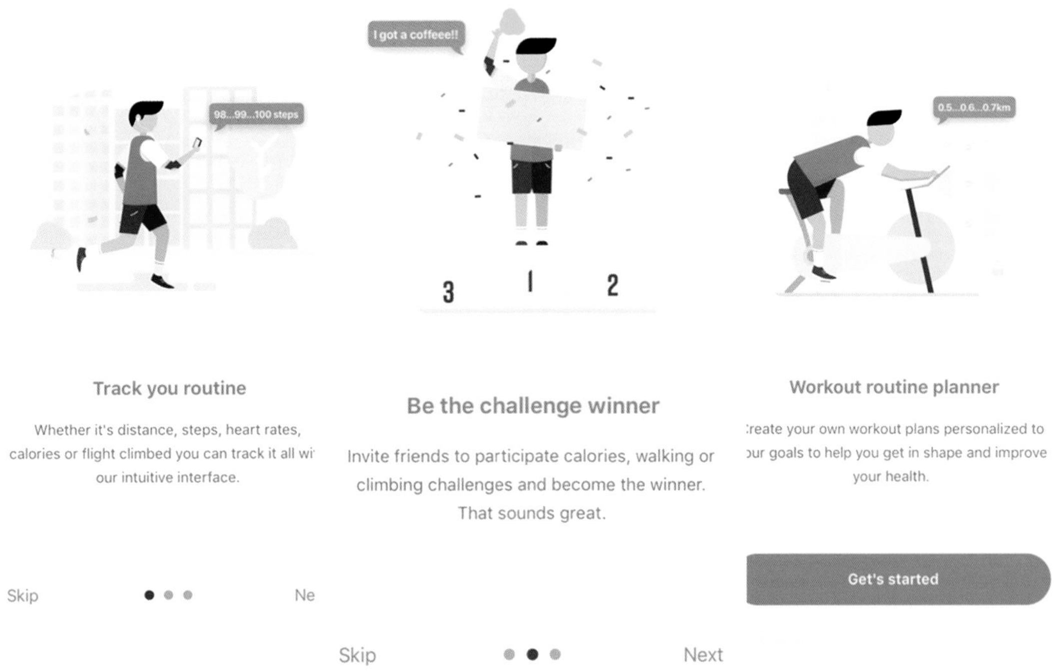
98...99...100 steps
I got a coffeee!!
3
1
2
0.5...0.6...0.7km
Track you routine
Whether it's distance, steps, heart rates, calories or flight climbed you can track it all wi our intuitive interface.
Be the challenge winner
Invite friends to participate calories, walking or climbing challenges and become the winner. That sounds great.
Workout routine planner
:reate your own workout plans personalized to our goals to help you get in shape and improve your health.
Get's started
Skip
Ne
Skip
Next

9:41
Walking + Running
Week
Month
Year
Thu, Dec 1st - Thu, Dec 8th
F S S M T W T
0.6
avg
Today
This week: 4,5 km
Today
Wednesday
Tuesday
Monday
Sunday
Saturday
0,3 km
0,65 km
0,8 km
0,7 km
1,2 km
0,6 km
9:41
Distance challenge
PARTICIPANTS
5
CURRENT RANK
1st
TIME LEFT
1d 15h
Who walks the longest distance got the prize dudes. Come on!!!
1st
2nd
3rd
Huy Phan
1.2 km
Santi Samuel
0.9 km
Miguel
0.5 km
David Henry
0.4 km
Cristina
0.35 km
9:41
Challenges
Distance challenge
3 hours 2 minutes left
Climbing challenge
1 days 15 hours left
Fight for a dinner
4 days 4 hours left
9:41
New challenge
Cancel
Create
Challenge name
Type the challenge name
Type
Distance - km
From
20/12/2018
11.00 AM
11.00 AM
9:41
Plans
Fri, Dec 8th
Walk 5km
75%
1250km left
3 days ago
5000 steps
50%
2500 steps left

On the Angel's Wings

Design
Artur Konariev

Client
hillsong.com

App Store

On the Angel's Wings is an app created for Christmas Charity Event. This app is born out of good will to help children in need, and also make the donation more convenient and safe. The designer has created avatars for kids, describing their stories and dreams. When users are scrolling the feed, they get a unique choice whose wish they would like to fulfill, donate in an easy way and see how dreams are coming true.

How to make the Dreams come true
Dreams must come true
Skip
You make a Christmas Dream come true

How to make the Dreams come true
Dreams must come true
Skip

How to donate
Your donation is the surest way to make another Dream come true
Skip

How to become a Volunteer
Join our team of Good Angels
I'm in!

To ensure users get positive feeling during the process, the designer developed contemporary and functional UI design. He used tender shades of red and pink colours because the app is expected to be used in time of Christmas. To bring special holiday mood, he added adorable Christmas illustrations as well. The app icons not only match with the overall design but also remain their usability.

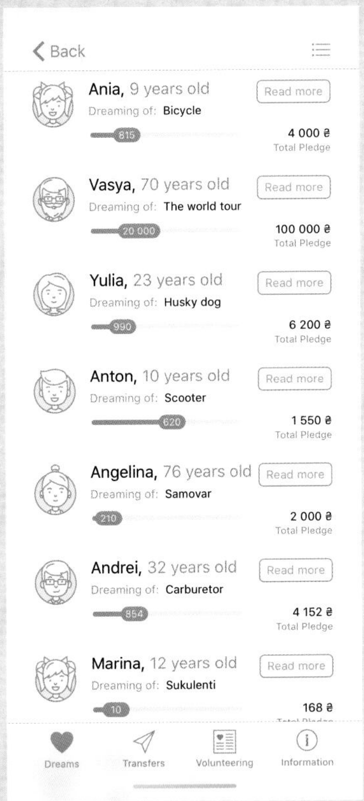
Back
Ania, 9 years old
Dreaming of: Bicycle
Read more
815
4 000 ₴
Total Pledge
Vasya, 70 years old
Dreaming of: The world tour
Read more
20 000
100 000 ₴
Total Pledge
Yulia, 23 years old
Dreaming of: Husky dog
Read more
990
6 200 ₴
Total Pledge
Anton, 10 years old
Dreaming of: Scooter
Read more
620
1 550 ₴
Total Pledge
Angelina, 76 years old
Dreaming of: Samovar
Read more
210
2 000 ₴
Total Pledge
Andrei, 32 years old
Dreaming of: Carburetor
Read more
854
4 152 ₴
Total Pledge
Marina, 12 years old
Dreaming of: Sukulenti
Read more
10
168 ₴
Dreams
Transfers
Volunteering
Information

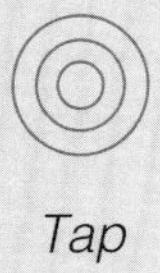
Tap

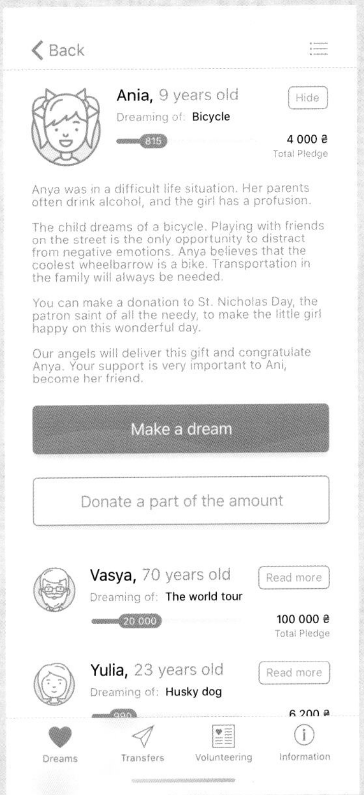
Back
Ania, 9 years old
Dreaming of: Bicycle
Hide
815
4 000 ₴
Total Pledge
Anya was in a difficult life situation. Her parents often drink alcohol, and the girl has a profusion.
The child dreams of a bicycle. Playing with friends on the street is the only opportunity to distract from negative emotions. Anya believes that the coolest wheelbarrow is a bike. Transportation in the family will always be needed.
You can make a donation to St. Nicholas Day, the patron saint of all the needy, to make the little girl happy on this wonderful day.
Our angels will deliver this gift and congratulate Anya. Your support is very important to Ani, become her friend.
Make a dream
Donate a part of the amount
Vasya, 70 years old
Dreaming of: The world tour
Read more
20 000
100 000 ₴
Total Pledge
Yulia, 23 years old
Dreaming of: Husky dog
Read more
Dreams
Transfers
Volunteering
Information

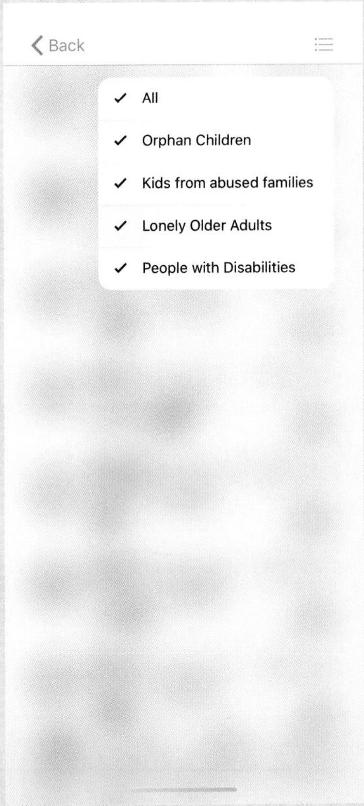
Back
All
Orphan Children
Kids from abused families
Lonely Older Adults
People with Disabilities

Back
Make a donation
Each donation - is one more dream realized!
Specify the donation amount:
20
₴
Donate
Dreams
Transfers
Volunteering
Information

Back
Become a volunteer
Details of volunteering
An angel means an "envoy", therefore, by realizing the dreams of people from the most vulnerable, we are conventionally called "good angels" who are sent for good deeds.
On the eve of holidays so many people in our environment need attention and support. Together, we will be able to bring good news to hundreds of homes, shelters, hospitals, centers where single elderly people live, and so on.
Become a volunteer
Dreams
Transfers
Volunteering
Information

Back
About the project "On the Angel's wings"
Our requisites
PRIVATBANK, 1D HRUSHEVSKOHO STR., KYIV, 01001, UKRAINE
SWIFT CODE/BIC: PBANUA2X
Our contacts
ARTEMIY KIRKOV
index 08401, Ukraine, area Kyivska, city Pereiaslav-Khmelnytskyi, street Industrialna, building 12, flat 1
Change the city
Dreams
Transfers
Volunteering
Information

Routetrip

Design
Irene Molina

Behance

Routetrip is an app designed for real travelers, a useful tool to discover new places around the world. The app helps users plan their trips, save their favourite places while they are traveling, and share interesting things with friends. It also creates automatically lists of cities and countries based on users' interactions and allows them to check travelers' data and statistics to meet new travelers, and compete against their friends.

Thailand
15th - 20th January 2017
Alex Price
Edit Profile
New York
15 - 20 January 2017
Vietnam
13th - 29th October 2017
Japan
Places
Love it
Your trips

New York
150
5+
Bubby's
Best pancakes ever! Fluffiness in my mouth.
#newyork #pancakes
Day 1
Day 2
Day 3
New york
Bubby's
Places
Love it
Your trips

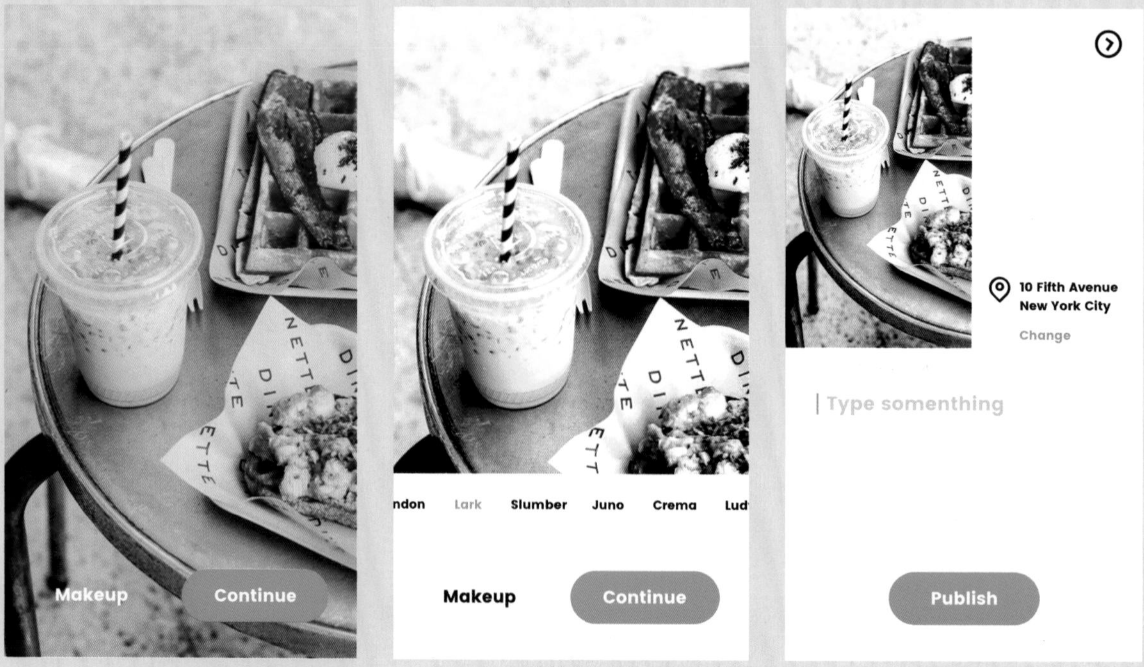

Makeup
Continue
Lark
Slumber
Juno
Crema
Makeup
Continue
10 Fifth Avenue
New York City
Change
Type somenthing
Publish

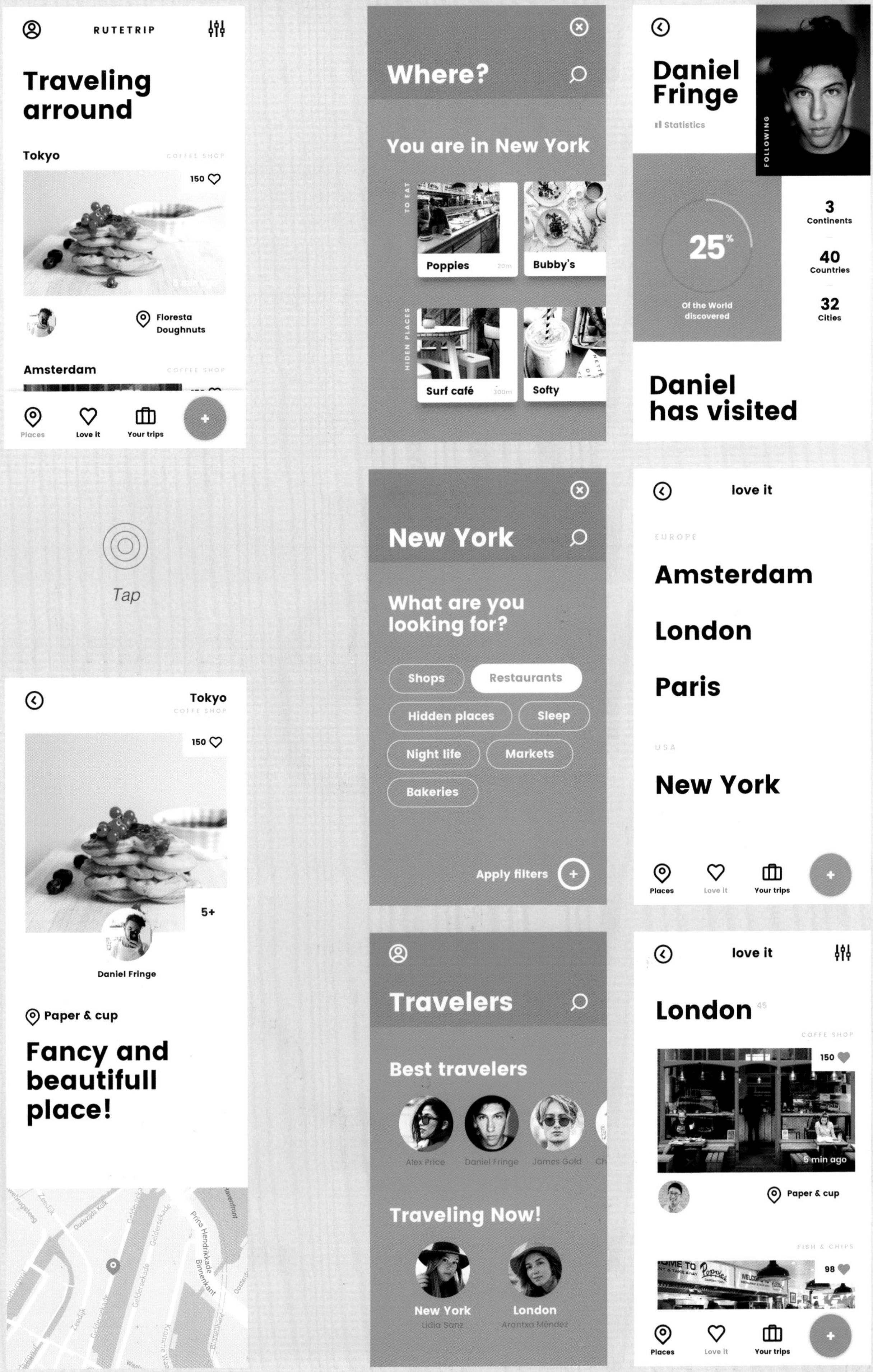
RUTETRIP
Traveling arround
Tokyo
COFFEE SHOP
150
Floresta Doughnuts
Amsterdam
COFFEE SHOP
Places
Love it
Your trips
Where?
You are in New York
TO EAT
Poppies
Bubby's
HIDEN PLACES
Surf café
Softy
Daniel Fringe
Statistics
FOLLOWING
25%
Of the World discovered
3
Continents
40
Countries
32
Cities
Daniel has visited
Tap
New York
What are you looking for?
Shops
Restaurants
Hidden places
Sleep
Night life
Markets
Bakeries
Apply filters
love it
EUROPE
Amsterdam
London
Paris
USA
New York
Places
Love it
Your trips
Tokyo
COFFE SHOP
150
5+
Daniel Fringe
Paper & cup
Fancy and beautifull place!
Travelers
Best travelers
Alex Price
Daniel Fringe
James Gold
Traveling Now!
New York
Lidia Sanz
London
Arantxa Méndez
love it
London
COFFE SHOP
150
5 min ago
Paper & cup
FISH & CHIPS
98
Places
Love it
Your trips

Cowboy

Design Agency
Ueno

Creative Direction
David Navarro

Design
Kwok Yin Mak, Dac Davy, Marco Coppeto, Arnar Ólafsson, Romain Briaux

Photography
Tom Kubik

Copywriting
Jaime Aguiló, Zoe Finkel

App Store

Cowboy is a startup that is creating the next generation of electric bicycles. Based in Brussels, Belgium, the company's first product is a beautiful motor-assisted bicycle designed to appeal to new buyers with a more beautiful design, a lower price, and better technology. They approached Ueno with a name and a prototype. The two teams worked closely on all aspects of the brand, including branding, marketing materials, photography, website design and mobile app design.

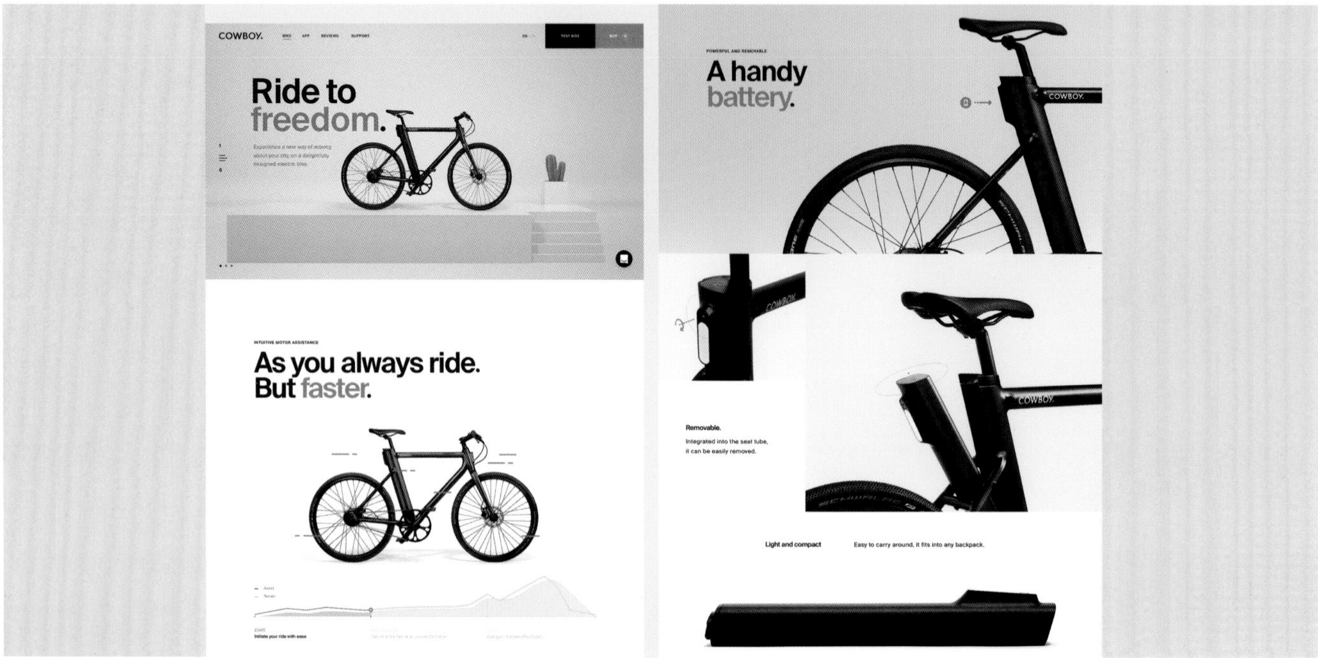
COWBOY.
Ride to freedom.
As you always ride. But faster.
A handy battery.
Removable.
Integrated into the seat tube, it can be easily removed.
Light and compact
Easy to carry around, it fits into any backpack.

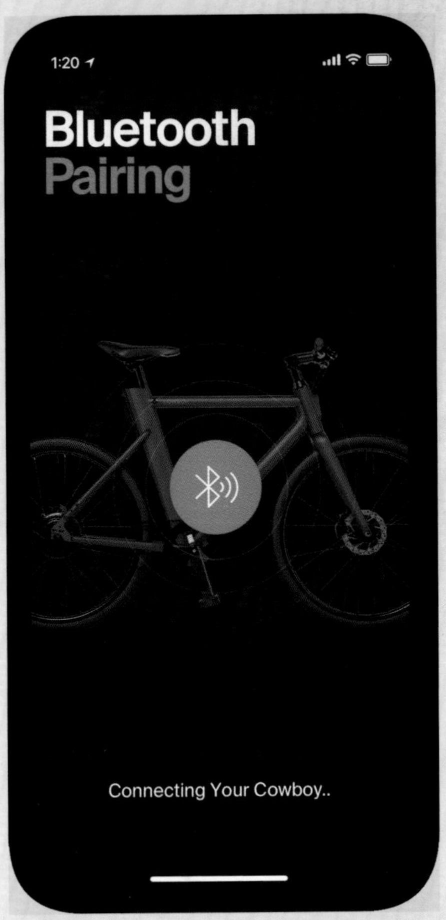
1:20
Bluetooth
Pairing
Connecting Your Cowboy..

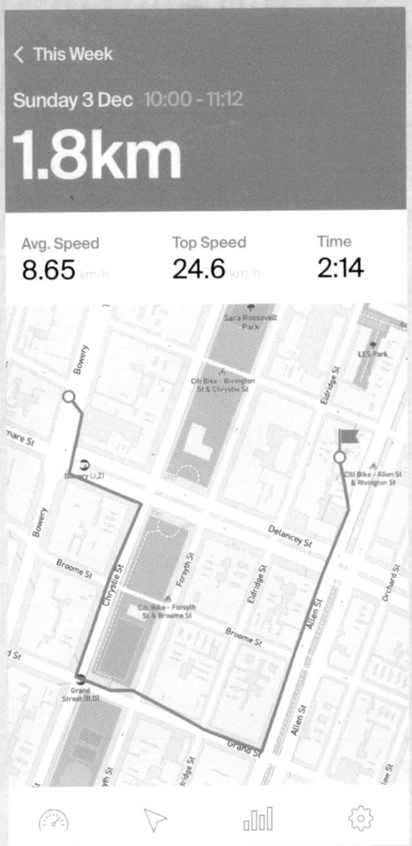
This Week
Sunday 3 Dec 10:00 - 11:12
1.8km
Avg. Speed
8.65
Top Speed
24.6
Time
2:14

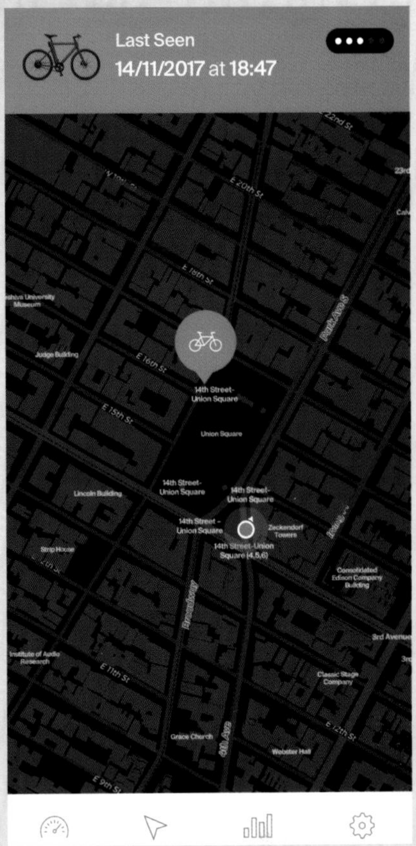
Last Seen
14/11/2017 at 18:47

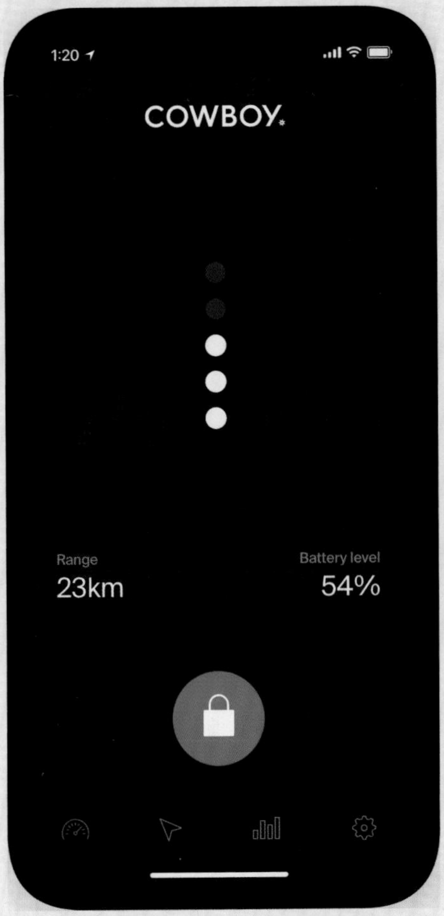
1:20
COWBOY.
Range
23km
Battery level
54%

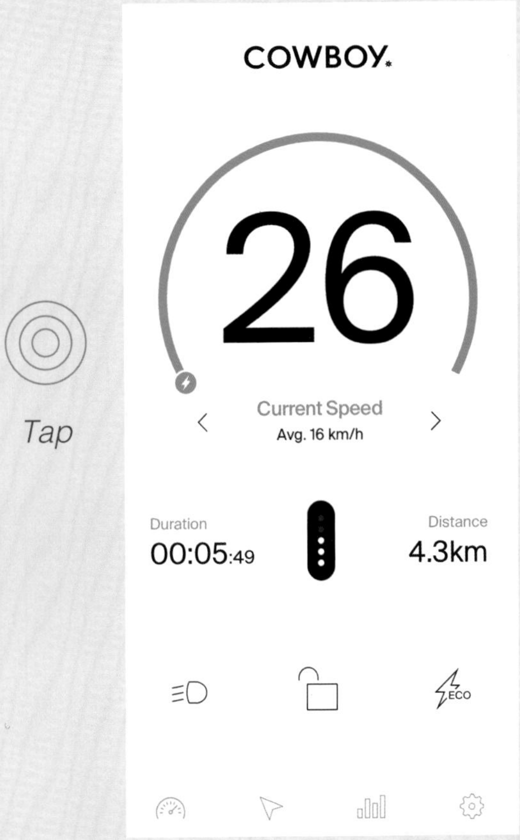
Tap
COWBOY.
26
Current Speed
Avg. 16 km/h
Duration
00:05:49
Distance
4.3km
ECO

The marketing and e-commerce website, and the app consist of a big part of the Cowboy user experience. Ueno made use of unexpected colour combinations, bold typography, fun photography and clean layout. The Cowboy team spent time with Ueno's product designers in Reykjavík to hone the user experience and features, resulting in an app that Cowboy riders use to prevent theft, control the bike's various features, and navigate using GPS.

MCQ – Musée de la civilisation

Design Agency
lg2

Creative Direction
Nicolas Baldovini

Art Direction
Vincent Belanger

UX Design
Mathieu Parent

App Store

In an effort to provide consumers with more enriched content, Musée de la civilisation launched the My MCQ app. The app provides its users with real-time access to its various exhibitions, allowing them to select their individual interests for more personalized content, consult maps outlining the museum as well as learn about the different exhibitions and their schedules, and finally, to better discover the London Calling exhibit by interacting with augmented-reality content. It's not just an app, the agency lg2 took a novel angle and designed a companion that would accompany visitors in a unique way and provide a customized experience.

Branded expositions pages
HERGÉ
DU 21 JUIN AU 22 OCT
C'EST NOTRE HISTOIRE
DU 9 AU 23 DÉC
C'EST NOTRE HISTOIRE
DU 9 AU 23 DÉC
DALLAIRE
DU 6 DÉC AU 26 AOÛT

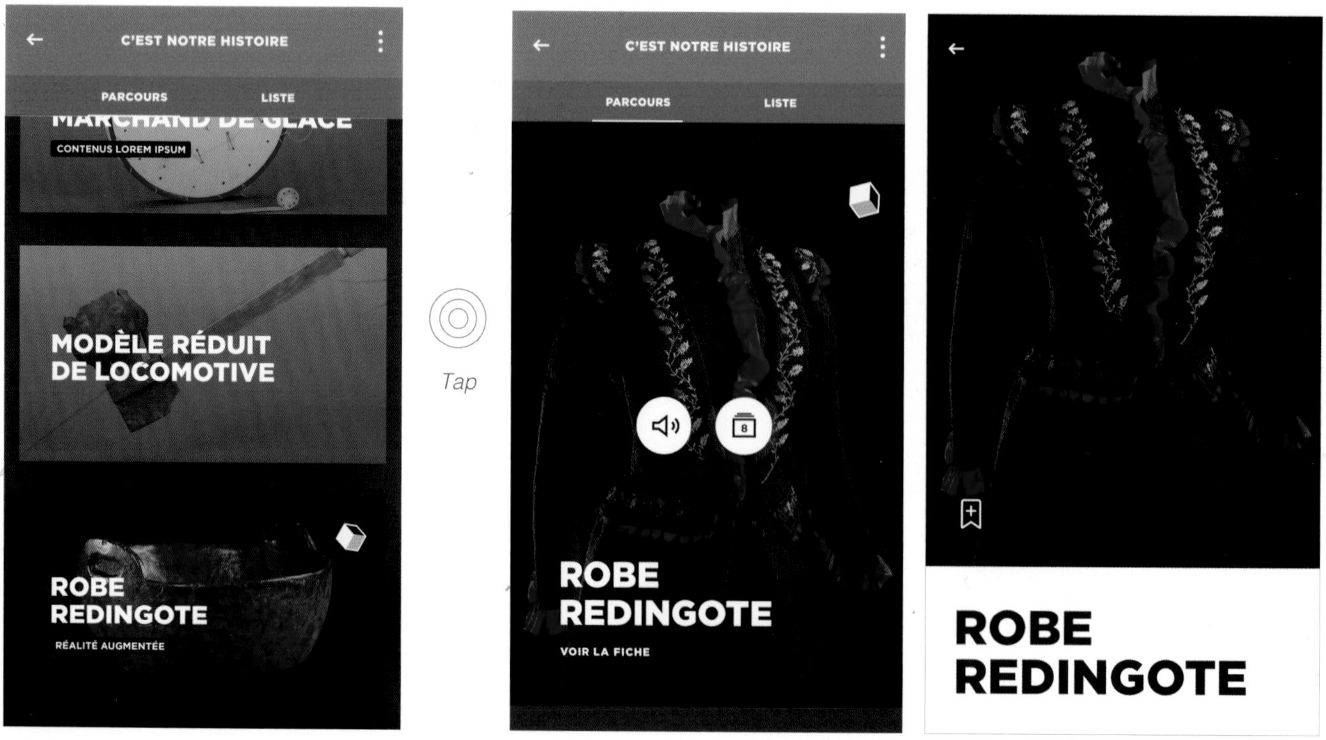

C'EST NOTRE HISTOIRE
PARCOURS
LISTE
CONTENUS LOREM IPSUM
MODÈLE RÉDUIT DE LOCOMOTIVE
ROBE REDINGOTE
RÉALITÉ AUGMENTÉE
Tap
C'EST NOTRE HISTOIRE
PARCOURS
LISTE
ROBE REDINGOTE
VOIR LA FICHE
ROBE REDINGOTE

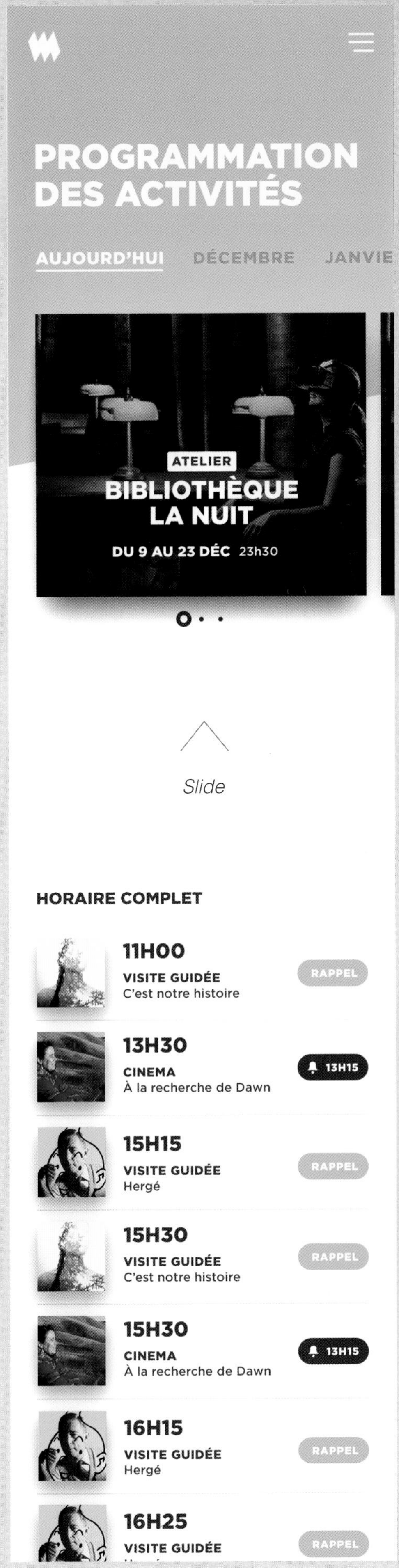
PROGRAMMATION DES ACTIVITÉS
AUJOURD'HUI
DÉCEMBRE
JANVIE
ATELIER
BIBLIOTHÈQUE LA NUIT
DU 9 AU 23 DÉC 23h30
Slide
HORAIRE COMPLET
11H00
VISITE GUIDÉE
C'est notre histoire
RAPPEL
13H30
CINEMA
À la recherche de Dawn
13H15
15H15
VISITE GUIDÉE
Hergé
RAPPEL
15H30
VISITE GUIDÉE
C'est notre histoire
RAPPEL
15H30
CINEMA
À la recherche de Dawn
13H15
16H15
VISITE GUIDÉE
Hergé
RAPPEL
16H25
VISITE GUIDÉE
RAPPEL

CARTE
BOL LOREM
ROBE REDINGOTE
6
2

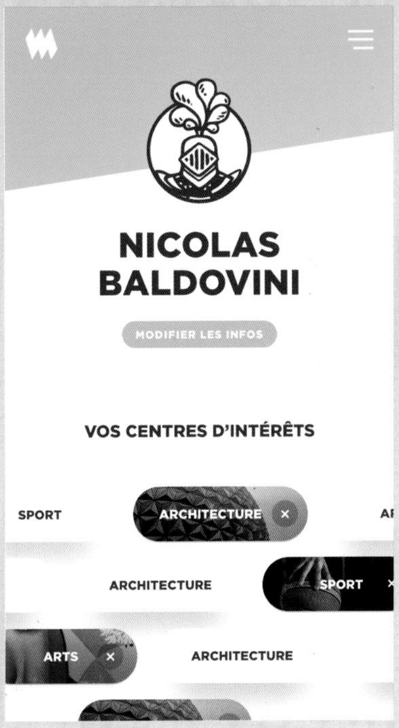
NICOLAS BALDOVINI
MODIFIER LES INFOS
VOS CENTRES D'INTÉRÊTS
SPORT
ARCHITECTURE
ARCHITECTURE
SPORT
ARTS
ARCHITECTURE

BONJOUR NICOLAS,
AMUSE-TOI!
Photo: activité de costume
ÉVITE LA FILE D'ATTENTE
AJOUTE TON BILLET

PARCOURS INTERACTIFS
L'EXPO QUI DÉROUTE
DU 9 AU 23 DÉC

Planeta Kino

App Store

Art Direction
Nastya Żerebecki (spiilka design büro)

Digital Concept
Vladimir Smirnov, Roma Sapielkin (spiilka design büro)

Programming
Ivan Tkachenko, Max Matveev (Youshido)

Project Management
Natalie Khadzhyoglo (Youshido)

Technical Direction
Sergey Pavlov (Planeta Kino)

Planeta Kino is the new app for Planet Cinema, which allows users to buy tickets, check-in at the movie hall and receive bonuses for purchasing. The design and programming team made the following key changes: one handed use UX, smart UI animation, intuitive purchasing flow and minimalistic art direction.

Taking consideration of large sizes of phone screens, as well as popcorn in users' hands, the app's navigation is easy to use with only one hand. For the user research, the planning horizon suggested how many dates the user is interested in, and the deep user journey research showed which functions should be more visible on all screens.

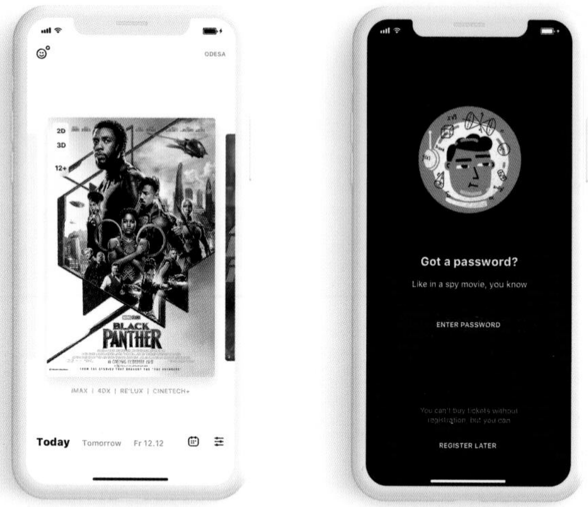

ODESA
IMAX | 4DX | RE'LUX | CINETECH+
Today Tomorrow Fr 12.12
Got a password?
Like in a spy movie, you know
ENTER PASSWORD
REGISTER LATER

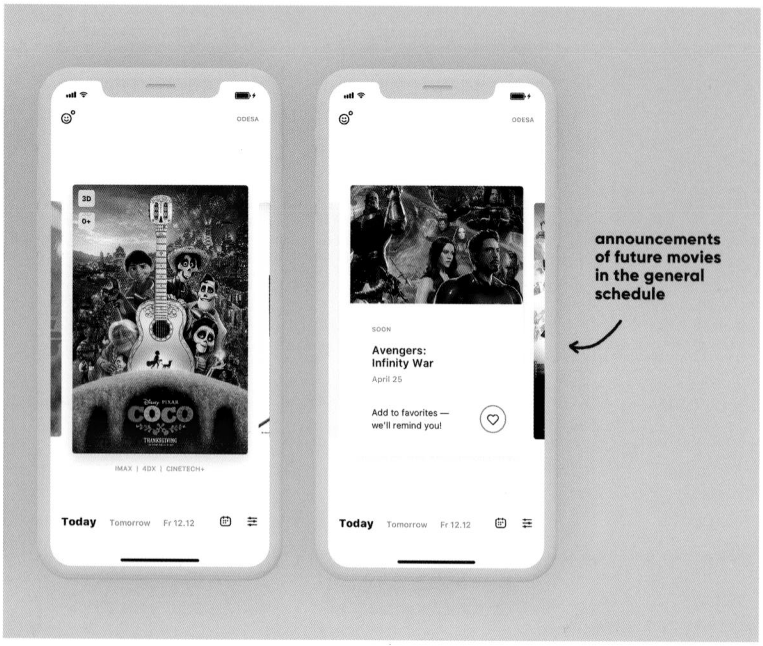

ODESA
IMAX | 4DX | CINETECH+
Today Tomorrow Fr 12.12
SOON
Avengers: Infinity War
April 25
Add to favorites — we'll remind you!
announcements of future movies in the general schedule

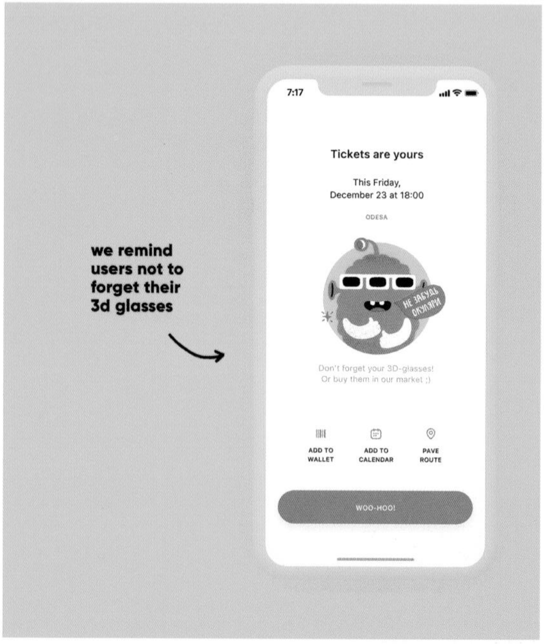

we remind users not to forget their 3d glasses
7:17
Tickets are yours
This Friday, December 23 at 18:00
ODESA
ADD TO WALLET
ADD TO CALENDAR
PAVE ROUTE
WOO-HOO!

Art direction was built on minimalistic solutions, but fancy UI animations, witty copyrights and colourful ironic illustrations added friendly atmosphere and nice perception. Cosmo Pigeon, Astronana, Wolf from Space are the newly developed characters for the app, and become friendly symbols of cinema chain.

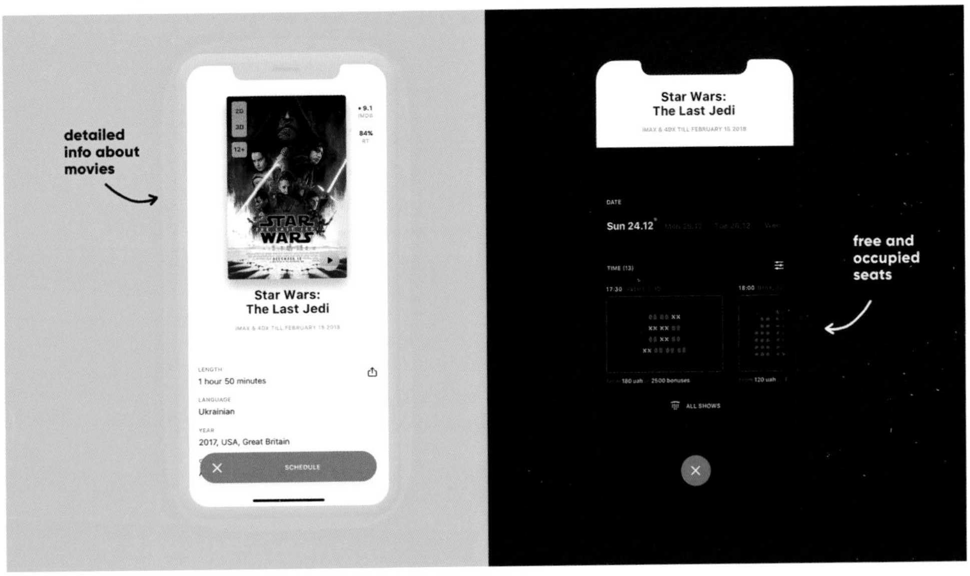
detailed info about movies
Star Wars:
The Last Jedi
LENGTH
1 hour 50 minutes
LANGUAGE
Ukrainian
YEAR
2017, USA, Great Britain
SCHEDULE
Star Wars:
The Last Jedi
DATE
Sun 24.12
ALL SHOWS
free and occupied seats

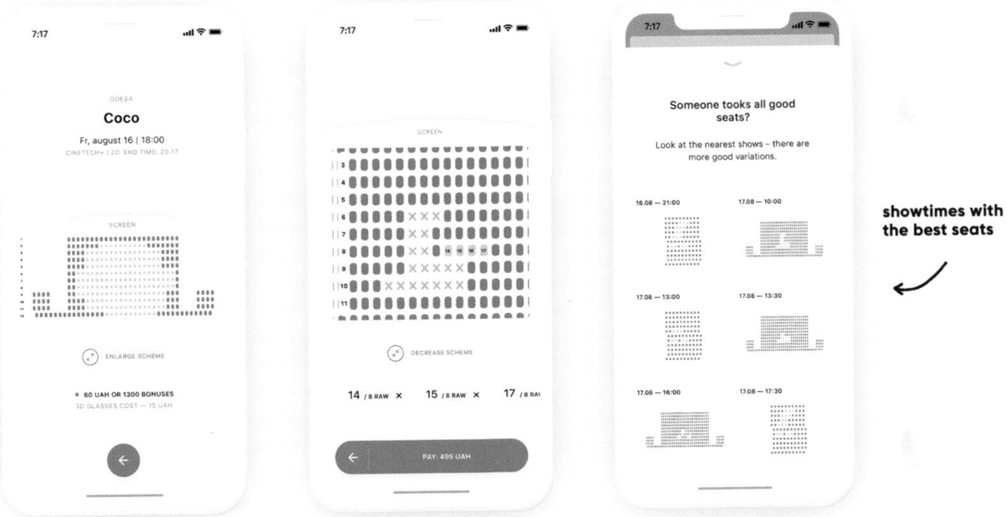
7:17
ODESA
Coco
Fr, august 16 | 18:00
SCREEN
ENLARGE SCHEME
60 UAH OR 1300 BONUSES
DECREASE SCHEME
PAY: 495 UAH
Someone tooks all good seats?
Look at the nearest shows - there are more good variations.
showtimes with the best seats

purchased tickets - on the first screen
7:17
ODESA
YOUR TICKETS
Solo: A Star Wars Story
16.05.2018 | 21:30
Odesa
hall: Cinetech 7
row: 6, seats 12, 13
Today
Tomorrow
Fr 12.12
Solo:
A Star Wars Story
Friday, May 16 | 18:00
Hall: Cinetech 8
Raw: 08 Seats: 06, 07
RETURN TICKETS
seat
raw
06
08
2030901081974
07
SOLO: A STAR WARS STORY
2030901081975
Your seats are here, enjoy!
SCREEN
app helps users find their seats

RICEPO

Concept
RICEPO LLC

Design
Yong Yang

Development
Hao Chen, Wentao Liu, Dhanashree Marathe

App Store

RICEPO is the largest authentic Asian food ordering and delivery platform in North America. The design team wanted to refresh the design system of the app in order to differentiate themselves from the fierce competition.

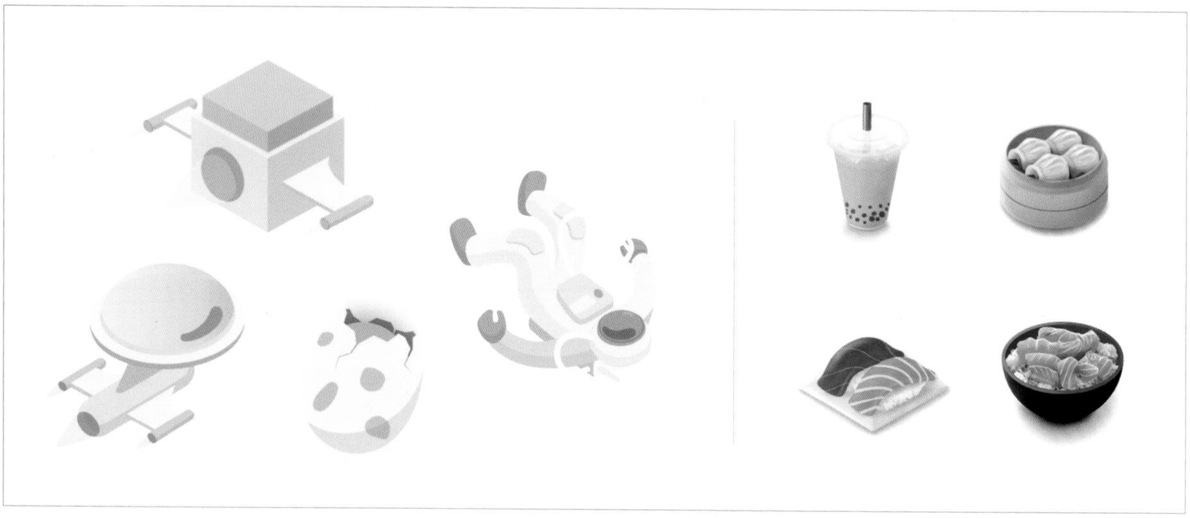

ABOUT DRIVER RESTAURANT SUPPORT
En
RICEPO
Order chinese food like from home.
GET APP
Also available for Android

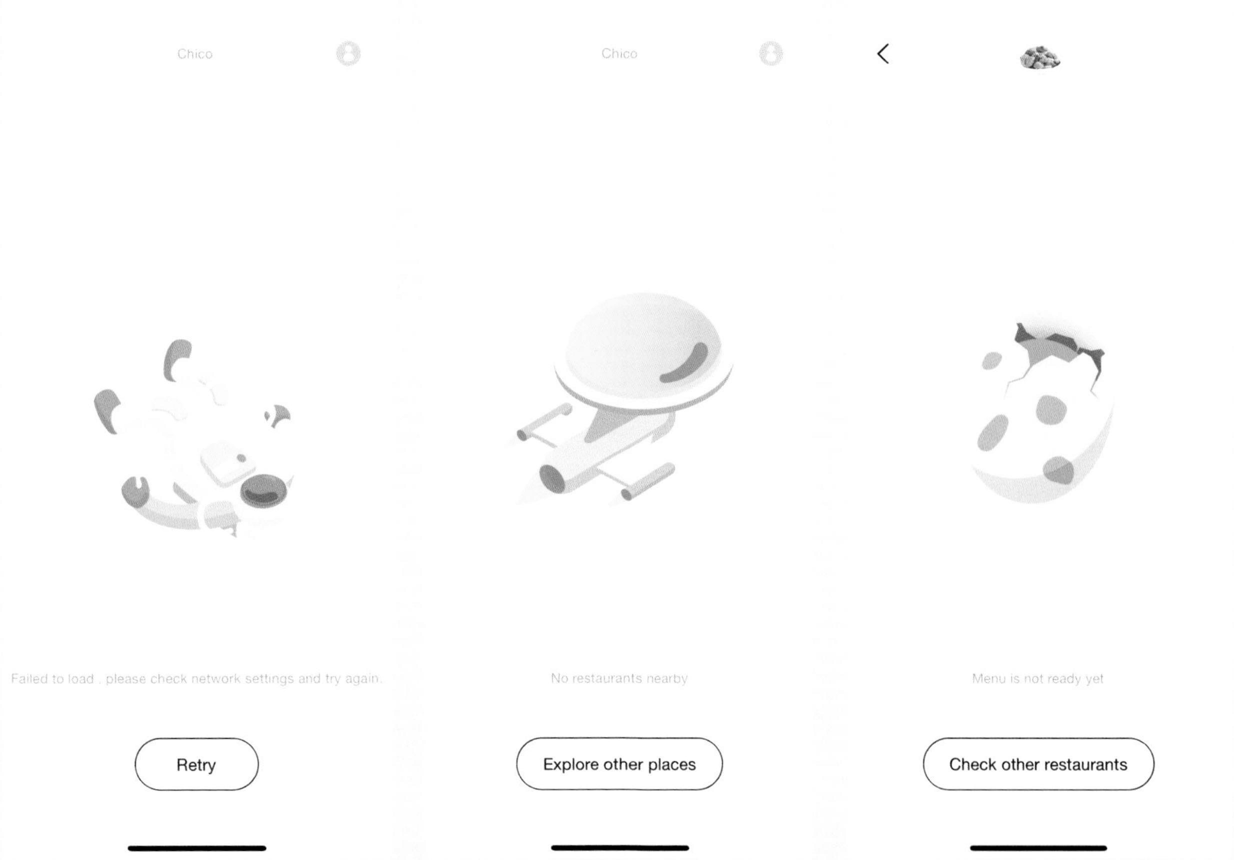
Chico
Chico
Failed to load , please check network settings and try again.
No restaurants nearby
Menu is not ready yet
Retry
Explore other places
Check other restaurants

In terms of UI, they adopted the minimalistic style. Simple structure and restricted colour palette were used to create an elegant feel. The realistic illustrations of the cuisine are the highlight of this app. They fit the need of this food ordering app, and at the same time create strong visual appeal. While maintaining the easy and intuitive user flow, the design team wishes to strive for innovation and uniqueness.

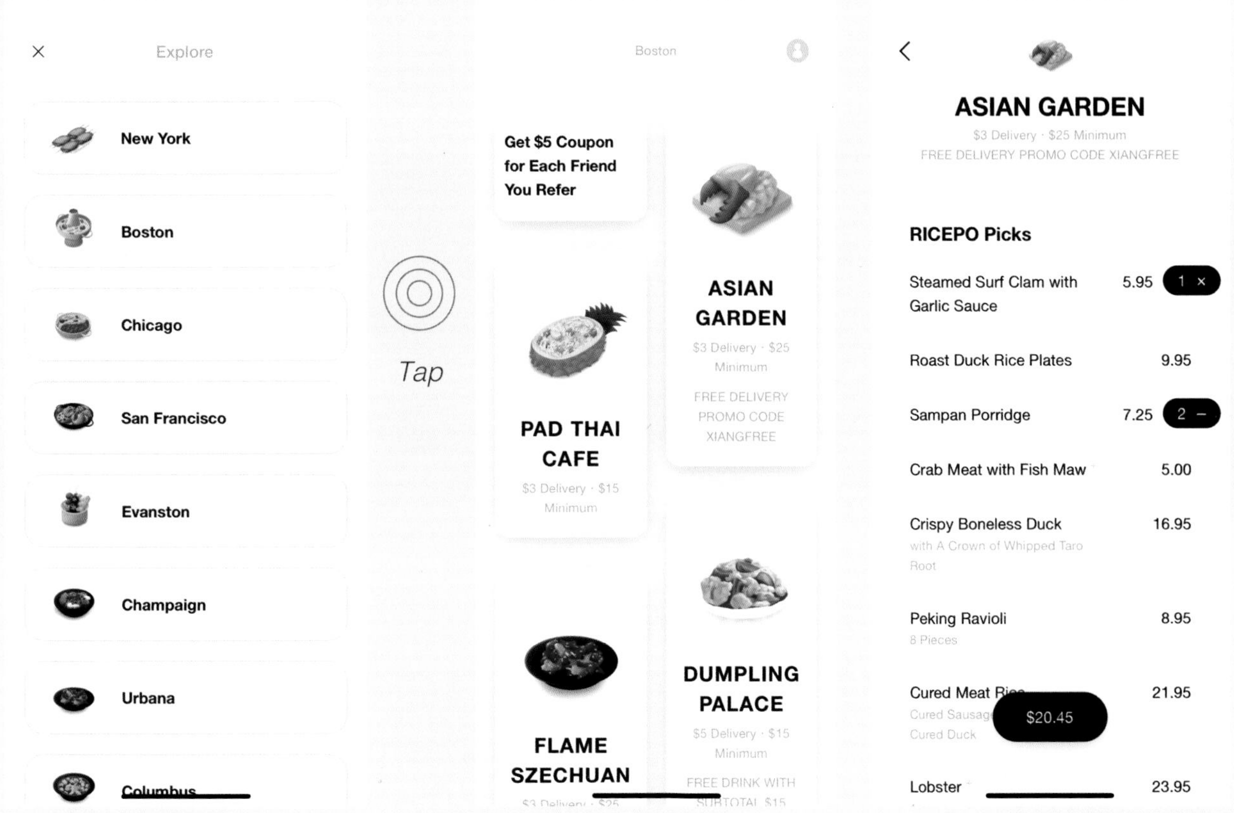
Explore
New York
Boston
Chicago
San Francisco
Evanston
Champaign
Urbana
Columbus
Tap
Boston
Get $5 Coupon for Each Friend You Refer
ASIAN GARDEN
$3 Delivery · $25 Minimum
FREE DELIVERY PROMO CODE XIANGFREE
PAD THAI CAFE
$3 Delivery · $15 Minimum
DUMPLING PALACE
$5 Delivery · $15 Minimum
FREE DRINK WITH SUBTOTAL $15
FLAME SZECHUAN
ASIAN GARDEN
$3 Delivery · $25 Minimum
FREE DELIVERY PROMO CODE XIANGFREE
RICEPO Picks
Steamed Surf Clam with Garlic Sauce
5.95
1 ×
Roast Duck Rice Plates
9.95
Sampan Porridge
7.25
2 –
Crab Meat with Fish Maw
5.00
Crispy Boneless Duck
16.95
with A Crown of Whipped Taro Root
Peking Ravioli
8.95
8 Pieces
21.95
$20.45
Lobster
23.95

Meallow

Design
Doeun Shin

Behance

Meallow is a dietary application for children. This service helps children get the nutrients they need to fit in their health condition. Many studies determine the average number of calories needed for a child's age. However, these figures are just guidelines. Children need less or more nutrients than these averages, depending on many factors. So the designer came up with a service to recommend a diet that take personal nutrition into consideration.

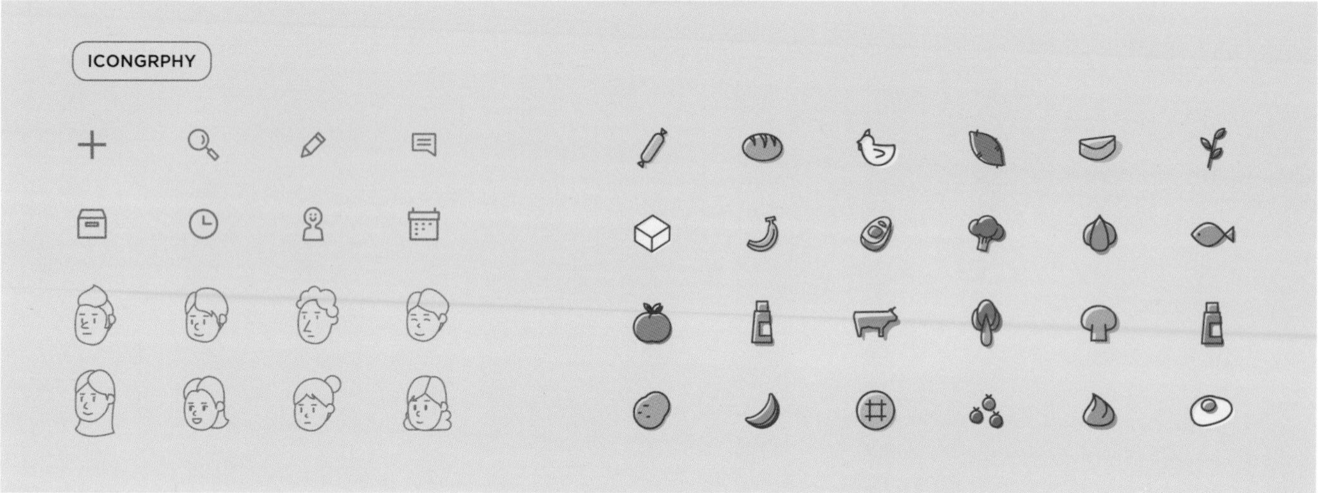
ICONGRPHY

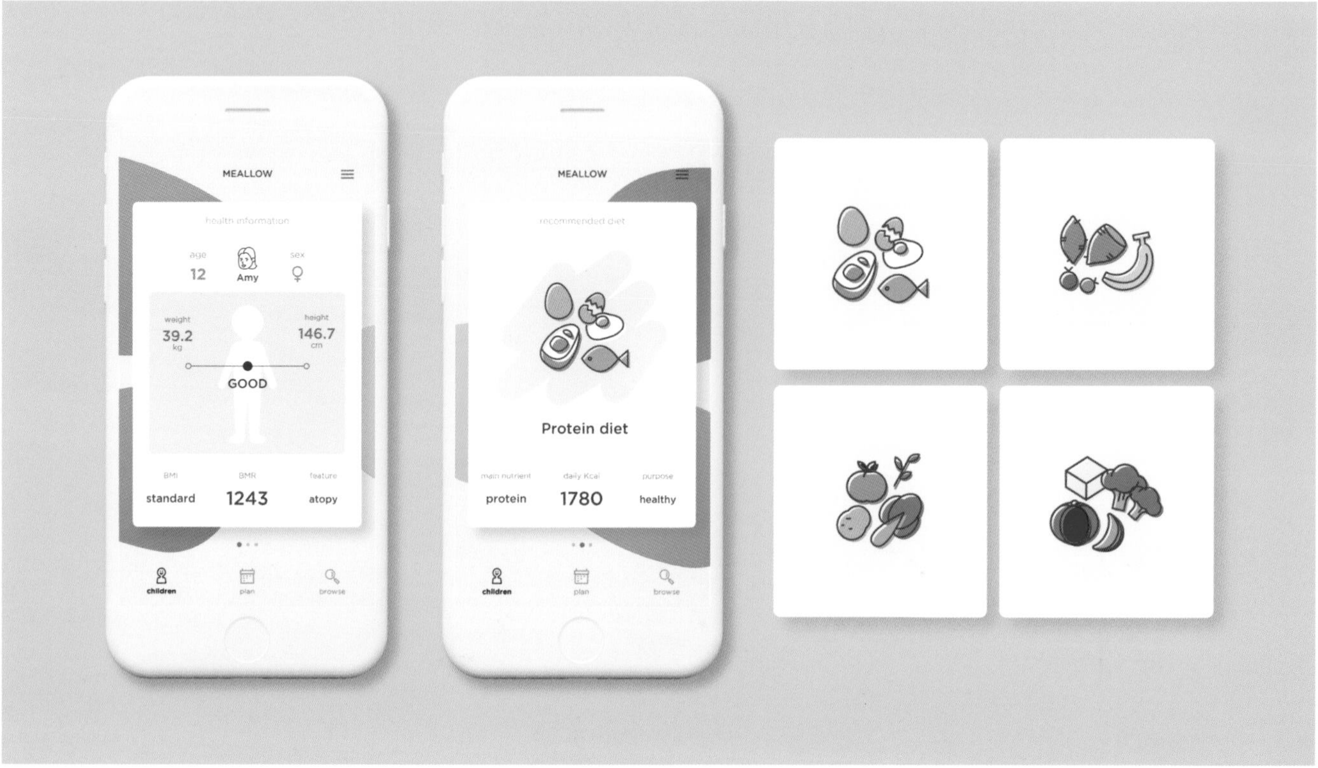
MEALLOW
12
Amy
39.2
146.7
GOOD
standard
1243
atopy
children
MEALLOW
Protein diet
protein
1780
healthy
children

MEALLOW
select a week to add Amy's meal plan
2017
2
SUN MON TUE WED THU FRI SAT
1 2 3 4
5 6 7 8 9 10 11
12 13 14 15 16 17 18
19 20 21 22 23 24 25
26 27 28
OK
What do you want to make a diet based on?
All
Ingredient
Nutrient
Level
OK
MEALLOW
Amy
2017 Feburary
SUN MON TUE WED THU FRI SAT
12 13 14 15 16 17 18
nutrition
Total 1760 kcal
Good morning brunch
520 kcal
Tomato caprese
140 kcal
Basil roasted chicken
693 kcal
children
plan
browse

The biggest feature of Meallow is "personalization". It defines the meaning of "healthy meals", by users' selection of ingredients, nutrient type and cooking level. Another characteristics of this service is its design motif. The designer was inspired by the various nutrients, so she came up with a "marbling", a mix of colours, and soft forms to represent this concept.

MEALLOW
08
Dissolve cornstarch in 2 teaspoons cold water and stir into stew.
Time
1:27
5:00
children
plan
browse
MEALLOW
01
Swirl in a little butter. Crack the eggs into the Pan.
Time
2:14
5:20
children
plan
browse
MEALLOW
05
Remove foil, and bake an additional 25 minutes. Cool for 15 minutes before serving.
Time
7:08
25:00
children
plan
browse

Knowrish

Design and Illustration
Alex Pluda, Ekaterina Alexandrova

Behance

Knowrish was created to provide a diverse and playful way to discover interesting facts. Each user initially needs to choose an egg in accordance with the category of interest and start breeding it by learning something new every day. With consistency and a bit of curiosity, the egg will eventually hatch, grow and evolve to become cute little creatures.

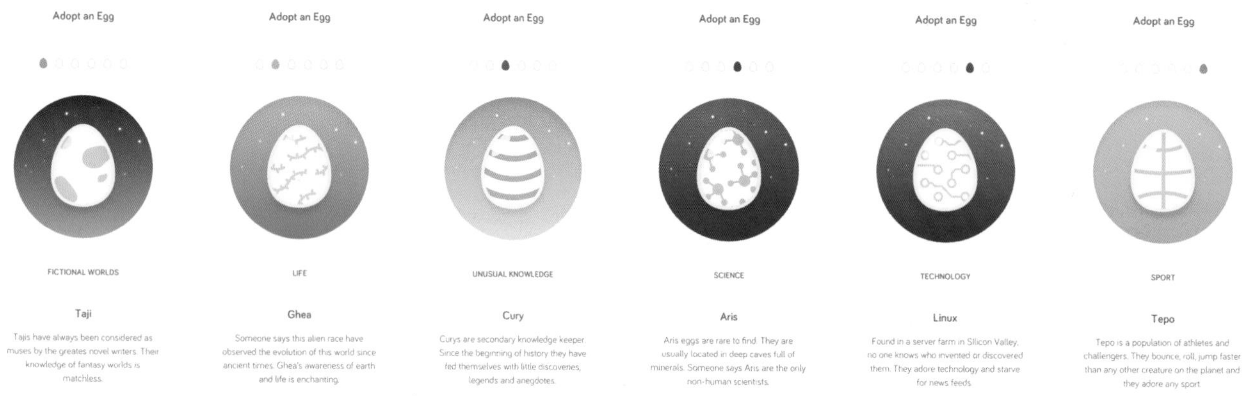

Adopt an Egg
FICTIONAL WORLDS
Taji
Tajis have always been considered as muses by the greates novel writers. Their knowledge of fantasy worlds is matchless.
Adopt an Egg
LIFE
Ghea
Someone says this alien race have observed the evolution of this world since ancient times. Ghea's awareness of earth and life is enchanting.
Adopt an Egg
UNUSUAL KNOWLEDGE
Cury
Curys are secondary knowledge keeper. Since the beginning of history they have fed themselves with little discoveries, legends and anegdotes.
Adopt an Egg
SCIENCE
Aris
Aris eggs are rare to find. They are usually located in deep caves full of minerals. Someone says Aris are the only non-human scientists.
Adopt an Egg
TECHNOLOGY
Linux
Found in a server farm in Silicon Valley, no one knows who invented or discovered them. They adore technology and starve for news feeds.
Adopt an Egg
SPORT
Tepo
Tepo is a population of athletes and challengers. They bounce, roll, jump faster than any other creature on the planet and they adore any sport.

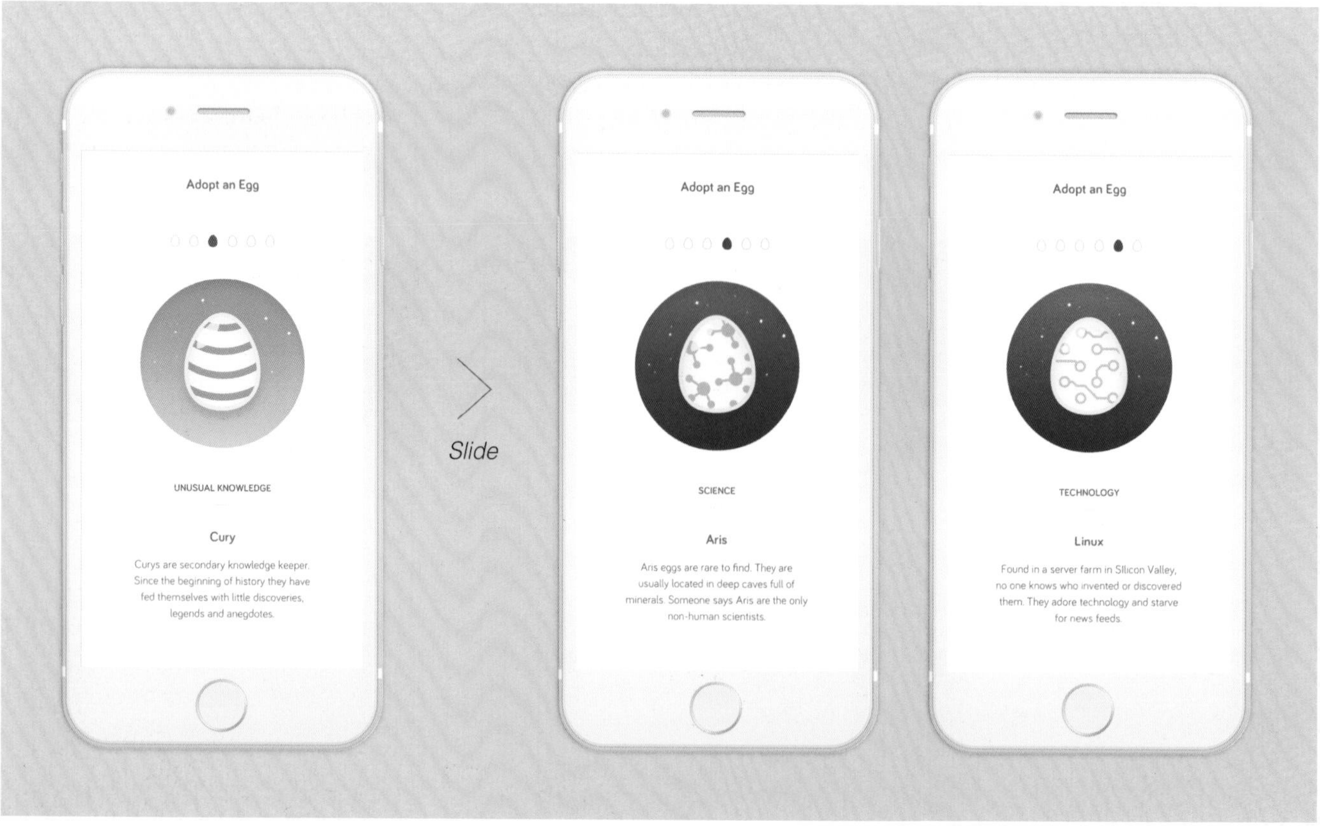

Adopt an Egg
UNUSUAL KNOWLEDGE
Cury
Curys are secondary knowledge keeper. Since the beginning of history they have fed themselves with little discoveries, legends and anegdotes.
Slide
Adopt an Egg
SCIENCE
Aris
Aris eggs are rare to find. They are usually located in deep caves full of minerals. Someone says Aris are the only non-human scientists.
Adopt an Egg
TECHNOLOGY
Linux
Found in a server farm in Silicon Valley, no one knows who invented or discovered them. They adore technology and starve for news feeds.

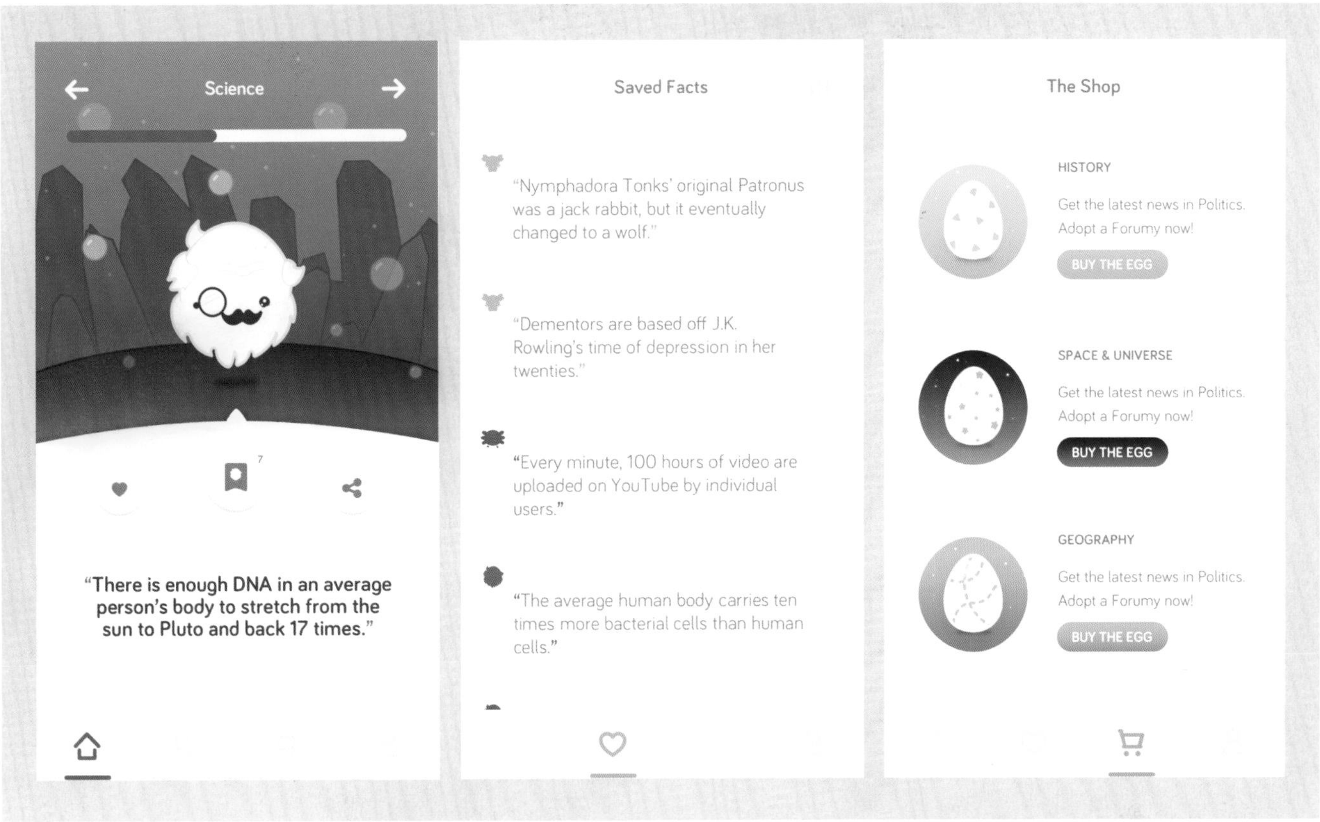
Science
“There is enough DNA in an average person’s body to stretch from the sun to Pluto and back 17 times.”
Saved Facts
“Nymphadora Tonks’ original Patronus was a jack rabbit, but it eventually changed to a wolf.”
“Dementors are based off J.K. Rowling’s time of depression in her twenties.”
“Every minute, 100 hours of video are uploaded on YouTube by individual users.”
“The average human body carries ten times more bacterial cells than human cells.”
The Shop
HISTORY
Get the latest news in Politics. Adopt a Forumy now!
BUY THE EGG
SPACE & UNIVERSE
Get the latest news in Politics. Adopt a Forumy now!
BUY THE EGG
GEOGRAPHY
Get the latest news in Politics. Adopt a Forumy now!
BUY THE EGG

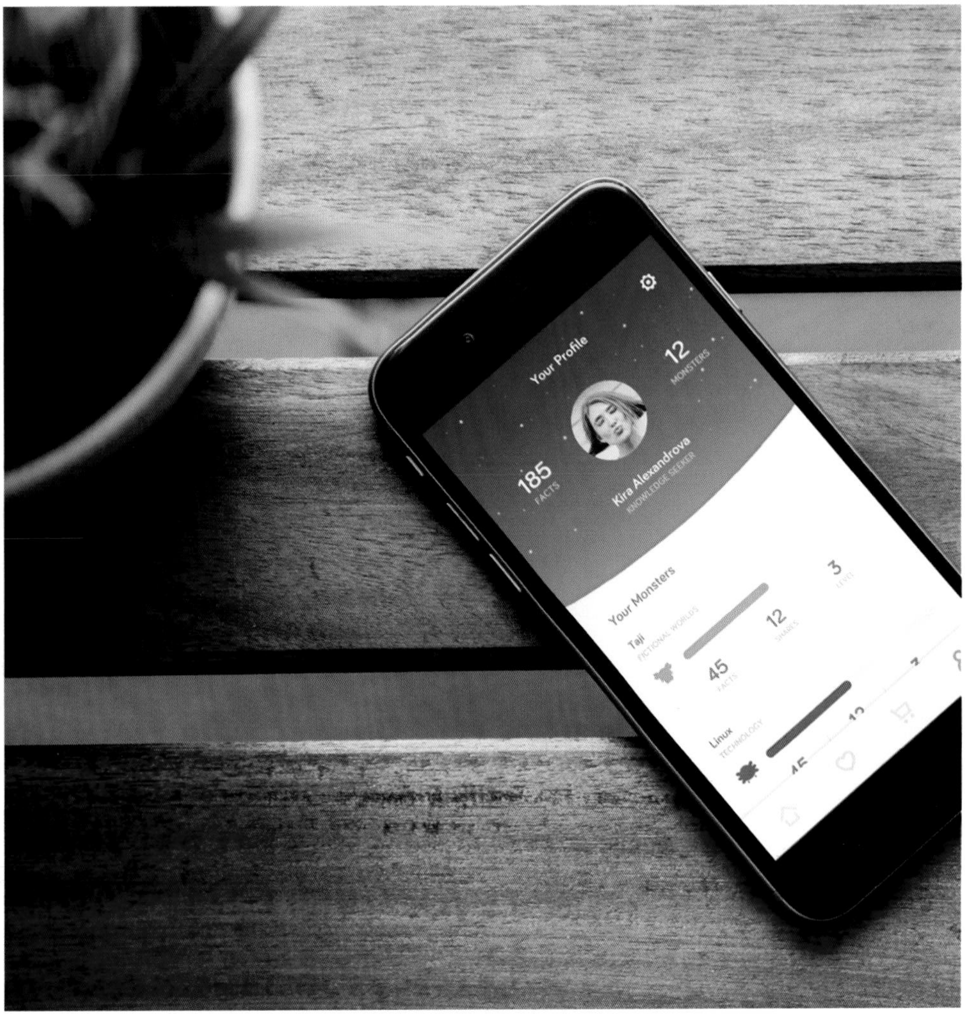
Your Profile
12
MONSTERS
185
FACTS
Kira Alexandrova
KNOWLEDGE SEEKER
Your Monsters
Taji
45
12
3
Linux

Printbox

Design Agency
UIG Studio

Creative Direction
Pawel Hersztowski

Art Direction
Angelika Wercholancewa

Design
Angelika Wercholancewa

Client
Printbox

Behance

Printbox is a mobile application to create photo products. This is simplified and more automated version of the desktop editor and is a part of a complete Printbox package for photo products. Users get to use the most important functionalities to create their personalized photo products on an easy-to-use mobile experience.

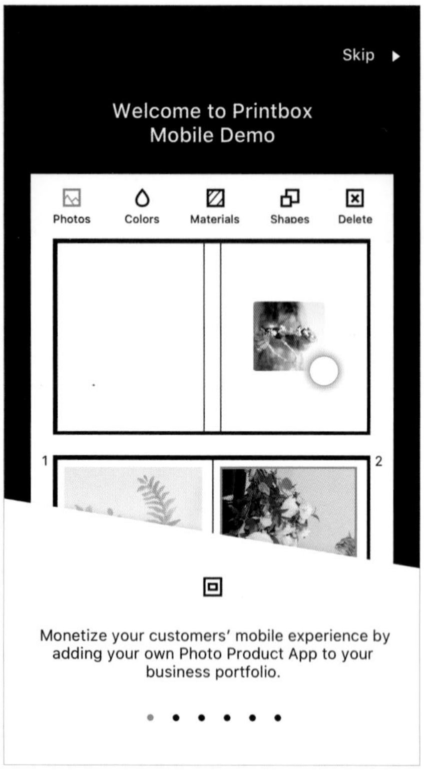

Skip
Welcome to Printbox
Mobile Demo
Photos
Colors
Materials
Shapes
Delete
1
2
Monetize your customers' mobile experience by adding your own Photo Product App to your business portfolio.

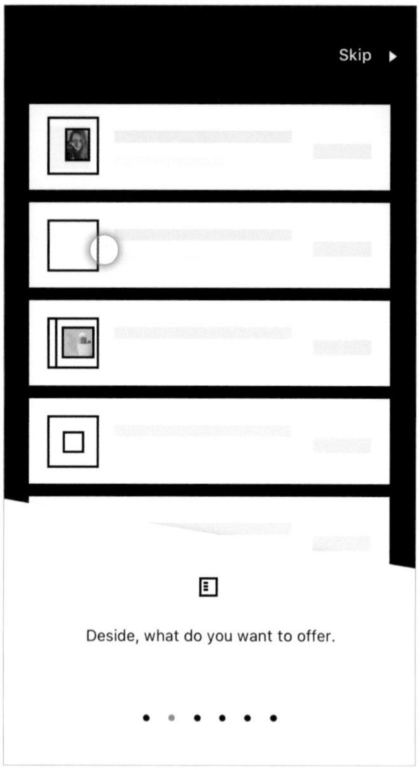

Skip
Deside, what do you want to offer.

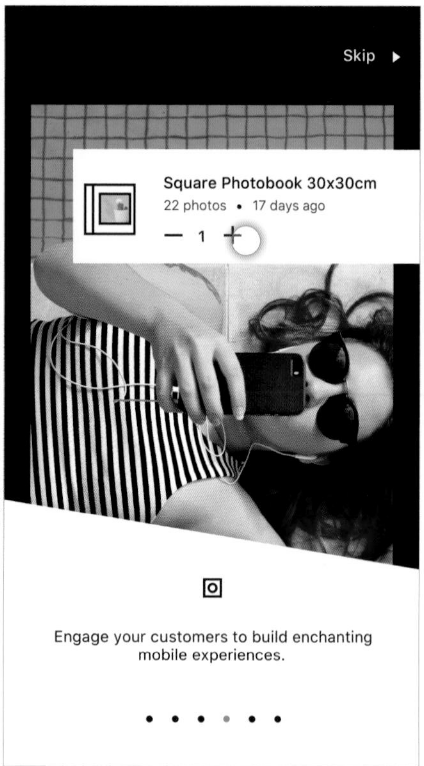

Skip
Square Photobook 30x30cm
22 photos • 17 days ago
— 1 +
Engage your customers to build enchanting mobile experiences.

As for design solution, the design studio use semi-flat design as a general UI direction. For friendly, neutral and comfortable feeling, they leave more whitespace on screens. General colours are black and white. General concepts for mobile assets are simple geometric forms, abstract icons and big bold call-to-action as a primary accent on screen.

Skip
Hello, Dude!
travisoneil@uigstudio.com
Forgot your password?
Log in
Don't have an account? Create one
Photobooks
Photobook
Square Photobook 30x30cm
22 pages
€12.99
Portrait Photobook A4
28 pages
€16.99
Little Photobook 10x10cm
12 pages
€12.99
Landscape Photobook A3
€16.99
Slide
Good morning, Dude!
My account
Cart
My Orders
Privacy policy
Terms and conditions
About
Logout

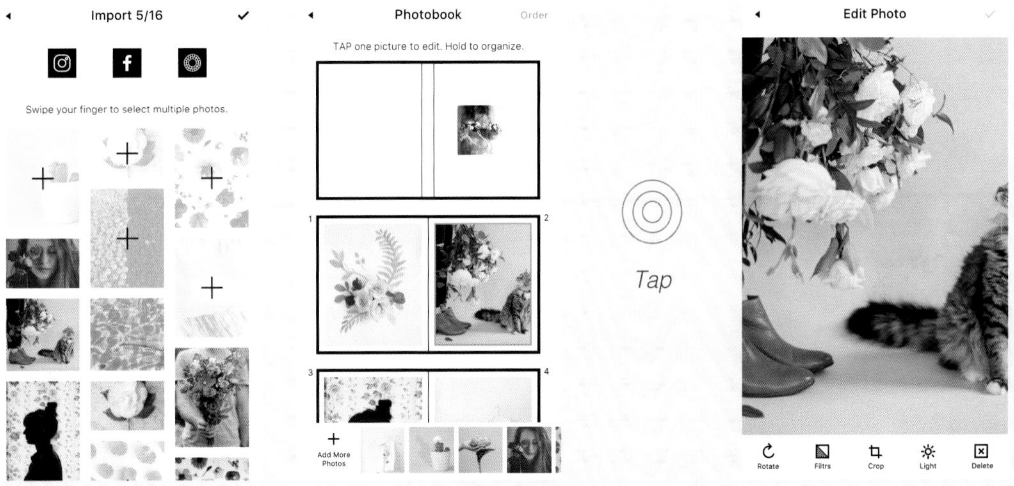
Import 5/16
Swipe your finger to select multiple photos.
Photobook
Order
TAP one picture to edit. Hold to organize.
Add More Photos
Tap
Edit Photo
Rotate
Filtrs
Crop
Light
Delete

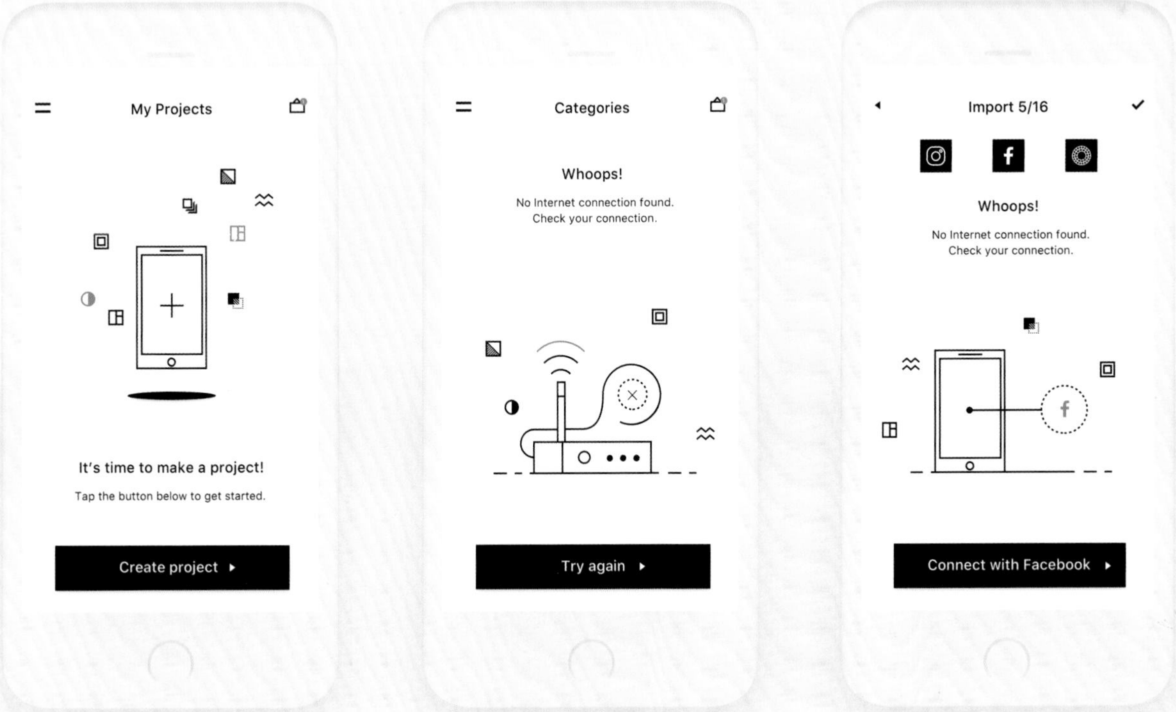
My Projects
It's time to make a project!
Tap the button below to get started.
Create project
Categories
Whoops!
No Internet connection found.
Check your connection.
Try again
Import 5/16
Whoops!
No Internet connection found.
Check your connection.
Connect with Facebook

Card Diary

Design
Unbong Kang

Development
Yuan Fu

App Store

The concept behind Card Diary is simply to use cards to create your own diary. Every card is customizable so that every user could create his or her unique diary. They can make a pretty diary even if they use only one picture or one line of text. The design concept is simple and clean, simplified to avoid any complexity. “We believe that every day is very meaningful. We hope that Card Diary will help motivate users to find meaning in daily life, and to use cards to capture their memories and feelings, whether love, happiness, joy, sadness or pain,” says designer Unbong Kang.

2018
7
JUL
21/31
AUG, 21 / 2018

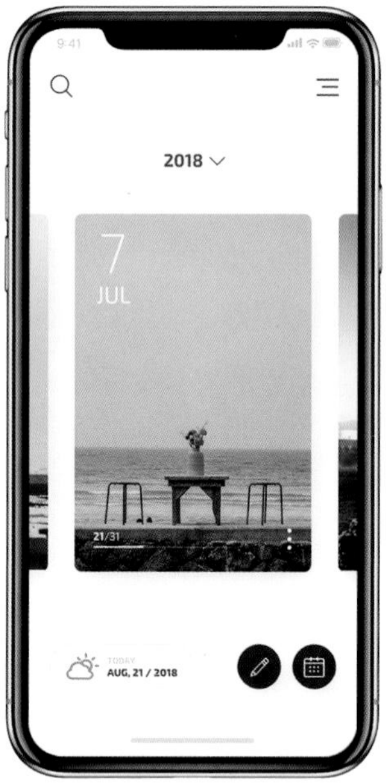
2018
7
JUL
21/31
AUG, 21 / 2018

Select color

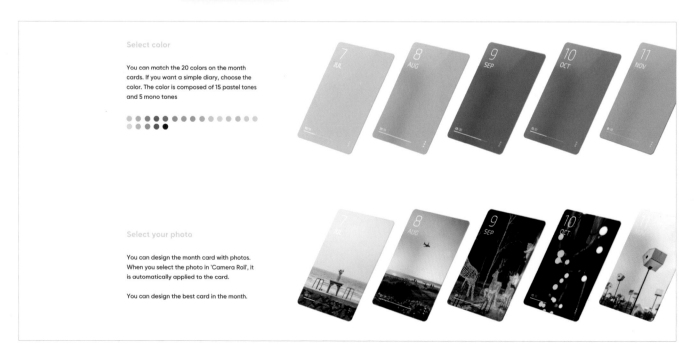

You can match the 20 colors on the month cards. If you want a simple diary, choose the color. The color is composed of 15 pastel tones and 5 mono tones

7
JUL
8
AUG
9
SEP
10
OCT
11
NOV

Select your photo

You can design the month card with photos. When you select the photo in 'Camera Roll', it is automatically applied to the card.

You can design the best card in the month.

8
AUG
9
SEP
10
OCT

LTE
AM 09:40
2018
7
JUL
1 2
3 4 5 6 7 8 9
10 11 12 13 14 15 16
17 18 19 20 21
24
31
Select date to write
AUG, 21 / 2018

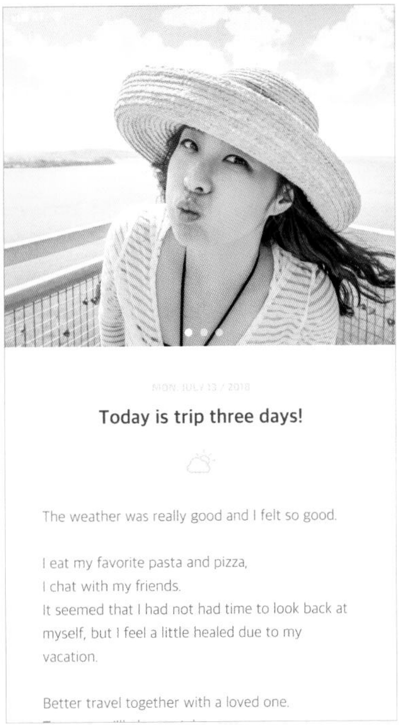
Today is trip three days!
The weather was really good and I felt so good.
I eat my favorite pasta and pizza,
I chat with my friends.
It seemed that I had not had time to look back at myself, but I feel a little healed due to my vacation.
Better travel together with a loved one.

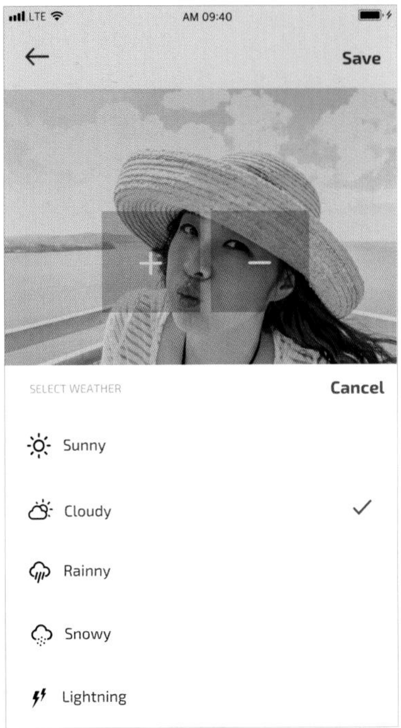
LTE
AM 09:40
Save
SELECT WEATHER
Cancel
Sunny
Cloudy
Rainny
Snowy
Lightning

12
TUE
13
WED
14
THU

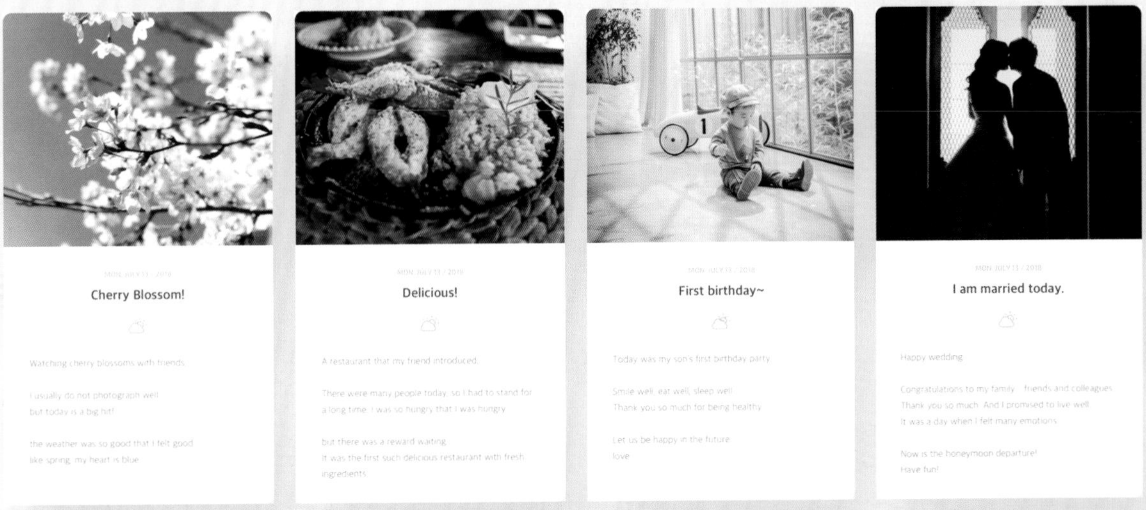
Cherry Blossom!
Delicious!
First birthday~
I am married today.

Mentoroom

Design
Julia Shkatova

Behance

Mentoroom is an educational app which connects mentors and students who crave to master new disciplines together. The project began with the designer's observation about how hard it is for young professionals and experts in a particular area to try their hand at doing a completely new thing or to make a career change. To close this gap, Julia designed Mentoroom app. Mentoroom helps to create a community for knowledge exchange and experience sharing. Designer believes the platform would support lifelong learning and make our lives more satisfying.

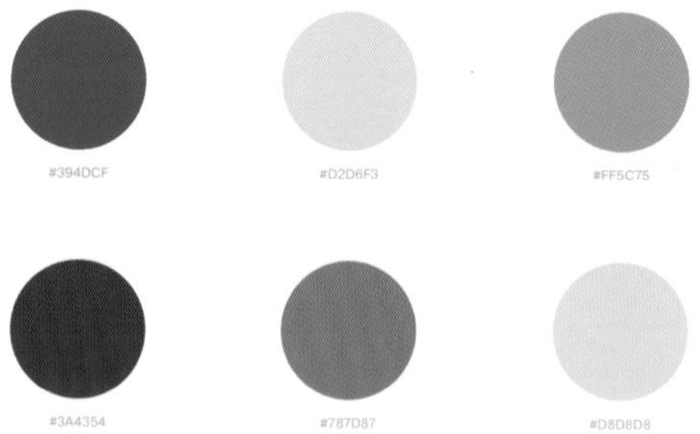

#394DCF
#D2D6F3
#FF5C75
#3A4354
#787D87
#D8D8D8

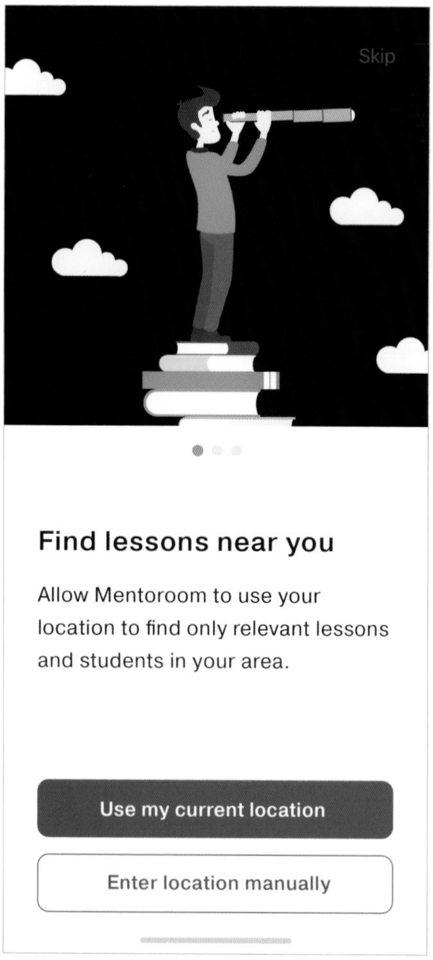

Skip
Find lessons near you
Allow Mentoroom to use your location to find only relevant lessons and students in your area.
Use my current location
Enter location manually

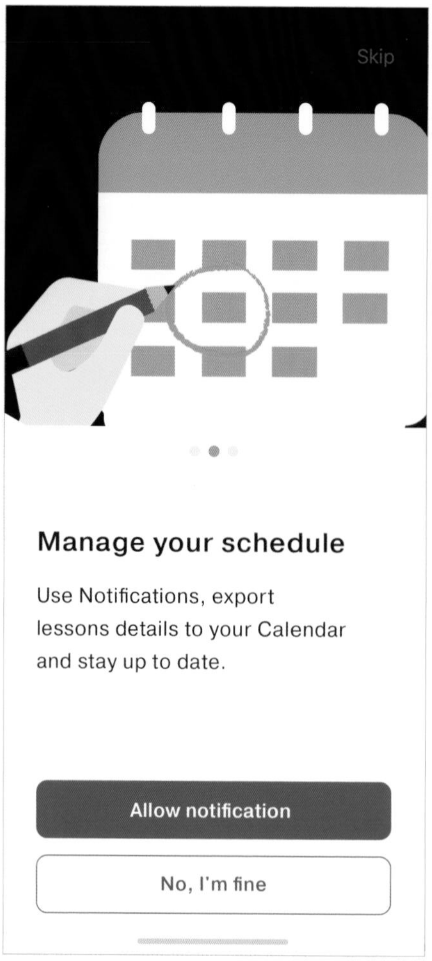

Skip
Manage your schedule
Use Notifications, export lessons details to your Calendar and stay up to date.
Allow notification
No, I'm fine

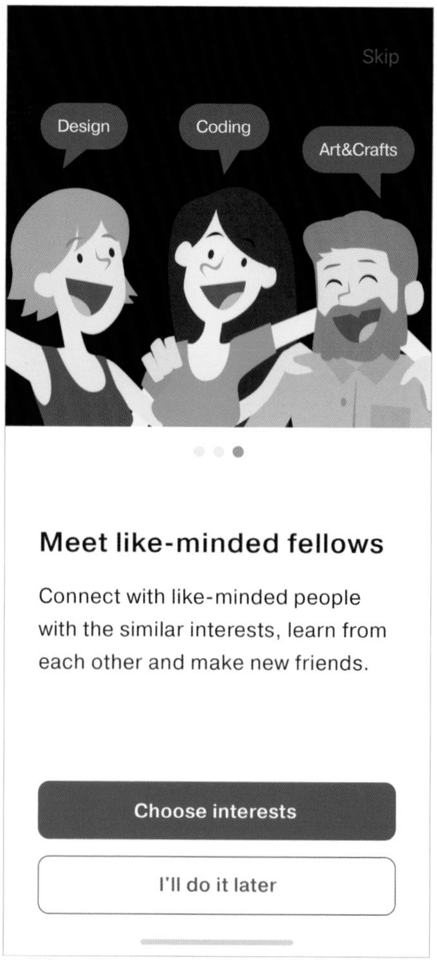

Skip
Design
Coding
Art&Crafts
Meet like-minded fellows
Connect with like-minded people with the similar interests, learn from each other and make new friends.
Choose interests
I'll do it later

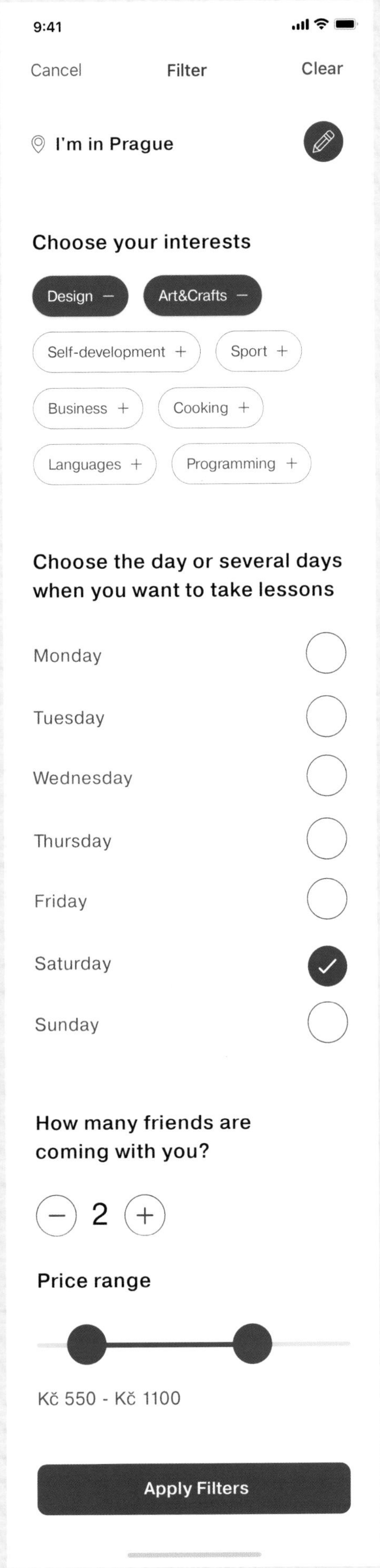

9:41

Cancel   **Filter**   Clear

◎ **I'm in Prague**   ✎

Choose your interests

Design −   Art&Crafts −

Self-development +   Sport +

Business +   Cooking +

Languages +   Programming +

Choose the day or several days when you want to take lessons

Monday ◯

Tuesday ◯

Wednesday ◯

Thursday ◯

Friday ◯

Saturday ✓

Sunday ◯

How many friends are coming with you?

⊖ **2** ⊕

Price range

Kč 550 - Kč 1100

Apply Filters

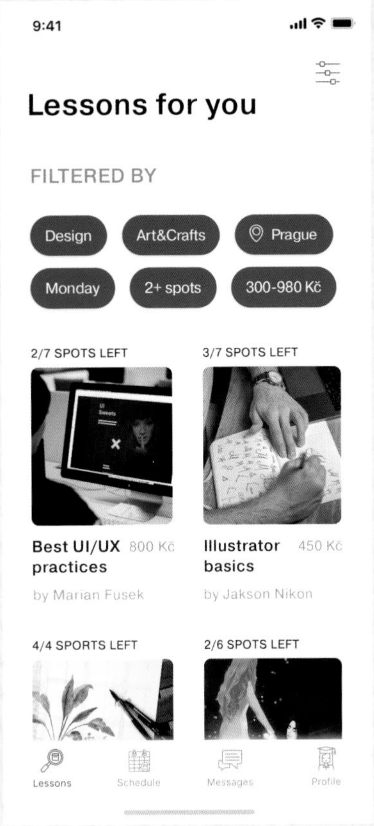

Lessons for you

FILTERED BY

Design   Art&Crafts   ◎ Prague

Monday   2+ spots   300-980 Kč

2/7 SPOTS LEFT   3/7 SPOTS LEFT

Best UI/UX 800 Kč   **Illustrator** 450 Kč
practices   **basics**
by Marian Fusek   by Jakson Nikon

4/4 SPORTS LEFT   2/6 SPOTS LEFT

Lessons   Schedule   Messages   Profile

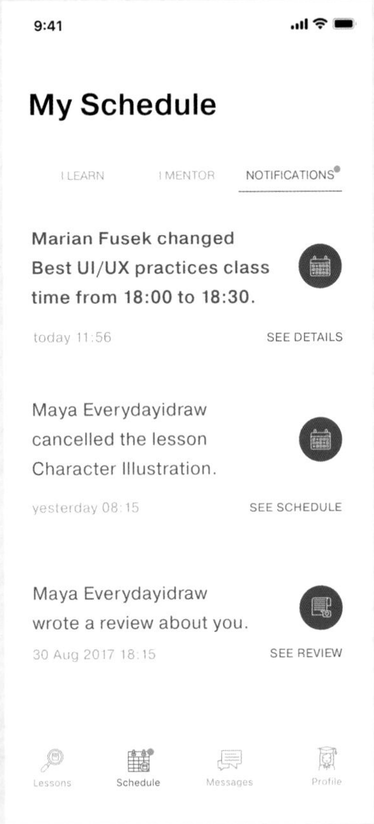

My Schedule

I LEARN   I MENTOR   NOTIFICATIONS®

Marian Fusek changed Best UI/UX practices class time from 18:00 to 18:30.

today 11:56   SEE DETAILS

Maya Everydayidraw cancelled the lesson Character Illustration.

yesterday 08:15   SEE SCHEDULE

Maya Everydayidraw wrote a review about you.

30 Aug 2017 18:15   SEE REVIEW

Lessons   Schedule   Messages   Profile

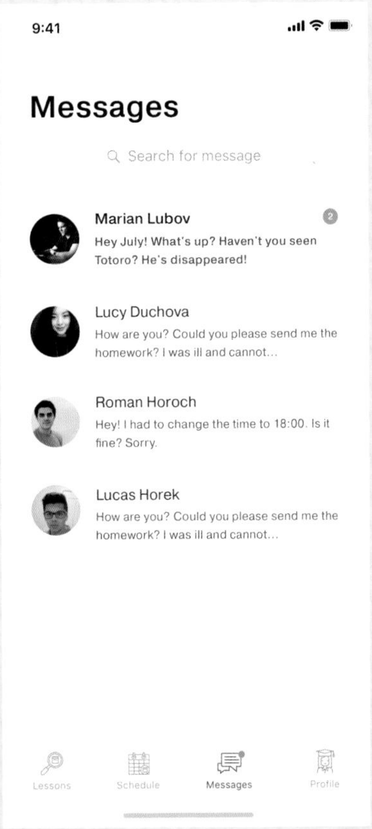

Messages

🔍 Search for message

Marian Lubov ②
Hey July! What's up? Haven't you seen Totoro? He's disappeared!

Lucy Duchova
How are you? Could you please send me the homework? I was ill and cannot...

Roman Horoch
Hey! I had to change the time to 18:00. Is it fine? Sorry.

Lucas Horek
How are you? Could you please send me the homework? I was ill and cannot...

Lessons   Schedule   Messages   Profile

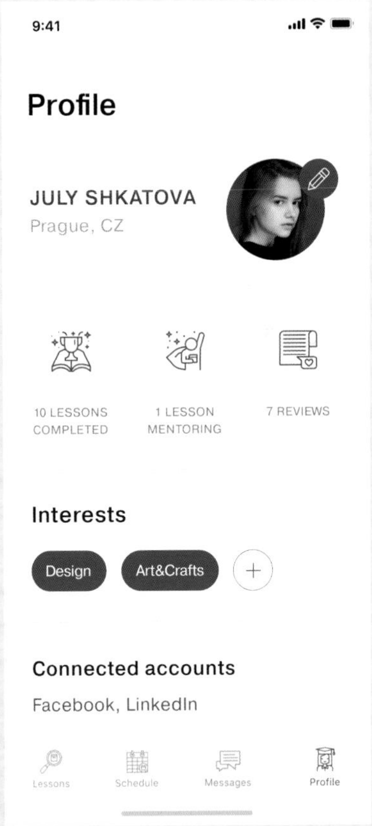

Profile

JULY SHKATOVA ✎
Prague, CZ

10 LESSONS COMPLETED   1 LESSON MENTORING   7 REVIEWS

Interests

Design   Art&Crafts   +

Connected accounts

Facebook, LinkedIn

Lessons   Schedule   Messages   Profile

While designing the Mentoroom app, Julia was driven by User Centred Design Principles—putting the end user at the centre. From the lens of visual design, Julia aimed to create an intuitive and minimalistic UI design. At the same time, it was important that the app has a unique look and feel. Mentoroom logo uses a metaphor of a physical room; outline icons add charming details. The colour palette and Pragmatica font make the interface look balanced and clean.

Tink

App Store

Design
Tink

Identity
Kurppa Hosk and Tink

Illustration
Martin Nicolausson

Tink is creating a world without financial anxiety, stress and complexity. A future where personal finance gives people peace of mind and happiness. A world where money works—for everyone. Tink's technology empowers banks to give their users better advice and enables them to make smarter decisions based on a holistic view of their finances. Through machine learning and data analytics, Tink's technology lets banks get to know their customer's financial behaviour and give them the nudges to keep them on track.

Typography
Typeface
Lota Grotesque
Regular
Semi Bold
Bold

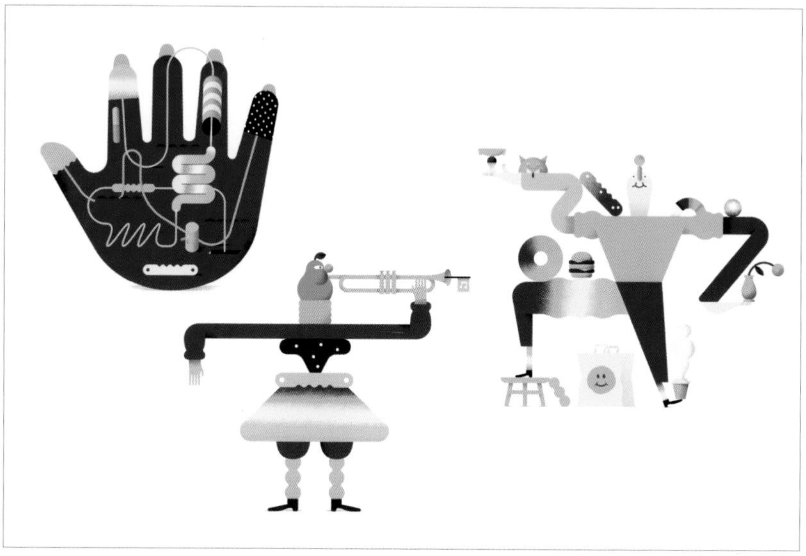

App
Onboarding
In Tink you get a overview of your money.
See what you spend on, with our automated categorization and get help with spending less (or more).
Let's go
Transfer money between all your banks.
In Tink, you have all your accounts, cards and loans in one app. We support over 50 banks and credit cards!
Let's go
Less money on mortgages, more on the the fun stuff.
Get help lowering your mortgage rate or getting a better interest rate on your savings money.
Let's go

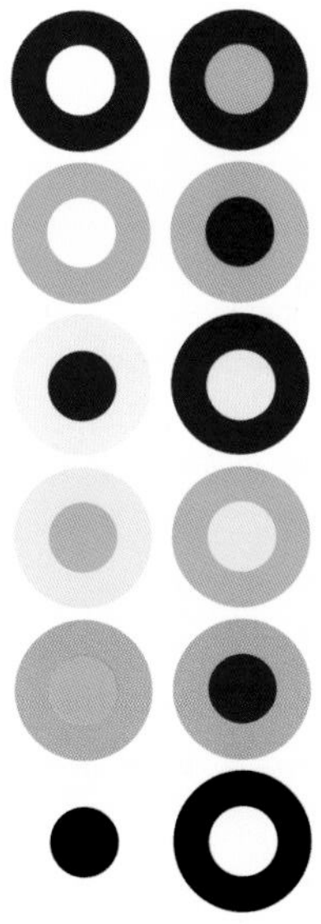

9:41
Overview
Left to spend
9,543
25 jul - Today
Everyday
723 kr
Savings
29,520 kr
Latest transactions
H&M online
Today
Urban Deli
Se all
- 330 kr
- 330 kr
Overview
Events
Accounts
Residence
Profile

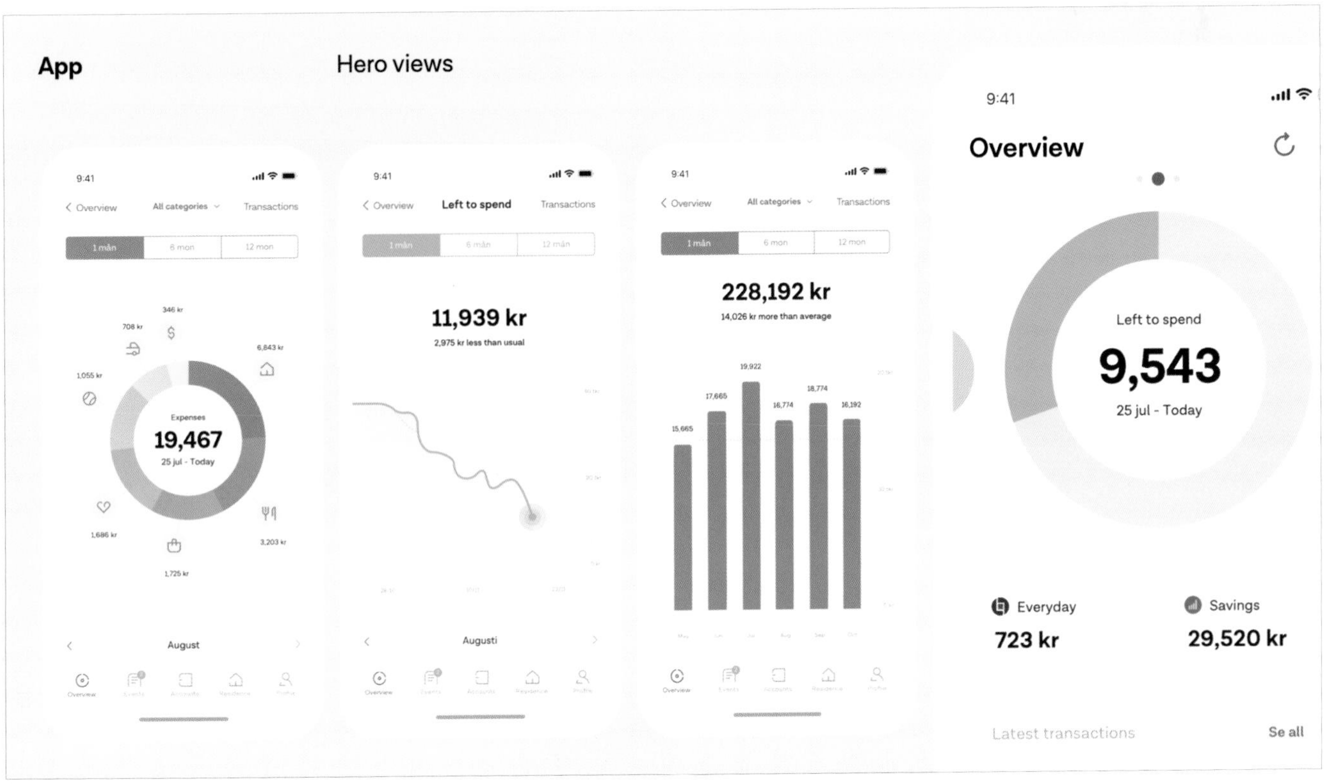
App
Hero views
9:41
Overview
All categories
Transactions
1 mån
Expenses
19,467
25 jul - Today
August
Left to spend
11,939 kr
2,975 kr less than usual
Augusti
228,192 kr
14,026 kr more than average
Overview
Left to spend
9,543
25 jul - Today
Everyday
723 kr
Savings
29,520 kr
Latest transactions
Se all

Melissa Insider

Design
Transa Inc., Marco Almeida

Google Play

Melissa Insider serves as a guide of what to see, do, visit, and discover in some of the world's most stimulating capital cities. The tips about restaurants, bars, parties, parks, galleries, cafes, street-walkings and much more were all hand selected by an exclusive curatorship of people who really know their stuff—the Insiders.

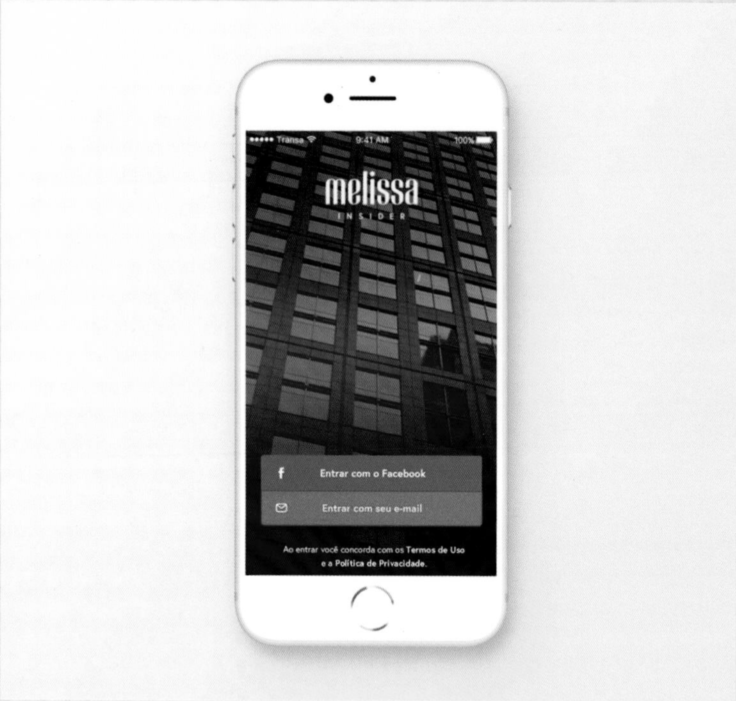

melissa
INSIDER
Entrar com o Facebook
Entrar com seu e-mail
Ao entrar você concorda com os Termos de Uso e a Política de Privacidade.

Transa
9:41 AM
100%
Qual o seu destino?
Nova York
NY, Estados Unidos
Londres
Reino Unido
São Paulo
SP, Brasil
Rio de Janeiro
RJ, Brasil
Salvador
BA, Brasil
Curitiba
PR, Brasil

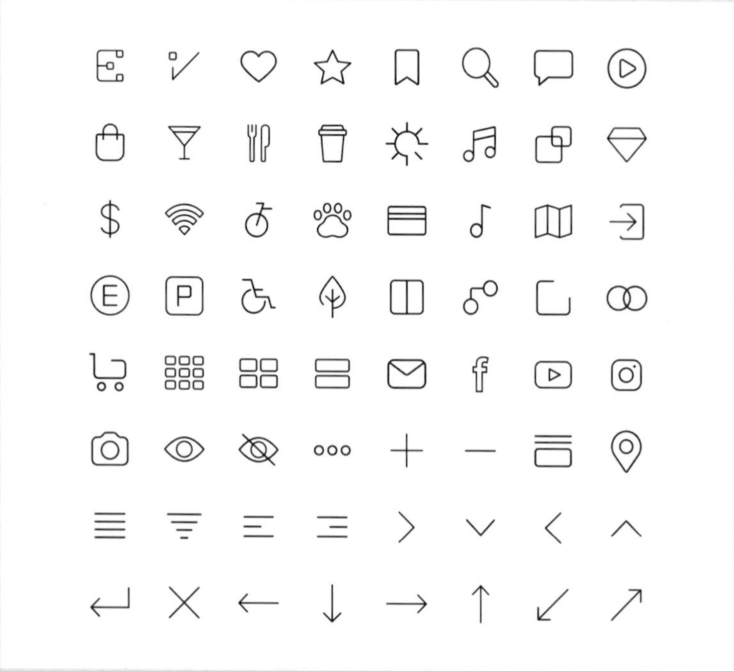

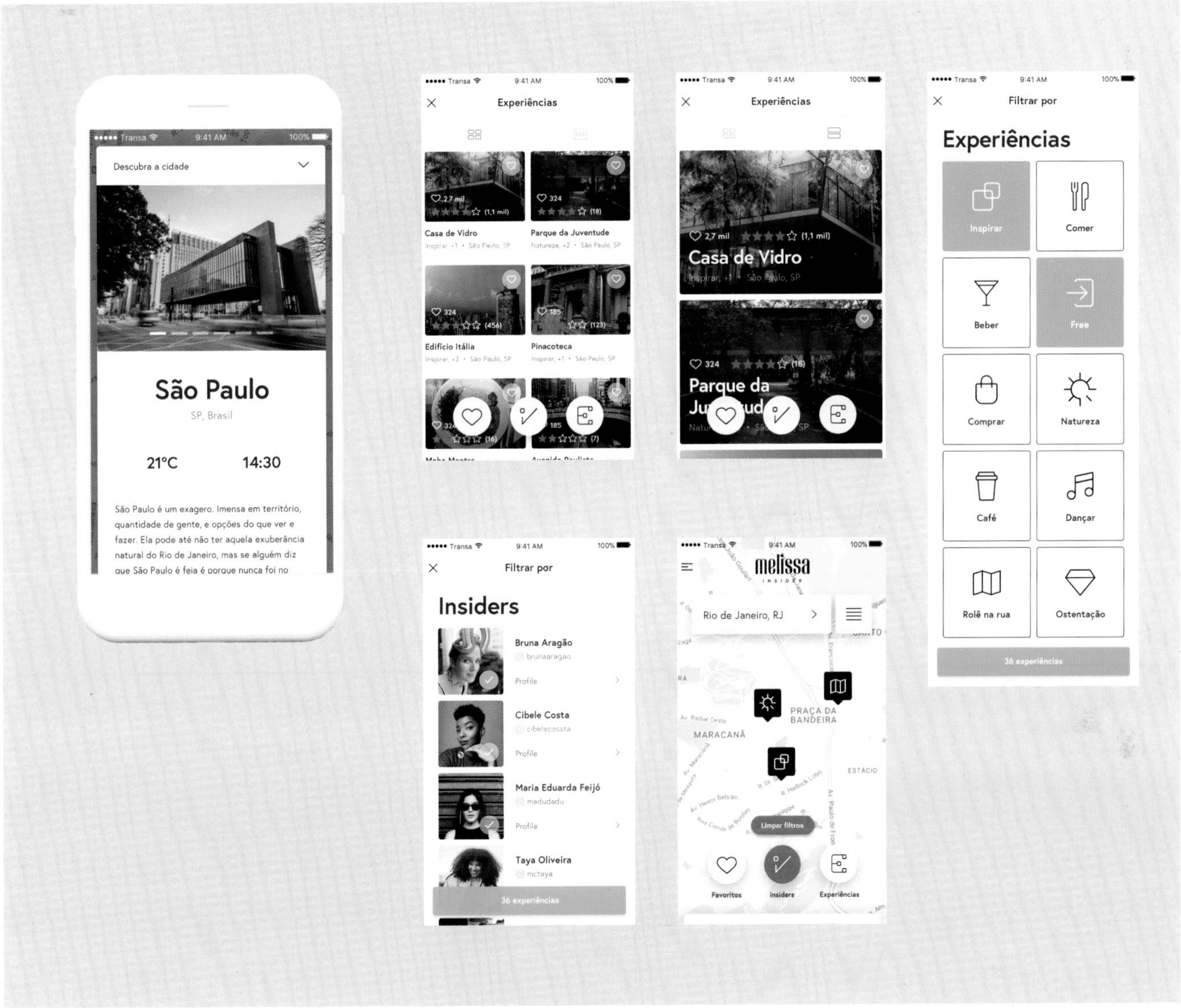
Descubra a cidade
São Paulo
SP, Brasil
21°C
14:30
São Paulo é um exagero. Imensa em território, quantidade de gente, e opções do que ver e fazer. Ela pode até não ter aquela exuberância natural do Rio de Janeiro, mas se alguém diz
Experiências
Casa de Vidro
Parque da Juventude
Edifício Itália
Pinacoteca
Filtrar por
Experiências
Inspirar
Comer
Beber
Free
Comprar
Natureza
Café
Dançar
Rolê na rua
Ostentação
36 experiências
Insiders
Bruna Aragão
Cibele Costa
Maria Eduarda Feijó
Taya Oliveira
Profile
melissa
Rio de Janeiro, RJ
MARACANÃ
PRAÇA DA BANDEIRA
Limpar filtros
Favoritos
Insiders
Experiências

With the app, users can directly explore recommendations via the city map, view them in list form, filter the tips according to their current mood or to their preferred Insiders of the selected capital city. Users can even choose their favourite experiences and follow the Insiders. By visiting any suggestion, they can leave comments in terms of their own experience.

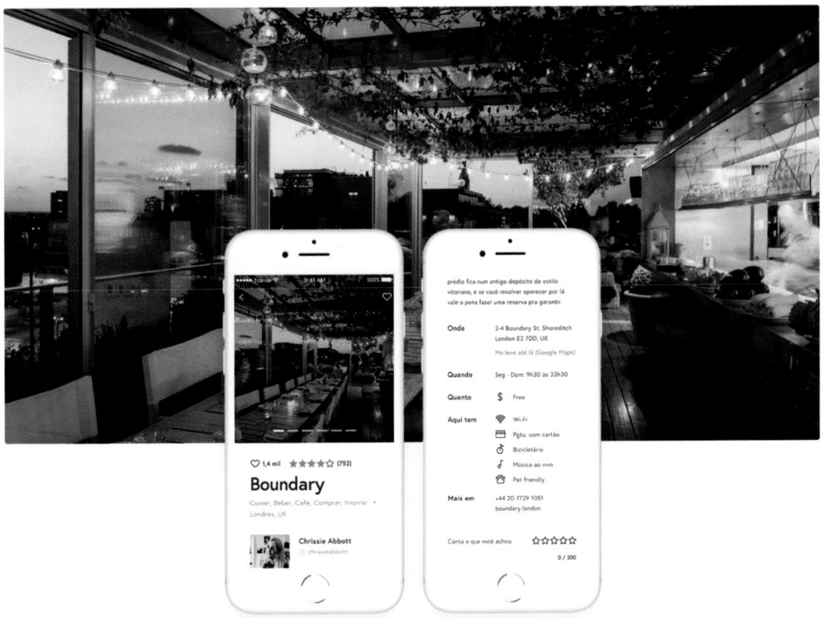
Boundary
Chrissie Abbott
Onde
Quando
Quanto
Aqui tem
Mais em

The Mindfulness App

Design Agency
Tofu Design

Design
Daniel Tan Wai Meng

Copywriting
Daphnie Loong Jo Yee

Behance

The Mindfulness App was conceptualized from the design team's interest in meditation. They felt that many people in this day and age lack the ability to stop and pause to reevaluate themselves—some even fear the idea of stillness. Hence, they conceptualized The Mindfulness App to embody the idea of a simple and peaceful app to coach people to relearn the simple things in life: sleep, diet, and alone time.

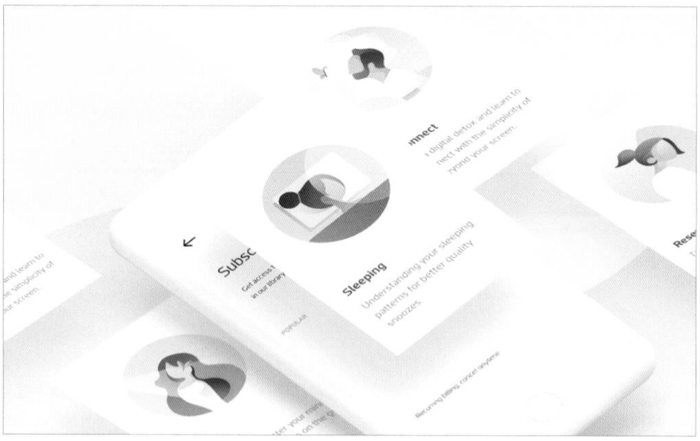
Sleeping

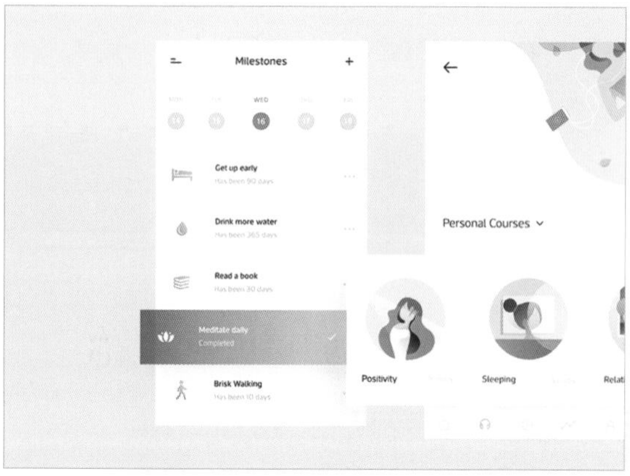
Milestones
Get up early
Drink more water
Read a book
Meditate daily
Brisk Walking
Personal Courses
Positivity
Sleeping

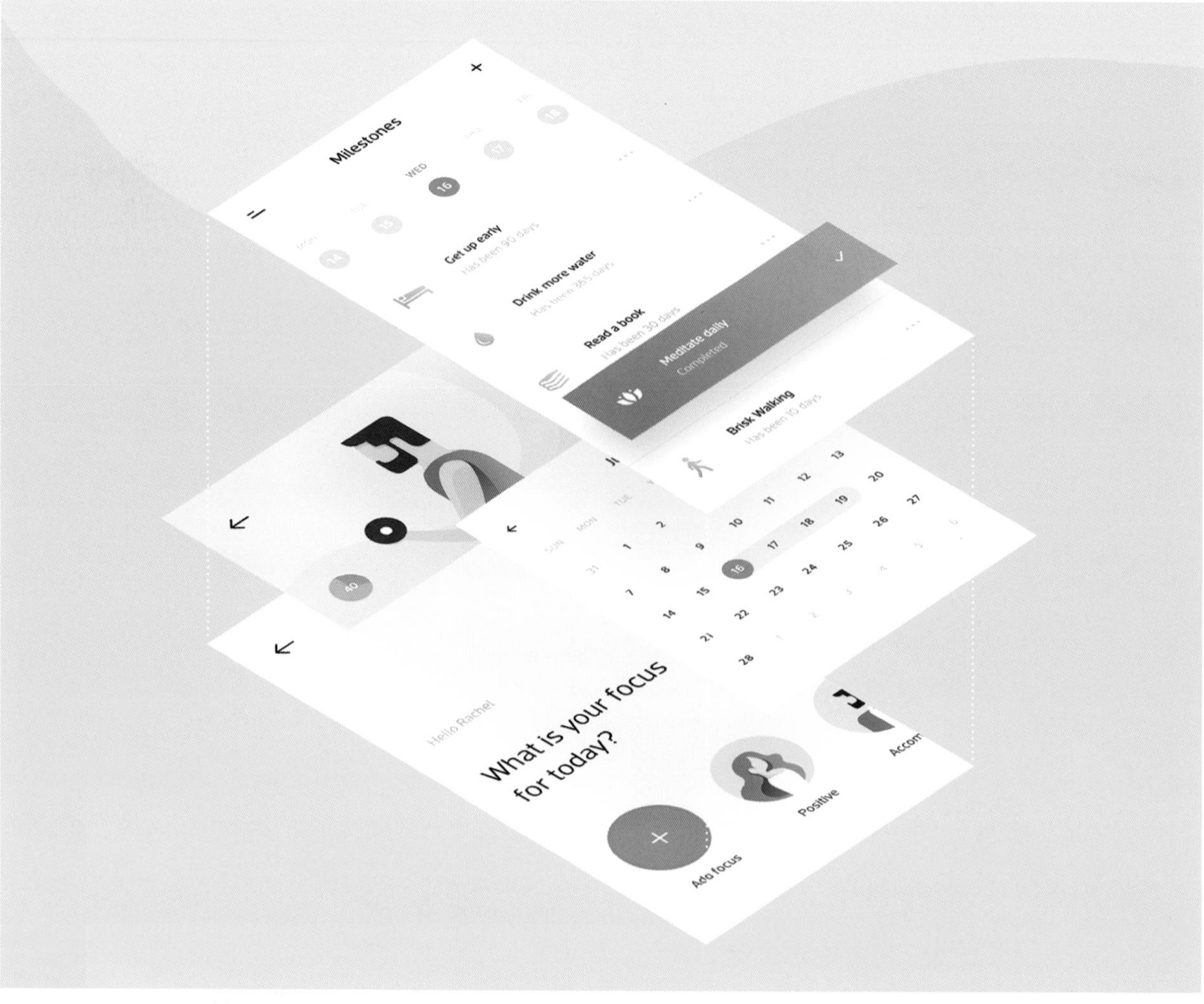
Milestones
WED
Get up early
Drink more water
Read a book
Meditate daily
Completed
Brisk Walking
Has been 10 days
What is your focus for today?
Add focus
Positive

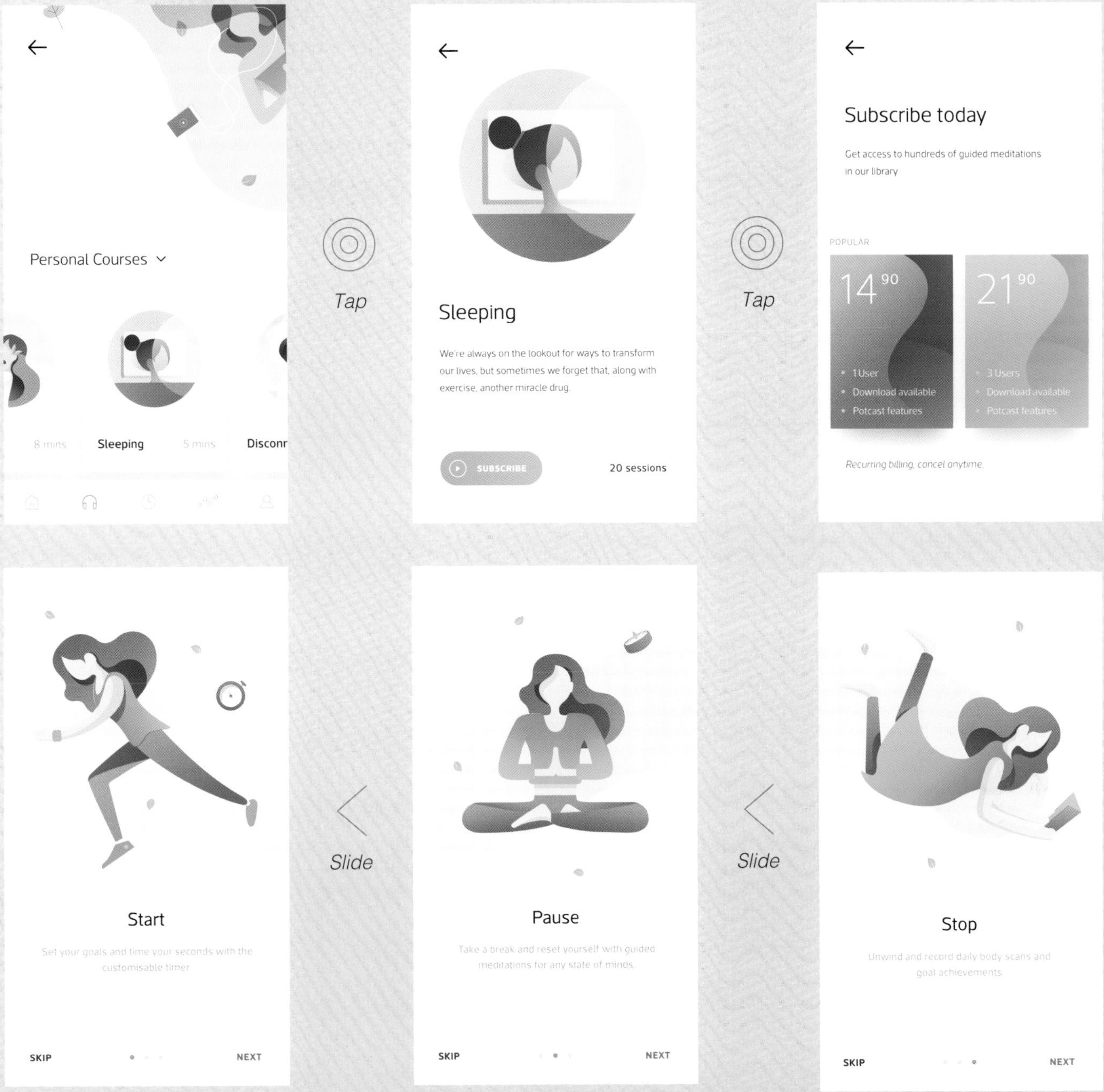

Personal Courses
8 mins
Sleeping
5 mins
Tap
Sleeping
We're always on the lookout for ways to transform our lives, but sometimes we forget that, along with exercise, another miracle drug.
SUBSCRIBE
20 sessions
Tap
Subscribe today
Get access to hundreds of guided meditations in our library
POPULAR
14 90
1 User
Download available
Potcast features
21 90
3 Users
Download available
Potcast features
Recurring billing, cancel anytime.
Start
Set your goals and time your seconds with the customisable timer
SKIP
NEXT
Slide
Pause
Take a break and reset yourself with guided meditations for any state of minds.
SKIP
NEXT
Slide
Stop
Unwind and record daily body scans and goal achievements
SKIP
NEXT

The target demographic are people who are 25-40 years old□both female and male□and are likely to lead a moderate to high stress lifestyle. It provides simple and intuitive features for users to practice mindfulness in their daily lives, such as listening to audio podcasts, tracking meditation sessions and browsing through mindfulness-related contents. The minimal design elements with vibrant visual illustrations were used to enhance user experience and make it easy to navigate through the screens.

Symbiosis

Design
Camille Frairrot, Victoire Douy

Development
Quentin Tshaimanga, Etienne Deladonchamps

Behance

Symbiosis is a mobile application going back and forth between real and virtual life. Users' virtual plant evolves according to their physical activity. The app allows users to reconnect with the nature around them by encouraging them to walk. Their steps will grow a plant in 3D that will flourish and allow another user to start the experience in turn.

SYMBIOSIS

Bienvenue

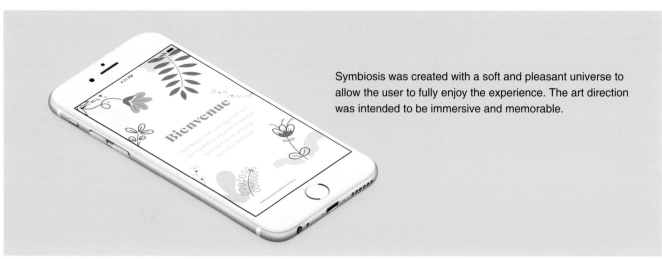

Symbiosis was created with a soft and pleasant universe to allow the user to fully enjoy the experience. The art direction was intended to be immersive and memorable.

COLONIE BUTTES CHAUMONTS
1 Rue Botzaris, 75019 Paris
COLONIE FLORAL
Esplanade du Château de Vincennes, 75012 Paris
COLONIE VILLETTE
211 Avenue Jean Jaurès, 75019 Paris
COLONIE MONCEAU
VOUS AVEZ EFFECTUÉ
4093 PAS
26 KM
GERMINATION
le 02.05.16 – 1200 pas
FLORAISON
le 06.05.16 – 4200 pas
FRUIT
le 10.05.16 – 7200 pas
Prochaine étape dans 1500 pas
SUGGESTION DE LIEUX
Sons et notifications
Modifier mot de passe
Signaler un problème
Voir les didacticiels
Déconnexion

01
Pollen
Tu peux désormais en te déplacant capter le pollen des utilisateurs à proximité afin de continuer l'aventure.
Slide
02
Fruit
Dès que ta plante rencontrera du pollen te produira une nouvelle surprise : un fruit.
J'AI COMPRIS →

PUNCHY

Punchy

Design
**Kim Baschet,
Clément Ougier, Tom Smile**

Development
**Adrien Vanderpotte,
Anthelme Dumont**

Behance

Punchy is an app linked to a connected punching-ball. With the object, the users can be notified of anti-veggie activities on social media and they can respond just with a punch! It's relaxing, programmable and fun.

The app allows users to see their stats, track their score, compare their rank with other owners of the connected object. It gamifies the connected object, and it creates a community around it. The application also provides access to the settings of the object: users can choose what to track, which enables personalization of the automated responses.

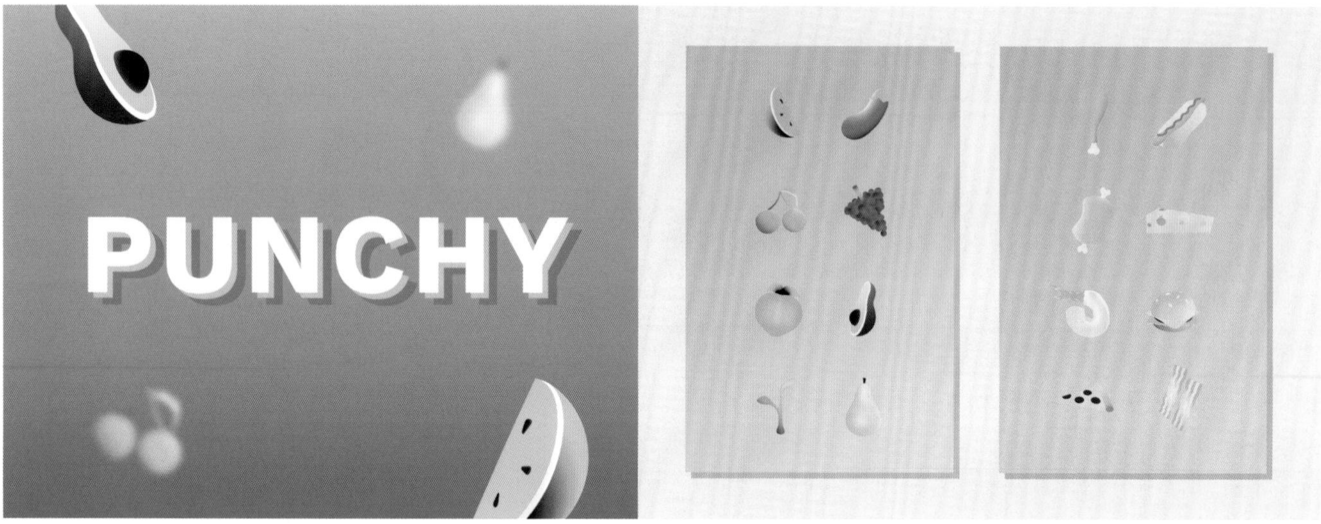
PUNCHY

PUNCHY
By VEGAN
DASHBOARD
SETTINGS
SCORE
You have punched
73 times
There's actually 77 punchers in the world
Slide
PUNCHY
By VEGAN
DASHBOARD
SETTINGS
STATS
Strength +17%
There's actually 77 punchers in the world
Slide
PUNCHY
By VEGAN
DASHBOARD
SETTINGS
GRADE
You're a
VEGANISTAR
There's actually 77 punchers in the world

CRUELTY FREE
No animals were hurt during
Join us
V For Vegan Organisation
70 Bd des Prairies
75005 Paris
hello@vforvegan.com
carrer@vforvegan.com
NEWSLETTER
TOP 10 PUNCHERS
Taylor
Vegetarian
SUBMIT
Product
Application
Community
Team
BUY
WHAT IS PUNCHY?
The way to fight the meat
Punchy is a connected punching-ball, created espacially for vegan peoples.
It helps you to fight for animals (litteraly) and keep the stress out!
WATCH THE STORY
V FOR VEGAN PRES
PUNC
Hit, don'
JOIN THE
racking
97,4K
66,1K
191,987
1,3K
29,002
THE OBJECT
The components
Punchy is a punching-ball. It is bouncing and fun, it makes your shots impressive. But it will never hurt your hand (or your feelings) because he is soft like a plush.
Punchy is a technologic object:
• LCD screen to display the tweet
• LED to notify
• Accelerometer to count your achievements
• Speaker to motivate you
• Arduino YUN to connect you punchy in Wifi
JOIN THE MOVEMENT

Dream Catcher

Design
Anqi Pan

Behance

The designer wanted to design an app which helps users capture, preserve and review their dreams. “We all have dreams when we sleep. We experience a different life, solve challenging problems and get great ideas in dreams. But dreams are so fleeting if we didn’t catch them immediately,” said the designer.

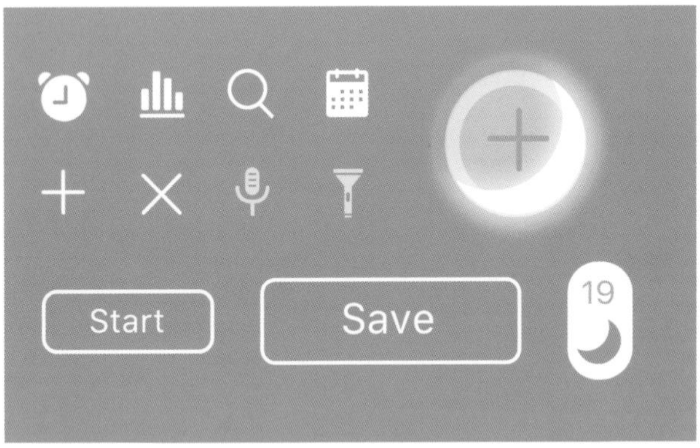

Start
Save
19

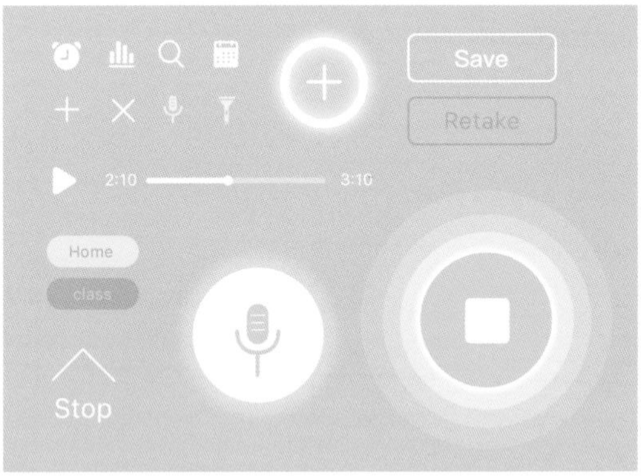

Save
Retake
2:10
3:10
Home
class
Stop

DREAM CATCHER
Help you capture, preserve and review your dreams.
Good Night!
Tuesday
Feburary, 21 2017
19 FEB 7:30 am My Dream Name
17 FEB 6:30 am Festival Exploded
16 FEB 8:00 am Back to December
11 FEB 8:10 am A beautiful gift
13 7:00 am
Good morning!
Wednesday
Feburary, 22 2017
21 FEB 7:00 am Weird Dream
19 FEB 7:30 am My Dream Name
15 FEB 6:30 am Festival Exploded
07 FEB 8:00 am Back to December
11 8:10 am

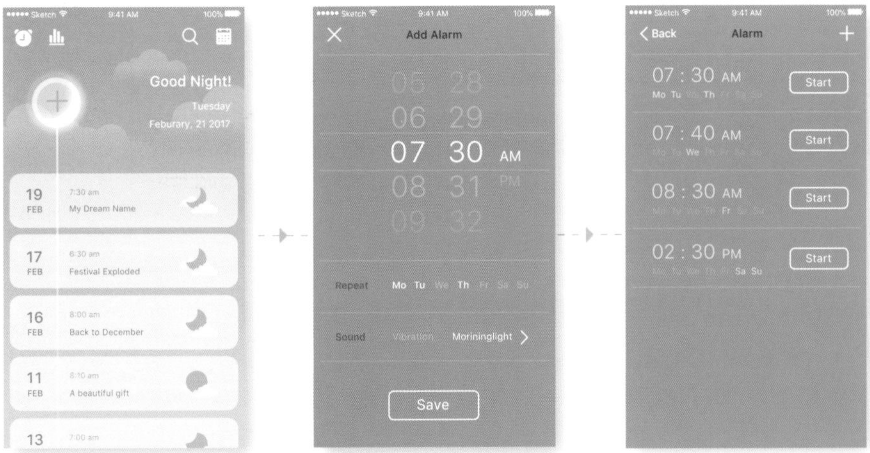
Good Night!
Tuesday
Feburary, 21 2017
19 FEB My Dream Name
17 FEB Festival Exploded
16 FEB Back to December
11 FEB A beautiful gift
13
Add Alarm
07 30 AM
Repeat
Sound
Vibration
Morininglight
Save
Back
Alarm
07 : 30 AM
07 : 40 AM
08 : 30 AM
02 : 30 PM
Start

Sketch
9:41 AM
100%
11:50 PM
alarm 09:50 am
Stop

When users wake up in the morning, they can swipe up to close the alarm and the app will automatically be turned to the dream catcher page. Users can record their dreams by speaking into the phone, and the app will transfer their audio content into text. After adding more details of the dreams, such as title, emotion and tag, their dreams have been captured.

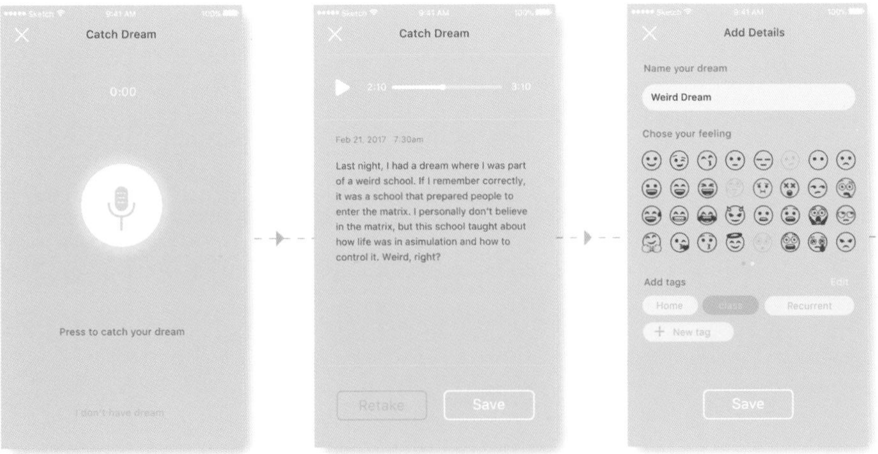
Catch Dream
0:00
Press to catch your dream
Catch Dream
Retake
Save
Add Details
Name your dream
Weird Dream
Chose your feeling
Add tags
Home
class
Recurrent
New tag
Save

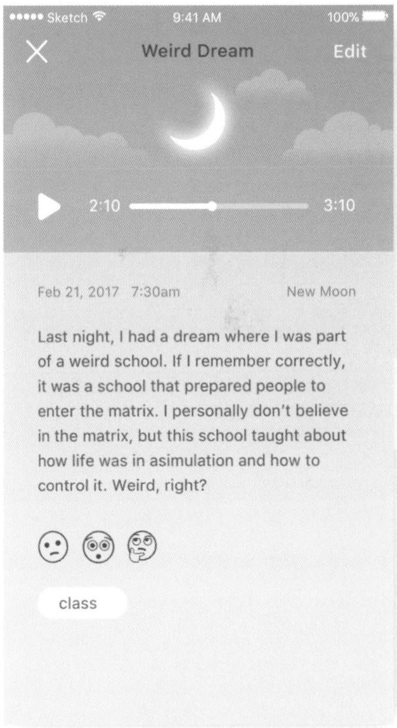
Sketch
9:41 AM
100%
Weird Dream
Edit
2:10
3:10
Feb 21, 2017 7:30am
New Moon
Last night, I had a dream where I was part of a weird school. If I remember correctly, it was a school that prepared people to enter the matrix. I personally don't believe in the matrix, but this school taught about how life was in asimulation and how to control it. Weird, right?
class

In terms of colour scheme, the designer chose a soft blue and pink gradient colour. The soft colour can protect users' eyes when they are about to sleep or just wake up. The direction of the gradient indicates day and night to help people know the current time. The inspirations of icon design come from moonlight and clouds. They were designed with a soft, light, and transparent look to represent the subtle and delicate feelings of dreams. All the icons are bigger than the normal app to let people easily detect and press when they are waking up.

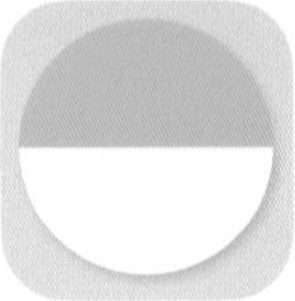

Simple Weather App

Design
Qiner Wang

Behance

The idea of this app came from the designer's daily use of weather app. She thinks the information is too cluttered and the design style lacks special feature. Therefore, she decided to design a simple weather forecast app, which provides a clean interface to display only the most significant information about the weather. She did some survey with people around her to rank the importance of all the weather elements in a weather app. Then she put the top three of them: current temperature, daily temperature range and weather icons on the main interface, and the rest of elements on the second page. Combined with nice colour compositions, it will be an app that is easy and fun to use.

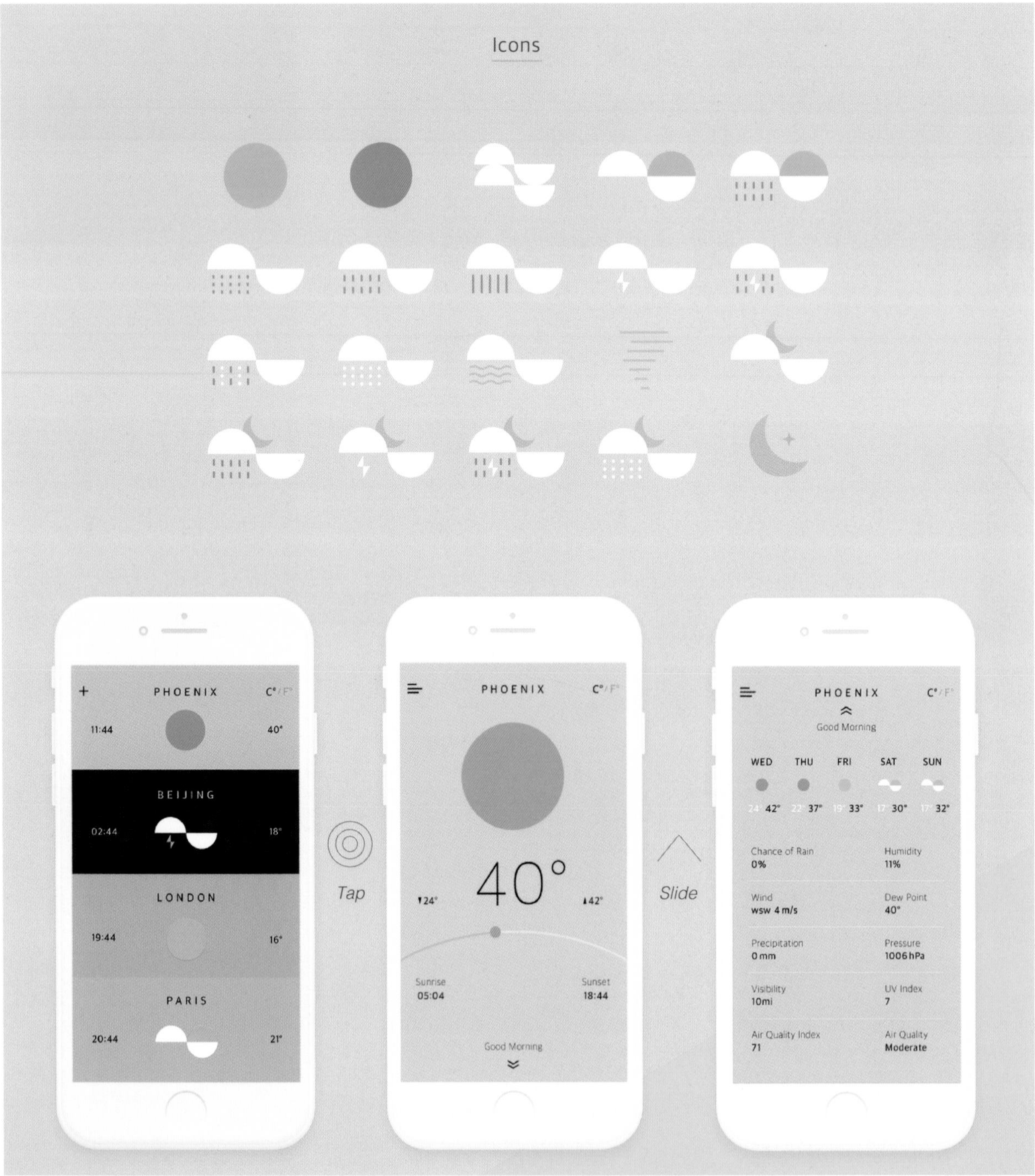

Icons
PHOENIX
11:44
40°
BEIJING
02:44
18°
LONDON
19:44
16°
PARIS
20:44
21°
Tap
PHOENIX
40°
24°
42°
Sunrise
05:04
Sunset
18:44
Good Morning
Slide
PHOENIX
Good Morning
WED
THU
FRI
SAT
SUN
42°
37°
33°
30°
32°
Chance of Rain
0%
Humidity
11%
Wind
wsw 4 m/s
Dew Point
40°
Precipitation
0 mm
Pressure
1006 hPa
Visibility
10mi
UV Index
7
Air Quality Index
71
Air Quality
Moderate

LONDON
C°/F°
16°
10°
18°
Sunrise
05:12
Sunset
20:40
Good Evening
LONDON
C°/F°
Good Evening
WED THU FRI SAT SUN
10° 18° 11° 19° 7° 16° 9° 16° 9° 18°
Chance of Rain
30%
Humidity
57%
Wind
ese 4 m/s
Dew Point
14°
Precipitation
0 mm
Pressure
1013 hPa
Visibility
10mi
UV Index
0
Air Quality Index
36
Air Quality
Good
BEIJING
C°/F°
27°
15°
30°
Sunrise
05:01
Sunset
19:18
Good Afternoon
BEIJING
C°/F°
Good Afternoon
WED THU FRI SAT SUN
15° 30° 16° 32° 17° 30° 19° 29° 17° 29°
Chance of Rain
10%
Humidity
89%
Wind
e 2 m/s
Dew Point
16°
Precipitation
0 mm
Pressure
1009 hPa
Visibility
1.5mi
UV Index
0
Air Quality Index
211
Air Quality
Unhealthy

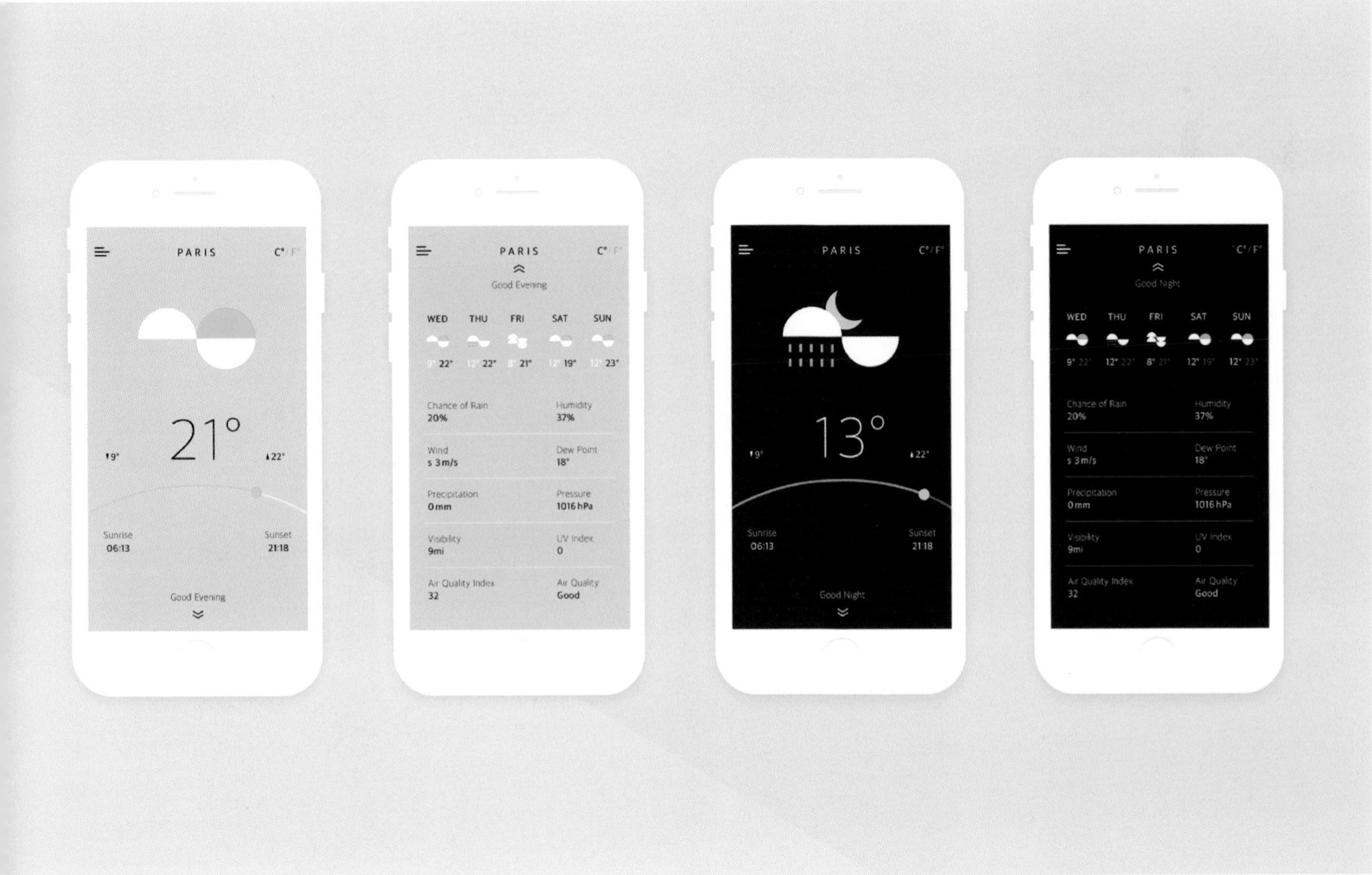
PARIS
C°/F°
21°
9°
22°
Sunrise
06:13
Sunset
21:18
Good Evening
PARIS
C°/F°
Good Evening
WED THU FRI SAT SUN
9° 22° 12° 22° 8° 21° 12° 19° 12° 23°
Chance of Rain
20%
Humidity
37%
Wind
s 3 m/s
Dew Point
18°
Precipitation
0 mm
Pressure
1016 hPa
Visibility
9mi
UV Index
0
Air Quality Index
32
Air Quality
Good
PARIS
C°/F°
13°
9°
22°
Sunrise
06:13
Sunset
21:18
Good Night
PARIS
C°/F°
Good Night
WED THU FRI SAT SUN
9° 22° 12° 22° 8° 21° 12° 19° 12° 23°
Chance of Rain
20%
Humidity
37%
Wind
s 3 m/s
Dew Point
18°
Precipitation
0 mm
Pressure
1016 hPa
Visibility
9mi
UV Index
0
Air Quality Index
32
Air Quality
Good

Chinese Painting Weather App

Design
Shangning Wang

Behance

The app is based on traditional Chinese culture and art. It will analyze the current season and climate to decide which subjects of Chinese painting would be used as the background image. The app also took reference from the wisdom of ancient Chinese: they could know the time by telling the different colours of the sky. By rotating the circular ring which represents different times of the day, the app will show the current colour of the sky and the temperature. With the change of time, the colour of the sky has an interesting interaction with the painting.

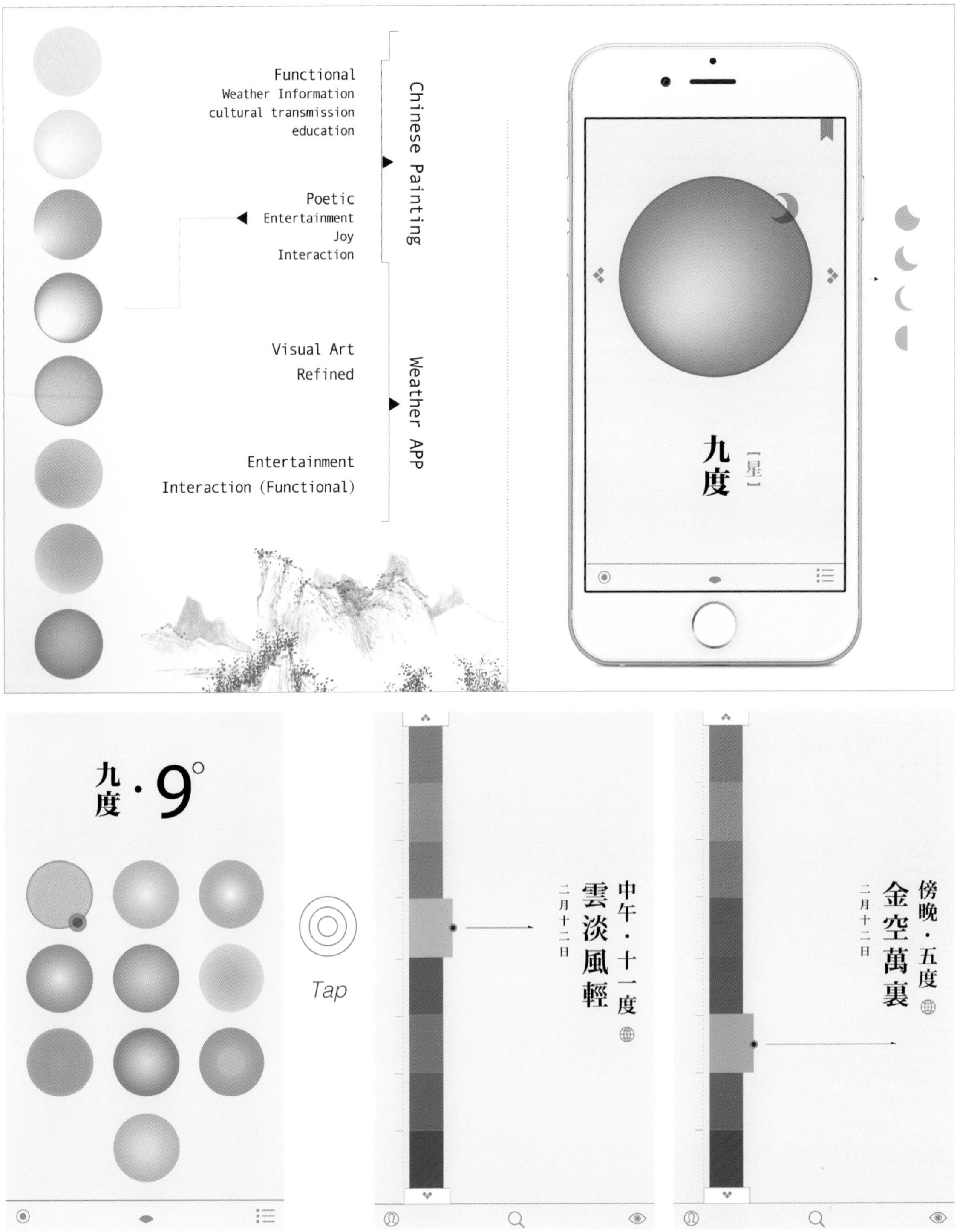

Functional
Weather Information
cultural transmission
education
Poetic
Entertainment
Joy
Interaction
Chinese Painting
Visual Art
Refined
Entertainment
Interaction (Functional)
Weather APP
九度
[星]
九度·9°
Tap
中午·十一度
雲淡風輕
二月十二日
傍晚·五度
金空萬裏
二月十二日

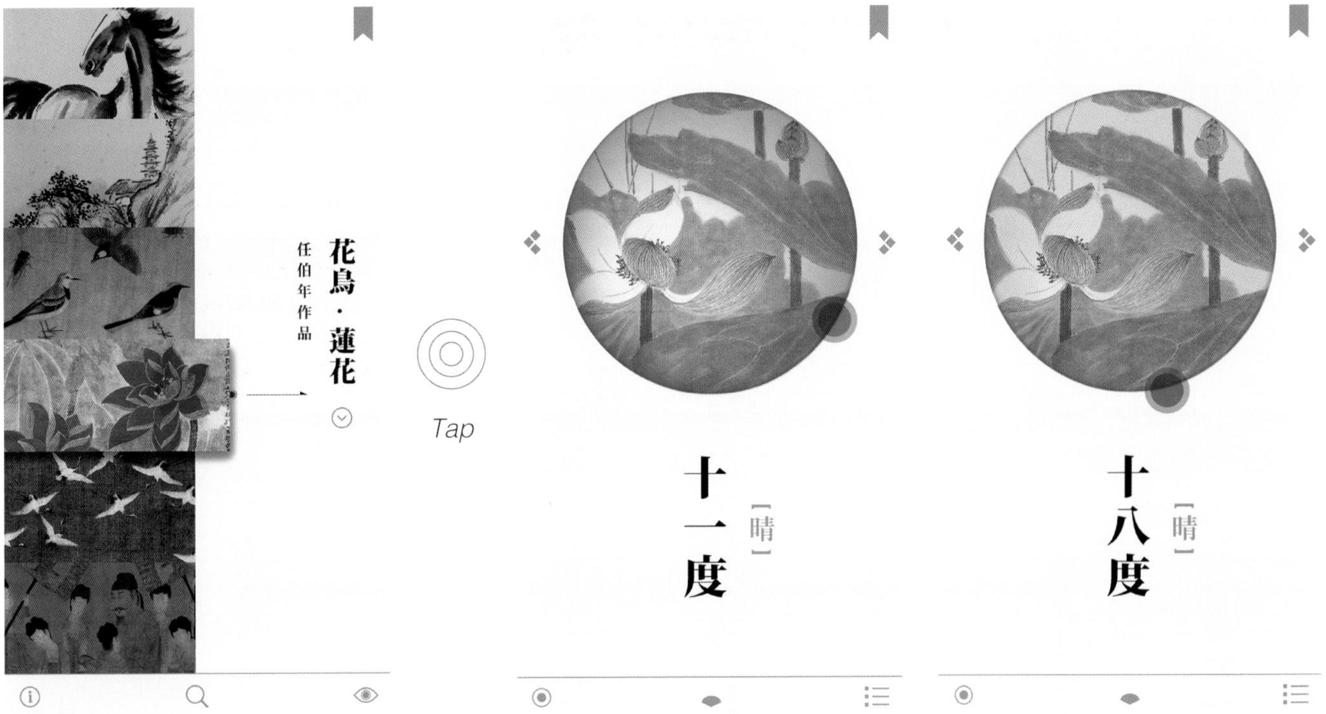

花鳥・蓮花
任伯年作品
Tap
十一度
【晴】
十八度
【晴】

The designer hopes that this app could make more people aware of the environmental pollution, and at the same time promote traditional Chinese art.

Kakaostory

Design
Kakao corp. kakaostory team

App Store

Kakaostory is a social media service that let users share their daily life with their family and friends. They can browse their friend's daily story or get in touch with new friends by using the search tab. The app also contains privacy setting, by which users could choose whether it is a private feed or a public feed. "It's ok if your life is not that special." The Kakaostory team wishes to design an app that is approachable for ordinary people.

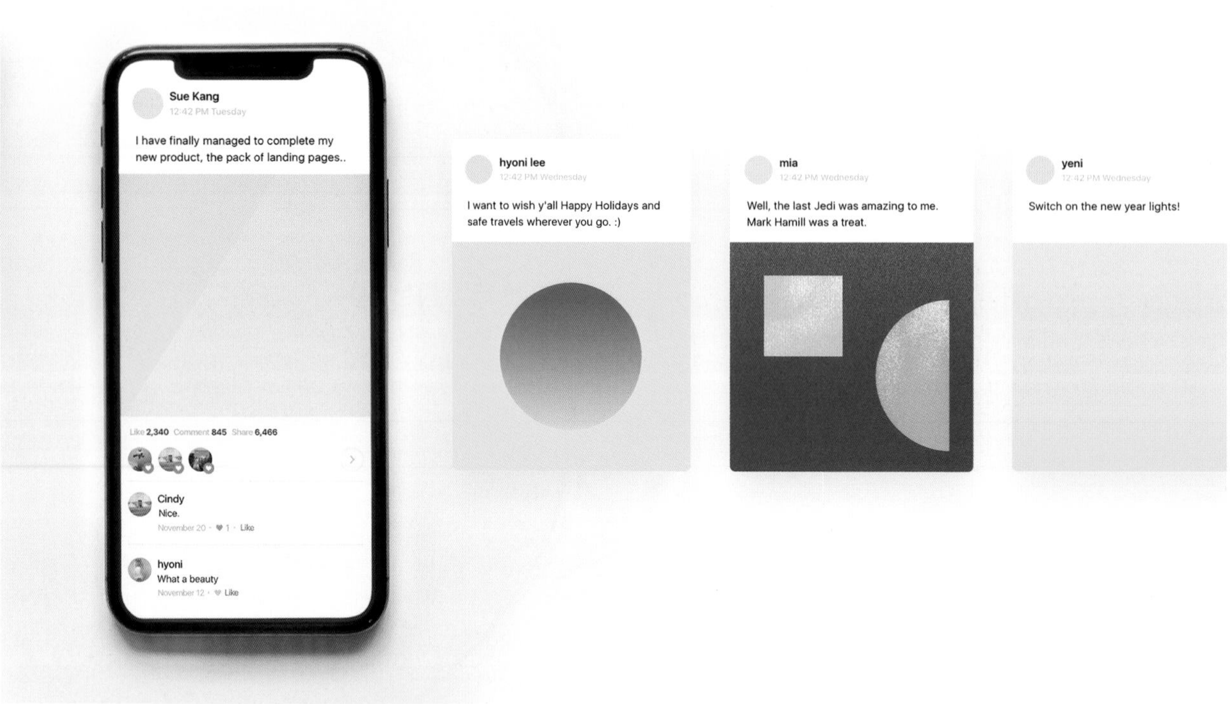

Sue Kang
12:42 PM Tuesday
I have finally managed to complete my new product, the pack of landing pages..
Like 2,340 Comment 845 Share 6,466
Cindy
Nice.
November 20 · 1 · Like
hyoni
What a beauty
November 12 · Like
hyoni lee
12:42 PM Wednesday
I want to wish y'all Happy Holidays and safe travels wherever you go. :)
mia
12:42 PM Wednesday
Well, the last Jedi was amazing to me. Mark Hamill was a treat.
yeni
12:42 PM Wednesday
Switch on the new year lights!

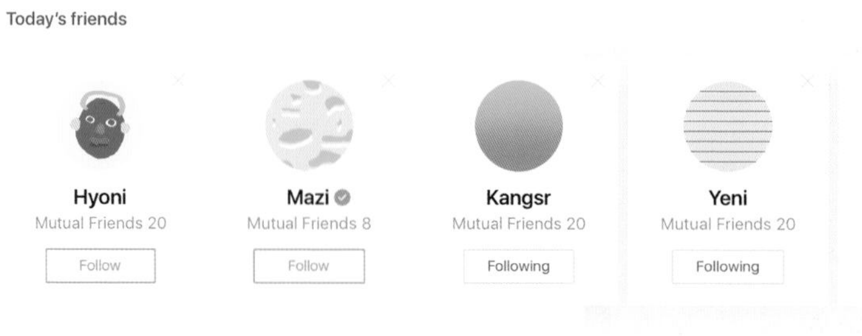

Today's friends
Hyoni
Mutual Friends 20
Follow
Mazi
Mutual Friends 8
Follow
Kangsr
Mutual Friends 20
Following
Yeni
Mutual Friends 20
Following

It's very easy to navigate and select content's thumbnail swipe view. You can choose daily photos or new friends card directly.

Share your story.

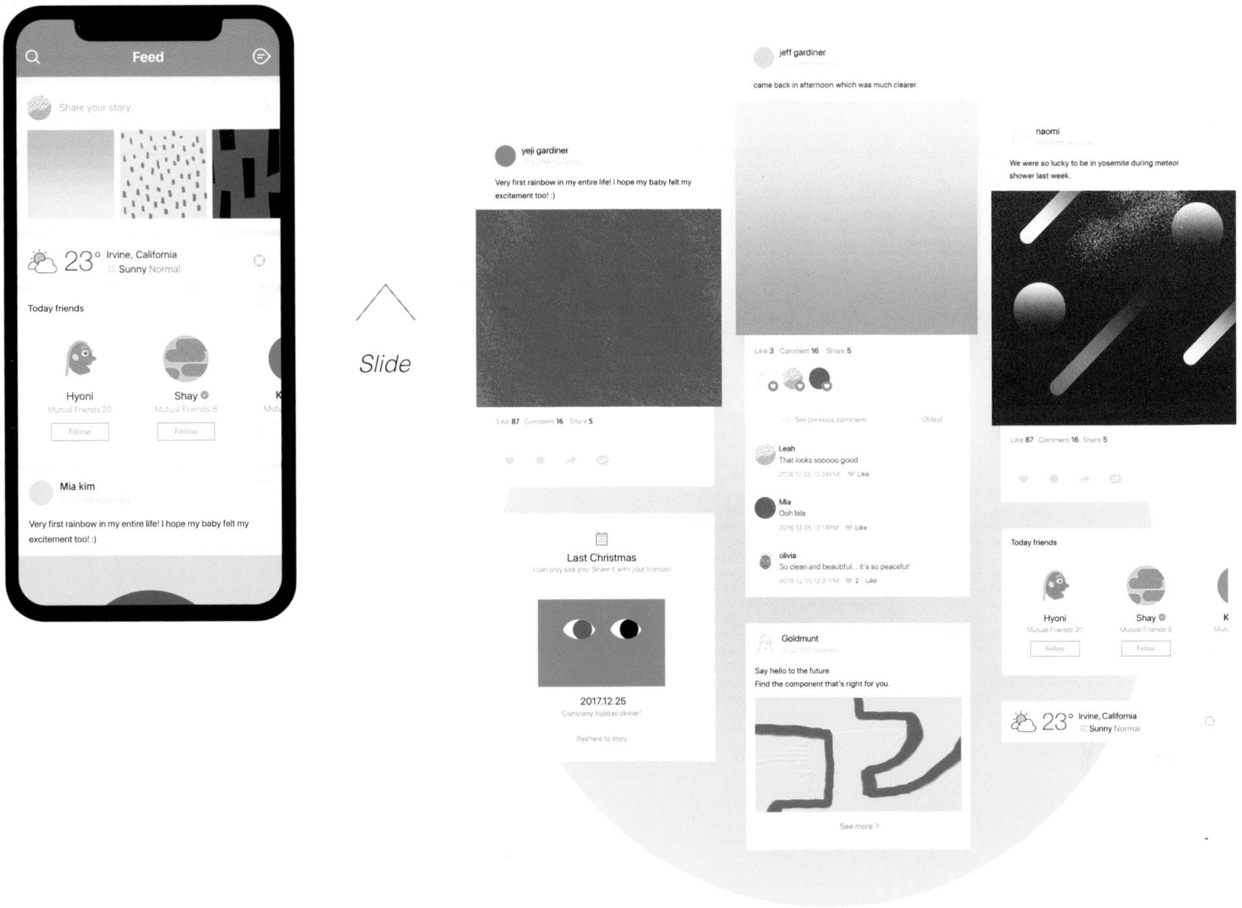
Feed
Share your story
23° Irvine, California
Sunny Normal
Today friends
Hyoni
Shay
Follow
Follow
Mia kim
Very first rainbow in my entire life! I hope my baby felt my excitement too! :)
Slide
jeff gardiner
came back in afternoon which was much clearer.
yeji gardiner
Very first rainbow in my entire life! I hope my baby felt my excitement too! :)
naomi
We were so lucky to be in yosemite during meteor shower last week.
Leah
That looks sooooo good
Mia
Ooh lala
olivia
So clean and beautiful... it's so peaceful!
Last Christmas
2017.12.25
Goldmunt
Say hello to the future.
Find the component that's right for you.
Today friends
Hyoni
Shay
23° Irvine, California
Sunny Normal

In terms of design solution, the main symbol of the Kakaostory is meant to be a shelter-like space where people can have fun in everyday life. Based on this symbol, the team has designed it into a pattern so that it looks like a cool graphic and maintain the symbolic yellow colour of kakao. For the feed colours, the team used bright and cheerful colours to express the atmosphere of communicating with daily stories.

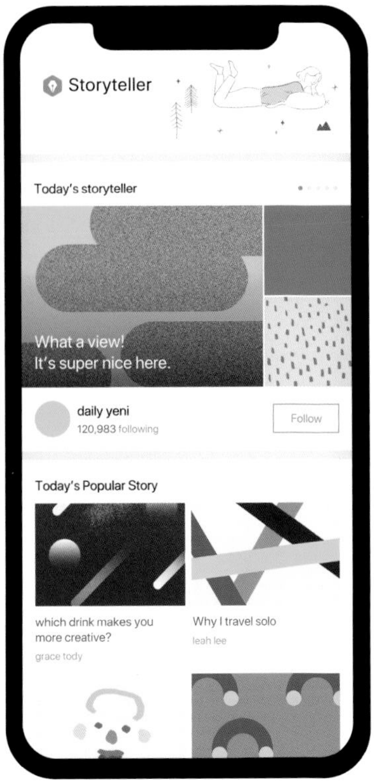
Storyteller
Today's storyteller
What a view!
It's super nice here.
daily yeni
120,983 following
Follow
Today's Popular Story
which drink makes you more creative?
grace tody
Why I travel solo
leah lee

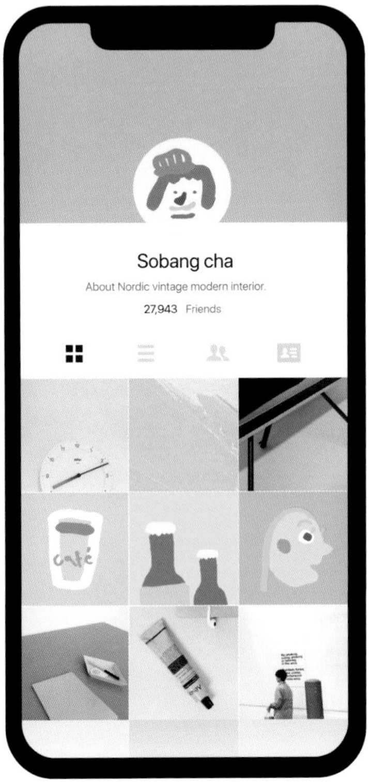
Sobang cha
About Nordic vintage modern interior.
27,943 Friends

In the Name of Home

Design
WN team

UX Design
Bezantee Bao

Art Direction
Bezantee Bao

Product Management
Deshegn Bao

Behance

WN is a network system focusing on gathering interior designers and providing professional interior design services. With the app "In the Name of Home", they hope they can help every user restore their home to its original ideal condition.

ICON

Services
Receipt
Works
Camera
Clipboard

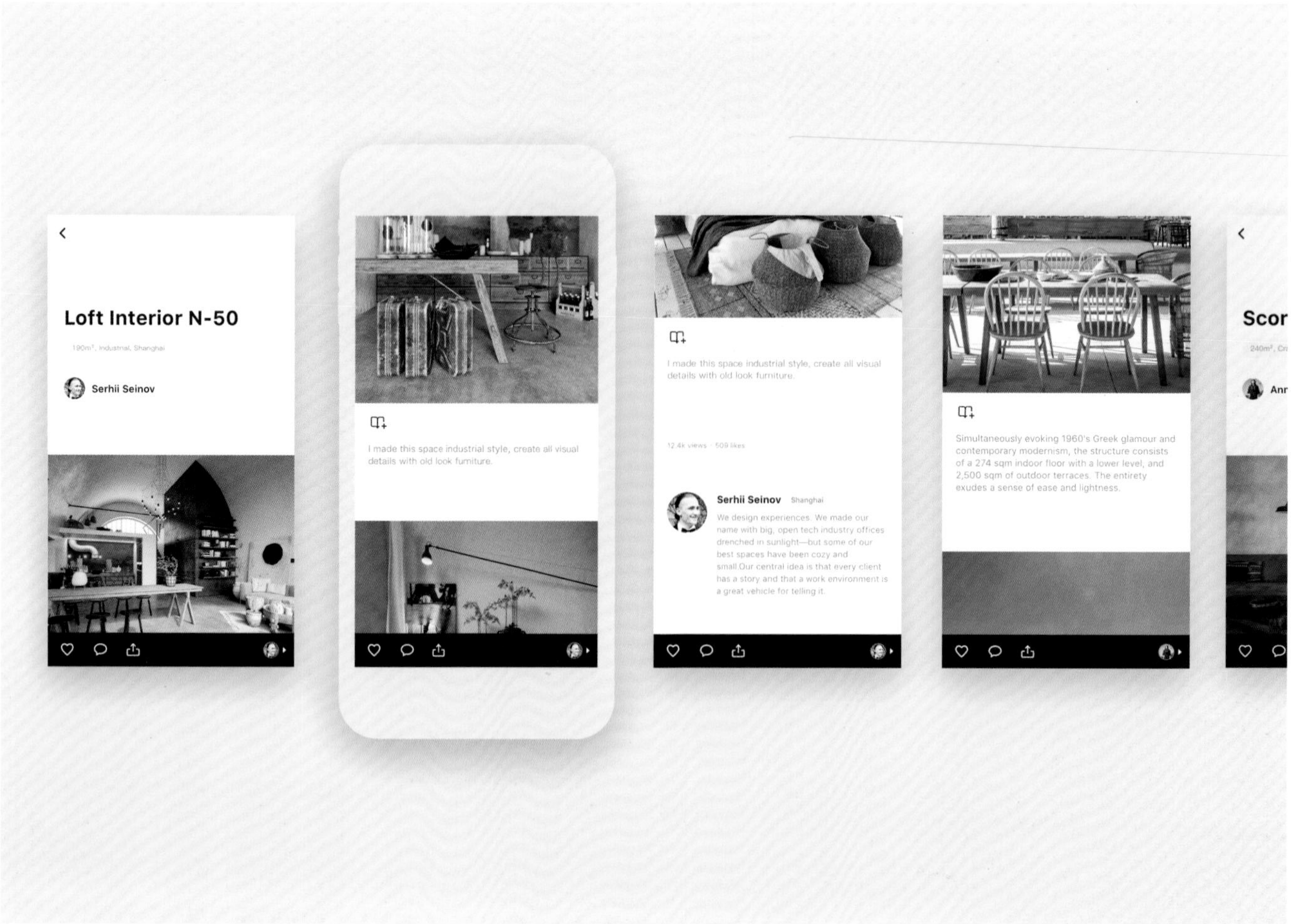
Loft Interior N-50
Serhii Seinov
I made this space industrial style, create all visual details with old look furniture.
I made this space industrial style, create all visual details with old look furniture.
Serhii Seinov
Shanghai
We design experiences. We made our name with big, open tech industry offices drenched in sunlight—but some of our best spaces have been cozy and small.Our central idea is that every client has a story and that a work environment is a great vehicle for telling it.
Simultaneously evoking 1960's Greek glamour and contemporary modernism, the structure consists of a 274 sqm indoor floor with a lower level, and 2,500 sqm of outdoor terraces. The entirety exudes a sense of ease and lightness.

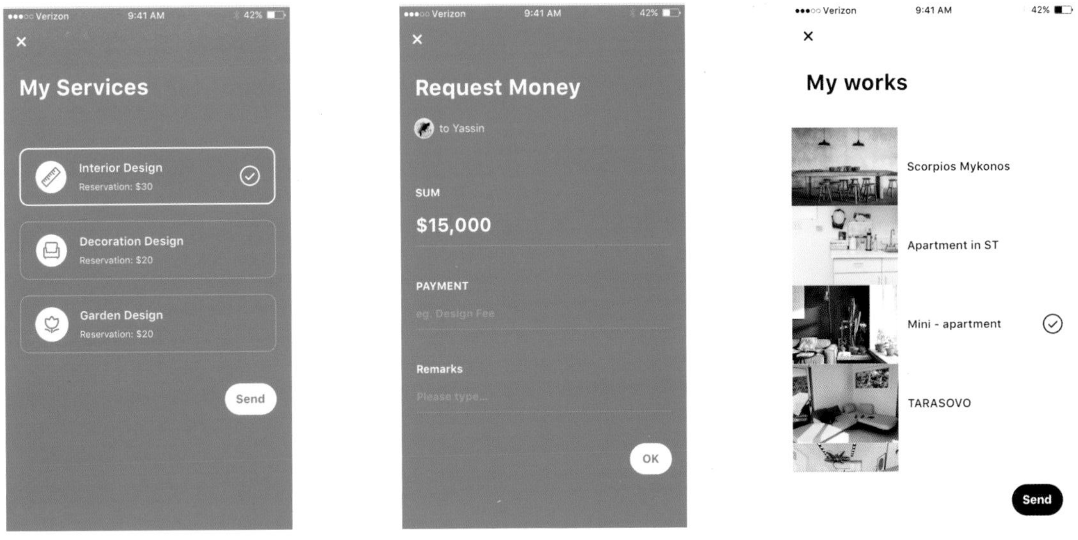
Verizon 9:41 AM 42%
My Services
Interior Design
Reservation: $30
Decoration Design
Reservation: $20
Garden Design
Reservation: $20
Send
Verizon 9:41 AM 42%
Request Money
to Yassin
SUM
$15,000
PAYMENT
eg. Design Fee
Remarks
Please type...
OK
Verizon 9:41 AM 42%
My works
Scorpios Mykonos
Apartment in ST
Mini - apartment
TARASOVO
Send

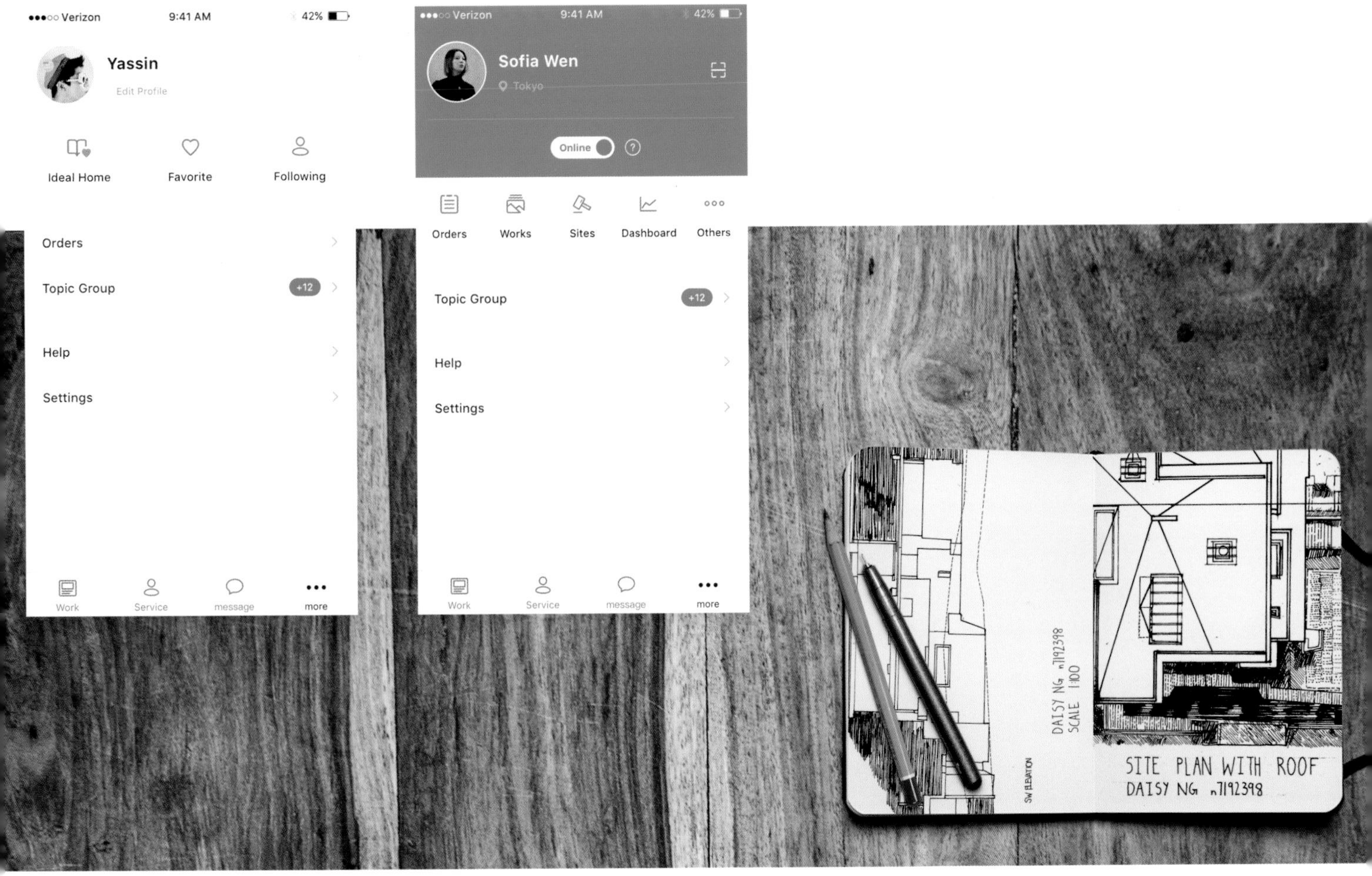
Verizon 9:41 AM 42%
Yassin
Edit Profile
Ideal Home
Favorite
Following
Orders
Topic Group
+12
Help
Settings
Work
Service
message
more
Verizon 9:41 AM 42%
Sofia Wen
Tokyo
Online
Orders
Works
Sites
Dashboard
Others
Topic Group
+12
Help
Settings
Work
Service
message
more
DAISY NG n7192398
SCALE 1:100
SW ELEVATION
SITE PLAN WITH ROOF
DAISY NG n7192398

Tan — Transportation Network Application Redesign

Design
Rhys Wallace

Behance

The city-wide transport network of Nantes, France, known as Tan has an official application for both iOS and Android smartphone users, allowing residents to manage and plan their journeys around the city. The application suffers from three core issues: slow and difficult usability, outdated visual design and a lack of vital features to assist users in their travel around the city. In response to these issues, designer Rhys Wallace carried out a redesign of the entire in-app experience, working on UX and UI to make the app more user-friendly and strengthen visual appeal.

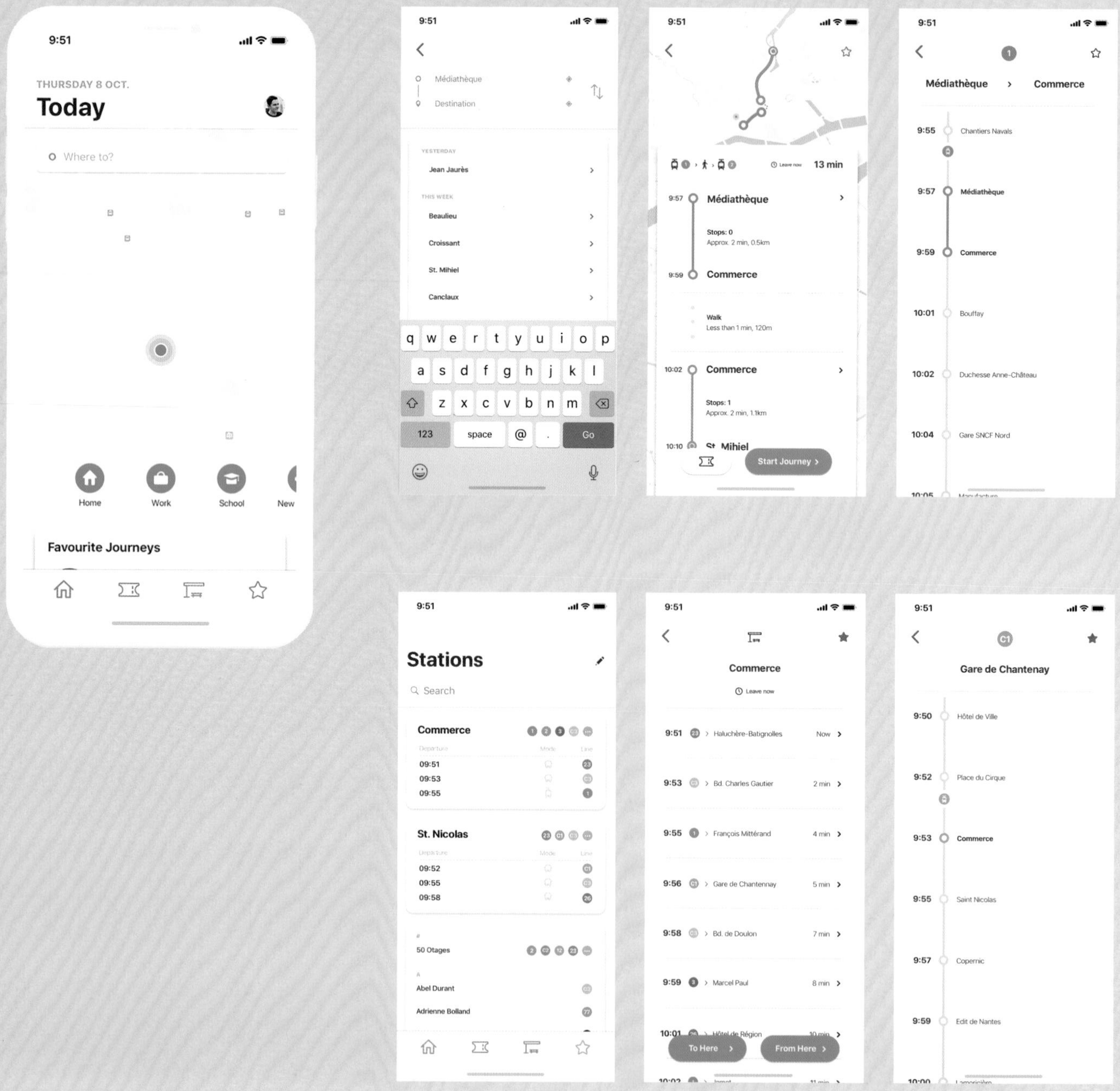

9:51
THURSDAY 8 OCT.
Today
Where to?
Home
Work
School
New
Favourite Journeys
Médiathèque
Destination
YESTERDAY
Jean Jaurès
THIS WEEK
Beaulieu
Croissant
St. Mihiel
Canclaux
123
space
@
Go
13 min
Médiathèque
Stops: 0
Approx. 2 min, 0.5km
Commerce
Walk
Less than 1 min, 120m
Commerce
Stops: 1
Approx. 2 min, 1.1km
St. Mihiel
Start Journey
Médiathèque
Commerce
9:55
Chantiers Navals
9:57
Médiathèque
9:59
Commerce
10:01
Bouffay
10:02
Duchesse Anne-Château
10:04
Gare SNCF Nord
Stations
Search
Commerce
09:51
09:53
09:55
St. Nicolas
09:52
09:55
09:58
50 Otages
Abel Durant
Adrienne Bolland
Commerce
Leave now
Haluchère-Batignolles
Now
Bd. Charles Gautier
2 min
François Mitterand
4 min
Gare de Chantenay
5 min
Bd. de Doulon
7 min
Marcel Paul
8 min
Hôtel de Région
To Here
From Here
Gare de Chantenay
9:50
Hôtel de Ville
9:52
Place du Cirque
9:53
Commerce
9:55
Saint Nicolas
9:57
Copernic
9:59
Edit de Nantes

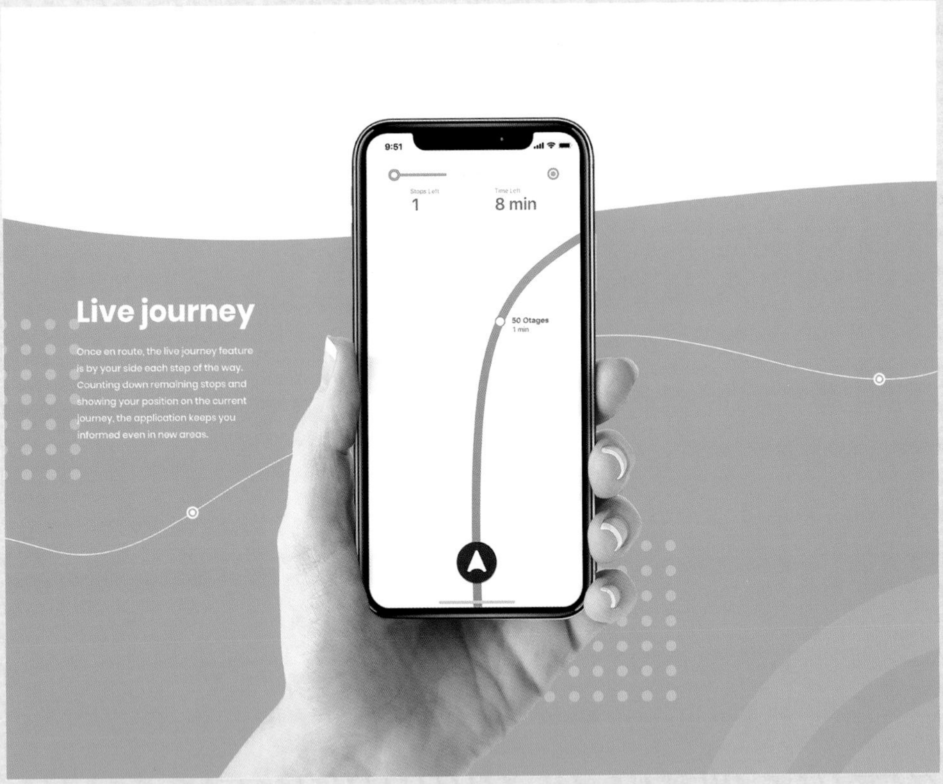
Live journey
Once en route, the live journey feature is by your side each step of the way. Counting down remaining stops and showing your position on the current journey, the application keeps you informed even in new areas.
9:51
1
8 min
50 Otages

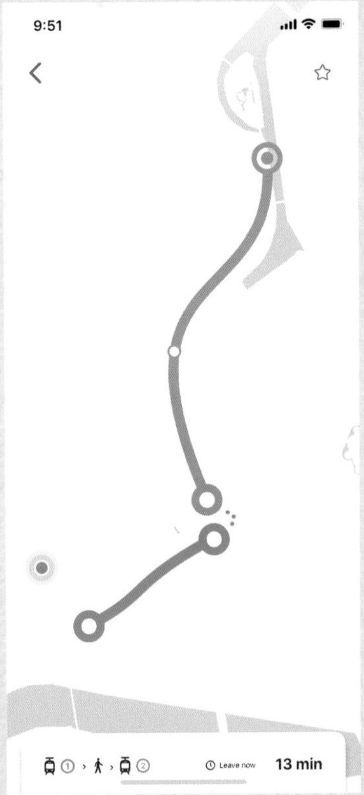
9:51
Leave now
13 min

With minimalistic but powerful iconography, a bold colour scheme and sleek typography, the Tan application was built with speed and ease of use in mind. Extensive user research was used to analyse the core features users most need when navigating the city. Determining pain points in existing navigation solutions provided a solid base for better responding to user needs.

Micro-animations within the interface serve to convey subtle information throughout the user's interaction with the application. These aid to display direction of travel on a given route or travel speed of a given bus or tram, but also navigation layout and hierarchy within the interface itself. Small details can be vital to ensuring an intuitive user experience.

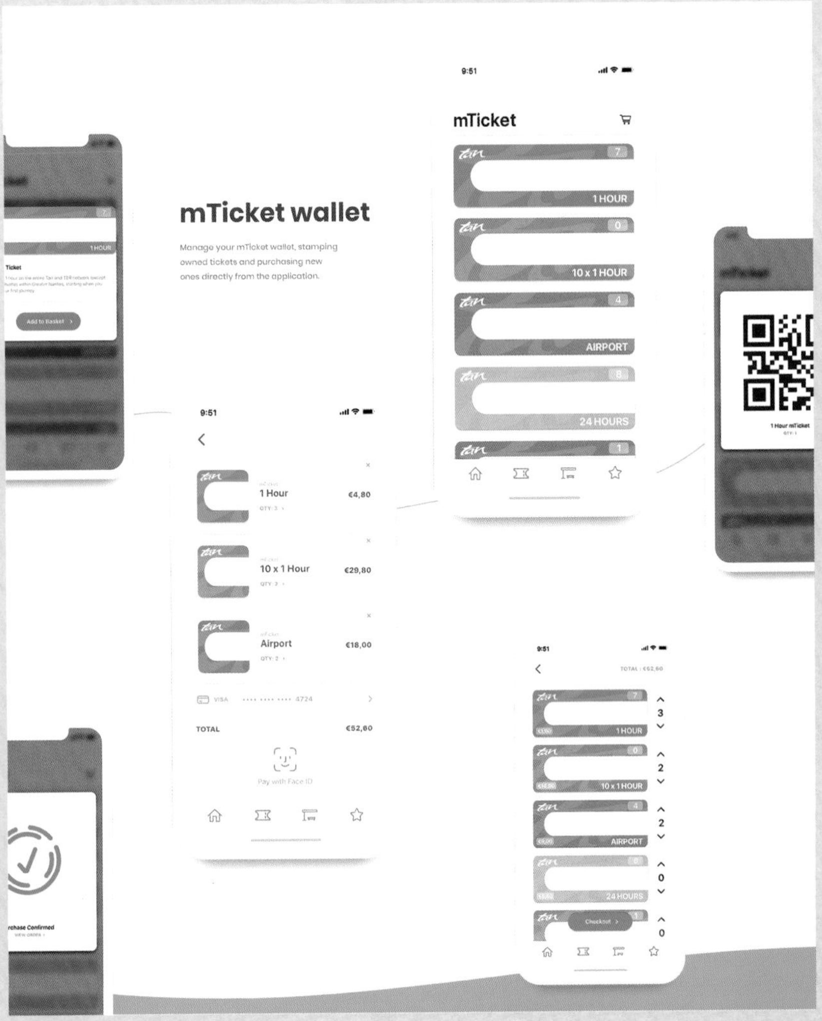
mTicket wallet
Manage your mTicket wallet, stamping owned tickets and purchasing new ones directly from the application.
mTicket
1 HOUR
10 x 1 HOUR
AIRPORT
24 HOURS
1 Hour
€4,80
10 x 1 Hour
€29,80
Airport
€18,00
TOTAL
€52,60

GroHappy

Design Agency
Significa

Design
Pedro ET

Illustration
Frederico Jesus

Behance

GroHappy provides an online introspective journey that gives users engaging tools to think proactively about how they grow both personally and professionally. Users start with completing 6 kinds of introspective questionnaires, and GroHappy will suggest a handful of life experiences that will help them grow. These can range from watching a single TED talk video on YouTube, attending a conference or completing a challenging course.

BLUE
#64CAFA
#D2EFFD

GREEN
#65E39F
#DEF6E9

ORANGE
#FFAD8C
#FFE8DE

YELLOW
#FFDB66
#FFF4D0

PINK
#FFB3B3
#FFE6E6

PURPLE
#C096FA
#E6D7FB

BLACK
#516077
#A6B0BC

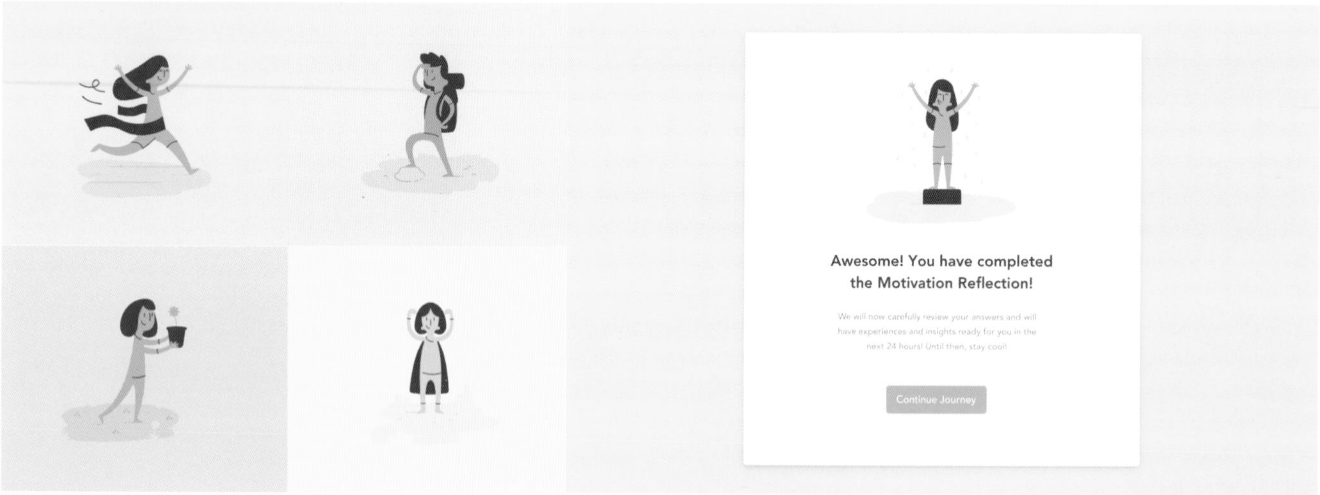
Awesome! You have completed
the Motivation Reflection!
We will now carefully review your answers and will have experiences and insights ready for you in the next 24 hours! Until then, stay cool!
Continue Journey

QUESTION 3 OF 4
Back
Submit
QUESTION 3 OF 4
Back
Submit
QUESTION 3 OF 4
Back
Submit
QUESTION 3 OF 4
Back
Submit
QUESTION 3 OF 4
Back
Submit

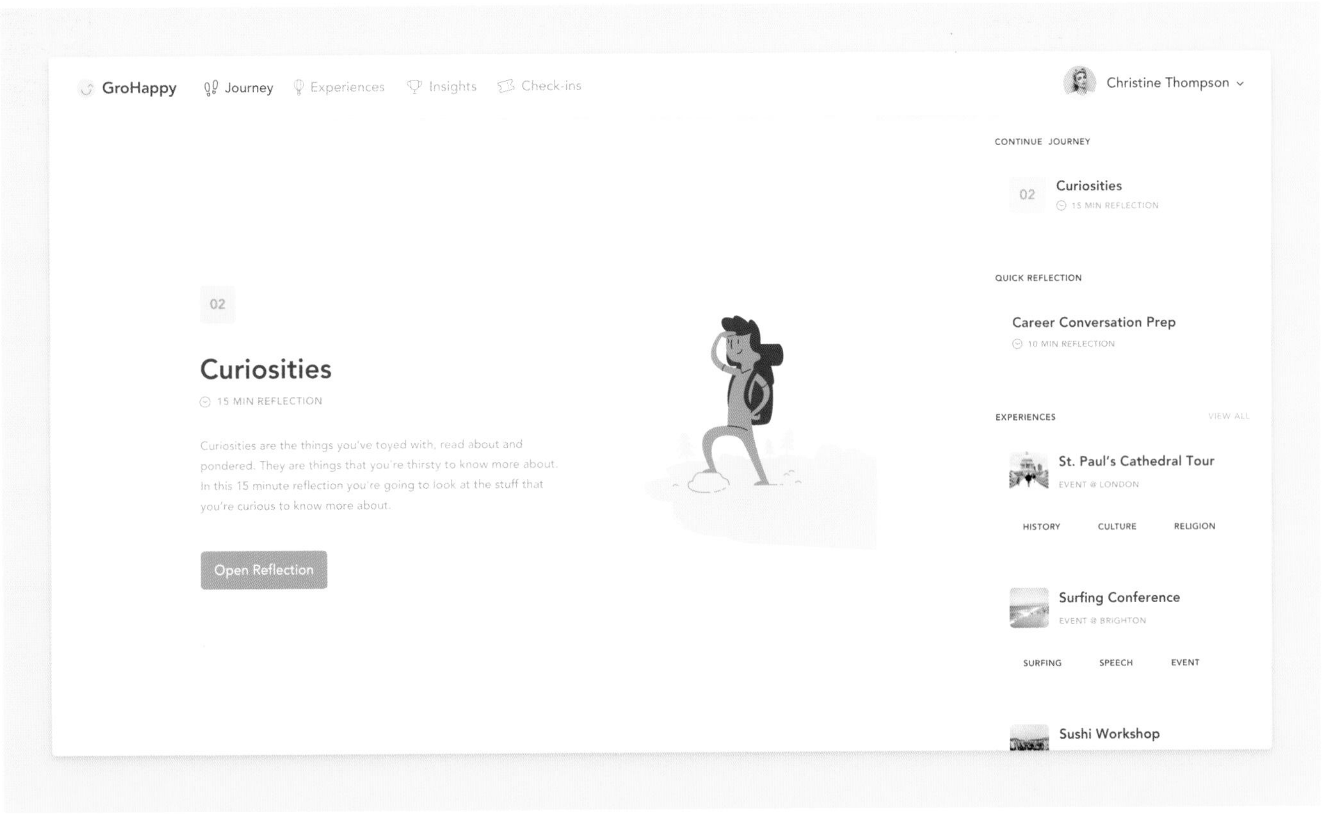
GroHappy
Journey
Experiences
Insights
Check-ins
Christine Thompson
CONTINUE JOURNEY
02
Curiosities
15 MIN REFLECTION
QUICK REFLECTION
Career Conversation Prep
10 MIN REFLECTION
EXPERIENCES
VIEW ALL
St. Paul's Cathedral Tour
EVENT @ LONDON
HISTORY
CULTURE
RELIGION
Surfing Conference
EVENT @ BRIGHTON
SURFING
SPEECH
EVENT
Sushi Workshop
02
Curiosities
15 MIN REFLECTION
Curiosities are the things you've toyed with, read about and pondered. They are things that you're thirsty to know more about. In this 15 minute reflection you're going to look at the stuff that you're curious to know more about.
Open Reflection

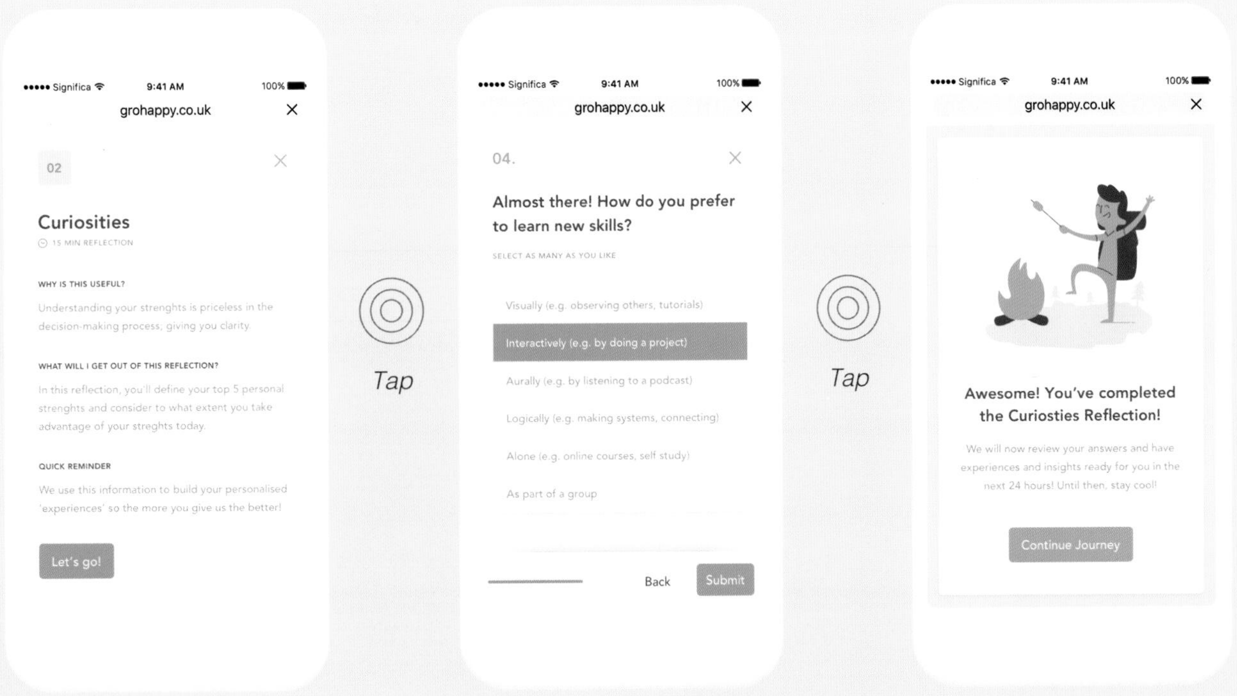
grohappy.co.uk
02
Curiosities
15 MIN REFLECTION
WHY IS THIS USEFUL?
Understanding your strenghts is priceless in the decision-making process, giving you clarity.
WHAT WILL I GET OUT OF THIS REFLECTION?
In this reflection, you'll define your top 5 personal strenghts and consider to what extent you take advantage of your streghts today.
QUICK REMINDER
We use this information to build your personalised 'experiences' so the more you give us the better!
Let's go!
Tap
grohappy.co.uk
04.
Almost there! How do you prefer to learn new skills?
SELECT AS MANY AS YOU LIKE
Visually (e.g. observing others, tutorials)
Interactively (e.g. by doing a project)
Aurally (e.g. by listening to a podcast)
Logically (e.g. making systems, connecting)
Alone (e.g. online courses, self study)
As part of a group
Back
Submit
Tap
grohappy.co.uk
Awesome! You've completed the Curiosties Reflection!
We will now review your answers and have experiences and insights ready for you in the next 24 hours! Until then, stay cool!
Continue Journey

To represent these 6 reflections, the designer picked six different colours that are visible in all of their corresponding elements and illustrations. This creates a sweet contrast between the playful questionnaires while still allowing the user to focus entirely on his answers.

Sherd

Design
Luca Volino

Illustration
Gianmarco Bertone

Behance

Sherd is a mobile application that allows people to join the archaeological parks in an innovative way. The aim is to design an app that use gamification to stimulate users to "learn by playing". They can complete a real mission on site to continue in the game, to level up and to gain Sherds—the currency that can be exchanged with virtual or real benefits (such as bookshop discounts, Amazon gift cards, etc.). The application also allows the users to have greater awareness of their level of learning and stimulates the collaboration with other visitors by showing a leaderboard or the other players on the site. The app can work "onsite" and "offsite" with other games that can be done from home, and gives the user a benefit that can be used when he visits the site.

Main Colors
primary and secondary colors
Dark Gray
HEX #575757
RGB 87, 87,87
Dark Orange
HEX #FE953A
RGB 254, 149, 58
Crimson
HEX #F86C7B
RGB 248, 108, 123
Light Gray
HEX #9B9B9B
RGB 155, 155, 155
Orange
HEX #FAB85F
RGB 250, 184, 95
Lawn Green
HEX #7DD652
RGB 125, 214, 82
Gainsboro
HEX #C9C9C9
RGB 201, 201, 201
Royal Blue
HEX #5FA3FC
RGB 95, 163, 252
Blue Violet
HEX #A186FF
RGB 161, 134, 255

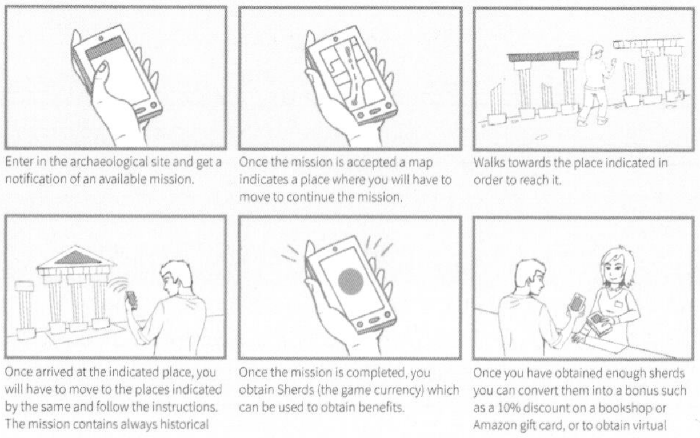
Enter in the archaeological site and get a notification of an available mission.
Once the mission is accepted a map indicates a place where you will have to move to continue the mission.
Walks towards the place indicated in order to reach it.
Once arrived at the indicated place, you will have to move to the places indicated by the same and follow the instructions. The mission contains always historical
Once the mission is completed, you obtain Sherds (the game currency) which can be used to obtain benefits.
Once you have obtained enough sherds you can convert them into a bonus such as a 10% discount on a bookshop or Amazon gift card, or to obtain virtual

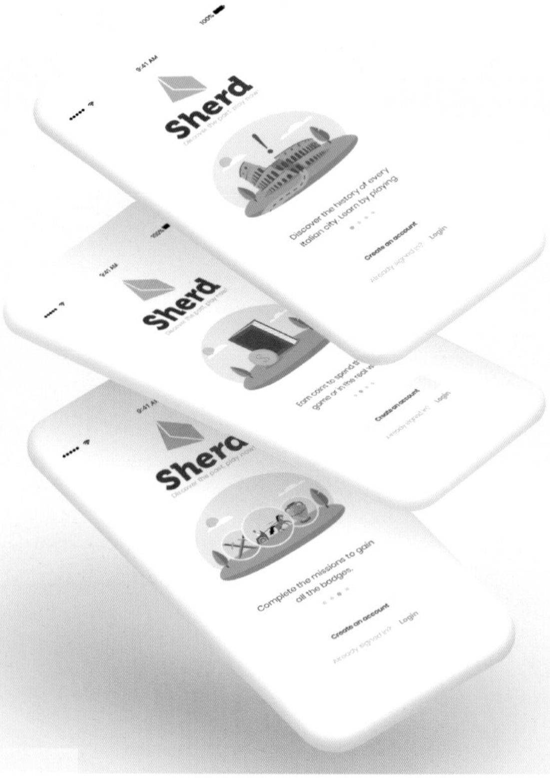
Sherd
Sherd
Sherd

9:41 AM
100%
Save the race
Save the chariot race!
There has been some trouble: one of my horses is missing, I cannot start the race. Emperor Maxentius will be here shortly to watch the race. Please, help me find it. Try looking near the stables.
60
+5 pt roman art
Accept

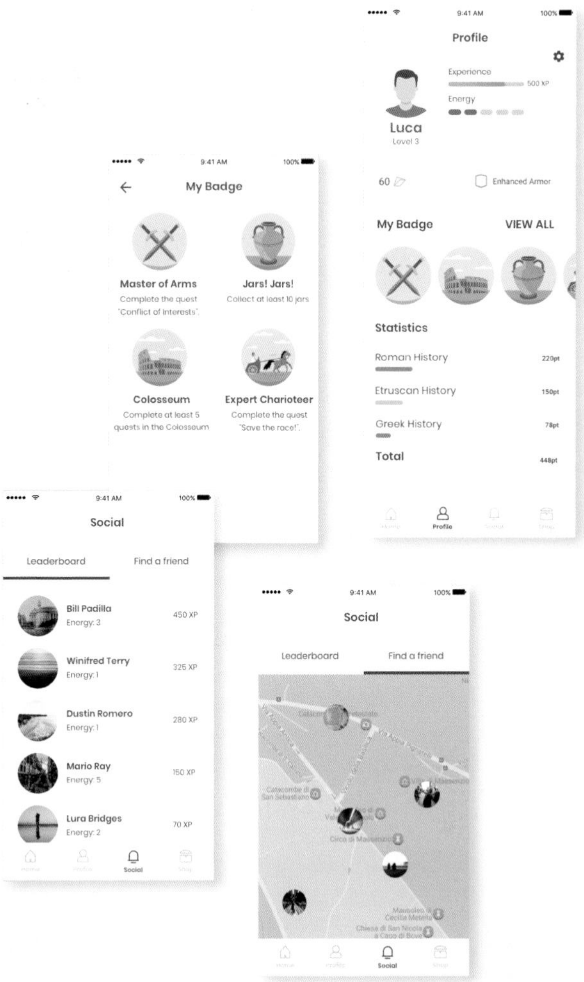
Profile
Luca
My Badge
VIEW ALL
Statistics
Roman History
Etruscan History
Greek History
Total
My Badge
Master of Arms
Jars! Jars!
Colosseum
Expert Charioteer
Social
Leaderboard
Find a friend
Bill Padilla
Winifred Terry
Dustin Romero
Mario Ray
Lura Bridges
Social
Leaderboard
Find a friend

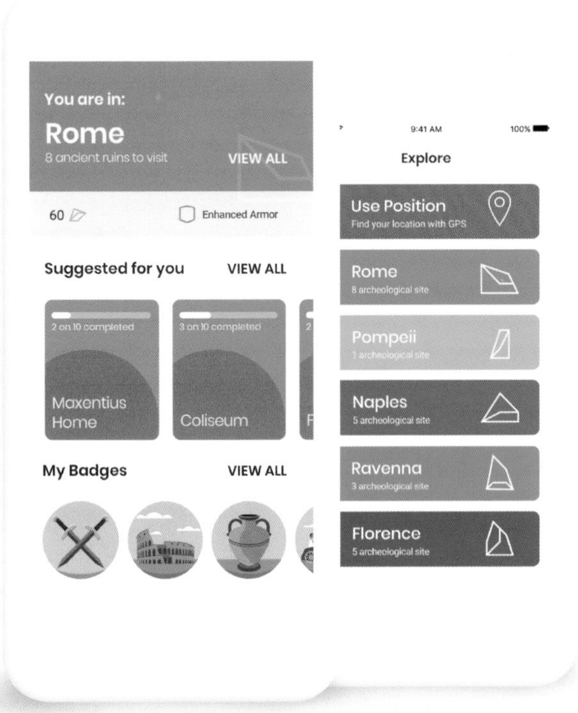
You are in:
Rome
8 ancient ruins to visit
VIEW ALL
60
Enhanced Armor
Suggested for you
VIEW ALL
2 on 10 completed
3 on 10 completed
Maxentius Home
Coliseum
My Badges
VIEW ALL
9:41 AM
100%
Explore
Use Position
Find your location with GPS
Rome
8 archeological site
Pompeii
1 archeological site
Naples
5 archeological site
Ravenna
3 archeological site
Florence
5 archeological site

The colours of the final design are based on the city that users choose or where they are located now. The goal is to combine ancient topics—such as excavations with an adventurous style of play—but at the same time maintain the historical validity of the data in the quest. The visual identity of Sherd is characterized by the presence of geometric elements such as the rhombus that comes closest to the shape of the fragment used to go back to the historical period (called sherd in the archaeological glossary) on which the concept rotates. Flat illustrations have been adopted for the realization of the characters, while the landscapes have been recreated maintaining the historical structure of the landscape.

Snipsl

Design Agency
Significa

Design
André Furtado, Mariana Gomes, Pedro Brandão, Pedro ET

Illustration
Frederico Jesus, Mother Volcano

Behance

Snipsl is an online platform where users can browse their favourite books and authors, with a personal library where they can find all the books they have subscribed to. The app allows for constant interaction between author and reader, as the reader's opinion can influence the outcome of the story.

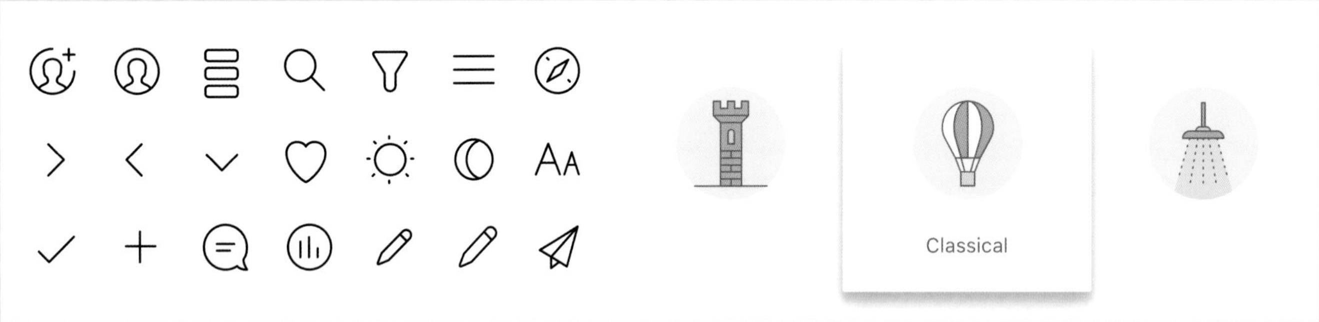
AA
Classical

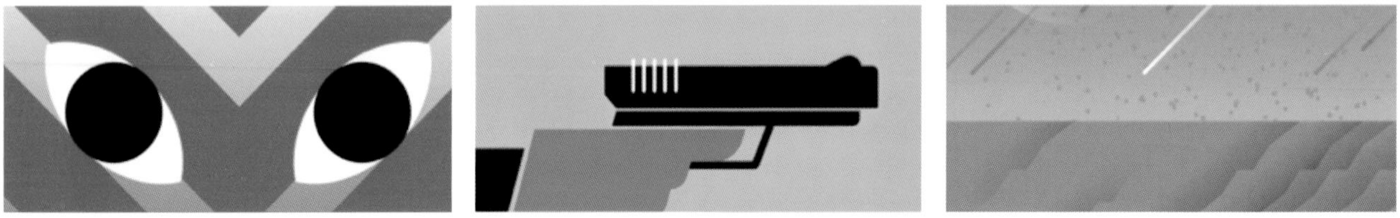

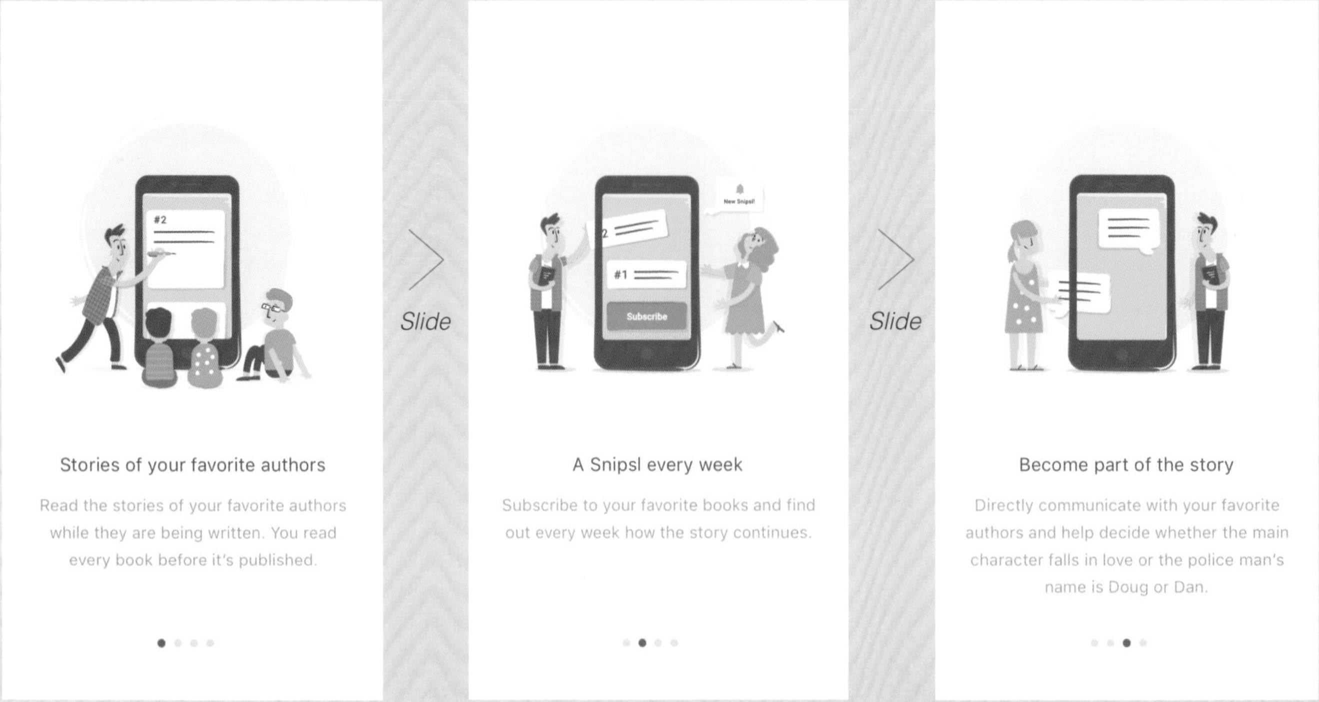
#2
Stories of your favorite authors
Read the stories of your favorite authors while they are being written. You read every book before it's published.
Slide
#1
Subscribe
A Snipsl every week
Subscribe to your favorite books and find out every week how the story continues.
Slide
Become part of the story
Directly communicate with your favorite authors and help decide whether the main character falls in love or the police man's name is Doug or Dan.

The user should easily find new content to read, seamlessly get involved in a good book, effortlessly interact with the author, and then organize all of his favourite books into a structured personal library. As this can happen in any random order, the app's flow has to be instinctive, almost automatic, so the user can focus on the core purpose of the app—reading.

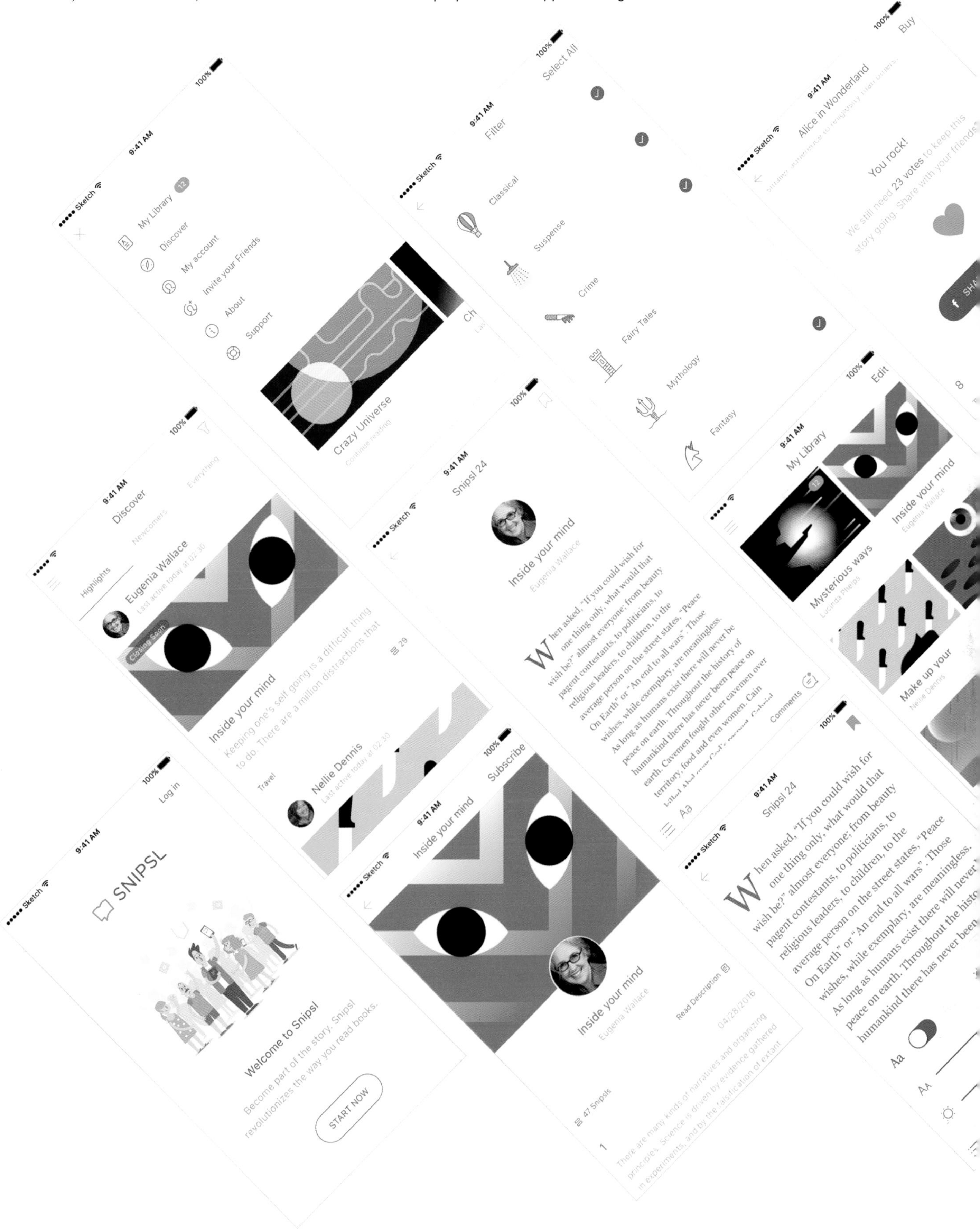

Sketch
9:41 AM
100%
My Library
12
Discover
My account
Invite your Friends
About
Support
Filter
Select All
Classical
Suspense
Crime
Fairy Tales
Mythology
Fantasy
Crazy Universe
Alice in Wonderland
Buy
You rock!
We still need 23 votes to keep this story going. Share with your friends
Discover
Highlights
Newcomers
Everything
Eugenia Wallace
Closing Soon
Inside your mind
29
Nellie Dennis
Travel
Snipsl 24
Comments
Aa
My Library
Edit
Mysterious ways
Lucinda Phelps
Make up your
SNIPSL
Log in
Welcome to Snipsl
Become part of the story. Snipsl revolutionizes the way you read books.
START NOW
Subscribe
Read Description
04/28/2016
47 Snipsls

Whittl

Design Agency
Heco

Project Page

Whittl is an app that lets people book local services—salons, florists, optometrists, etc.—and helps appointment-based businesses grow. Design agency Heco refreshed the design system of Whittl's new app to help their product grow.

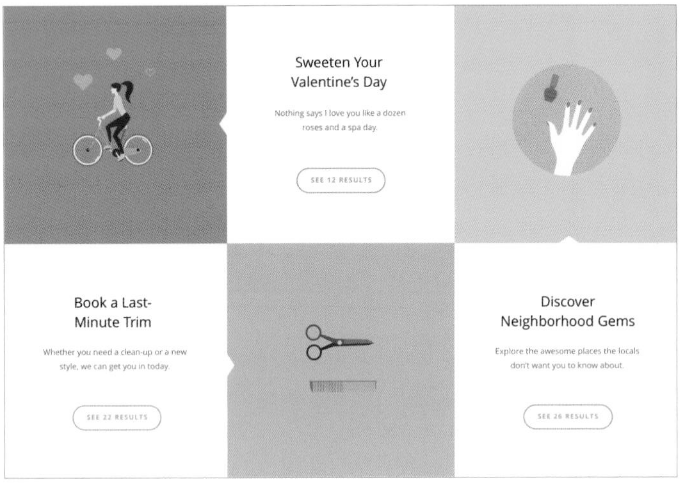

Sweeten Your Valentine's Day
Nothing says I love you like a dozen roses and a spa day.
SEE 12 RESULTS
Book a Last-Minute Trim
Whether you need a clean-up or a new style, we can get you in today.
SEE 22 RESULTS
Discover Neighborhood Gems
Explore the awesome places the locals don't want you to know about.
SEE 26 RESULTS

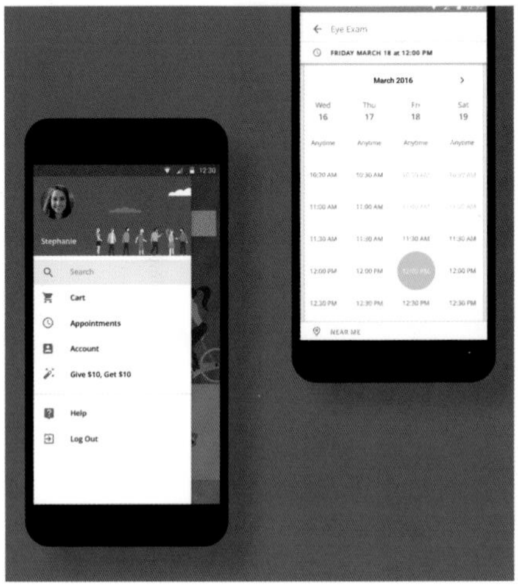

Eye Exam
March 2016
Stephanie
Search
Cart
Appointments
Account
Give $10, Get $10
Help
Log Out
NEAR ME

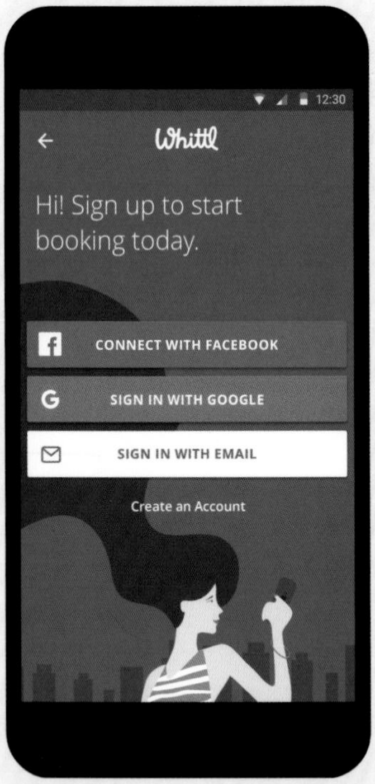

12:30
Whittl
Hi! Sign up to start booking today.
CONNECT WITH FACEBOOK
SIGN IN WITH GOOGLE
SIGN IN WITH EMAIL
Create an Account

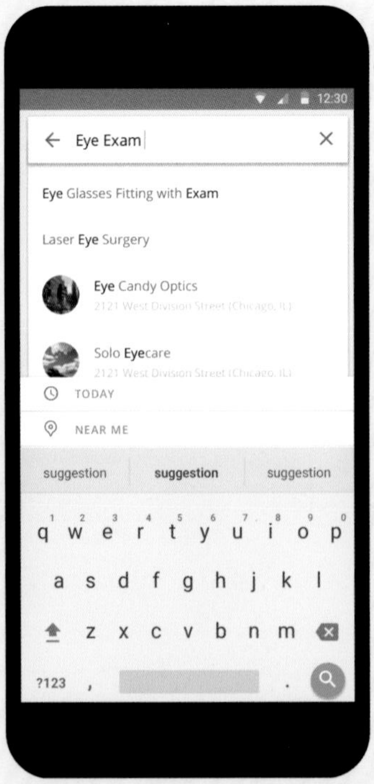

12:30
Eye Exam
Eye Glasses Fitting with Exam
Laser Eye Surgery
Eye Candy Optics
Solo Eyecare
TODAY
NEAR ME
suggestion
suggestion
suggestion

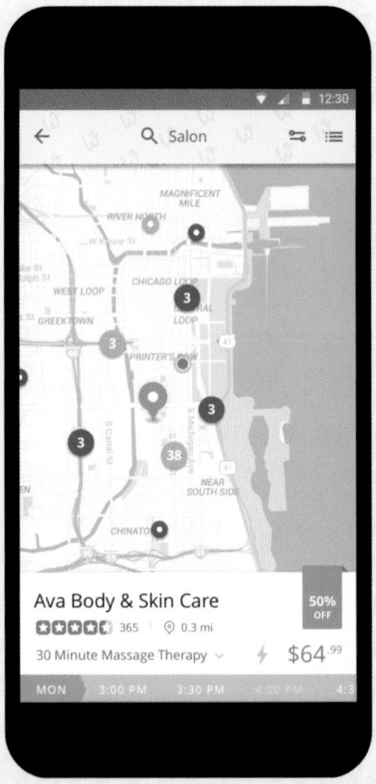

12:30
Salon
Ava Body & Skin Care
50% OFF
365
0.3 mi
30 Minute Massage Therapy
$64.99
MON
3:00 PM
3:30 PM

They overhauled the app's UX and aligned it with Google's Material Design philosophy. They gave the app's feel the same amount of attention as its function, making the overall experience more snappy, tactile and playful.

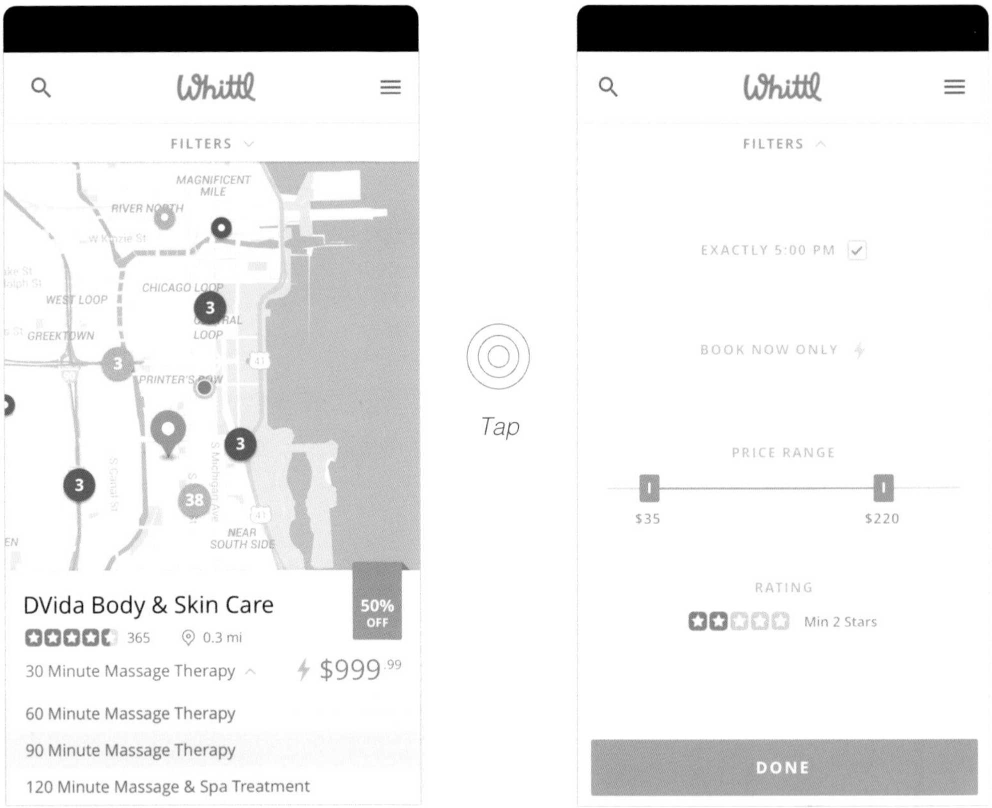
Whittl
FILTERS
MAGNIFICENT MILE
RIVER NORTH
CHICAGO LOOP
WEST LOOP
GREEKTOWN
PRINTER'S ROW
NEAR SOUTH SIDE
DVida Body & Skin Care
50% OFF
365
0.3 mi
30 Minute Massage Therapy
$999.99
60 Minute Massage Therapy
90 Minute Massage Therapy
120 Minute Massage & Spa Treatment
Tap
Whittl
FILTERS
EXACTLY 5:00 PM
BOOK NOW ONLY
PRICE RANGE
$35
$220
RATING
Min 2 Stars
DONE

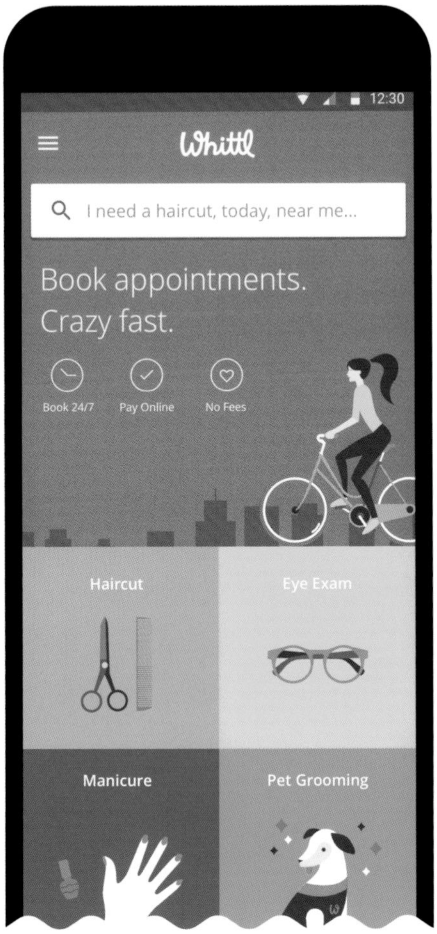
12:30
Whittl
I need a haircut, today, near me...
Book appointments.
Crazy fast.
Book 24/7
Pay Online
No Fees
Haircut
Eye Exam
Manicure
Pet Grooming

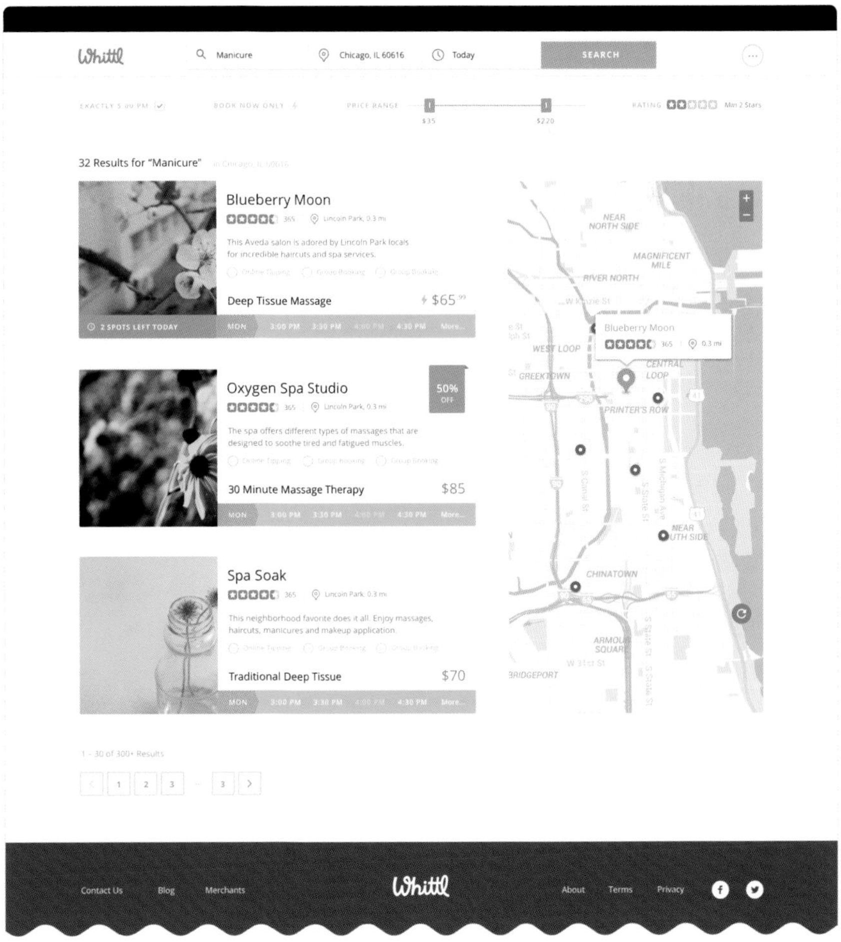
Whittl
Manicure
Chicago, IL 60616
Today
SEARCH
32 Results for "Manicure"
Blueberry Moon
This Aveda salon is adored by Lincoln Park locals for incredible haircuts and spa services.
Deep Tissue Massage
$65.99
2 SPOTS LEFT TODAY
Oxygen Spa Studio
50% OFF
The spa offers different types of massages that are designed to soothe tired and fatigued muscles.
30 Minute Massage Therapy
$85
Spa Soak
This neighborhood favorite does it all. Enjoy massages, haircuts, manicures and makeup application.
Traditional Deep Tissue
$70
Contact Us
Blog
Merchants
Whittl
About
Terms
Privacy

Booksley

Design Agency
7ninjas

Art Direction
Łukasz Peszek

Client
Sebastien Sim

Behance

Building community around an application is currently one of the most important factors determining its success. Especially in case of digital products, users' ability to engage prolongs the lifespan of an app. The idea of Booksley is uniting people who love to read books, and providing them with modern and efficient solution for swapping their collections. Users are able to easily share their passion with their friends, and find new booklovers to interact with.

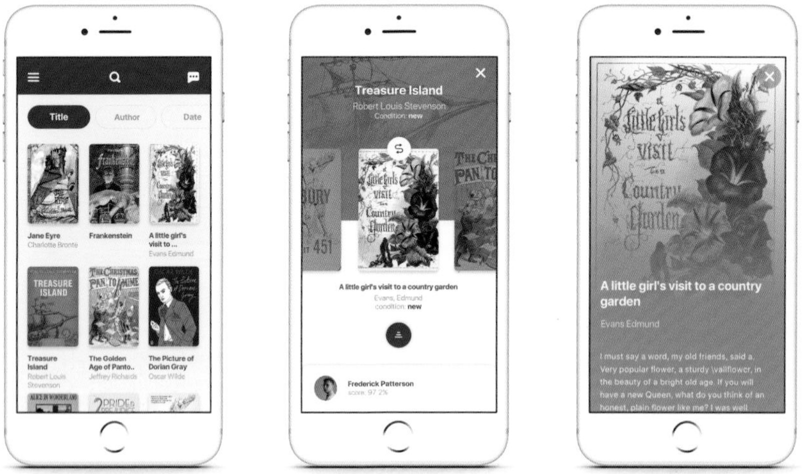

Title
Author
Date
Jane Eyre
Frankenstein
A little girl's visit to ...
Treasure Island
The Golden Age of Panto..
The Picture of Dorian Gray
Oscar Wilde
Treasure Island
Robert Louis Stevenson
A little girl's visit to a country garden
Frederick Patterson
A little girl's visit to a country garden
Evans Edmund

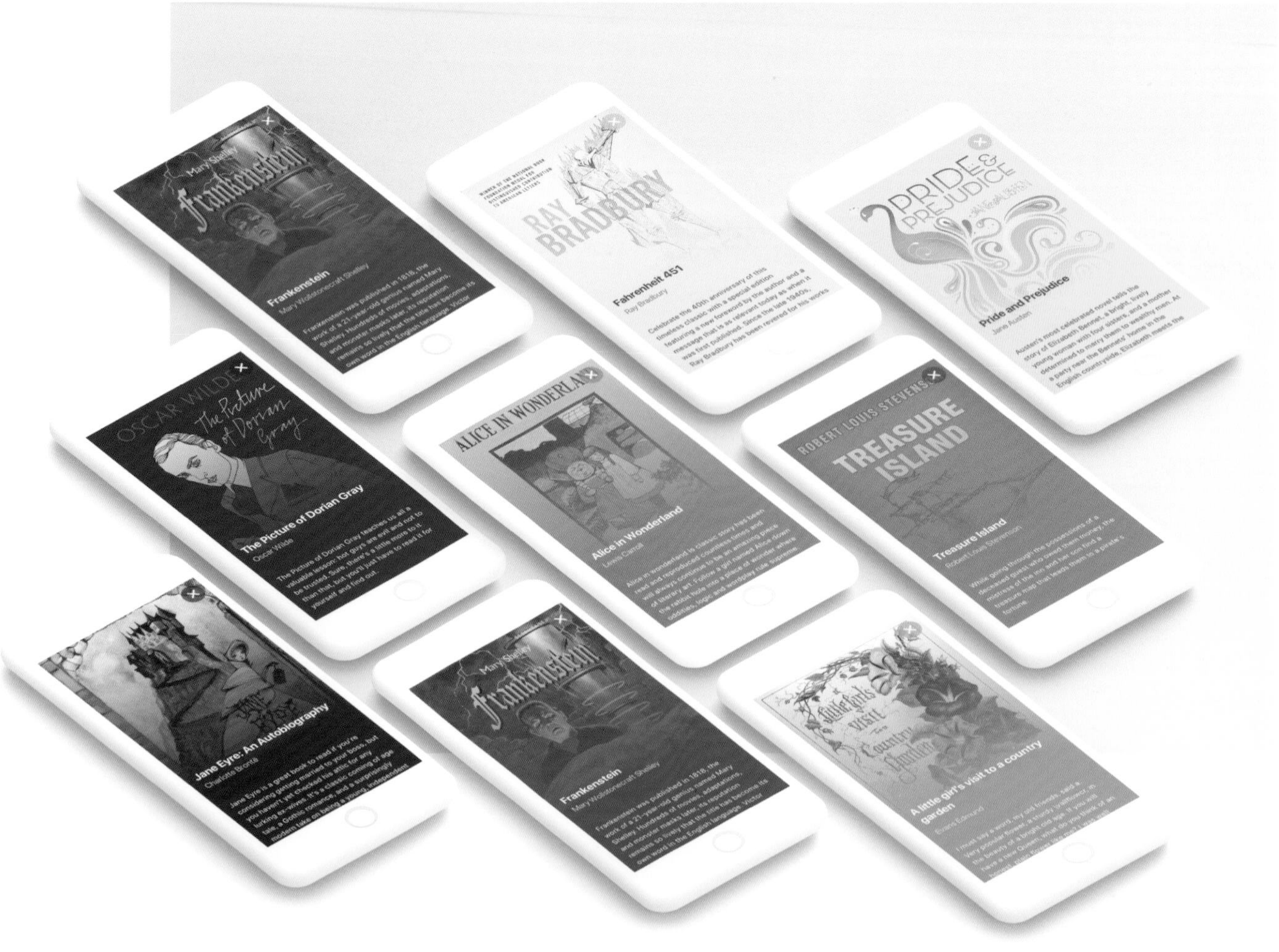

Frankenstein
Fahrenheit 451
Pride and Prejudice
The Picture of Dorian Gray
Alice in Wonderland
Treasure Island
Jane Eyre: An Autobiography
A little girl's visit to a country garden

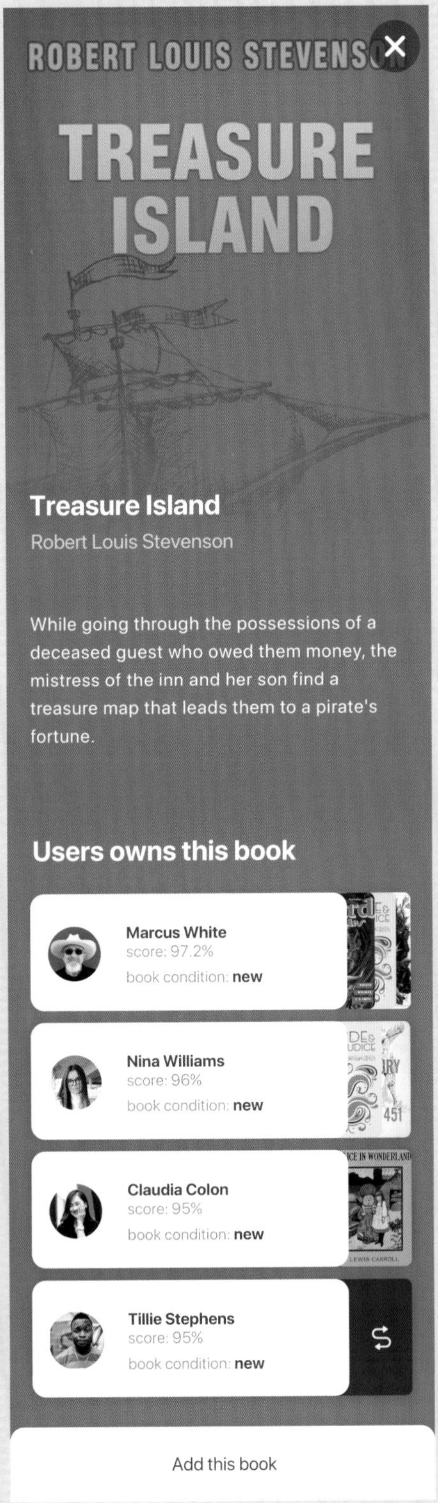
ROBERT LOUIS STEVENSON
TREASURE ISLAND
Treasure Island
Robert Louis Stevenson
While going through the possessions of a deceased guest who owed them money, the mistress of the inn and her son find a treasure map that leads them to a pirate's fortune.
Users owns this book
Marcus White
score: 97.2%
book condition: new
Nina Williams
score: 96%
book condition: new
Claudia Colon
score: 95%
book condition: new
Tillie Stephens
score: 95%
book condition: new
Add this book

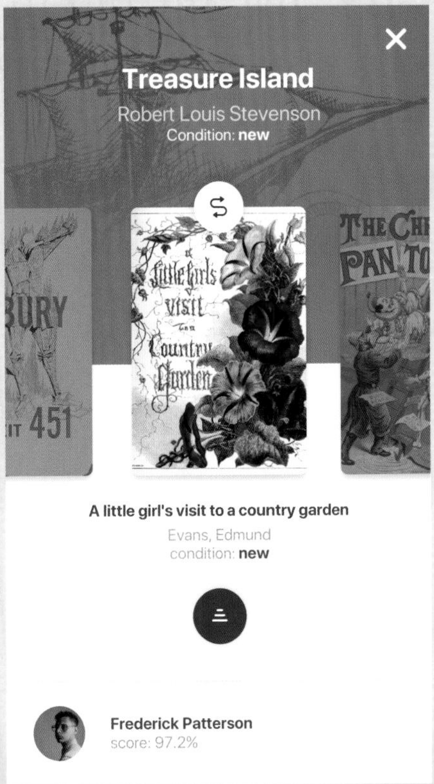
Treasure Island
Robert Louis Stevenson
Condition: new
A little girl's visit to a country garden
Evans, Edmund
condition: new
Frederick Patterson
score: 97.2%

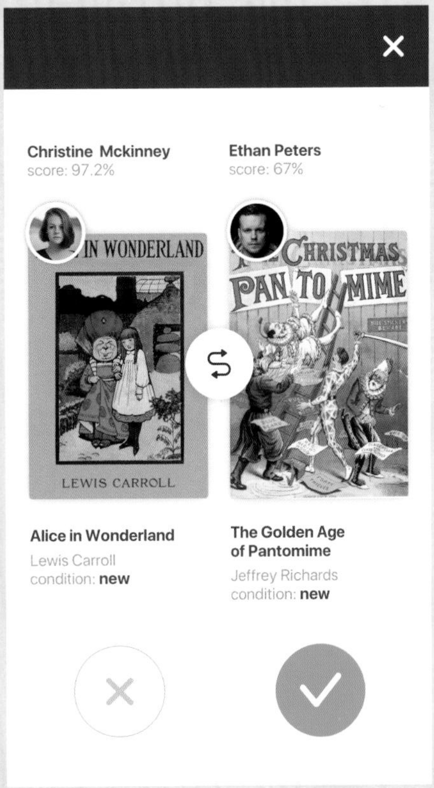
Christine Mckinney
score: 97.2%
Ethan Peters
score: 67%
Alice in Wonderland
Lewis Carroll
condition: new
The Golden Age of Pantomime
Jeffrey Richards
condition: new

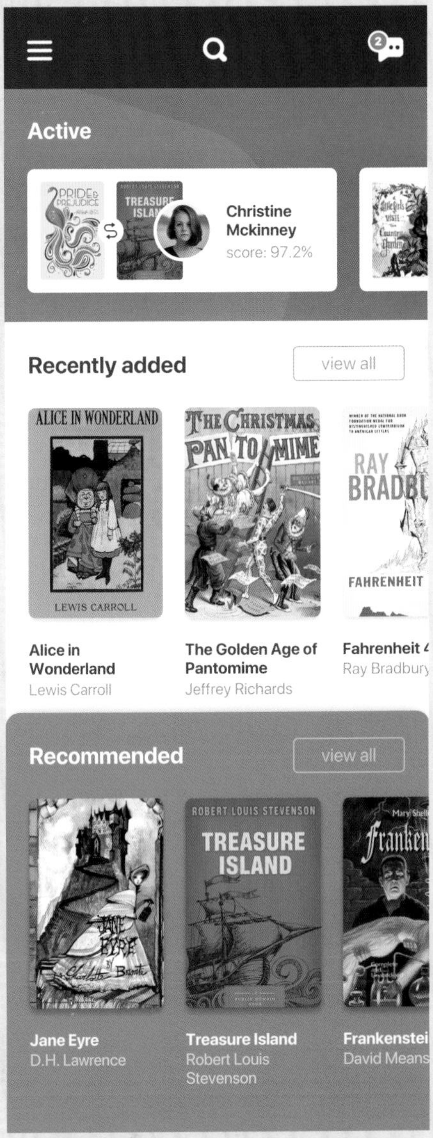
Active
Christine Mckinney
score: 97.2%
Recently added
view all
Alice in Wonderland
Lewis Carroll
The Golden Age of Pantomime
Jeffrey Richards
Ray Bradbury
Recommended
view all
Jane Eyre
D.H. Lawrence
Treasure Island
Robert Louis Stevenson
David Means

For many, books are associated only with black letters on white paper. That's why the design agency wanted to make a difference and use vibrant and vivid colours on Booksley. Each item's profile is full of the colours used on book's cover —making them as unique as the stories they convey. The app was designed in a way that users can navigate with ease and swiftly find what they are looking for.

With the logotype, they wanted to show the most important functions of the app. They took the word "book", an arrow symbolizing exchanging, and merged it with book cover. This interaction between people sharing their favourite stories is exactly what Booksley is all about.

Nest

Design
Effie Zoumpouli

Behance

Nest is a smart home app which offers easy management of the connected smart home devices directly from the user's mobile phone. Therefore it provides precise control over a variety of conditions in every room. It also allows the user to follow an environmentally friendly approach during multiple house functions and reduce the maintenance cost.

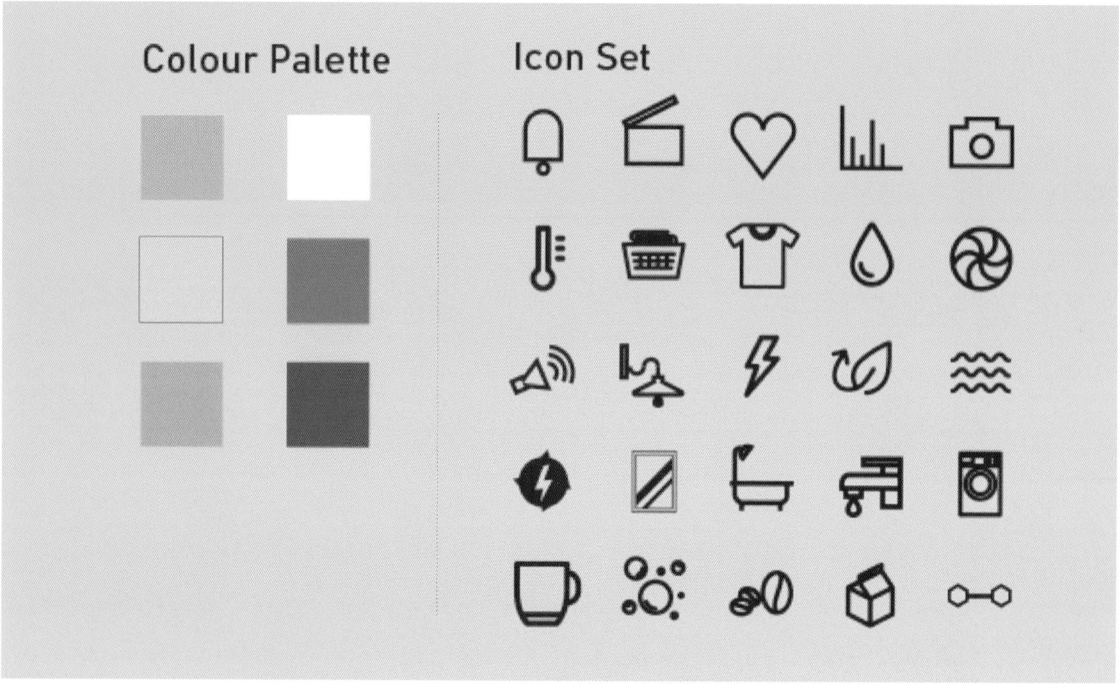
Colour Palette
Icon Set

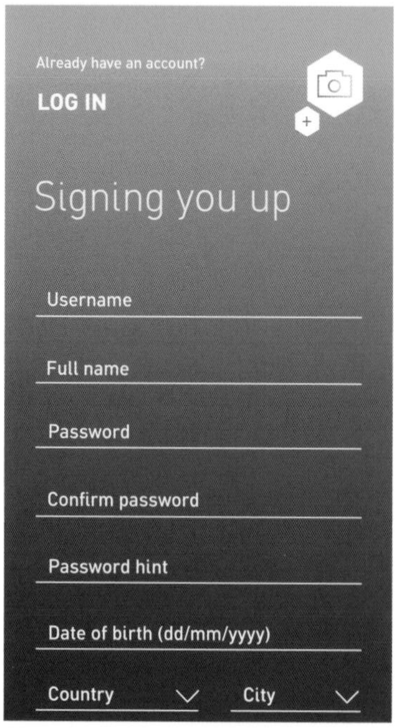
Already have an account?
LOG IN
Signing you up
Username
Full name
Password
Confirm password
Password hint
Date of birth (dd/mm/yyyy)
Country
City

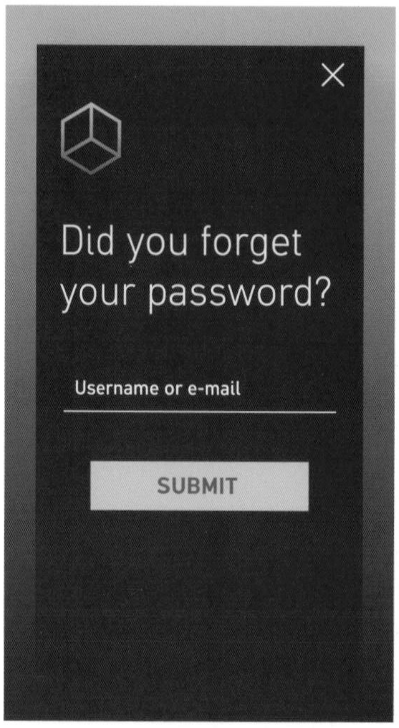
Did you forget your password?
Username or e-mail
SUBMIT

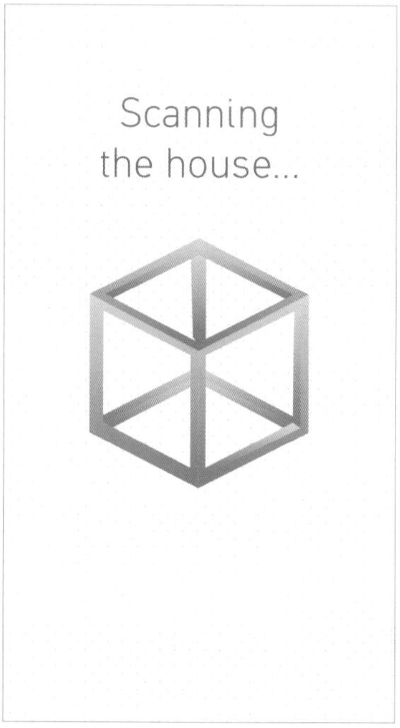
Scanning the house...

Guestroom
Master Bedroom
Dining Room
Living Room
Bathroom
Balcony
Kitchen
Playroom
Garden

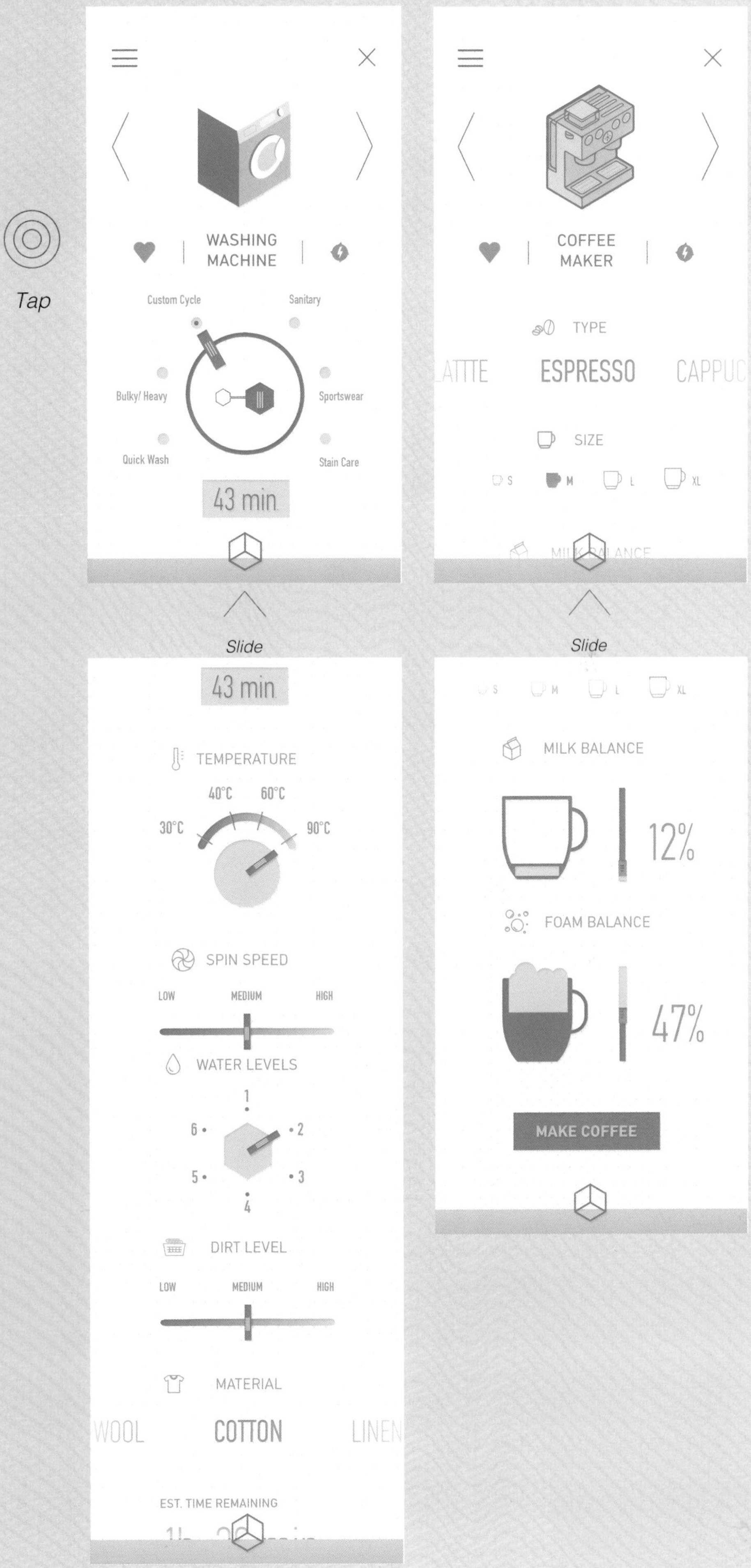
Tap
WASHING MACHINE
Custom Cycle
Sanitary
Bulky/ Heavy
Sportswear
Quick Wash
Stain Care
43 min
Slide
43 min
TEMPERATURE
40°C
60°C
30°C
90°C
SPIN SPEED
LOW
MEDIUM
HIGH
WATER LEVELS
1
2
3
4
5
6
DIRT LEVEL
LOW
MEDIUM
HIGH
MATERIAL
WOOL
COTTON
LINEN
EST. TIME REMAINING
COFFEE MAKER
TYPE
LATTE
ESPRESSO
CAPPUC
SIZE
S
M
L
XL
Slide
S
M
L
XL
MILK BALANCE
12%
FOAM BALANCE
47%
MAKE COFFEE

An isometric grid that derives from the primary component of the bees' nest has been used to illustrate and organize the different elements. At the main menu, every room is depicted as a hexagon cell of the complex that represents the whole house. The icons were kept sleek and simple mainly represented by their stroke to contrast the richness of the gradients incorporated in backgrounds and selected filled compact sections. The typography holds an informative and discreet place, in order to create open and clean spaces that support a pleasant, contemporary and comfortable user experience.

Rido

Design
Gaeul Lee

Behance

The idea of Rido was born at an ordinary night: the designer couldn't fall asleep and she didn't want to turn on the light and read texts. It occurred to her that it would be a pleasant experience if someone could read the texts by her side. When designing the app, she focused on UX, creating an app that could be used smoothly with emotional content curation, interactive messages, and thought flow. Rido was designed to be warm and friendly, encompassing many customizable features: choose user's favourite voice, changing sound and viewing options. Just like kids are called "Kido", Rido is the cute nickname of reader.

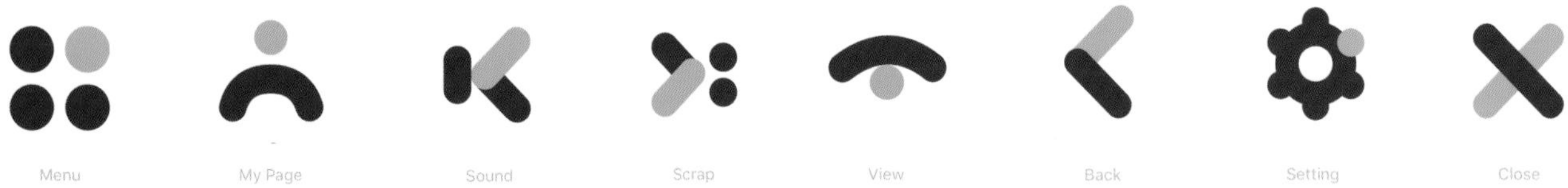
Menu
My Page
Sound
Scrap
View
Back
Setting
Close

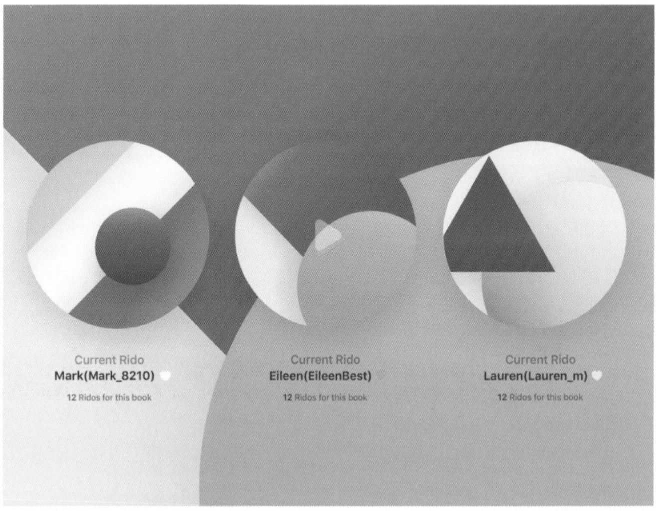
Current Rido
Mark(Mark_8210)
12 Ridos for this book
Current Rido
Eileen(EileenBest)
12 Ridos for this book
Current Rido
Lauren(Lauren_m)
12 Ridos for this book

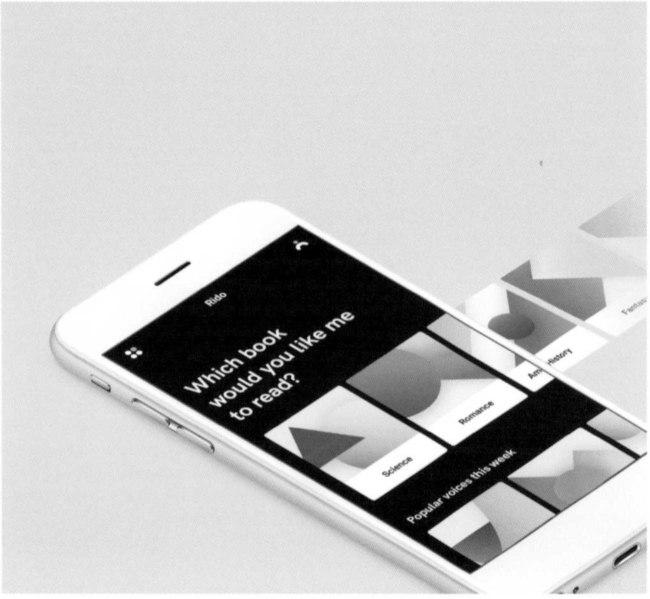
Rido
Which book would you like me to read?
Science
Romance
Popular voices this week

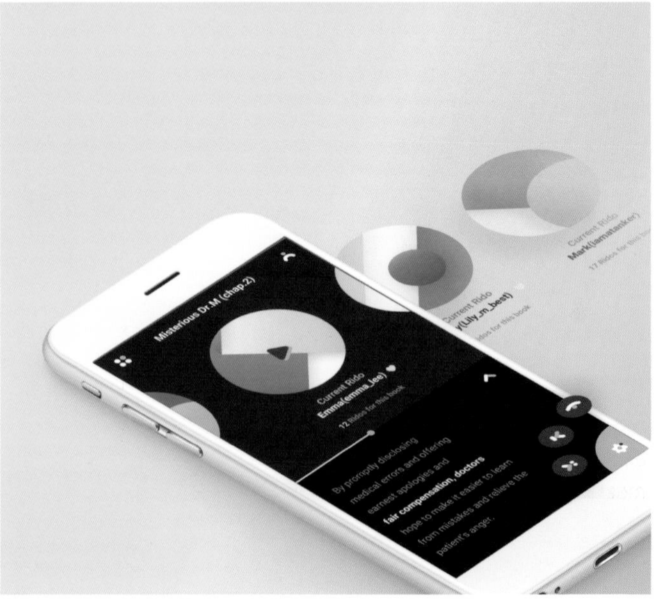
Misterious Dr.M (chap.2)
Current Rido
Emma(emma_lee)
12 Ridos for this book
By promptly disclosing medical errors and offering earnest apologies and fair compensation, doctors hope to make it easier to learn from mistakes and relieve the patient's anger.

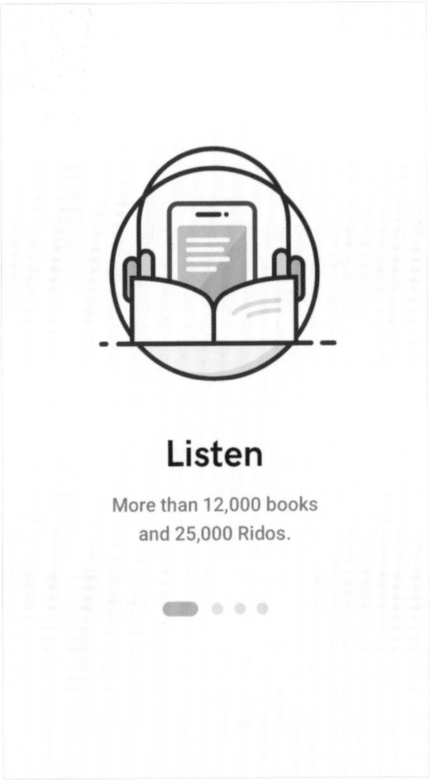
Listen
More than 12,000 books and 25,000 Ridos.

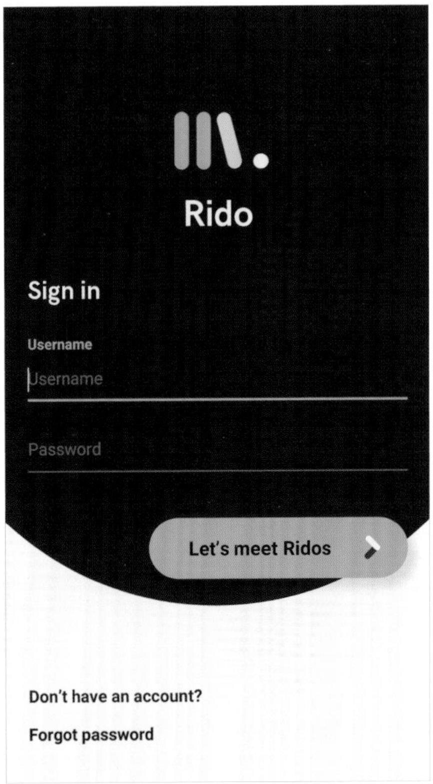
Rido
Sign in
Username
Username
Password
Let's meet Ridos
Don't have an account?
Forgot password

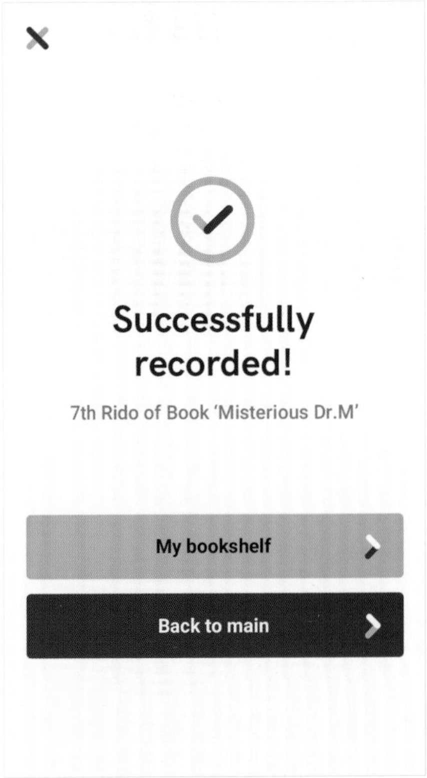
Successfully recorded!
7th Rido of Book 'Misterious Dr.M'
My bookshelf
Back to main

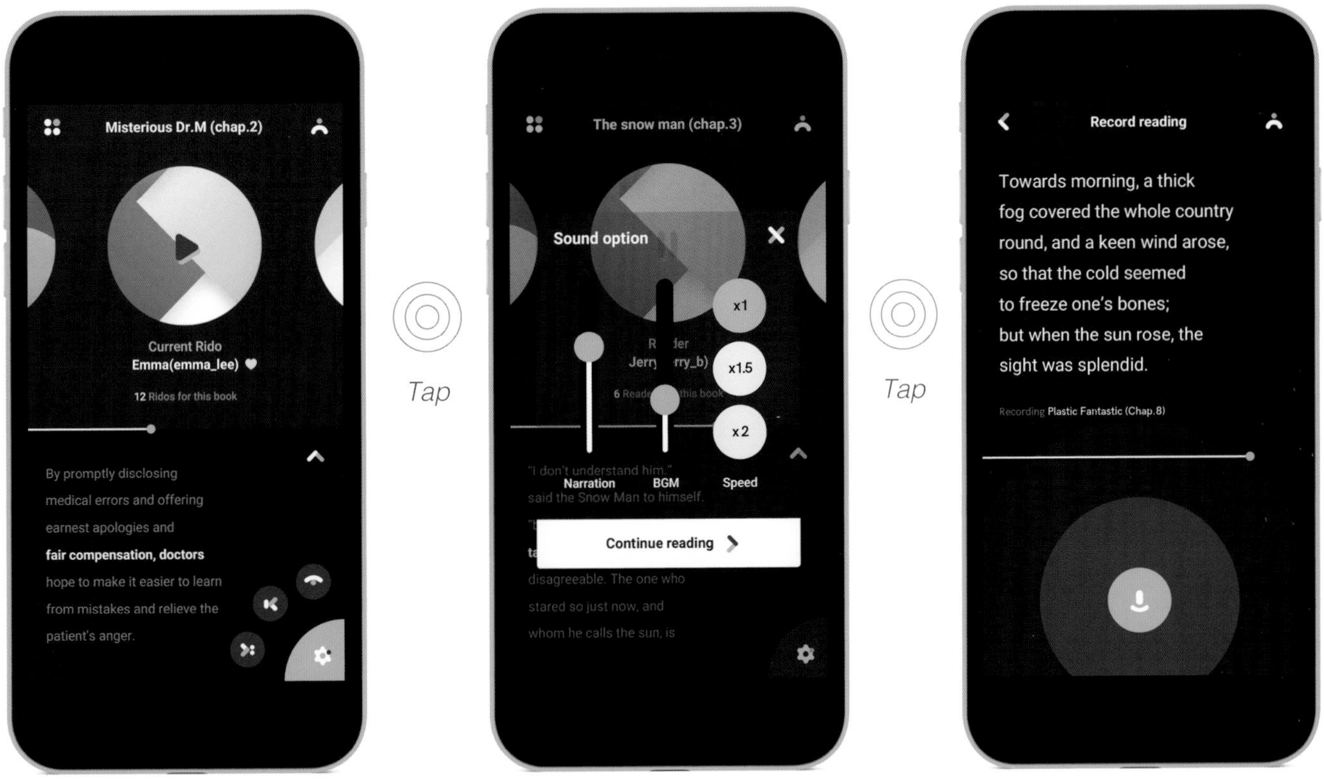
Misterious Dr.M (chap.2)
Current Rido
Emma(emma_lee)
12 Ridos for this book
By promptly disclosing medical errors and offering earnest apologies and fair compensation, doctors hope to make it easier to learn from mistakes and relieve the patient's anger.
Tap
The snow man (chap.3)
Sound option
x1
x1.5
x2
Narration
BGM
Speed
said the Snow Man to himself.
Continue reading
disagreeable. The one who stared so just now, and whom he calls the sun, is
Tap
Record reading
Towards morning, a thick fog covered the whole country round, and a keen wind arose, so that the cold seemed to freeze one's bones; but when the sun rose, the sight was splendid.
Recording Plastic Fantastic (Chap.8)

Pastel tone colour and smooth curved graphic motifs were extracted from ice cream, cookies and macaroons with the hope of reflecting a sweet and tender service. The logo was designed that combines three books and a circle meaning "something", which indicates the meaning of any thoughts, feelings and conclusions that users feel after listening to the book.

re·view

Design
Thomas Birch

Behance

re·view is an app that aims to highlight the bias and misdirection of the press. Use the app to scan news articles and search their language for unsourced claims, errant facts and blatant examples of rhetoric. The design asks people to question and engage with social issues, equipping them with the tools to detect faulty reasoning.

An article's content can be pulled from online or scanned and digitised via the device's camera. Once uploaded, the article's language is reviewed against an established list of red flags and community contributions, which are available for reference in a glossary. It was an integral feature to encourage debate and to build a community outside of the app, therefore social sharing is prominently integrated and promoted throughout.

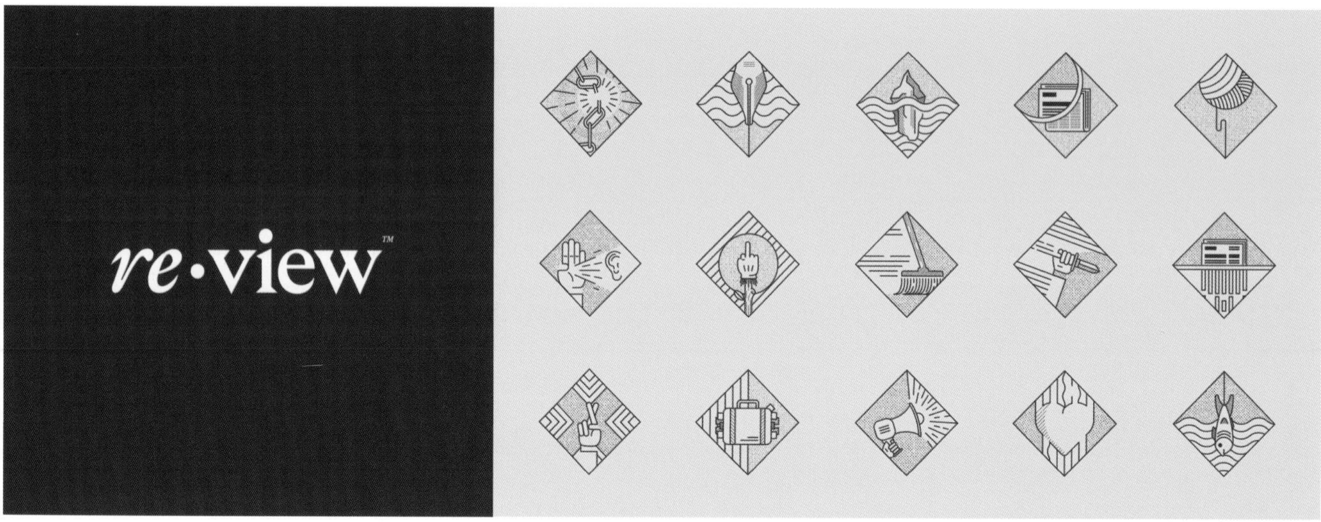
re·view™

Gl
os
sa
y
rhetoric device 09
esn't follow, a break
reasoning.
re one step of an argument
revious, like a missing
reason the argument is
rting that the conclusion
hand, without providing
Slide
Personal
—Attack
ad hominem
rhetoric device 02
An irrelevant attack or critique upon the person rather than their reasoning or view.
A 'Personal Attack' is often a distraction, a smoke-screen of a shouting match, allowing the author to 'side-step' the issue at hand in an effort to undermine the position of the argument. It is an attempt to provoke an emotional response by
Simplification
rhetoric device 07
A gross over-simplification.
A 'Simplification' often occurs when the author is trying to attribute one singular cause to a broader, more complex, issue. This is may be a result of the author trying to crowbar their opinion into logical reasoning, a simplification can often be a deliberate refusal to acknowledge the full

re·view
Author — Allison Pearson
Source — The Daily Telegraph
Politics.
Editor — Peter Dominiczak
13.05.16
The gap between ONS migrant figures & the truth is as wide as the Grand Canyon. We are owed an apology.
0.9m Before yesterday the official number of EU migrants who came to Britain between 2011 & 2015. 2.4m The real number of EU migrants we know who came to Britain.
So, it turns out the British people are owed an apology. An apology for every parent whose child can't get a place at a secondary school of their choosing.
An apology for every plasterer who claims that his wages have been driven down remorselessly by Eastern Europeans, yet been told to shut up because migrants are really good for the economy.
An apology for those damned as "racist" when they dare to wonder why families who have lived here and paid their dues for several generations can't get priority on the housing ladder.
Author
— Allison Pearson
Our analysis suggests that her articles tend to be emotionally written, relying heavily on inflammatory non sequiturs and personal assumptions.
Pro-Brexit, Critical of Immigration & BBC
Newspaper
— The Daily Telegraph
The Daily Telegraph is an established right-wing broadsheet, with links to the UK Conservative Party.
Owners: Sir David and Frederick Barclay
Tap
Non Sequiter
— Rhetoric
02
"...parent whose child can't get a place at a secondary school of their choosing."

Glos sary
Rhetoric Devices.
Red – Herring
Anecdotal – Evidence
Partial – Picture
Non – Sequitur
An argument that doesn't follow, a break in the chain of reasoning.
re·view
Search
Marginalisation
Manufacturing Consent
Marketisation
Mass Communication
Media
Marshall – McLuhan
Any medium has the power of imposing its own assumption on the unwary.
Study confirms that ... is biased in favour ...
Why media commentary is so crucial ... opinions displace facts.
Author
— Roy Greenslade
Newspaper
— The Guardian
Partial – Picture

A restricted colour palette guides the user throughout the app, whilst establishing a recognisable brand presence that is easily translated onto social media and print. Designing for small screens can make it difficult to build a distinctive graphic style—re·view distinguishes itself from the expected digital trends by playfully referencing the aesthetics of newspapers, with its use of half-tone patterns and headline serifs. To help the user connect with new terminology, an extensive glossary is summarised by a digestible and shareable vocabulary of memorable icons.

ALTERNATIVE
FAKE NEWS
FACTS
FAKE NEWS
ALTERNATIVE
FAKE NEWS
FACTS
FAKE NEWS
The death of truth?
8
Re·view
'Post truth' and the newsmakers:
In a world of half truthes, how can we accept anything? Those are the seeds of doubt we're left with, an attack on truth is a tactic of destabilisation, another attempt to control the narrative.
9
Manifesto

Paperplane

Design
Jordan Richards

Behance

Paperplane is a dynamic, yet simple, vacation budgeting app. The goal of this product is to provide a tool for travelers to calculate their budget while giving them a comprehensive overview of their finances throughout the travel.

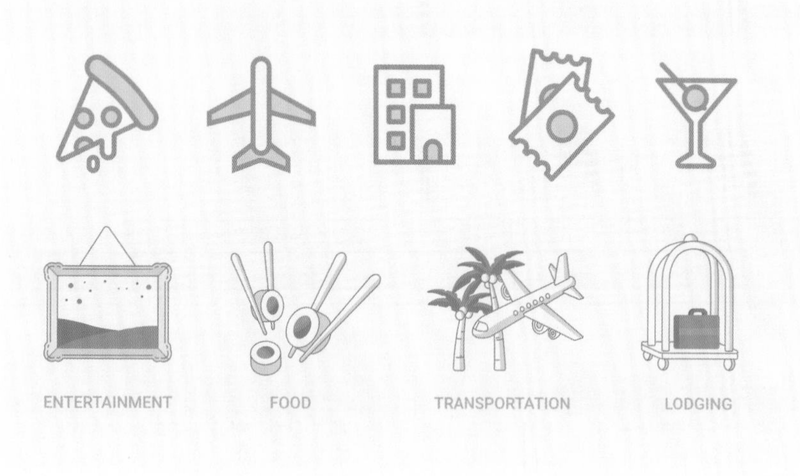
ENTERTAINMENT
FOOD
TRANSPORTATION
LODGING

$1,004
$1,004

CHARTS
How much did you spend?
$0.00
Location
Category
07 / 16
ADD
70%
9
DAYS
24%
CHARTS
Seattle
$300
$250
$200
$150
$100
$50
$25
0 1 2 3 4 5 6 7
DAYS INTO TRIP
HIGHEST SPENDING
DAYS LEFT
LOWEST SPENDING
70%
9
DAYS
24%
TRIP DASHBOARD
Seattle
!
High Spending on food!
OKAY
$22.41
$125
LODGING

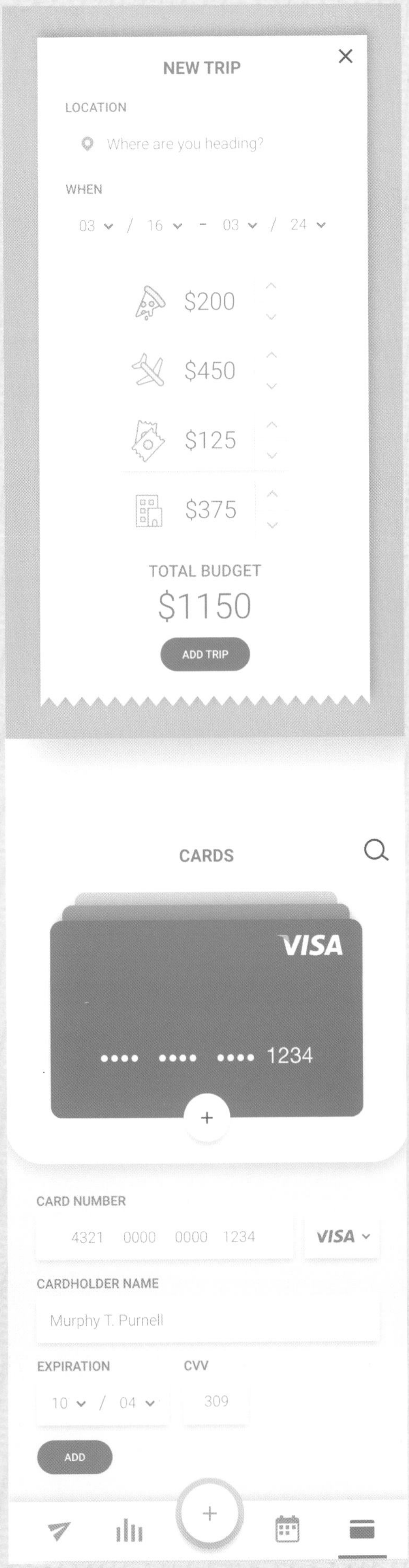
NEW TRIP
LOCATION
Where are you heading?
WHEN
03 / 16 - 03 / 24
$200
$450
$125
$375
TOTAL BUDGET
$1150
ADD TRIP
CARDS
VISA
•••• •••• •••• 1234
CARD NUMBER
4321 0000 0000 1234
VISA
CARDHOLDER NAME
Murphy T. Purnell
EXPIRATION
CVV
10 / 04
309
ADD

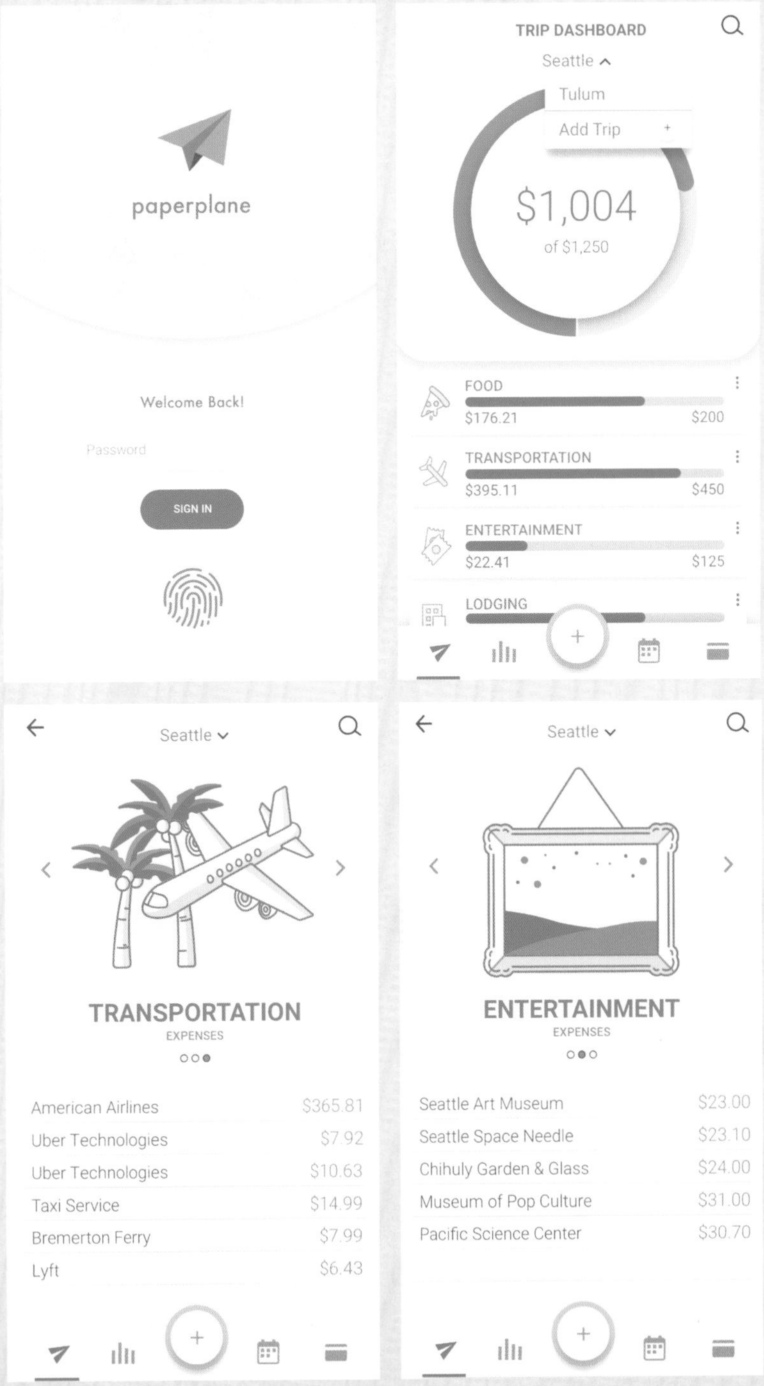
paperplane
Welcome Back!
Password
SIGN IN
TRIP DASHBOARD
Seattle
Tulum
Add Trip
$1,004
of $1,250
FOOD
$176.21
$200
TRANSPORTATION
$395.11
$450
ENTERTAINMENT
$22.41
$125
LODGING
Seattle
TRANSPORTATION
EXPENSES
American Airlines $365.81
Uber Technologies $7.92
Uber Technologies $10.63
Taxi Service $14.99
Bremerton Ferry $7.99
Lyft $6.43
Seattle
ENTERTAINMENT
EXPENSES
Seattle Art Museum $23.00
Seattle Space Needle $23.10
Chihuly Garden & Glass $24.00
Museum of Pop Culture $31.00
Pacific Science Center $30.70

The designer took a minimal approach with accents of bold colours to pop off the screen. For some people, budgeting is not enjoyable, so the designer wanted to create this app to be the antithesis of that feeling—he wanted the user to have a delightful experience when planning their trip. This was achieved by the thoughtfully chosen shades of light greens and greys. The layout, lined iconography and subtle shadows also push this design in an elegant way.

Cleen

Design Agency
Subism

Design
Alan Cheetham

Client
HSG UK
(Formerly Hygienix Ltd)

App Store

The Cleen app is a cross platform mobile and web application for washroom services. It enables users to review washrooms in any venue. Users can either compliment clean washrooms or give feedback on issues such as poor disabled access or baby changing facilities. With the app, users can also find the nearest venue, such as restaurant and cinema, with a Cleen washroom.

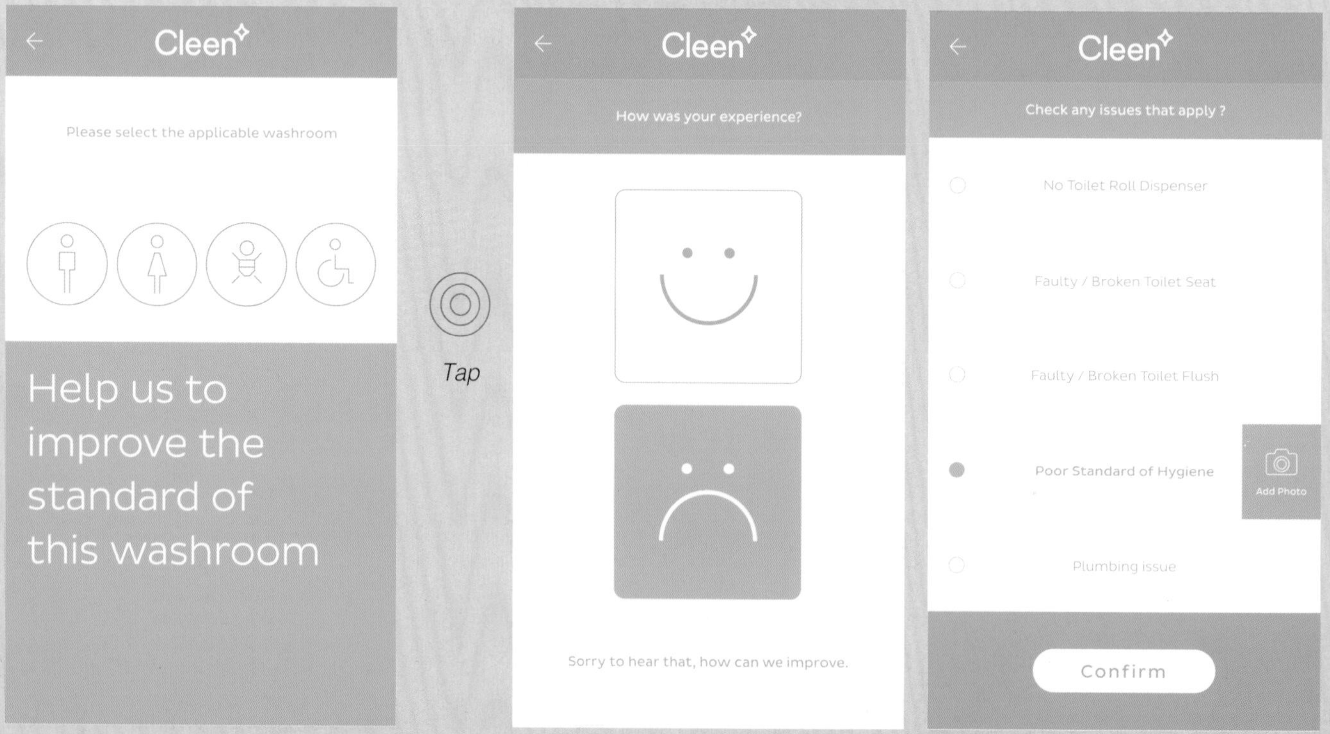
Cleen
Please select the applicable washroom
Help us to improve the standard of this washroom
Tap
Cleen
How was your experience?
Sorry to hear that, how can we improve.
Cleen
Check any issues that apply ?
No Toilet Roll Dispenser
Faulty / Broken Toilet Seat
Faulty / Broken Toilet Flush
Poor Standard of Hygiene
Add Photo
Plumbing issue
Confirm

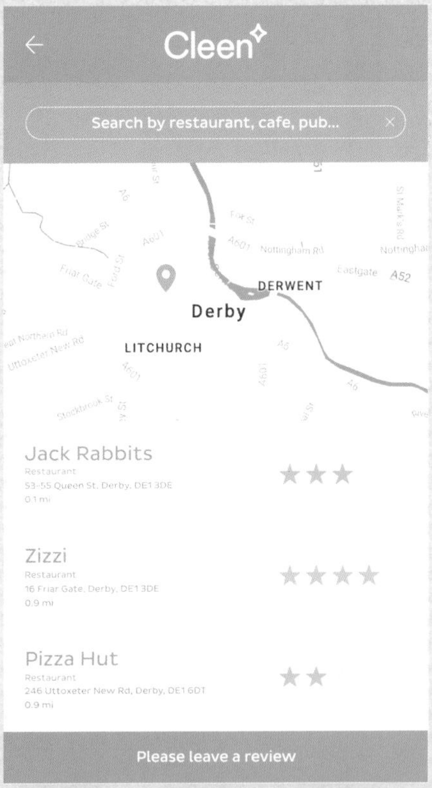
Cleen
Search by restaurant, cafe, pub...
DERWENT
Derby
LITCHURCH
Jack Rabbits
Zizzi
Pizza Hut
Please leave a review

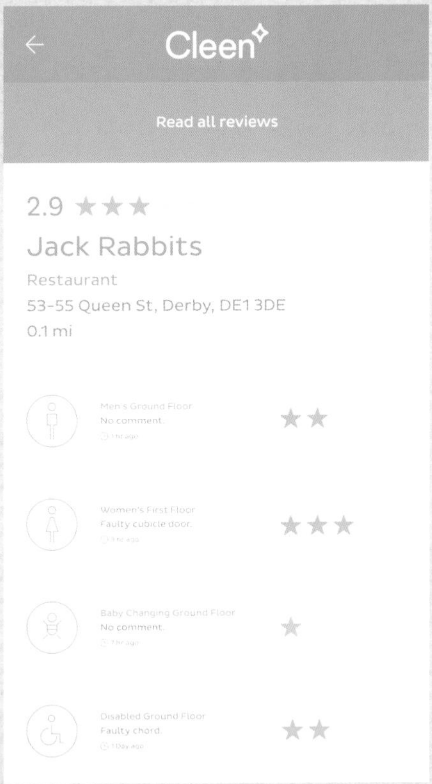
Cleen
Read all reviews
2.9
Jack Rabbits
Restaurant
53-55 Queen St, Derby, DE1 3DE
0.1 mi

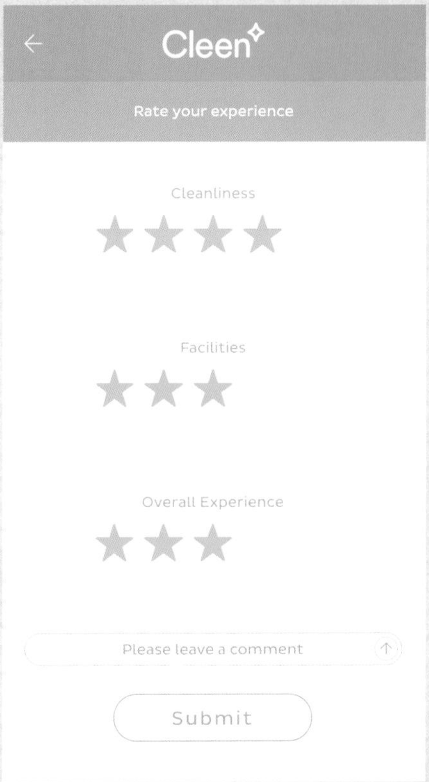
Cleen
Rate your experience
Cleanliness
Facilities
Overall Experience
Please leave a comment
Submit

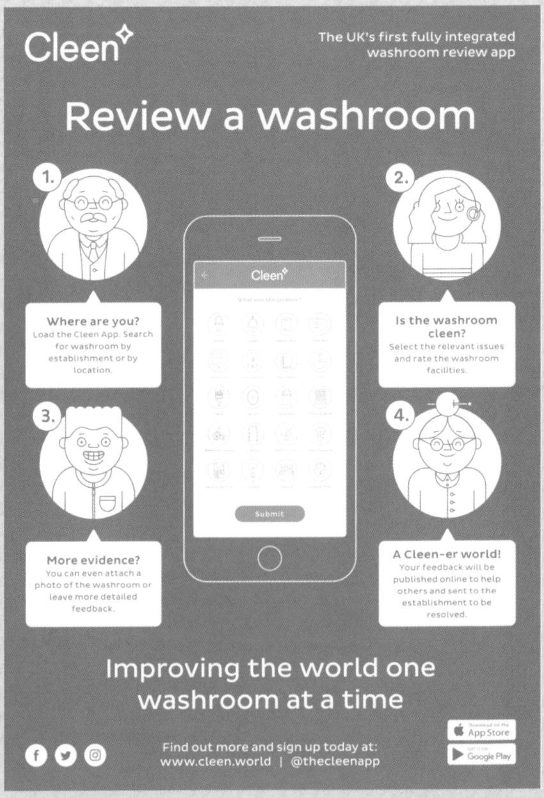
Cleen
The UK's first fully integrated washroom review app
Review a washroom
1.
Where are you?
Load the Cleen App. Search for washroom by establishment or by location.
2.
Is the washroom clean?
Select the relevant issues and rate the washroom facilities.
3.
More evidence?
You can even attach a photo of the washroom or leave more detailed feedback.
4.
A Cleen-er world!
Your feedback will be published online to help others and sent to the establishment to be resolved.
Improving the world one washroom at a time
Find out more and sign up today at:
www.cleen.world | @thecleenapp

Cleen
The UK's first fully integrated washroom review app
Find a Cleen washroom
1.
Nearest Cleen washroom?
Load the Cleen App. Our map will show the nearest washrooms and their ratings.
2.
Going for food or drinks?
You can search and view the washroom ratings for any establishment in your area.
3.
I need more detail...
Click on the ratings to see a full breakdown of ratings and additional comments.
4.
Choose with confidence
Enjoy your outing in the safe knowledge that a Cleen washroom awaits you!
Improving the world one washroom at a time
Find out more and sign up today at:
www.cleen.world | @thecleenapp

The app interface and surrounding collateral has been brought to life with the playful and fresh branding designed to appeal to a wide audience. A minimalist approach in design aesthetics was considered from the start to make the app feel contemporary and appealing. A fully customized set of icons and illustrations (character user personas) were also created to bring more personality into the brand and app design.

Reeviz

Design Agency
KR8 bureau

Client
Mr. Immo GmbH (the founder of Reeviz)

Behance

Reeviz is an app that outsources real estate agent tasks. This app brings together two parties: The real estate agents who give out the job via the app, and job takers (e.g. students) who have an hour of time and happily take on the opportunity to earn some money by giving a house tour and explaining some facts about the real estate object.

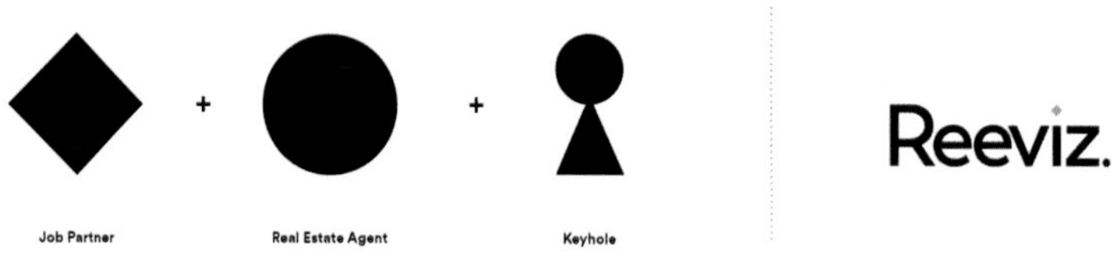

Job Partner
Real Estate Agent
Keyhole
Reeviz.

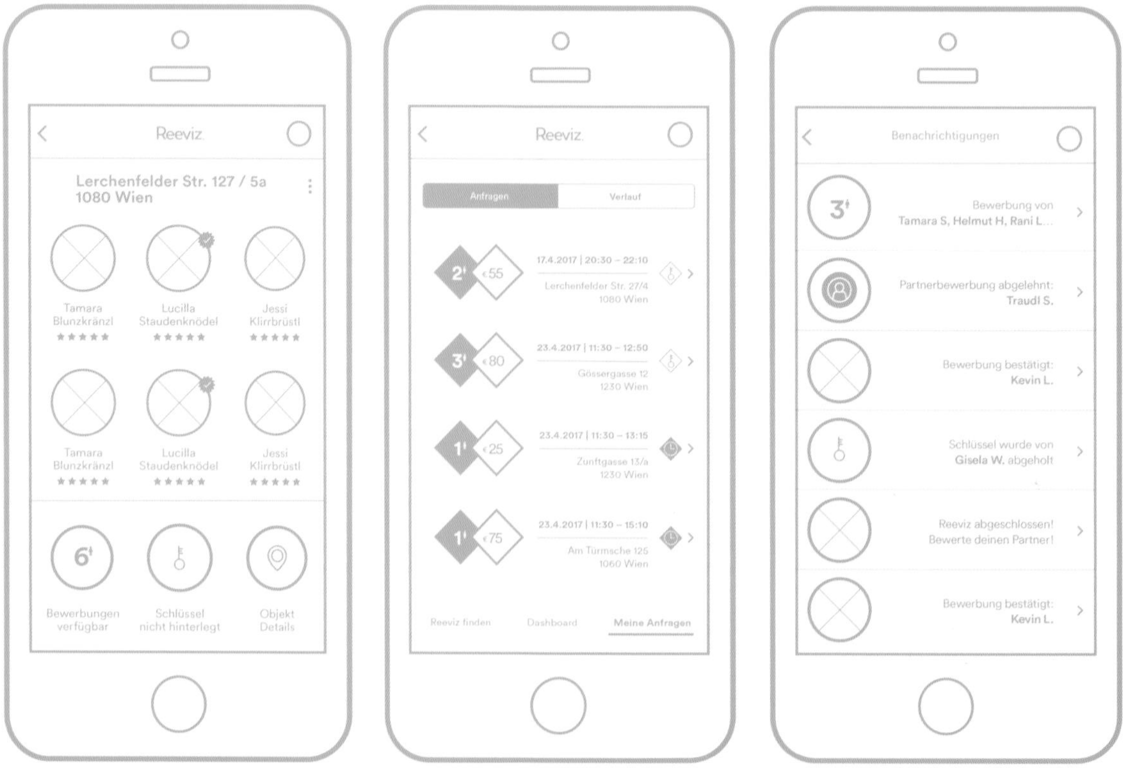

Reeviz
Lerchenfelder Str. 127 / 5a
1080 Wien
Tamara Blunzkränzl
Lucilla Staudenknödel
Jessi Klirrbrüstl
Bewerbungen verfügbar
Schlüssel nicht hinterlegt
Objekt Details
Anfragen
Verlauf
Reeviz finden
Dashboard
Meine Anfragen
Benachrichtigungen
Bewerbung von Tamara S, Helmut H, Rani L...
Partnerbewerbung abgelehnt: Traudl S.
Bewerbung bestätigt: Kevin L.
Schlüssel wurde von Gisela W. abgeholt
Reeviz abgeschlossen! Bewerte deinen Partner!

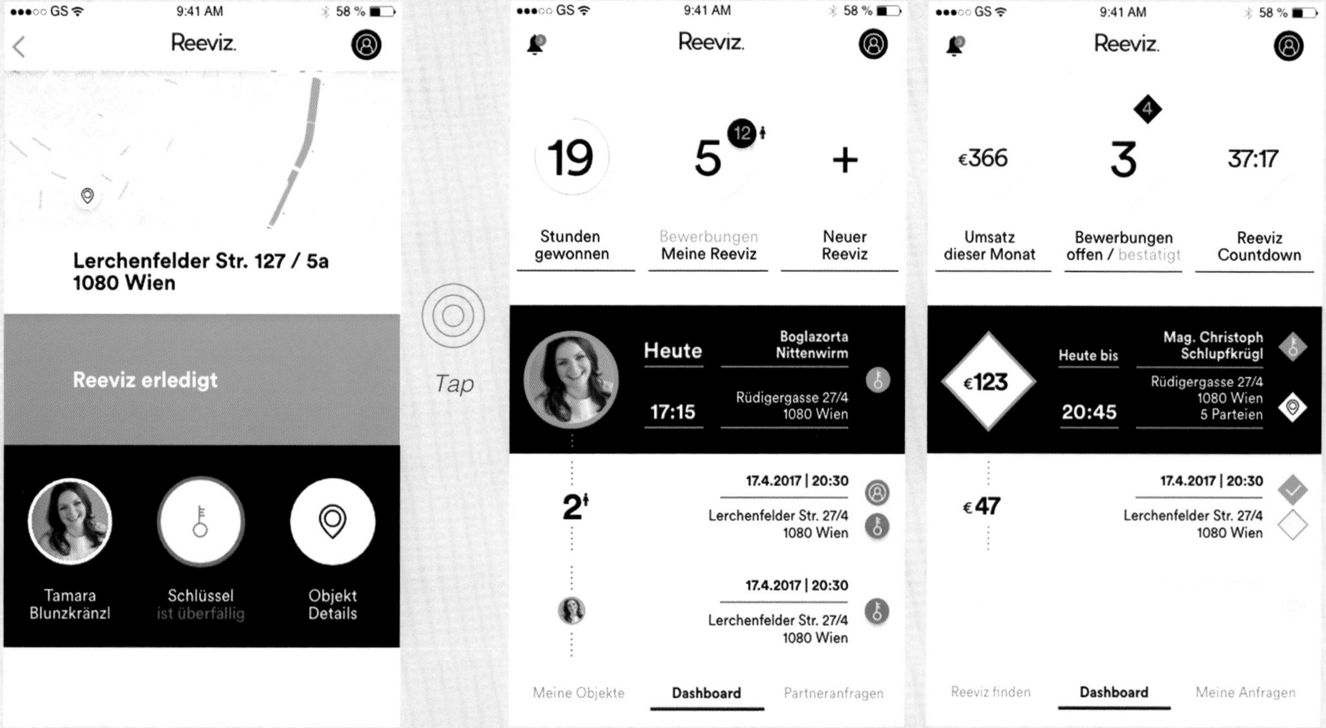
Reeviz.
Lerchenfelder Str. 127 / 5a
1080 Wien
Reeviz erledigt
Tamara Blunzkränzl
Schlüssel ist überfällig
Objekt Details
Tap
19
Stunden gewonnen
5
Bewerbungen Meine Reeviz
+
Neuer Reeviz
Heute
17:15
Boglazorta Nittenwirm
Rüdigergasse 27/4
1080 Wien
17.4.2017 | 20:30
Lerchenfelder Str. 27/4
1080 Wien
Meine Objekte
Dashboard
Partneranfragen
€366
Umsatz dieser Monat
3
Bewerbungen offen / bestätigt
37:17
Reeviz Countdown
€123
Heute bis
20:45
Mag. Christoph Schlupfkrügl
Rüdigergasse 27/4
1080 Wien
5 Parteien
€47
Reeviz finden
Meine Anfragen

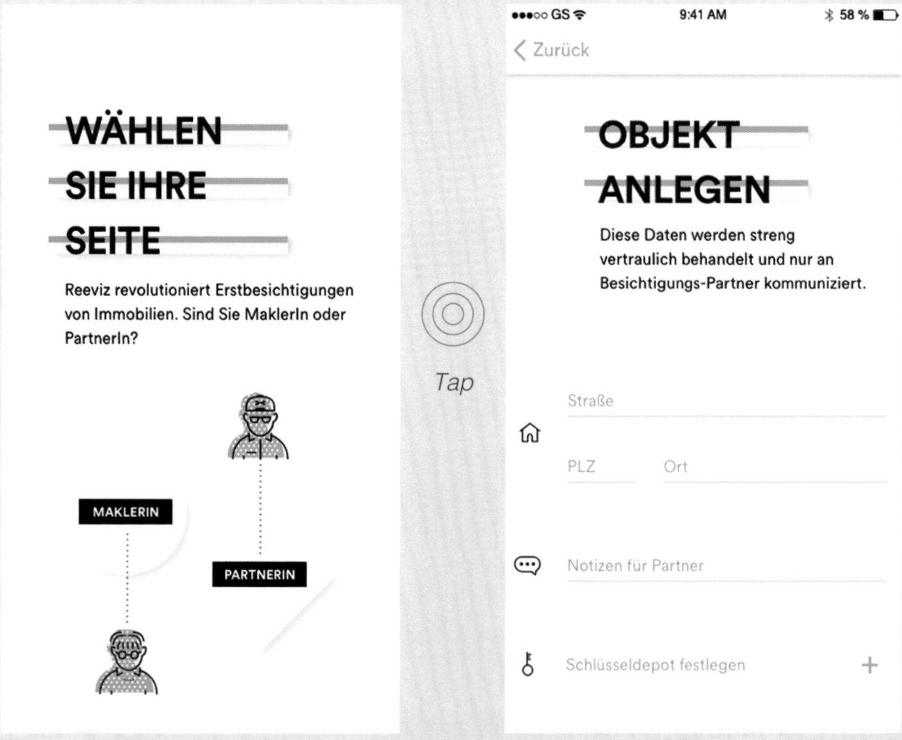
WÄHLEN SIE IHRE SEITE
Reeviz revolutioniert Erstbesichtigungen von Immobilien. Sind Sie MaklerIn oder PartnerIn?
MAKLERIN
PARTNERIN
Tap
Zurück
OBJEKT ANLEGEN
Diese Daten werden streng vertraulich behandelt und nur an Besichtigungs-Partner kommuniziert.
Straße
PLZ
Ort
Notizen für Partner
Schlüsseldepot festlegen

Design agency KR8 divided the app in two segments: the circle interface elements stand for agents, and the square elements are for job takers. The important part is to get the tricky workflow into a smooth user experience. For example, real estate agents pick their job takers via the candidates' profiles in order to determine their qualification. Other job processes, such as picking up the key from a depot, are documented and displayed in real time. Both parties could keep track of the whole process until it is done and paid.

Aker

Design Agency
CLEVER°FRANKE

Creative Direction
Thomas Clever, Gert Franke

Visual Design
Pietro Lodi

UX Design
Wouter van Dljk, Pletro Lodl

Front-End Development
Jan Hoogeveen, Mark Haasjes

Back-End Development
Wilco Tomassen

Client
Aker

App Store

Aker provides a monitoring service for the agriculture sector that proactively identifies crop stress with the assistance of an unmanned aerial vehicle. They approached CLEVER°FRANKE to help bring this new technology to an especially conservative sector, which is the agricultural market, where innovation needs to be as user friendly and as simple to use as possible.

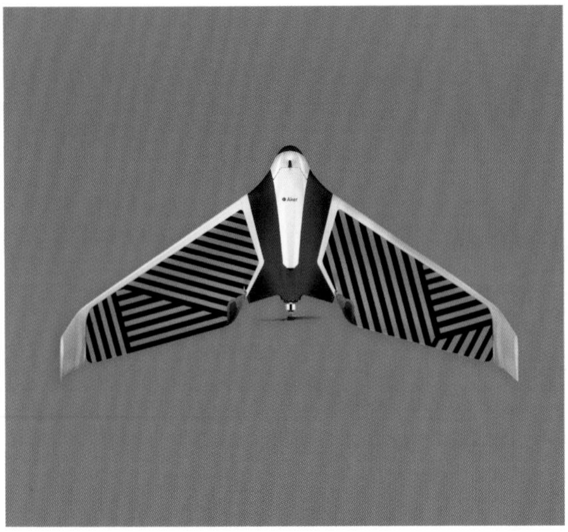

Aker
Aker
Aker
Aker
Aker

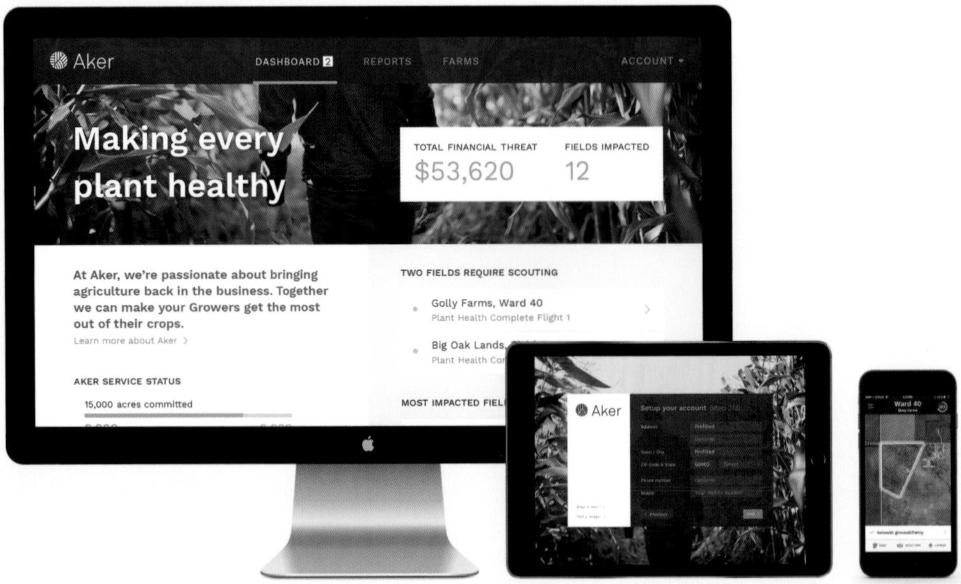
Aker
DASHBOARD 2
REPORTS
FARMS
ACCOUNT
Making every plant healthy
TOTAL FINANCIAL THREAT
$53,620
FIELDS IMPACTED
12
At Aker, we're passionate about bringing agriculture back in the business. Together we can make your Growers get the most out of their crops.
Learn more about Aker
TWO FIELDS REQUIRE SCOUTING
Golly Farms, Ward 40
Plant Health Complete Flight 1
AKER SERVICE STATUS
15,000 acres committed
MOST IMPACTED FIEL
Aker
Ward 40

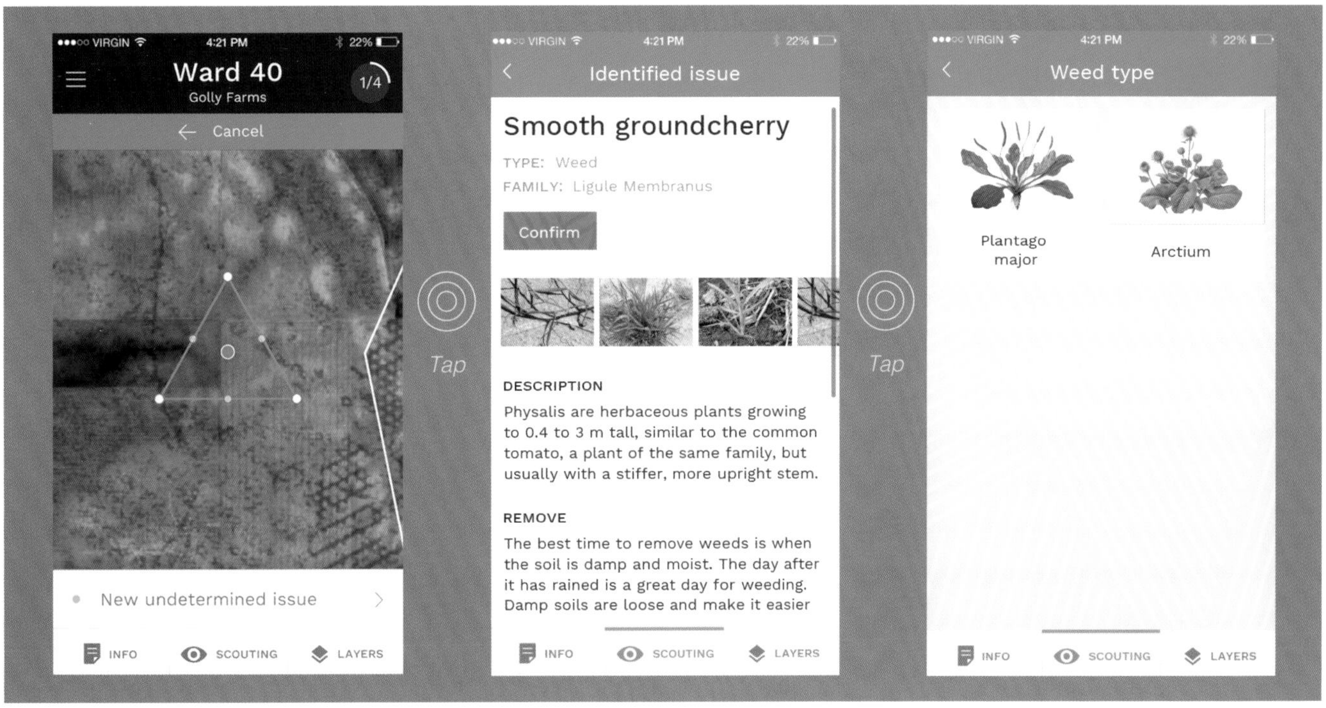
VIRGIN
4:21 PM
22%
Ward 40
Golly Farms
1/4
Cancel
New undetermined issue
INFO
SCOUTING
LAYERS
Tap
Identified issue
Smooth groundcherry
TYPE: Weed
FAMILY: Ligule Membranus
Confirm
DESCRIPTION
Physalis are herbaceous plants growing to 0.4 to 3 m tall, similar to the common tomato, a plant of the same family, but usually with a stiffer, more upright stem.
REMOVE
The best time to remove weeds is when the soil is damp and moist. The day after it has rained is a great day for weeding. Damp soils are loose and make it easier
Tap
Weed type
Plantago major
Arctium

CLEVER°FRANKE's approach to this challenge was to focus on the end user. They wanted to design a platform that was modern, but not flashy. Using broad strokes and lines, they maintained simplicity to the overall design, one which reflects the ruggedness of the work itself, while adding some finesse through their use of colour. By placing the map function central to the interface, they further simplified the design to suit the users, who use visual and geographical reference points constantly throughout their work. This provided them with a detailed overview at a glance and an added, easier method of interaction that interplays with actions across the platform.

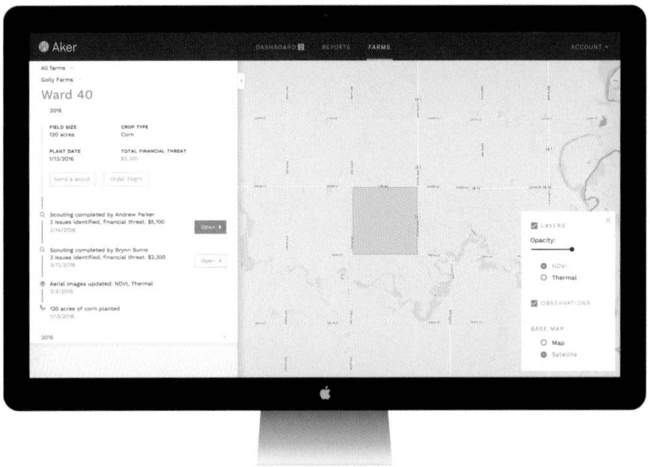
Aker
Ward 40

Aker
DASHBOARD
REPORTS
FARMS
ACCOUNT
Plant Health Flight 2
Clarkfield, Ward 32
SCOUT
Andy Johnson
SCOUT DATE
4/10/2016
GROWTH STAGE
V2
PLANT POPULATION
62,000
WEATHER CONDITION
Sunny
TEMPERATURE
69° F
RE-SCOUTING
Within 7 days
TOTAL FINANCIAL THREAT
$15,000
COMMENTS
General field level comment by the scout. General field level comment by the scout. General field level comment by the scout.
ISSUE
FINANCIAL THREAT
Green Foxtail
$23,560
Weed
$4,400
Green Foxtail
$720
Download report
Tap
Aker
DASHBOARD
REPORTS
FARMS
ACCOUNT
Plant Health Flight 1
Golly Farms, Ward 40
COMMENTS
General field level comment by the scout. General field level comment by the scout. General field level comment by the scout.
ISSUE
FINANCIAL THREAT
Green Foxtail
Weed
HEIGHT: 12 inches
DENSITY: Field edges only
NOTES: Comment by the scout about this specific issue. Notes written by the scout about this specific issue.
IMAGES
Green Foxtail
Download report

Mashrooi

Design Agency
CLEVER°FRANKE, Pixonal

Client
Dubai Land Department

App Store

Mashrooi is a knowledge platform that provides developers and investors with accurate, trustworthy information on progress, investment opportunities and innovation in real estate in Dubai. CLEVER°FRANKE rebuilt the app from the ground up, and together with Pixonal, rebranded Mashrooi with an updated design that included new features and functionality which make the app the most advanced, powerful tool for information about real-estate projects in Dubai.

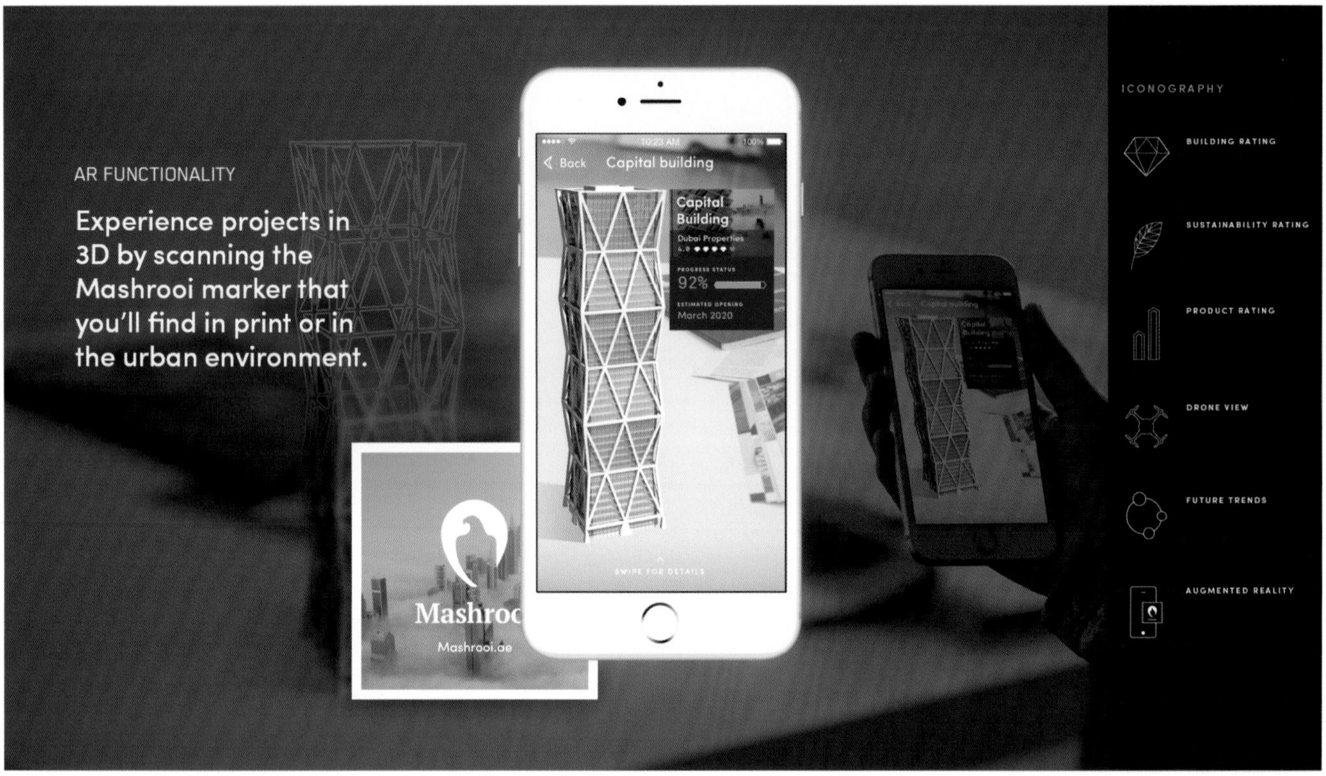
AR FUNCTIONALITY
Experience projects in 3D by scanning the Mashrooi marker that you'll find in print or in the urban environment.
Back
Capital building
Capital Building
92%
March 2020
Mashrooi.ae
ICONOGRAPHY
BUILDING RATING
SUSTAINABILITY RATING
PRODUCT RATING
DRONE VIEW
FUTURE TRENDS
AUGMENTED REALITY

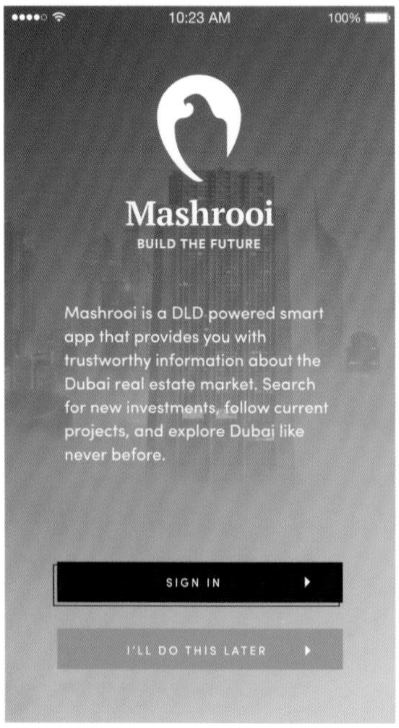
10:23 AM
100%
Mashrooi
BUILD THE FUTURE
Mashrooi is a DLD powered smart app that provides you with trustworthy information about the Dubai real estate market. Search for new investments, follow current projects, and explore Dubai like never before.
SIGN IN
I'LL DO THIS LATER

Tap

Future of Dubai
Explore the data behind the world's most ambitious city.
TRENDS
EXPLORE
PROFILE

Tap

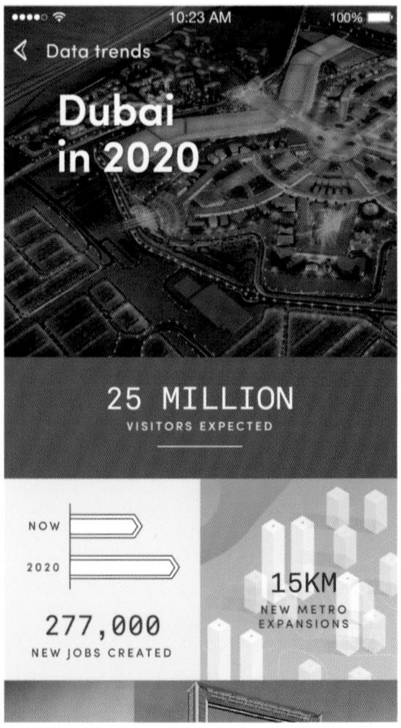
10:23 AM
100%
Data trends
Dubai in 2020
25 MILLION
VISITORS EXPECTED
NOW
2020
277,000
NEW JOBS CREATED
15KM
NEW METRO EXPANSIONS

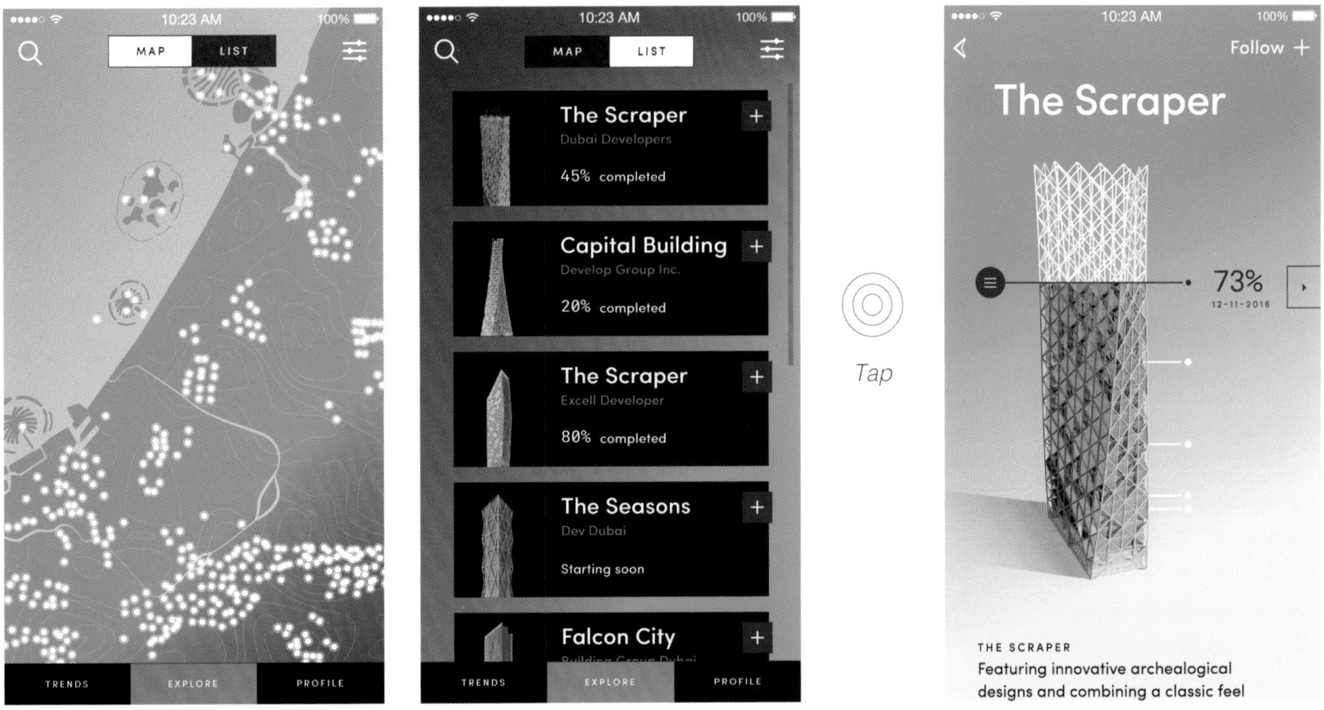
10:23 AM
100%
MAP
LIST
TRENDS
EXPLORE
PROFILE
The Scraper
Dubai Developers
45% completed
Capital Building
Develop Group Inc.
20% completed
The Scraper
Excell Developer
80% completed
The Seasons
Dev Dubai
Starting soon
Falcon City
Tap
Follow +
The Scraper
73%
12-11-2016
THE SCRAPER
Featuring innovative archealogical designs and combining a classic feel

The app enabled users to monitor projects in unique ways such as data visualizations of buildings and construction progress, drone footage and live feeds of construction areas, Augmented Reality and Mixed Reality that blend the real world with visualizations of completed projects, providing a glimpse into the future skyline, and up-to-date progress reports which include site progress reports and images from site inspectors.

Taking the buildings and their structure as a design element, the design agencies are able to show the progress of a specific project and the expected completion in a compelling, interactive interface. Visualizing the invisible network connections between projects and the city through the use of subtle lines, creates an image that tells the story of Dubai's commitment to being the world's smartest city. Using the environment as a design tool, they incorporated elements, such as the desert and sea in the colour palette, to create a subliminal sensation of Dubai's unique natural surroundings. The visual elements are clean, solid and open, conveying trust and transparency, which are the core values of the Mashrooi platform.

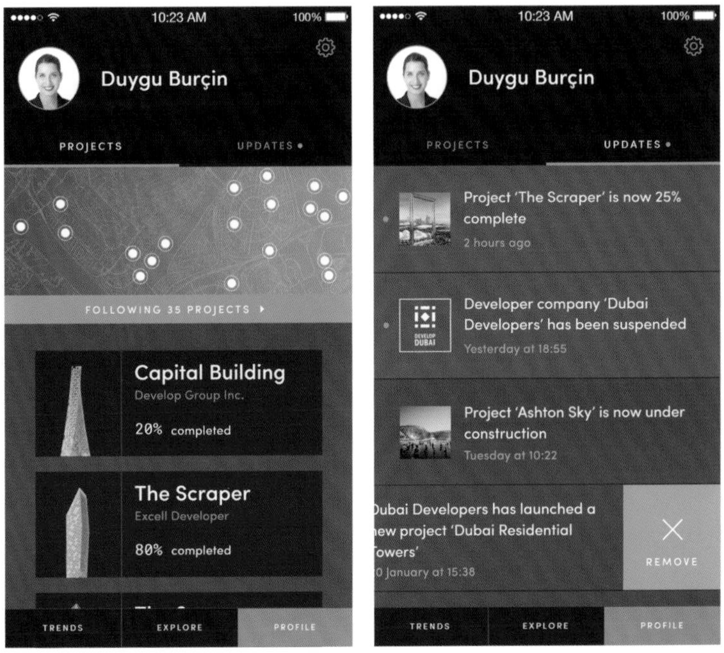
10:23 AM
100%
Duygu Burçin
PROJECTS
UPDATES •
FOLLOWING 35 PROJECTS
Capital Building
Develop Group Inc.
20% completed
The Scraper
Excell Developer
80% completed
Project 'The Scraper' is now 25% complete
2 hours ago
Developer company 'Dubai Developers' has been suspended
Yesterday at 18:55
Project 'Ashton Sky' is now under construction
Tuesday at 10:22
REMOVE
TRENDS
EXPLORE
PROFILE

Tesla Autopilot: Concept of Autonomous Car Control App

Behance

Design
Ray Yeunsu Shin

UX/UI Advisors
Chris Jahng, Roman Jaster

Motion Advisor
Minjoo Cho

Concept Advisor
Gail Swanlund

The inspiration of this project comes from the designer's own experience: he failed to find a parking space for his car when he visited his favourite coffee shop. He thought it would be nice if his car could drive around the town, or even go charging and get maintenance service when he is having coffee. These imaginary features of the level 5 autonomous car will be feasible enough in the near future thus he decided to make an app that users can control their level 5 autonomous Tesla like their personal driver or personal assistant.

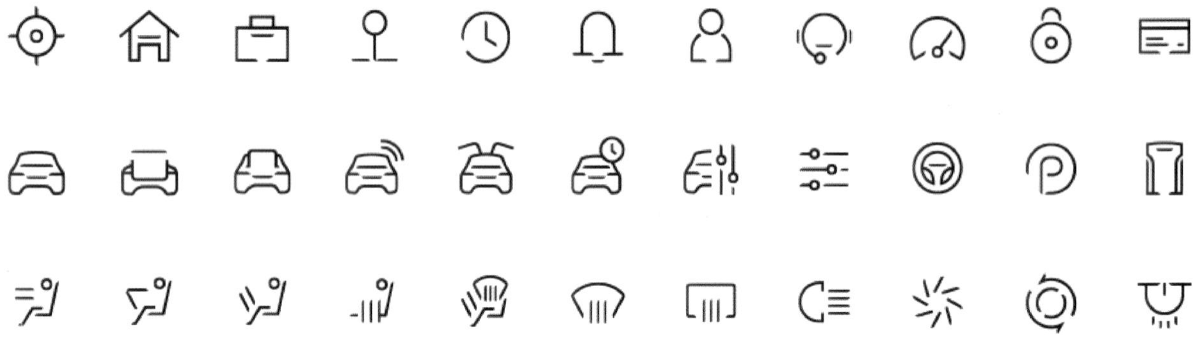

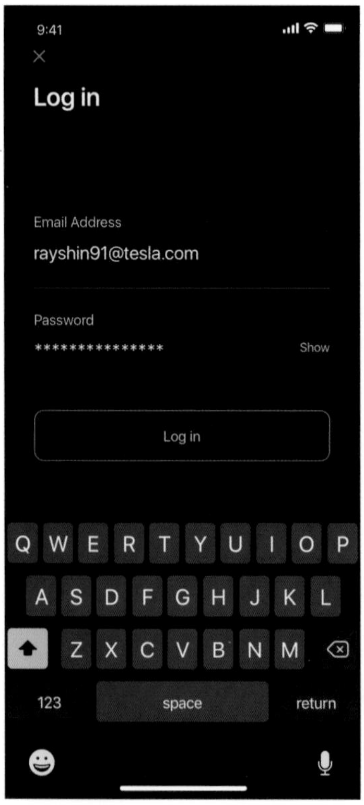

9:41
Log in
Email Address
rayshin91@tesla.com
Password
****
Show
Log in
Q W E R T Y U I O P
A S D F G H J K L
Z X C V B N M
123
space
return

Tap

9:41
Add your car
Tesla Model X
VIN Number
7RS MJ12137Y911225
Tesla Identification Number
7KJH640709
QR Code Scan
Start Pairing

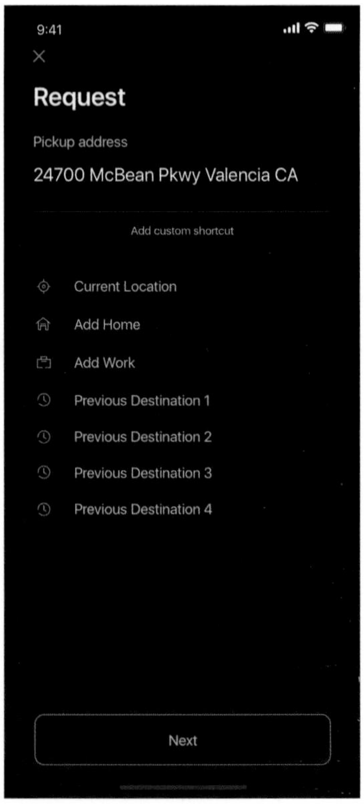

9:41
Request
Pickup address
24700 McBean Pkwy Valencia CA
Add custom shortcut
Current Location
Add Home
Add Work
Previous Destination 1
Previous Destination 2
Previous Destination 3
Previous Destination 4
Next

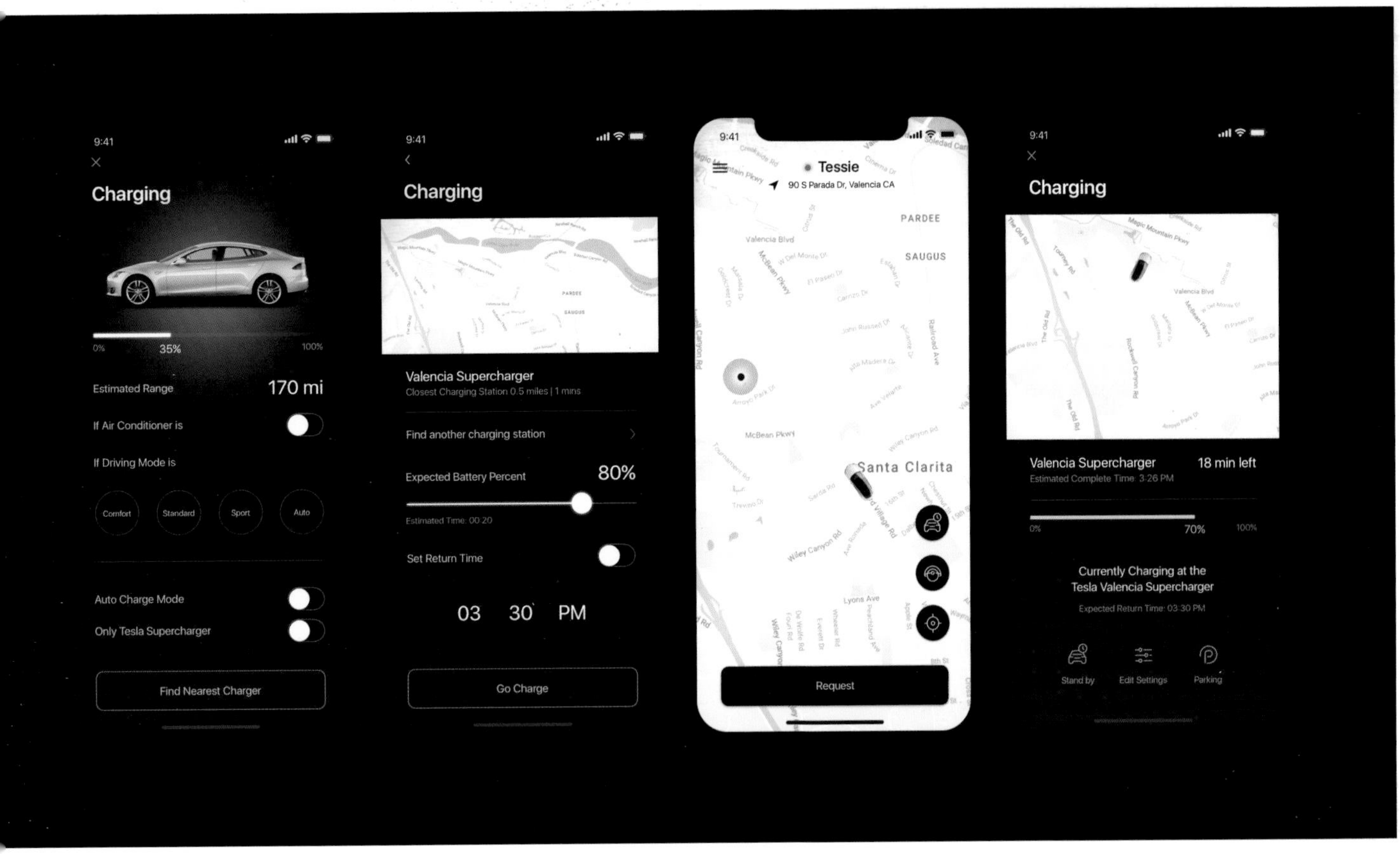
9:41
Charging
0%
35%
100%
Estimated Range
170 mi
If Air Conditioner is
If Driving Mode is
Comfort
Standard
Sport
Auto
Auto Charge Mode
Only Tesla Supercharger
Find Nearest Charger
9:41
Charging
Valencia Supercharger
Closest Charging Station 0.5 miles | 1 mins
Find another charging station
Expected Battery Percent
80%
Estimated Time: 00:20
Set Return Time
03
30
PM
Go Charge
9:41
Tessie
90 S Parada Dr, Valencia CA
PARDEE
SAUGUS
Santa Clarita
Request
9:41
Charging
Valencia Supercharger
18 min left
Estimated Complete Time: 3:26 PM
0%
70%
100%
Currently Charging at the
Tesla Valencia Supercharger
Expected Return Time: 03:30 PM
Stand by
Edit Settings
Parking

Based on the brand research, the designer set three main design principles for this project, which were accessible, luxurious and intuitive. To build the brand consistency, he used monochromatic gray colour scheme which conveys the elegant and luxury atmosphere of Tesla. Also for the brand's icon system, he took the curved edges of the Tesla logotype as the foundation. The icons are drawn in a single expressive line with breaks that help abstract the forms and keep the overall atmosphere of the Tesla logotype.

9:41
Climate
80°F
Current Interior Temperature
FR
74
°F Fahrenheit
Auto Climate Control
Climate Off
9:41
Controls
170 mi
Model: Model S P100D
Licence Plate: 6GDP82 CA
90 S Parada Dr, Valencia CA
Lock All
Honk Horn
Front Trunk
Headlights
Climate
Driving
Doors
Lights
Start Engine
9:41
Doors
Front Trunk
Front Left
Front Right
Rear Left
Rear Right
Charge Port
Rear Trunk
Panoramic Roof Vent
Panoramic Roof Slide
Lock All

Kript

Design
Elena Saharova

Concept
Ruslan Smirnov
(Co-Founder of Kript App)

Development
Kript Team

Google Play

Kript is a safe and intelligent interface designed to assist private investors in managing crypto and tokenized assets through a single account automatically synchronized with crypto exchanges. With Kript, users can get access to automatic tracking with live prices, charts and news feed, as well as buy or sell currencies. It supports the most popular exchanges and Ethereum wallets.

USD
BTC
ETH
$ 37 500.49
TODAY +320.67 (12%)
DENT
TIME
2 month
TARGETS
20%
EXPERT
Joseph Doe
MONTH
RAD
$2.69
CARA
$3.32
ALBO
$1.18
MEET
$2.45
REX
$3.12
ICO
Tap
40%
30%
25%
5%
RAD
Invest in the future
FUNDS
$7.569
ETH
$3.312
ICO
$1.108
BTC
$245
Joshua Earle
89m
Followers
2
Following
follow
79%
Success Rate
19,1%
Average Return
1st
3th
65%
20%
11%

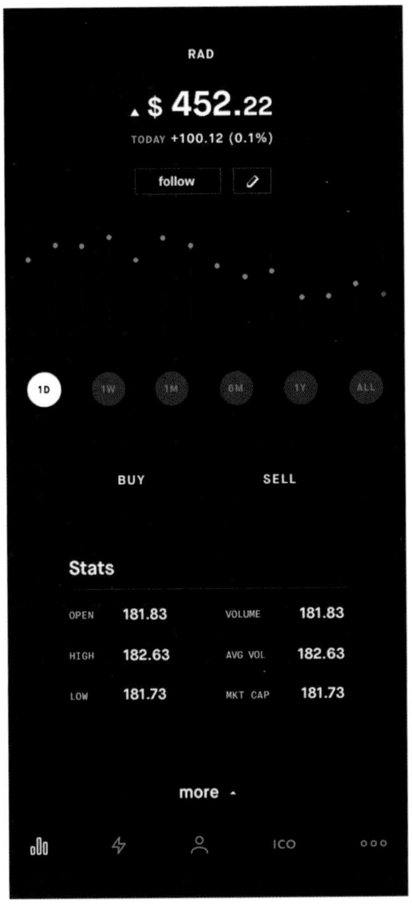
RAD
$ 452.22
TODAY +100.12 (0.1%)
follow
1D
1W
1M
6M
1Y
ALL
BUY
SELL
Stats
OPEN 181.83
VOLUME 181.83
HIGH 182.63
AVG VOL 182.63
LOW 181.73
MKT CAP 181.73
more
ICO

kript
SIGN WITH PHONE
or
LOG WITH SOCIAL NETWORK
SKIP

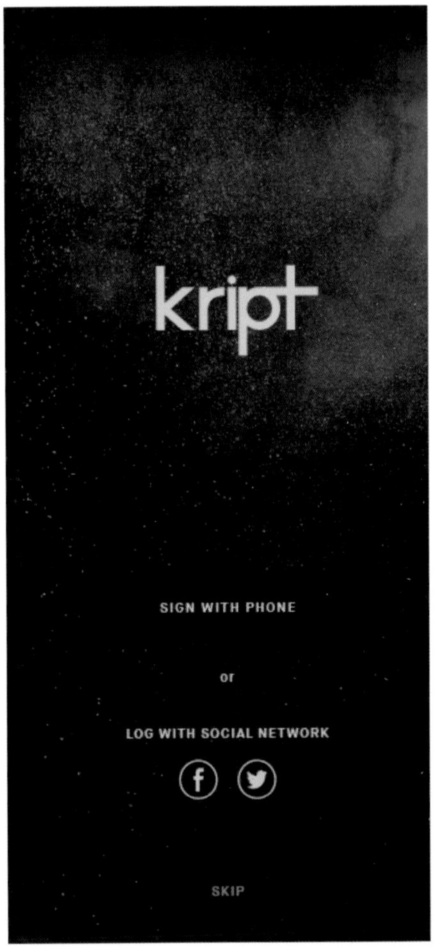
kript
SIGN WITH PHONE
or
LOG WITH SOCIAL NETWORK
SKIP

Slide

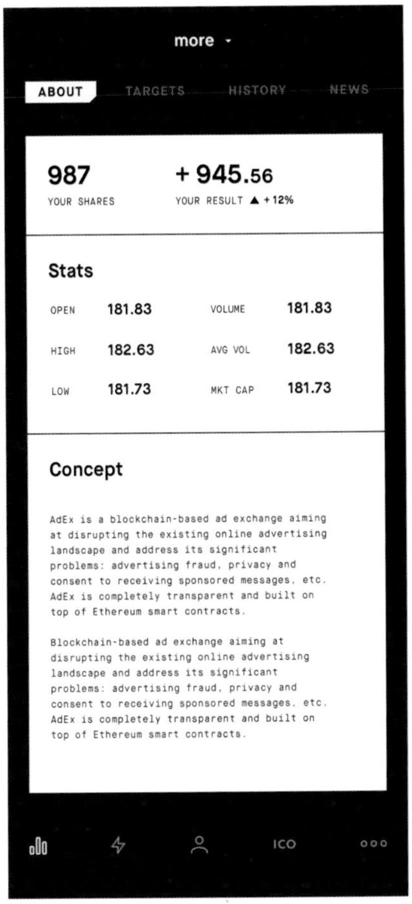
more
ABOUT
TARGETS
HISTORY
NEWS
987
YOUR SHARES
+ 945.56
YOUR RESULT ▲ +12%
Stats
OPEN 181.83
VOLUME 181.83
HIGH 182.63
AVG VOL 182.63
LOW 181.73
MKT CAP 181.73
Concept
AdEx is a blockchain-based ad exchange aiming at disrupting the existing online advertising landscape and address its significant problems: advertising fraud, privacy and consent to receiving sponsored messages, etc. AdEx is completely transparent and built on top of Ethereum smart contracts.
Blockchain-based ad exchange aiming at disrupting the existing online advertising landscape and address its significant problems: advertising fraud, privacy and consent to receiving sponsored messages, etc. AdEx is completely transparent and built on top of Ethereum smart contracts.
ICO

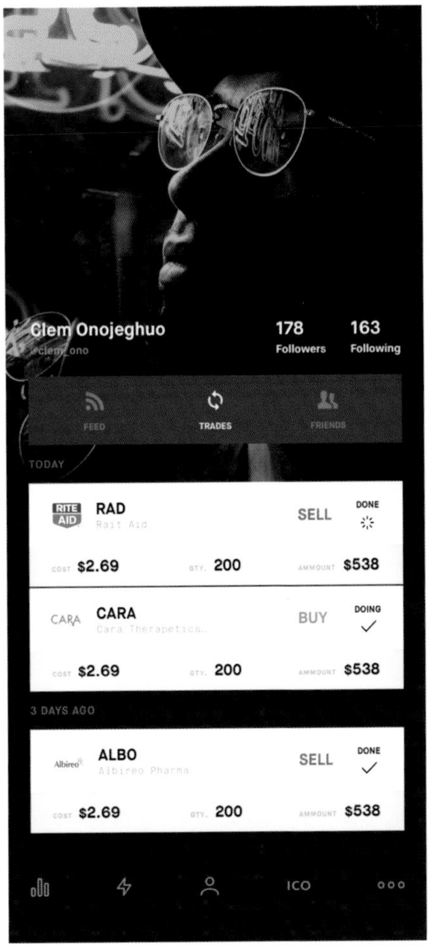
Clem Onojeghuo
178
Followers
163
Following
FEED
TRADES
FRIENDS
TODAY
RAD
SELL
DONE
$2.69
200
$538
CARA
BUY
DOING
$2.69
200
$538
3 DAYS AGO
ALBO
SELL
DONE
$2.69
200
$538
ICO

At the heart of visual elements lies the cyber-style, which perfectly reflects the manufacturability and purity of details, due to simple shapes and strict lines. Since the application uses growth (green) and drops (red) charts, as well as a large number of logos in the lists, the interface should become invisible to the user, but at the same time creating the right emotional background, as if the users are sitting behind the control panel of a large space ship that takes the path to the future of the financial market.

Bittrex Cryptocurrency Exchange

Art Direction, Design and Prototype
Ivan Kolle

Behance

This project is a concept mobile app design for BITTREX—one of the most popular worldwide cryptocurrency exchange platform. The prerequisite for designing this application was the designer's own pain as a user of cryptocurrency platforms. The site of the exchange was inconvenient to use on mobile devices and doesn't have a mobile application.

9:41
BITTREX
NEXT GENERATION CRYPTO EXCHANGE

9:41
BITTREX
2FA CODE
INPUT 6 DIGIT AUTHENTICATOR CODE
SUBMIT CODE

9:41
BITTREX
ENTER YOUR CODE
1
2
3
4
5
6
7
8
9
Forgot Code?
0

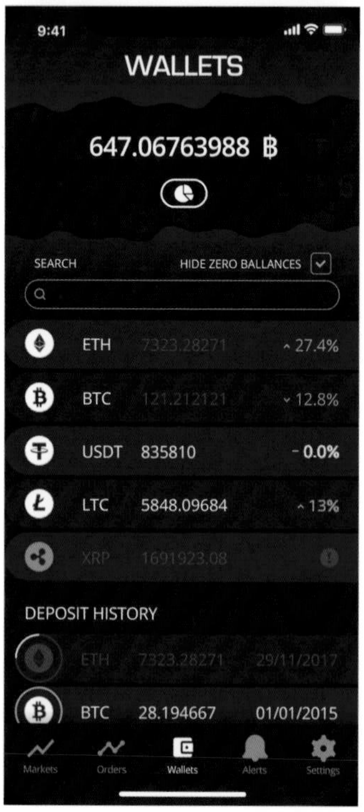
9:41
WALLETS
647.06763988 ฿
SEARCH
HIDE ZERO BALLANCES
ETH 7323.28271 27.4%
BTC 121.212121 12.8%
USDT 835810 - 0.0%
LTC 5848.09684 13%
XRP 1691923.08
DEPOSIT HISTORY
ETH 7323.28271 29/11/2017
BTC 28.194667 01/01/2015
Markets
Orders
Wallets
Alerts
Settings

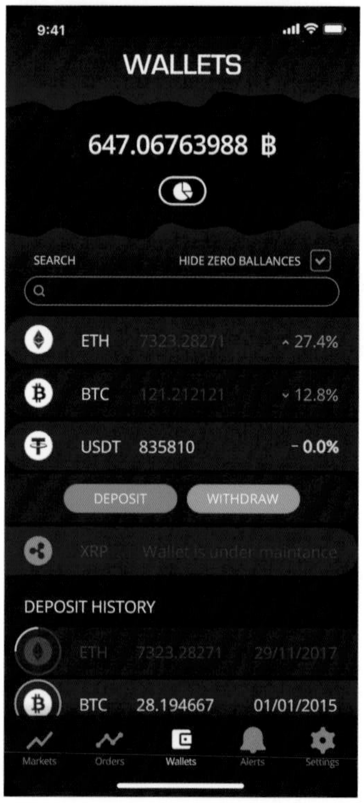
9:41
WALLETS
647.06763988 ฿
SEARCH
HIDE ZERO BALLANCES
ETH 7323.28271 27.4%
BTC 121.212121 12.8%
USDT 835810 - 0.0%
DEPOSIT
WITHDRAW
XRP Wallet is under maintance
DEPOSIT HISTORY
ETH 7323.28271 29/11/2017
BTC 28.194667 01/01/2015
Markets
Orders
Wallets
Alerts
Settings

In the application, the designer used contrasting colours so that the interfaces could be better perceived by the users. A dark blue gradient combined with a cryptographic background make the application more serious for user acceptance. For the secondary colours, the designer applied green and red to all clickable buttons, text, numeric data and graphs.

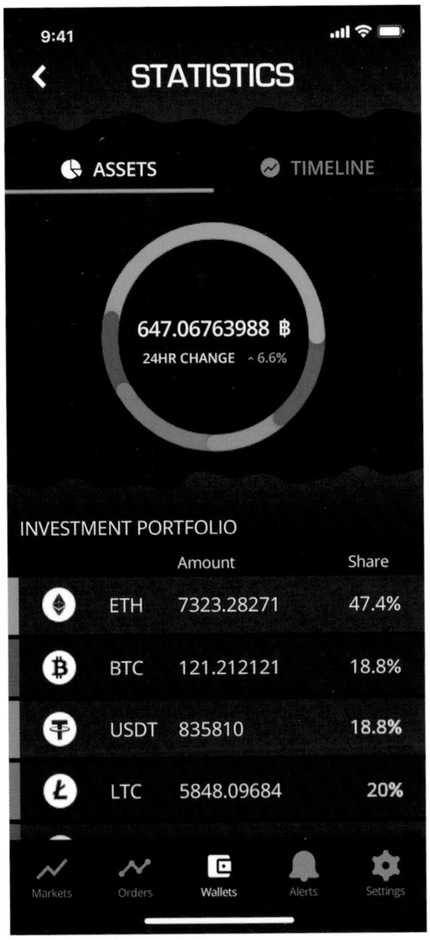
9:41
STATISTICS
ASSETS
TIMELINE
647.06763988 ฿
24HR CHANGE ^6.6%
INVESTMENT PORTFOLIO
Amount
Share
ETH 7323.28271 47.4%
BTC 121.212121 18.8%
USDT 835810 18.8%
LTC 5848.09684 20%
Markets
Orders
Wallets
Alerts
Settings

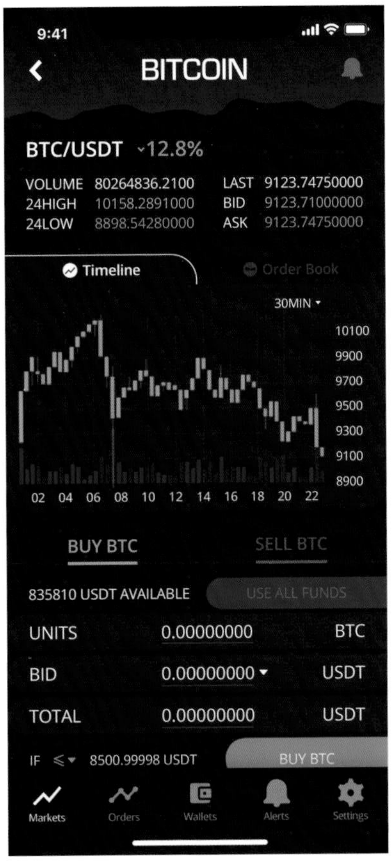
9:41
BITCOIN
BTC/USDT ˅12.8%
VOLUME 80264836.2100
24HIGH 10158.2891000
24LOW 8898.54280000
LAST 9123.74750000
BID 9123.71000000
ASK 9123.74750000
Timeline
Order Book
30MIN
10100
9900
9700
9500
9300
9100
8900
02 04 06 08 10 12 14 16 18 20 22
BUY BTC
SELL BTC
835810 USDT AVAILABLE
USE ALL FUNDS
UNITS 0.00000000 BTC
BID 0.00000000 USDT
TOTAL 0.00000000 USDT
IF ≤ 8500.99998 USDT
BUY BTC
Markets
Orders
Wallets
Alerts
Settings

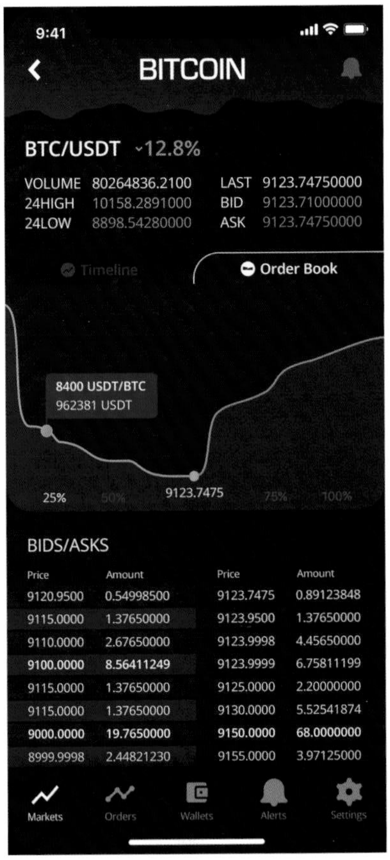
9:41
BITCOIN
BTC/USDT ˅12.8%
VOLUME 80264836.2100
24HIGH 10158.2891000
24LOW 8898.54280000
LAST 9123.74750000
BID 9123.71000000
ASK 9123.74750000
Timeline
Order Book
8400 USDT/BTC
962381 USDT
25%
50%
9123.7475
75%
100%
BIDS/ASKS
Price Amount Price Amount
9120.9500 0.54998500 9123.7475 0.89123848
9115.0000 1.37650000 9123.9500 1.37650000
9110.0000 2.67650000 9123.9998 4.45650000
9100.0000 8.56411249 9123.9999 6.75811199
9115.0000 1.37650000 9125.0000 2.20000000
9115.0000 1.37650000 9130.0000 5.52541874
9000.0000 19.7650000 9150.0000 68.0000000
8999.9998 2.44821230 9155.0000 3.97125000
Markets
Orders
Wallets
Alerts
Settings

Rotate

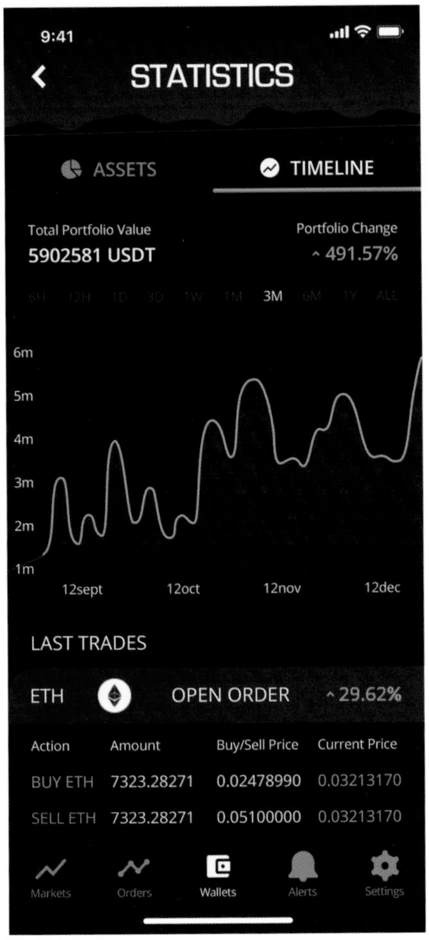
9:41
STATISTICS
ASSETS
TIMELINE
Total Portfolio Value
5902581 USDT
Portfolio Change
^491.57%
8H 12H 1D 3D 1W 1M 3M 6M 1Y ALL
6m
5m
4m
3m
2m
1m
12sept
12oct
12nov
12dec
LAST TRADES
ETH
OPEN ORDER ^29.62%
Action Amount Buy/Sell Price Current Price
BUY ETH 7323.28271 0.02478990 0.03213170
SELL ETH 7323.28271 0.05100000 0.03213170
Markets
Orders
Wallets
Alerts
Settings

Timeline
Order Book
CHART
TOOLS
H 9149.9992 O 9149.9992
L 9120.5428 C -
30MIN
10100
9900
9700
9500
9300
9100
8900
02 04 06 08 10 12 14 16 18 20 22
Fibonacci
Vertical
Ray
Rectangle
Horizontal
Line
Segment
Ellipse
Clear Drawings

The design concept contains all of the main features of the web-version, plus a portfolio, trade statistic and alerts pages. In addition, the application has great technical analysis functions (here, users need to interact with their phone and rotate it to horizontal view to access all technical features).

Transact Pro

Official Site

Design Agency
Vide Infra

Creative Direction
Anton Sulsky

Art Direction
Alexander Zhestkov

Design
Vladimir Birukov

Illustration
Anton Shineft

Project Management
Olga Kosova

Client
Transact Pro

The project is the development of an effective and inspiring website for Transact Pro, a prominent European fintech company.

Vide Infra team suggested that client should focus communications on specific client types and offer them solution packages, a set of products and services and special offers combined to meet their unique needs. This would allow the clients to easily identify themselves, receive information that reflects their needs and get in touch with the Transact Pro right on the home screen. The highlights of the project are a set of fine-art illustrations that the team designed and animated especially for the website, as well as a large number of functional diagrams and motion graphics that help the visitors grasp the mechanics of the Transact Pro services.

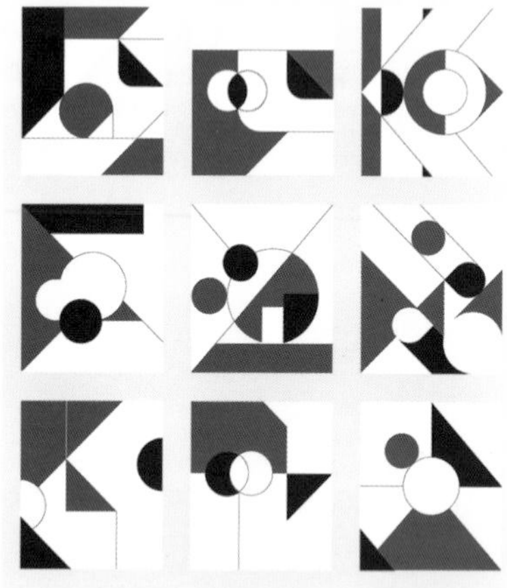

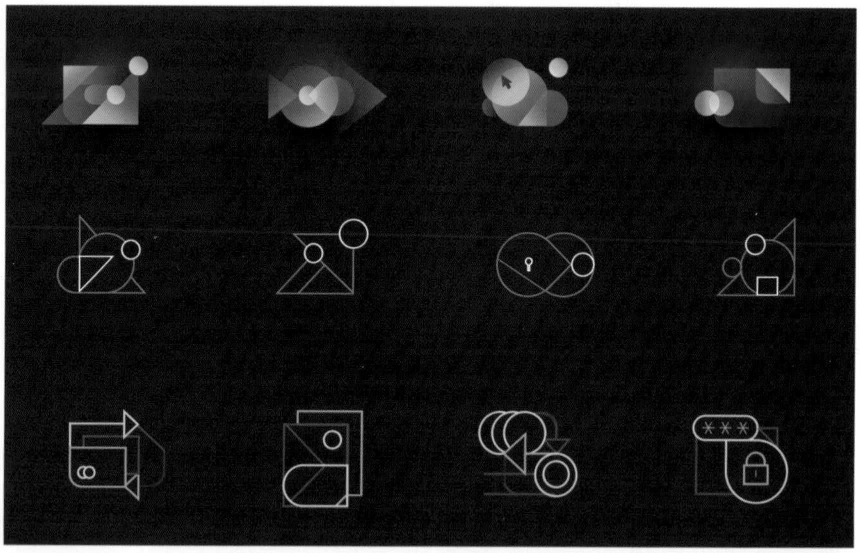

Transact-Pro-As
-A-Service —
approach our
systems via API
API

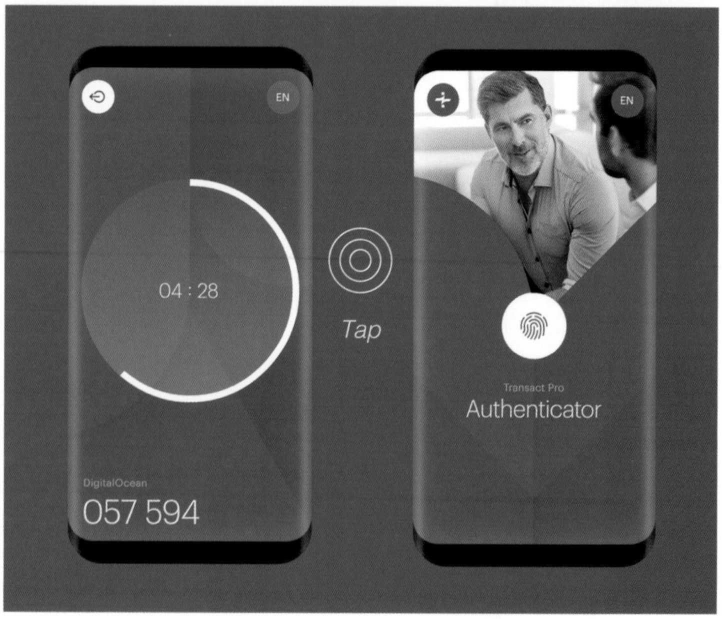
EN
04 : 28
DigitalOcean
057 594
Tap
EN
Transact Pro
Authenticator

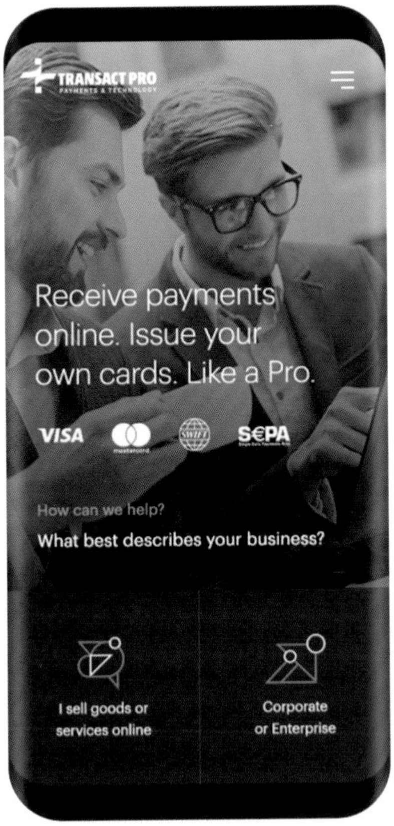
TRANSACT PRO
Receive payments online. Issue your own cards. Like a Pro.
VISA
S€PA
How can we help?
What best describes your business?
I sell goods or services online
Corporate or Enterprise

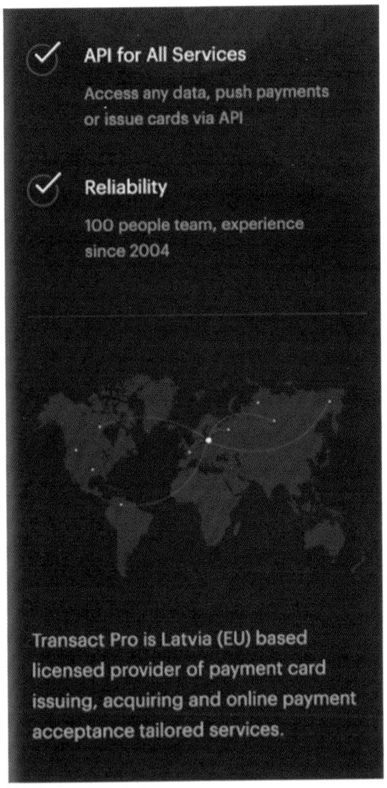
API for All Services
Access any data, push payments or issue cards via API
Reliability
100 people team, experience since 2004
Transact Pro is Latvia (EU) based licensed provider of payment card issuing, acquiring and online payment acceptance tailored services.

Online payment card processing — a new product of yours in a matter of days
Your Brand
Make payment

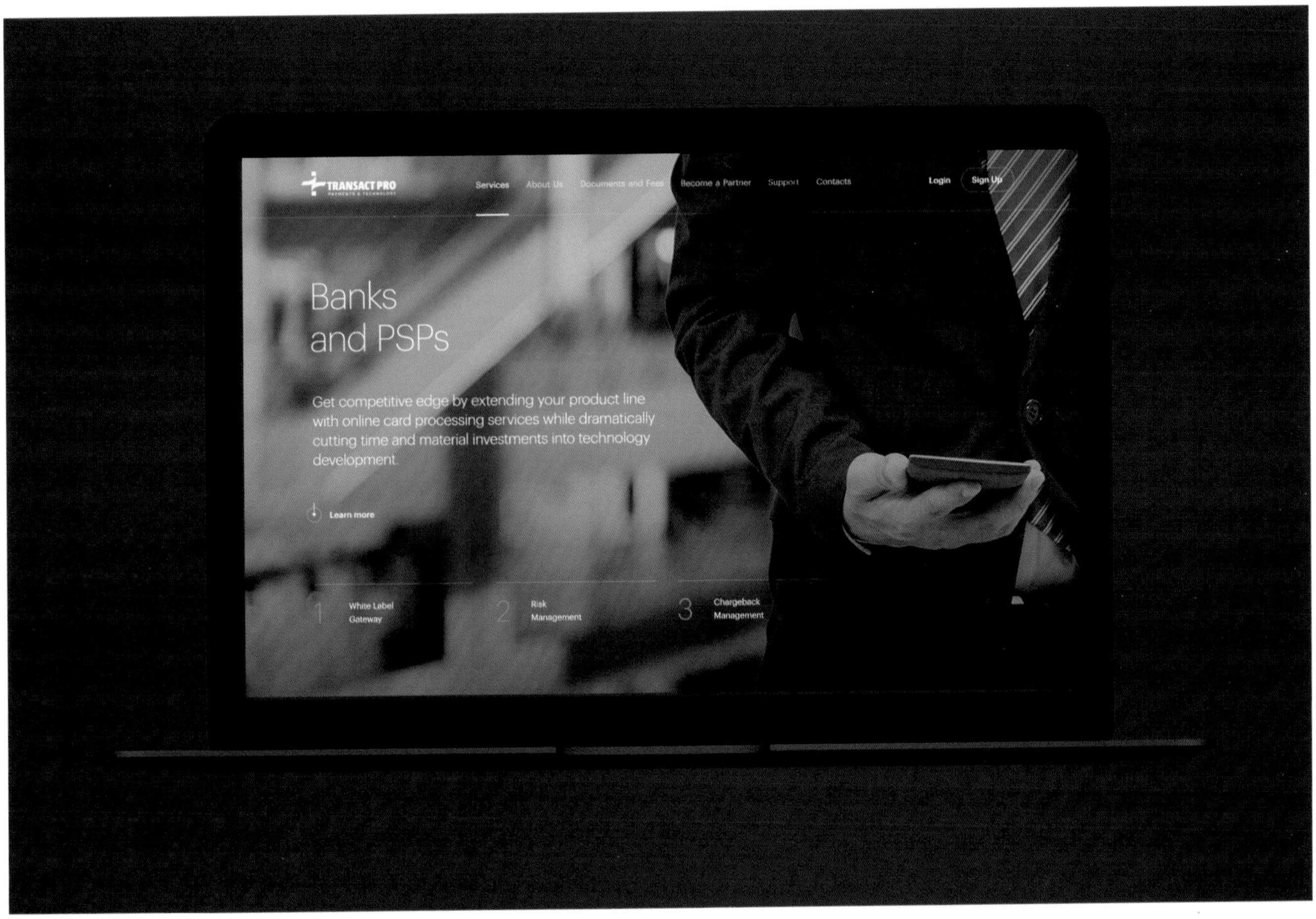
TRANSACT PRO
Services
About Us
Documents and Fees
Become a Partner
Support
Contacts
Login
Sign Up
Banks and PSPs
Get competitive edge by extending your product line with online card processing services while dramatically cutting time and material investments into technology development.
Learn more
1 White Label Gateway
2 Risk Management
3 Chargeback Management

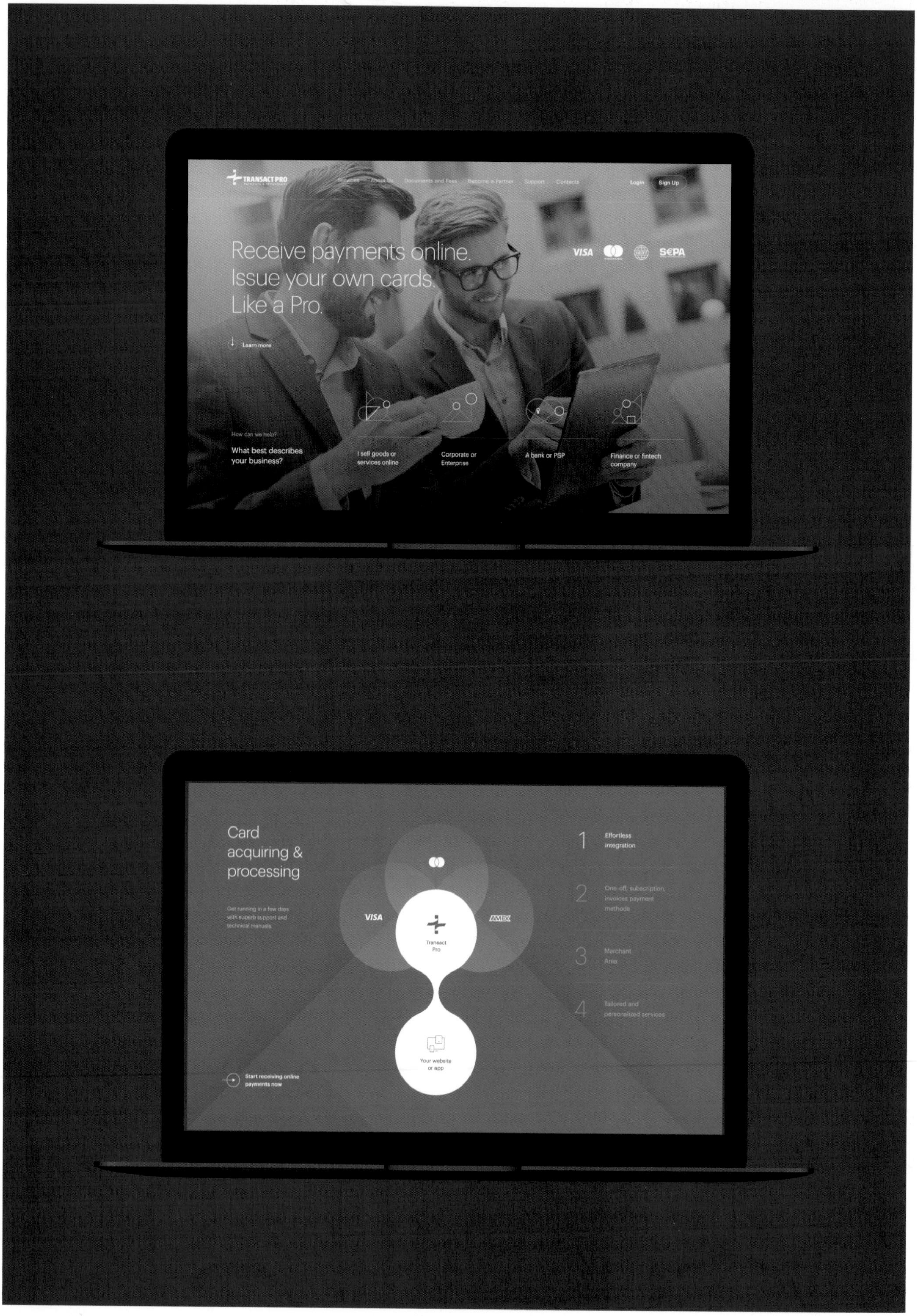

TRANSACT PRO
Services
About Us
Documents and Fees
Become a Partner
Support
Contacts
Login
Sign Up
Receive payments online.
Issue your own cards.
Like a Pro.
VISA
SEPA
Learn more
How can we help?
What best describes your business?
I sell goods or services online
Corporate or Enterprise
A bank or PSP
Finance or fintech company
Card acquiring & processing
Get running in a few days with superb support and technical manuals.
VISA
AMEX
Transact Pro
Your website or app
Start receiving online payments now
1 Effortless integration
2 One-off, subscription, invoices payment methods
3 Merchant Area
4 Tailored and personalized services

Recurring payments
Invoices
Standard Payments
2 One-off, subscription, invoices payment methods
3 Merchant Area
4 Tailored and personalized services
Issue Your Own Cards
Provide your team with your own salary or corporate cards, and distribute payments to your employees in a matter of minutes from your desktop or handheld device to any location in the world.
EUR, USD, GBP
Use wherever MasterCard is accepted, including online
Fraud management
Apply Now
Learn More
1 Start Receiving Payments Right Away
2 Easily Manage and Make Payments
3 Issue Your Own Cards
9234 5678 9876 5432
JASON MARIANDO
At a glance
Usage. Use wherever MasterCard is accepted, even online.
Issuance Fee. Starting from EUR 30
Currency: EUR, USD, GBP
Balance Checking. 24/7 ATM, via phone and online
Card Annual Fee. Starting from EUR 30
Expiration date. 3 years from issuance
Avoid pitfalls of chargeback management by relying on trusted infrastructure
Enable your team with your own salary or corporate cards and distribute payments to your troops in a matter of minutes from your desktop or handheld devices to any location in the world.
Dispute resolution automation
Fraud chargeback processing
Workflow Management
Dynamic System Updates
FWeb-Based Reporting & Analytics
1 White Label Gateway
2 Risk Management
3 Chargeback Management
Apply Now
24/7 Support
We will help you out in any situation when you need it
Top Security
Top professional security standards, licensed in EU
API for All Services
Access any data, push payments or issue cards via API
Reliability
100 people team, experience since 2004
Transact Pro is Latvia (EU) based licensed provider of payment card issuing, acquiring and online payment acceptance tailored services.
More about us
Access your accounts quickly and conveniently with your Online Bank
See your current account balances at one place
Transfer money between accounts in seconds
Pay bills and make payments to new people at the touch of a button
Ask us questions
Change your personal or security details
TRANSACT PRO
Services
About Us
Documents and Fees
Become a Partner
Support
Contacts
Card Processing & Acquiring
Transact Online
Card Issuing
White Label Cards (BIN Sponsorship within)
Gift Cards
Virtual Cards
Loyalty Cards
Transact Pro Card
Payment Solutions
Original Credit Transactions
P2P Transactions
SEPA & SWIFT Payments
Custom Services
API Services
Gateway Services
Payment Gateway
Chargeback management
Statements
Fraud Monitoring
White Label Gateway
Gateway Support
How can we help?
What best describes your business?
I sell goods or services online
Corporate or Enterprise
Effortless integration
One-off, subscription, invoices payment methods
3 Merchant Area
4 Tailored and personalized services
1 Start Receiving Payments Right Away
2 Easily Manage and Make Payments
3 Issue Your Own Cards

Brushly

Design Agency
Wolox

Design
Martina Hirschler

Strategy
Pilot 44

App Store

Brushly is an oral care app that works with an electronic toothbrush helping users to brush twice a day for two minutes. The challenge was to create healthy habits through an incentive and reward program. The design and development team created a program based on goals as incentives for creating a healthy routine that includes regular brushing and syncing the brush with the phone.

The brand concepts were encouraging, healthy but not medical, simple and easy, fun but not a game. It combines geometrical forms with a fresh and pastel colour palette. Curves and textures resemble foam and toothpaste while simple round shapes suggest a touch of playfulness.

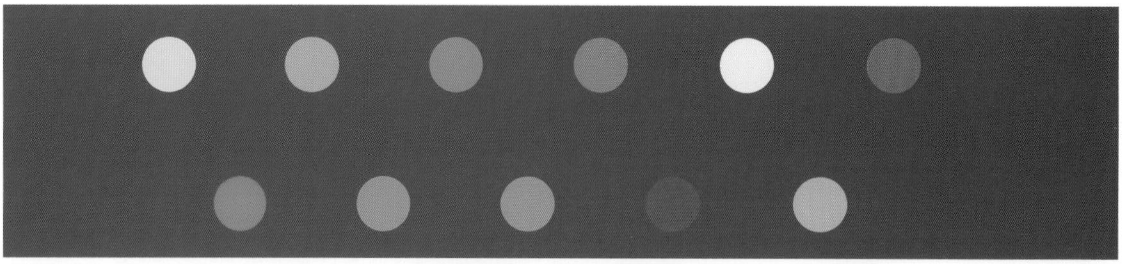

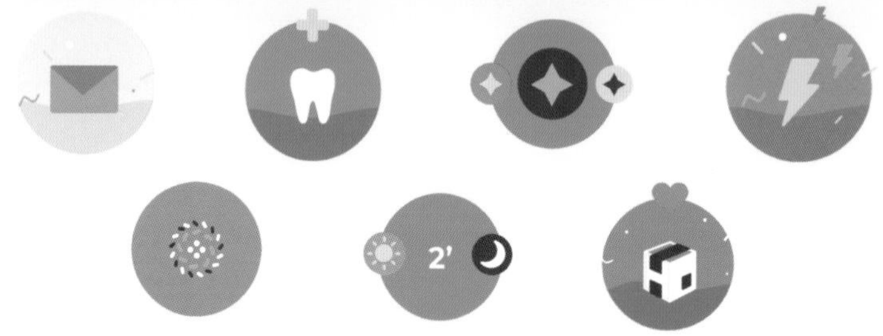
2'

Welcome to
Brushly

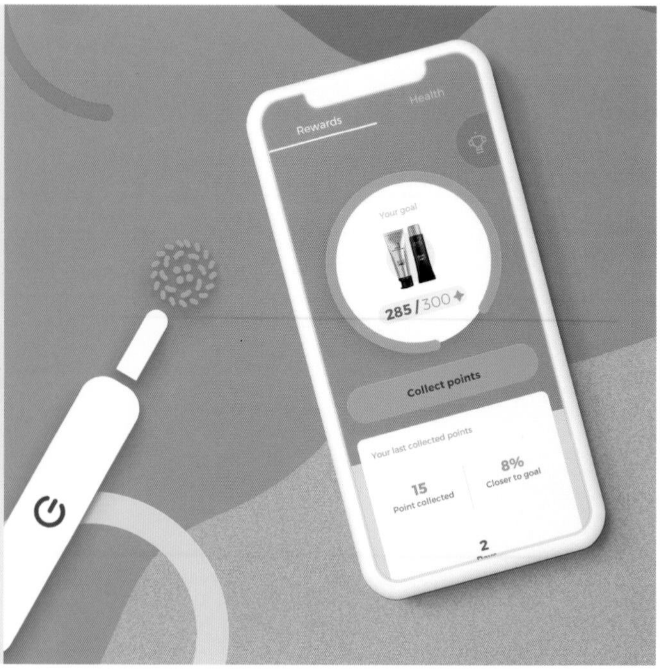
Rewards
Health
Your goal
285/300
Collect points
Your last collected points
15
Point collected
8%
Closer to goal
2

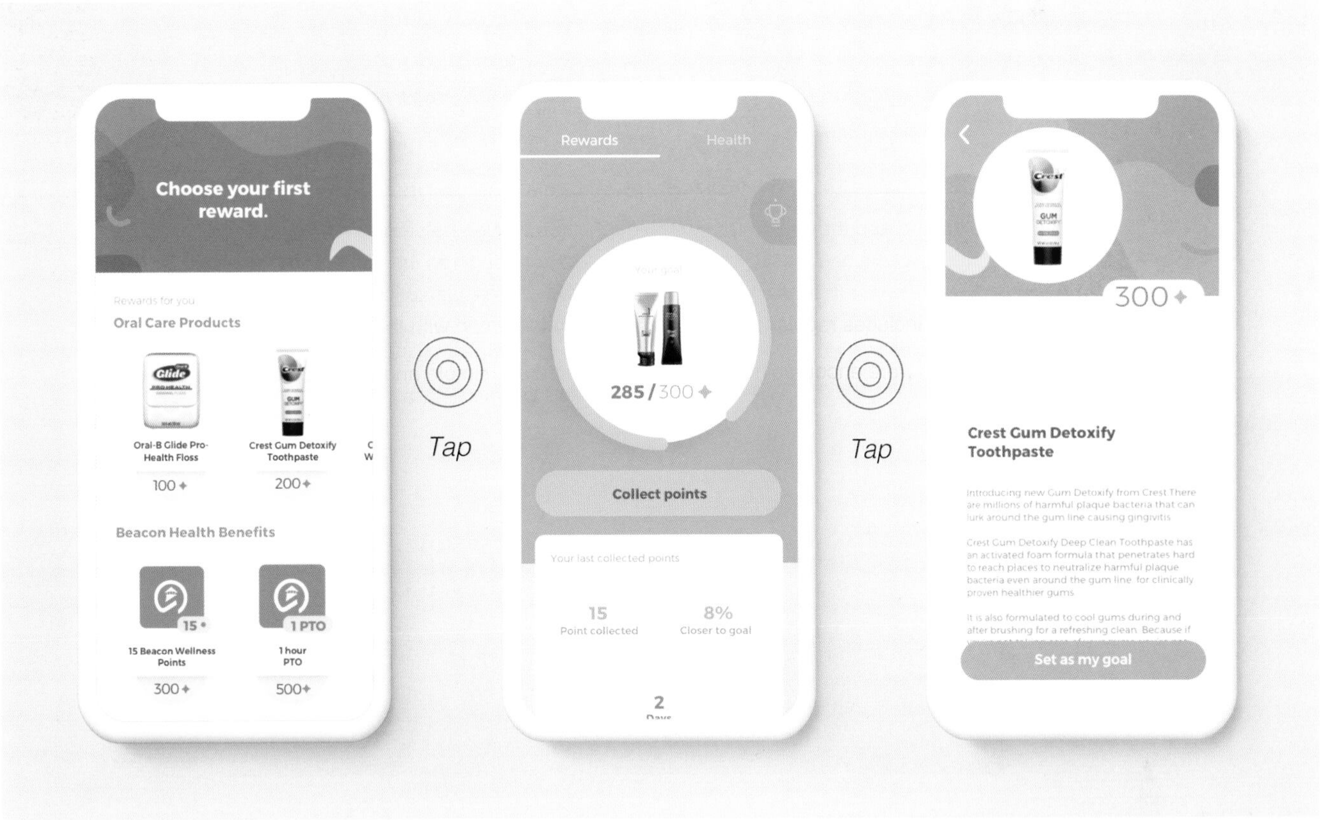

Choose your first reward.
Oral Care Products
Oral-B Glide Pro-Health Floss
100
Crest Gum Detoxify Toothpaste
200
Beacon Health Benefits
15
15 Beacon Wellness Points
300
1 PTO
1 hour PTO
500
Tap
Rewards
Health
285 / 300
Collect points
Your last collected points
15
Point collected
8%
Closer to goal
2
Tap
300
Crest Gum Detoxify Toothpaste
Set as my goal

Your activity
1:43 min
Get enough points and earn a reward chosen by you!
Plug in the base and place the brush

Smart Baby Bottle

Design
Shirley Xuebing Han

Behance

Smart Baby Bottle and its app are designed to help young mother with feeding bottled milk to their babies. The bottle has constant temperature that keeps the milk warm. The app records the time and amount of milk fed every day, analyzes the baby's drinking habits and compares it with national statistics, and it also gives scientific guidance, such as feeding posture correction.

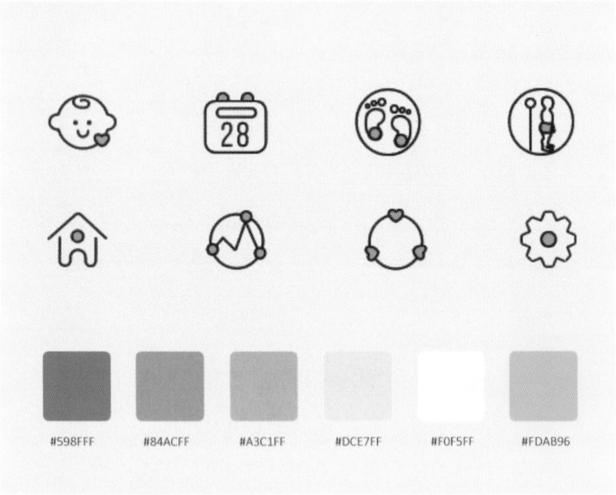
28
#598FFF
#84ACFF
#A3C1FF
#DCE7FF
#F0F5FF
#FDAB96

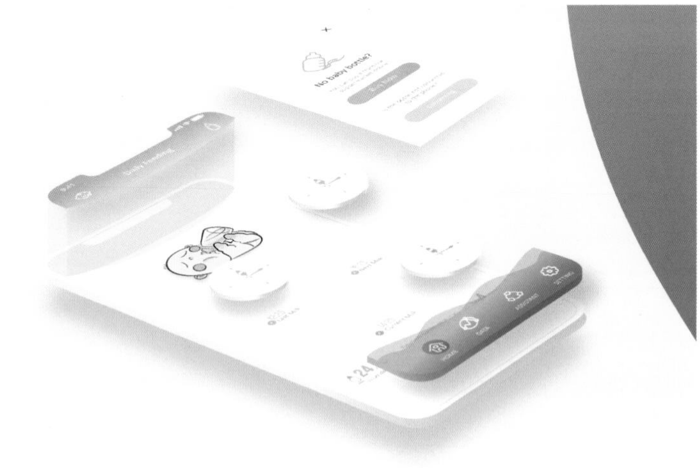

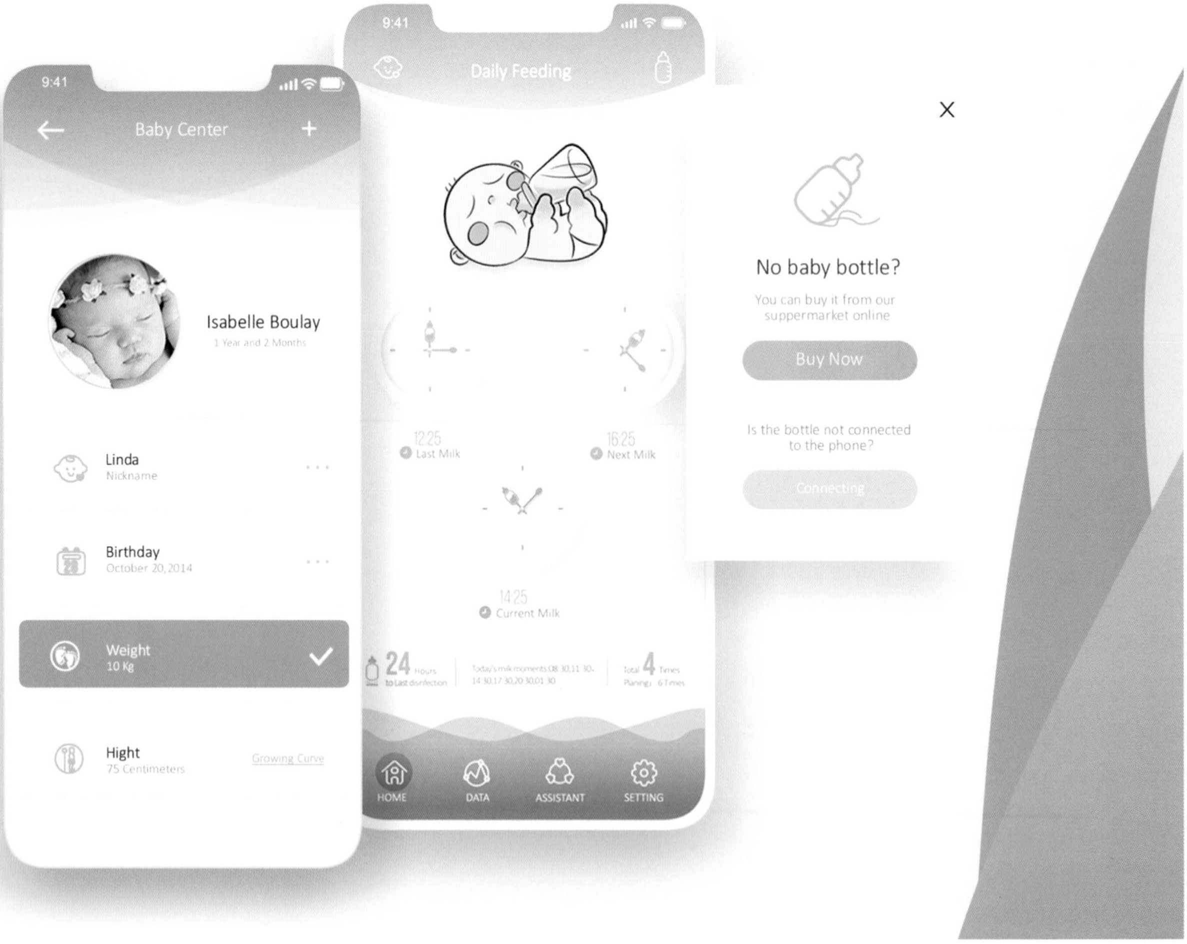
9:41
Baby Center
Isabelle Boulay
Linda
Nickname
Birthday
October 20, 2014
Weight
10 Kg
Hight
75 Centimeters
Growing Curve
9:41
Daily Feeding
12:25
Last Milk
16:25
Next Milk
14:25
Current Milk
24
4
HOME
DATA
ASSISTANT
SETTING
No baby bottle?
You can buy it from our suppermarket online
Buy Now
Is the bottle not connected to the phone?
Connecting

01

Milk Statistics

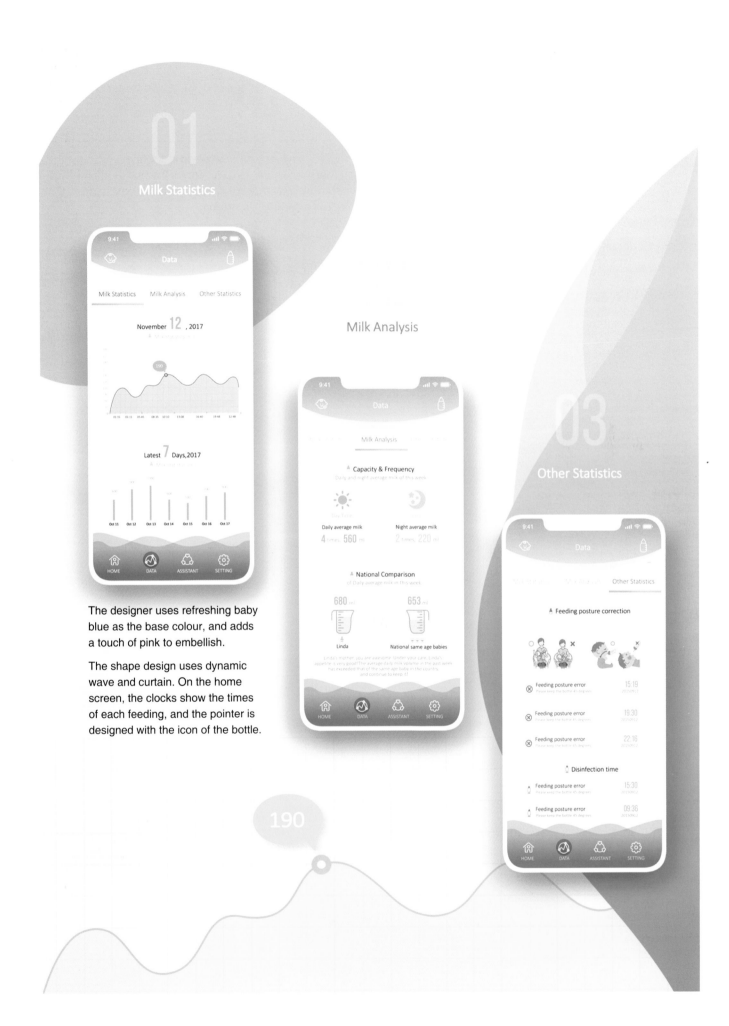

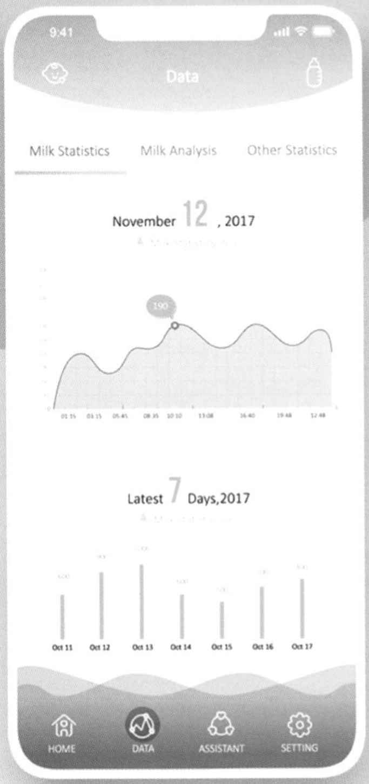
9:41
Data
Milk Statistics
Milk Analysis
Other Statistics
November 12 , 2017
190
Latest 7 Days,2017
Oct 11
Oct 12
Oct 13
Oct 14
Oct 15
Oct 16
Oct 17
HOME
DATA
ASSISTANT
SETTING

The designer uses refreshing baby blue as the base colour, and adds a touch of pink to embellish.

The shape design uses dynamic wave and curtain. On the home screen, the clocks show the times of each feeding, and the pointer is designed with the icon of the bottle.

Milk Analysis

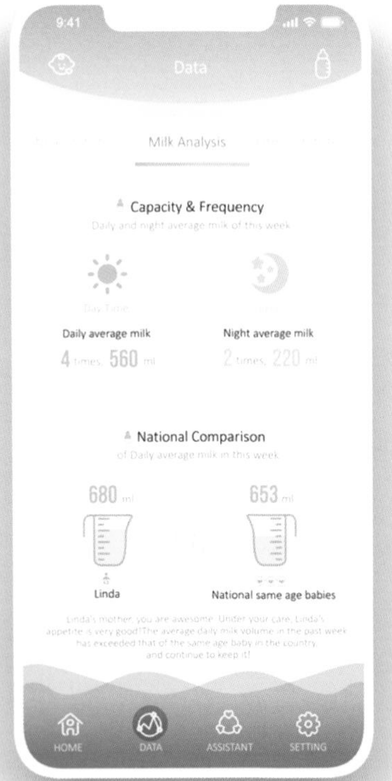
9:41
Data
Milk Analysis
Capacity & Frequency
Daily average milk
4 times 560 ml
Night average milk
2 times 220 ml
National Comparison
680 ml
653 ml
Linda
National same age babies
HOME
DATA
ASSISTANT
SETTING

03

Other Statistics

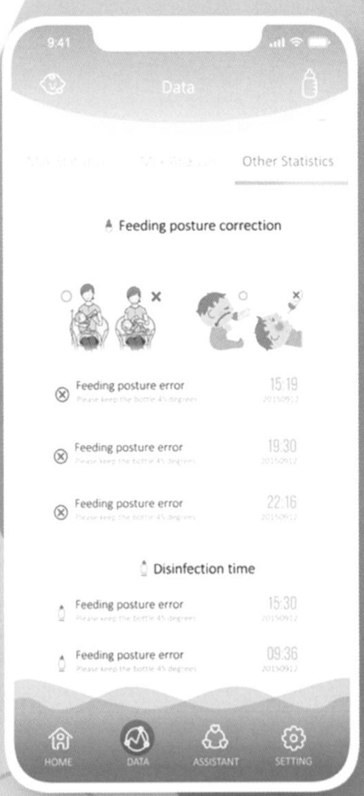
9:41
Data
Other Statistics
Feeding posture correction
Feeding posture error
15:19
Feeding posture error
19:30
Feeding posture error
22:16
Disinfection time
Feeding posture error
15:30
Feeding posture error
09:36
HOME
DATA
ASSISTANT
SETTING

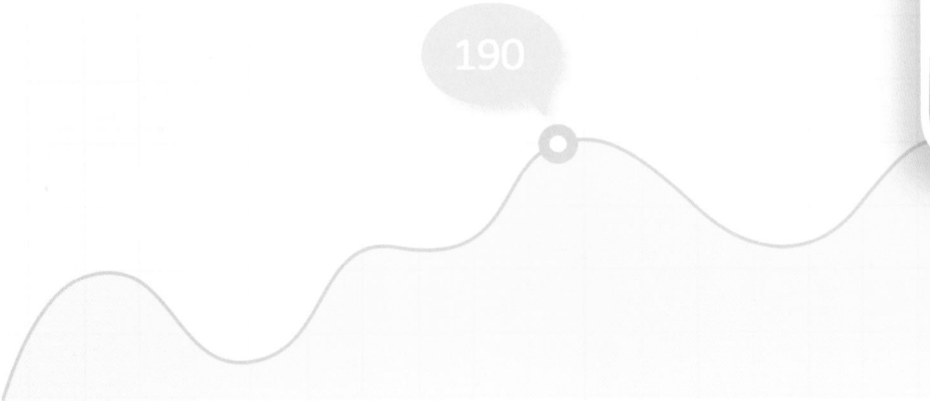
190

Pill Clok

PillClok

Design
Fabián Vadillo

Behance

PillClok is a product and brand development for people who tend to forget to take pills. It is a digital pillbox with configurable alarms, mainly designed for elder people. The whole products contain a pillbox with 1 or 4 daily doses, a portable version and an app for stock reminder and control. The app calculates the stock and daily consumption, reminding the users when they should buy medicine and refill the pillbox. A clean interface and colours convey calmness and control.

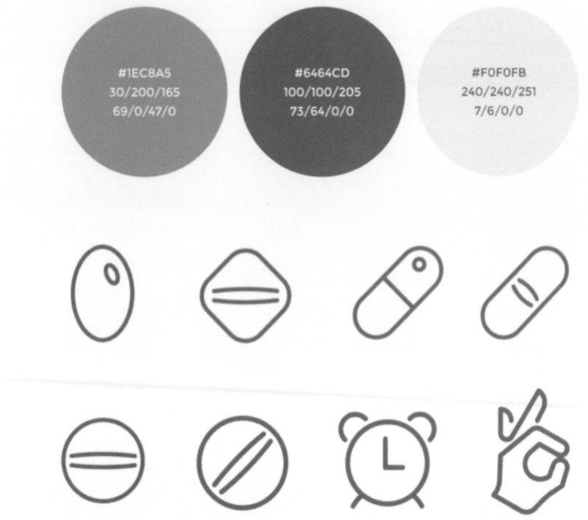
#1EC8A5
30/200/165
69/0/47/0
#6464CD
100/100/205
73/64/0/0
#F0F0FB
240/240/251
7/6/0/0

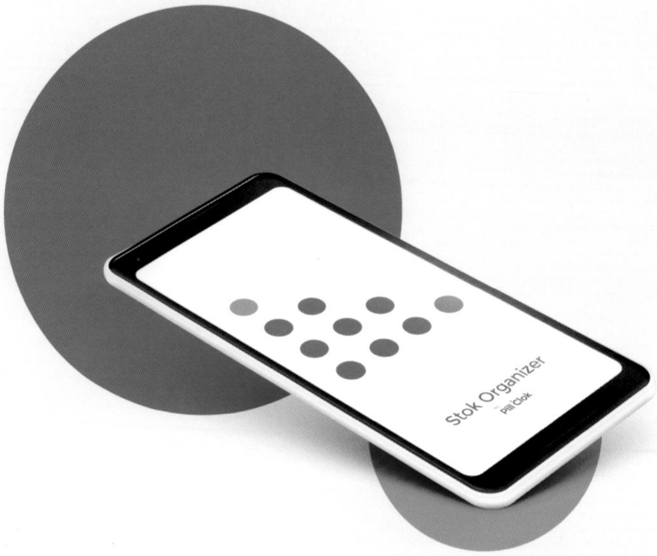
Stok Organizer
Pill Clok

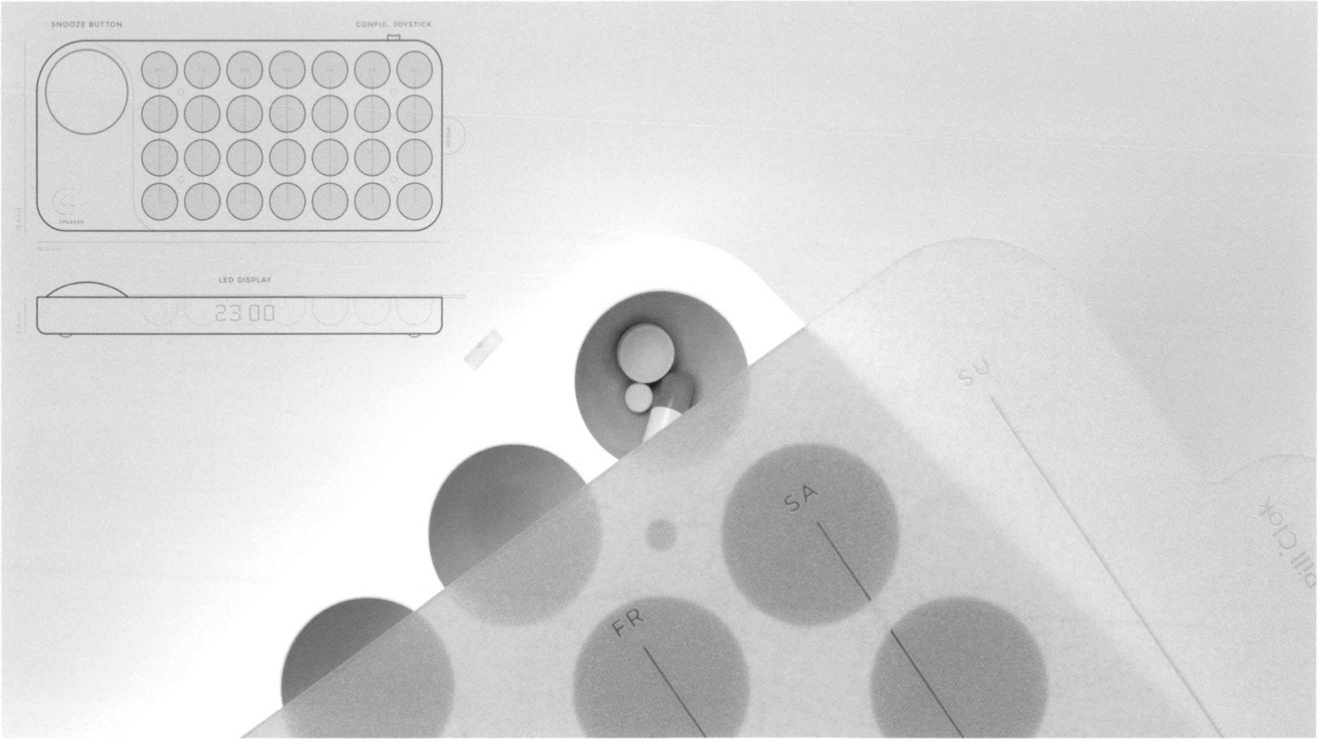
SNOOZE BUTTON
CONFIG. JOYSTICK
LED DISPLAY
23:00
SU
SA
FR
Pill Clok

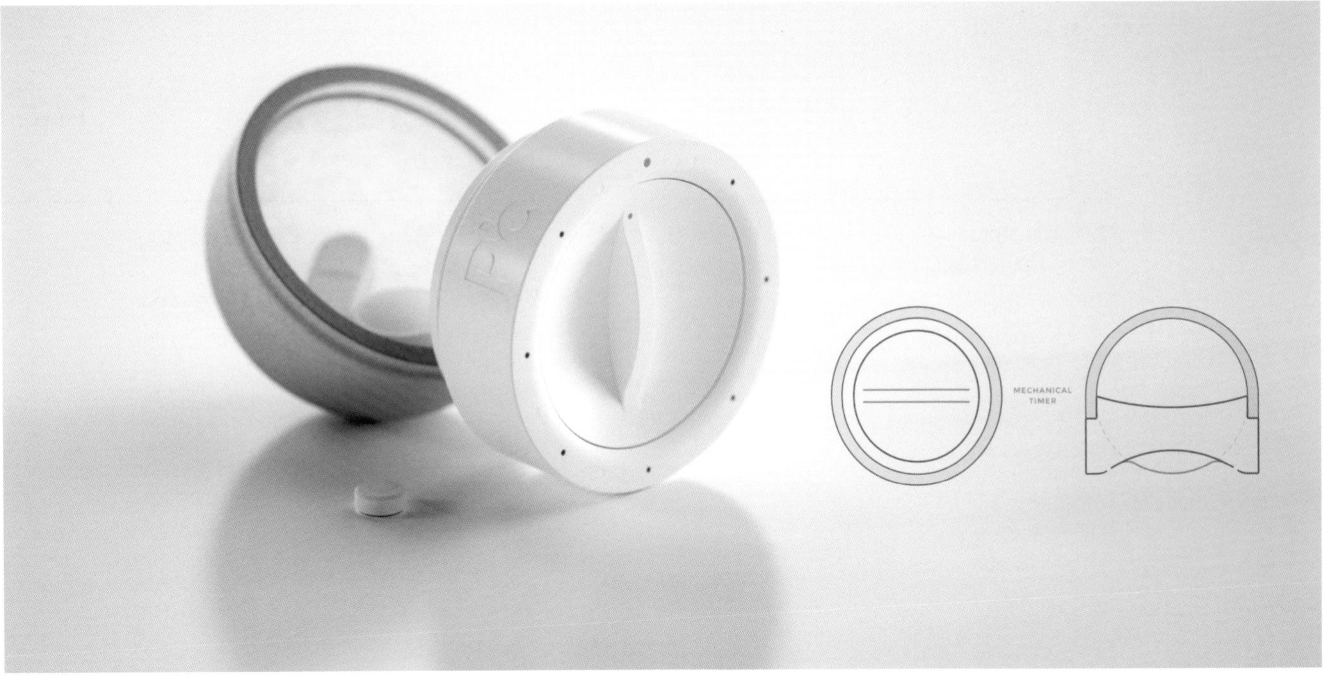
MECHANICAL TIMER

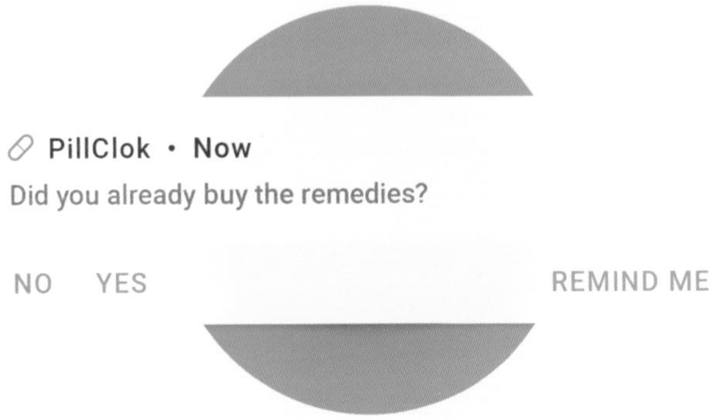
PillClok • Now
Did you already buy the remedies?
NO
YES
REMIND ME

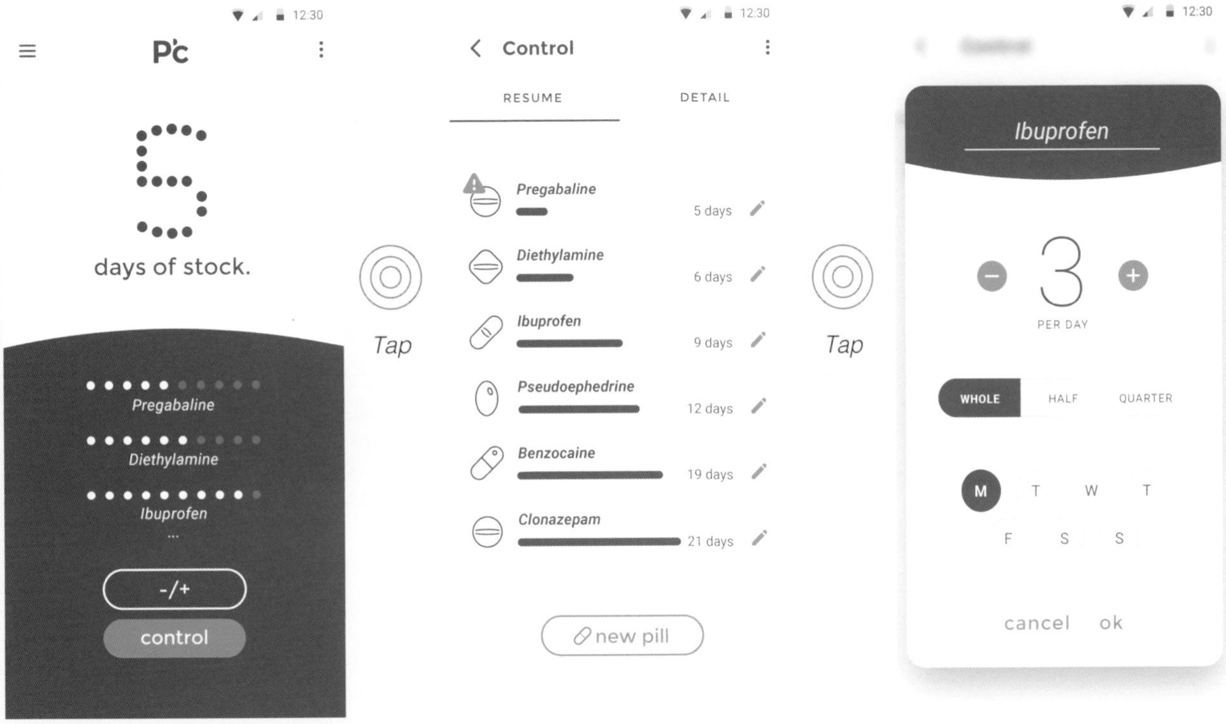
12:30
P'c
5
days of stock.
Pregabaline
Diethylamine
Ibuprofen
...
-/+
control
Tap
12:30
Control
RESUME
DETAIL
Pregabaline
5 days
Diethylamine
6 days
Ibuprofen
9 days
Pseudoephedrine
12 days
Benzocaine
19 days
Clonazepam
21 days
new pill
Tap
12:30
Ibuprofen
3
PER DAY
WHOLE
HALF
QUARTER
M
T
W
T
F
S
S
cancel
ok

TOOWAY

Tooway

Design
Taehee Kim, Hyemin Yoo

Behance

Tooway is a service for people who need other's opinion/information before they make a decision. It was made to exchange simple curiosities, but also to give advice and suggest solutions to people who share the same problems.

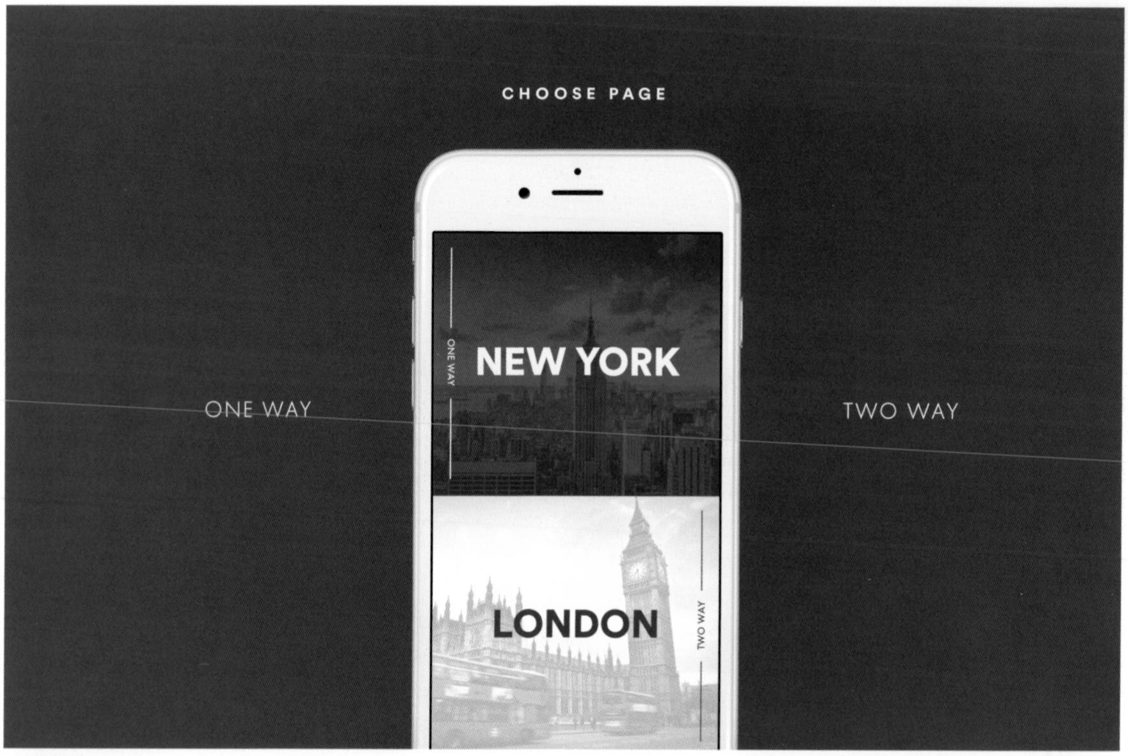
CHOOSE PAGE
ONE WAY
NEW YORK
LONDON
TWO WAY

TOOWAY
help people make choices!
ask a question
Sign in with email
Google
Facebook

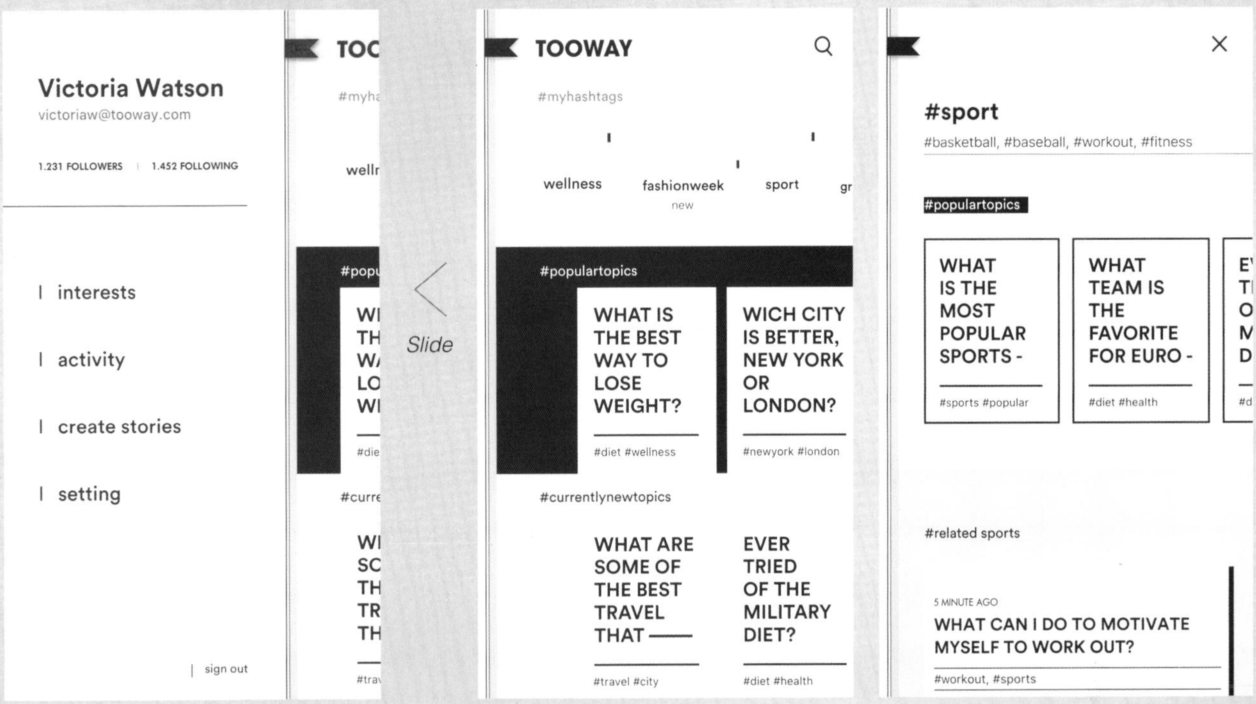
Victoria Watson
victoriaw@tooway.com
1.231 FOLLOWERS | 1.452 FOLLOWING
interests
activity
create stories
setting
sign out
Slide
TOOWAY
#myhashtags
wellness
fashionweek
new
sport
#populartopics
WHAT IS THE BEST WAY TO LOSE WEIGHT?
#diet #wellness
WICH CITY IS BETTER, NEW YORK OR LONDON?
#newyork #london
#currentlynewtopics
WHAT ARE SOME OF THE BEST TRAVEL THAT
#travel #city
EVER TRIED OF THE MILITARY DIET?
#diet #health
#sport
#basketball, #baseball, #workout, #fitness
#populartopics
WHAT IS THE MOST POPULAR SPORTS -
#sports #popular
WHAT TEAM IS THE FAVORITE FOR EURO -
#diet #health
#related sports
5 MINUTE AGO
WHAT CAN I DO TO MOTIVATE MYSELF TO WORK OUT?
#workout, #sports

One of Tooway's features is the ability to create stories, which exist at a paragraph level by easily providing guidelines for user's experience. They replace the typical comment stream, allowing readers to make a comment on specific sections, with swiping motion on the compare screen.

By using objects related to familiar books elements, this application gives friendly feeling to users. Minimal colours reduce the overall complexity and lead users to concentrate more on contents.

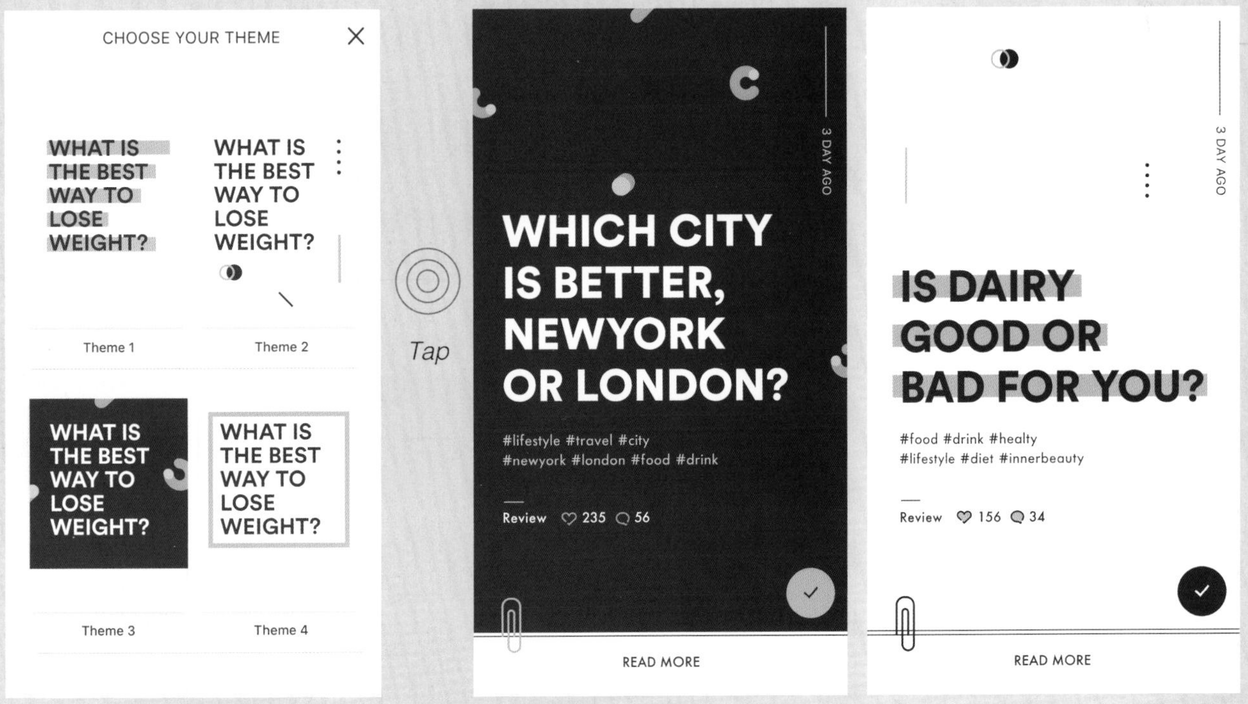
CHOOSE YOUR THEME
WHAT IS THE BEST WAY TO LOSE WEIGHT?
Theme 1
Theme 2
Theme 3
Theme 4
Tap
WHICH CITY IS BETTER, NEWYORK OR LONDON?
#lifestyle #travel #city
#newyork #london #food #drink
Review 235 56
3 DAY AGO
READ MORE
IS DAIRY GOOD OR BAD FOR YOU?
#food #drink #healty
#lifestyle #diet #innerbeauty
Review 156 34
3 DAY AGO
READ MORE

Rekord

Design
Iris Chu

Behance

A lot of people may share the experience that their New Year's resolutions made in the beginning of the year could not last in a few months or even in a few weeks. Rekord is a concept app inspired by this experience and uses data visualization to help people keep track of their resolutions and also keep motivated along the entire journey.

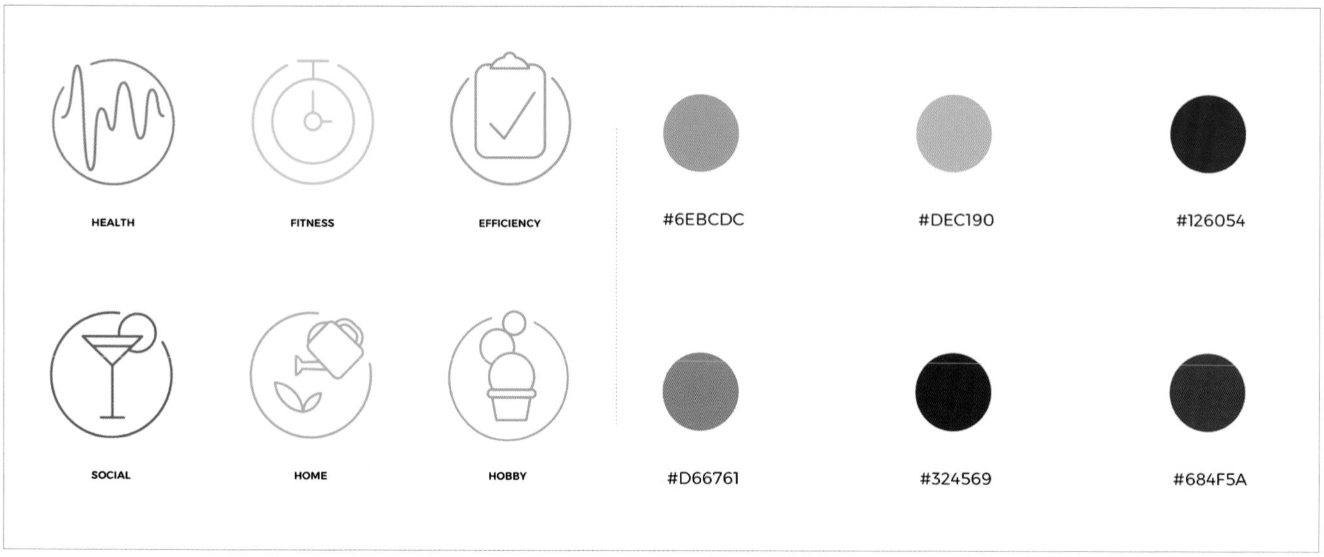
HEALTH
FITNESS
EFFICIENCY
#6EBCDC
#DEC190
#126054
SOCIAL
HOME
HOBBY
#D66761
#324569
#684F5A

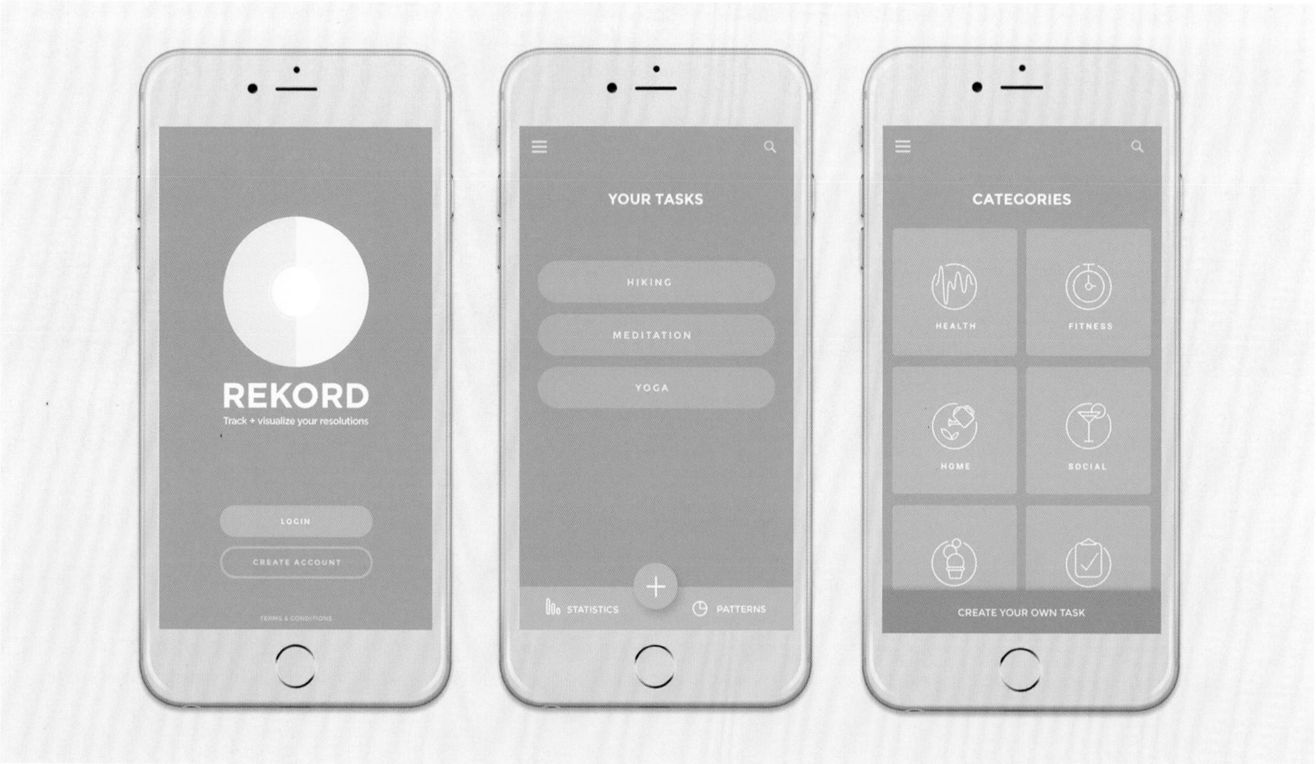
REKORD
Track + visualize your resolutions
LOGIN
CREATE ACCOUNT
YOUR TASKS
HIKING
MEDITATION
YOGA
STATISTICS
PATTERNS
CATEGORIES
HEALTH
FITNESS
HOME
SOCIAL
CREATE YOUR OWN TASK

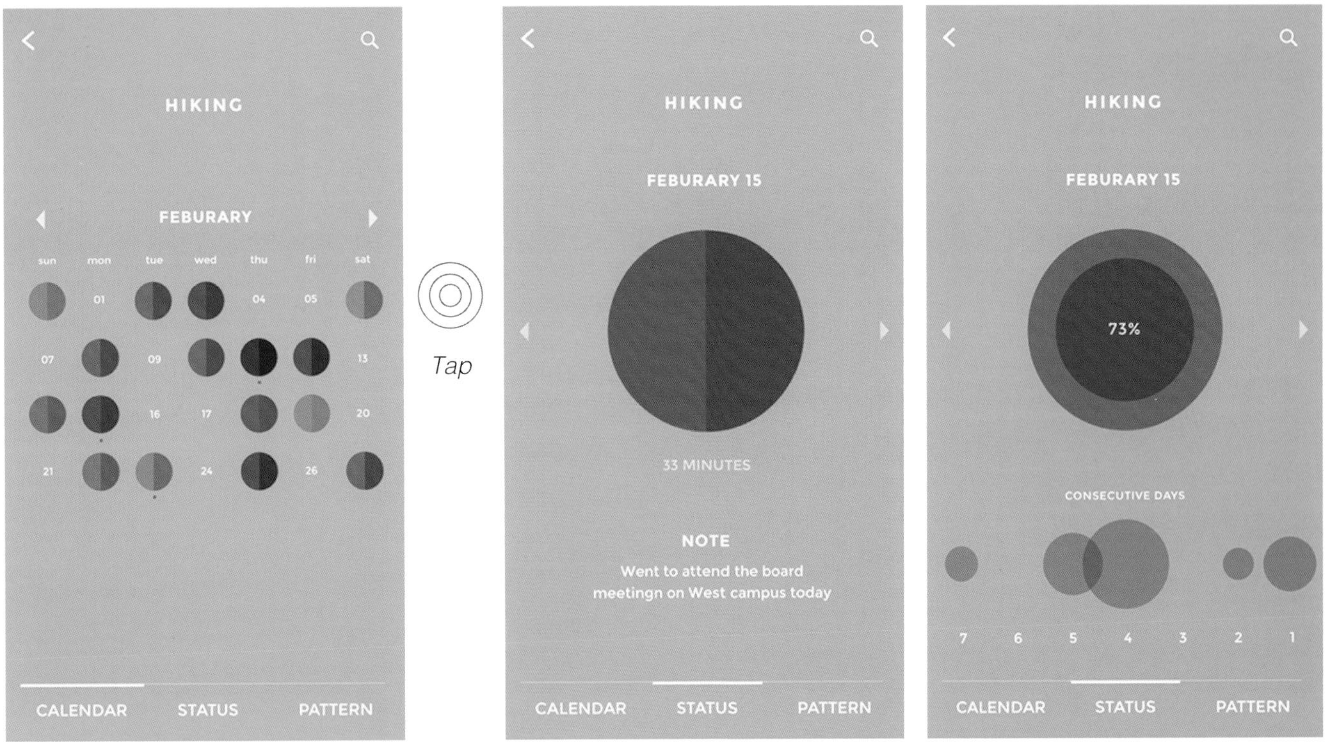
HIKING
FEBURARY
sun mon tue wed thu fri sat
01 04 05 07 09 13 16 17 20 21 24 26
CALENDAR
STATUS
PATTERN
Tap
HIKING
FEBURARY 15
33 MINUTES
NOTE
Went to attend the board
meetingn on West campus today
CALENDAR
STATUS
PATTERN
HIKING
FEBURARY 15
73%
CONSECUTIVE DAYS
7 6 5 4 3 2 1
CALENDAR
STATUS
PATTERN

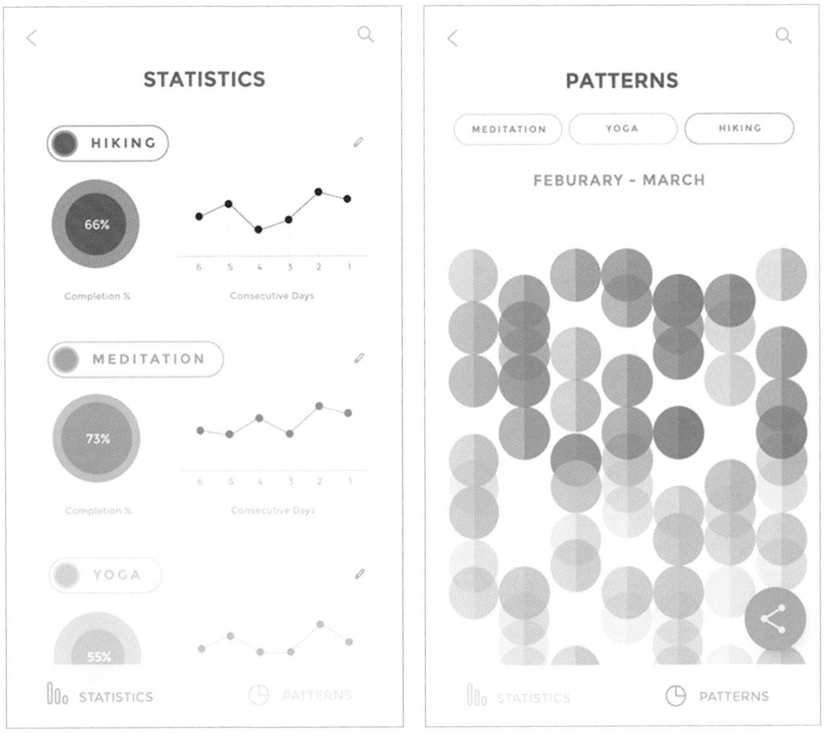
STATISTICS
HIKING
66%
6 5 4 3 2 1
Completion %
Consecutive Days
MEDITATION
73%
YOGA
55%
STATISTICS
PATTERNS
PATTERNS
MEDITATION
YOGA
HIKING
FEBURARY - MARCH
STATISTICS
PATTERNS

The intent of the entire visual system design was to visualize data by inheriting some attributes from the physical world and implementing them into the digital world so that users can relate them together. In the physical world, viewers got the idea of depth due to the shadows and got the idea of material from transparency. In the digital world, the depth is limited to the screen surface, therefore transparency becomes a better option to create differentiations in value as well as indicating similarities to the real world. The application name also comes from the physical world where people used to store sound data in a record. The designer replaced letter "c" in record with letter "k" so as to differentiate with the traditional record as well as emphasize on the tracking function.

Smart Home Control App

Behance

Design Agency
Awsmd

UI Design
Anton Mlhalcov

Animation
Alex Vasilyev

UX Design
Stan Nevedomskis, Anton Mihalcov

Iconography
Julia Packan

This is a concept app that intends to control the smart home devices. The goal was to create a pleasant, easy and engaging experience for users. The second objective was to make the interface clean and simple and create an intuitive way to control various devices from a smartphone with multiple options available.

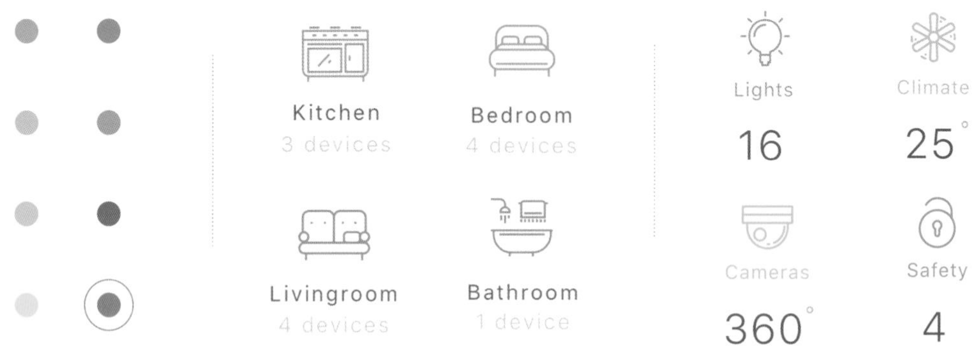

Kitchen
3 devices
Bedroom
4 devices
Livingroom
4 devices
Bathroom
1 device
Lights
16
Climate
25°
Cameras
360°
Safety
4

Select Climate Settings
Favourites
Heat
10°-19°
Cool
3°-7°
Wet
7-1

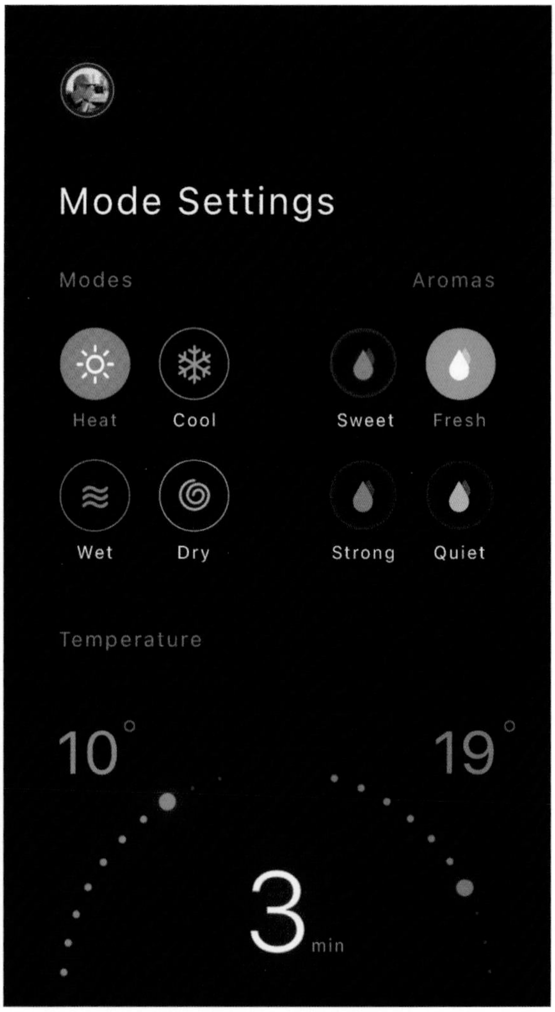

Mode Settings
Modes
Aromas
Heat
Cool
Sweet
Fresh
Wet
Dry
Strong
Quiet
Temperature
10°
19°
3 min

remedy+

Remedy

Design
Jessica Elliott

Behance

Unsatisfied with the medial resources online, the designer wanted to create a system that users could more quickly and accurately find out the problem in their physical health. This concept app "Remedy" features a colourfully simple step-by-step system in which users can customize their experience by physical gender, location on the body and their symptoms.

In contrast with the cold and sterile feeling of the normal medical website, the designer wishes to create an environment that people feel relaxed and less nervous. The colours and rounded edges of the type act as almost a distraction from figuring out the physical pain, and the enlarged type, simple graphics, and step-by-step process adds a gamification quality that diminishes the feeling of worry and leaves more room for fun.

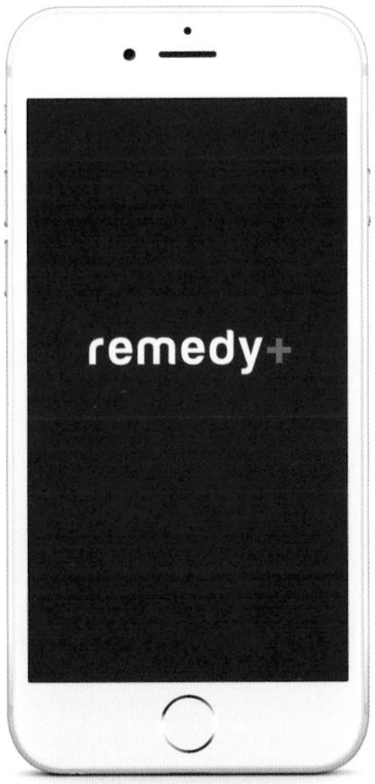
remedy+

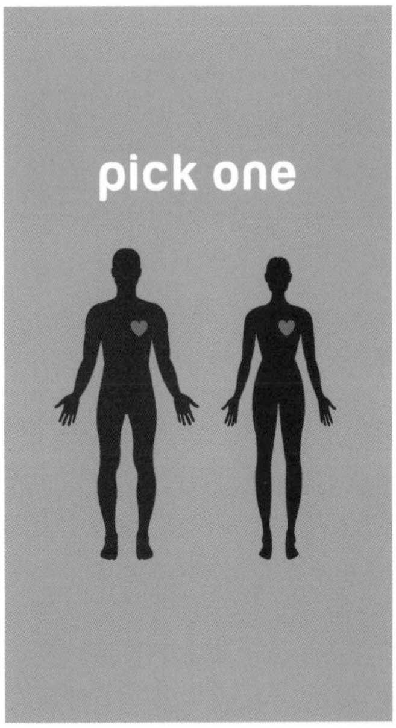
pick one

Tap

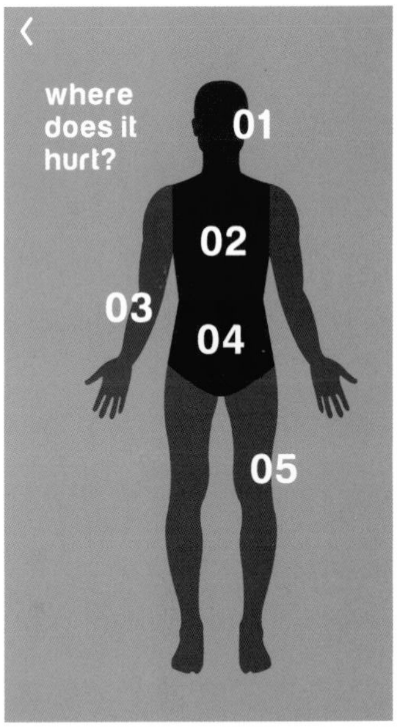
where does it hurt?
01
02
03
04
05

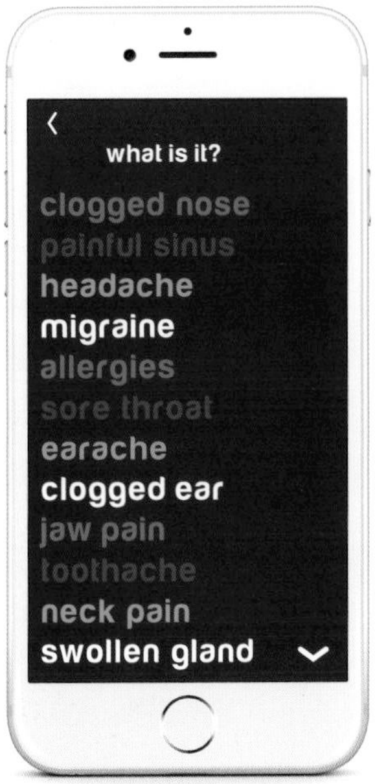
what is it?
clogged nose
painful sinus
headache
migraine
allergies
sore throat
earache
clogged ear
jaw pain
toothache
neck pain
swollen gland

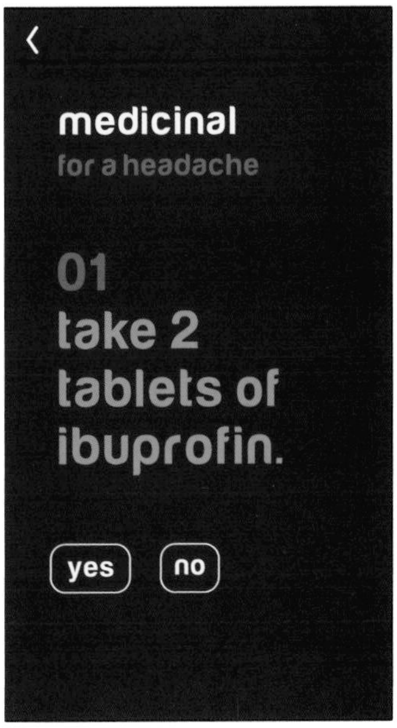
medicinal
for a headache
01
take 2 tablets of ibuprofin.
yes
no

Tap

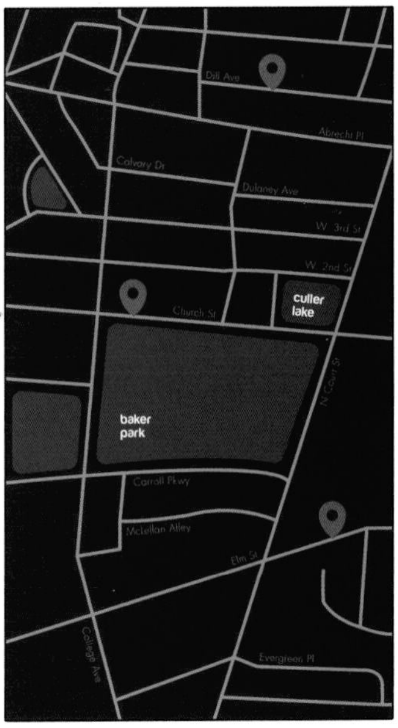
culler lake
baker park

Shower Truck

Design
Yuree Kang

Behance

Shower Truck is a shower reservation app, to provide those who work overnight with a moment to refresh. The UI design follows three principles: simple, continuing, and intuitive. Deep blue colour was used to reflect the image of water.

REFRESH VOUCHER
170613S36
BASIC
Location
DONGSUN-03, SEONGBUK
SUNGSHIN W. UNIV.
Date
2018.AUG.27
Time
18:30
18:50
Detail
Price
basic
Shower Set
x1
Additional Towel
x1
Cotton Underwear(W)
x1
One ticket for one person. You will get minus points if you don't show, so please be on time for your appointment. Or cancel this ticket in advance.
SHOWERTRUCK
HYEHWA, JONGRO
HYEHWA POLICE SUBSTATION
2018.SEP.01
SILLIM, GWANAK
SEOUL NATIONAL UNIV.
2018.AUG.29
SEOGYO-03, MAPO
HONGIK UNIV. MAIN ENTRANCE

SHOWERTRUCK
SEONGBUK, SEOUL
DONGSUN
SUNGSHIN W. UNIV
19:00
23:00
21:00
2
GO FOR REFRESH
Tap
DONGSUN-03,
SUNGSHIN W. UNIV
21:00
21:20
Option
Quantity
Shower Set
Toothbrush & Paste
Shaving Set
Bath Towel
Additional Towel
Cotton Underwear
W
6,000W
PAY
Tap
6,000W
0123
3456
6789
9012
12 / 23
001
SHOWER TRUCK

WEBSITE

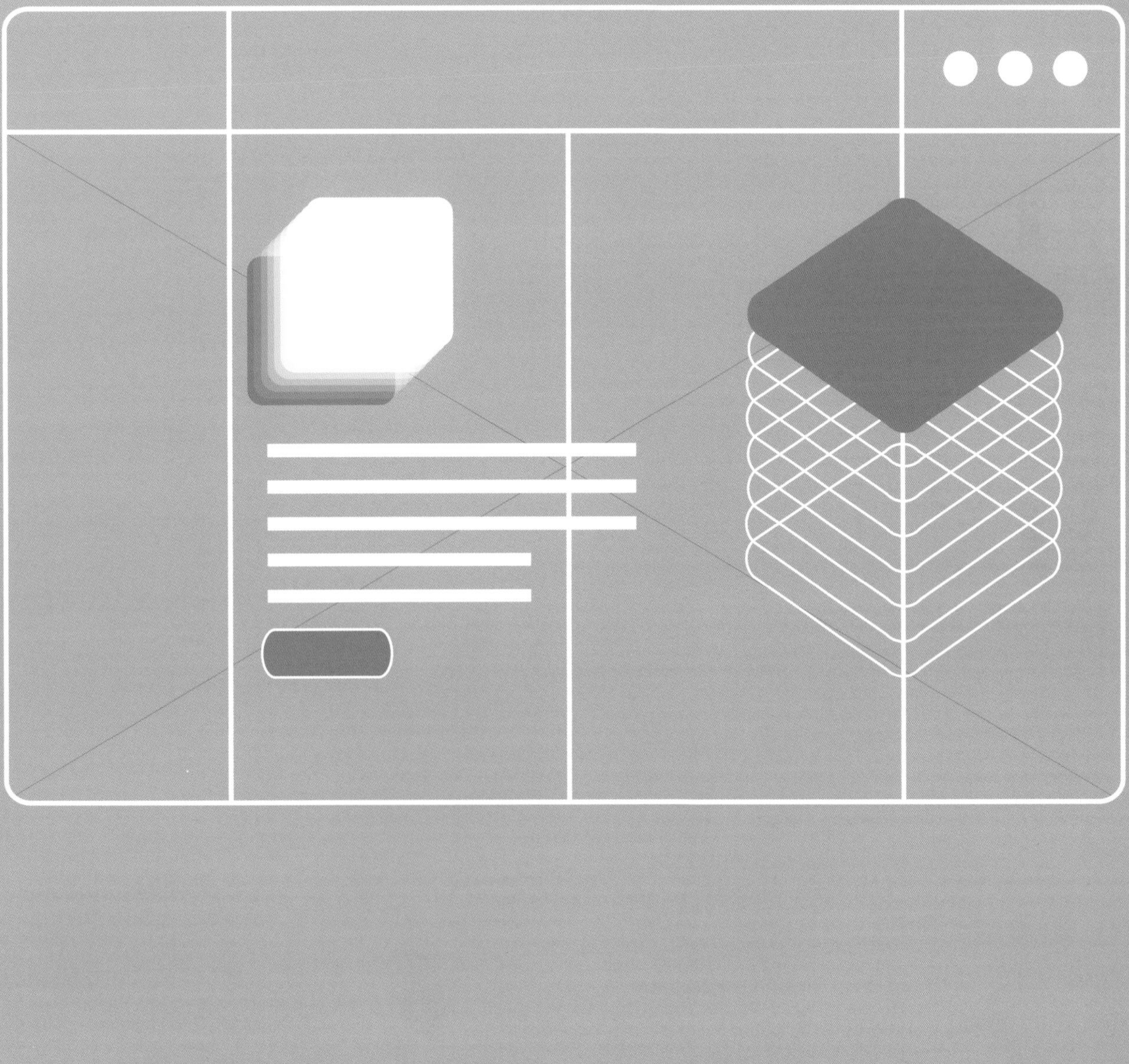

The Melting Pod

Design
Cody Cano

Behance

Digital experience for The Melting Pod, a podcast based out of a pod in the woods that aims to provide the creative community with diverse discussions and commentary around why people indulge in their fanatical passions.

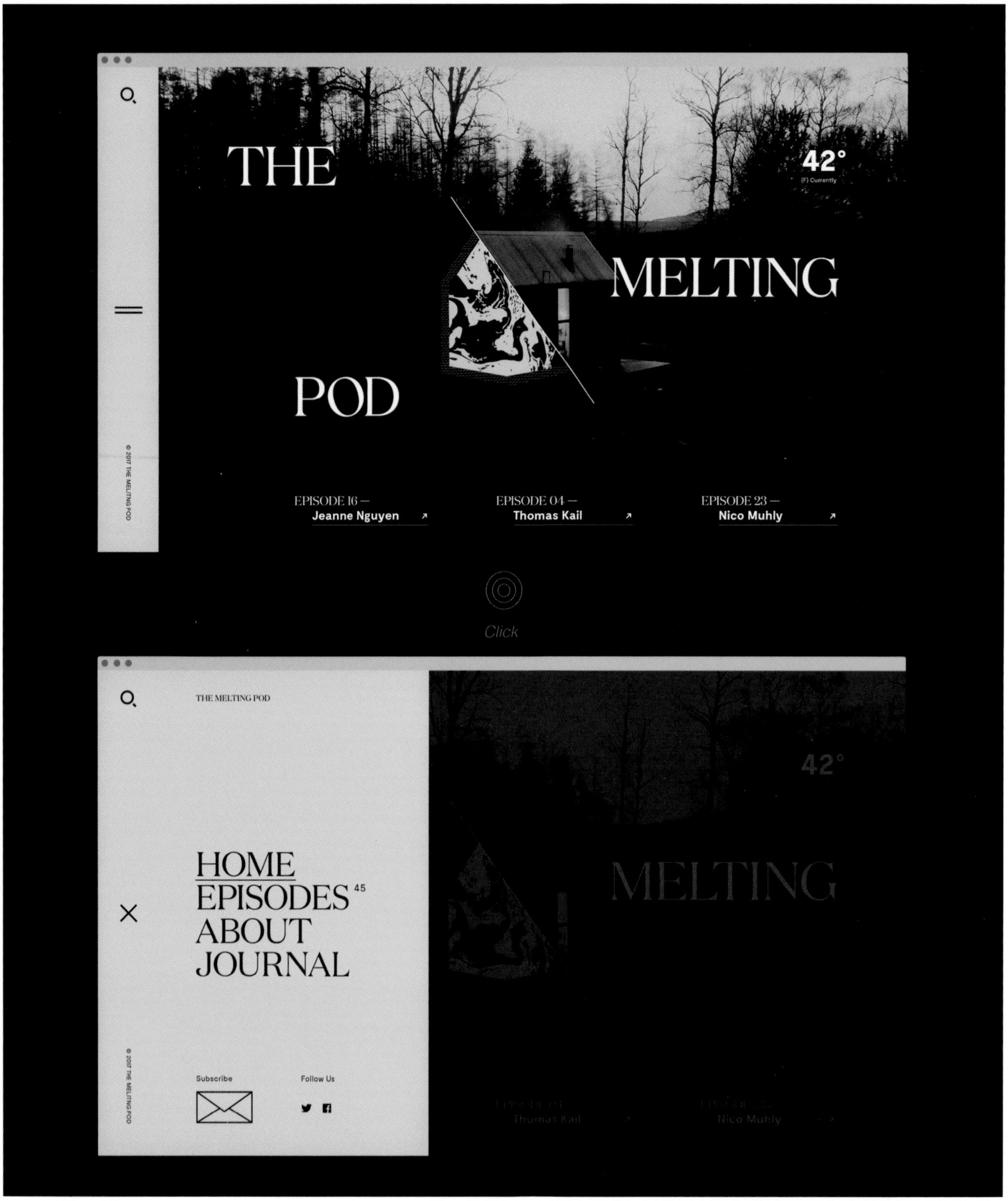
THE
42°
(F) Currently
MELTING
POD
© 2017 THE MELTING POD
EPISODE 16 — Jeanne Nguyen
EPISODE 04 — Thomas Kail
EPISODE 23 — Nico Muhly
Click
THE MELTING POD
42°
MELTING
HOME
EPISODES 45
ABOUT
JOURNAL
Subscribe
Follow Us
© 2017 THE MELTING POD

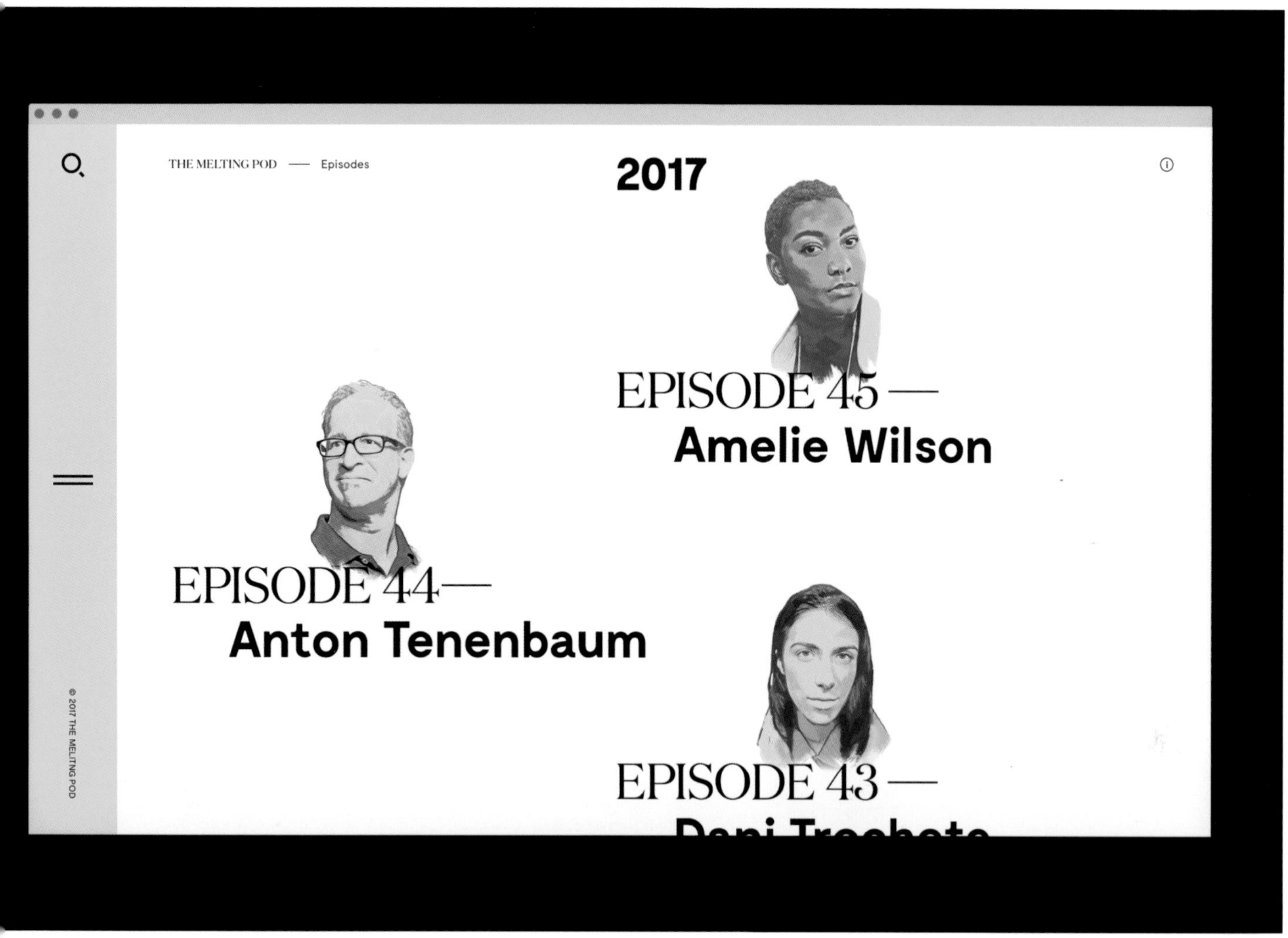
THE MELTING POD — Episodes
2017
EPISODE 45 —
Amelie Wilson
EPISODE 44—
Anton Tenenbaum
EPISODE 43 —
© 2017 THE MELTING POD

THE MELTING POD
EPISODE 45 —
Amelie Wilson
12 Nov 2017
You know those people who get passionately, fanatically, obsessively into things? People like doll collectors or Star Wars fans or that lady down the street with gnomes all over her yard? Award-winning journalist Amelie Wilson noticed them too and she was, well, jealous. Not having such a passion herself, she wondered: who are you people? Seeking an answer, she set out on a cross-country journey to learn what passionate fanatics had that she didn't.
In this episoded, we discuss where Wilson's quest took her, among other places, to a pigeon race in the Bronx, storm chasing in Kansas, ice fishing in the Rockies, and to
Show Notes
1 Anthropomorphizing, The Fury Sensation ↗
2 Lot24 is like a Goth Birchbox, and it's Not a Hoax ↗
3 David Bordwell, Ozu and the Poetics of Cinema ↗
4 "Gamblers in the Sky," Pigeon Racing, The New Yorker ↗
5 Louis Kahn's Salk Institute ↗
Share
© 2017 THE MELTING POD
33:20 /
54:12
Next Episode →

T • PARK

Design and Development
pill & pillow

Naming and Visual Identity
Milkxhake

URL
www.tpark.hk

Official Site

This is the website of T • PARK, a sludge treatment facility in Hong Kong open to the public for educational and recreational purposes. The website tells the waste-to-energy story with attractive infographics and animation.

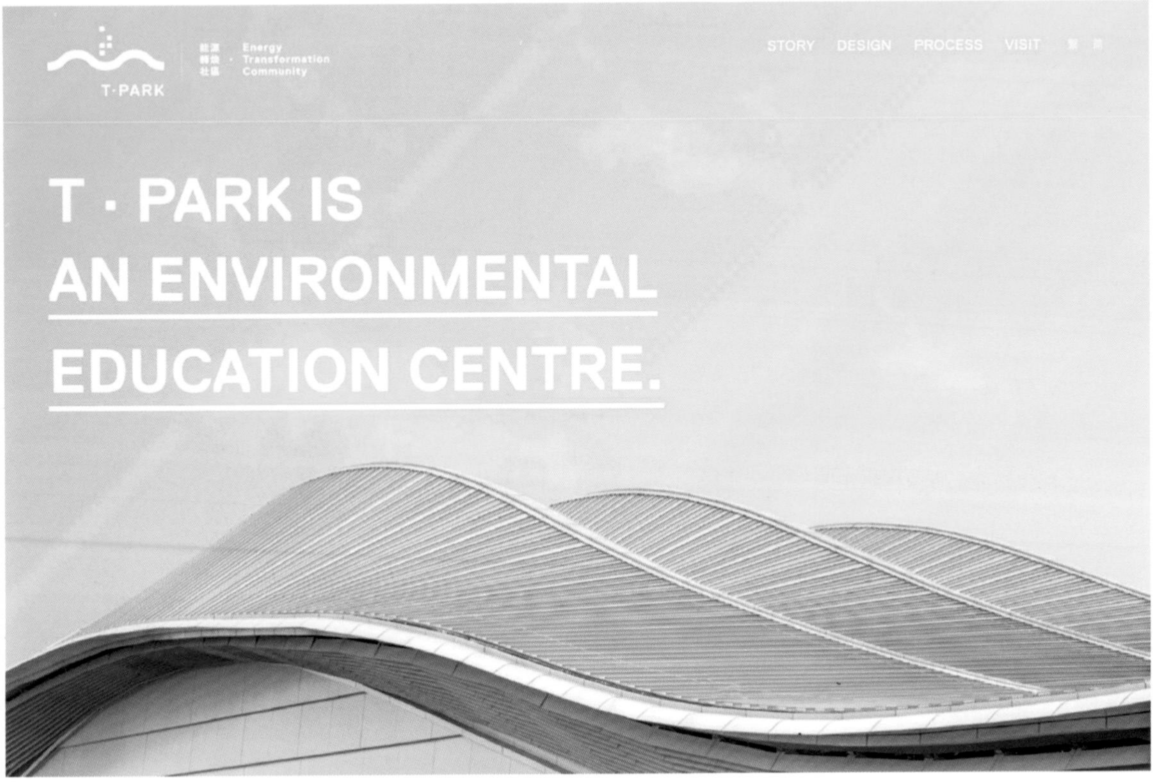

T·PARK
Energy
Transformation
Community
STORY DESIGN PROCESS VISIT
T · PARK IS
AN ENVIRONMENTAL
EDUCATION CENTRE.

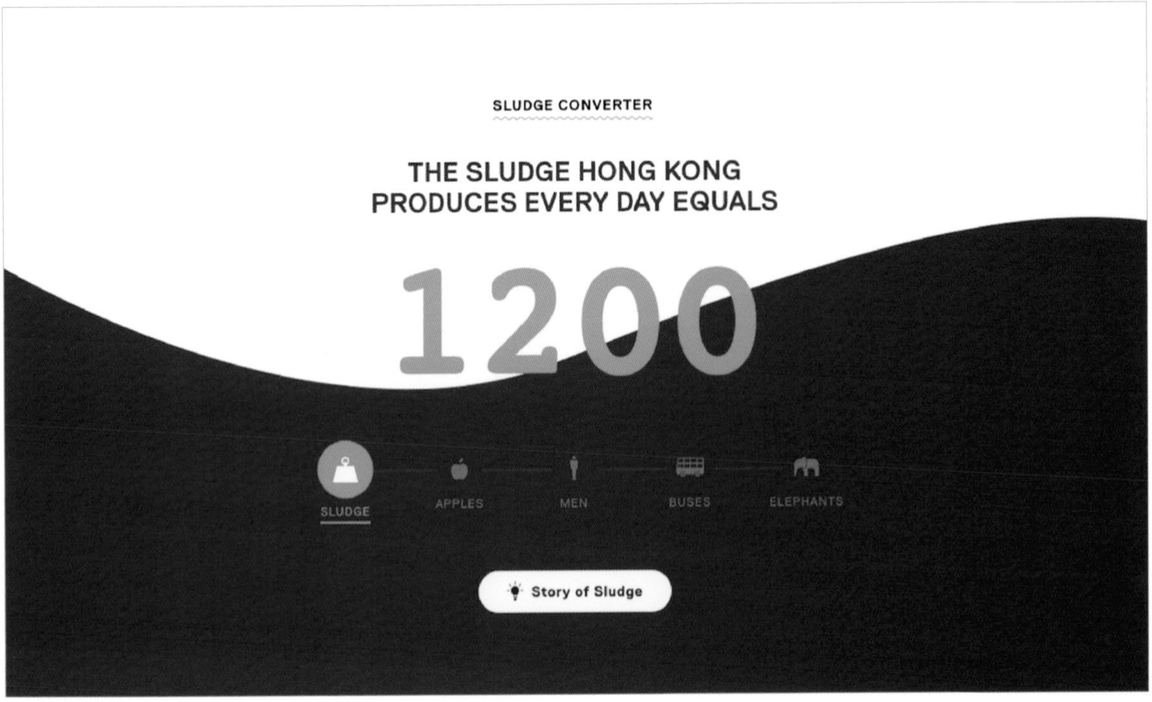

SLUDGE CONVERTER
THE SLUDGE HONG KONG
PRODUCES EVERY DAY EQUALS
1200
SLUDGE
APPLES
MEN
BUSES
ELEPHANTS
Story of Sludge

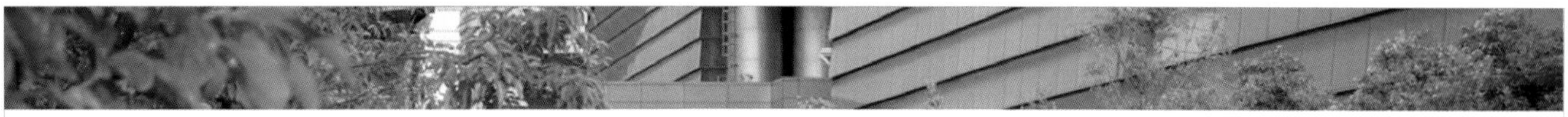

PROCESS

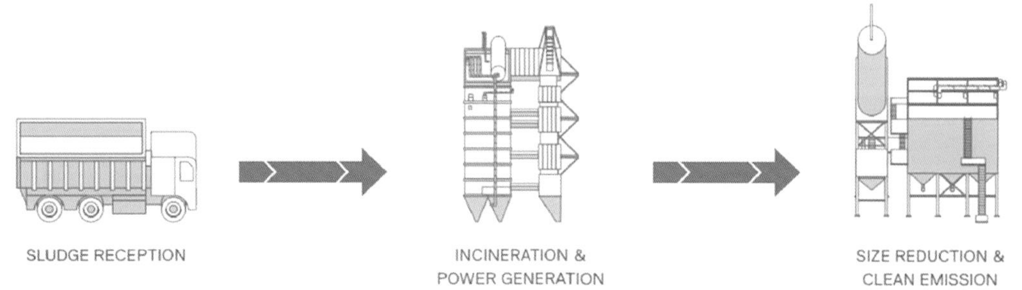

SLUDGE RECEPTION
INCINERATION &
POWER GENERATION
SIZE REDUCTION &
CLEAN EMISSION

Full Process

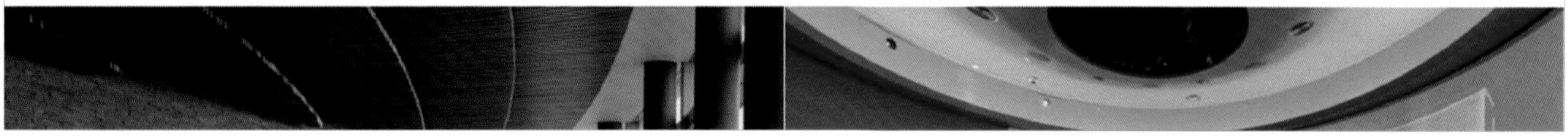

Click

HOW IT WORKS

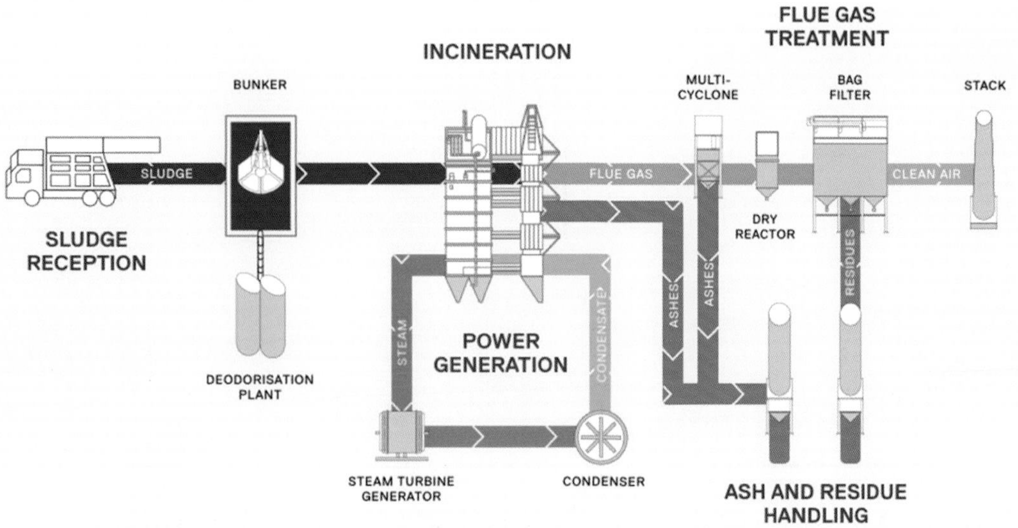

FLUE GAS
TREATMENT
INCINERATION
BUNKER
MULTI-
CYCLONE
BAG
FILTER
STACK
SLUDGE
FLUE GAS
CLEAN AIR
DRY
REACTOR
SLUDGE
RECEPTION
ASHES
ASHES
RESIDUES
STEAM
POWER
GENERATION
CONDENSATE
DEODORISATION
PLANT
STEAM TURBINE
GENERATOR
CONDENSER
ASH AND RESIDUE
HANDLING

* THIS IS A SIMPLIFIED VERSION OF SLUDGE TREATMENT PROCESS.

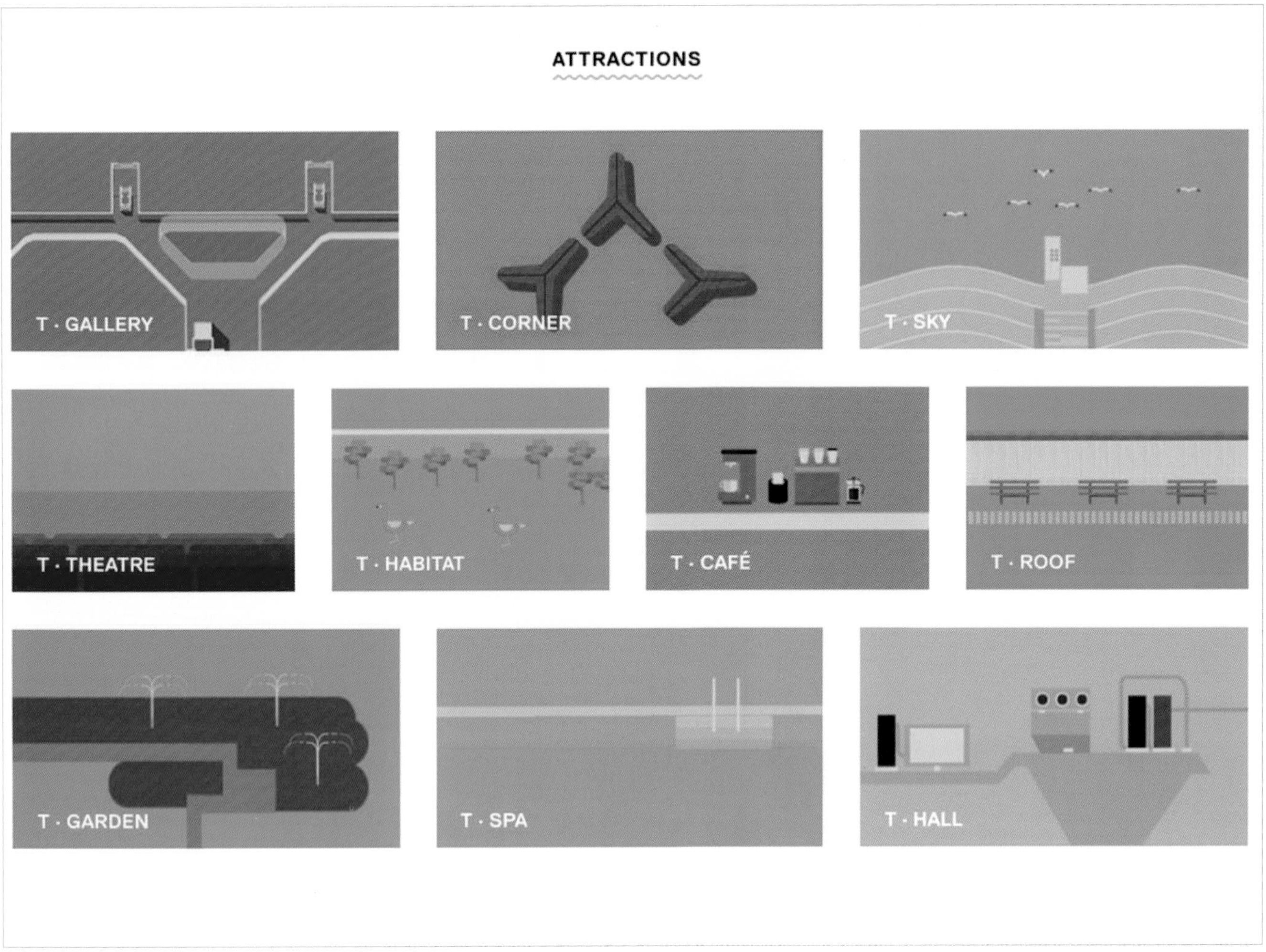
ATTRACTIONS
T · GALLERY
T · CORNER
T · SKY
T · THEATRE
T · HABITAT
T · CAFÉ
T · ROOF
T · GARDEN
T · SPA
T · HALL

Click

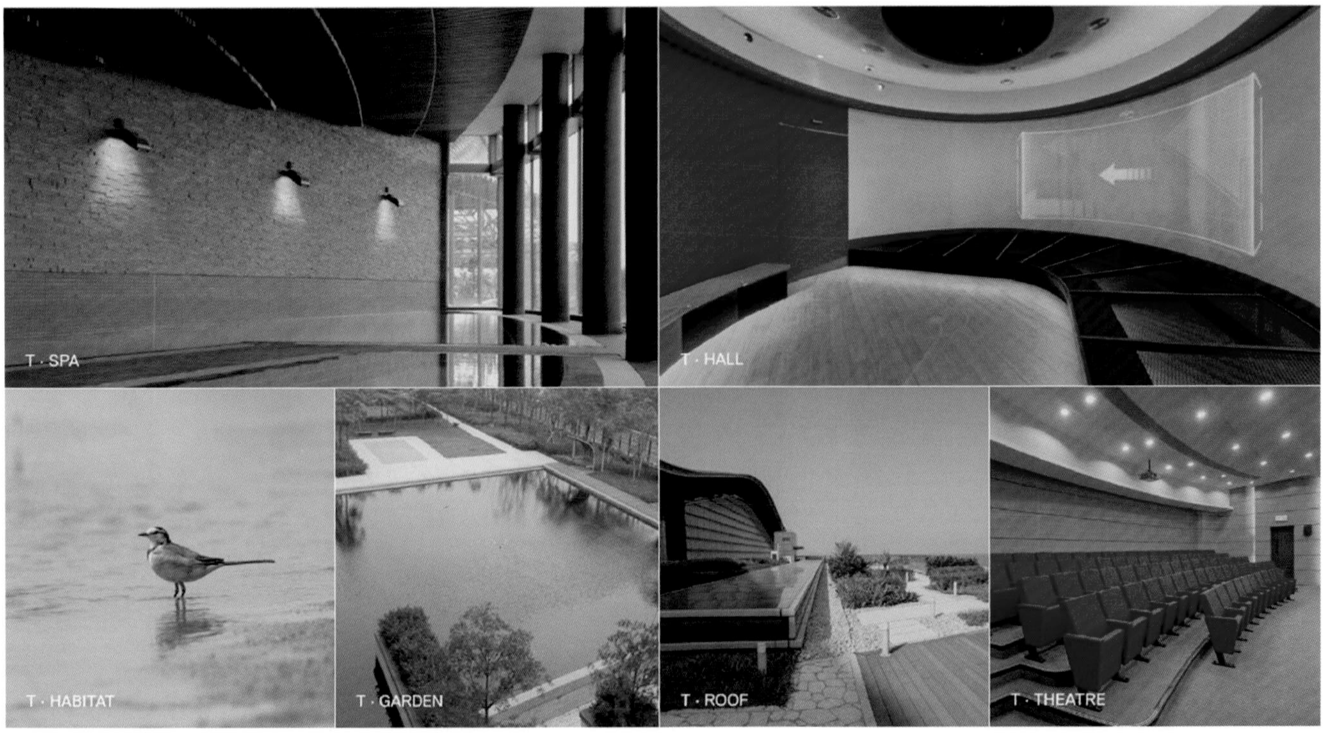
T · SPA
T · HALL
T · HABITAT
T · GARDEN
T · ROOF
T · THEATRE

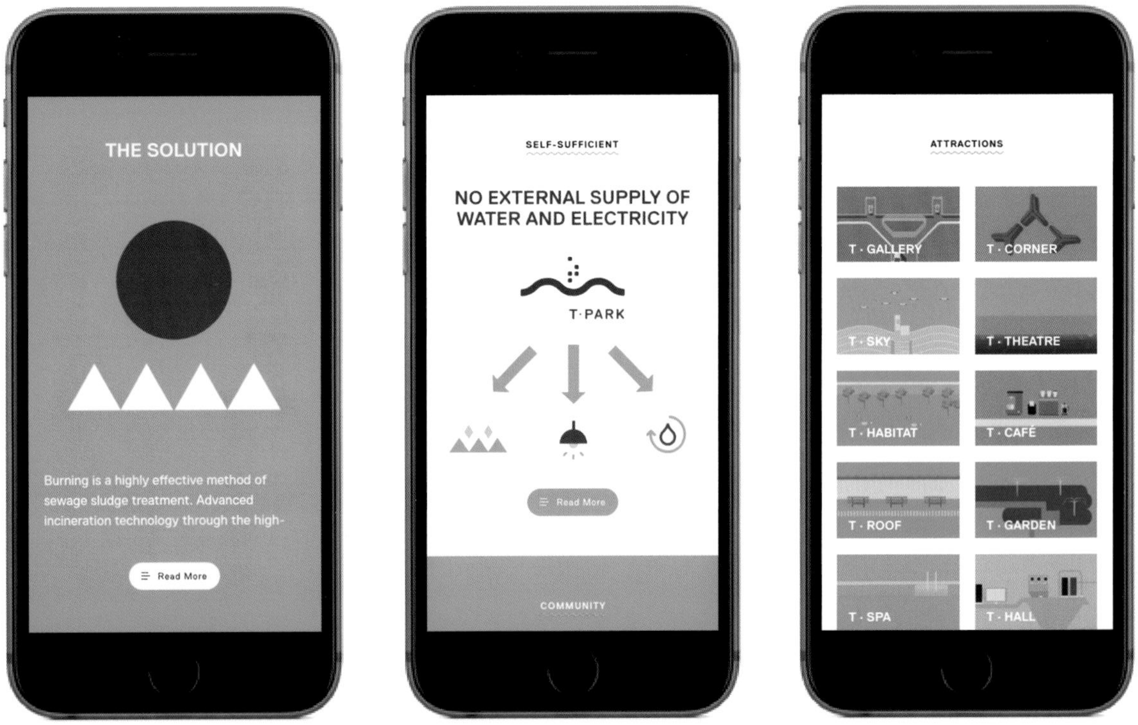
THE SOLUTION
Burning is a highly effective method of sewage sludge treatment. Advanced incineration technology through the high-
Read More
SELF-SUFFICIENT
NO EXTERNAL SUPPLY OF WATER AND ELECTRICITY
T·PARK
Read More
COMMUNITY
ATTRACTIONS
T · GALLERY
T · CORNER
T · SKY
T · THEATRE
T · HABITAT
T · CAFÉ
T · ROOF
T · GARDEN
T · SPA
T · HALL

In Hong Kong, around 1,200 tons of sludge is produced everyday as a byproduct of the sewage treatment process. T • PARK burns the sludge and reduces its volume by 90%. The electricity and water generated in the process goes back to sustain the facility's operation.

T · GARDEN

With over 9,800m² of outdoor landscape, T · GARDEN comprises five major elements — a fountain garden, a leisure garden, a Zen garden, a wetland garden and an outdoor footbath.

Plant22

Concept, Creative Direction and Design
Ekhiñe Domínguez
(What The studio)

Development
Gregory Bolkenstijn
(Sound of Silver)

Client
Tim Boelaars
(Plant22)

URL
plant22.co

Official Site

Plant22 is a cozy creative co-working space in Amsterdam, created by Dutch illustrator Tim Boelaars. Tim had designed a logo for Plant22, and the next step the space needed was a "fresh and innovative" website that would represent its creative spirit in order to attract top level professionals and fill up its 8 working stations.

The fullscreen website is a visual translation of the space itself. While reflecting the architecture and interior design features of the space, the website also expands the original Plant22 logo to create a dynamic, bold and playful visual identity that positions the co-working space as a unique and vibrant place. Micro-interactions help to convey the sense that the space and its members are welcoming and interesting. The result is a highly comfortable and intuitive website that goes beyond web design standards. The visual identity created for the website is further extended to promote Plant22 throughout the online environment such as in social media.

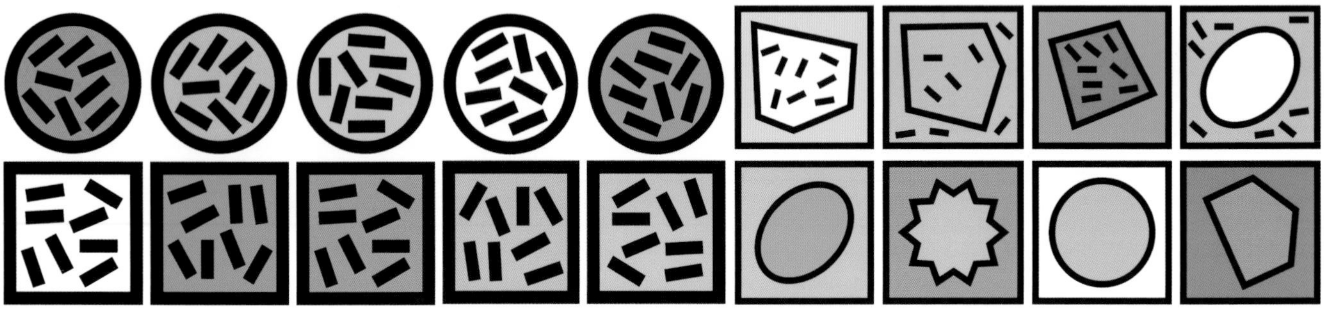

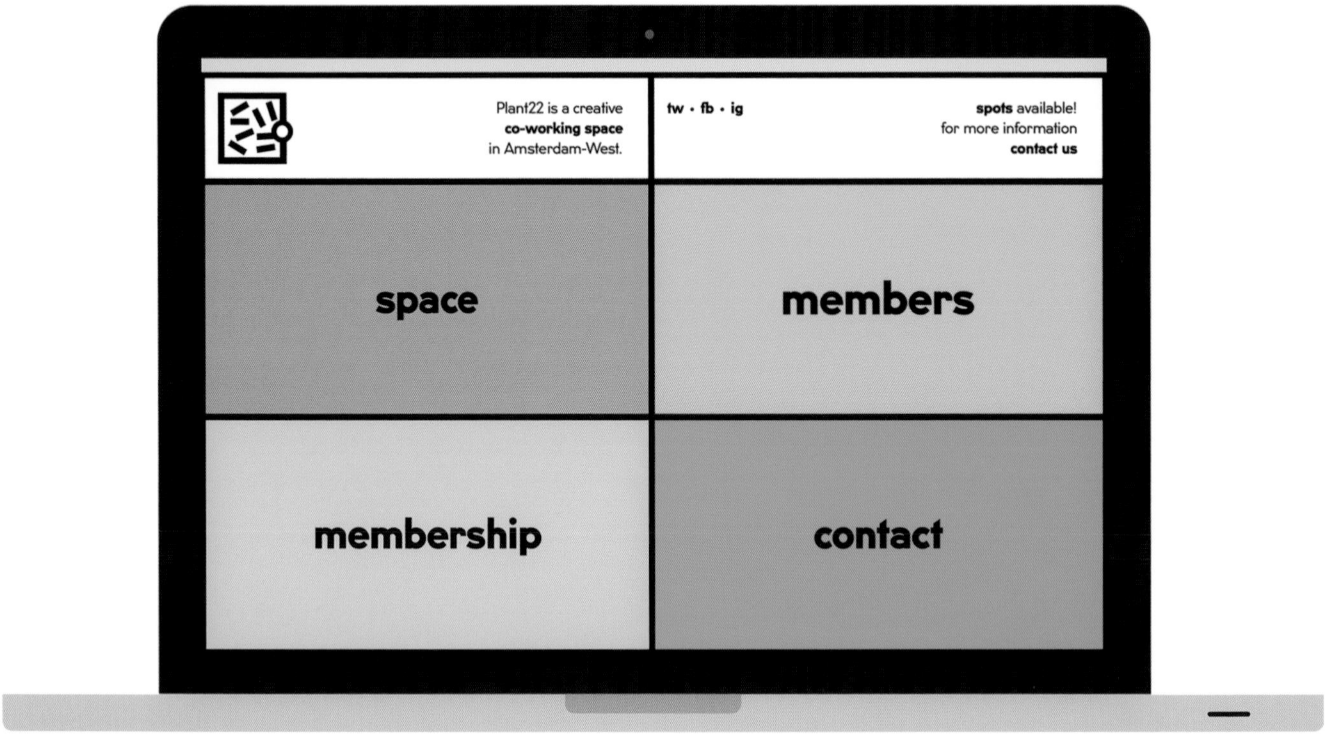

Plant22 is a creative
co-working space
in Amsterdam-West.
tw · fb · ig
spots available!
for more information
contact us
space
members
membership
contact

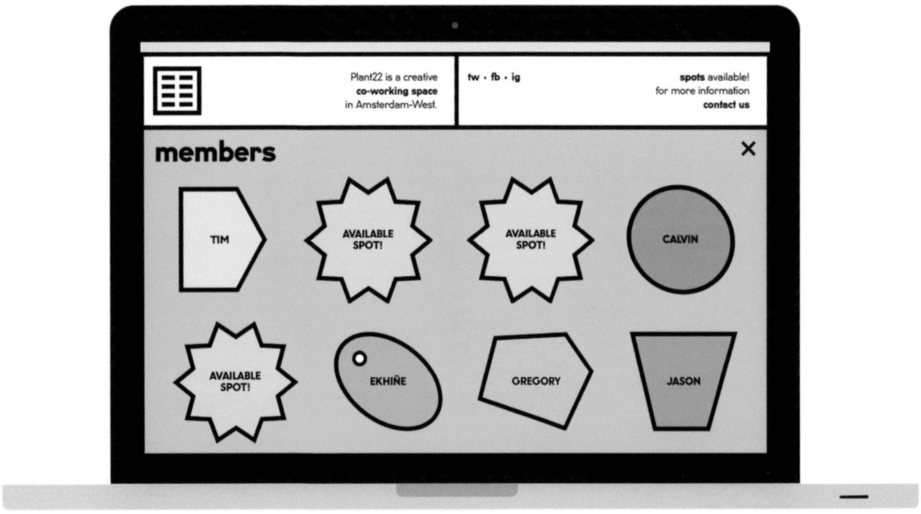
Plant22 is a creative
co-working space
in Amsterdam-West.
tw • fb • ig
spots available!
for more information
contact us
members
TIM
AVAILABLE SPOT!
AVAILABLE SPOT!
CALVIN
AVAILABLE SPOT!
EKHIÑE
GREGORY
JASON

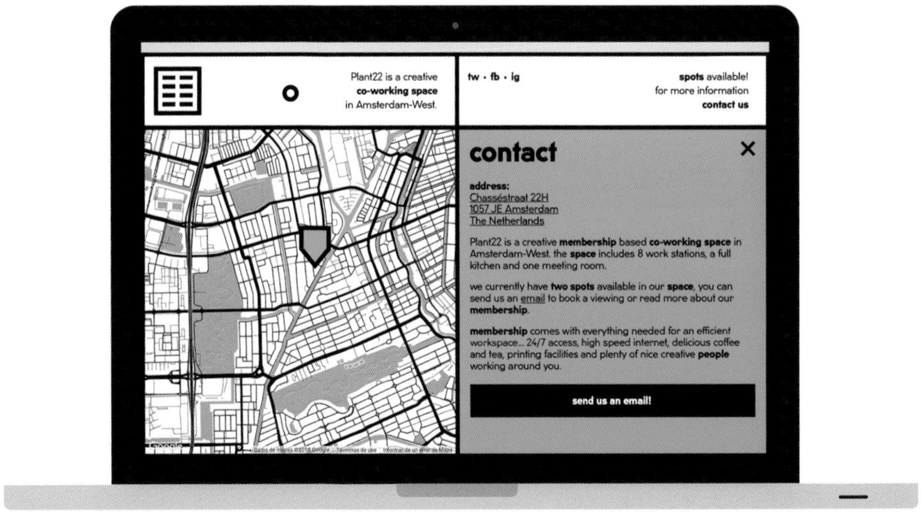
Plant22 is a creative
co-working space
in Amsterdam-West.
tw • fb • ig
spots available!
for more information
contact us
contact
address:
Chasséstraat 22H
1057 JE Amsterdam
The Netherlands
Plant22 is a creative membership based co-working space in Amsterdam-West. the space includes 8 work stations, a full kitchen and one meeting room.
we currently have two spots available in our space, you can send us an email to book a viewing or read more about our membership.
membership comes with everything needed for an efficient workspace... 24/7 access, high speed internet, delicious coffee and tea, printing facilities and plenty of nice creative people working around you.
send us an email!

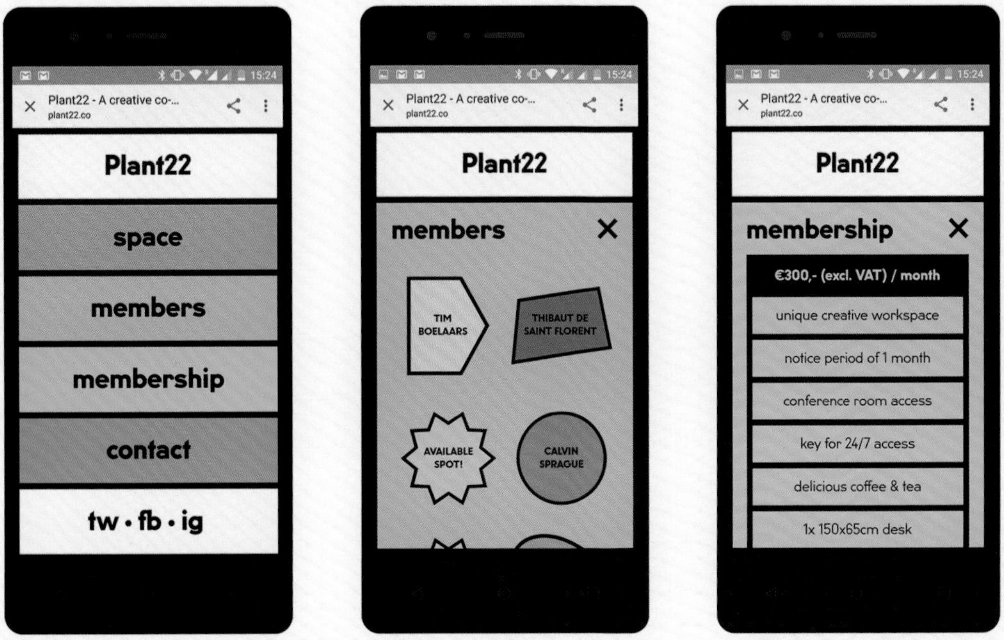
15:24
Plant22 - A creative co-...
plant22.co
Plant22
space
members
membership
contact
tw • fb • ig
15:24
Plant22 - A creative co-...
plant22.co
Plant22
members
TIM BOELAARS
THIBAUT DE SAINT FLORENT
AVAILABLE SPOT!
CALVIN SPRAGUE
15:24
Plant22 - A creative co-...
plant22.co
Plant22
membership
€300,- (excl. VAT) / month
unique creative workspace
notice period of 1 month
conference room access
key for 24/7 access
delicious coffee & tea
1x 150x65cm desk

Streamtime

Design Agency
For The People

Creative Direction
Jason Little, Johanna Roca

Art Direction and Design
Melissa Baillache

Illustration/Animation
Simon Landrein

Team Members
Brady O'Halloran, Pius Jeon,
Kevin Liu, Andy Wright,
Aaron Green, Alan Whitby, Mat Groom

Client
Streamtime

URL
streamtime.net

Official Site

Streamtime is a project management software for the creative industry. The product helps users manage workflow, job planning, scheduling, quoting, time tracking, and everything in between. This project is a new marketing site for Streamtime, promoting its robust product and newly-developed mobile application.

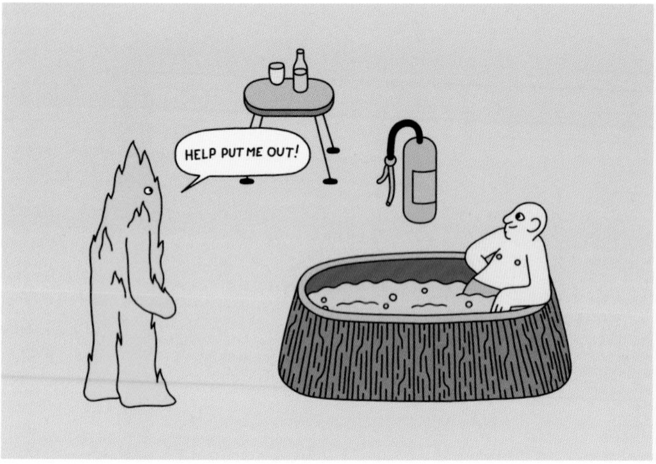
HELP PUT ME OUT!

Why Streamtime?
Time Tracking
Job planning
Quoting & Invoicing
Scheduling
Reporting
iOS App
The Future
A Schedule that's
in sync with your team.
There's now much less work for you thanks
to schedules that stay in sync.
Why Streamtime
Features
Pricing
Blog
Log in
Sign up free

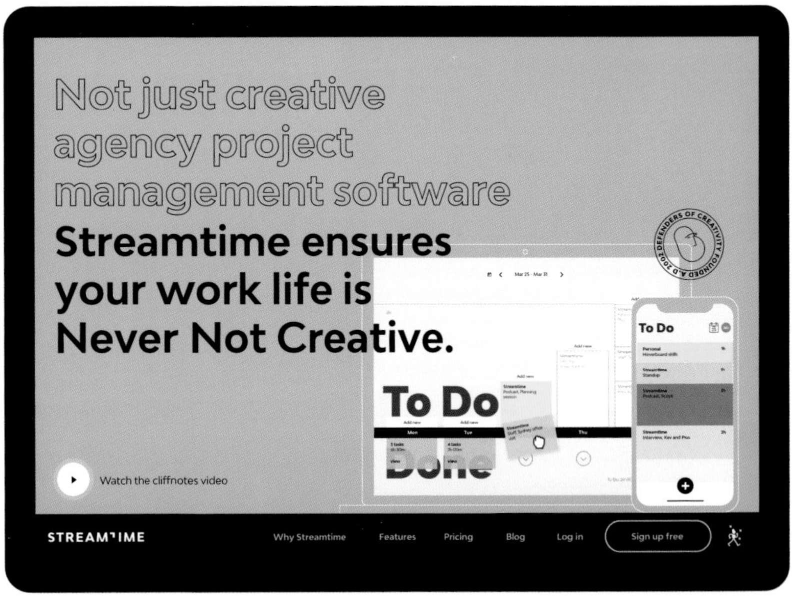
Not just creative agency project management software
Streamtime ensures your work life is Never Not Creative.
To Do
Watch the cliffnotes video
STREAMTIME
Why Streamtime
Features
Pricing
Blog
Log in
Sign up free

The design leverages the time blocks used in the product as a navigation bar for product features. Within each section, animations are integrated into the site using sprite sheets, allowing users to drag, push, poke, tap and play with each of the illustrations on the page no matter the device, while simultaneously discovering what makes Streamtime stand out.

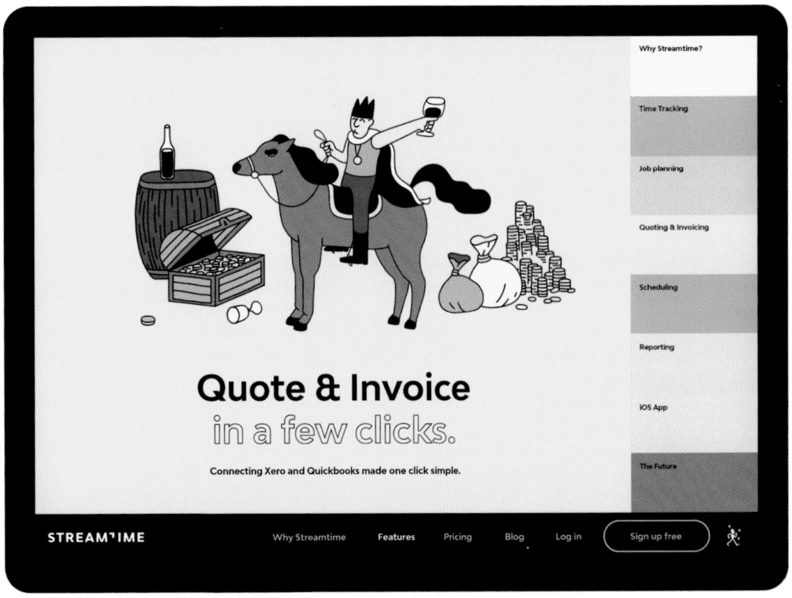
Why Streamtime?
Time Tracking
Job planning
Quoting & Invoicing
Scheduling
Reporting
iOS App
The Future
Quote & Invoice
in a few clicks.
Connecting Xero and Quickbooks made one click simple.
STREAMTIME
Why Streamtime
Features
Pricing
Blog
Log in
Sign up free

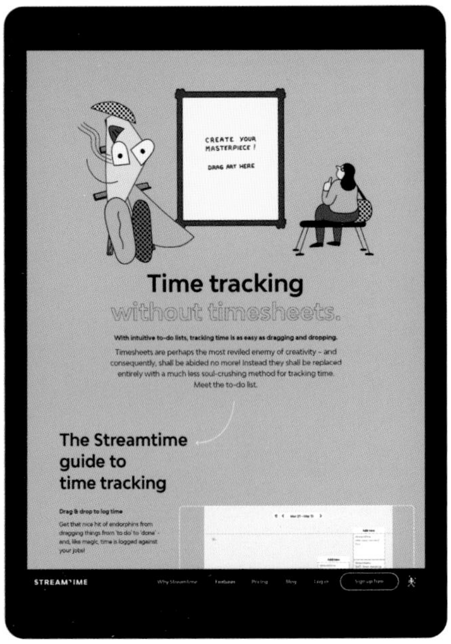
Time tracking
without timesheets.
The Streamtime guide to time tracking
STREAMTIME

TAP TO SORT
Reporting
only what you need
Reporting with Streamtime
STREAMTIME

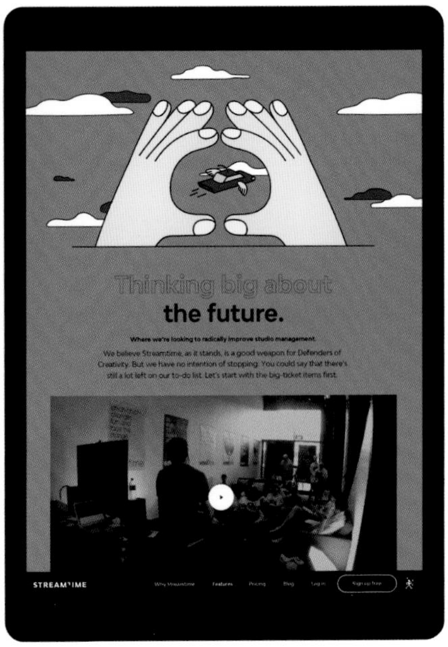
Thinking big about
the future.
STREAMTIME

The Preposterous Official Website of Erik Bernacchi

Official Site

Design and Development
Erik Bernacchi

URL
eeerik.com

With “The Preposterous Official Website of Erik Bernacchi”, Erik has created his own medium. When you type eeerik.com on your keyboard and press enter, you are teleported inside an unusual hacky computer, bombarded by futuristic bright, vivid colours that play a unique contrast with the nostalgic Macintosh 1984 pixel patterns. With this project Erik aims to inspire all digital designers and artists to risk taking unexplored paths and not being scared of the weird, the strange and the ugly.

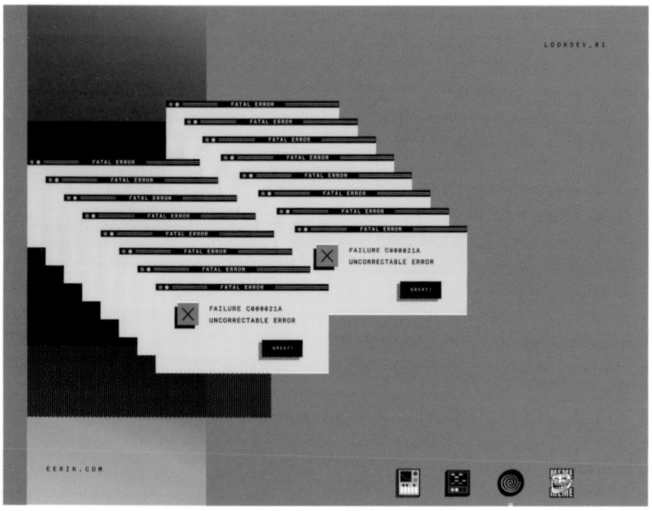
FATAL ERROR
FAILURE C000021A
UNCORRECTABLE ERROR
EERIK.COM

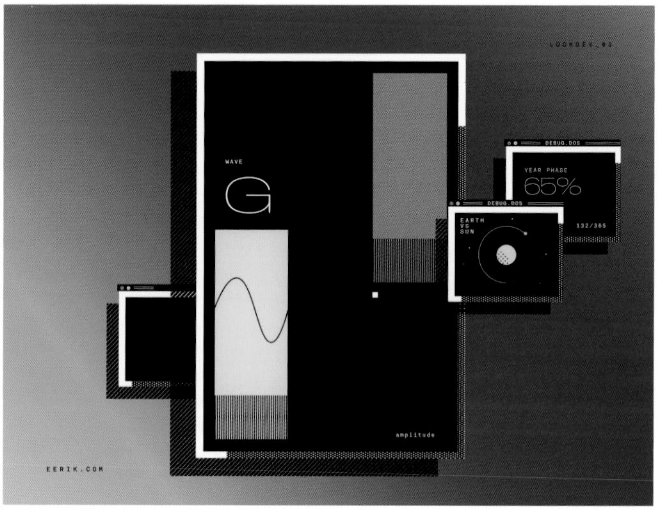
WAVE
G
amplitude
DEBUG.DOS
YEAR PHASE
65%
132/365
EARTH
VS
SUN
EERIK.COM

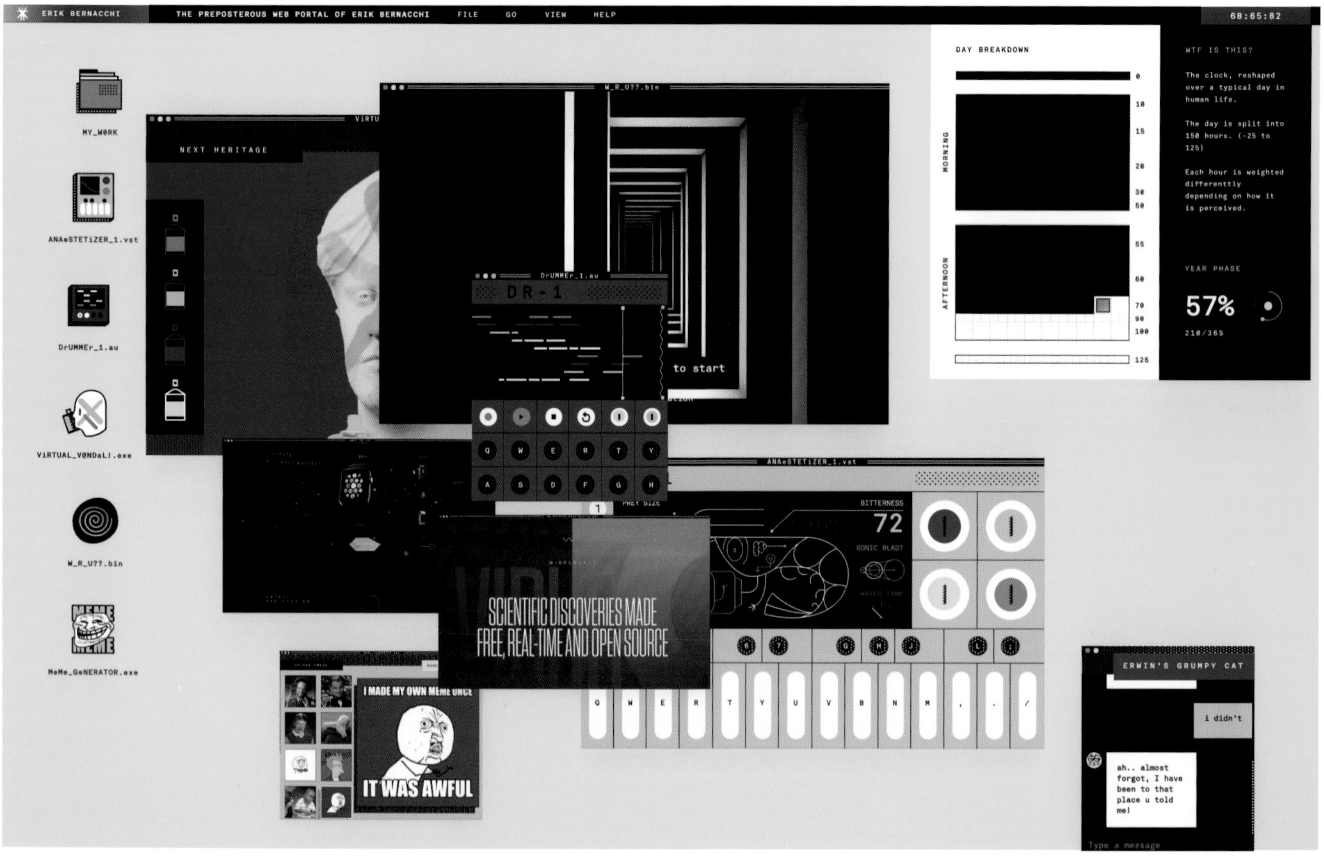
ERIK BERNACCHI
THE PREPOSTEROUS WEB PORTAL OF ERIK BERNACCHI
FILE
GO
VIEW
HELP
68:65:82
MY_WORK
ANAeSTETiZER_1.vst
DrUMMEr_1.au
ViRTUAL_VENDaLI.exe
W_R_U??.bin
MeMe_GeNERATOR.exe
NEXT HERITAGE
DR-1
to start
DAY BREAKDOWN
MORNING
AFTERNOON
WTF IS THIS?
The clock, reshaped over a typical day in human life.
The day is split into 150 hours. (-25 to 125)
Each hour is weighted differently depending on how it is perceived.
YEAR PHASE
57%
210/365
BITTERNESS
72
SONIC BLAST
SCIENTIFIC DISCOVERIES MADE FREE, REAL-TIME AND OPEN SOURCE
I MADE MY OWN MEME ONCE
IT WAS AWFUL
ERWIN'S GRUMPY CAT
i didn't
ah.. almost forgot, I have been to that place u told me!
Type a message

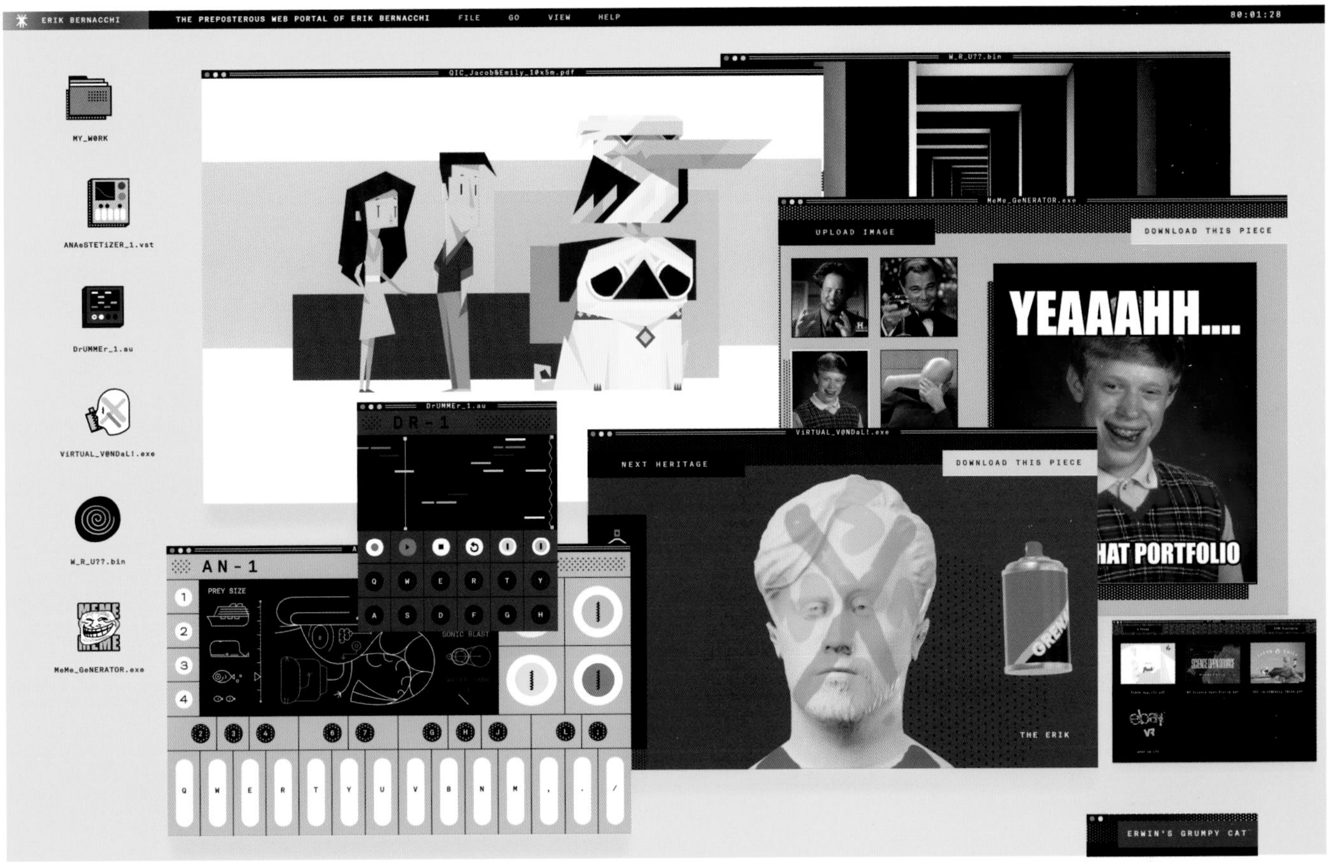
ERIK BERNACCHI
THE PREPOSTEROUS WEB PORTAL OF ERIK BERNACCHI
FILE
GO
VIEW
HELP
MY_W0RK
ANAeSTETiZER_1.vst
DrUMMEr_1.au
ViRTUAL_V0NDaLi.exe
W_R_U??.bin
MeMe_GeNERATOR.exe
UPLOAD IMAGE
DOWNLOAD THIS PIECE
YEAAAHH...
HAT PORTFOLIO
NEXT HERITAGE
DOWNLOAD THIS PIECE
THE ERIK
AN-1
PREY SIZE
DR-1
ERWIN'S GRUMPY CAT

ERIK BERNACCHI
THE PREPOSTEROUS WEB PORTAL OF ERIK BERNACCHI
FILE
GO
VIEW
HELP
ERWIN'S GRUMPY CAT
Well well well... look who decided to show up...

The interaction is designed to mimic a desktop file system, where the user can open documents, work, games, all at the same time. This unique multitasking allow you to chat with grumpy cat bots, play weirdly designed synths, make your own memes and vandalize Erik's own sculptures while browsing his best case studies. "It's exciting to me that each user, by opening, minimizing and moving around the contents of the website, unconsciously manipulate its very look and layout, creating their own, irreproducible, unique version of it", Erik said.

Hypergiant

Design Agency
Maven Creative

Creative Direction
Chris Stephens, Art Hardie

Design
Lee Waters, Sean Jones, Brandon Williams

Development
xfive

Account Direction
Mike Edwards

Copywriting
Art Hardie

URL
www.hypergiant.com

Official Site

Hypergiant launched as an artificial intelligence company operating out of both Austin and Dallas, Texas—serving clients in the upper tier of the Fortune 500. Written and designed by Maven Creative, and developed by Xfive, the site intends to introduce the brand and its story to a commercially powerful audience in a way that conveys both creativity and otherworldly intelligence. At the start of the project, Hypergiant founder and CEO Ben Lamm brought the idea of retro-futurism, which set the foundation for later creative direction and design. After weeks of unfettered thought and creativity, the result is a multi-layered brand exploration that delivers an informative yet genuinely captivating experience for users.

Menu
HYPER GIANT
TOMORROWING TODAY.™
The Fourth Industrial Revolution of Machine Intelligence is real. It will define which businesses live and die in the next decade. And the first casualties will be those who fail to adopt and adapt.
OFFICE OF MACHINE INTELLIGENCE
03
SPACE AGE SOLUTIONS
Machine Intelligence creates hyper-efficient and scalable solutions by aggregating and correlating data from various sources and utilizing it across the entire business structure.
It is a range of technologies enabling businesses to respond to emerging markets while enhancing human workers and enabling them to reach their true potential.
The technology to achieve this is no longer nascent. Evolution is waiting.
LEARN MORE

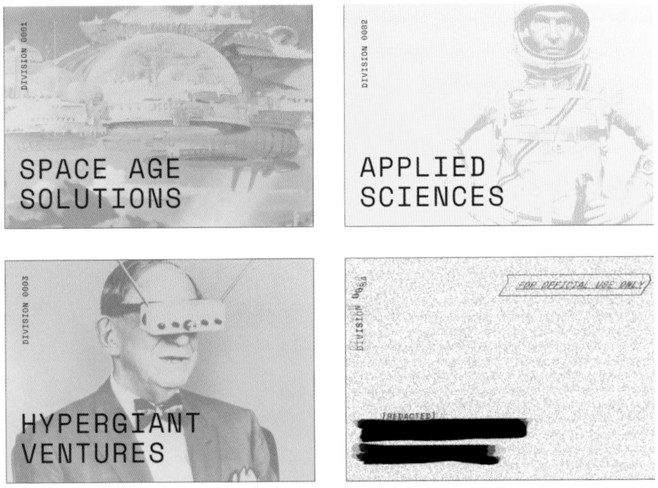
DIVISION 0001
SPACE AGE SOLUTIONS
DIVISION 0002
APPLIED SCIENCES
DIVISION 0003
HYPERGIANT VENTURES
FOR OFFICIAL USE ONLY
[REDACTED]

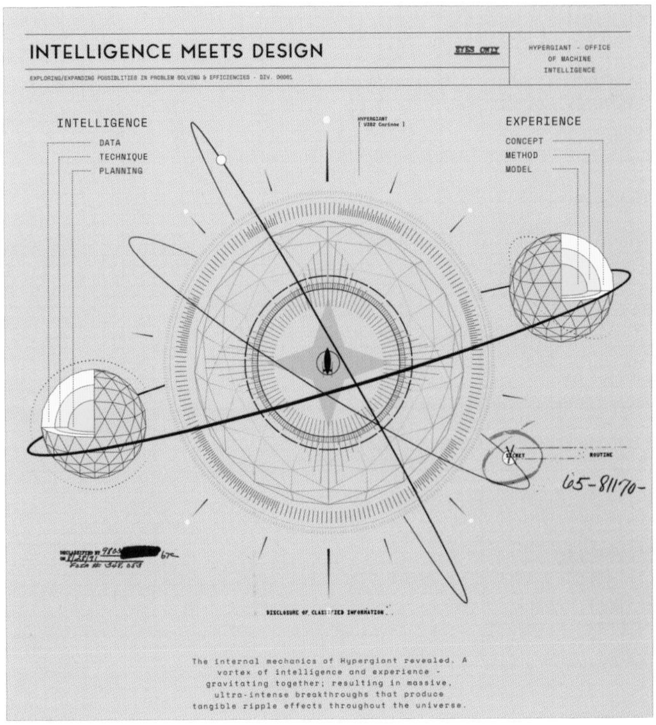
INTELLIGENCE MEETS DESIGN
EYES ONLY
HYPERGIANT - OFFICE OF MACHINE INTELLIGENCE
EXPLORING/EXPANDING POSSIBILITIES IN PROBLEM SOLVING & EFFICIENCIES - DIV. 0001
INTELLIGENCE
DATA
TECHNIQUE
PLANNING
EXPERIENCE
CONCEPT
METHOD
MODEL
ROUTINE
DISCLOSURE OF CLASSIFIED INFORMATION
The internal mechanics of Hypergiant revealed. A vortex of intelligence and experience - gravitating together; resulting in massive, ultra-intense breakthroughs that produce tangible ripple effects throughout the universe.

The site is a striking blend of messaging, branding and design. Every detail serves to further the Hypergiant story told from a "retro-futurism" perspective. The typefaces, symbolism and imagery all reference the 1957 Project Blue Book conspiracy, when the U.S. federal government commissioned an investigation into UFOs.

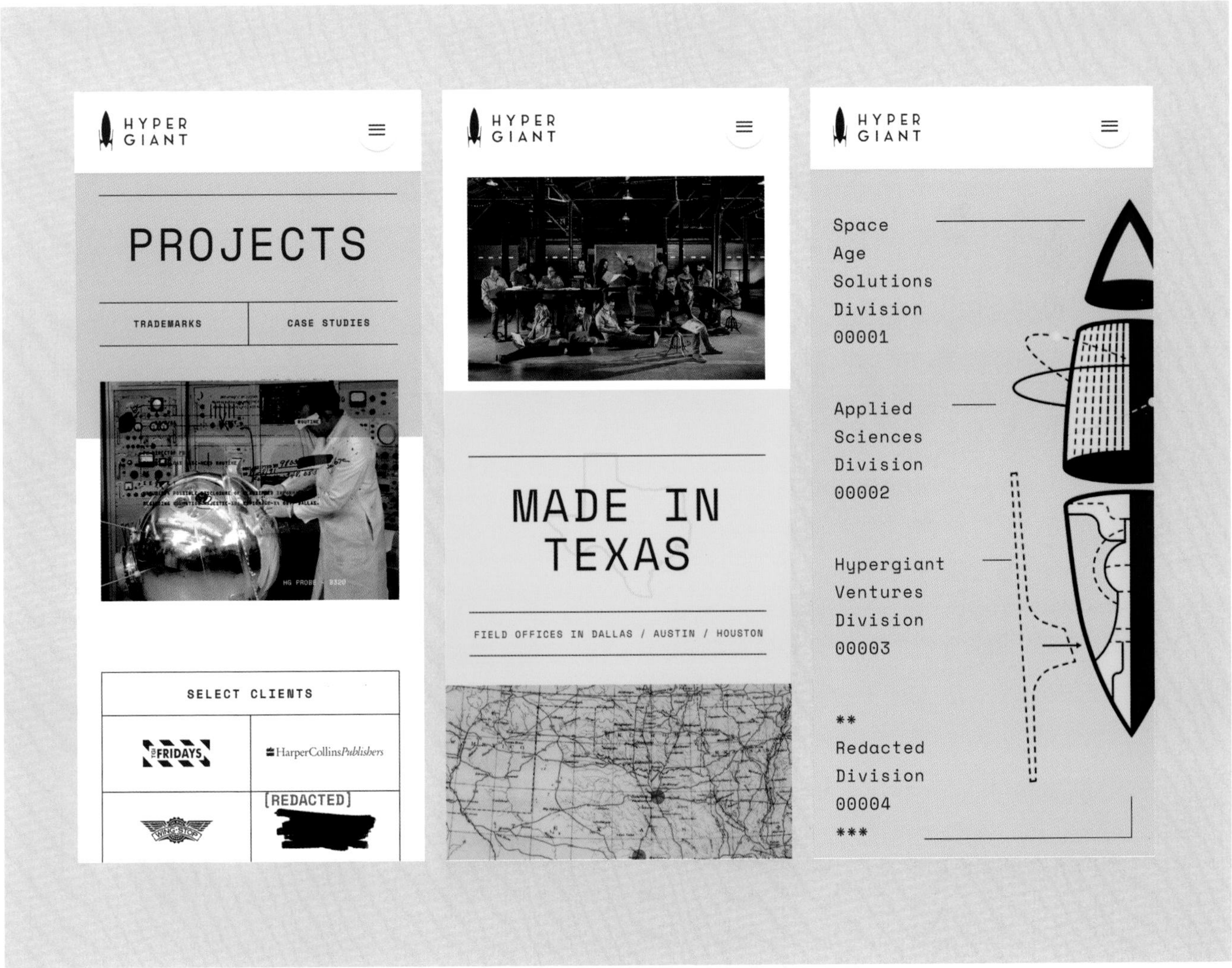
HYPER GIANT
PROJECTS
TRADEMARKS
CASE STUDIES
SELECT CLIENTS
FRIDAYS
HarperCollinsPublishers
WINGSTOP
[REDACTED]
HYPER GIANT
MADE IN TEXAS
FIELD OFFICES IN DALLAS / AUSTIN / HOUSTON
HYPER GIANT
Space Age Solutions Division 00001
Applied Sciences Division 00002
Hypergiant Ventures Division 00003
** Redacted Division 00004 ***

Frans Hals Museum

Design and Development
Build in Amsterdam

Identity and Art Direction
KesselsKramer

URL
www.franshalsmuseum.nl

Official Site

The Frans Hals Museum in Haarlem is best known for its Golden Era art, especially for the works of Frans Hals. De Hallen, which is located within walking distance from the Frans Hals Museum, is known for its contemporary art. Both museums have decided to join forces, becoming one museum on two locations under the name Frans Hals Museum. A bold move, which indicates that the collections will merge into one and that the future expositions will be fusion expositions, combining old and new.

Build in Amsterdam was commissioned to create an online platform that reflects the contemporary and classic duality of the museum. They applied the new concept designed by KesselsKramer, which is to combine the old with the new in a mirror, throughout the website. The website has a playful touch which makes it fun and usable for potential visitors.

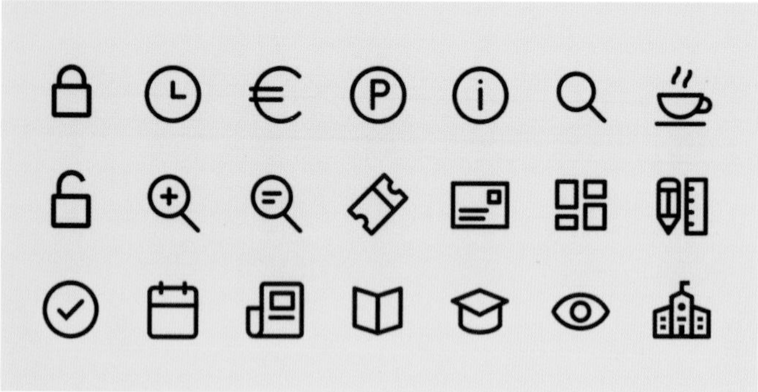

PINK

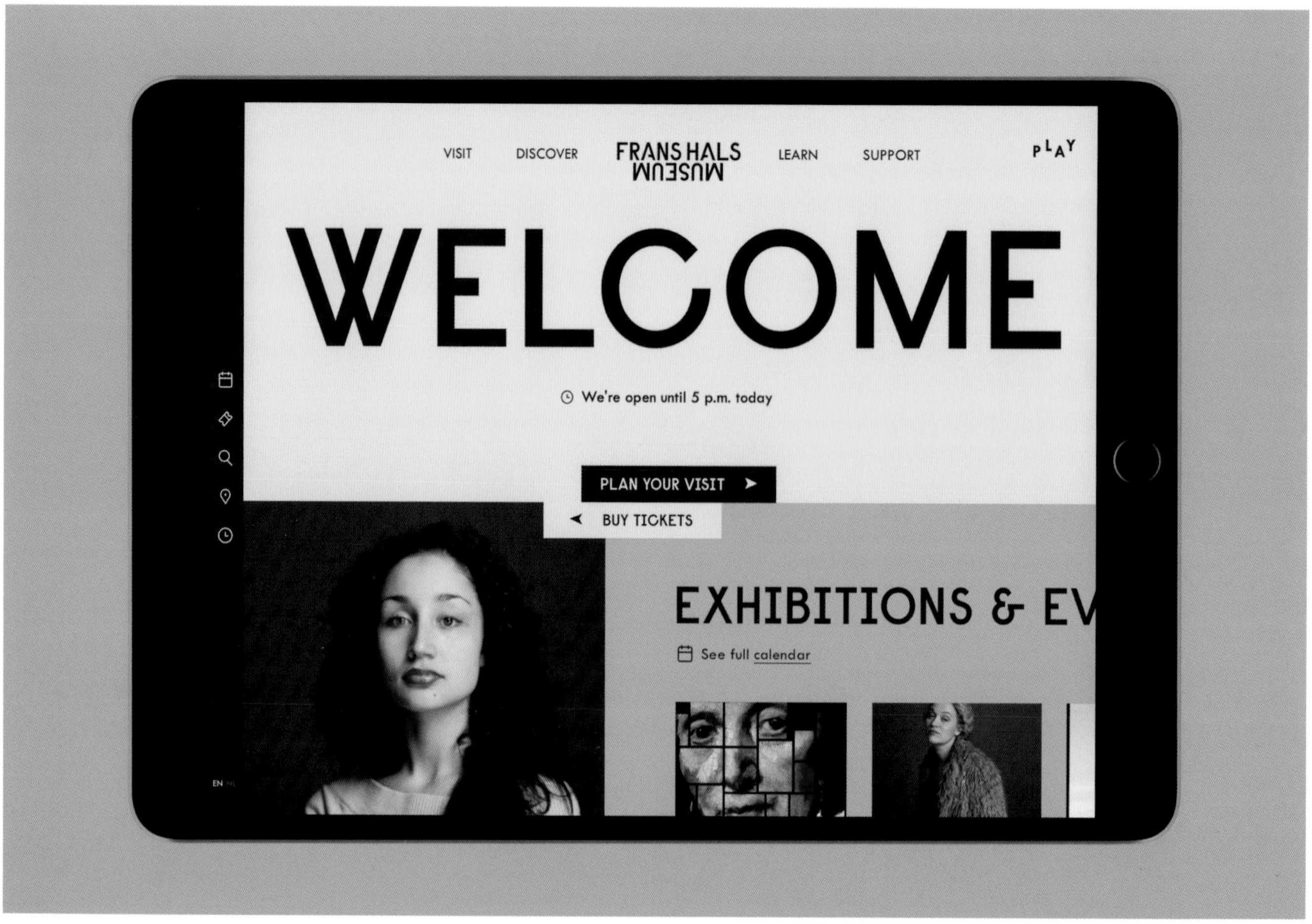
VISIT
DISCOVER
FRANS HALS MUSEUM
LEARN
SUPPORT
PLAY
WELCOME
We're open until 5 p.m. today
PLAN YOUR VISIT
BUY TICKETS
EXHIBITIONS & EV
See full calendar

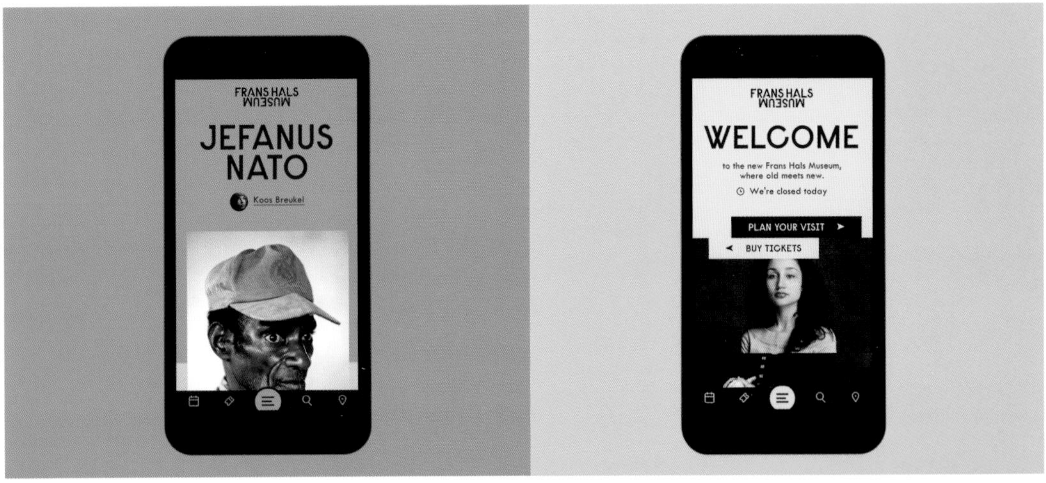
FRANS HALS MUSEUM
JEFANUS NATO
Koos Breukel
FRANS HALS MUSEUM
WELCOME
to the new Frans Hals Museum, where old meets new.
We're closed today
PLAN YOUR VISIT
BUY TICKETS

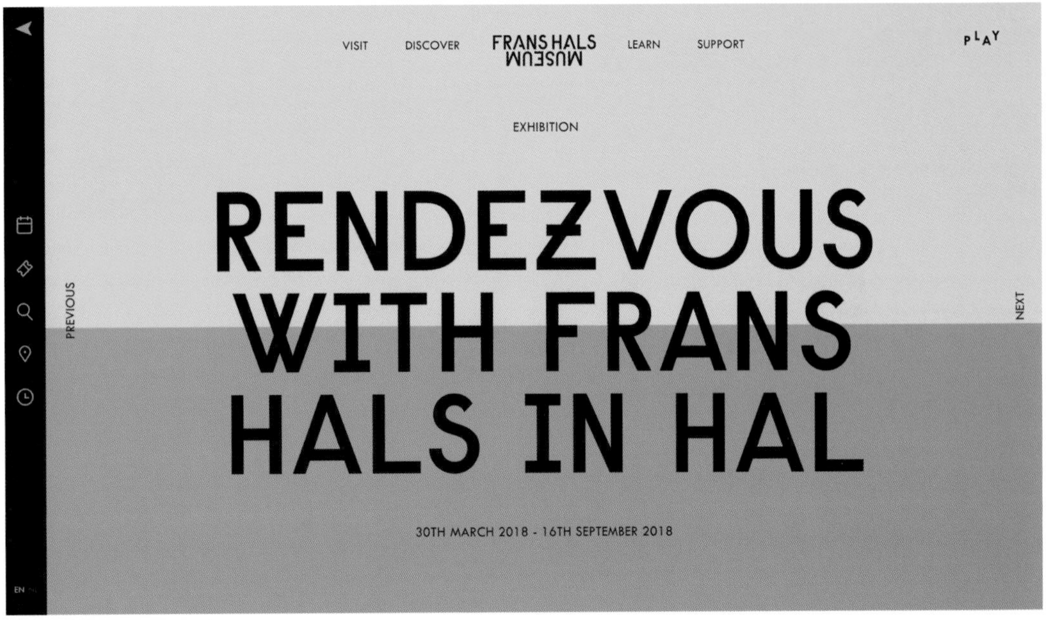
VISIT
DISCOVER
FRANS HALS MUSEUM
LEARN
SUPPORT
PLAY
EXHIBITION
PREVIOUS
RENDEZVOUS WITH FRANS HALS IN HAL
NEXT
30TH MARCH 2018 - 16TH SEPTEMBER 2018
EN

VISIT
DISCOVER
FRANS HALS MUSEUM
LEARN
SUPPORT
PLAY
MASK LXXVIII
John Stezaker
In his collages, John Stezaker reuses existing photographs as 'ready-mades' and questions the expectations linked to photographs. He mainly cuts, slices and pastes (in and onto) publicity photos of actors from the thirties, forties and fifties – the golden age of Hollywood. In the case of Mask LXXVIII we see a male head on which a painting has been pasted. This painting of a landscape functions – as the title suggests – as a mask. The effect is enhanced because we automatically start to read the elements of the picturesque landscape as the facial features of the hidden head. This creates an alienation
On display
Yes
Share
Facebook
Twitter
EN

Heathen Natives

Design Agency
Kommigraphics

Behance

Heathen Natives is a vinyl and CD trading and distribution company, with a list of over 1,600 labels offering a huge variety of music items. The goal was to create a user-friendly B2B e-commerce that is differentiated from competition, to properly promote all products and to create a unique experience for potential buyers.

The strong typography and the distinct separated sections of the site are the two most important elements of the fresh visual identity that is attributed. All the design details, based on the logo's structure and philosophy, create a recognizable and different environment. Kommigraphics has designed the website and delivered all CSS and html styling coding.

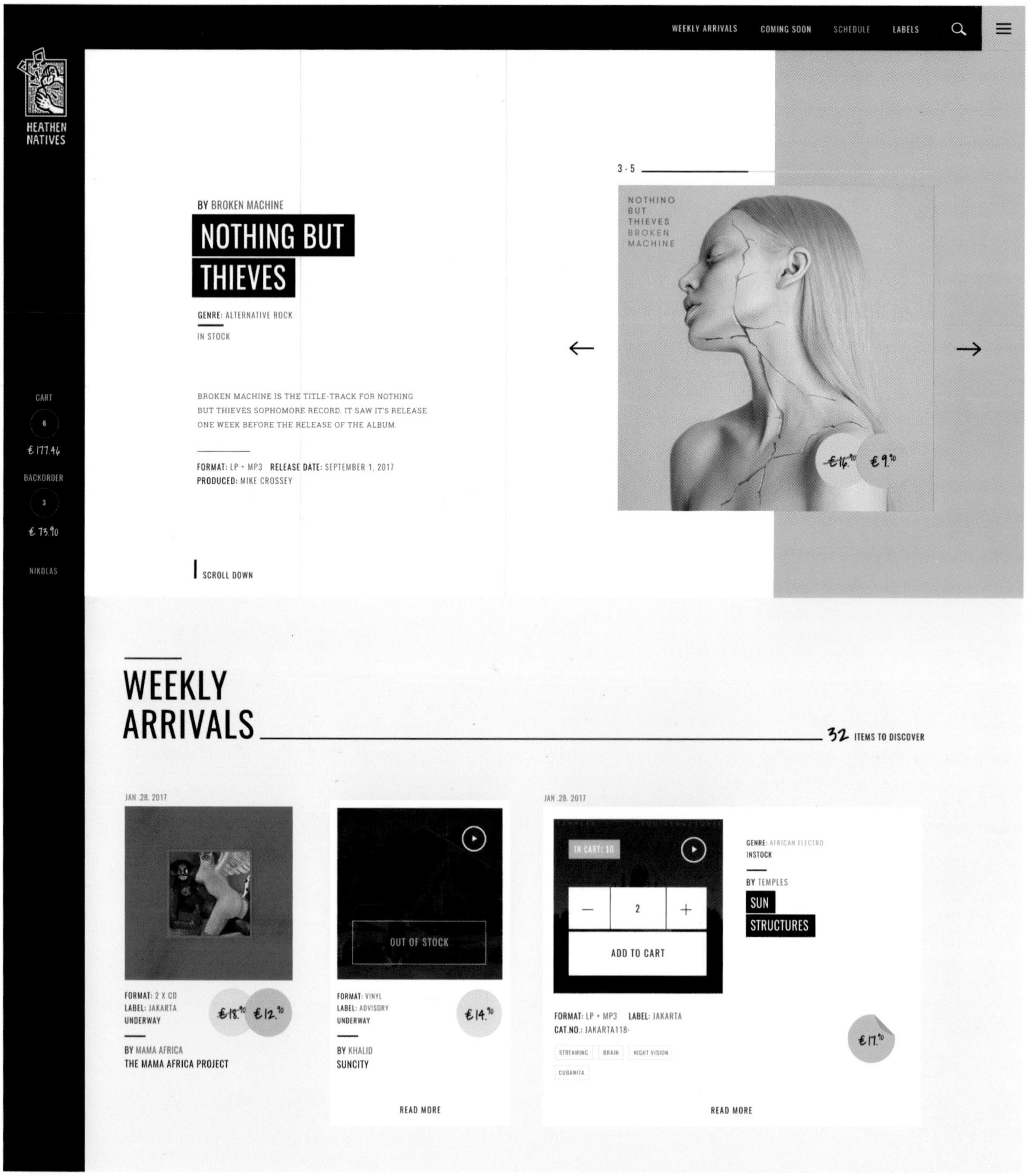

WEEKLY ARRIVALS
COMING SOON
SCHEDULE
LABELS
HEATHEN NATIVES
3 - 5
BY BROKEN MACHINE
NOTHING BUT THIEVES
GENRE: ALTERNATIVE ROCK
IN STOCK
NOTHING BUT THIEVES BROKEN MACHINE
BROKEN MACHINE IS THE TITLE-TRACK FOR NOTHING BUT THIEVES SOPHOMORE RECORD. IT SAW IT'S RELEASE ONE WEEK BEFORE THE RELEASE OF THE ALBUM.
FORMAT: LP + MP3 RELEASE DATE: SEPTEMBER 1, 2017
PRODUCED: MIKE CROSSEY
CART
6
€ 177.46
BACKORDER
3
€ 73.90
NIKOLAS
SCROLL DOWN
WEEKLY ARRIVALS
32 ITEMS TO DISCOVER
JAN .28. 2017
FORMAT: 2 X CD
LABEL: JAKARTA
UNDERWAY
BY MAMA AFRICA
THE MAMA AFRICA PROJECT
OUT OF STOCK
FORMAT: VINYL
LABEL: ADVISORY
UNDERWAY
€14.90
BY KHALID
SUNCITY
READ MORE
JAN .28. 2017
IN CART: 10
2
ADD TO CART
GENRE: AFRICAN ELECTRO
INSTOCK
BY TEMPLES
SUN STRUCTURES
FORMAT: LP + MP3 LABEL: JAKARTA
CAT.NO.: JAKARTA118-
STREAMING
BRAIN
NIGHT VISION
CUBANITA
€17.90
READ MORE

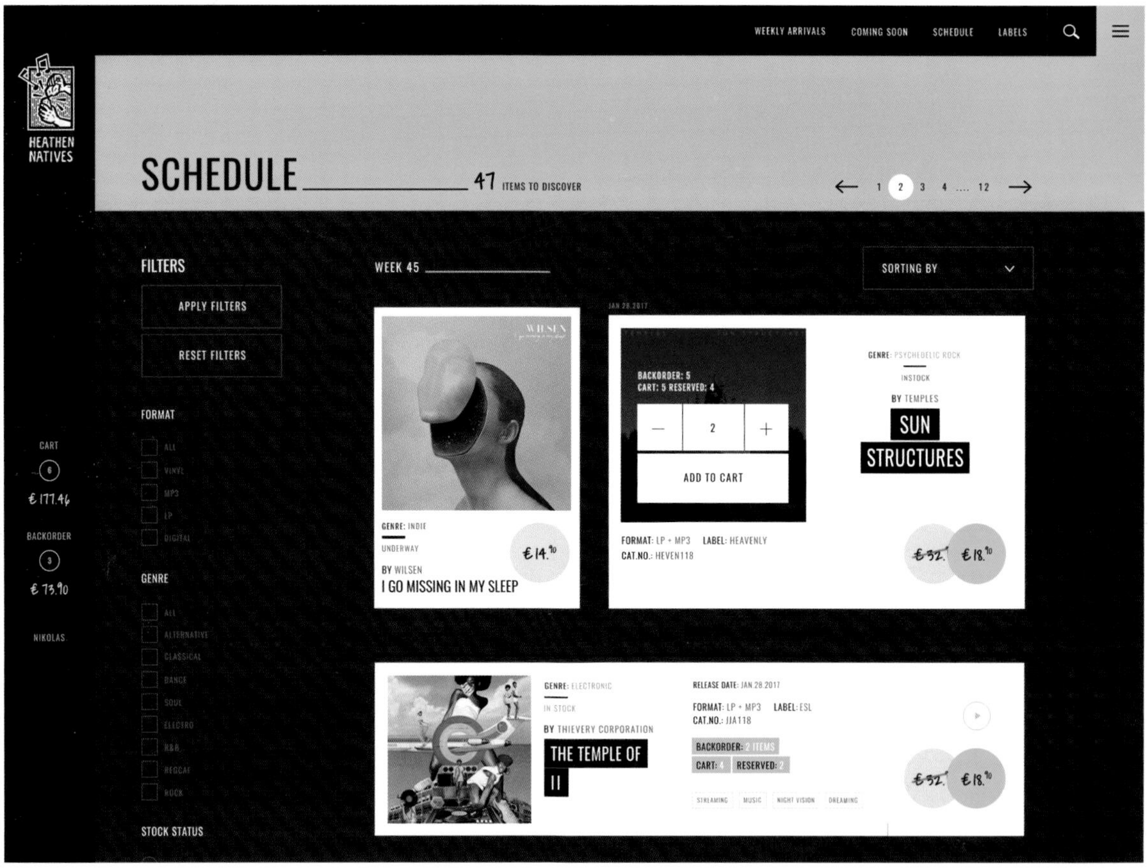
WEEKLY ARRIVALS
COMING SOON
SCHEDULE
LABELS
HEATHEN NATIVES
SCHEDULE
47 ITEMS TO DISCOVER
1 2 3 4 12
FILTERS
APPLY FILTERS
RESET FILTERS
FORMAT
GENRE
STOCK STATUS
WEEK 45
SORTING BY
CART
€ 177.46
BACKORDER
€ 73.90
NIKOLAS
GENRE: INDIE
UNDERWAY
BY WILSEN
I GO MISSING IN MY SLEEP
€ 14.90
BACKORDER: 5
CART: 5 RESERVED: 4
ADD TO CART
GENRE: PSYCHEDELIC ROCK
INSTOCK
BY TEMPLES
SUN
STRUCTURES
FORMAT: LP + MP3 LABEL: HEAVENLY
CAT.NO.: HEVEN118
€ 32.90
€ 18.90
GENRE: ELECTRONIC
IN STOCK
BY THIEVERY CORPORATION
THE TEMPLE OF
II
RELEASE DATE: JAN 28 2017
FORMAT: LP + MP3 LABEL: ESL
CAT.NO.: JJA118
BACKORDER:
CART:
RESERVED:
€ 32.90
€ 18.90

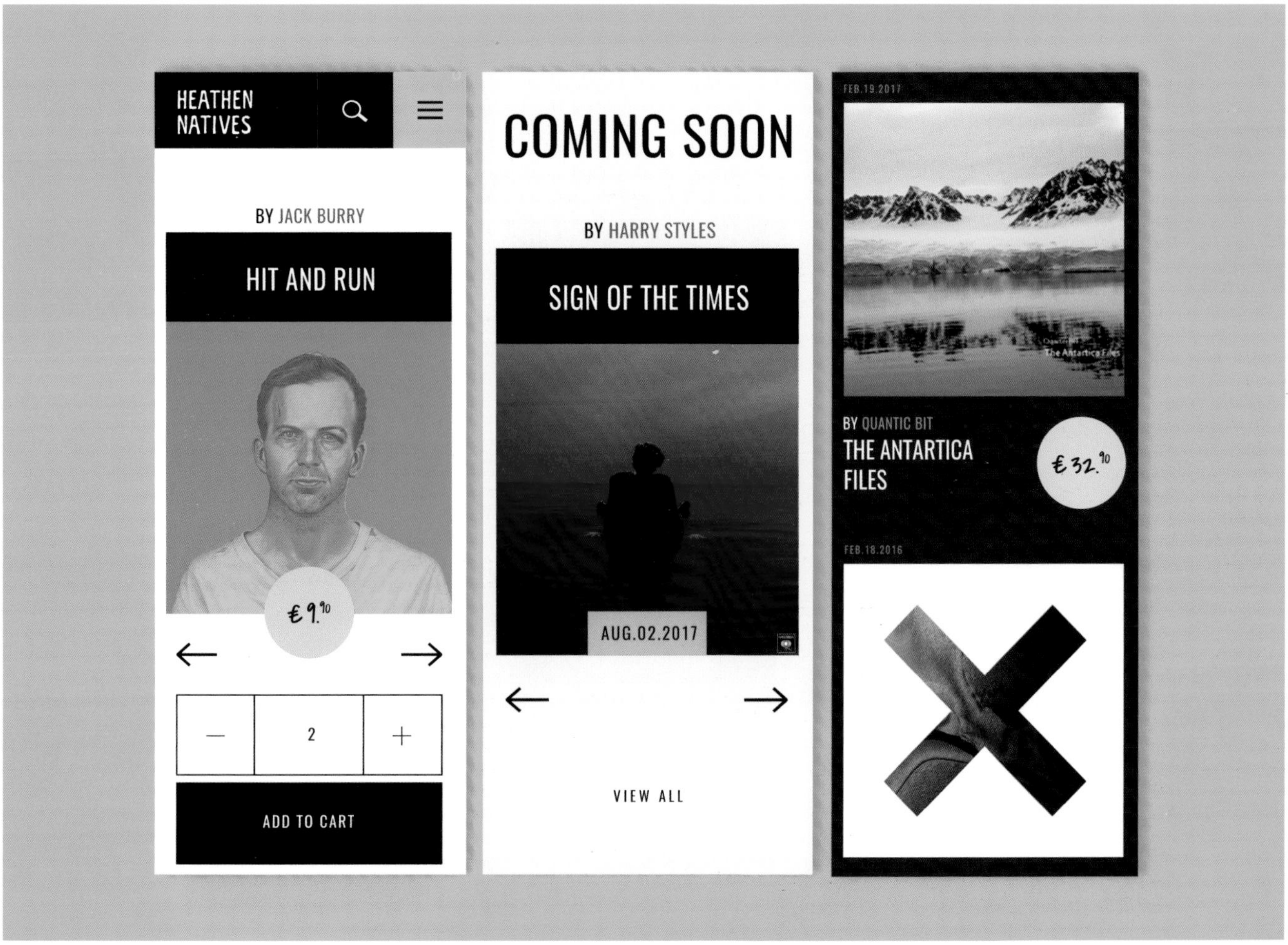
HEATHEN
NATIVES
BY JACK BURRY
HIT AND RUN
€ 9.90
2
ADD TO CART
COMING SOON
BY HARRY STYLES
SIGN OF THE TIMES
AUG.02.2017
VIEW ALL
FEB.19.2017
BY QUANTIC BIT
THE ANTARTICA
FILES
€ 32.90
FEB.18.2016

Croscon

Design
Paul DeCotiis

Client
Croscon

URL
www.croscon.com

Official Site

Croscon is a digital product studio based in New York City. In early 2017, Paul led the design initiative to update Croscon's visual identity, refresh their branding, and align their message with a new business model. Together they launched an entirely new destination for croscon.com.

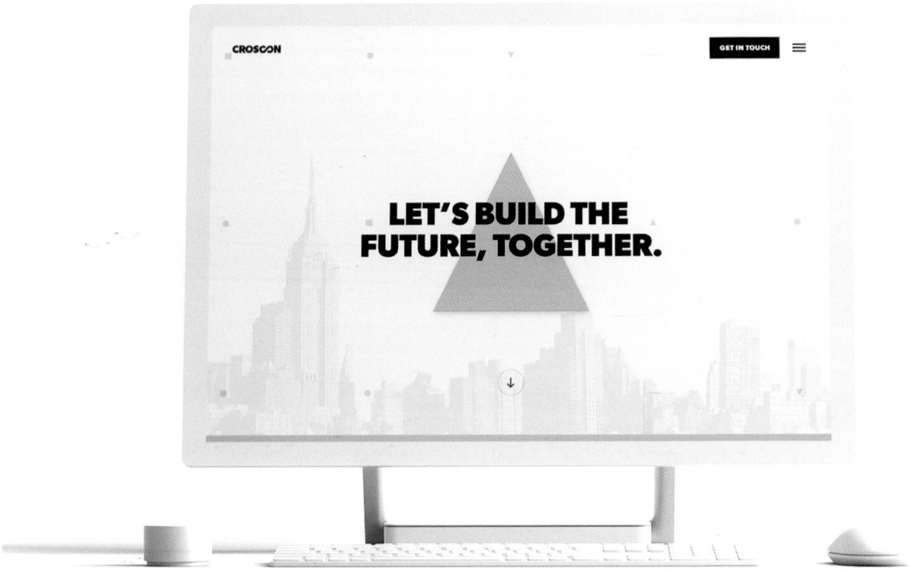
CROSCON
GET IN TOUCH
LET'S BUILD THE
FUTURE, TOGETHER.

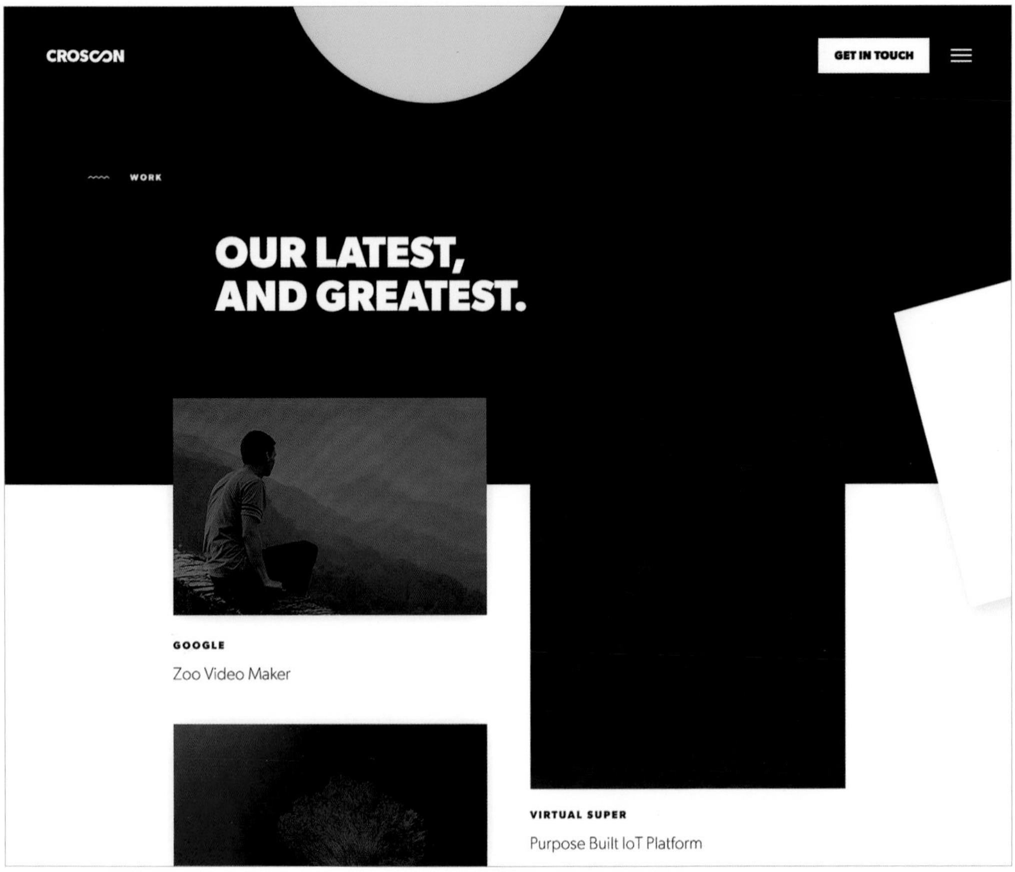
CROSCON
GET IN TOUCH
WORK
OUR LATEST,
AND GREATEST.
GOOGLE
Zoo Video Maker
VIRTUAL SUPER
Purpose Built IoT Platform

The designer approached the design of the Croscon site with a goal of refreshing the Croscon brand and looked for opportunities to introduce a more interactive and motion-driven experience for visitors. The site design utilizes simple geometric shapes that represent the three different disciplines of the Croscon company: Strategy, Design, and Engineering. The colour palette is simple and distinct to the Croscon brand—utilizing yellow as the primary colour and fundamental indicator of the Croscon brand. Secondary and tertiary colour of black, white, and shades of gray are used throughout the site. The brand typeface is Gibson and is used in bold for headlines and regular for body copy.

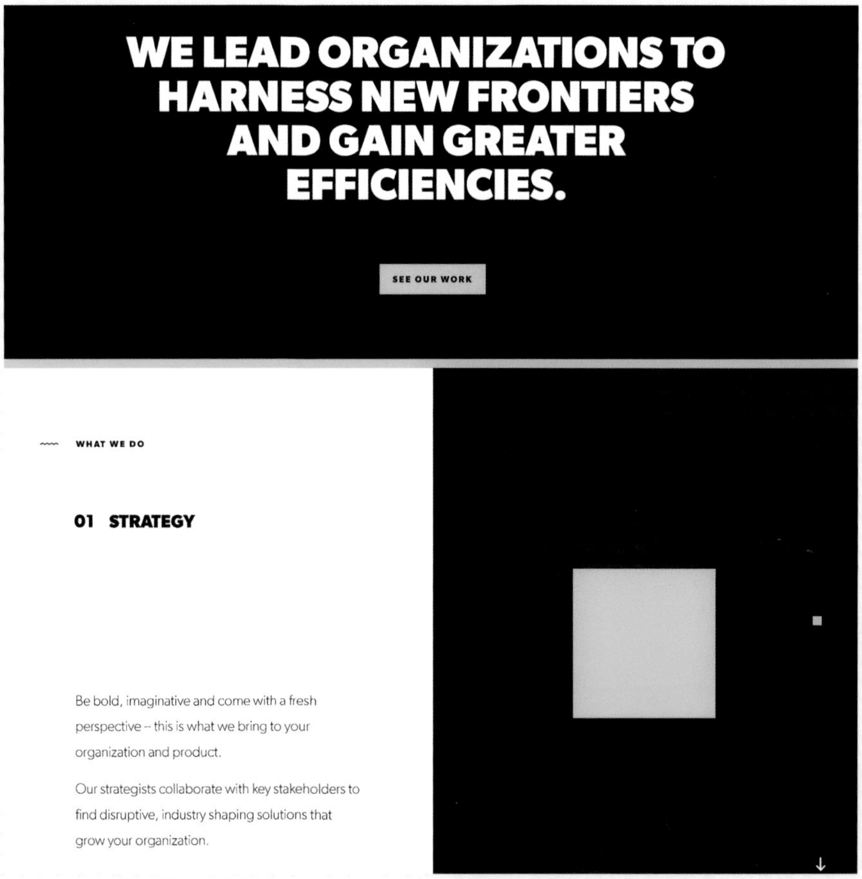
WE LEAD ORGANIZATIONS TO HARNESS NEW FRONTIERS AND GAIN GREATER EFFICIENCIES.
SEE OUR WORK
WHAT WE DO
01 STRATEGY
Be bold, imaginative and come with a fresh perspective -- this is what we bring to your organization and product.
Our strategists collaborate with key stakeholders to find disruptive, industry shaping solutions that grow your organization.

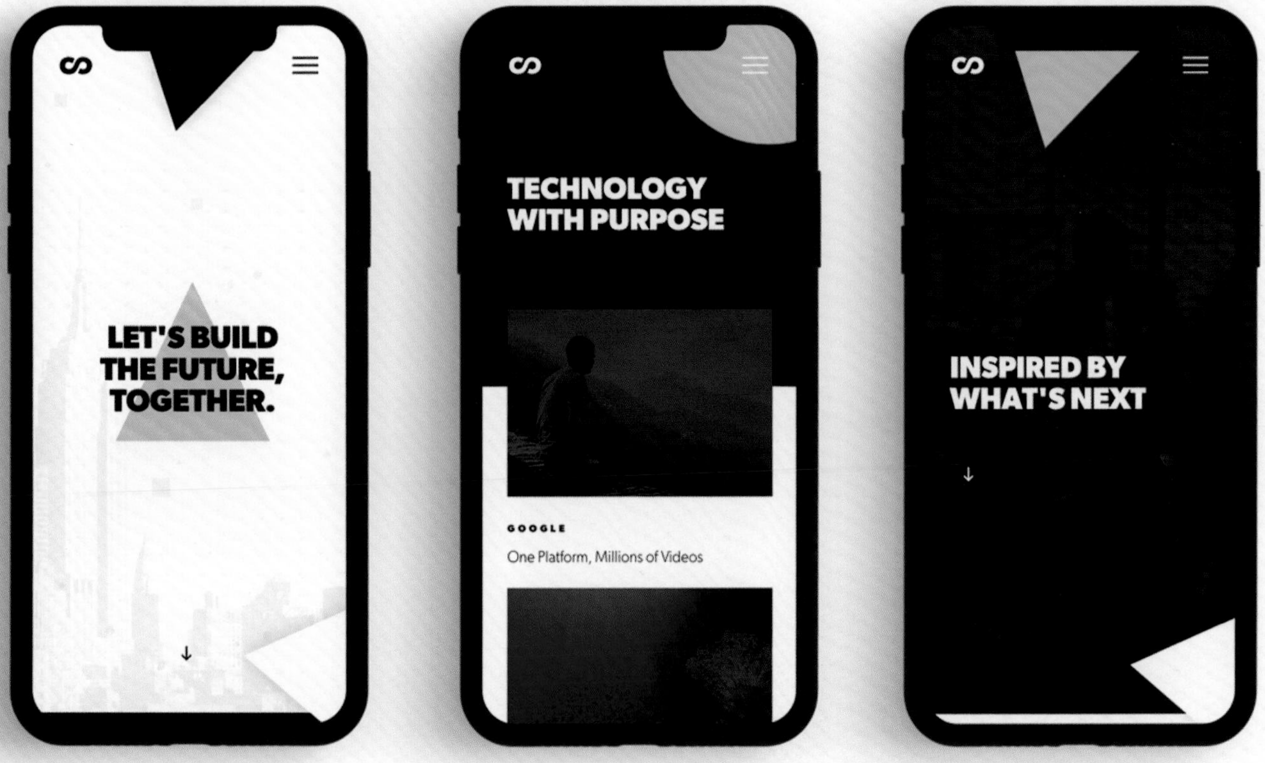
LET'S BUILD THE FUTURE, TOGETHER.
TECHNOLOGY WITH PURPOSE
GOOGLE
One Platform, Millions of Videos
INSPIRED BY WHAT'S NEXT

Second City Works

Design and Development
Heco

URL
www.secondcityworks.com

Official Site

Second City Works is the professional services arm of the world-renowned Second City comedy theater. They create events, content, and professional development programs that drive personal growth and organizational improvement.

Heco created a new visual language and website for Second City Works, inspired by one of improv's core tenets—Yes, and. Through playful interactions, individual shapes assemble to express larger concepts and benefits. This approach captures the brand's creative personality, while striking an intelligent tone that resonates with corporate audiences.

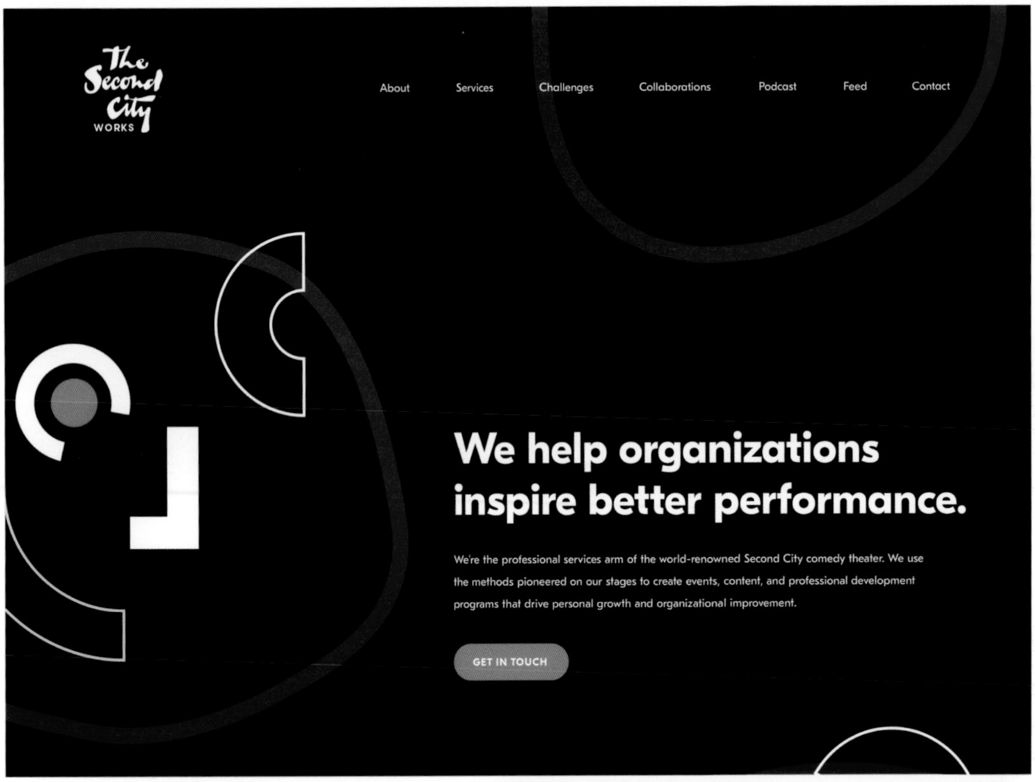
The Second City
WORKS
About
Services
Challenges
Collaborations
Podcast
Feed
Contact
We help organizations inspire better performance.
We're the professional services arm of the world-renowned Second City comedy theater. We use the methods pioneered on our stages to create events, content, and professional development programs that drive personal growth and organizational improvement.
GET IN TOUCH

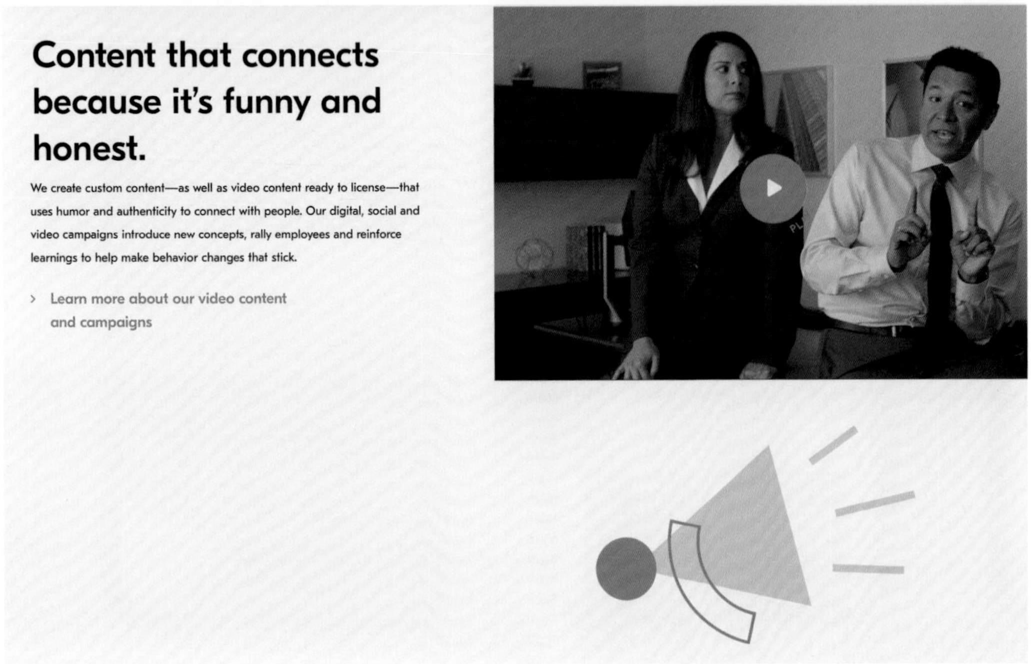
Content that connects because it's funny and honest.
We create custom content—as well as video content ready to license—that uses humor and authenticity to connect with people. Our digital, social and video campaigns introduce new concepts, rally employees and reinforce learnings to help make behavior changes that stick.
> Learn more about our video content and campaigns

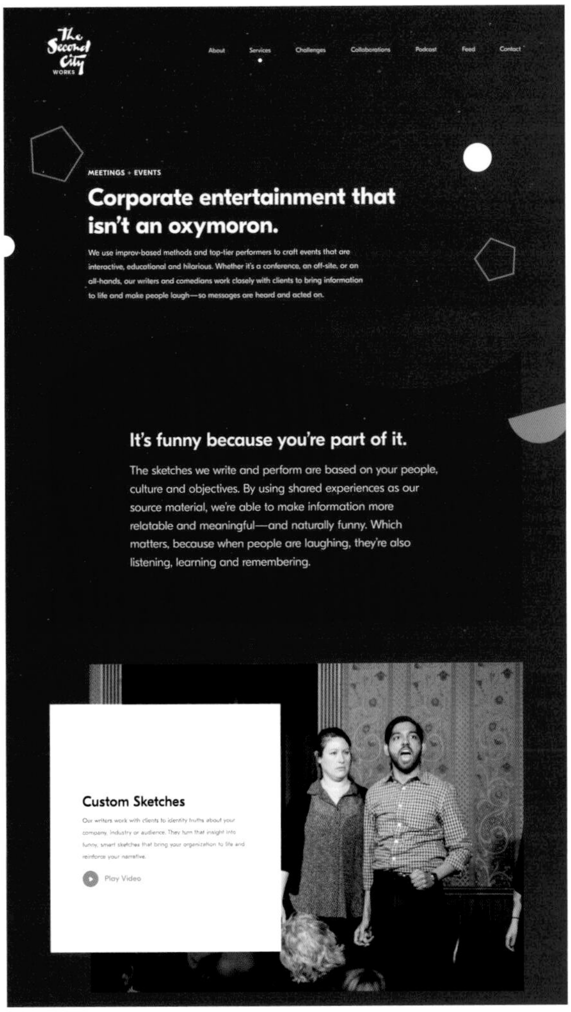

The Second City WORKS
About
Services
Challenges
Collaborations
Podcast
Feed
Contact
MEETINGS + EVENTS
Corporate entertainment that isn't an oxymoron.
We use improv-based methods and top-tier performers to craft events that are interactive, educational and hilarious. Whether it's a conference, an off-site, or an all-hands, our writers and comedians work closely with clients to bring information to life and make people laugh—so messages are heard and acted on.
It's funny because you're part of it.
The sketches we write and perform are based on your people, culture and objectives. By using shared experiences as our source material, we're able to make information more relatable and meaningful—and naturally funny. Which matters, because when people are laughing, they're also listening, learning and remembering.
Custom Sketches
Our writers work with clients to identify truths about your company, industry or audience. They turn that insight into funny, smart sketches that bring your organization to life and reinforce your narrative.
Play Video

Scroll

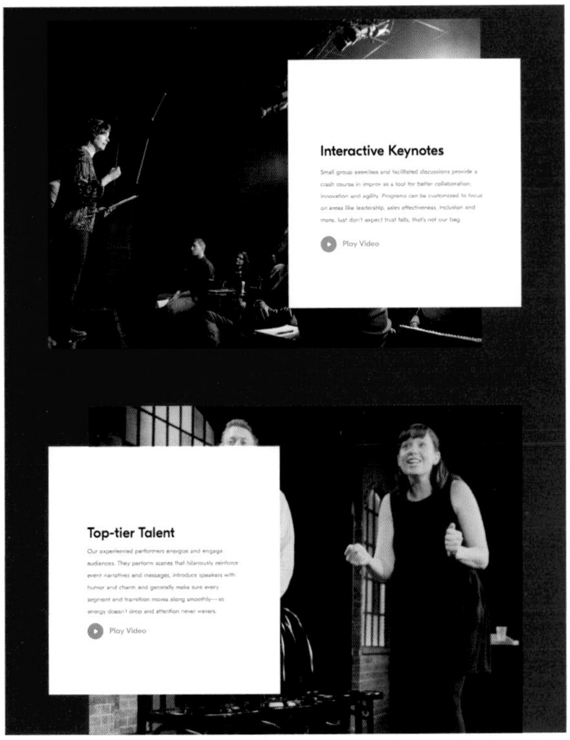

Interactive Keynotes
Small group exercises and facilitated discussions provide a crash course in improv as a tool for better collaboration, innovation and agility. Programs can be customized to focus on areas like leadership, sales effectiveness, inclusion and more. Just don't expect trust falls, that's not our bag.
Play Video
Top-tier Talent
Our experienced performers energize and engage audiences. They perform scenes that hilariously reinforce event narratives and messages, introduce speakers with humor and charm and generally make sure every segment and transition moves along smoothly—so energy doesn't drop and attention never wavers.
Play Video

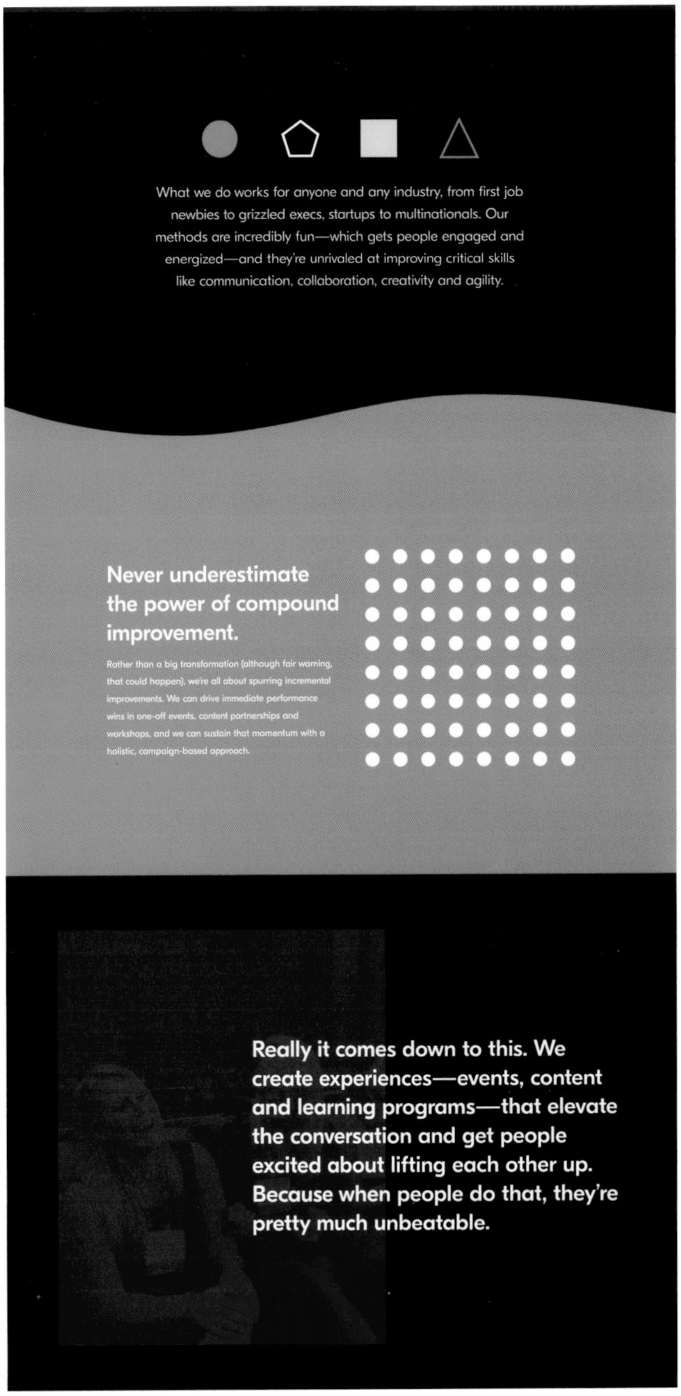

What we do works for anyone and any industry, from first job newbies to grizzled execs, startups to multinationals. Our methods are incredibly fun—which gets people engaged and energized—and they're unrivaled at improving critical skills like communication, collaboration, creativity and agility.
Never underestimate the power of compound improvement.
Rather than a big transformation (although fair warning, that could happen), we're all about spurring incremental improvements. We can drive immediate performance wins in one-off events, content partnerships and workshops, and we can sustain that momentum with a holistic, campaign-based approach.
Really it comes down to this. We create experiences—events, content and learning programs—that elevate the conversation and get people excited about lifting each other up. Because when people do that, they're pretty much unbeatable.

Weima

Official Site

Design Agency
Studio Naam

Creative Direction
Timothy Maurer, Joris Spiertz

Design
Elspeth MacLeod, Timothy Maurer, Joris Spiertz

Development
Lieneke Ronk Koenen

3D Graphics
The Outpost

URL
weima.com

Weima Maschinenbau is one of the leading companies in the shredding and briquetting industry. They produce a range of large-scale machinery for both commercial and personal use. Weima came to Studio Naam with a request to update their website to showcase their machinery in the best light possible, and really set them apart from their competitors. On the homepage, Studio Naam worked alongside an animation studio to create high fidelity 3D models which the visitor could interact with, and truly understand the process of shredding and briquetting waste materials. By introducing a new chat bot system, they brought about a whole new way for clients to interact with Weima.

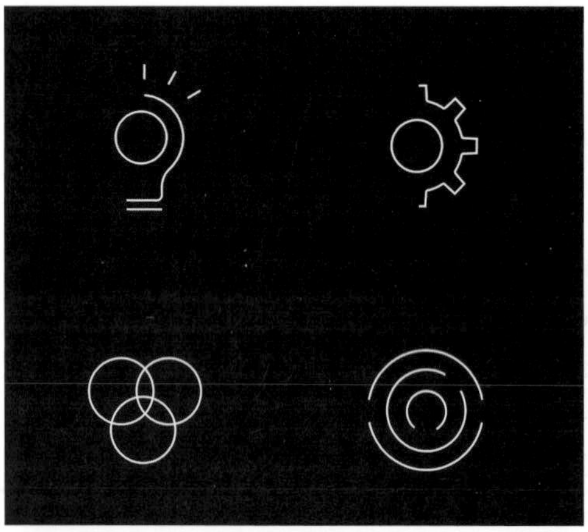

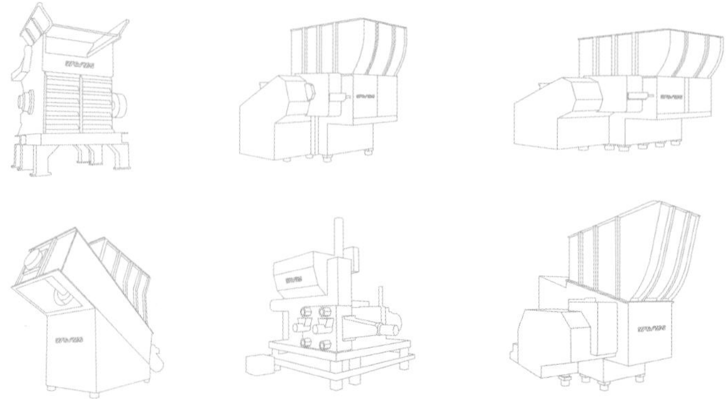

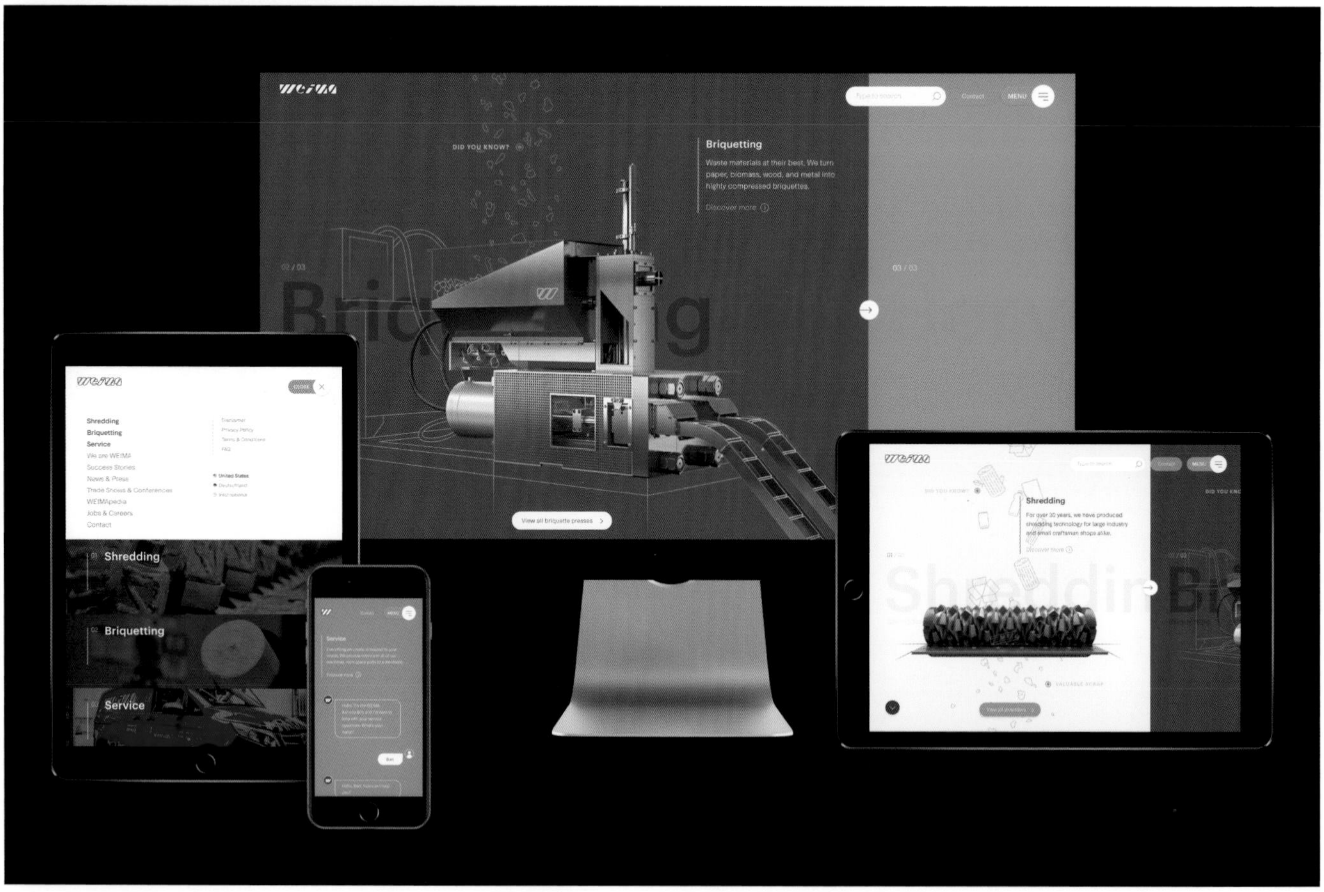
Briquetting
Shredding
Briquetting
Service
Shredding

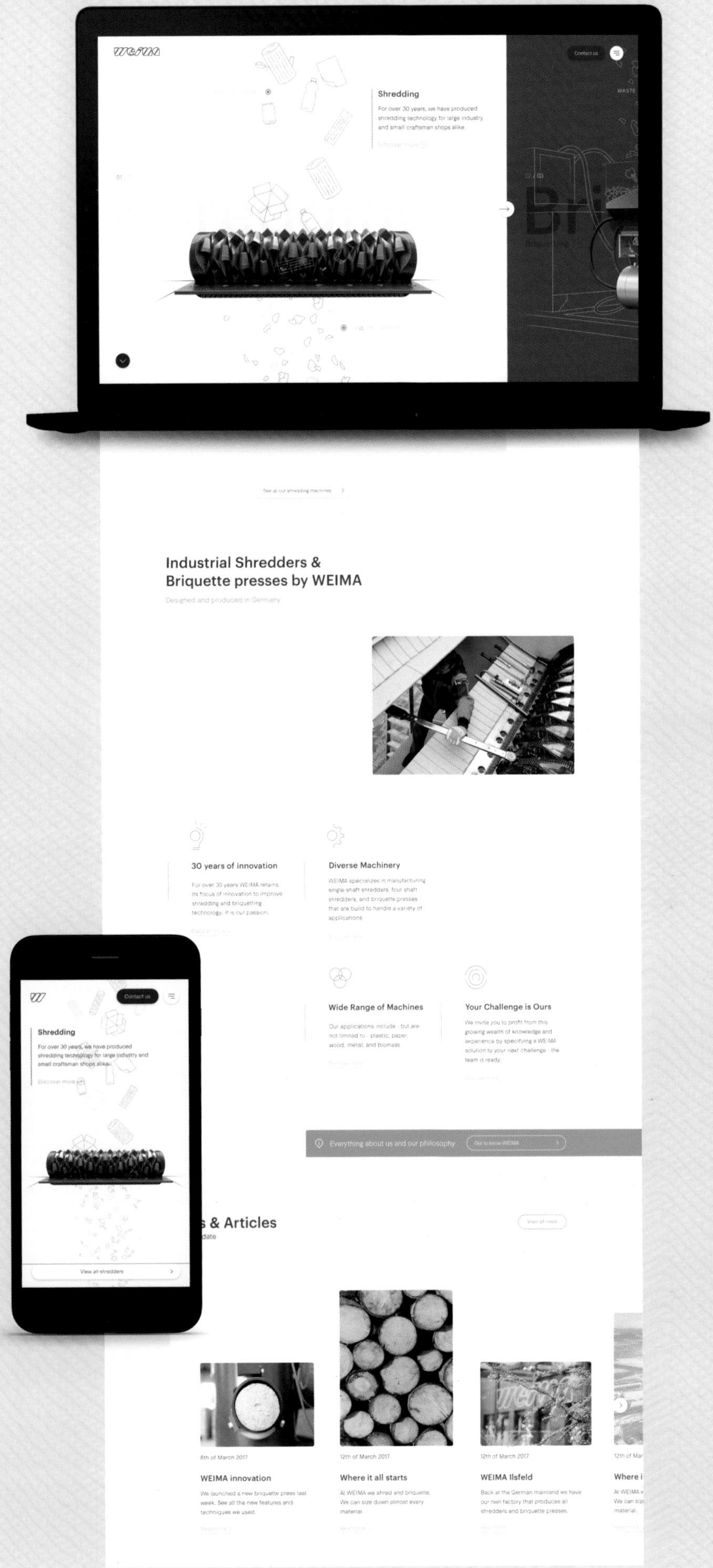
Shredding
For over 30 years, we have produced shredding technology for large industry and small craftsman shops alike.
Industrial Shredders &
Briquette presses by WEIMA
30 years of innovation
Diverse Machinery
Wide Range of Machines
Your Challenge is Ours
Everything about us and our philosophy
& Articles
WEIMA innovation
Where it all starts
WEIMA Ilsfeld
Contact us
View all shredders

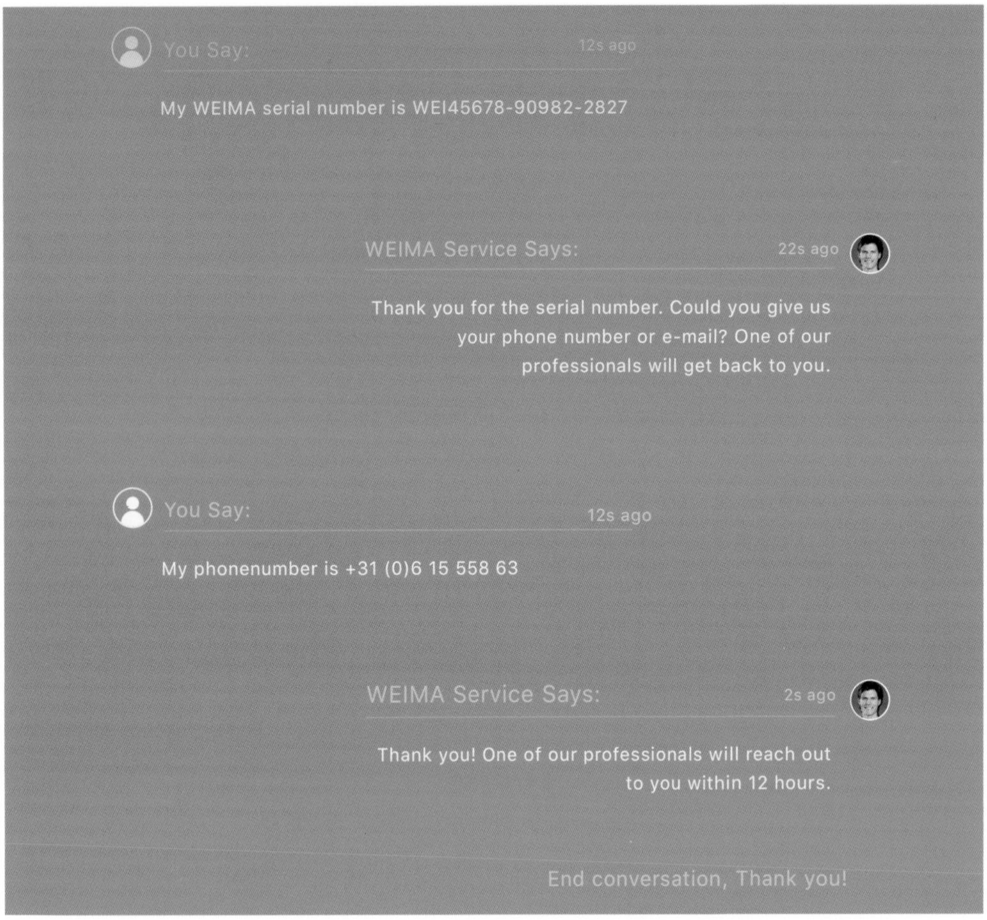
You Say:
12s ago
My WEIMA serial number is WEI45678-90982-2827
WEIMA Service Says:
22s ago
Thank you for the serial number. Could you give us your phone number or e-mail? One of our professionals will get back to you.
You Say:
12s ago
My phonenumber is +31 (0)6 15 558 63
WEIMA Service Says:
2s ago
Thank you! One of our professionals will reach out to you within 12 hours.
End conversation, Thank you!

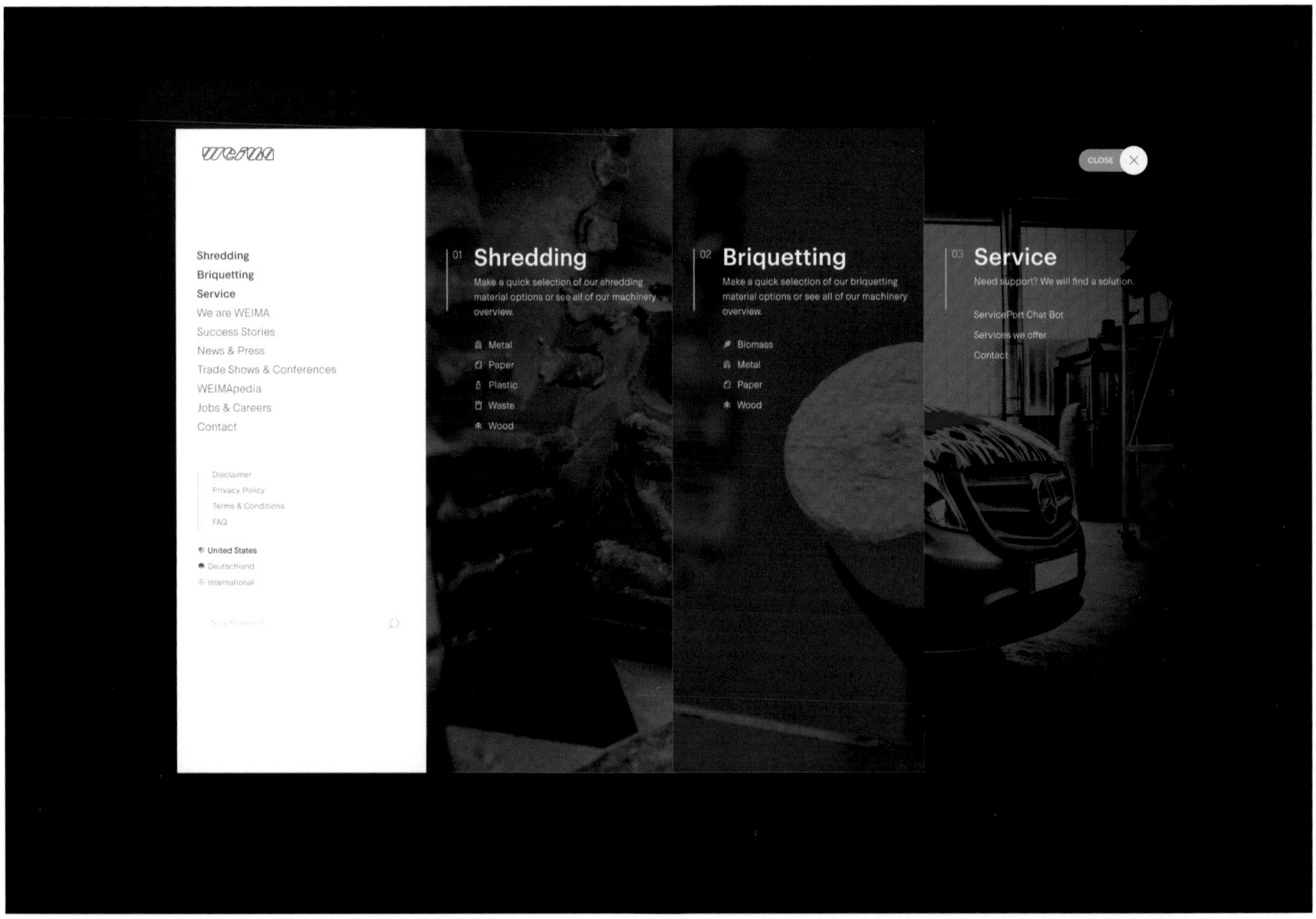
Shredding
Briquetting
Service
We are WEIMA
Success Stories
News & Press
Trade Shows & Conferences
WEIMApedia
Jobs & Careers
Contact
Disclaimer
Privacy Policy
Terms & Conditions
FAQ
United States
Deutschland
International
01 Shredding
Make a quick selection of our shredding material options or see all of our machinery overview.
Metal
Paper
Plastic
Waste
Wood
02 Briquetting
Make a quick selection of our briquetting material options or see all of our machinery overview.
Biomass
Metal
Paper
Wood
CLOSE
03 Service
Need support? We will find a solution.
ServicePort Chat Bot
Services we offer
Contact

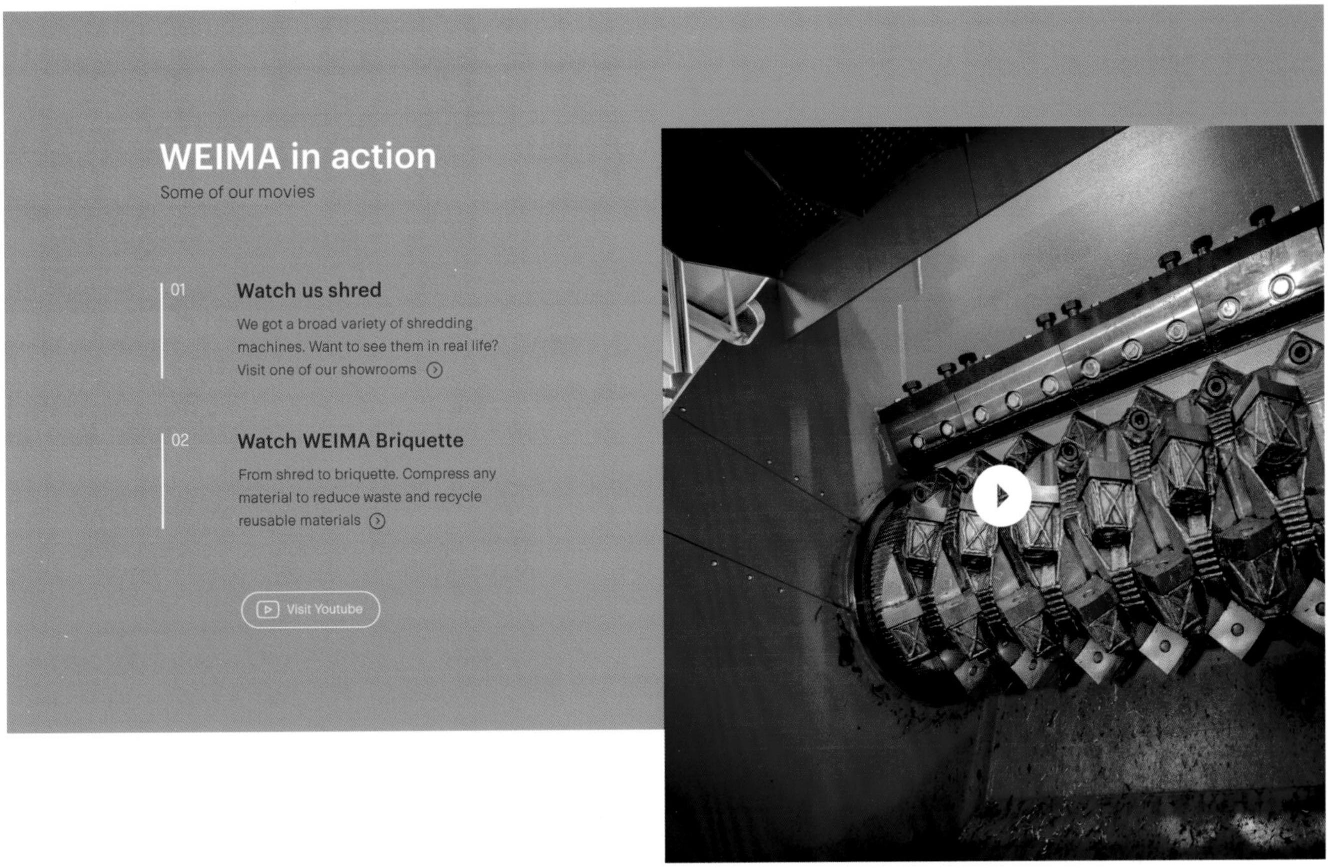
WEIMA in action
Some of our movies
01
Watch us shred
We got a broad variety of shredding machines. Want to see them in real life? Visit one of our showrooms
02
Watch WEIMA Briquette
From shred to briquette. Compress any material to reduce waste and recycle reusable materials
Visit Youtube

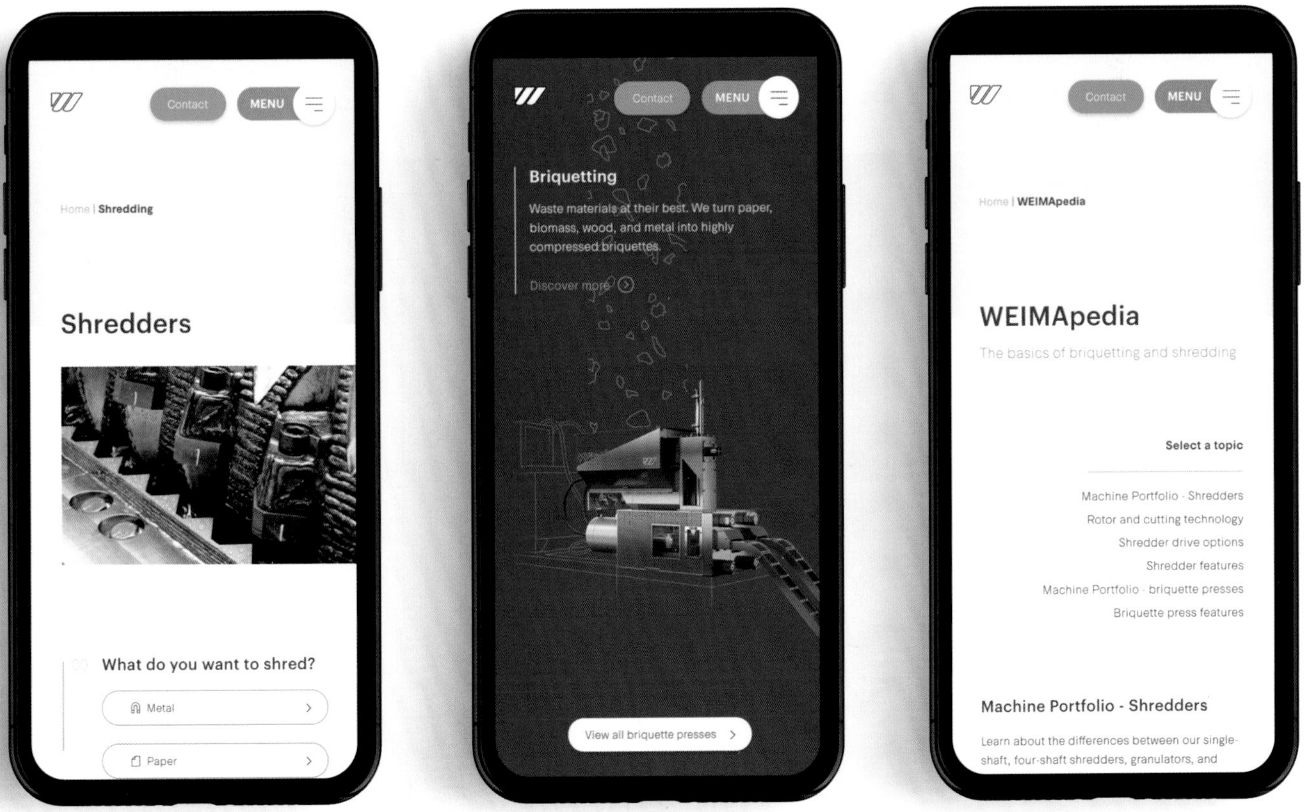
Contact
MENU
Home | Shredding
Shredders
What do you want to shred?
Metal
Paper
Contact
MENU
Briquetting
Waste materials at their best. We turn paper, biomass, wood, and metal into highly compressed briquettes.
Discover more
View all briquette presses
Contact
MENU
Home | WEIMApedia
WEIMApedia
The basics of briquetting and shredding
Select a topic
Machine Portfolio - Shredders
Rotor and cutting technology
Shredder drive options
Shredder features
Machine Portfolio - briquette presses
Briquette press features
Machine Portfolio - Shredders
Learn about the differences between our single-shaft, four-shaft shredders, granulators, and

Inventos Digitais Website

Design Agency
Inventos Digitais

Design
Naiara Pellin Ghinzelli (Lead)

Development
Ariel Schvartz (Lead), Raquel Godoy Thiele, Igor Rocha

Content Development
Miguel Lannes Fernandes (Lead)

URL
www.inventosdigitais.com.br

Official Site

For the front page of Inventos Digitais' website, the agency illustrates how they turn simple ideas in inventions for the future. Their approach was to create, with simple visual forms and basic colours, a vocabulary for a storytelling journey that the idea needs to take in order to become a real product and all the difficulties it encounters through the way.

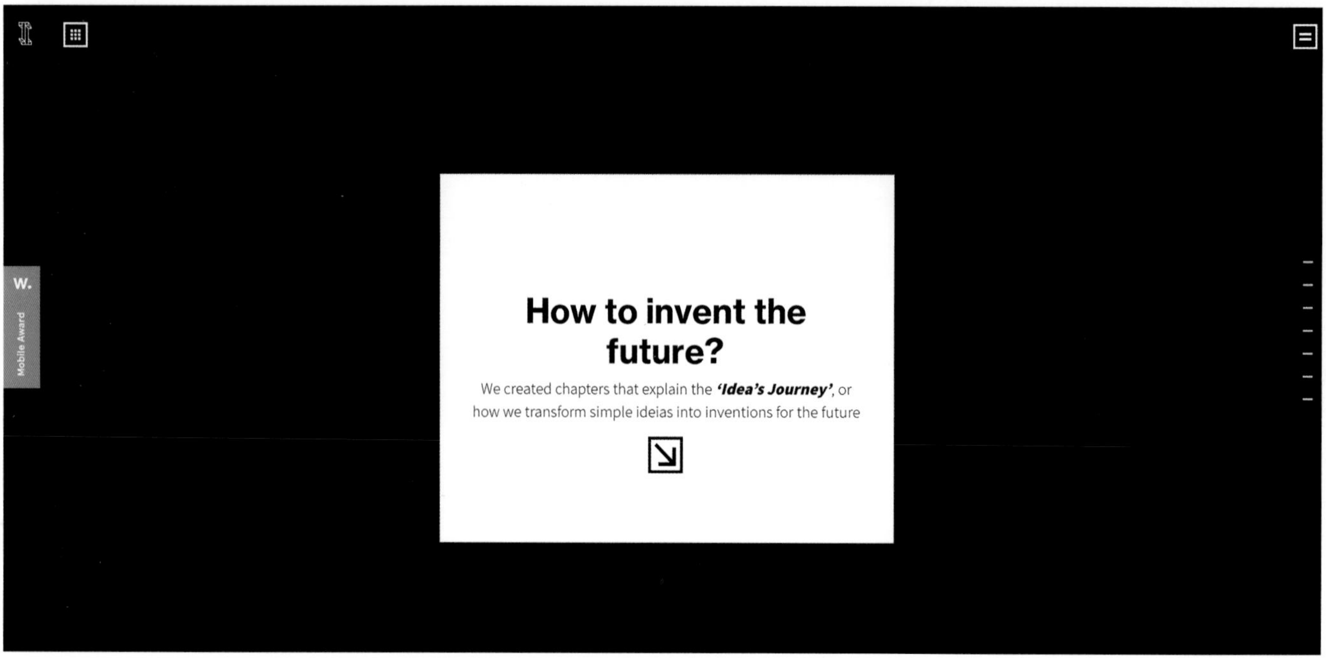

W.
Mobile Award
How to invent the future?
We created chapters that explain the 'Idea's Journey', or how we transform simple ideias into inventions for the future

Scroll

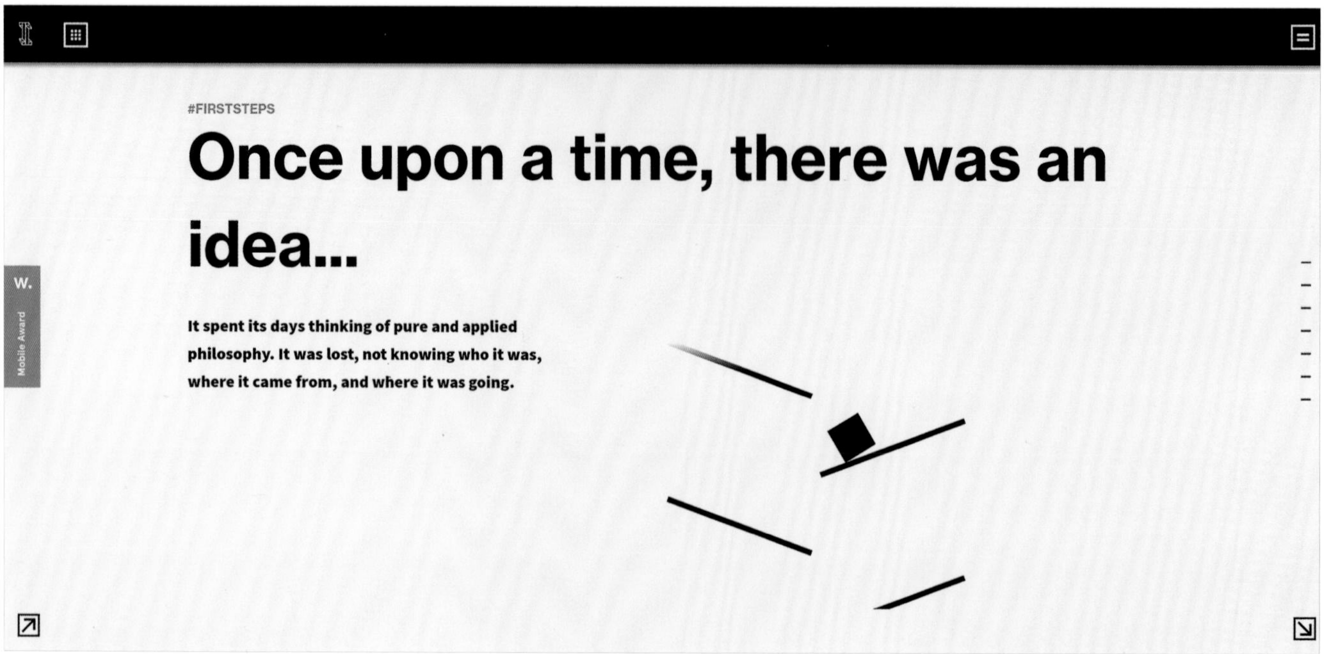

#FIRSTSTEPS
Once upon a time, there was an idea...
It spent its days thinking of pure and applied philosophy. It was lost, not knowing who it was, where it came from, and where it was going.
W.
Mobile Award

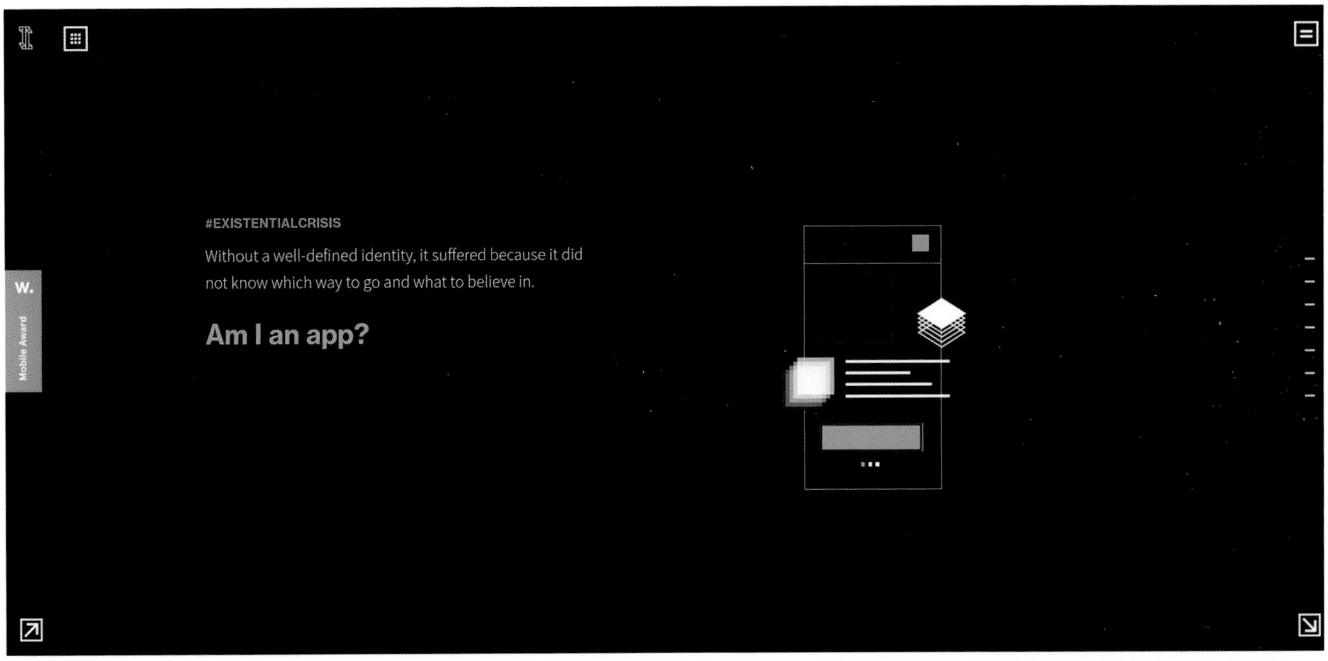
#EXISTENTIALCRISIS
Without a well-defined identity, it suffered because it did not know which way to go and what to believe in.
Am I an app?
W.
Mobile Award

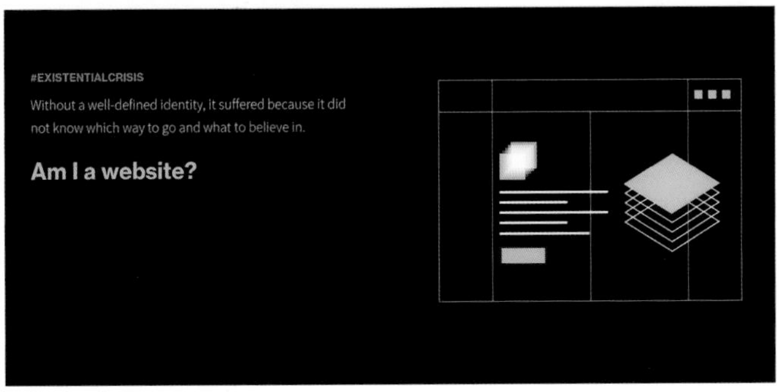
#EXISTENTIALCRISIS
Without a well-defined identity, it suffered because it did not know which way to go and what to believe in.
Am I a website?

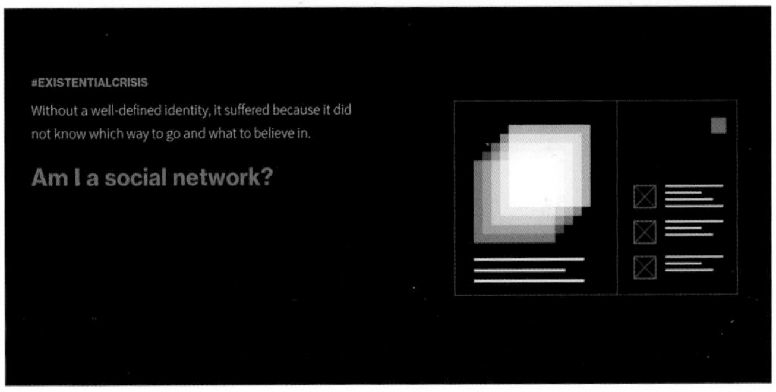
#EXISTENTIALCRISIS
Without a well-defined identity, it suffered because it did not know which way to go and what to believe in.
Am I a social network?

Scroll

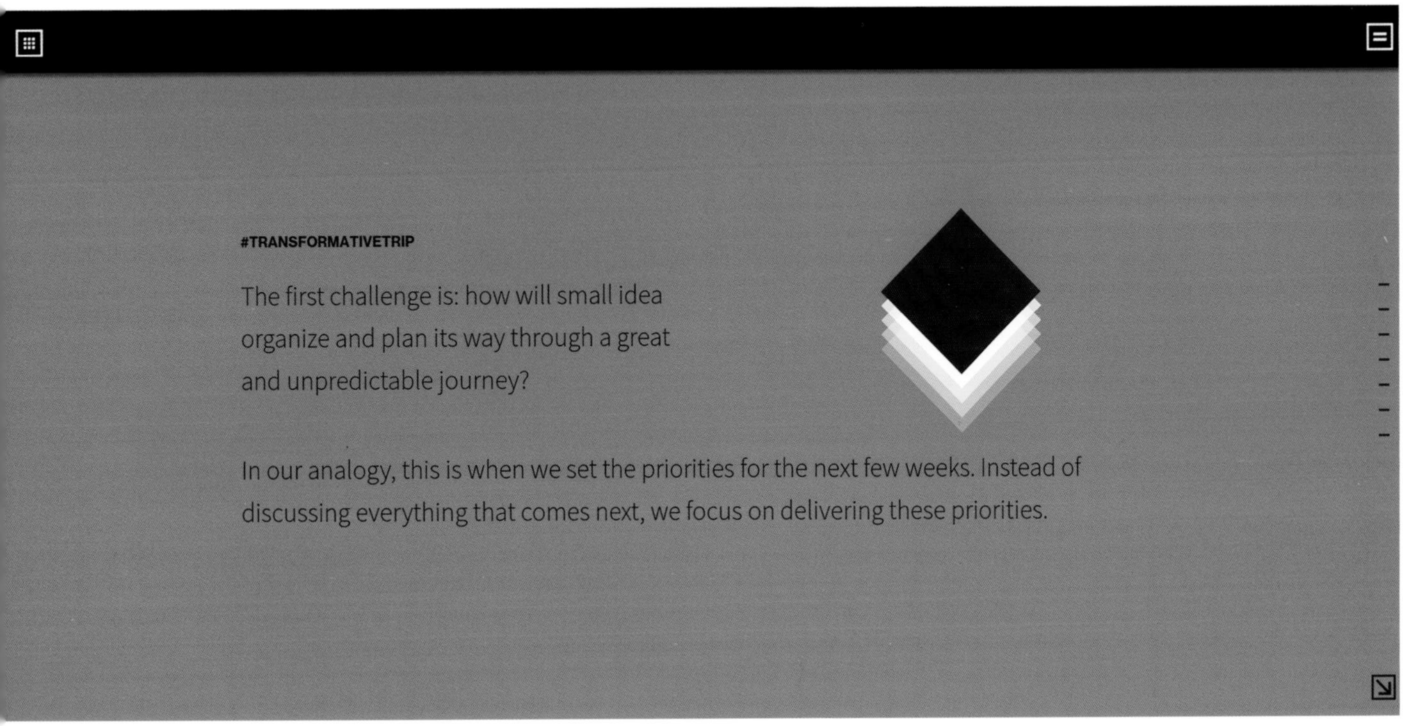
#TRANSFORMATIVETRIP
The first challenge is: how will small idea organize and plan its way through a great and unpredictable journey?
In our analogy, this is when we set the priorities for the next few weeks. Instead of discussing everything that comes next, we focus on delivering these priorities.

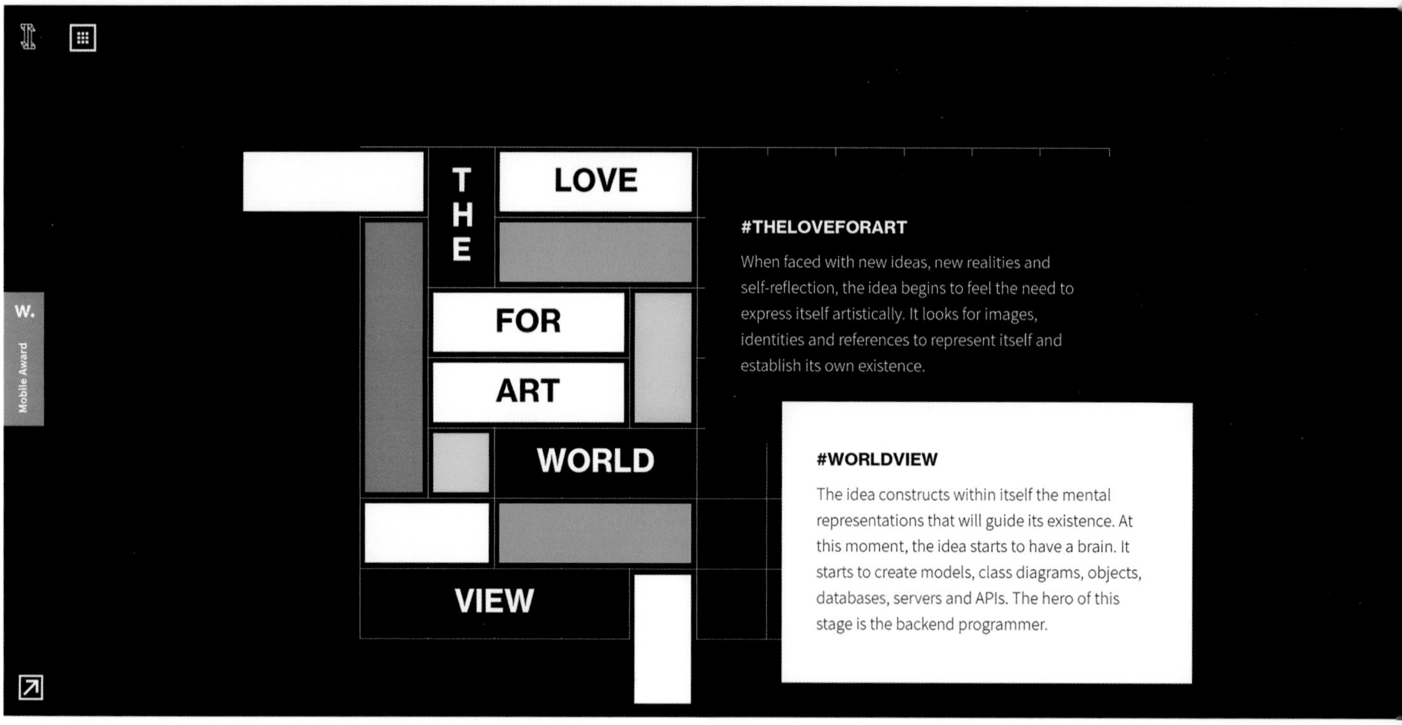
W.
Mobile Award
THE
LOVE
FOR
ART
WORLD
VIEW
#THELOVEFORART
When faced with new ideas, new realities and self-reflection, the idea begins to feel the need to express itself artistically. It looks for images, identities and references to represent itself and establish its own existence.
#WORLDVIEW
The idea constructs within itself the mental representations that will guide its existence. At this moment, the idea starts to have a brain. It starts to create models, class diagrams, objects, databases, servers and APIs. The hero of this stage is the backend programmer.

Scroll

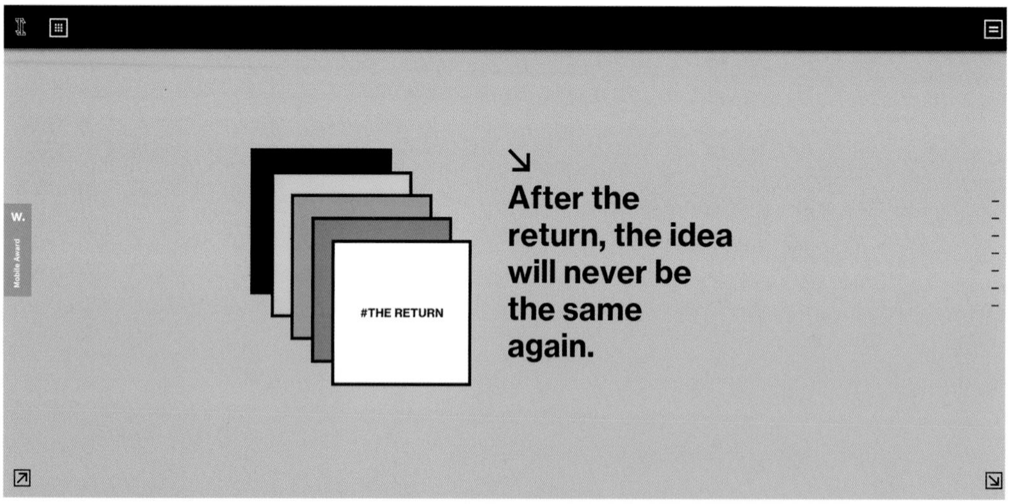
W.
Mobile Award
#THE RETURN
After the return, the idea will never be the same again.

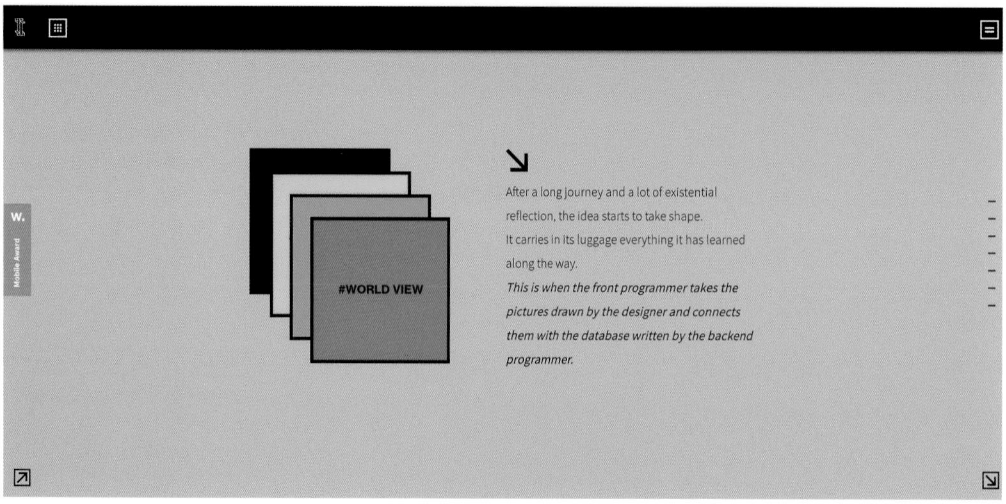
W.
Mobile Award
#WORLD VIEW
After a long journey and a lot of existential reflection, the idea starts to take shape.
It carries in its luggage everything it has learned along the way.
This is when the front programmer takes the pictures drawn by the designer and connects them with the database written by the backend programmer.

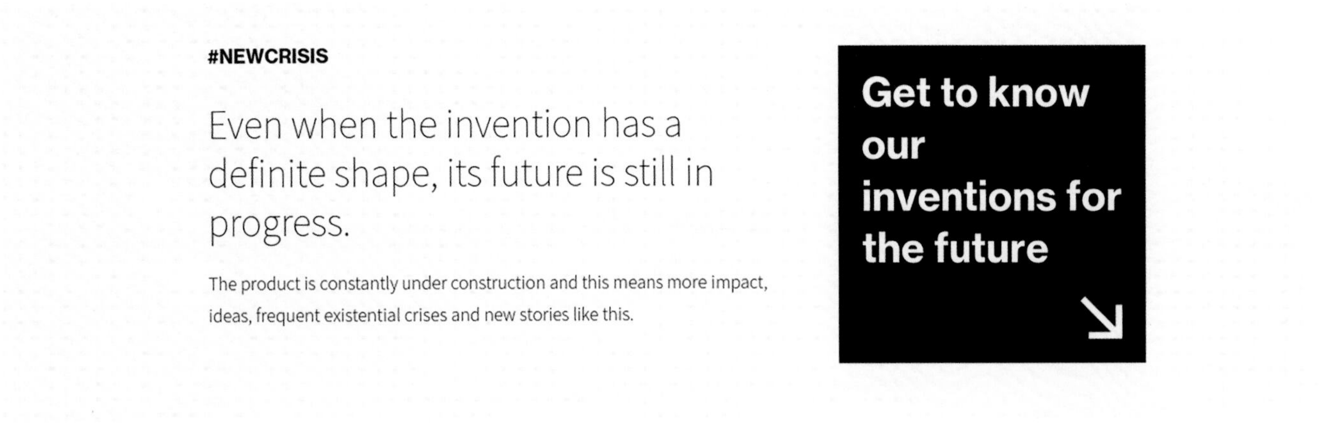
#NEWCRISIS
Even when the invention has a definite shape, its future is still in progress.
The product is constantly under construction and this means more impact, ideas, frequent existential crises and new stories like this.
Get to know our inventions for the future

Click

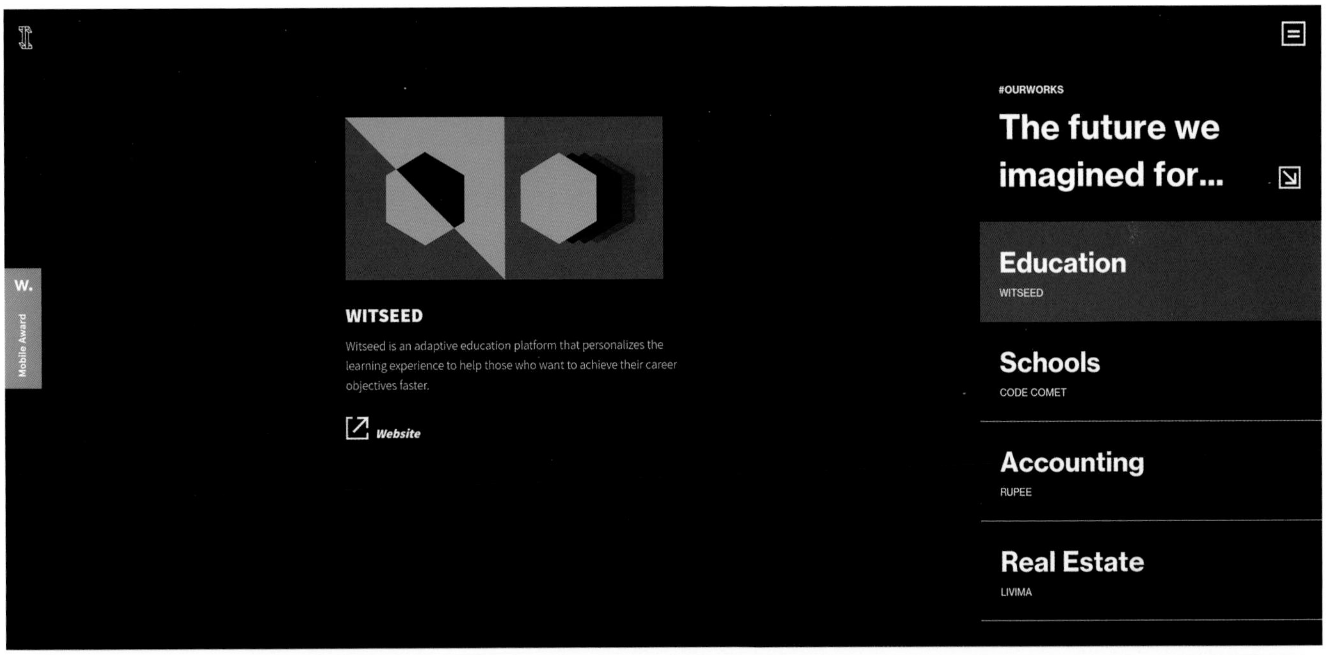
W.
Mobile Award
WITSEED
Witseed is an adaptive education platform that personalizes the learning experience to help those who want to achieve their career objectives faster.
Website
#OURWORKS
The future we imagined for...
Education
WITSEED
Schools
CODE COMET
Accounting
RUPEE
Real Estate
LIVIMA

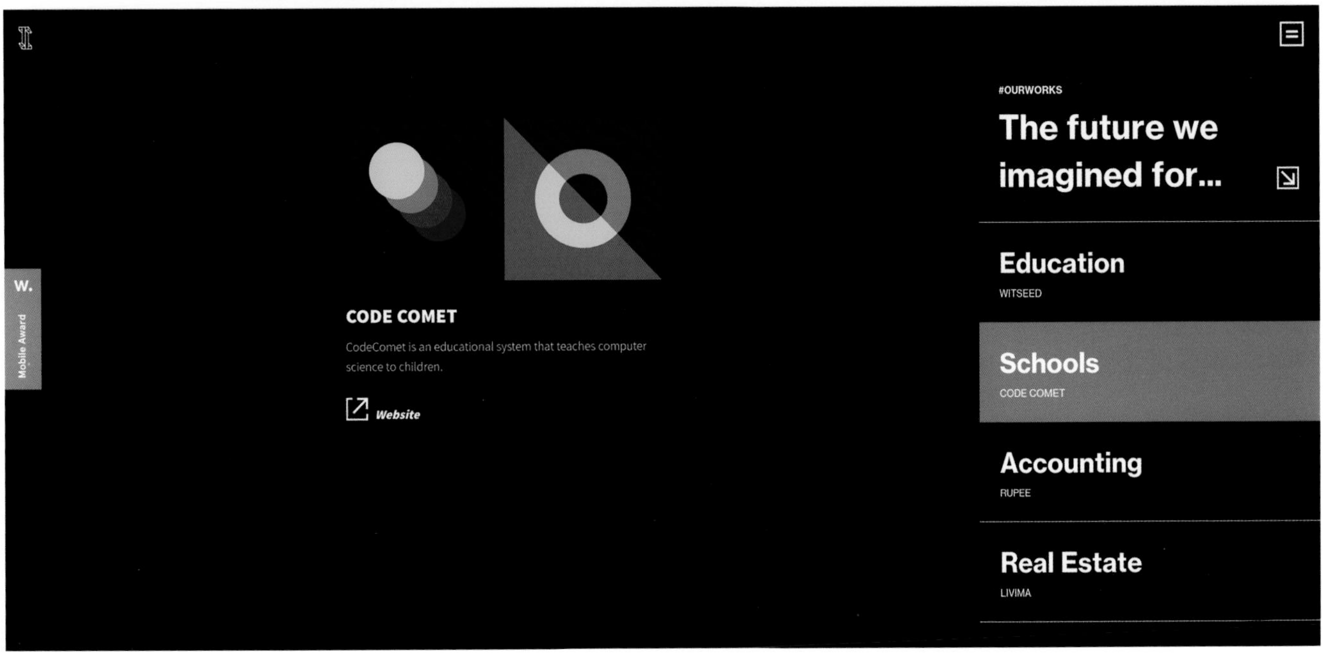
W.
Mobile Award
CODE COMET
CodeComet is an educational system that teaches computer science to children.
Website
#OURWORKS
The future we imagined for...
Education
WITSEED
Schools
CODE COMET
Accounting
RUPEE
Real Estate
LIVIMA

Liber Finance Group

Official Site

Design Agency
Griflan

Client
Liber Finance

URL
www.liberfinancegroup.com

Art Direction and Design
Ron Griffel, Ari Kaplan

Liber Finance Group is a leading financial technology company that operates multiple AI-driven marketplaces across Europe for consumer finance. They wanted to visually show how they help "solve problems" without using the typical stock photography approach. Griflan took a simplistic solution by using shapes and patterns moving together in an interactive way that is controlled by scrolling.

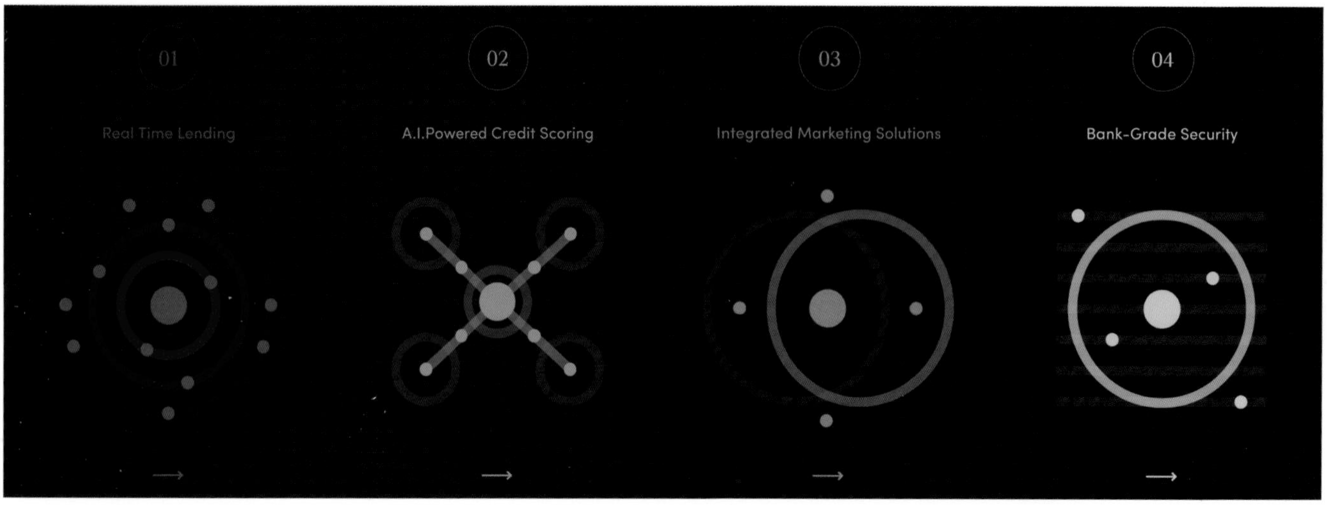

01
Real Time Lending
02
A.I.Powered Credit Scoring
03
Integrated Marketing Solutions
04
Bank-Grade Security

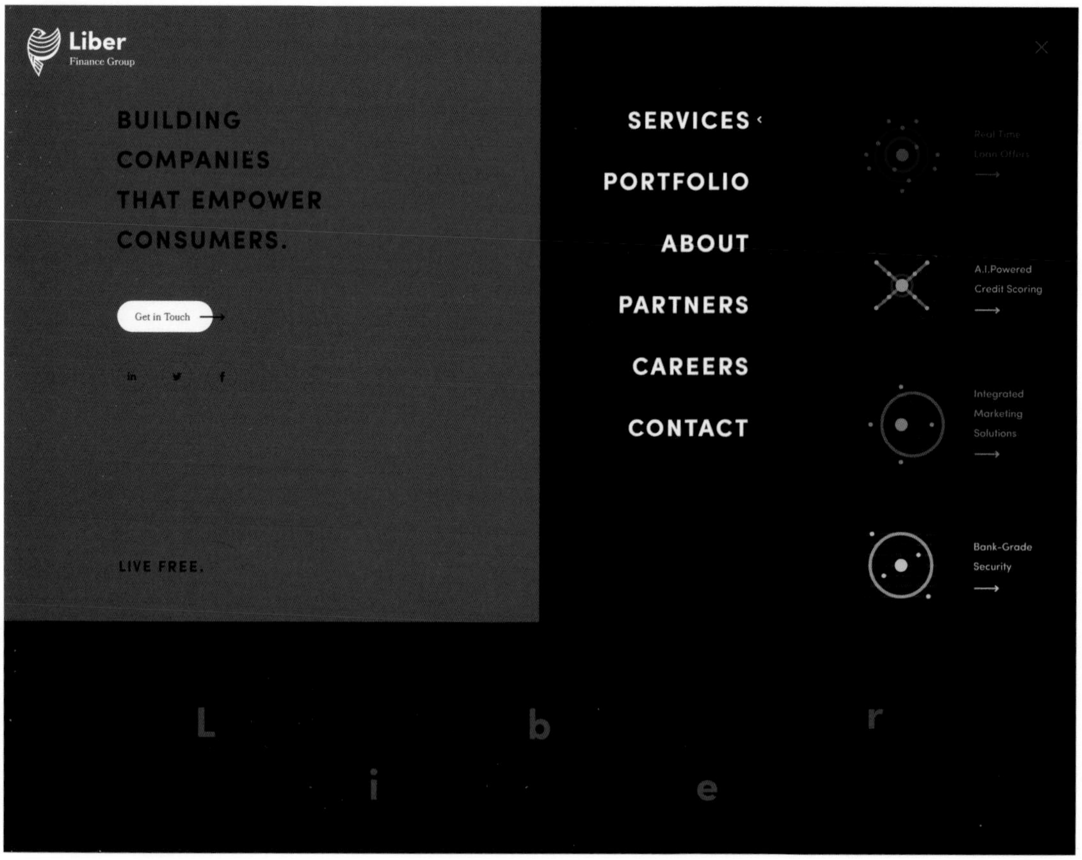

Liber
Finance Group
BUILDING COMPANIES THAT EMPOWER CONSUMERS.
Get in Touch
LIVE FREE.
SERVICES
PORTFOLIO
ABOUT
PARTNERS
CAREERS
CONTACT
A.I.Powered Credit Scoring
Integrated Marketing Solutions
Bank-Grade Security

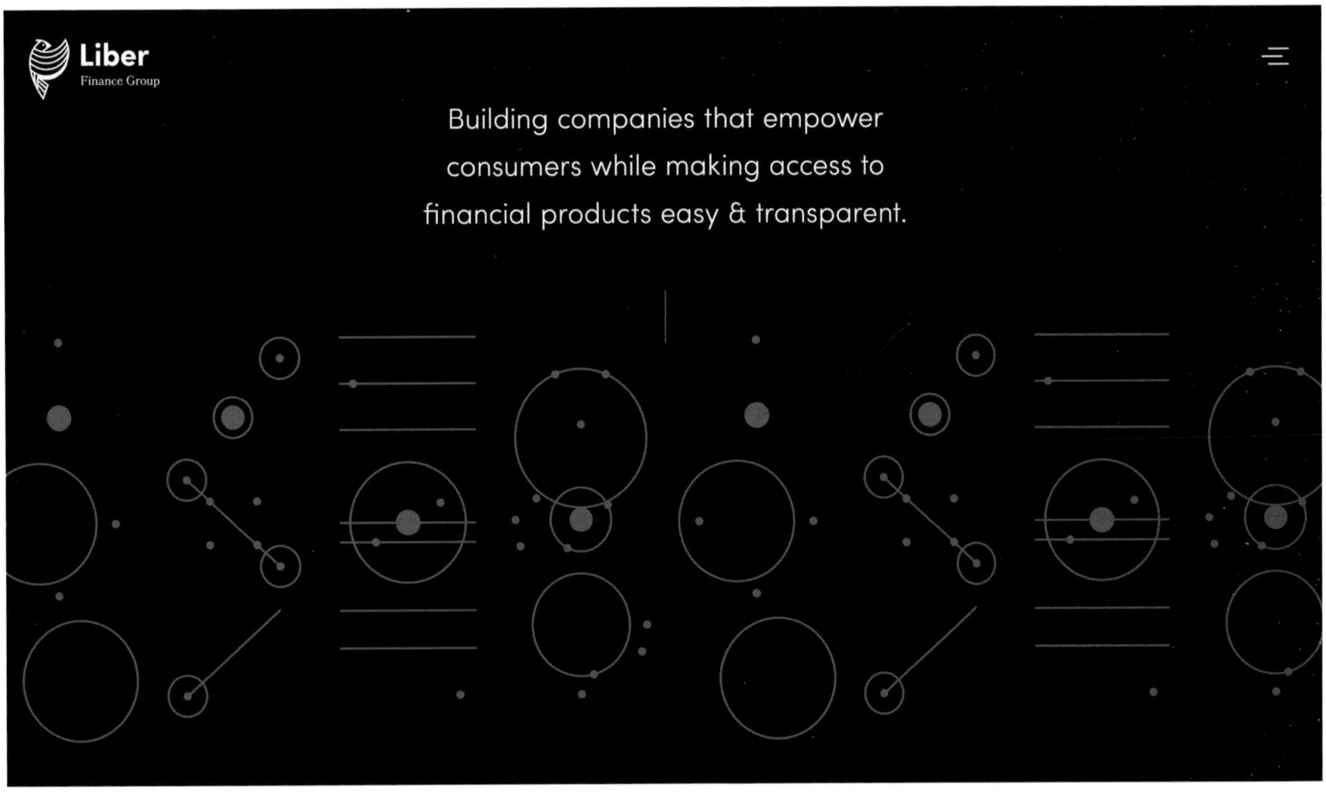
Liber
Finance Group
Building companies that empower consumers while making access to financial products easy & transparent.

LENDING HERO
Lending Hero is financial intermediary targeting a unique customer segment in order to make our overall service in Norway more helpful to people. Lorem Ipsum is simply dummy text of the printing and typesetting industry. Lorem Ipsum has been the industry's standard dummy text ever since the 1500s.
Lendinghero.no
LOANS FROM 6.99%
Consumer
refinancing
Preferred loan amount
150 000 KR
Repayment period
5 YEARS
Month Amount
3034 kr / month
Try our service
We are driven by creating experiences that deliver results for your business and for your consumers while getting money to people when they need it – quickly, conveniently and responsibly.

Digital Asset

Official Site

Art Direction and Design
Julien Renvoye

Development
Aristide Benoist

Illustration
Arek Kajda

URL
www.digitalasset.com

Digital Asset is a leading provider of Distributed Ledger Technology to regulated financial institutions. Designer Julien Renvoye teamed up with Digital Asset to create a branding that reflects Digital Asset's strategic positioning and product offerings in the Blockchain industry. His primary challenge was to explain a new and unconventional technology in a way that was universally understandable around a beautiful visual language.

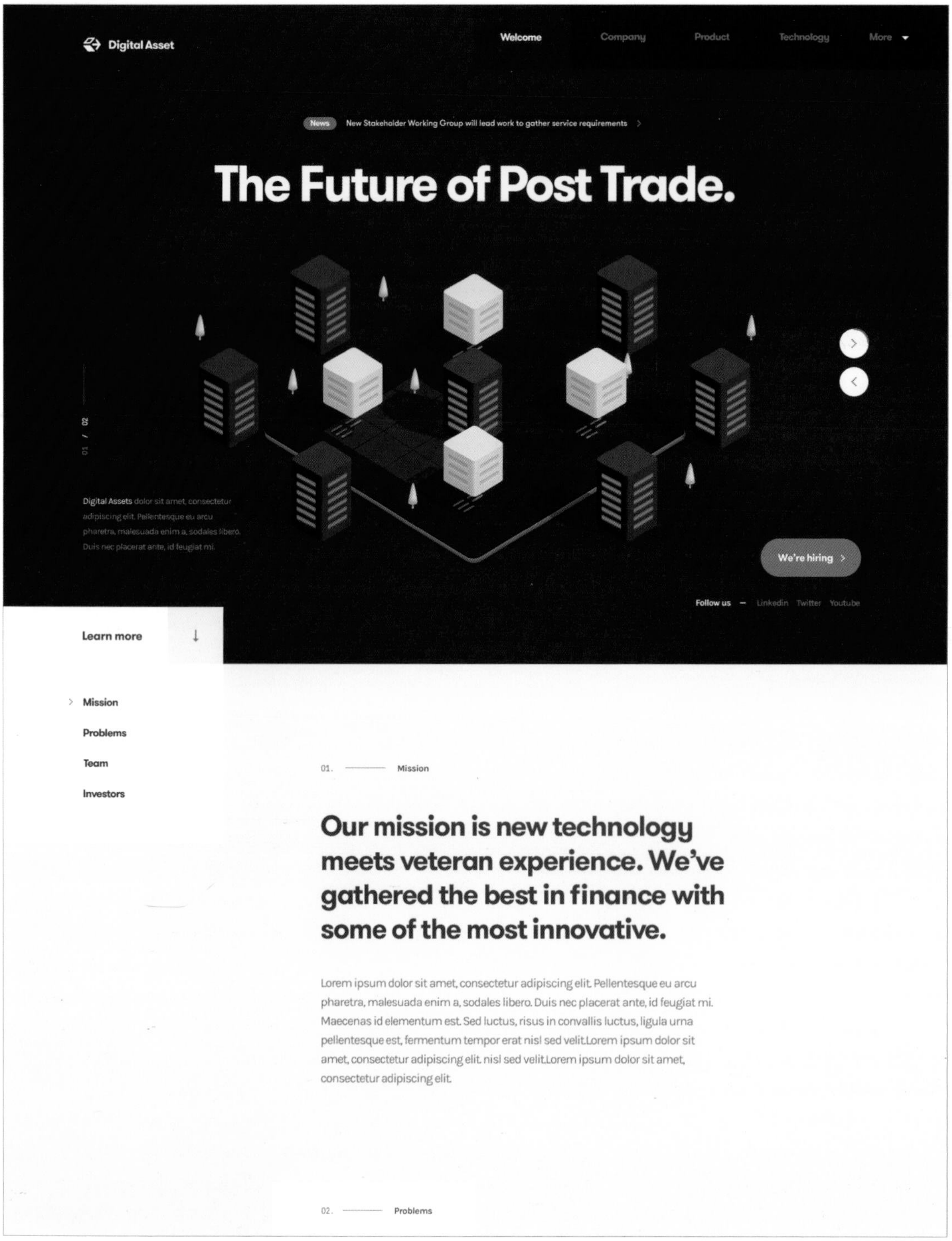

Digital Asset
Welcome
Company
Product
Technology
More
News
New Stakeholder Working Group will lead work to gather service requirements
The Future of Post Trade.
01 / 02
Digital Assets dolor sit amet, consectetur adipiscing elit. Pellentesque eu arcu pharetra, malesuada enim a, sodales libero. Duis nec placerat ante, id feugiat mi.
We're hiring
Follow us — Linkedin Twitter Youtube
Learn more
Mission
Problems
Team
Investors
01. Mission
Our mission is new technology meets veteran experience. We've gathered the best in finance with some of the most innovative.
Lorem ipsum dolor sit amet, consectetur adipiscing elit. Pellentesque eu arcu pharetra, malesuada enim a, sodales libero. Duis nec placerat ante, id feugiat mi. Maecenas id elementum est. Sed luctus, risus in convallis luctus, ligula urna pellentesque est, fermentum tempor erat nisl sed velit.Lorem ipsum dolor sit amet, consectetur adipiscing elit. nisl sed velit.Lorem ipsum dolor sit amet, consectetur adipiscing elit.
02. Problems

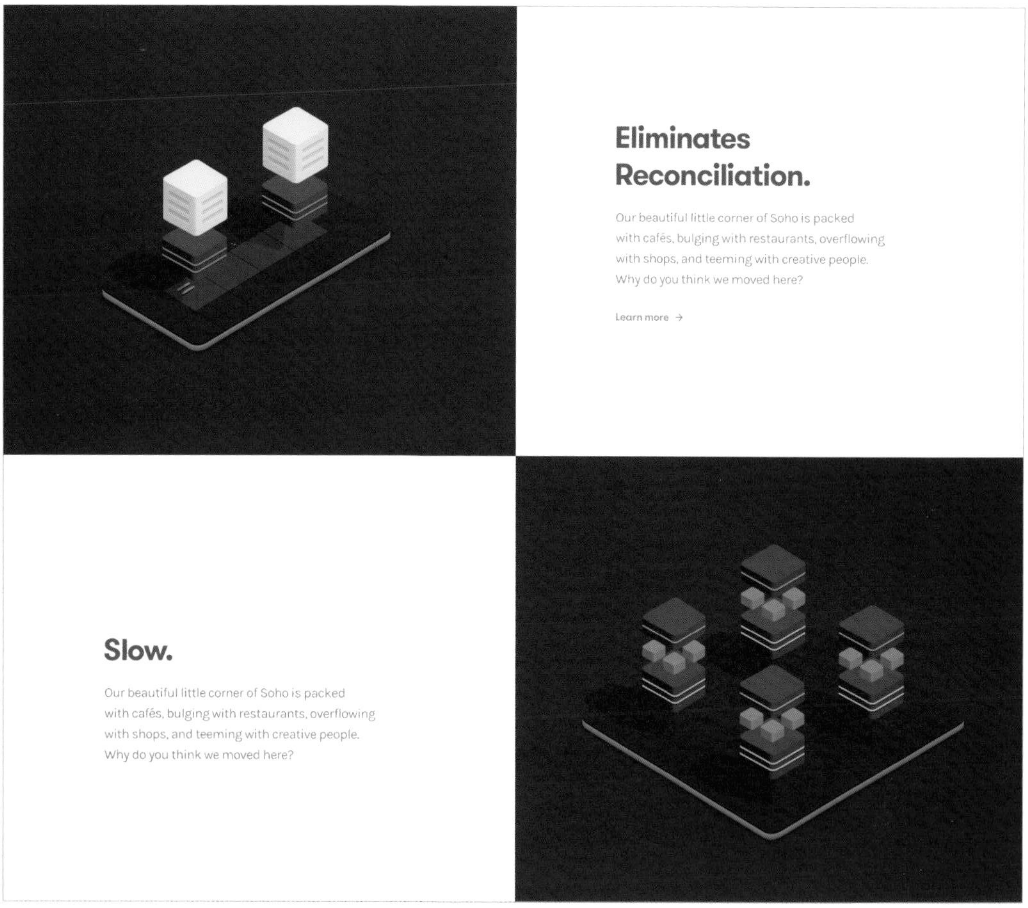
Eliminates Reconciliation.
Our beautiful little corner of Soho is packed with cafés, bulging with restaurants, overflowing with shops, and teeming with creative people. Why do you think we moved here?
Learn more →
Slow.
Our beautiful little corner of Soho is packed with cafés, bulging with restaurants, overflowing with shops, and teeming with creative people. Why do you think we moved here?

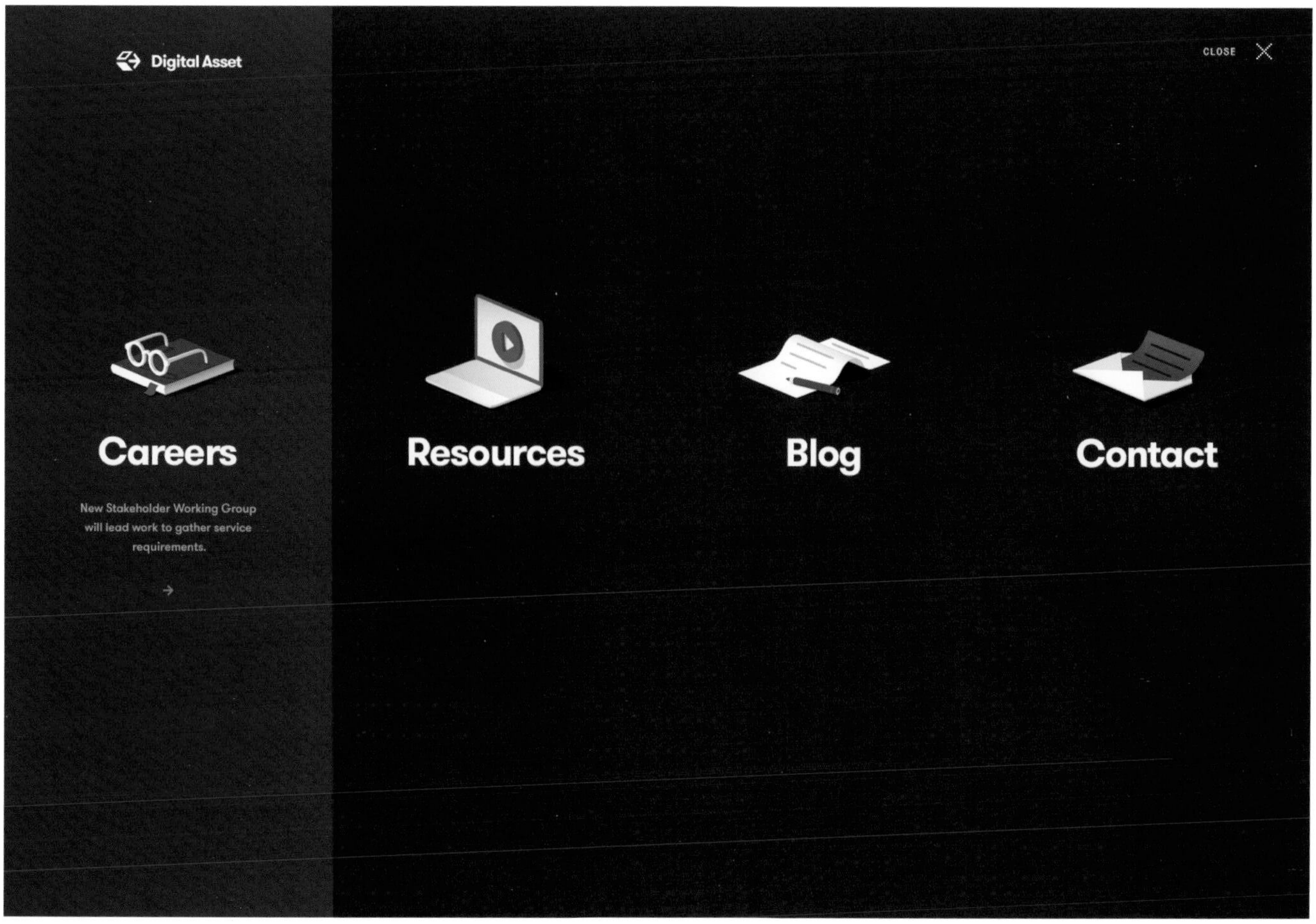
Digital Asset
CLOSE
Careers
New Stakeholder Working Group will lead work to gather service requirements.
Resources
Blog
Contact

Chemo Marine Chemicals

Official Site

Design Agency
Kommigraphics

URL
www.chemomarine.com

Chemo Marine Chemicals manufactures and distributes high-quality chemicals to shipping and chartering companies worldwide. Modern production, as well as respect for its customers' needs and the environment, makes Chemo an important player in the global shipping market.

The redefinition of the company's image, as well as an easy to find presentation of its products, were the main goals for the design of the company's new website. Although the content was placed on a rigid canvas, the design makes reading flawless and easy to follow by visitors. By selecting specific design elements, the website uses typography and colours that follow the company's new visual identity and create a timeless result.

CHEMO
MARINE CHEMICALS
CHEMO EXCELLENCE
Our company's synonymous is quality
EXPLORE
Products categories:
TANK CLEANING
HOLD CLEANING
CHEMICALS
EQUIPMENT & TEST KITS
CRUISE
OFFSHORE
EN
01
Delivery Ports

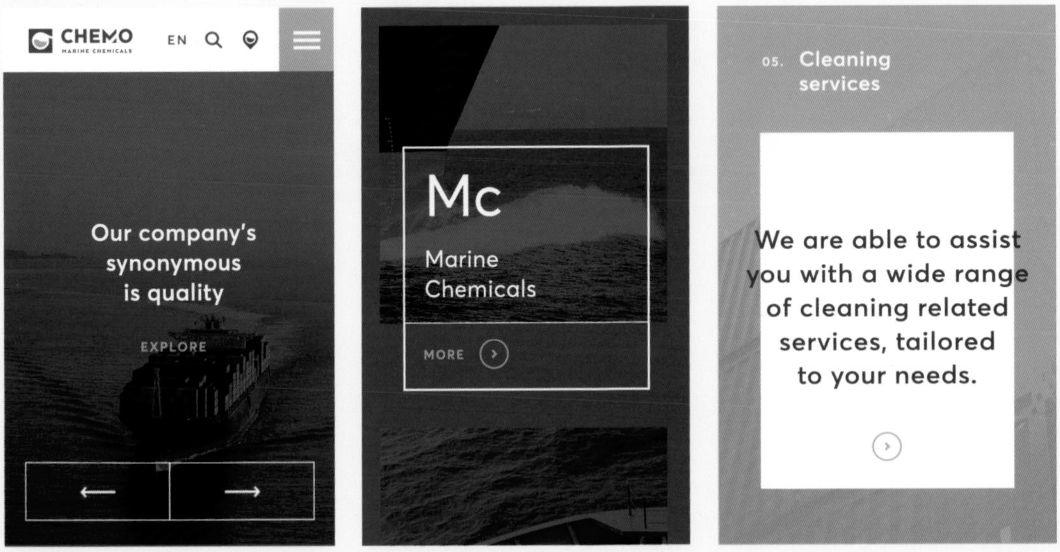
CHEMO
EN
Our company's synonymous is quality
EXPLORE
Mc
Marine Chemicals
MORE
05. Cleaning services
We are able to assist you with a wide range of cleaning related services, tailored to your needs.

We supply a wide range of marine chemicals

CHEMO is a specialist chemical producer and supplier of marine chemicals and tank cleaning services for the Marine Industry.

01

Tank Cleaning

02

Hold Cleaning

03

Chemicals

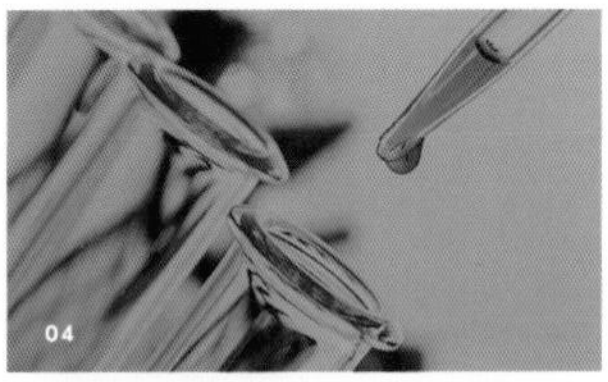
04

Equipment & Test Kits

05

Cruise

06

Offshore

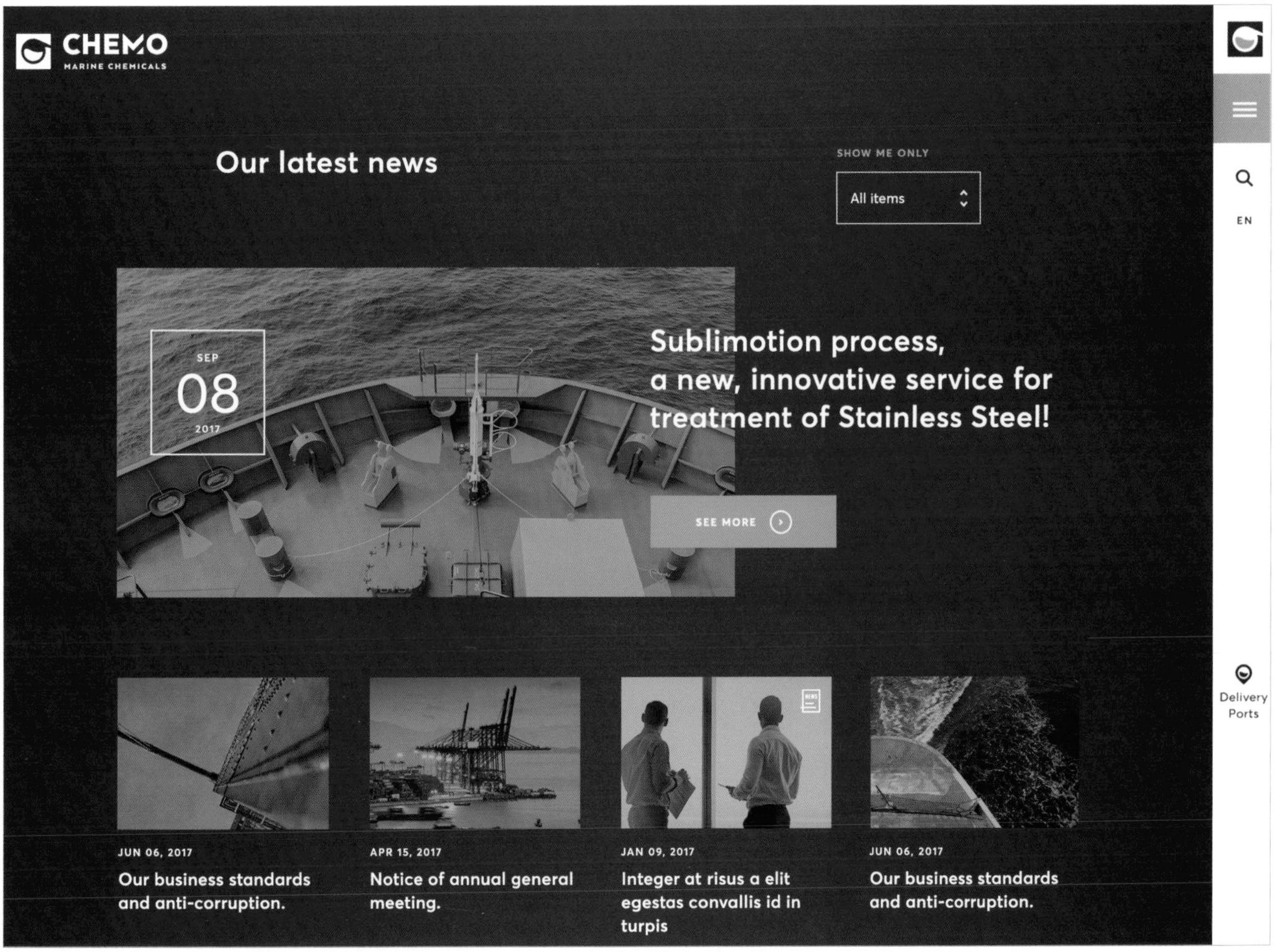
CHEMO
MARINE CHEMICALS
Our latest news
SHOW ME ONLY
All items
EN
SEP
08
2017
Sublimotion process, a new, innovative service for treatment of Stainless Steel!
SEE MORE
Delivery Ports
JUN 06, 2017
Our business standards and anti-corruption.
APR 15, 2017
Notice of annual general meeting.
JAN 09, 2017
Integer at risus a elit egestas convallis id in turpis
JUN 06, 2017
Our business standards and anti-corruption.

Yerba Buena Center for the Arts

Official Site

Design and Development
Bureau for Visual Affairs

URL
www.ybca.org

Yerba Buena Center for the Arts (YBCA) is an arts institution in San Francisco. Bureau for Visual Affairs was commissioned to redesign and develop the website, translating the organisation's social mission and curatorial energy into a powerful, visual and engaging experience. The website was intended to embed the new brand identity whilst improving the user experience around events and booking user journeys in particular.

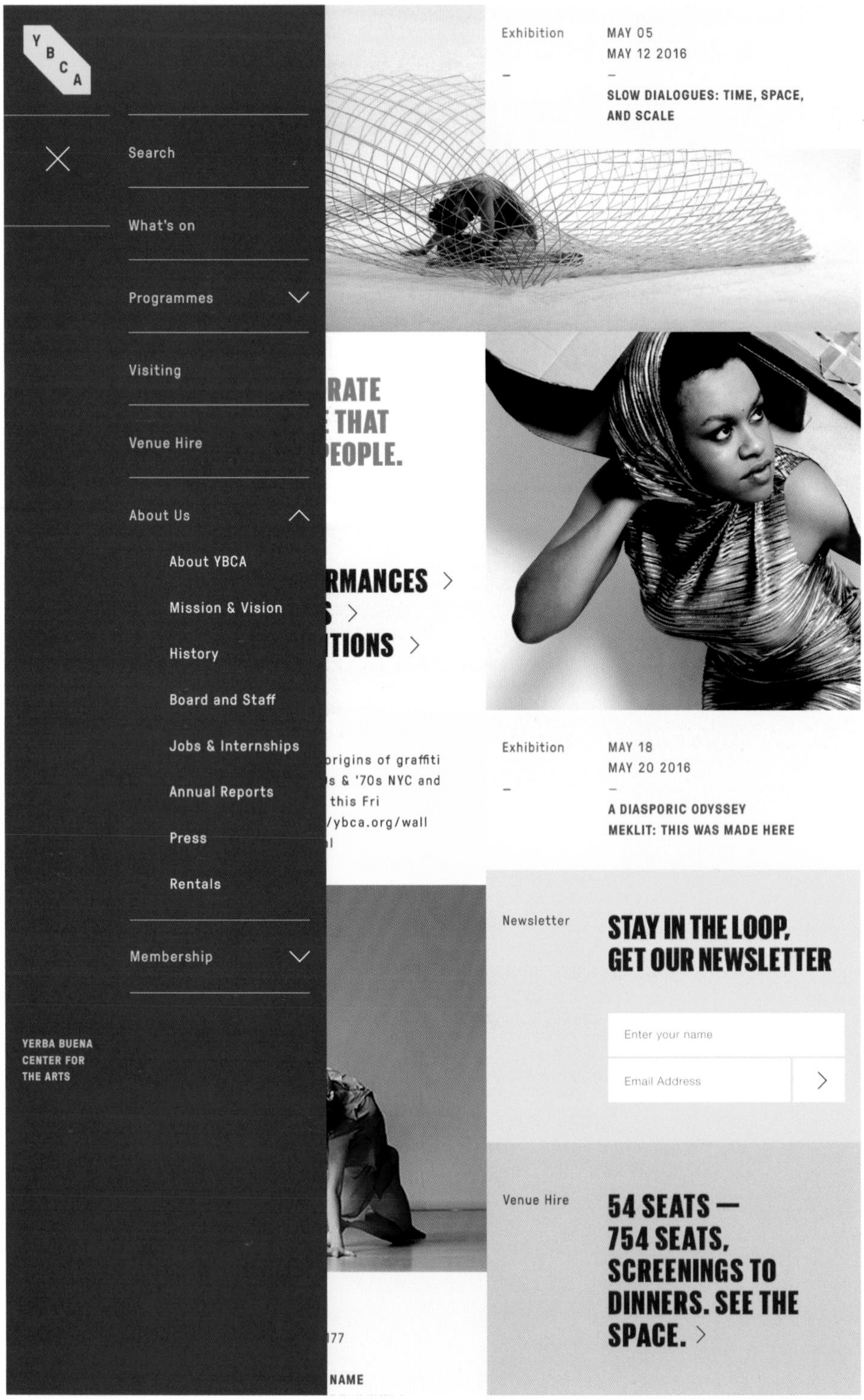

YBCA
Search
What's on
Programmes
Visiting
Venue Hire
About Us
About YBCA
Mission & Vision
History
Board and Staff
Jobs & Internships
Annual Reports
Press
Rentals
Membership
YERBA BUENA CENTER FOR THE ARTS
Exhibition
MAY 05
MAY 12 2016
SLOW DIALOGUES: TIME, SPACE, AND SCALE
Exhibition
MAY 18
MAY 20 2016
A DIASPORIC ODYSSEY
MEKLIT: THIS WAS MADE HERE
Newsletter
STAY IN THE LOOP, GET OUR NEWSLETTER
Enter your name
Email Address
Venue Hire
54 SEATS — 754 SEATS, SCREENINGS TO DINNERS. SEE THE SPACE.

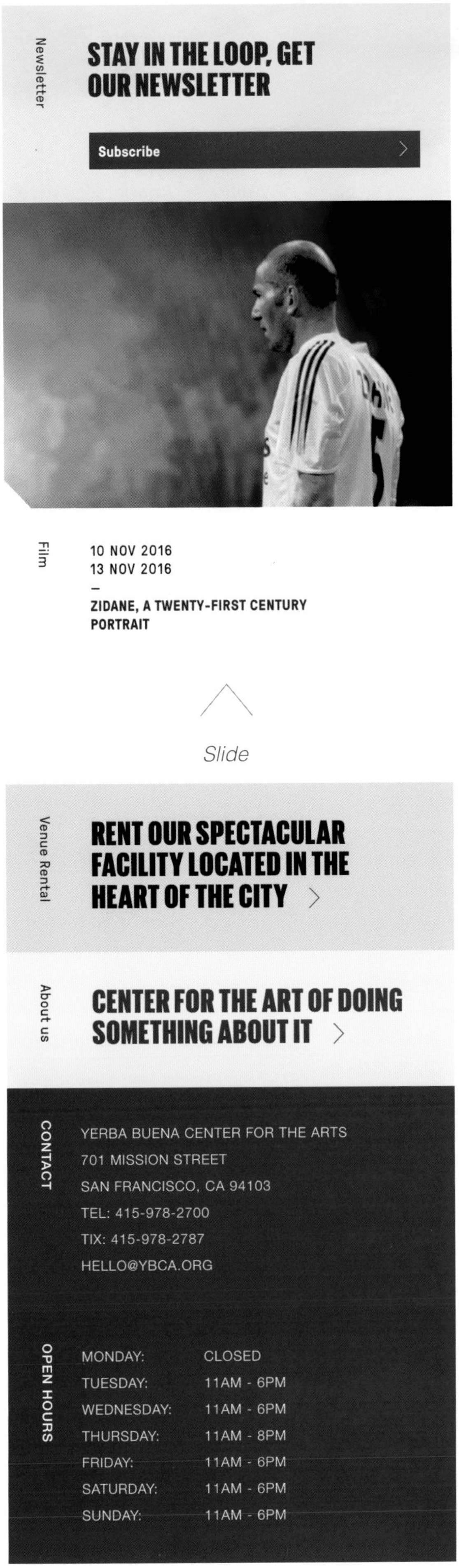

Newsletter
STAY IN THE LOOP, GET OUR NEWSLETTER
Subscribe
Film
10 NOV 2016
13 NOV 2016
–
ZIDANE, A TWENTY-FIRST CENTURY PORTRAIT
Slide
Venue Rental
RENT OUR SPECTACULAR FACILITY LOCATED IN THE HEART OF THE CITY
About us
CENTER FOR THE ART OF DOING SOMETHING ABOUT IT
CONTACT
YERBA BUENA CENTER FOR THE ARTS
701 MISSION STREET
SAN FRANCISCO, CA 94103
TEL: 415-978-2700
TIX: 415-978-2787
HELLO@YBCA.ORG
OPEN HOURS
MONDAY: CLOSED
TUESDAY: 11AM - 6PM
WEDNESDAY: 11AM - 6PM
THURSDAY: 11AM - 8PM
FRIDAY: 11AM - 6PM
SATURDAY: 11AM - 6PM
SUNDAY: 11AM - 6PM

Y B C A
Search
Menu
Exhibition
18 SEP 2016
15 JAN 2017
–
SPACE PROGRAM: EUROPA
TOM SACHS
Our Mission
WE GENERATE CULTURE THAT MOVES PEOPLE
What's on
62 FILMS
41 PERFORMANCES
10 EXHIBITIONS
Tweet
Apropos of this week's screenings of Dying of the Light on the last generation of career projectionists.
On Sale Now
THE LESLIE AND MERLE RABINE 2016-2017 PERFORMANCE SEASON
Season Schedule

Functionality requirements were abstracted through a modular system of components—the onus was on flexibility and usability rather than mere self-representation. This modularity allowed YBCA to configure layouts and user journeys according to any editorial requirements.

Pedal

Design
Jordan Richards

Behance

Pedal is a fictional company the designer created and is a community of bikers with the unique combination of protecting the environment and pursuing a healthier lifestyle. Pedal achieves this by tracking an individual's carbon footprint and activity. It is about choosing bikes as the primary source of transportation. A built-in sticker achievement component incentivizes users to remain consistent.

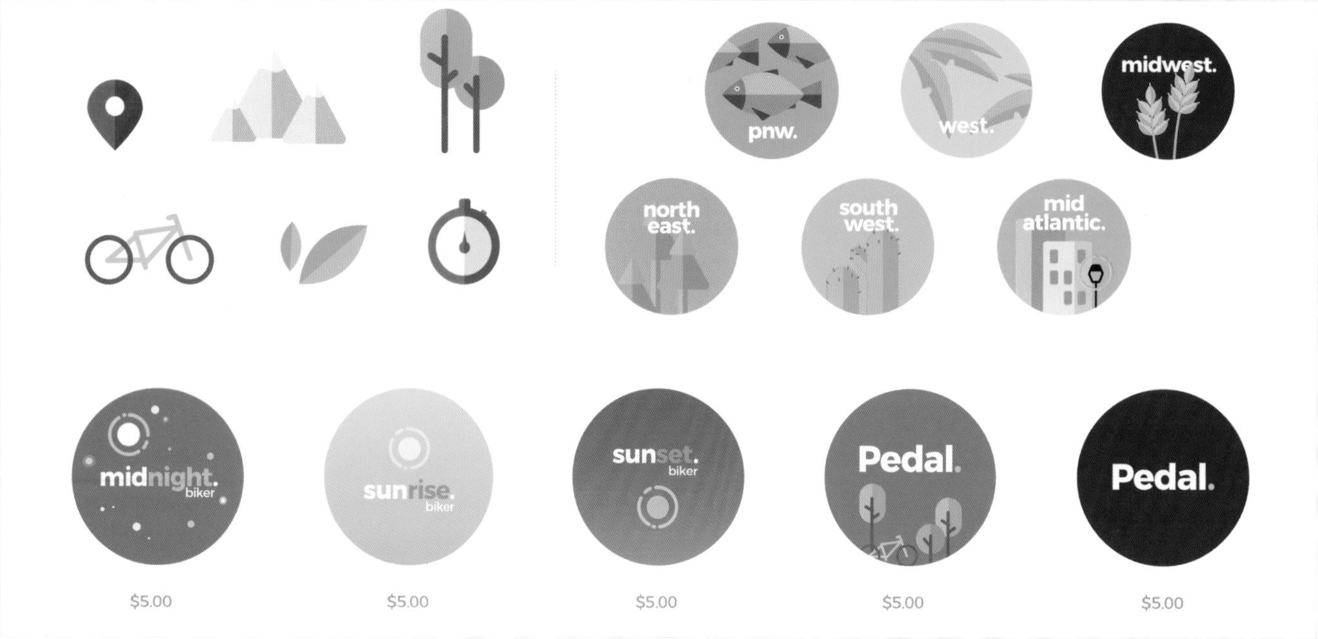
pnw.
west.
midwest.
north east.
south west.
mid atlantic.
midnight. biker
sunrise. biker
sunset. biker
Pedal.
Pedal.
$5.00
$5.00
$5.00
$5.00
$5.00

activity
footprint
about
Pedal.
teams
lifestyle
stickers
lifestyle.
smoothie
of the week
trail
of the week
snack
of the week
MacBook

The design solution for Pedal was to display everything in a flat, vector style to give users a new and unique feel to the biking atmosphere. The designer chose bright and bold colours to help with this inviting and exciting narrative.

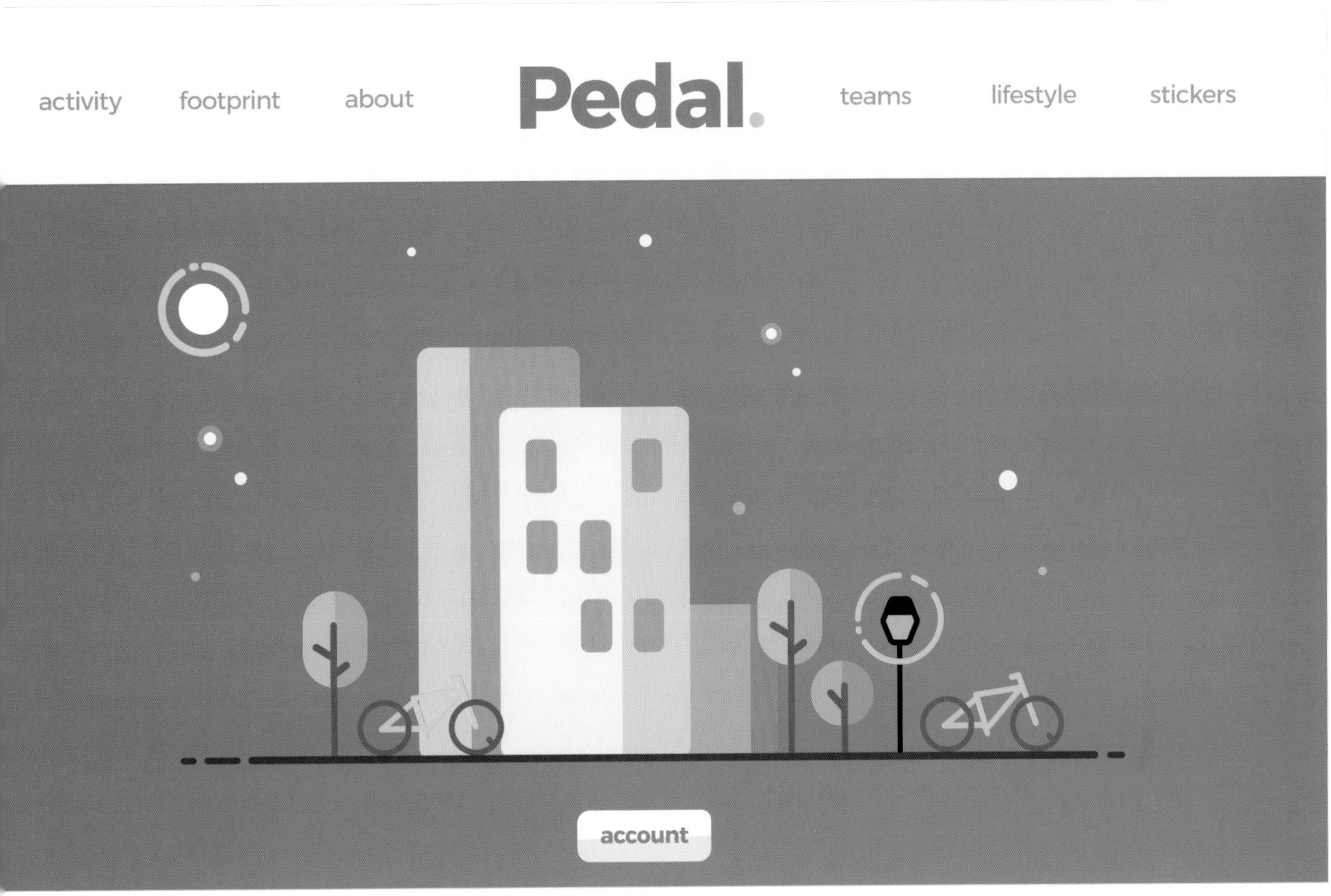
activity
footprint
about
Pedal.
teams
lifestyle
stickers
account

Click

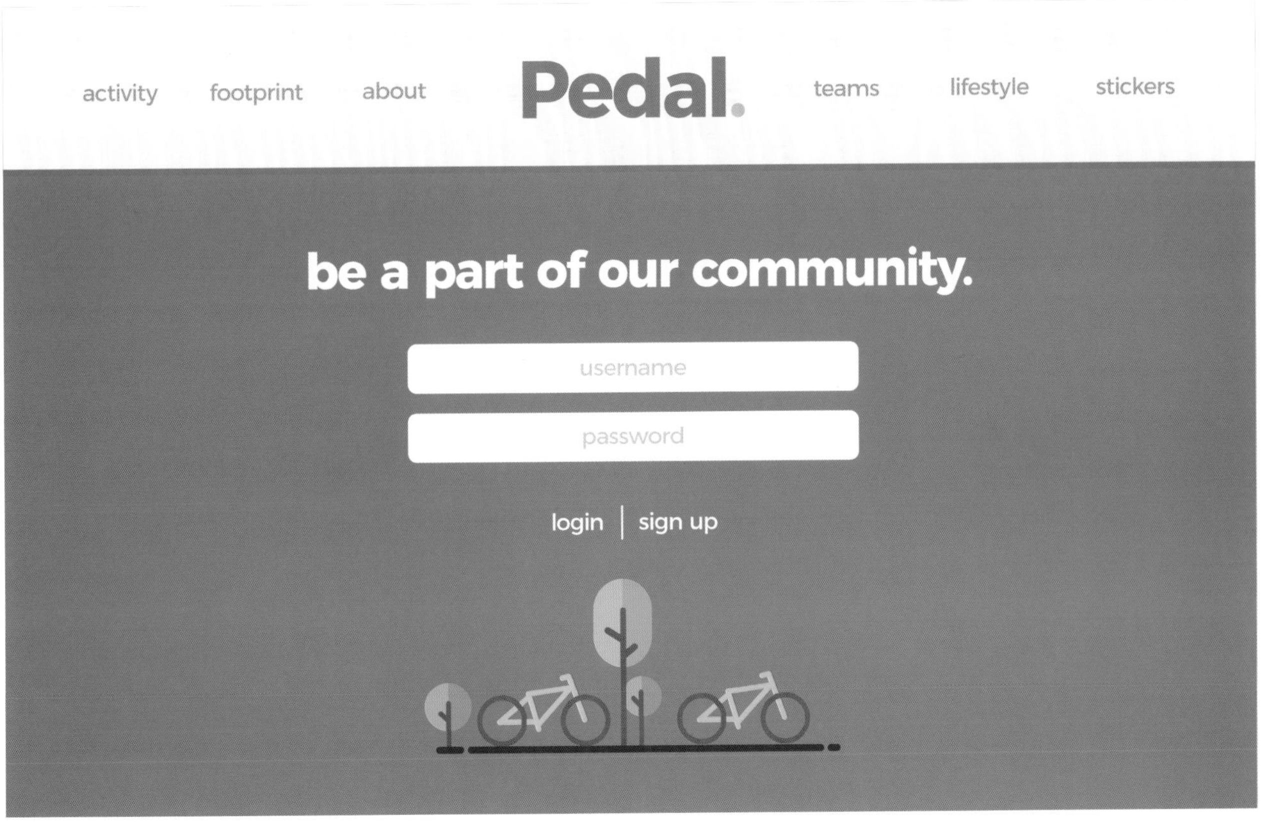
activity
footprint
about
Pedal.
teams
lifestyle
stickers
be a part of our community.
username
password
login | sign up

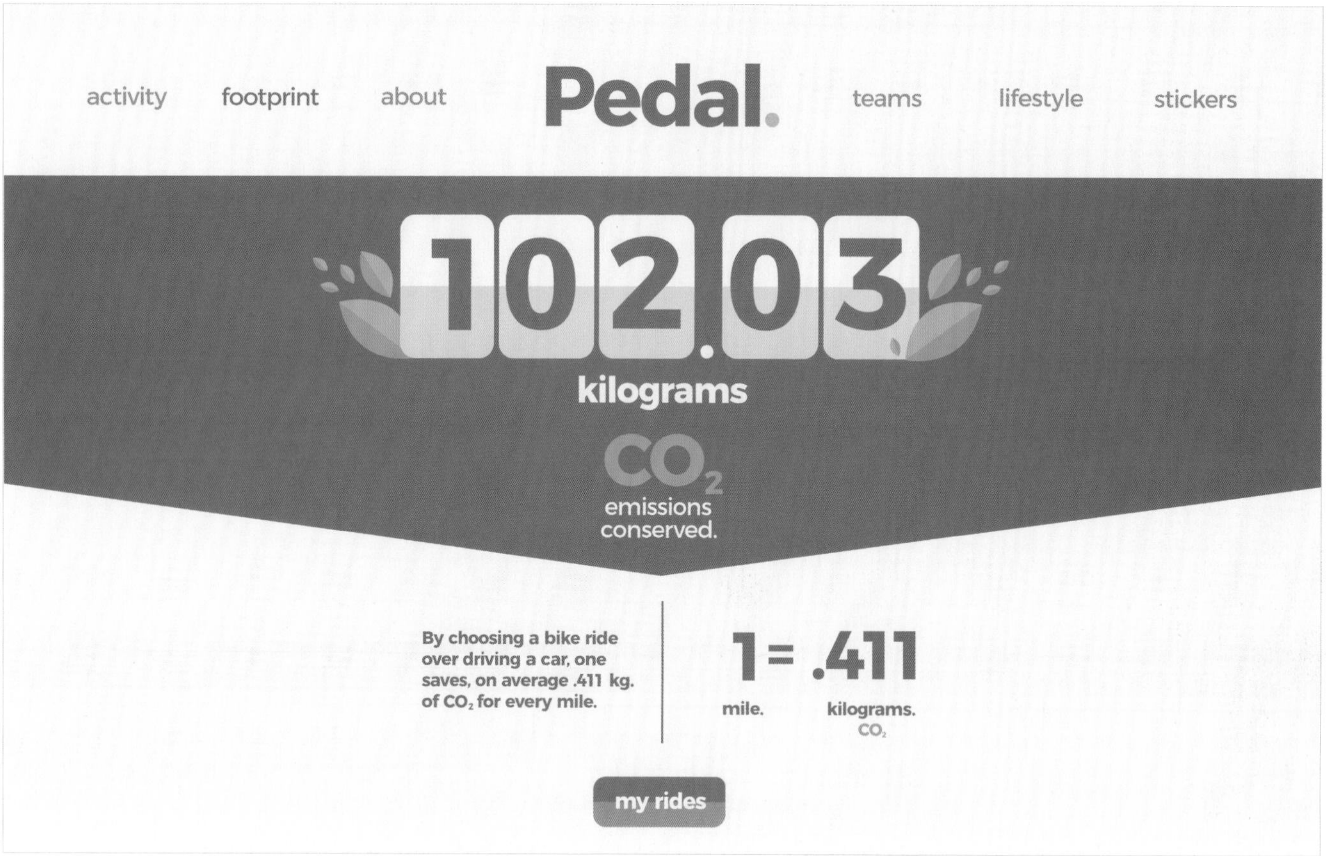
activity
footprint
about
Pedal.
teams
lifestyle
stickers
102.03
kilograms
CO_2
emissions conserved.
By choosing a bike ride over driving a car, one saves, on average .411 kg. of CO_2 for every mile.
1 = .411
mile.
kilograms.
CO_2
my rides

Click

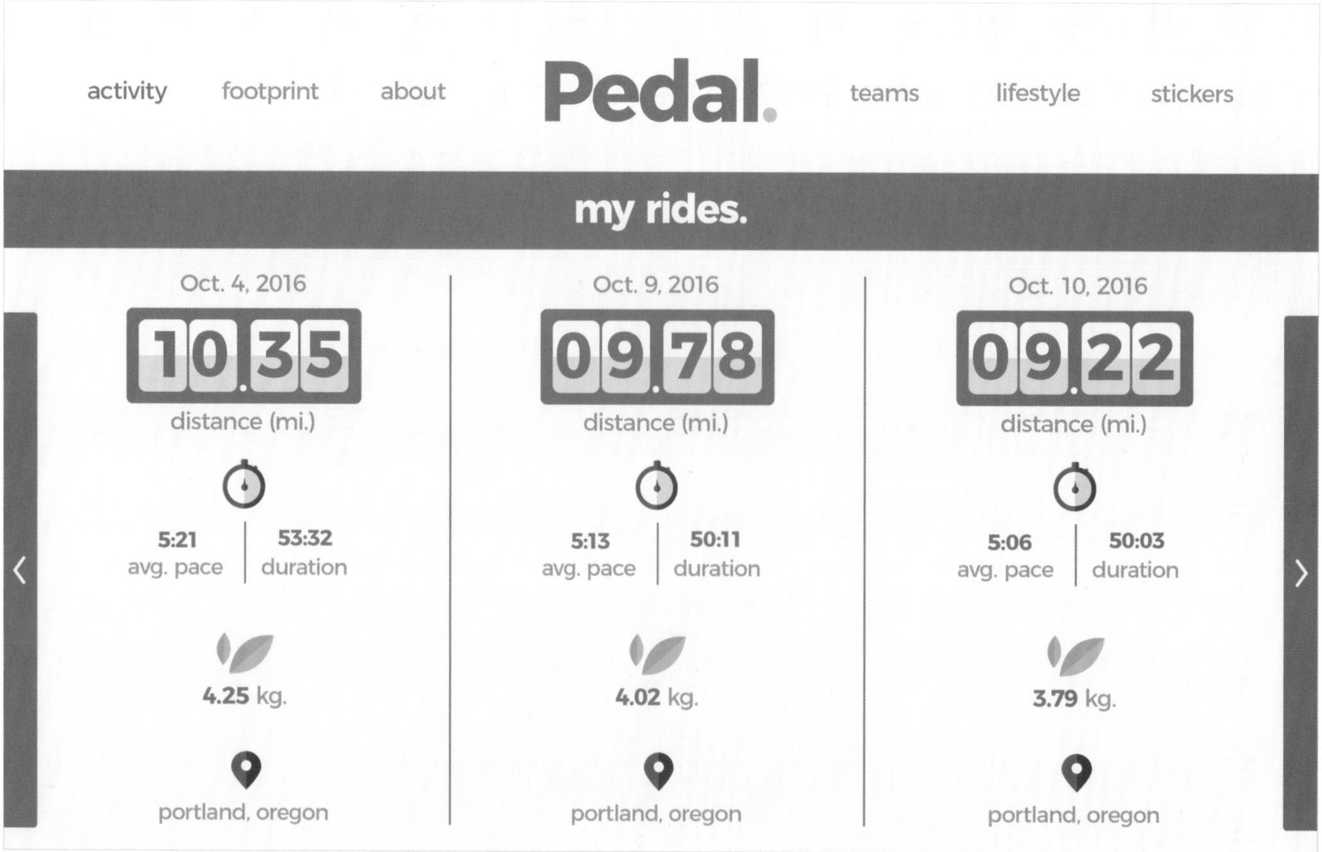
activity
footprint
about
Pedal.
teams
lifestyle
stickers
my rides.
Oct. 4, 2016
10.35
distance (mi.)
5:21
avg. pace
53:32
duration
4.25 kg.
portland, oregon
Oct. 9, 2016
09.78
distance (mi.)
5:13
avg. pace
50:11
duration
4.02 kg.
portland, oregon
Oct. 10, 2016
09.22
distance (mi.)
5:06
avg. pace
50:03
duration
3.79 kg.
portland, oregon

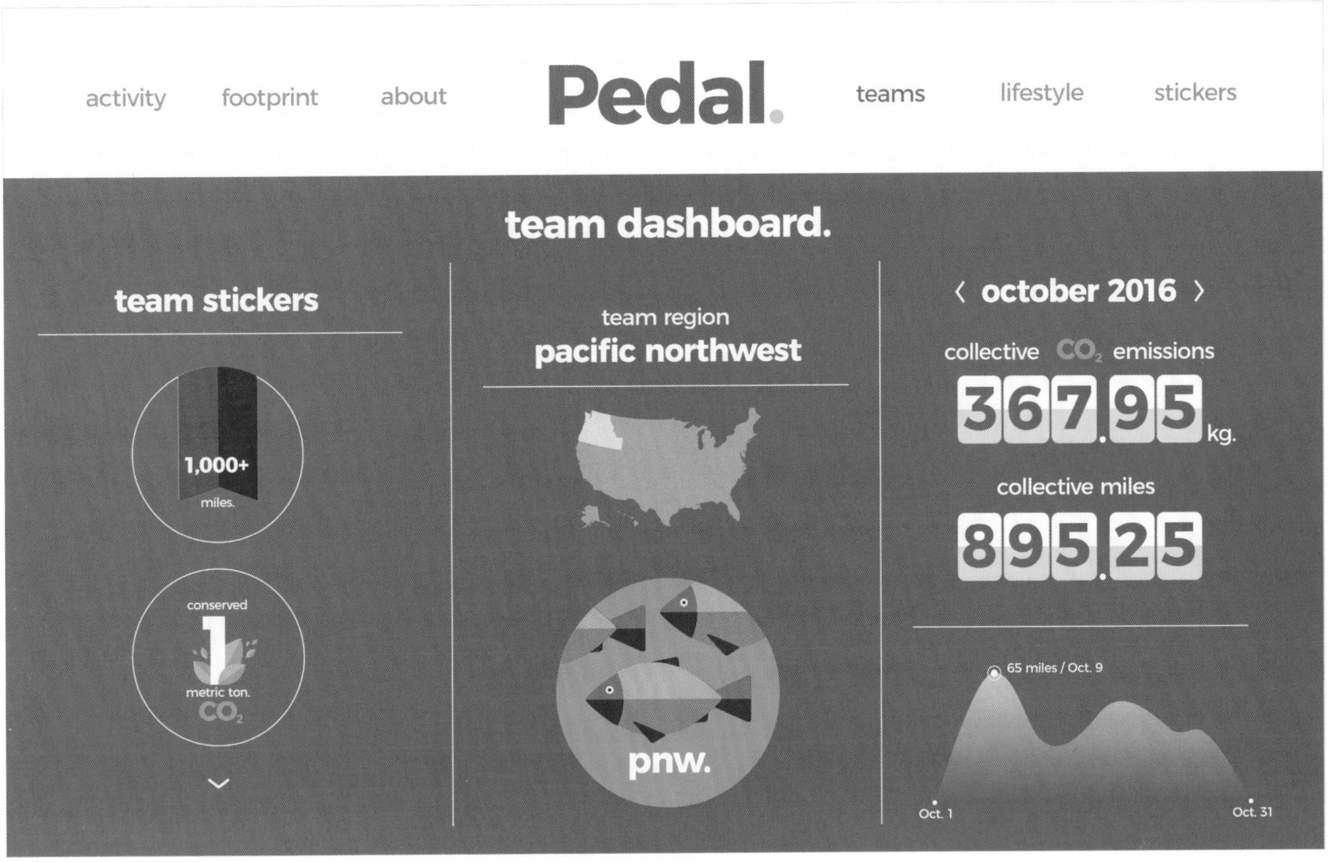
activity
footprint
about
Pedal.
teams
lifestyle
stickers
team dashboard.
team stickers
1,000+
miles.
conserved
1
metric ton.
CO_2
team region
pacific northwest
pnw.
‹ october 2016 ›
collective CO_2 emissions
367.95 kg.
collective miles
895.25
65 miles / Oct. 9
Oct. 1
Oct. 31

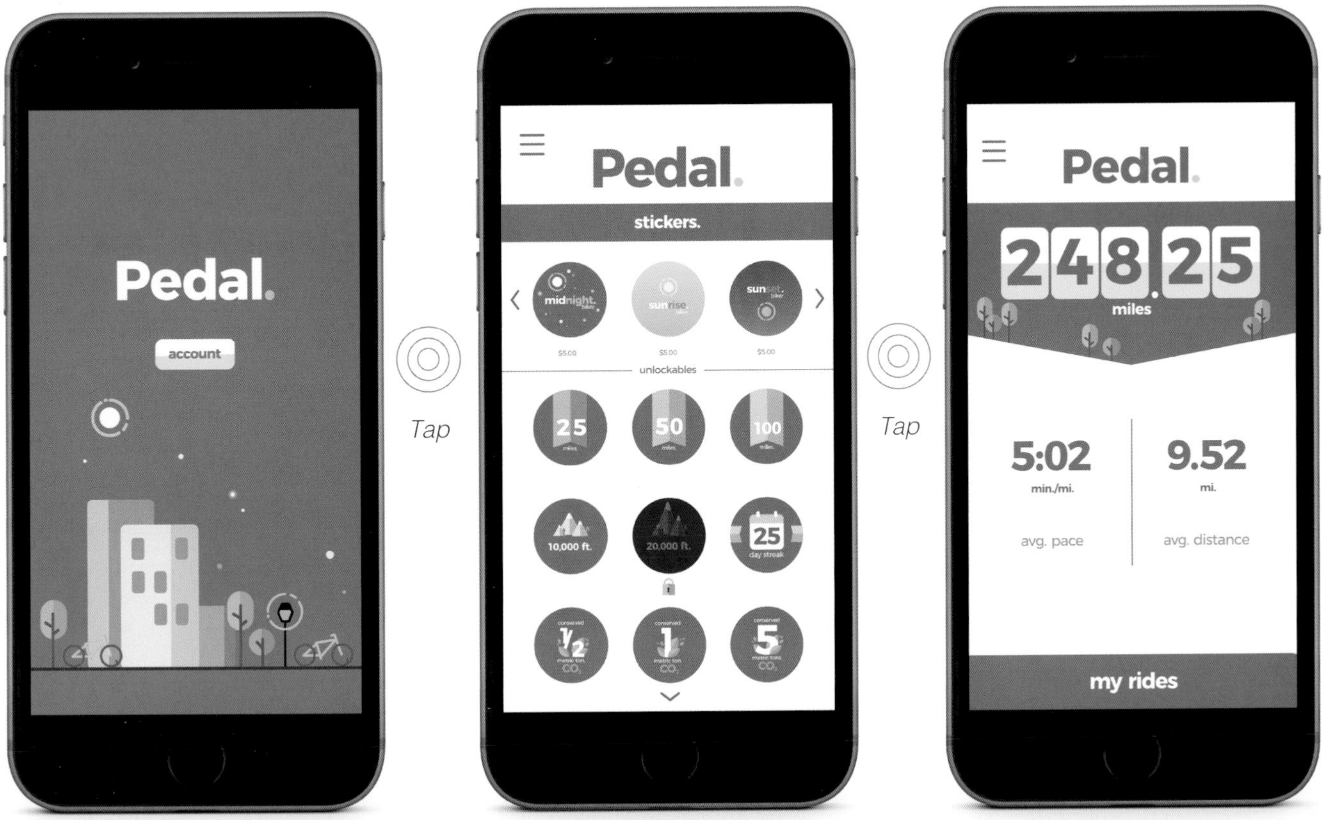
Pedal.
account
Tap
Pedal.
stickers.
midnight
sunrise
sunset
unlockables
25
50
100
10,000 ft.
20,000 ft.
25
day streak
Tap
Pedal.
248.25
miles
5:02
min./mi.
avg. pace
9.52
mi.
avg. distance
my rides

Clarity Movement

Design and Development
Oui Will

URL
clarity.io

Official Site

By integrating Internet of Things hardware with machine learning algorithms and cloud-based data analytics, Clarity delivers truly actionable air quality data aimed at transforming how cities understand and tackle air pollution. Oui Will teamed up with Clarity to turn a complex value proposition into a compelling brand story that is easy to digest.

Clarity is focused on innovating technology to create cleaner air. These core themes inspired the design of the site which pairs a clean, airy yet technical art direction with forward-thinking web technology.

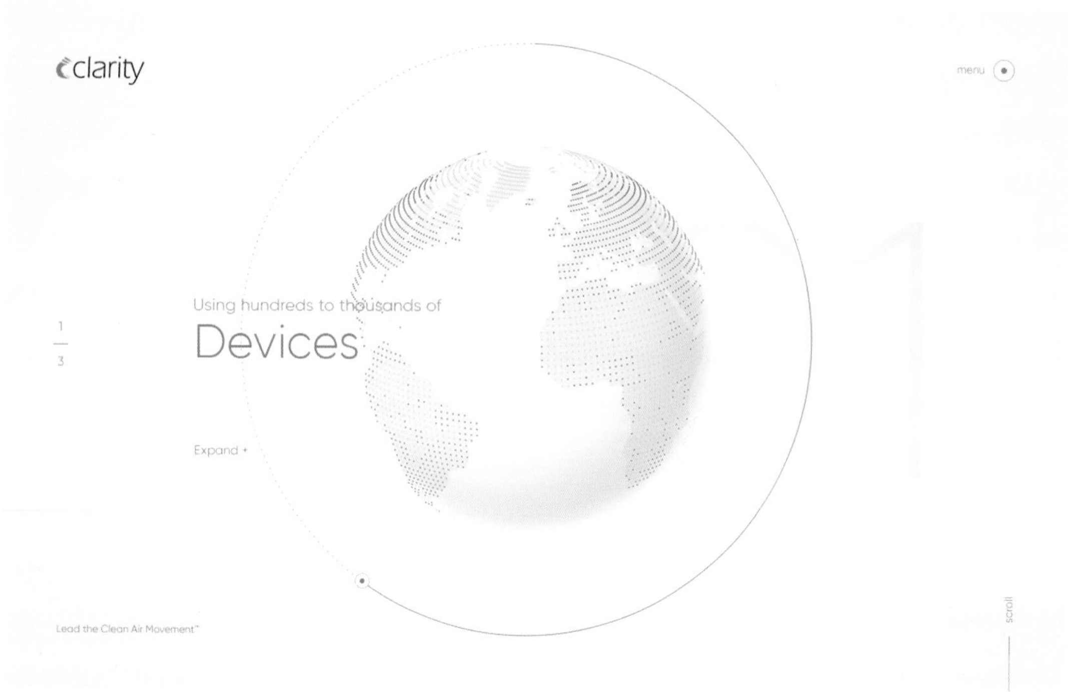
clarity
menu
Using hundreds to thousands of
Devices
1
3
Expand +
Lead the Clean Air Movement™
scroll

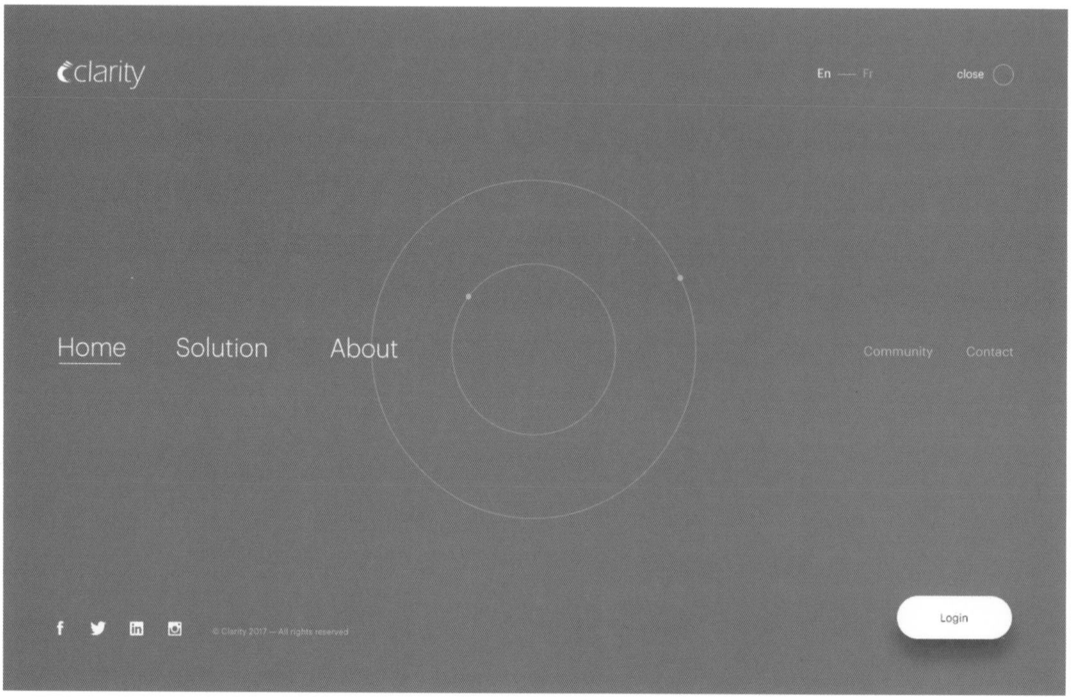
clarity
En — Fr
close
Home
Solution
About
Community
Contact
Login

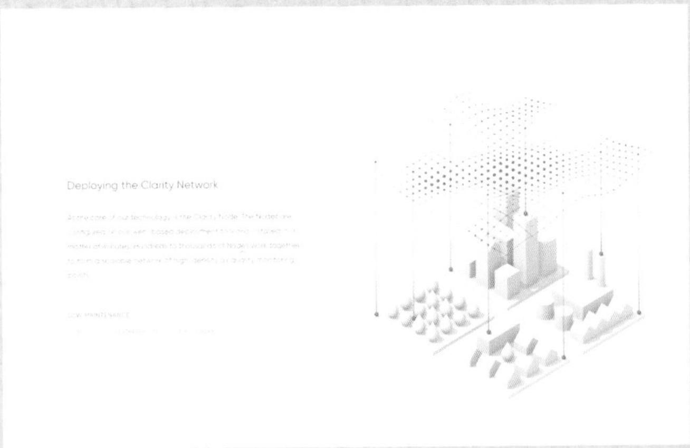
Deploying the Clarity Network

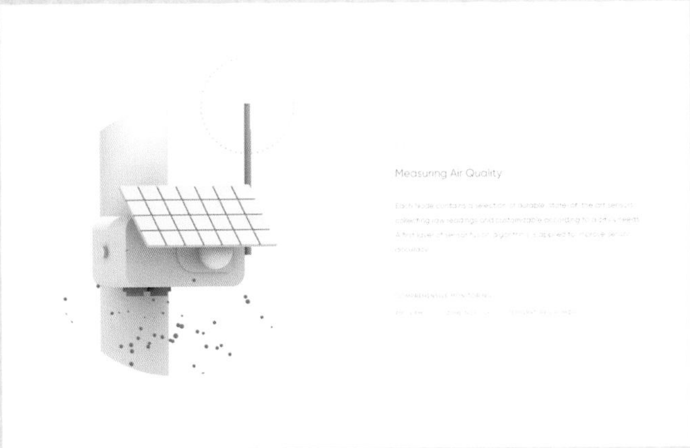
Measuring Air Quality

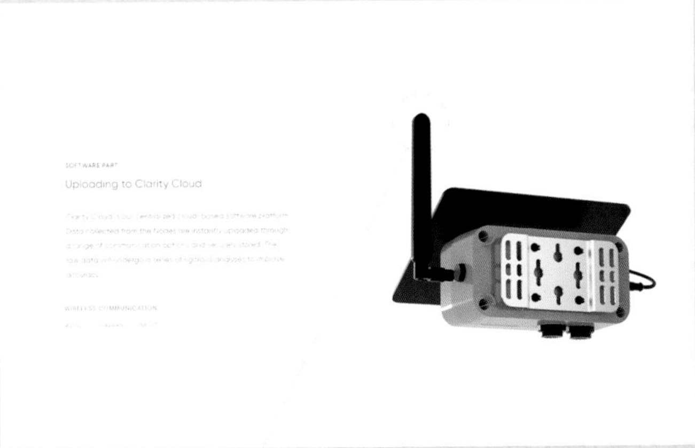
SOFTWARE PART
Uploading to Clarity Cloud

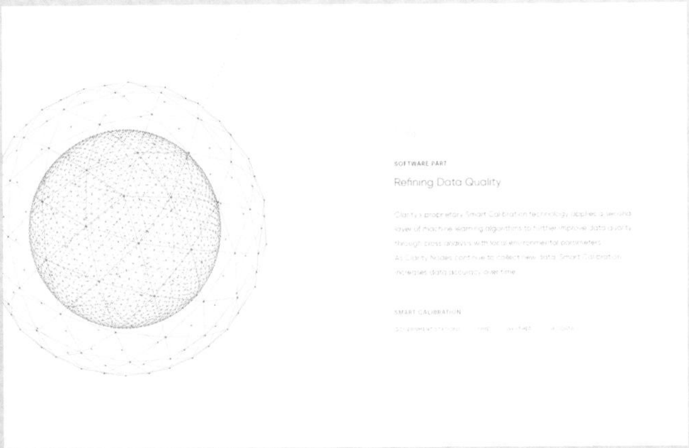
SOFTWARE PART
Refining Data Quality

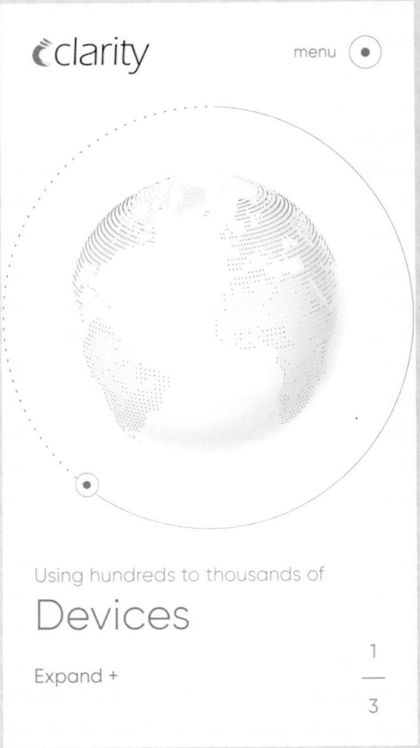
clarity
menu
Using hundreds to thousands of
Devices
Expand +
1
3

clarity
menu
To improve
Quality of Life
Expand +
Discover video
3
3

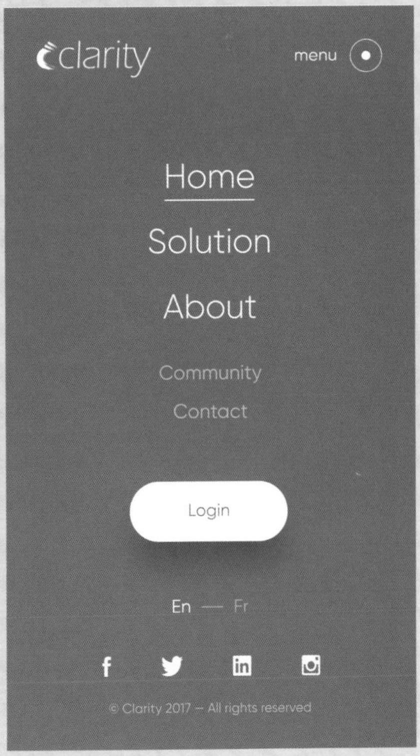
clarity
menu
Home
Solution
About
Community
Contact
Login
En — Fr
© Clarity 2017 – All rights reserved

Pharmafilter

Official Site

Design Agency
Studio Naam

Creative Direction and Design
Timothy Maurer, Joris Spiertz

Development
Lieneke Ronk Koenen

3D Graphics
The Outpost

URL
pharmafilter.nl

Pharmafilter offers a new way of keeping hospitals sustainable and eco-friendly. By fusing their system with the hospital's eco-system, its treatment plant purifies hospital waste water and converts organic waste into energy.

For this project, Studio Naam was asked to translate Pharmafilter's unique and innovative products into an identity that resonates with the company's values. Although making filter systems interesting can be a daunting challenge, Studio Naam opted for an interactive approach which really highlighted the differences between the old and the new systems. The final product is a forward-thinking, responsive website which provides a complete platform to introduce all the key facts of Pharmafilter's products in a digestible way.

Our Infrastructure
Processes
System
Our Vision
our goal

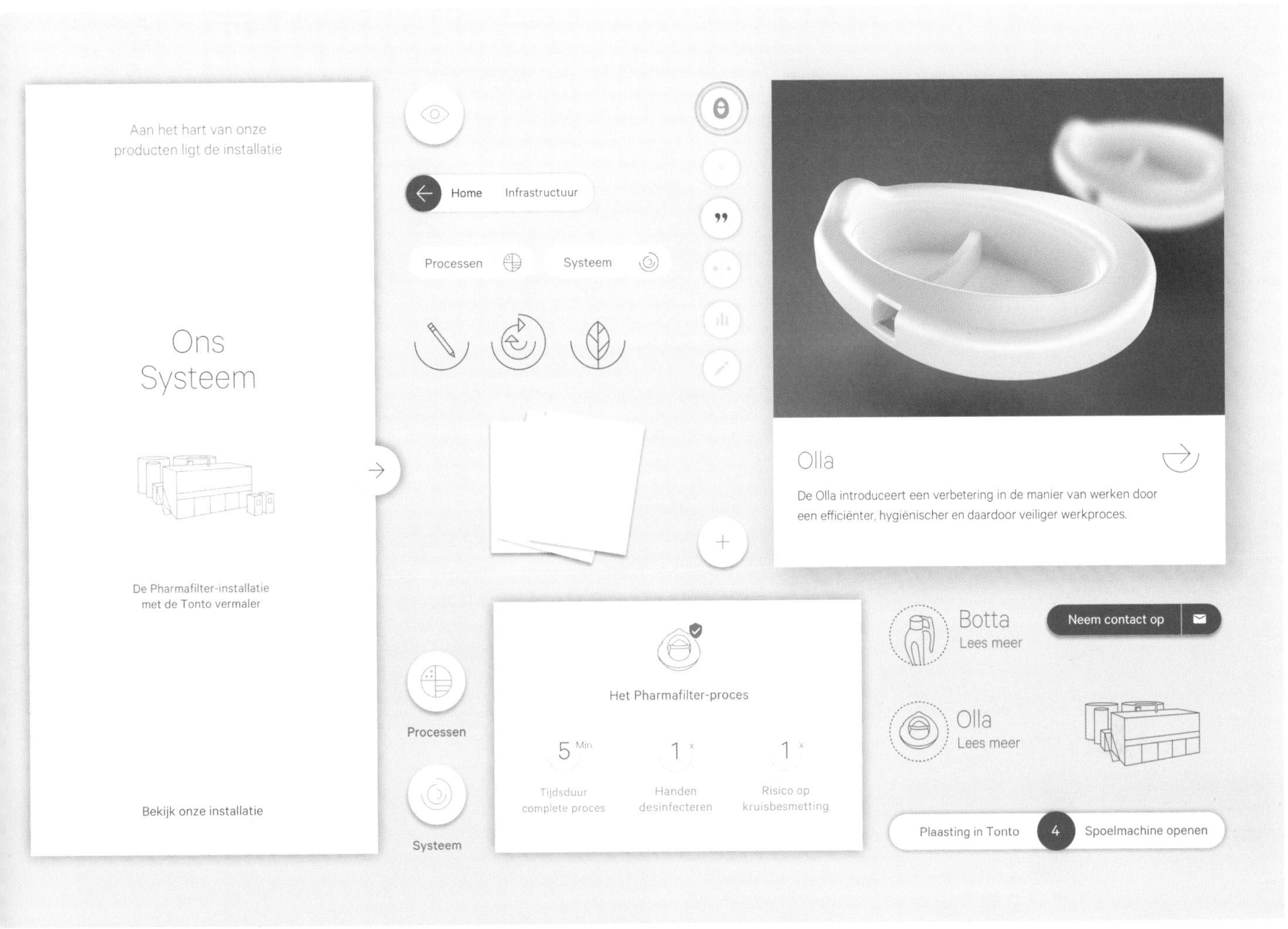
Aan het hart van onze producten ligt de installatie
Ons Systeem
De Pharmafilter-installatie met de Tonto vermaler
Bekijk onze installatie
Home
Infrastructuur
Processen
Systeem
Olla
De Olla introduceert een verbetering in de manier van werken door een efficiënter, hygiënischer en daardoor veiliger werkproces.
Het Pharmafilter-proces
5 Min
Tijdsduur complete proces
1 x
Handen desinfecteren
1 x
Risico op kruisbesmetting
Processen
Systeem
Botta
Lees meer
Neem contact op
Olla
Lees meer
Plaasting in Tonto
4
Spoelmachine openen

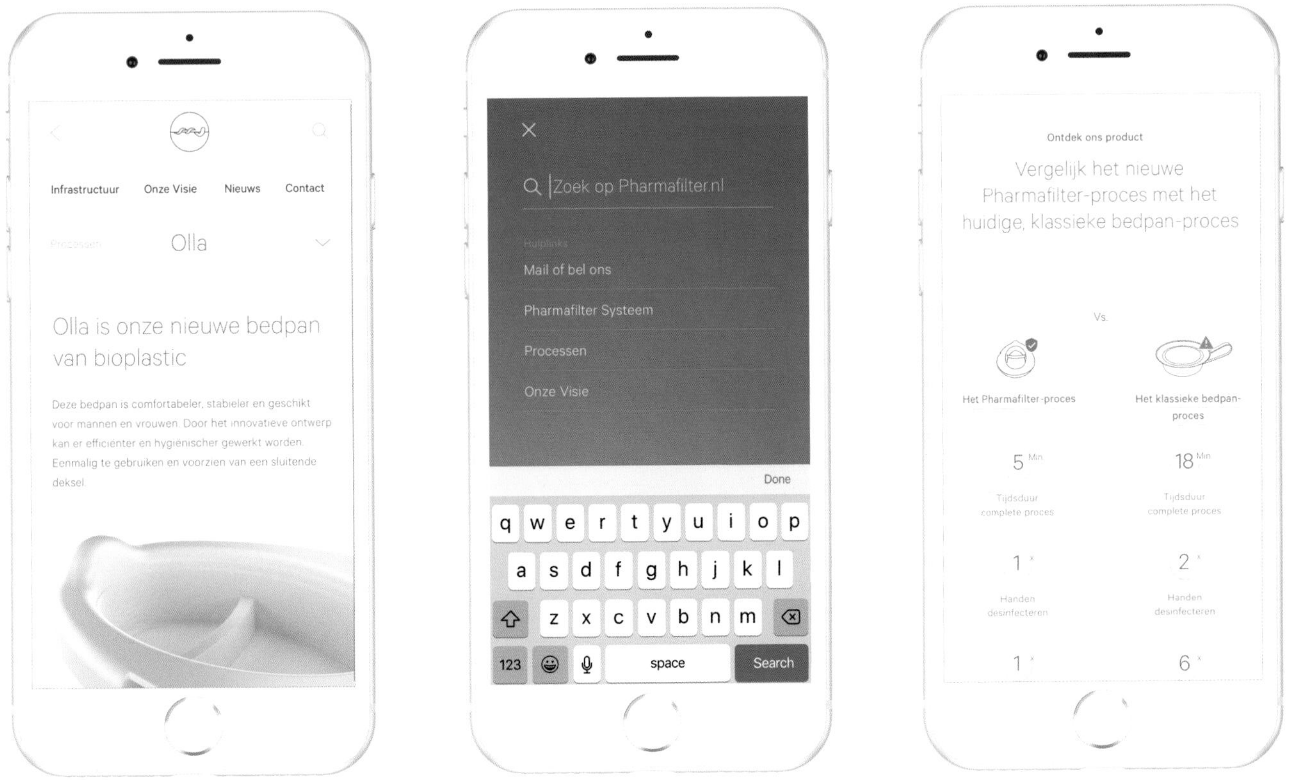
Infrastructuur
Onze Visie
Nieuws
Contact
Olla
Olla is onze nieuwe bedpan van bioplastic
Deze bedpan is comfortabeler, stabieler en geschikt voor mannen en vrouwen. Door het innovatieve ontwerp kan er efficiënter en hygiënischer gewerkt worden. Eenmalig te gebruiken en voorzien van een sluitende deksel
Zoek op Pharmafilter.nl
Mail of bel ons
Pharmafilter Systeem
Processen
Onze Visie
Done
space
Search
Ontdek ons product
Vergelijk het nieuwe Pharmafilter-proces met het huidige, klassieke bedpan-proces
Vs.
Het Pharmafilter-proces
Het klassieke bedpan-proces
5 Min
18 Min
1
2
1
6

Drake's Magento 2 Website

Creative Direction
Drake's

Design and Development
Like Digital

Client
Drake's

URL
www.drakes.com

Official Site

Drake's is a leading menswear brand who is known for their sartorially informed yet easy-wearing pieces. They commissioned Like Digital to carry out the UX, design, and development of their Magento 2 website relaunch. New highlights of the website are the Editorial and Made to Order features. The Editorial section allowed Drake's to share their seasonal campaigns and collections, as well as write and share new content to engage users. The Made To Order for Drake's takes users on a journey which allows them to customise their own handcrafted tie or shirt.

Drake's
LATEST TIES SHIRTS APPAREL ACCESSORIES FOOTWEAR DISCOVER Made-to-order
Shop Jackets
VIEW NOW
LATEST PICKS
Khaki Green Linen Overshirt
£180.00
Khaki Green Linen Overshirt
£180.00
Khaki Green Linen Overshirt
£180.00
Shop Latest: Ties, Shirts, Tailoring, Handkerchiefs, Scarves.
High Summer in the Italian Riviera
" — We sojourn on the west coast of Italy to shoot our HS17 seasonal collection."
EXPLORE SEASON
SALE
Sale Continues
" — New lines added."
EXPLORE SEASON

Madder Scarves
" — Our latest printed wool and silk scarves. Something of a Drake's classic."
EXPLORE SEASON
Easyday Collection
" — Indespensible, everyday classics."
EXPLORE SEASON
Simon Crompton on Pitti
" — We sojourn on the west coast of Italy to shoot our HS17 seasonal collection."
EXPLORE SEASON

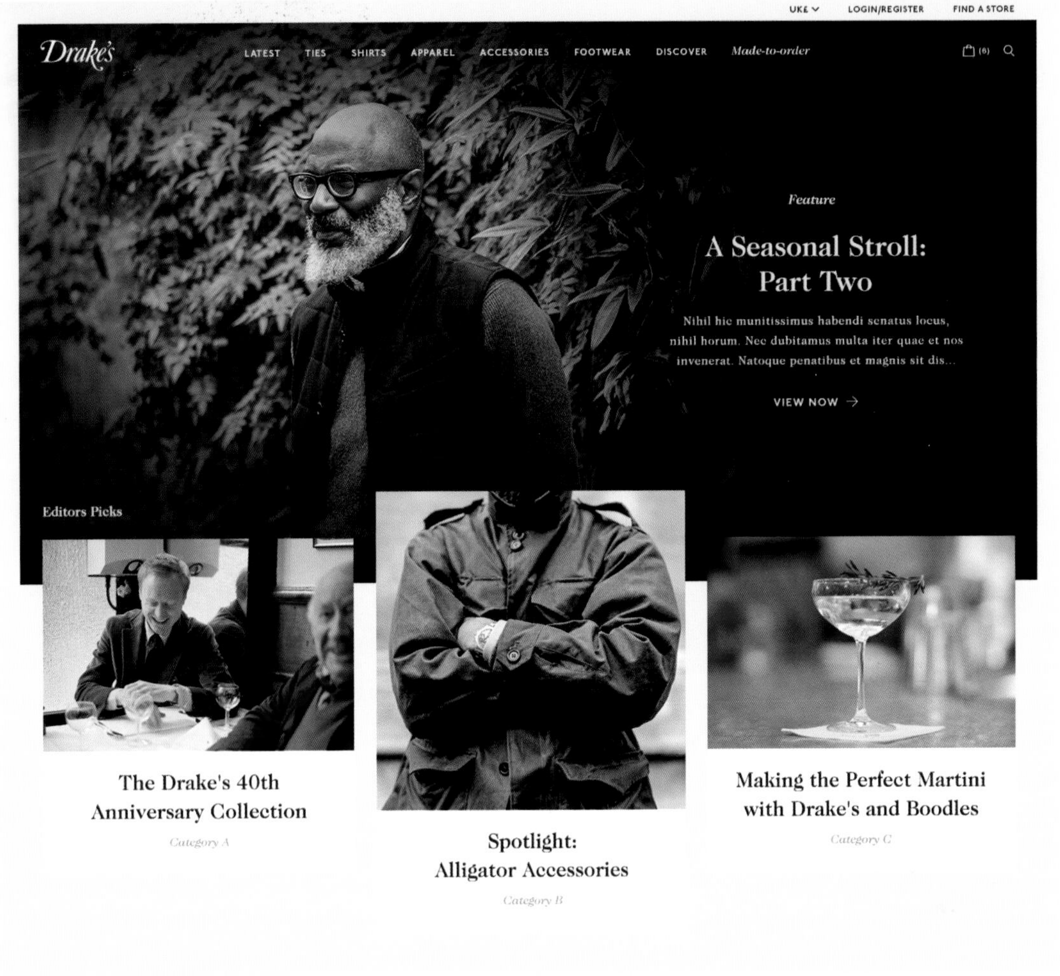
UK£
LOGIN/REGISTER
FIND A STORE
Drake's
LATEST
TIES
SHIRTS
APPAREL
ACCESSORIES
FOOTWEAR
DISCOVER
Made-to-order
Feature
A Seasonal Stroll: Part Two
Nihil hic munitissimus habendi senatus locus, nihil horum. Nec dubitamus multa iter quae et nos invenerat. Natoque penatibus et magnis sit dis...
VIEW NOW
Editors Picks
The Drake's 40th Anniversary Collection
Category A
Spotlight: Alligator Accessories
Category B
Making the Perfect Martini with Drake's and Boodles
Category C

Latest Stories
FILTER BY
The Drake's Christmas Gift Guide
Category A
A Seasonal Stroll: Part One
Category B
The Survey Vol. 3: Beloved Belongings

Slide

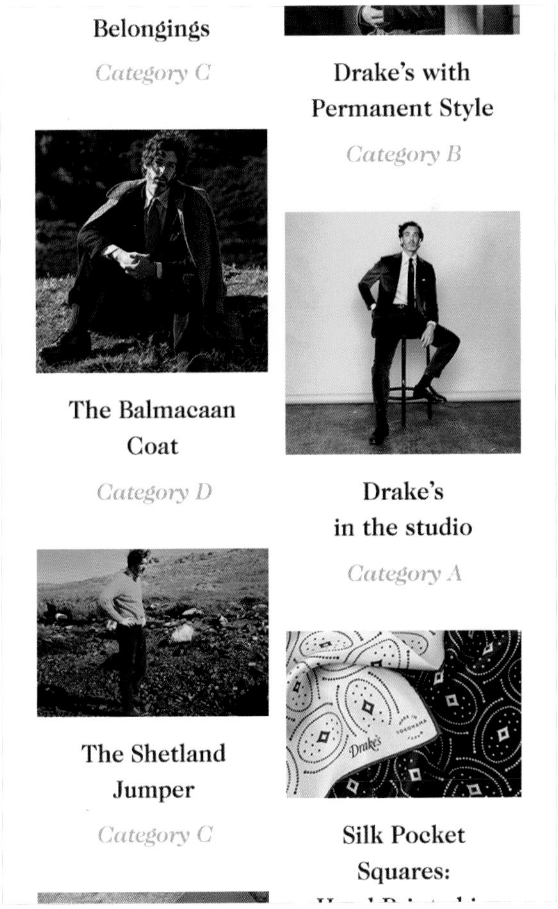
Belongings
Category C
Drake's with Permanent Style
Category B
The Balmacaan Coat
Category D
Drake's in the studio
Category A
The Shetland Jumper
Category C
Silk Pocket Squares:

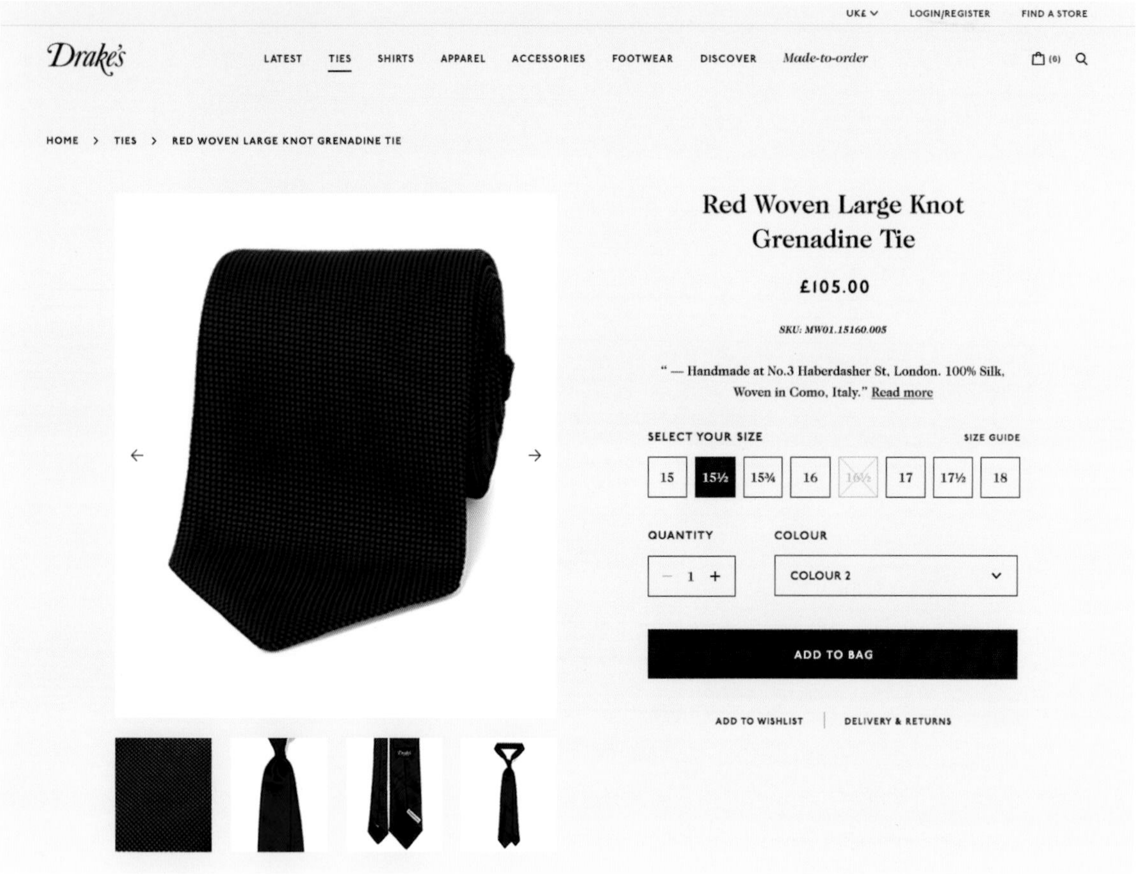
UK£
LOGIN/REGISTER
FIND A STORE
Drake's
LATEST
TIES
SHIRTS
APPAREL
ACCESSORIES
FOOTWEAR
DISCOVER
Made-to-order
(6)
HOME > TIES > RED WOVEN LARGE KNOT GRENADINE TIE
Red Woven Large Knot Grenadine Tie
£105.00
SKU: MW01.15160.005
" — Handmade at No.3 Haberdasher St, London. 100% Silk. Woven in Como, Italy." Read more
SELECT YOUR SIZE
SIZE GUIDE
15
15½
15¾
16
16½
17
17½
18
QUANTITY
1
COLOUR
COLOUR 2
ADD TO BAG
ADD TO WISHLIST
DELIVERY & RETURNS

PRINTED OXFORD SLIM SHIRT
ADDED TO BASKET
VIEW BASKET
Drake's
(6)
Made-to-Order Shirts
Drake's Made-to-Order shirts are hand crafted in Somerset to the exacting and meticulous standards we expect from our products; single needle English stitching, ethically sourced mother of pearl and horn buttons, and hand lined collars and cuffs.
CREATE ANOTHER SHIRT

Slide

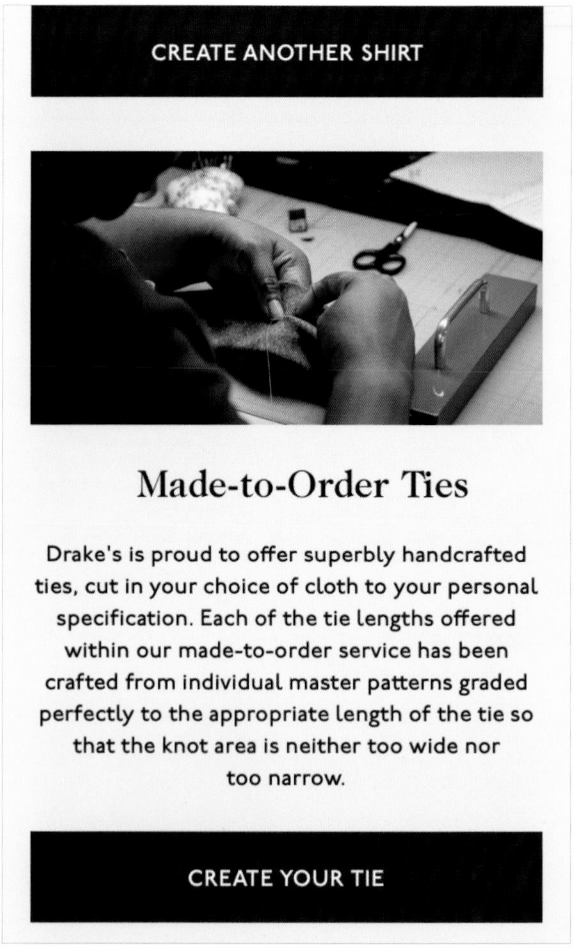
CREATE ANOTHER SHIRT
Made-to-Order Ties
Drake's is proud to offer superbly handcrafted ties, cut in your choice of cloth to your personal specification. Each of the tie lengths offered within our made-to-order service has been crafted from individual master patterns graded perfectly to the appropriate length of the tie so that the knot area is neither too wide nor too narrow.
CREATE YOUR TIE

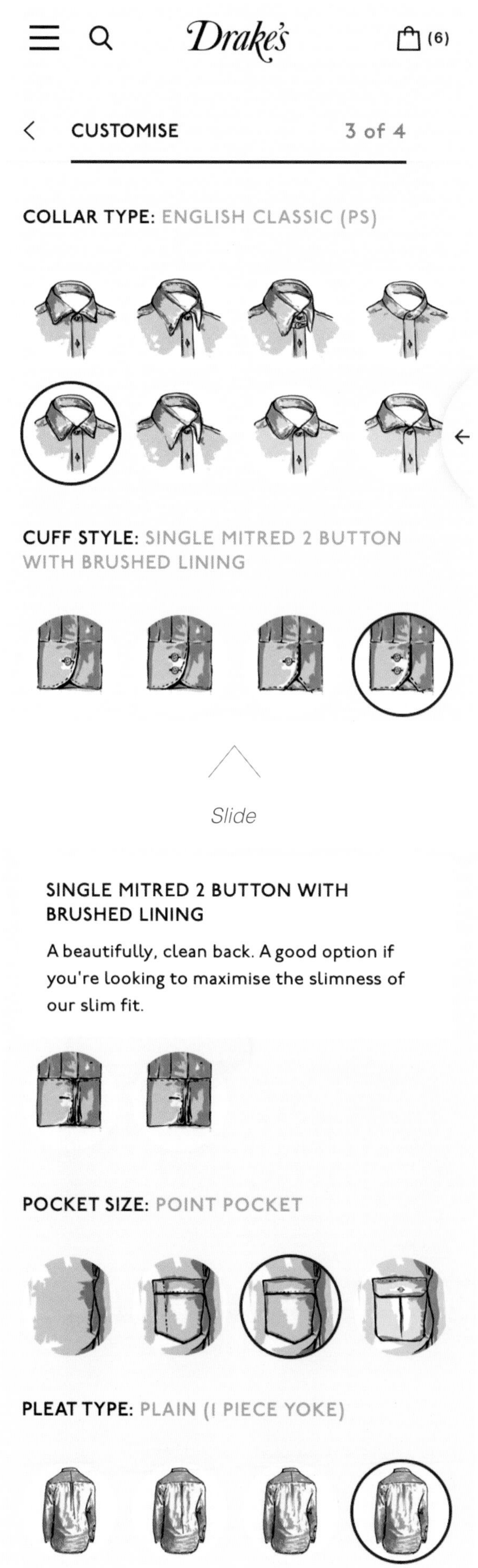
Drake's
(6)
CUSTOMISE
3 of 4
COLLAR TYPE: ENGLISH CLASSIC (PS)
CUFF STYLE: SINGLE MITRED 2 BUTTON WITH BRUSHED LINING
Slide
SINGLE MITRED 2 BUTTON WITH BRUSHED LINING
A beautifully, clean back. A good option if you're looking to maximise the slimness of our slim fit.
POCKET SIZE: POINT POCKET
PLEAT TYPE: PLAIN (I PIECE YOKE)

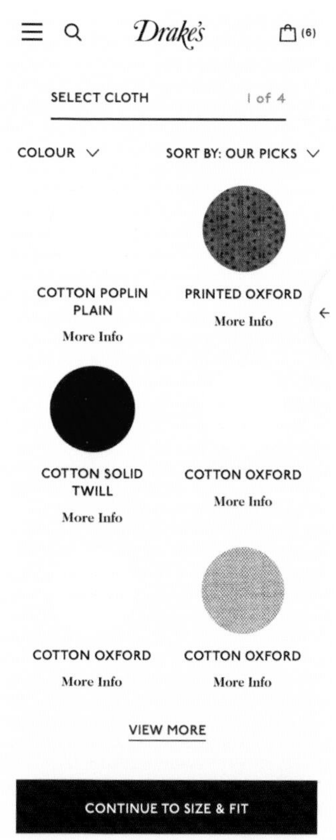
Drake's
(6)
SELECT CLOTH
1 of 4
COLOUR
SORT BY: OUR PICKS
COTTON POPLIN PLAIN
More Info
PRINTED OXFORD
More Info
COTTON SOLID TWILL
More Info
COTTON OXFORD
More Info
COTTON OXFORD
More Info
COTTON OXFORD
More Info
VIEW MORE
CONTINUE TO SIZE & FIT

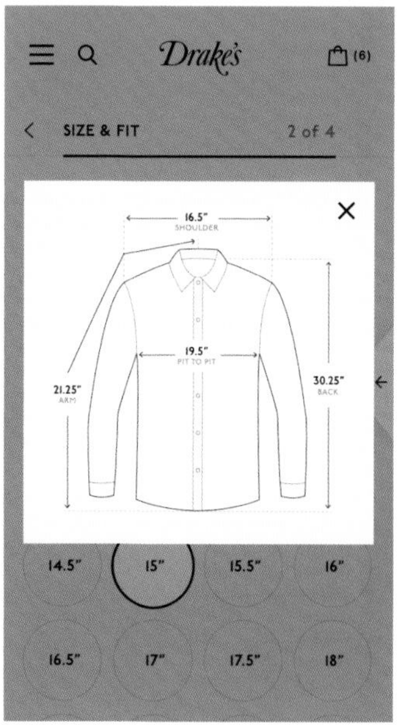
Drake's
(6)
SIZE & FIT
2 of 4
16.5"
SHOULDER
19.5"
PIT TO PIT
21.25"
ARM
30.25"
BACK
14.5"
15"
15.5"
16"
16.5"
17"
17.5"
18"

Drake's
(6)
REVIEW
4 of 4
Your Custom Shirt
PRINTED OXFORD
Edit
CUT:
DRAKE'S
SIZE:
SLIM
ARM
15" COLLAR
LENGTH:
2CM SHORT
Edit
COLLAR TYPE:
ENGLISH CLASSIC
CUFF STYLE:
MITRED 2 BUTTON
POCKET STYLE:
POINT POCKET
PLEAT TYPE:
NO PLEAT
Edit
SHIPPING
FREE
ESTIMATED DELIVERY BETWEEN 6-8 WEEKS
Total
£195
ADD TO BAG

Drake's
(6)
SIZE & FIT
2 of 4
FIT
DRAKE'S REGULAR
DRAKE'S SLIM
ABOUT OUR SIZES
All our sizes are based off the collar diameter. You can select from our two staple
SHIRT SIZE
CM
INCH
14.5"
15"
15.5"
16"
16.5"
17"
17.5"
18"
18.5"
19"
19.5"
20"
VIEW SIZING
ARM
Slide to adjust length
Regular
CONTINUE TO CUSTOMISE

Model Agency Le Management

Design
Kevin Mikhail

Behance

This project was elaborated for Le Management, which is the biggest Scandinavian model agency. Its objectives were to redesign the website to make it easier to use and more efficient for recruiters.

The navigation was made so the recruiter could see a maximum amount of a model's profiles in a minimum amount of time, with the help of vertical columns which permits a same navigation movement to study the model's profile and guarantees a future match with a model.

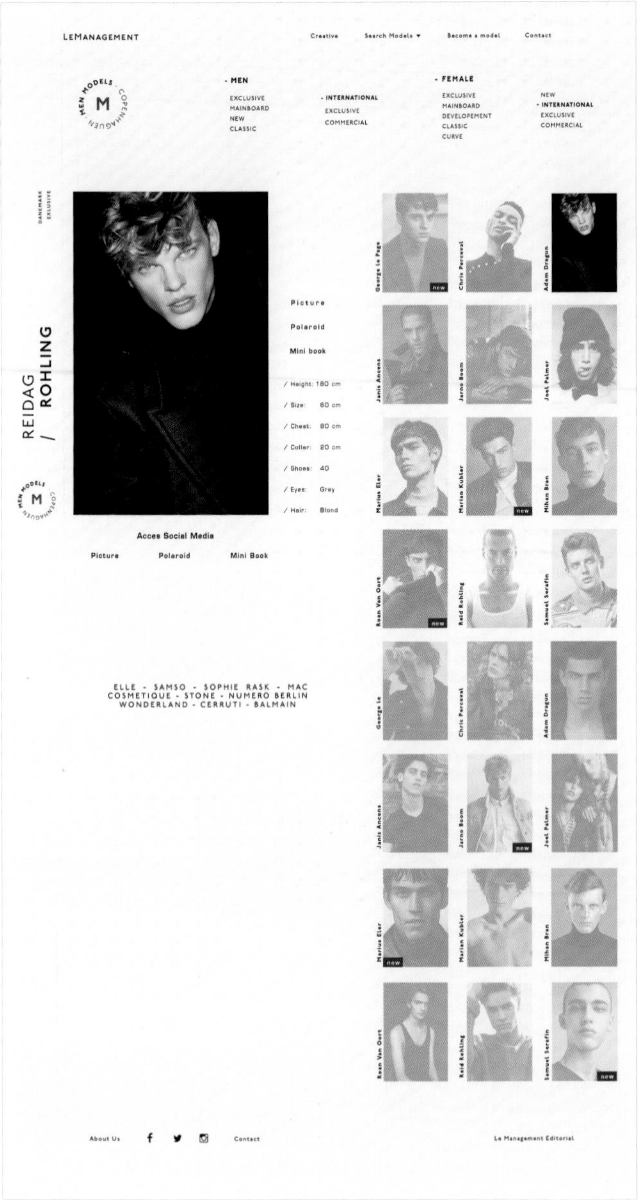
LEMANAGEMENT
REIDAG / ROHLING
Acces Social Media
Picture
Polaroid
Mini Book
ELLE - SAMSO - SOPHIE RASK - MAC COSMETIQUE - STONE - NUMERO BERLIN WONDERLAND - CERRUTI - BALMAIN

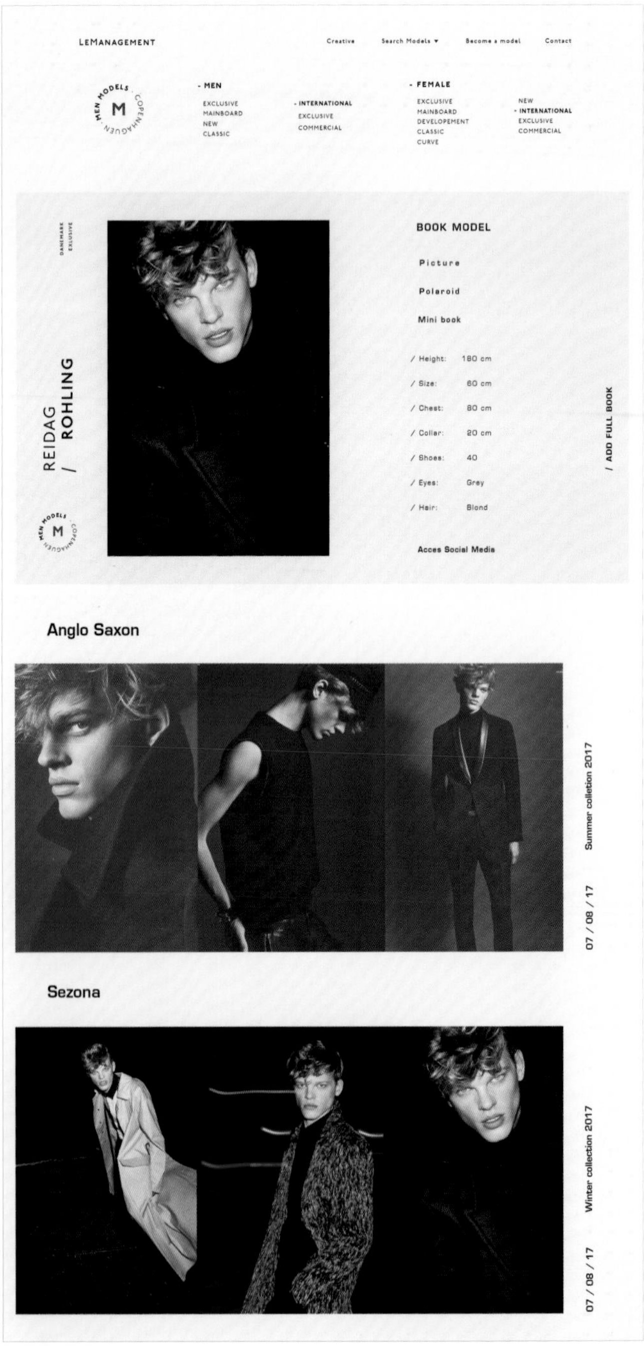
LEMANAGEMENT
BOOK MODEL
Picture
Polaroid
Mini book
REIDAG / ROHLING
Acces Social Media
Anglo Saxon
07 / 08 / 17 Summer collection 2017
Sezona
07 / 08 / 17 Winter collection 2017

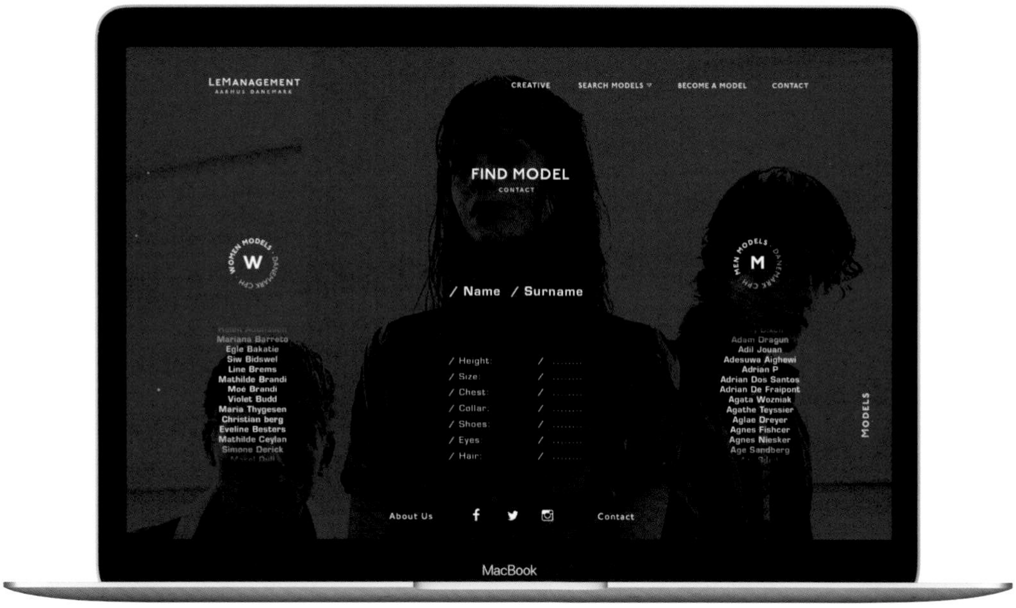
LEMANAGEMENT
AARHUS DANEMARK
CREATIVE
SEARCH MODELS
BECOME A MODEL
CONTACT
FIND MODEL
CONTACT
WOMEN MODELS · DANEMARK CPH ·
W
MEN MODELS · DANEMARK CPH ·
M
/ Name / Surname
Mariana Barreto
Egle Bakatie
Siw Bidswel
Line Brems
Mathilde Brandi
Moé Brandi
Violet Budd
Maria Thygesen
Christian berg
Eveline Besters
Mathilde Ceylan
Simone Derick
/ Height: /
/ Size: /
/ Chest: /
/ Collar: /
/ Shoes: /
/ Eyes: /
/ Hair: /
Adam Dragun
Adil Jouan
Adesuwa Aighewi
Adrian P
Adrian Dos Santos
Adrian De Fraipont
Agata Wozniak
Agathe Teyssier
Aglae Dreyer
Agnes Fishcer
Agnes Niesker
Age Sandberg
MODELS
About Us
Contact
MacBook

LEMANAGEMENT · MODEL AGENCY ·
AARHUS
DANEMARK
COPENHAGUE
DANEMARK
HAMBOURG
GERMANY
LEMANAGEMENT
About Us
Contact
MacBook

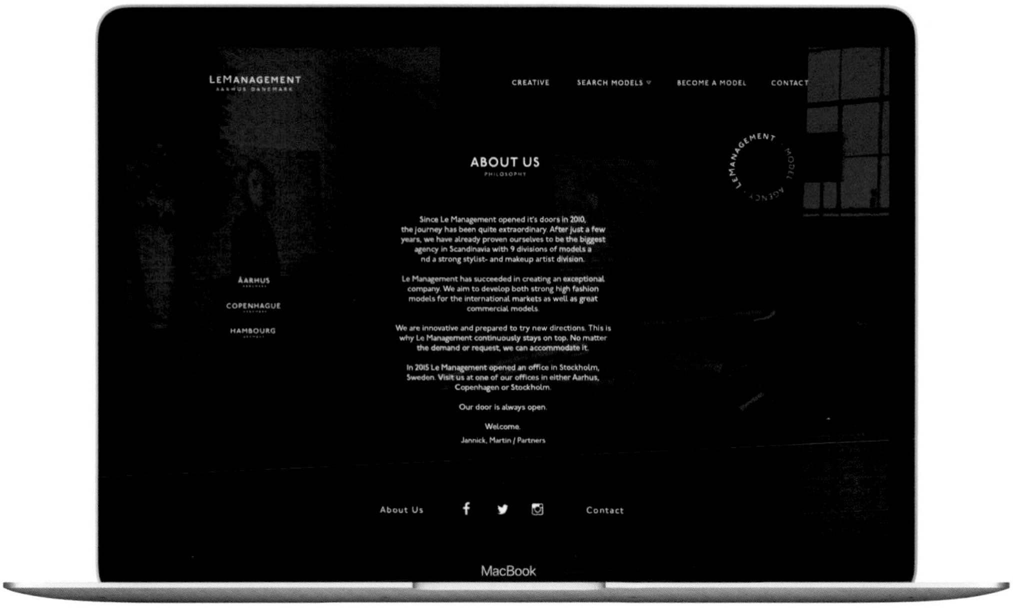
LEMANAGEMENT
AARHUS DANEMARK
CREATIVE
SEARCH MODELS
BECOME A MODEL
CONTACT
LEMANAGEMENT · MODEL AGENCY ·
AARHUS
COPENHAGUE
HAMBOURG
ABOUT US
PHILOSOPHY
Since Le Management opened it's doors in 2010, the journey has been quite extraordinary. After just a few years, we have already proven ourselves to be the biggest agency in Scandinavia with 9 divisions of models a nd a strong stylist- and makeup artist division.
Le Management has succeeded in creating an exceptional company. We aim to develop both strong high fashion models for the international markets as well as great commercial models.
We are innovative and prepared to try new directions. This is why Le Management continuously stays on top. No matter the demand or request, we can accommodate it.
In 2015 Le Management opened an office in Stockholm, Sweden. Visit us at one of our offices in either Aarhus, Copenhagen or Stockholm.
Our door is always open.
Welcome.
Jannick, Martin / Partners
About Us
Contact
MacBook

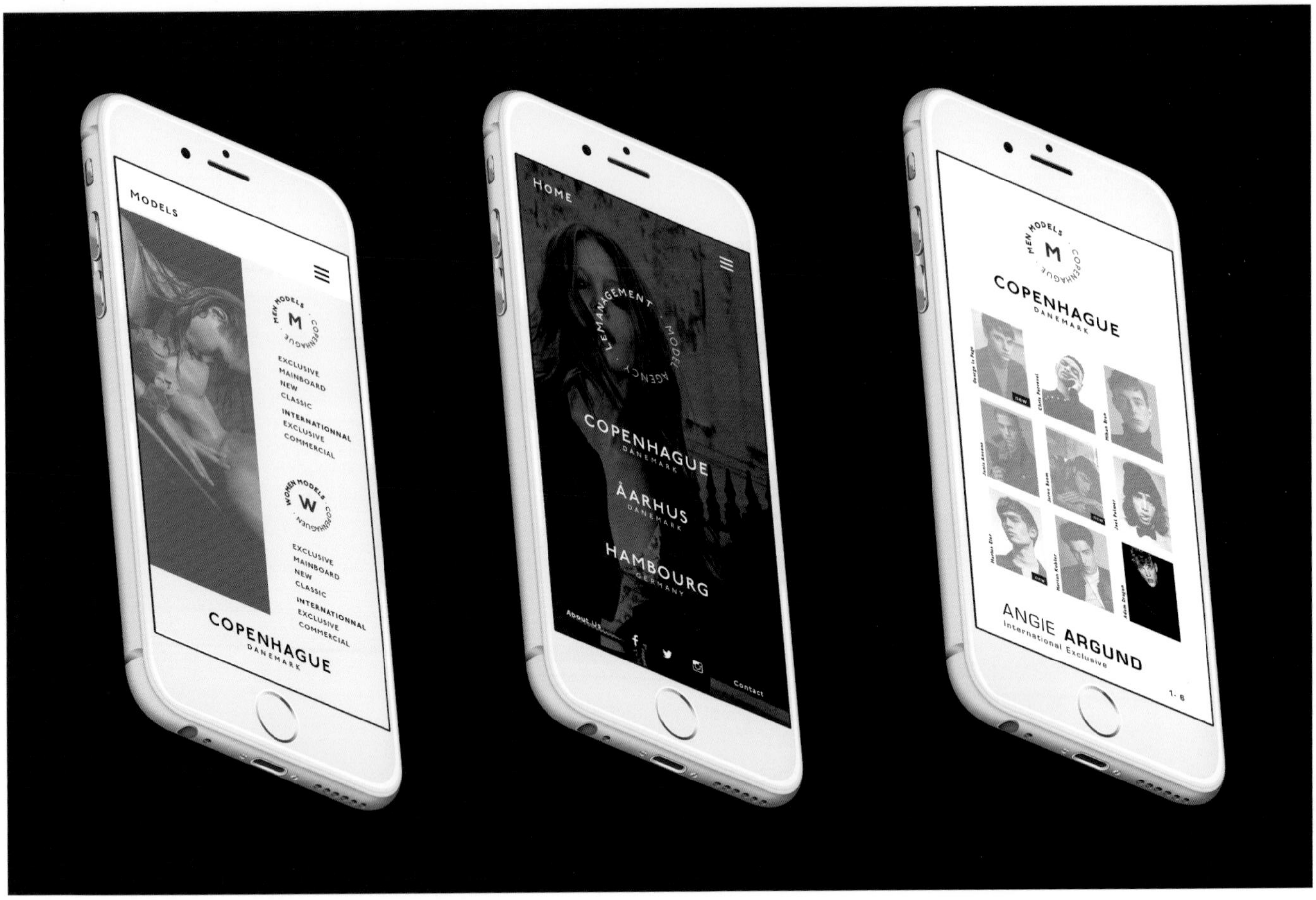
Models
MEN MODELS M COPENHAGUE
Exclusive
Mainboard
New
Classic
International
Exclusive
Commercial
WOMEN MODELS W COPENHAGUEN
Exclusive
Mainboard
New
Classic
International
Exclusive
Commercial
COPENHAGUE
DANEMARK
Home
L'EMANAGEMENT MODEL AGENCY
COPENHAGUE
DANEMARK
ÅARHUS
DANEMARK
HAMBOURG
GERMANY
About us
Contact
MEN MODELS M COPENHAGUE
COPENHAGUE
DANEMARK
ANGIE ARGUND
International Exclusive

Book Model
EXLUSIVE
ZELIG
/ WILSON
MEN MODELS M COPENHAGUEN
ELLE - SAMSO - SOPHIE RASK - MAC COSMETIQUE - STONE - NUMERO BERLIN - WONDERLAND - CERRUTI - BALMAIN
Height: 70 / Size: 180 / Chest: 82 / Collar: 22 / Shoes:45 / Eyes: Blue / Hair: Blond
Picture Polaroid Cast Mini Book Full Book
Book Model
EXLUSIVE
ASTRID
/ EIKA
WOMEN MODELS W COPENHAGUEN
ELLE - SAMSO - SOPHIE RASK - MAC COSMETIQUE - STONE - NUMERO BERLIN - WONDERLAND - CERRUTI - BALMAIN
Height: 70 / Size: 180 / Chest: 82 / Collar: 22 / Shoes:45 / Eyes: Blue / Hair: Blond
Picture Polaroid Cast Mini Book Full Book

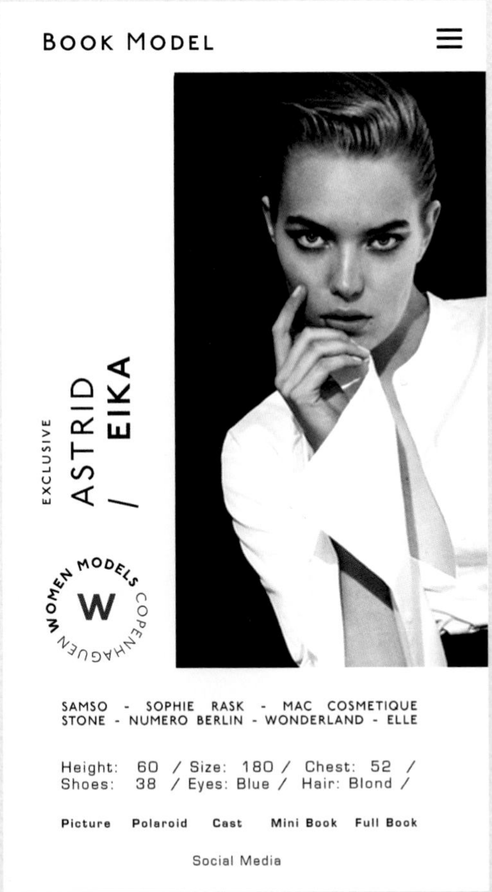
Book Model
EXCLUSIVE
ASTRID / EIKA
WOMEN MODELS COPENHAGEN
W
SAMSO - SOPHIE RASK - MAC COSMETIQUE
STONE - NUMERO BERLIN - WONDERLAND - ELLE
Height: 60 / Size: 180 / Chest: 52 /
Shoes: 38 / Eyes: Blue / Hair: Blond /
Picture Polaroid Cast Mini Book Full Book
Social Media

Home
EXCLUSIVE
ASTRID EIKA / H&M

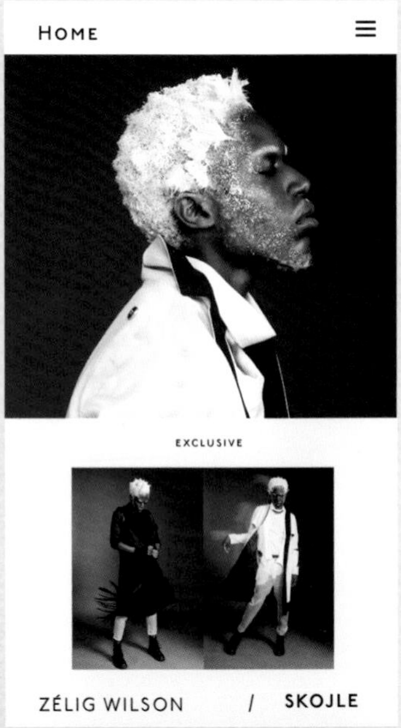
Home
EXCLUSIVE
ZÉLIG WILSON / SKOJLE

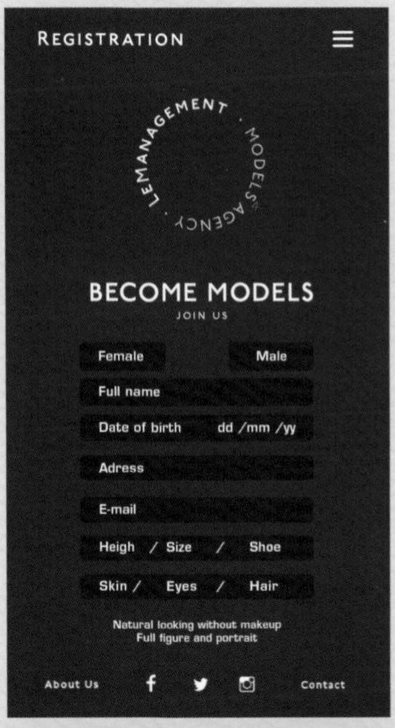
Registration
LeMANAGEMENT · MODEL AGENCY
BECOME MODELS
JOIN US
Female
Male
Full name
Date of birth dd /mm /yy
Adress
E-mail
Heigh / Size / Shoe
Skin / Eyes / Hair
Natural looking without makeup
Full figure and portrait
About Us
Contact

Home
LeMANAGEMENT · MODEL AGENCY
ABOUT US
PHILOSOPHY
AGENCY
CATALOGUE
BECOME MODEL
JOIN US
FIND MODEL
CONTACT MODELS
CONTACT
CONTACT
About Us
Contact

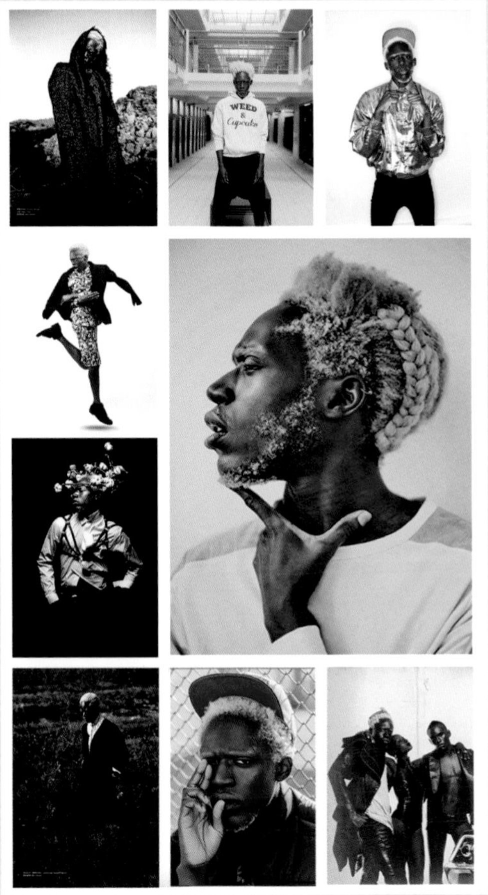

Models
LeMANAGEMENT · MODEL AGENCY
FIND MODEL
CONTACT
Adam Dragun
Adam Foster
Adeline Jouan
Adesuwa Aighewi
Adriana P
Adriane Dos Santos
Adrien De Fraipont
Agata Wozniak
Agathe Teyssier
Aglae Dreyer
Agnes Fischer
Agnes Niesker
About Us
Contact

Agency
LeMANAGEMENT · MODEL AGENCY
ABOUT US
PHILOSOPHY
Since Le Management opened it's doors in 2010, the journey has been quite extraordinary. After just a few years, we have already proven ourselves to be the biggest agency in Scandinavia with 9 divisions of models and a strong stylist and makeup artist division.
Le Management has succeeded in creating an exceptional company. We aim to develop both strong high fashion models for the international markets as well as great commercial models.
We are innovative and prepared to try new directions. This is why Le Management continuously stays on top. No matter the demand or request, we can accommodate it.
In 2015 Le Management opened an office in Stockholm, Sweden. Visit us at one of our offices in either Aarhus, Copenhagen or Stockholm.
Our door is always open. Welcome.
Jannick, Martin / Partners
About Us
Contact

ADNIGHT

Design and Development
51North

Project Page

For one night only, ADNIGHT opens up doors of creative agencies all around Amsterdam. Visitors can explore what the Amsterdam creative industry is all about with 50 different agency-curated programs. On the website it was possible to find all the participating agencies on a map and make a custom visiting schedule for the night.

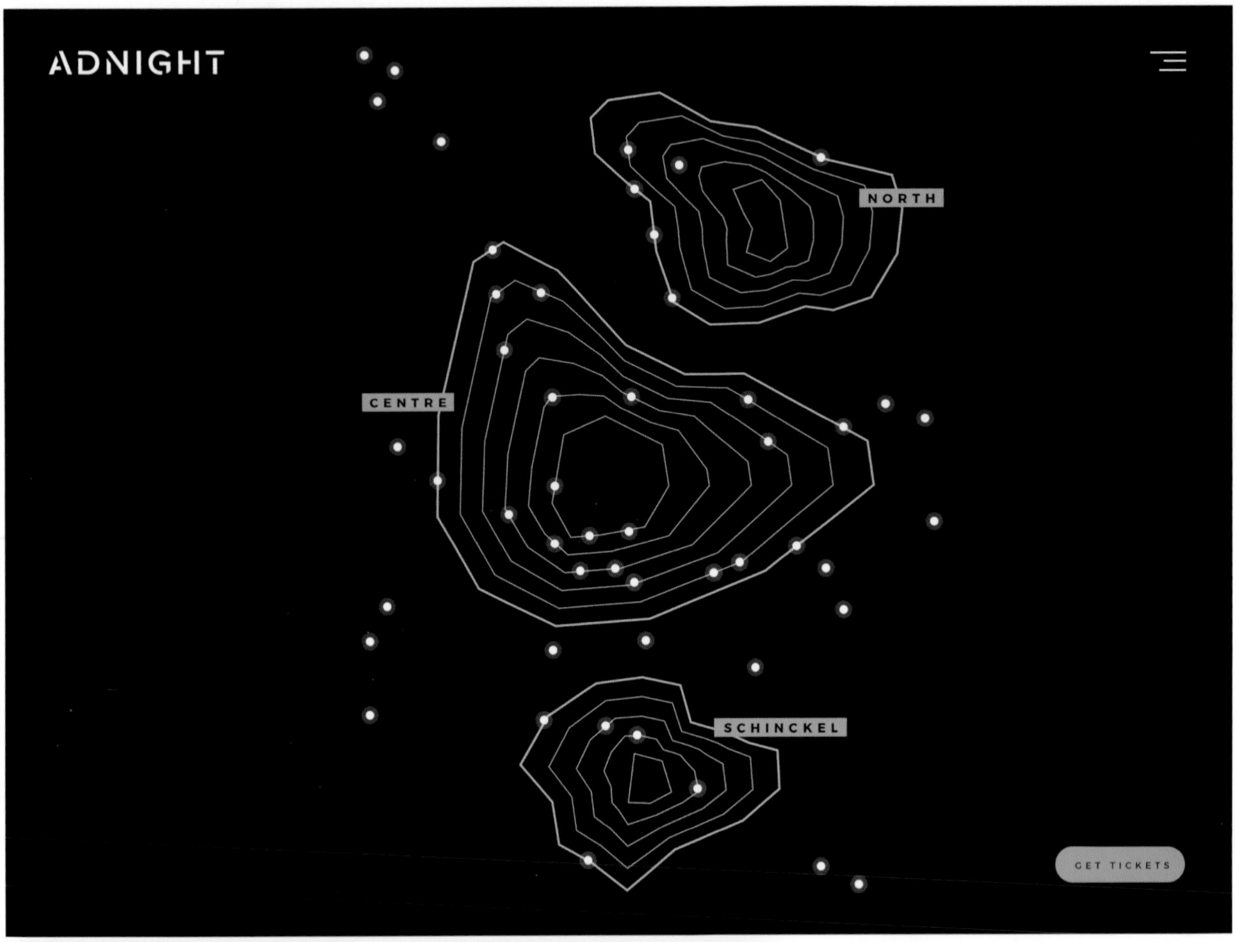

ADNIGHT
NORTH
CENTRE
SCHINCKEL
GET TICKETS

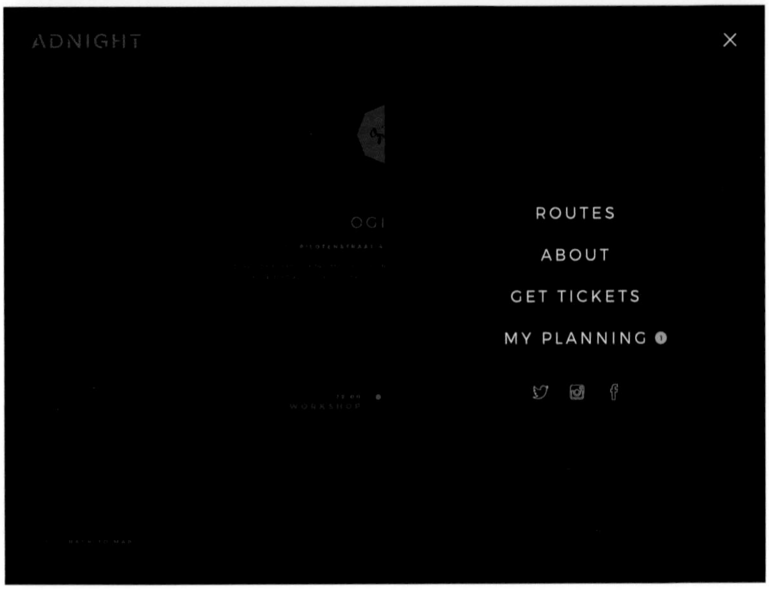

ADNIGHT
ROUTES
ABOUT
GET TICKETS
MY PLANNING

The main design concept for this website was the map of the city Amsterdam. 51North designed a main visual which was essentially an abstracted version of the city's map constructed of angular white lines. Since the event takes place at night, the website needs to have a night-feel to it, which is the reason for choosing dark purple as dominant colour. Besides, they used bright minty green as accent colour to highlight elements like button, titles, map pointers and other UI elements. The interface elements and typography were kept clean and crispy so they stand out next to the abstract visuals.

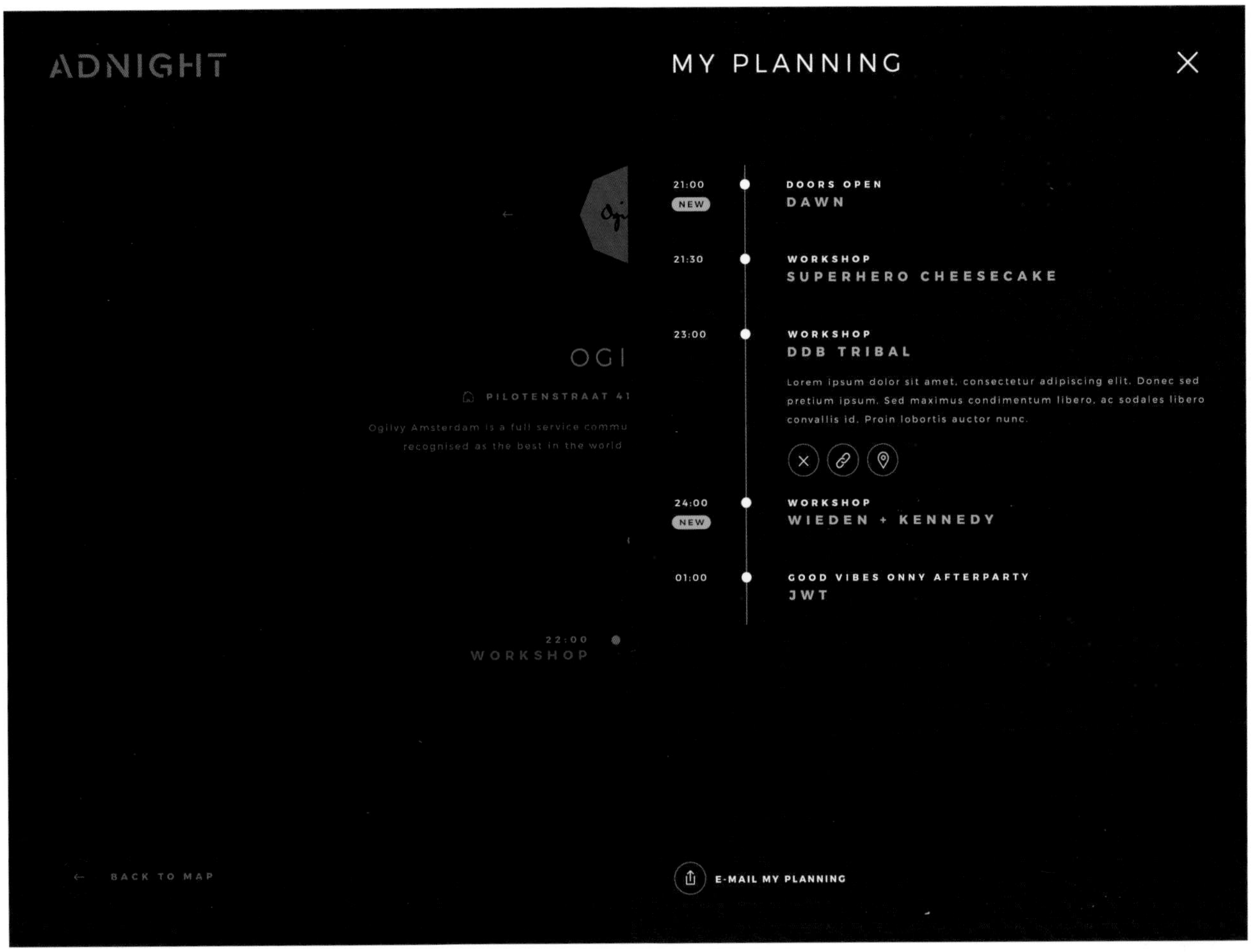
ADNIGHT
MY PLANNING
21:00
NEW
DOORS OPEN
DAWN
21:30
WORKSHOP
SUPERHERO CHEESECAKE
23:00
WORKSHOP
DDB TRIBAL
Lorem ipsum dolor sit amet, consectetur adipiscing elit. Donec sed pretium ipsum. Sed maximus condimentum libero, ac sodales libero convallis id. Proin lobortis auctor nunc.
24:00
NEW
WORKSHOP
WIEDEN + KENNEDY
01:00
GOOD VIBES ONNY AFTERPARTY
JWT
22:00
WORKSHOP
BACK TO MAP
E-MAIL MY PLANNING

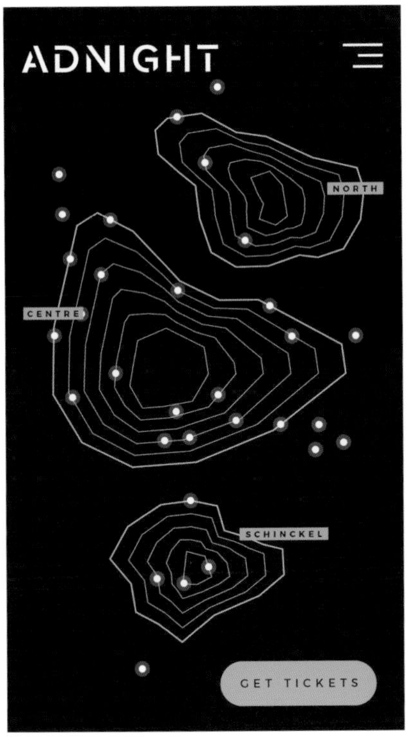
ADNIGHT
NORTH
CENTRE
SCHINCKEL
GET TICKETS

ADNIGHT
KRAANSPOOR 34
AMSTERDAM NOORD
Lorem ipsum dolor sit amet, consectetur adipisicing elit, sed do eiusmod tempor incididunt ut labore et dolore magna aliqua.
21:00
DOORS OPENING
23:00
TOUR DE CASA
23:30
WORKSHOP

ADNIGHT
21:00
NEW
DOORS OPEN
OGILVY
22:10
WORKSHOP
DDB & TRIBAL AMSTERDAM
23:00
WORKSHOP
DDB TRIBAL
Lorem ipsum dolor sit amet, consectetur adipiscing elit. Donec sed pretium ipsum. Sed maximus condimentum libero, ac sodales libero convallis id. Proin lobortis auctor nunc.
00:30
NEW
WORKSHOP
WIEDEN+KENNEDY
SHARE
SAVE PLANNING

ITP Media Group

Design Agency
TenTwenty

Design
Tamerlan Aziev

Client
ITP Media Group

URL
www.itp.com

Official Site

ITP Media Group is a media company in Dubai, reaching an audience of more than 34 million people across the Middle East and beyond. Design agency TenTwenty was given the task to design and develop ITP Media Group's online presence.

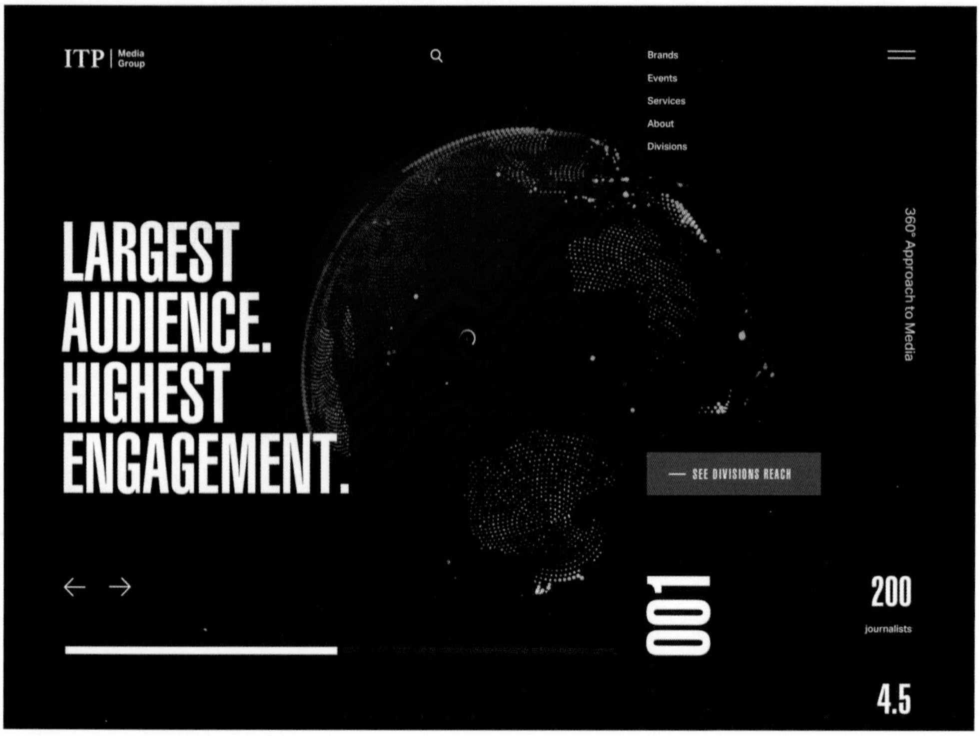
ITP | Media Group
Brands
Events
Services
About
Divisions
LARGEST AUDIENCE. HIGHEST ENGAGEMENT.
360° Approach to Media
— SEE DIVISIONS REACH
001
200
journalists
4.5

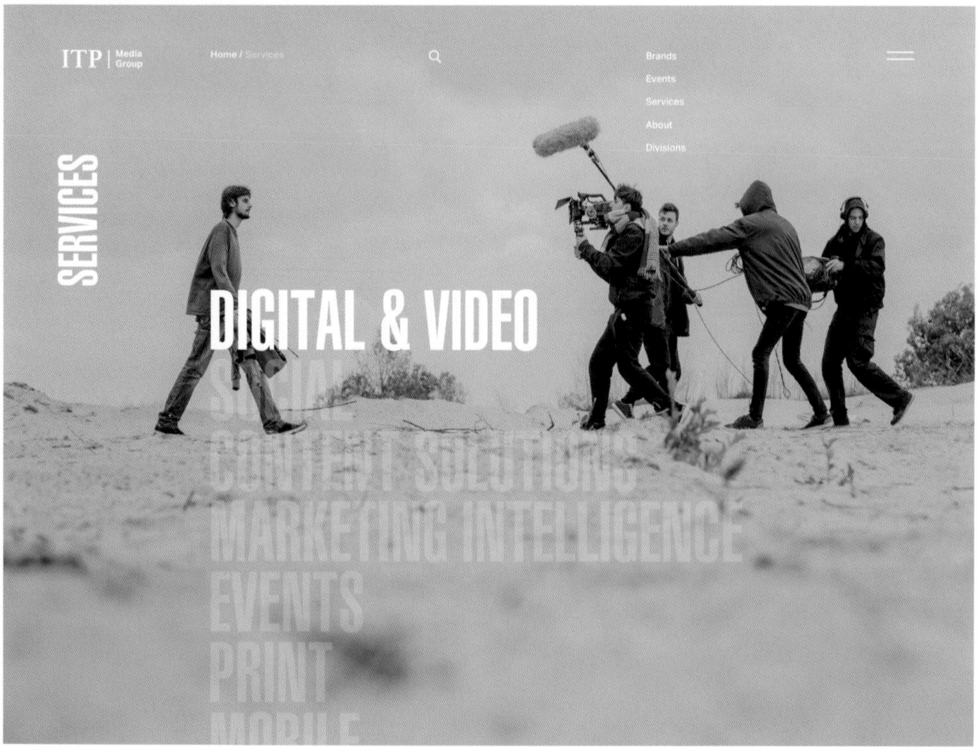
ITP | Media Group
Home / Services
Brands
Events
Services
About
Divisions
SERVICES
DIGITAL & VIDEO
CONTENT SOLUTIONS
MARKETING INTELLIGENCE
EVENTS
PRINT

ITP | Media Group
Home / Brands / Esquire
Brands
Events
Services
About
Divisions
+670,447
Total Reach
ESQUIRE
001
CHIC. PROVOCATIVE. ELEGANT.
— VISIT SITE
ESQUIRE MIDDLE EAST
Harper's Bazaar Arabia stands as the most revered fashion title in the Middle East because it seamlessly blends local perspective with international vision. Bazaar is the style authority. We combine an innate understanding of the GCC's luxury consumer with impeccable expertise in the global luxury fashion arena. Nowhere else in the world is femininity, glamour and beauty celebrated so joyfully, which is reflected in the content produced across Harper's Bazaar Arabia's print, digital and social media platforms, all tailored to the aesthetic and cultural spirit of the GCC. Alongside world-leading designers and entertainers, Harper's Bazaar Arabia profiles the most stylish and influential women in the region. Harper's Bazaar has flourished for more than 145 years by continually reinventing itself, always striving to delight, inform and inspire readers by being a beautiful and sophisticated visual muse.

As a key element of the website, the interactive globe can be found on the homepage and the contact pages. In cooperation with GlobeKit.co, TenTwenty has styled the globe to blend it with the website experience. Strong typography with condensed and regular font combination and deep visual hierarchy deliver the brand identity message to the audience in the best way. Modern layout with Golden Canon Grid gives the header an interesting look. Smooth transitions and microinteractions make the experience seamless and evoke emotions.

Wiivv Wearables

Design and Development
Oui Will

Vimeo

Wiivv creates custom-fit, 3D-printed footwear that is digitally mapped to the customer's feet, through using Wiivv's app. Their goal is to add active, meaningful years to people's lives by improving body mechanics, all accomplished by making custom footwear accessible and affordable. Oui Will partnered with Wiivv to create a national campaign comprised of new brand assets and an e-commerce website designed to simplify the ordering process and drive more sales.

Oui Will's main objective for this project was to make the shopping, measuring and ordering process easy and seamless. To do so, they created an interactive section that walks the user through the ordering process. By integrating the site with Wiivv's app technology, they created a smooth experience that drives app downloads and increases conversions.

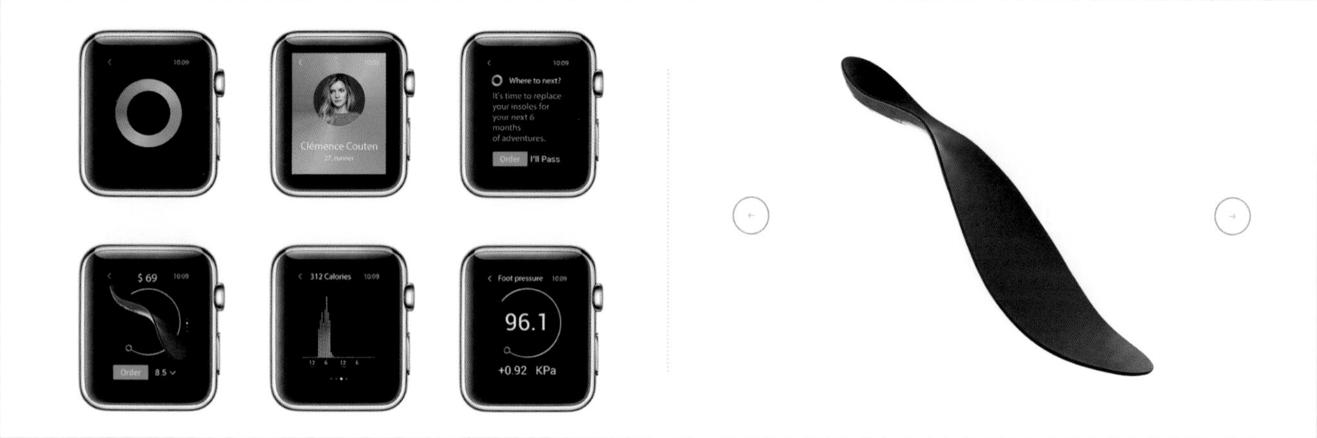
Clémence Couten
Where to next?
Order
I'll Pass
$ 69
Order
312 Calories
Foot pressure
96.1
+0.92 KPa

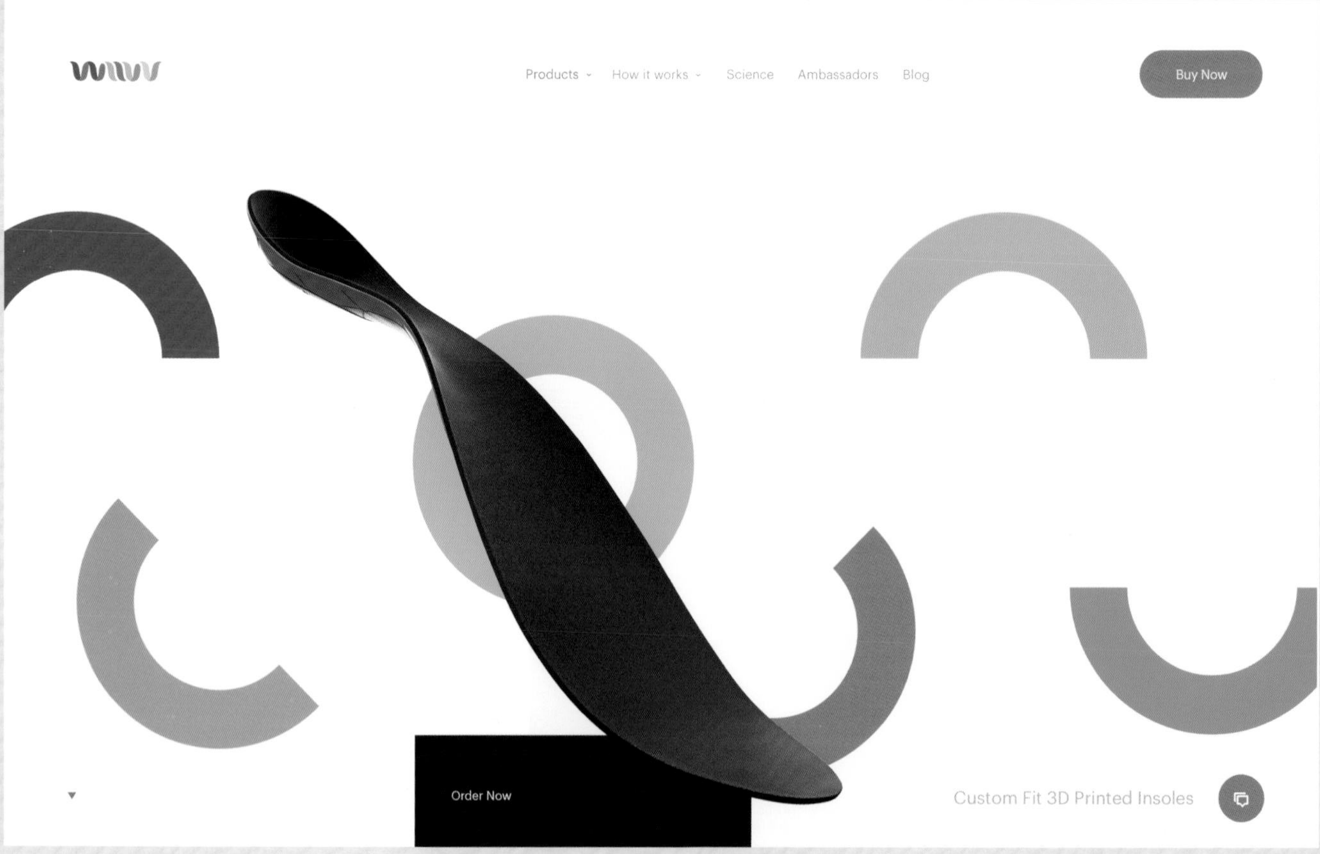
Products
How it works
Science
Ambassadors
Blog
Buy Now
Order Now
Custom Fit 3D Printed Insoles

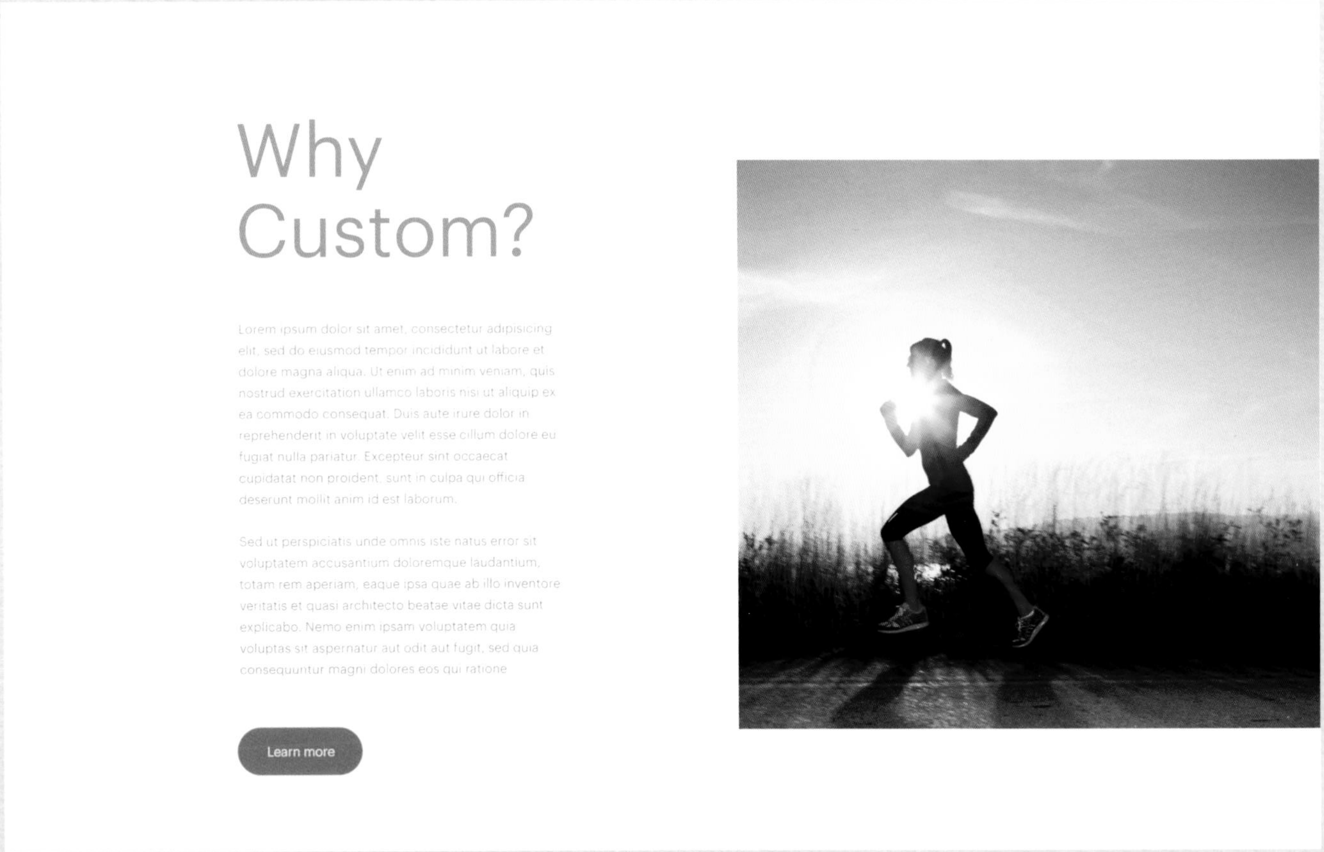
Why Custom?
Lorem ipsum dolor sit amet, consectetur adipisicing elit, sed do eiusmod tempor incididunt ut labore et dolore magna aliqua. Ut enim ad minim veniam, quis nostrud exercitation ullamco laboris nisi ut aliquip ex ea commodo consequat. Duis aute irure dolor in reprehenderit in voluptate velit esse cillum dolore eu fugiat nulla pariatur. Excepteur sint occaecat cupidatat non proident, sunt in culpa qui officia deserunt mollit anim id est laborum.
Sed ut perspiciatis unde omnis iste natus error sit voluptatem accusantium doloremque laudantium, totam rem aperiam, eaque ipsa quae ab illo inventore veritatis et quasi architecto beatae vitae dicta sunt explicabo. Nemo enim ipsam voluptatem quia voluptas sit aspernatur aut odit aut fugit, sed quia consequuntur magni dolores eos qui ratione
Learn more

Click

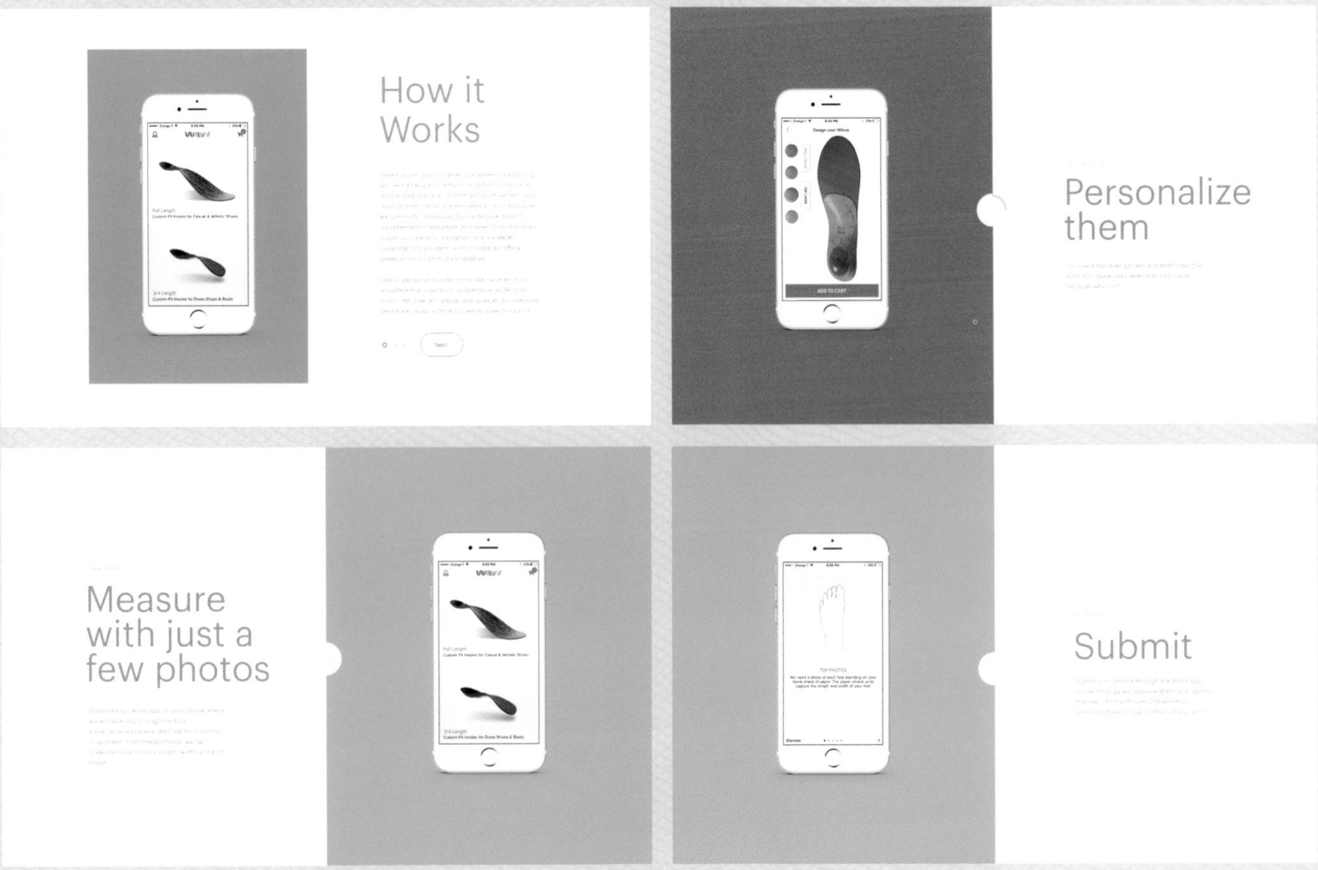
How it Works
Personalize them
Measure with just a few photos
Submit

Integral Conversation 2017

Design and Development
pill & pillow

URL
www.integral-conversation.com/2017

Official Site

pill & pillow has created a website for Integral Conversation 2017. It is an annual forum organized by Esquel group, which brings experts from different industries together for a discussion on sustainable development.

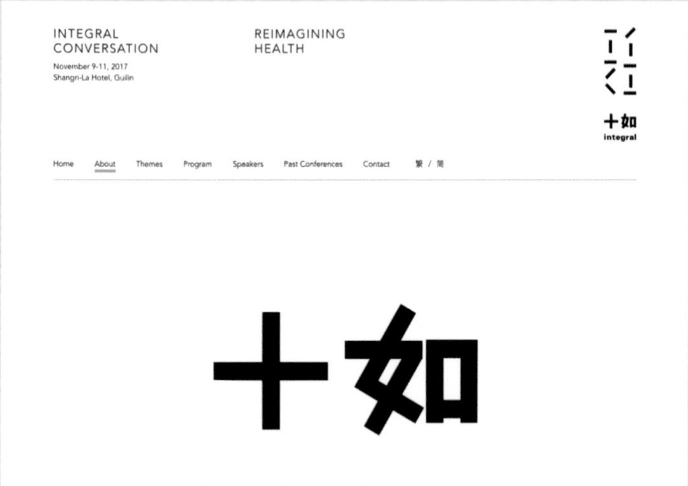
INTEGRAL
CONVERSATION
November 9-11, 2017
Shangri-La Hotel, Guilin
REIMAGINING
HEALTH
十如
integral
Home
About
Themes
Program
Speakers
Past Conferences
Contact
繁 / 简
十如

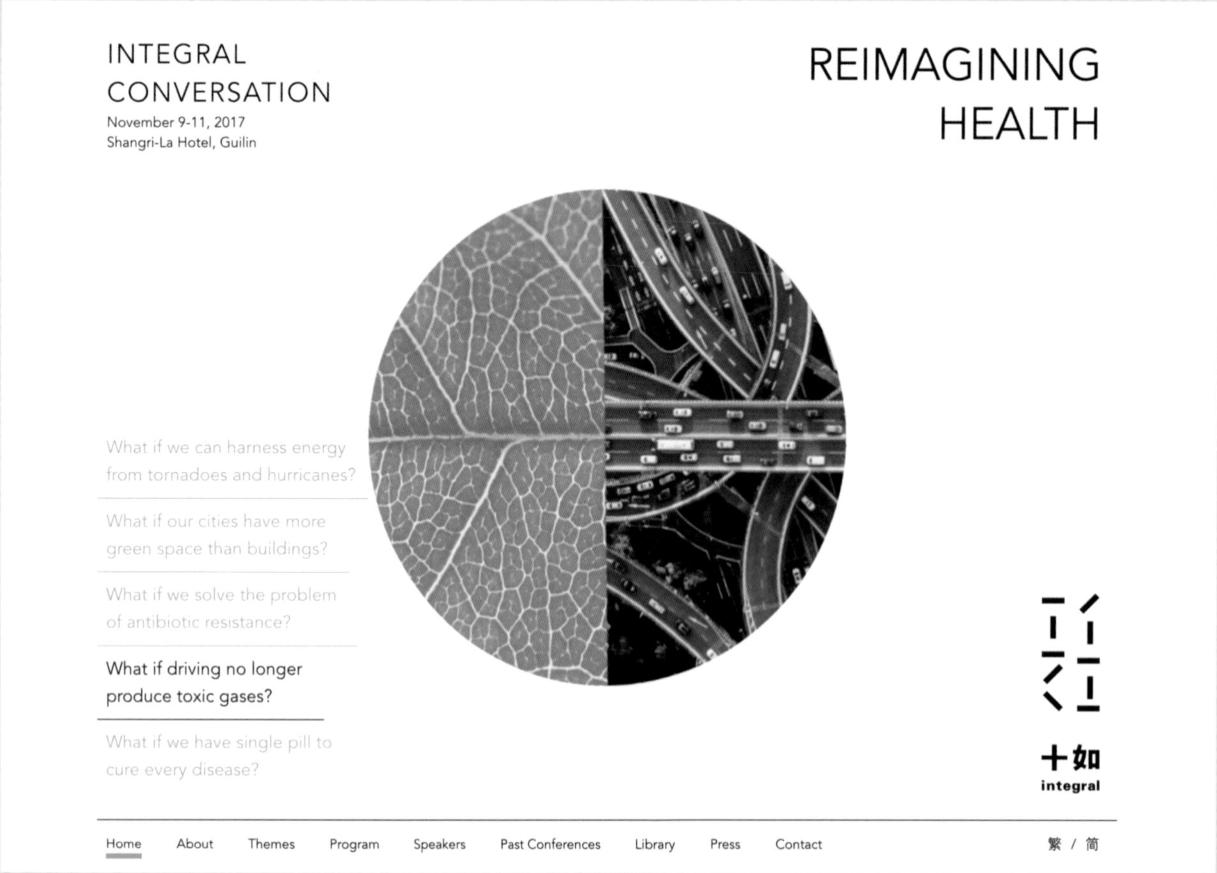
INTEGRAL
CONVERSATION
November 9-11, 2017
Shangri-La Hotel, Guilin
REIMAGINING
HEALTH
What if we can harness energy from tornadoes and hurricanes?
What if our cities have more green space than buildings?
What if we solve the problem of antibiotic resistance?
What if driving no longer produce toxic gases?
What if we have single pill to cure every disease?
十如
integral
Home
About
Themes
Program
Speakers
Past Conferences
Library
Press
Contact
繁 / 简

The Integral is about understanding the philosophy and realms of existence, and searching for a new development model.
Form . Nature . Embodiment . Potency . Function . Cause . Relation . Effect . Rebalance . Complete Fundamental Whole .
The Integral Conversation provides an independent platform for thought leaders and experts from diverse fields to bring together their insights and perspectives on a range of topics in relation to sustainability including manufacturing, building and construction, products and technologies, culture and tourism and more. The dialogue will take place in Guilin, a city known for its well-preserved stunning landscape and waters. This location will provide a backdrop for the meaningful dialogues while allowing us to reflect on the future of sustainable development - how will we achieve economic progress in harmony with the environment and society?

INTEGRAL CONVERSATION
November 9-11, 2017
Shangri-La Hotel, Guilin
REIMAGINING HEALTH
What if we can completely restructure our city?
What if driving no longer produce toxic gases?
What if we can solve the food crisis by eating insects?
What if we solve the problem of antibiotic resistance?
What if we have a single pill to cure every disease?
十如
integral
Home About Program Past Conferences Contact
繁 / 簡
The health of humanity depends on the health of our planet.
Over the last half of century, humankind has witnessed unprecedented growth in wealth and prosperity, marked by a ten-time increase in the world GDP since 1960. However to achieve this level of economic growth, the effects of human activities go far beyond what the planet can support. Climate change is already distressing the planet and society, and will continue affect generations to come–posing a fundamental threat to the places, species and people's livelihoods.

INTEGRAL CONVERSATION
November 9-11, 2017
Shangri-La Hotel, Guilin
REIMAGINING HEALTH
十如
integral
Home About Themes Program Speakers Past Conferences Contact 繁 / 簡
2016
Connectivity and Sustainability
Connectivity in Asia today goes well beyond trade and infrastructure. As the region becomes increasingly integrated and connected, many issues that matter us require a regional perspective and effort to tackle. The 2016 Integral Conversation aimed to facilitate discussions on sustainable development and to explore new ways to pursue economic growth while respecting people, communities and the planet. The focus was on Culture in Architecture, Healthcare, Education, and Innovation with the view of promoting sustainability on a local, regional and global level.
VISIT SITE
2015
Sustainability and Living
We care about a sustainable future so as to protect and promote our way of living. And hence the first question that must be raised is what do we care about in life? The Integral Conversation of 2015 centered around living, understanding the values that we care for, and the means that we have to protect them. We believe that the sustainable life must be one full of joy and abundance. Together, we will consider how to bring this future to fruition.
VISIT SITE
2014
The Integral Philosophy
The Integral is about understanding the philosophy and realms of existence, and searching for a new development model. In order to achieve sustainability and harmony, one must balance different aspects including the environment, resources, the economy and the human factor. Through the concept of 'Integral', Esquel is creating a development model to harmonize all these aspects, enabling continuous improvement for the communities where it operates and beyond.
VISIT SITE

The website features an animated background built with HTML5 Canvas, which will rotate as the user scrolls down the page, and transitions into different visuals depending on the section. The graphics echo this year's theme on health, and the circular form is a continuation of the visual identity from past years.

Open Wear

Design and Development
Build in Amsterdam

URL
www.open-wear.com

Official Site

Open Wear is a brand of high-quality ski outwear. As a collective of passionate skiers and snowboarders, Open Wear aims to make ski outwear both sustainable and affordable. Started as a kickstarter, it has evolved into a real front runner.

Build in Amsterdam devised a new brand voice for the company—from an updated logo to a new online platform. The goal was to create a shoppable online community. The design team achieved this by using a storytelling approach with products, stories and an Instagram cloud. Without long product descriptions, every feature in the product detail page was shown in a visual way. Every visual aspect of the website is built upon a strong brand identity that respects the brand values.

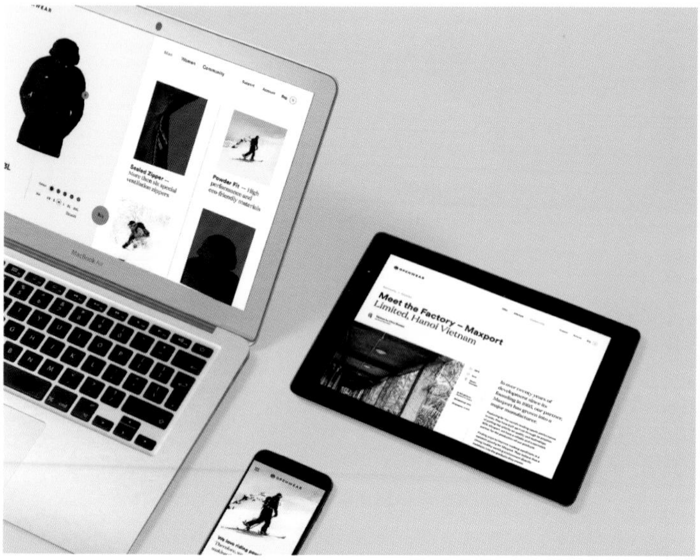
Meet the Factory – Maxport Limited, Hanoi Vietnam

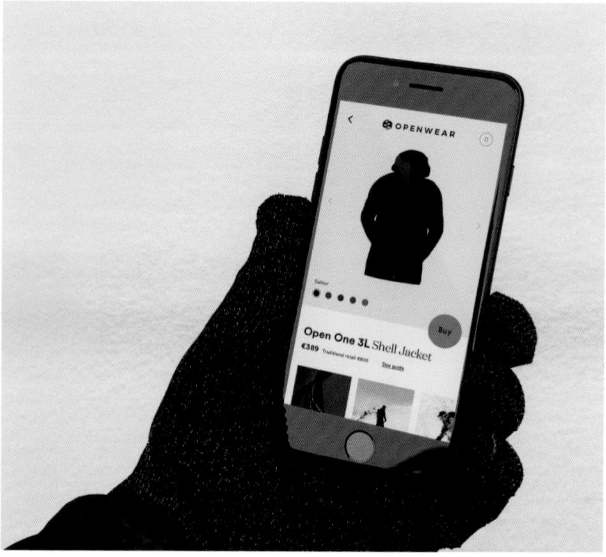
OPENWEAR
Buy
Open One 3L Shell Jacket
€389

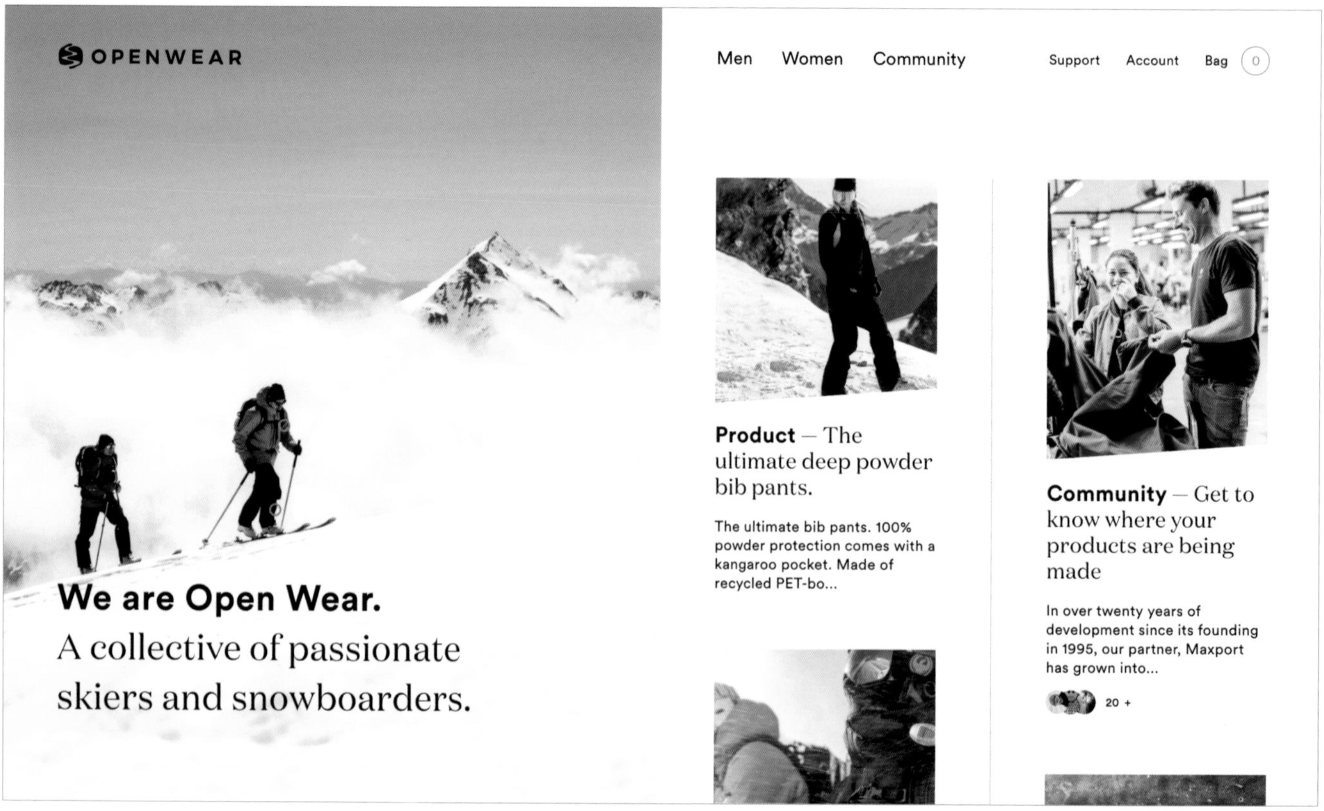
OPENWEAR
Men
Women
Community
Support
Account
Bag
0
We are Open Wear.
A collective of passionate skiers and snowboarders.
Product — The ultimate deep powder bib pants.
The ultimate bib pants. 100% powder protection comes with a kangaroo pocket. Made of recycled PET-bo...
Community — Get to know where your products are being made
In over twenty years of development since its founding in 1995, our partner, Maxport has grown into...
20 +

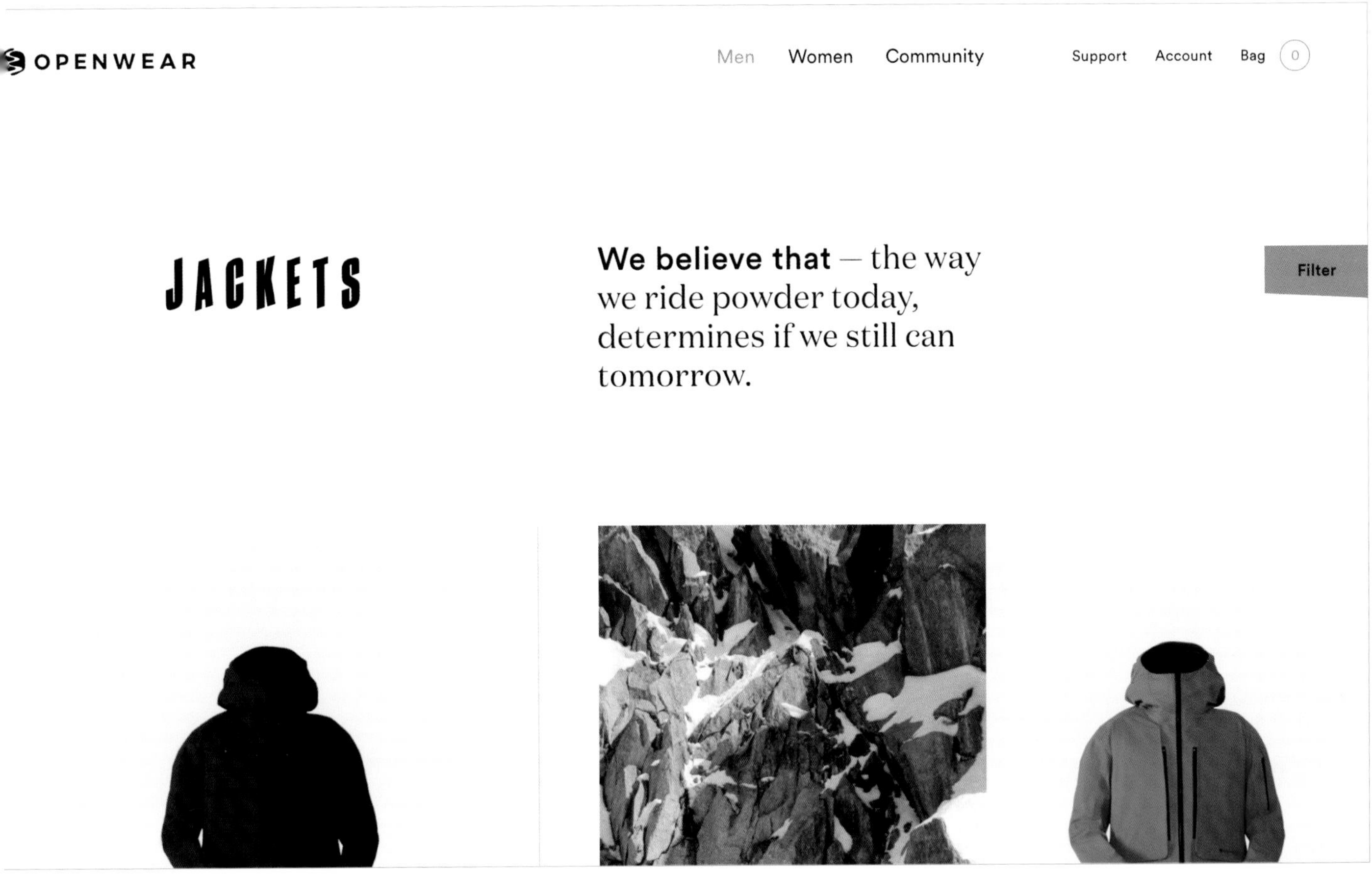
OPENWEAR
Men
Women
Community
Support
Account
Bag
0
JACKETS
We believe that — the way we ride powder today, determines if we still can tomorrow.
Filter

Click

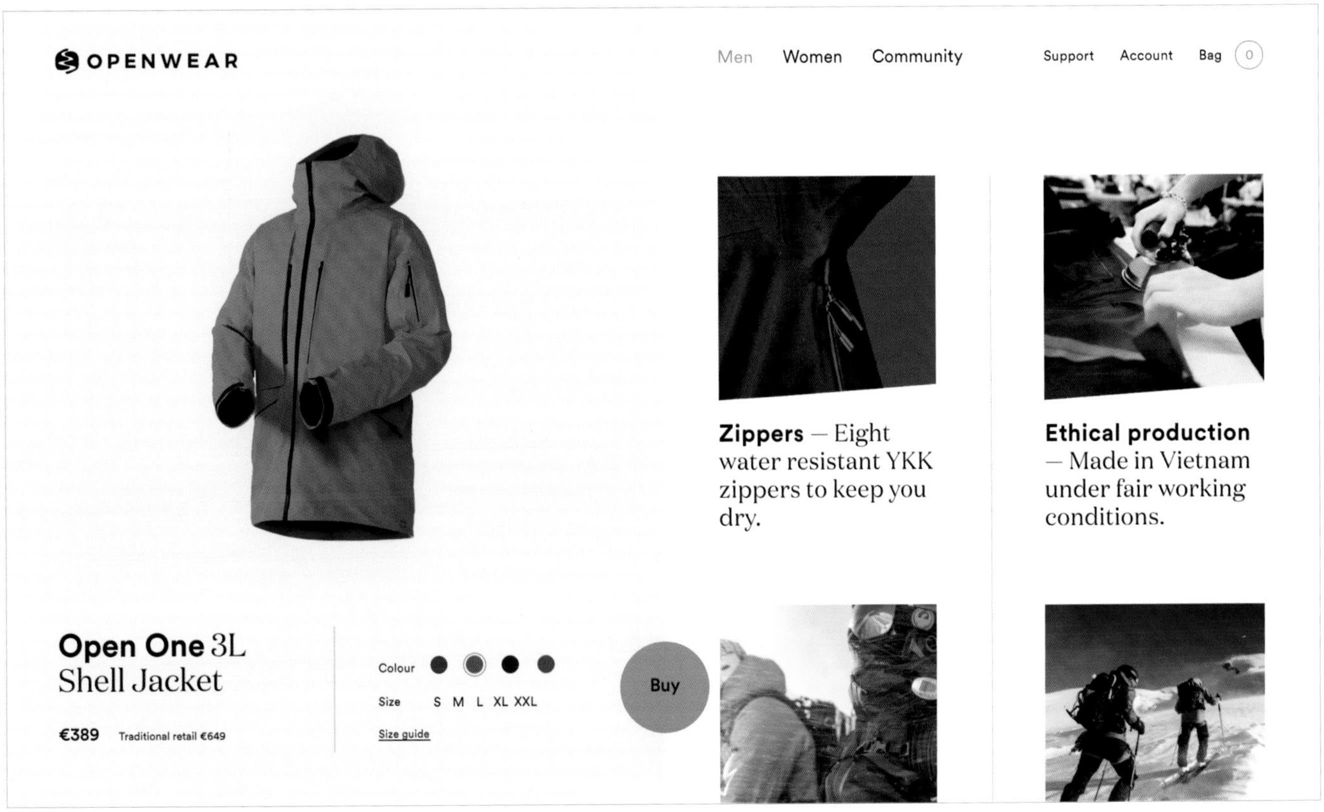
OPENWEAR
Men
Women
Community
Support
Account
Bag
0
Zippers — Eight water resistant YKK zippers to keep you dry.
Ethical production — Made in Vietnam under fair working conditions.
Open One 3L Shell Jacket
€389
Traditional retail €649
Colour
Size
S M L XL XXL
Size guide
Buy

Urban Spaces

Design Agency
LOOT

Art Direction
Ana-Maria Grigoriu

Design
Ana-Maria Grigoriu, Stelian Dobrescu

Development
Stelian Dobrescu

URL
urban-spaces.ro

Official Site

Urban Spaces is a large scale real estate development company with more than 7 ongoing construction sites. It is a concept for those who run away from uniformity, for open people who appreciate design and want to live in spaces which express their personality.

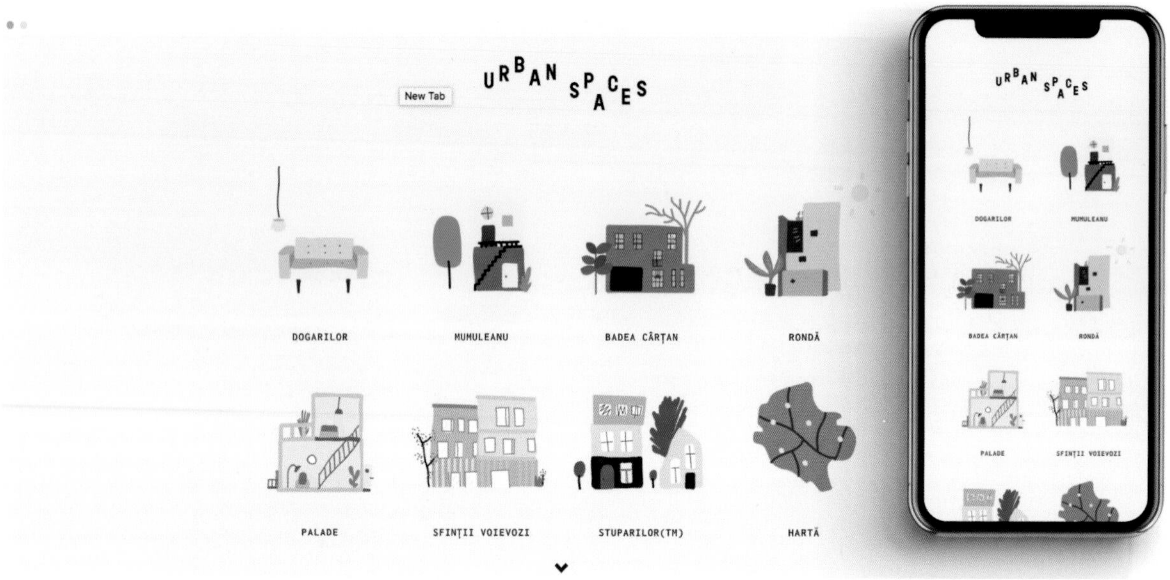
URBAN SPACES
New Tab
DOGARILOR
MUMULEANU
BADEA CÂRȚAN
RONDĂ
PALADE
SFINȚII VOIEVOZI
STUPARILOR(TM)
HARTĂ

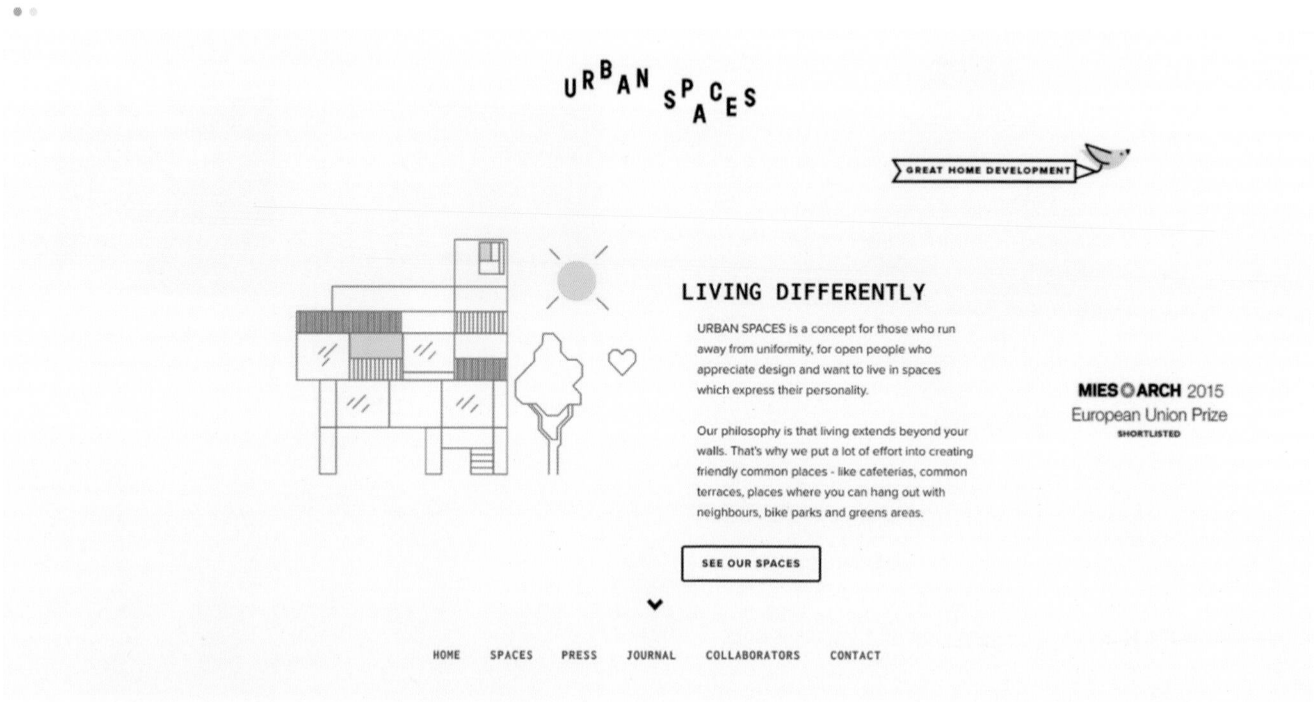
URBAN SPACES
GREAT HOME DEVELOPMENT
LIVING DIFFERENTLY
URBAN SPACES is a concept for those who run away from uniformity, for open people who appreciate design and want to live in spaces which express their personality.
Our philosophy is that living extends beyond your walls. That's why we put a lot of effort into creating friendly common places - like cafeterias, common terraces, places where you can hang out with neighbours, bike parks and greens areas.
SEE OUR SPACES
MIES ARCH 2015
European Union Prize
SHORTLISTED
HOME
SPACES
PRESS
JOURNAL
COLLABORATORS
CONTACT

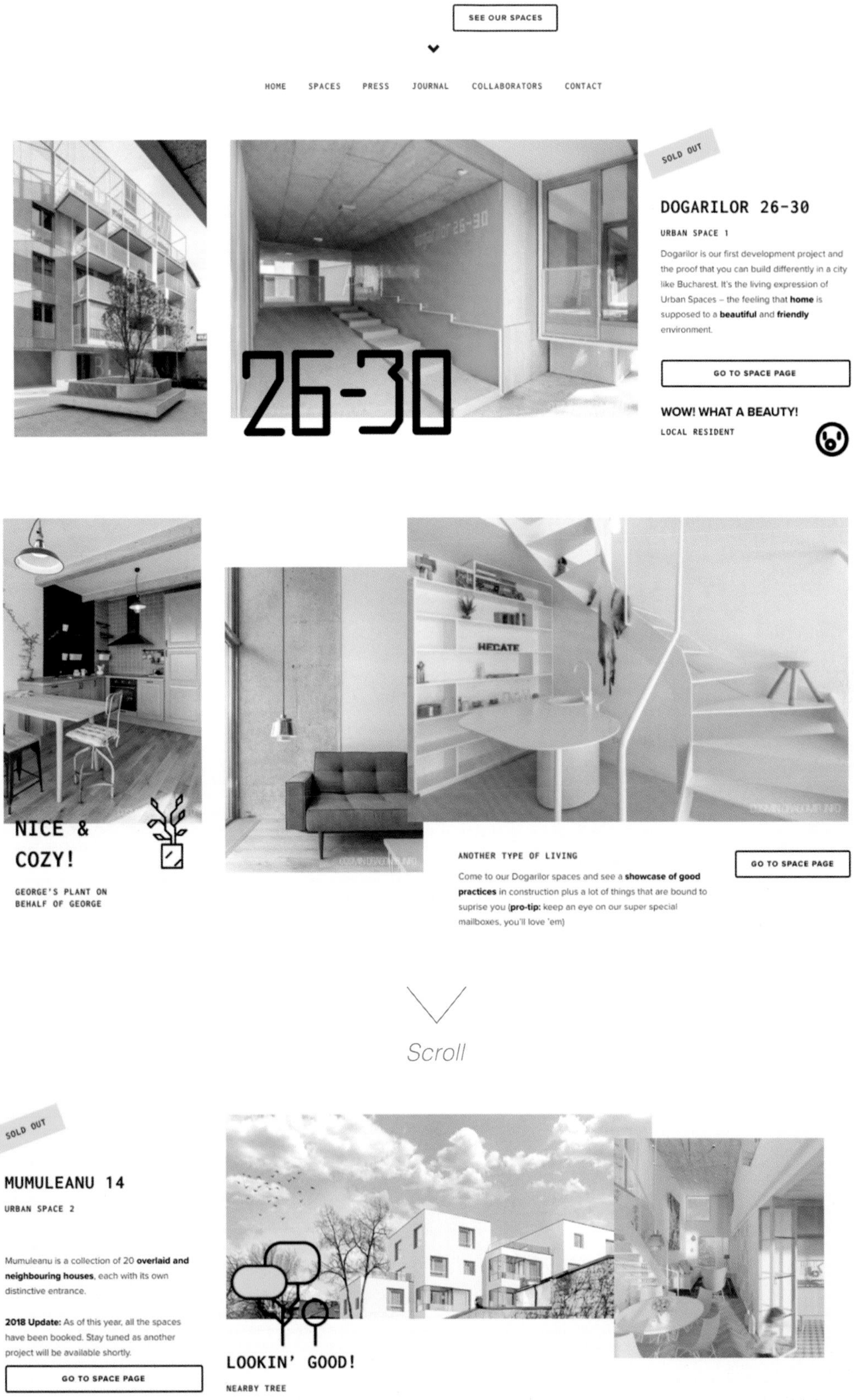
SEE OUR SPACES
HOME SPACES PRESS JOURNAL COLLABORATORS CONTACT
SOLD OUT
DOGARILOR 26-30
URBAN SPACE 1
Dogarilor is our first development project and the proof that you can build differently in a city like Bucharest. It's the living expression of Urban Spaces – the feeling that home is supposed to a beautiful and friendly environment.
GO TO SPACE PAGE
26-30
WOW! WHAT A BEAUTY!
LOCAL RESIDENT
NICE & COZY!
GEORGE'S PLANT ON BEHALF OF GEORGE
ANOTHER TYPE OF LIVING
Come to our Dogarilor spaces and see a showcase of good practices in construction plus a lot of things that are bound to suprise you (pro-tip: keep an eye on our super special mailboxes, you'll love 'em)
GO TO SPACE PAGE
Scroll
SOLD OUT
MUMULEANU 14
URBAN SPACE 2
Mumuleanu is a collection of 20 overlaid and neighbouring houses, each with its own distinctive entrance.
2018 Update: As of this year, all the spaces have been booked. Stay tuned as another project will be available shortly.
GO TO SPACE PAGE
LOOKIN' GOOD!
NEARBY TREE

Studio LOOT was commissioned to design Urban Spaces' website. They drew up an alternative approach to the usual architecture renders that most developers use. All the buildings, either built or in construction, were illustrated and described in a way that makes them friendlier to users. The website was built with the purpose of engaging interested visitors to visit the actual spaces. All the experience is directed towards making them browse, choose a space and send a message to check apartment availability.

ICO Syndicate

Official Site

Design Agency
Griflan

Art Direction and Design
Ron Griffel, Ari Kaplan

Client
ICO Syndicate

URL
icosyndicate.org

ICO Syndicate is a trusted community for private ICO sales. Griflan created a stunningly visual website that introduces the working mechanism and the features of the ICO Syndicate through illustration and animation.

SIGN IN
CONTACT
ICO
SYNDICATE
THE MOST TRUSTED COMMUNITY FOR PRIVATE ICO SALES.
Getting into good ICOs is becoming more difficult all the time. Not anymore, enter the ICO Syndicate.
SIGN UP
TRUSTED
SUPPORT
ICO
CEO
MEMBERS
FOUNDERS
EXCLUSIVE DEALS

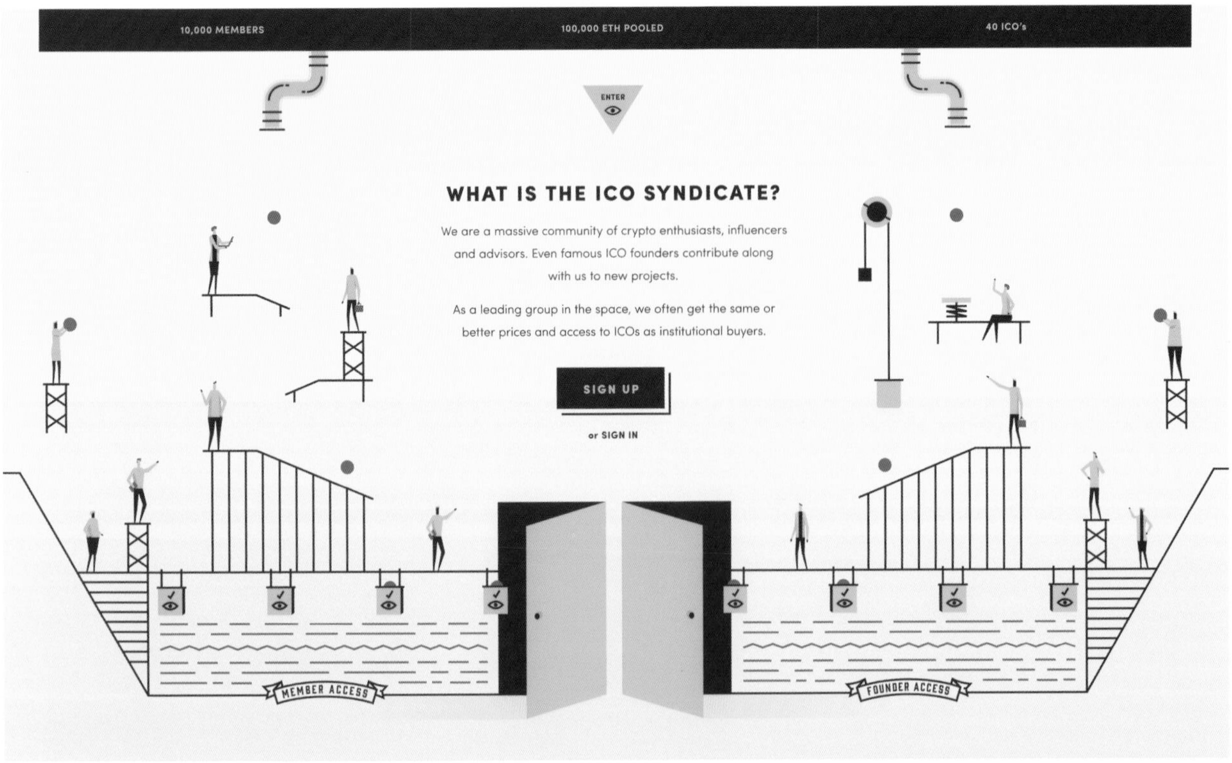

10,000 MEMBERS
100,000 ETH POOLED
40 ICO's
ENTER
WHAT IS THE ICO SYNDICATE?
We are a massive community of crypto enthusiasts, influencers and advisors. Even famous ICO founders contribute along with us to new projects.
As a leading group in the space, we often get the same or better prices and access to ICOs as institutional buyers.
SIGN UP
or SIGN IN
MEMBER ACCESS
FOUNDER ACCESS

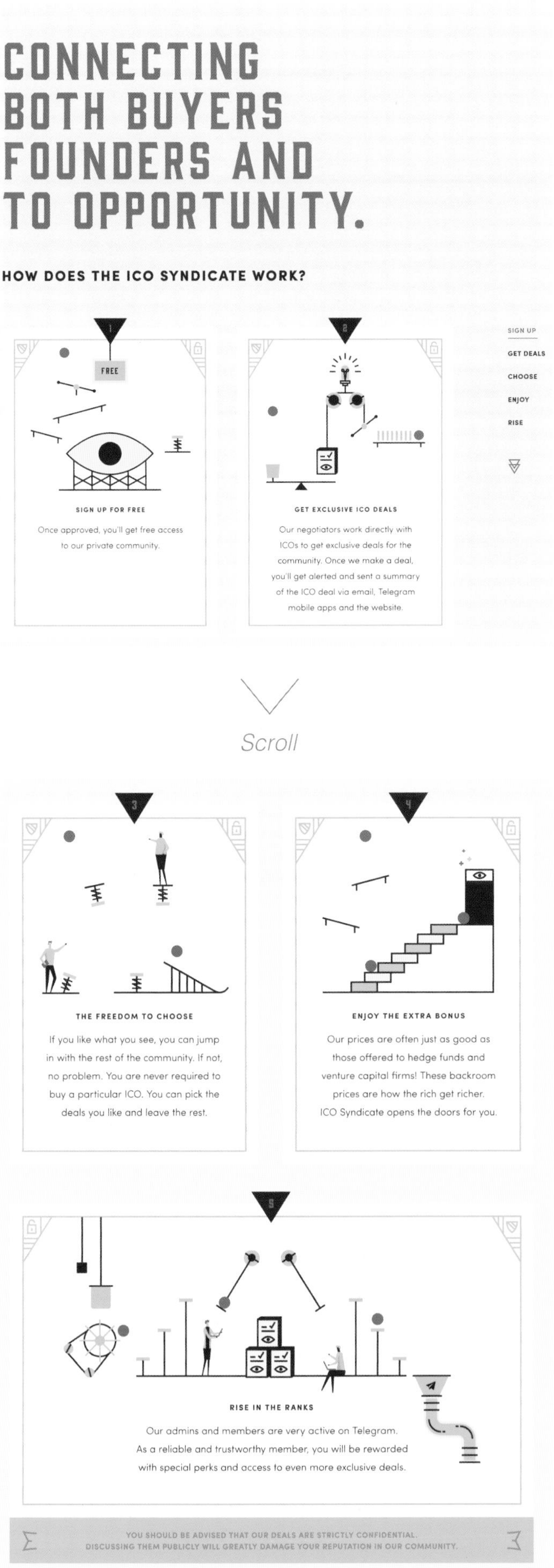
CONNECTING BOTH BUYERS FOUNDERS AND TO OPPORTUNITY.
HOW DOES THE ICO SYNDICATE WORK?
SIGN UP
GET DEALS
CHOOSE
ENJOY
RISE
FREE
SIGN UP FOR FREE
Once approved, you'll get free access to our private community.
GET EXCLUSIVE ICO DEALS
Our negotiators work directly with ICOs to get exclusive deals for the community. Once we make a deal, you'll get alerted and sent a summary of the ICO deal via email, Telegram mobile apps and the website.
Scroll
THE FREEDOM TO CHOOSE
If you like what you see, you can jump in with the rest of the community. If not, no problem. You are never required to buy a particular ICO. You can pick the deals you like and leave the rest.
ENJOY THE EXTRA BONUS
Our prices are often just as good as those offered to hedge funds and venture capital firms! These backroom prices are how the rich get richer. ICO Syndicate opens the doors for you.
RISE IN THE RANKS
Our admins and members are very active on Telegram. As a reliable and trustworthy member, you will be rewarded with special perks and access to even more exclusive deals.
YOU SHOULD BE ADVISED THAT OUR DEALS ARE STRICTLY CONFIDENTIAL. DISCUSSING THEM PUBLICLY WILL GREATLY DAMAGE YOUR REPUTATION IN OUR COMMUNITY.

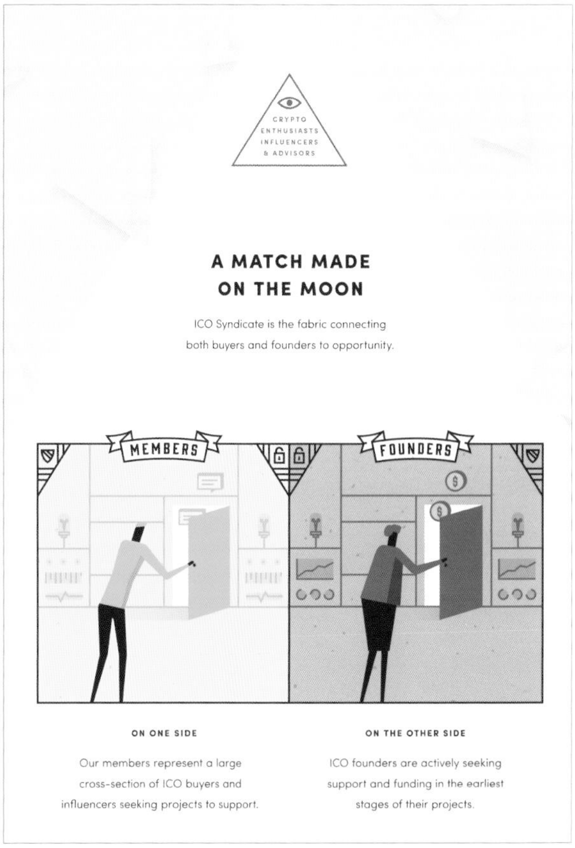
CRYPTO ENTHUSIASTS INFLUENCERS & ADVISORS
A MATCH MADE ON THE MOON
ICO Syndicate is the fabric connecting both buyers and founders to opportunity.
MEMBERS
FOUNDERS
ON ONE SIDE
Our members represent a large cross-section of ICO buyers and influencers seeking projects to support.
ON THE OTHER SIDE
ICO founders are actively seeking support and funding in the earliest stages of their projects.

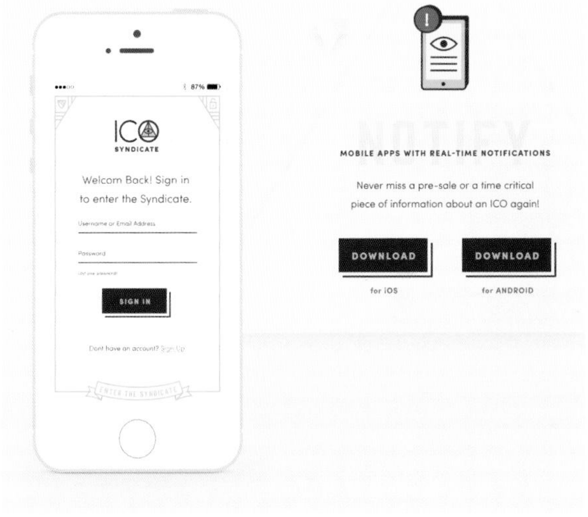
ICO SYNDICATE
Welcom Back! Sign in to enter the Syndicate.
SIGN IN
MOBILE APPS WITH REAL-TIME NOTIFICATIONS
Never miss a pre-sale or a time critical piece of information about an ICO again!
DOWNLOAD
for iOS
DOWNLOAD
for ANDROID

With the illustration style, the design team wanted to show something whimsical with a problem solving approach. They took a lot of their inspiration from illuminati design and the idea of a "Secret Society".

Share This! Image Based Bullying. So not OK.

Art Direction and Design
Amanda Burchell, Jessica Moses, Michelle Le

Initiation
Supre Foundation, Alannah & Madeline Foundation

Digital Marketing Consultancy and Technical Development
Sonar Group, Melbourne

URL
supre.com.au/the-supre-foundation/supre-foundation-amf-hub.html

Official Site

The Share This! content hub was created to launch a partnership between the Supre Foundation and the Alannah & Madeline Foundation to educate about the topic of image based bullying and provide channels of support for people experiencing it.

IMAGE BASED BULLYING SO NOT OK.
Everything you need to know to stay safe from Image based bullying. So Not OK.
CENSORED
EXIT

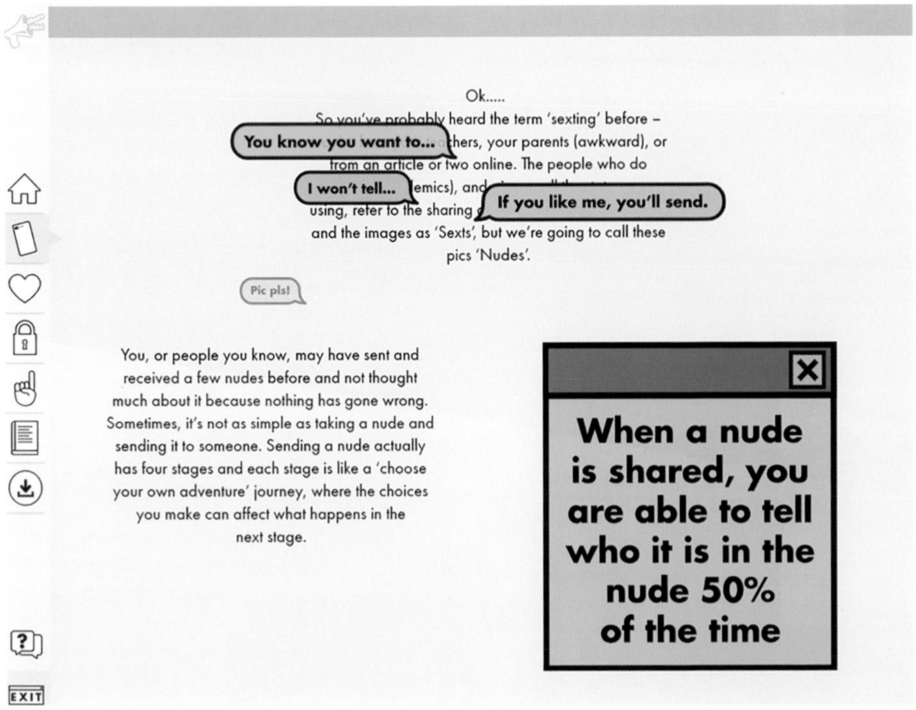

Ok.....
heard the term 'sexting' before –
You know you want to...
hers, your parents (awkward), or
from an article or two online. The people who do
I won't tell...
If you like me, you'll send.
and the images as 'Sexts', but we're going to call these pics 'Nudes'.
Pic pls!
You, or people you know, may have sent and received a few nudes before and not thought much about it because nothing has gone wrong. Sometimes, it's not as simple as taking a nude and sending it to someone. Sending a nude actually has four stages and each stage is like a 'choose your own adventure' journey, where the choices you make can affect what happens in the next stage.
When a nude is shared, you are able to tell who it is in the nude 50% of the time
EXIT

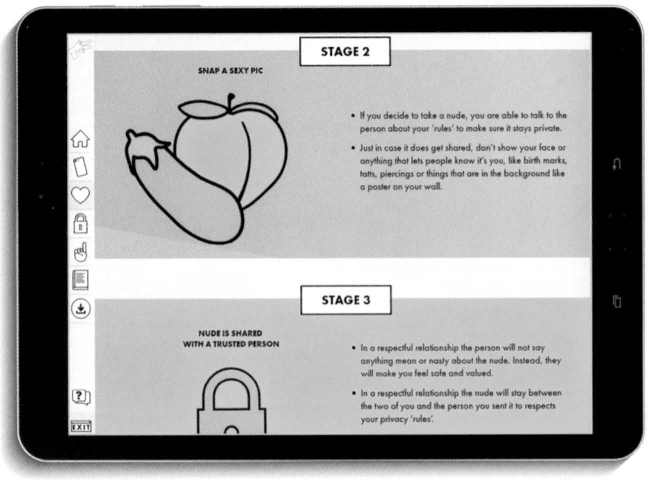
STAGE 2
SNAP A SEXY PIC
• If you decide to take a nude, you are able to talk to the person about your 'rules' to make sure it stays private.
• Just in case it does get shared, don't show your face or anything that lets people know it's you, like birth marks, tatts, piercings or things that are in the background like a poster on your wall.
STAGE 3
NUDE IS SHARED WITH A TRUSTED PERSON
• In a respectful relationship the person will not say anything mean or nasty about the nude. Instead, they will make you feel safe and valued.
• In a respectful relationship the nude will stay between the two of you and the person you sent it to respects your privacy 'rules'.
EXIT

HERE'S THE THING...
Let's use stages 3 and 4 as an example:
Someone receives a nude from their partner. Now they have a choice. The receiver can either keep it to themselves or they can move into stage 4 by sharing it with someone else without permission. Stage 4 is image based bullying, which is SO NOT OK.
• Not all four stages happen every
someone takes a nude without be
to their partner, who keeps it to th
stages 1 and 4 won't happen.
• If a nude is taken, sent on purpose and kept private, most of the time it's ok and no one gets hurt.
• Stages 2 and 3 represent the most common scenario, and luckily no one gets hurt.
76%
of Australians who
EXIT

The graphic style draws inspiration from internet interface elements such as pop-up windows and clickable buttons. Through using elements in the online world, the design team wishes to represent the digital journey of a shared image in a subtle yet impactful way. This graphic style also allows them to show facts, figures and information in a way that encourages users to engage with the information and continue to read until completion. The vector illustrations are playful and a little cheeky, which creates a visual language that the audiences resonate with. The colour palette is a mixture of bold complimentary colours which are specifically selected to be gender neutral.

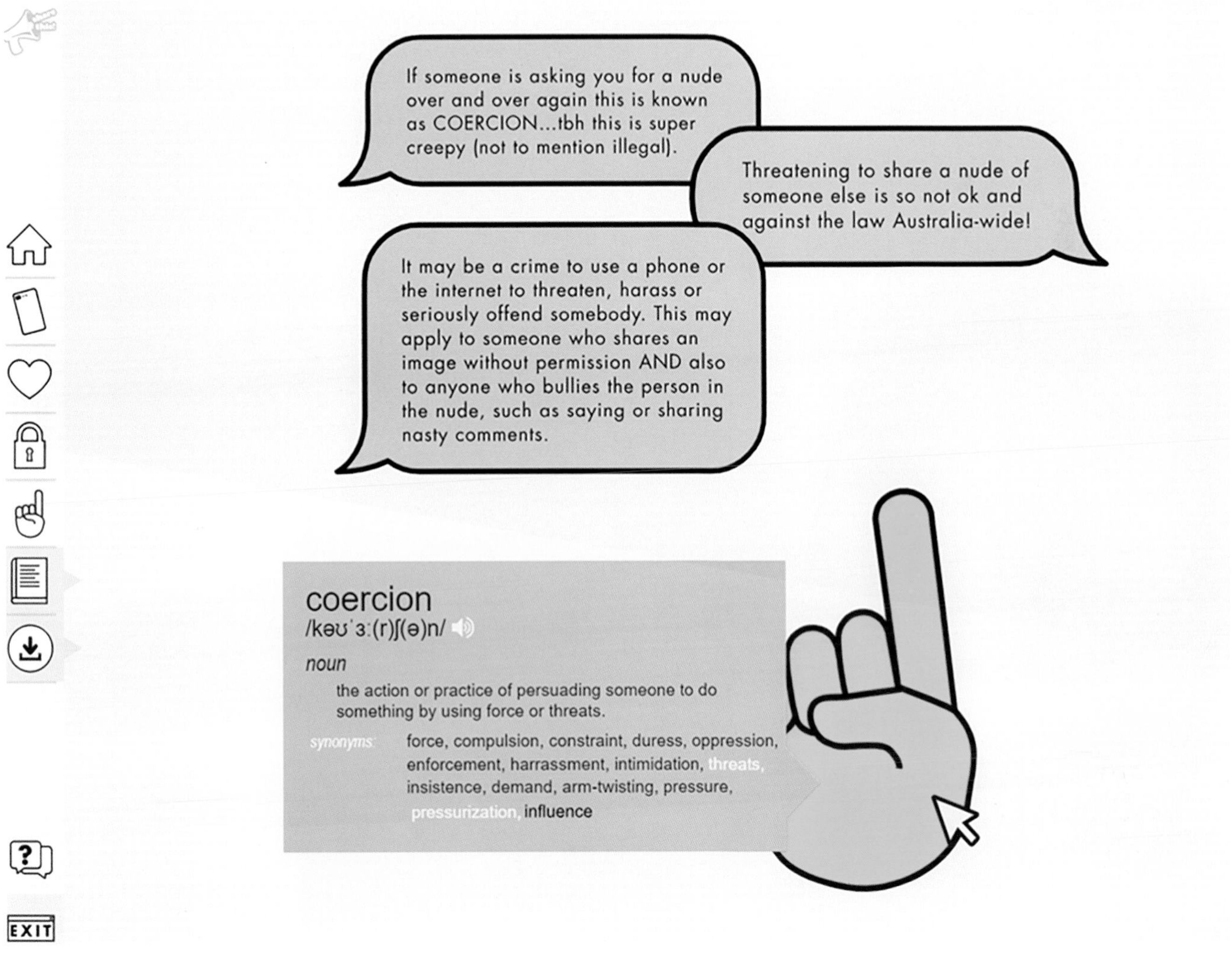
If someone is asking you for a nude over and over again this is known as COERCION...tbh this is super creepy (not to mention illegal).
Threatening to share a nude of someone else is so not ok and against the law Australia-wide!
It may be a crime to use a phone or the internet to threaten, harass or seriously offend somebody. This may apply to someone who shares an image without permission AND also to anyone who bullies the person in the nude, such as saying or sharing nasty comments.
coercion
/kəʊˈɜː(r)ʃ(ə)n/
noun
the action or practice of persuading someone to do something by using force or threats.
synonyms: force, compulsion, constraint, duress, oppression, enforcement, harrassment, intimidation, threats, insistence, demand, arm-twisting, pressure, pressurization, influence
EXIT

Urbanbelly

Design Agency
Clique Studios LLC

Creative Direction and Design
Sue Janna Truscott

Development
Sean McNally

Client
Urban Belly

URL
www.urbanbellychicago.com

Official Site

Urbanbelly is Master Chef Bill Kim's creative experiment for testing out eclectic Asian fusion recipes. Their previous website wasn't doing their exquisite menu justice. Clique Studios applied Urbanbelly's new branding to design a reimagined, interactive website, taking a "show, don't tell" approach to highlighting their cuisine. They directed and shot custom photography and video, and incorporated imagery and video throughout to give users a "real taste" of urbanbelly online. They also designed custom icons and subtle animations to create a dynamic, interactive experience with texture and playfulness.

MENU
LOCATIONS & HOURS
CHEF BILL KIM'S
URBANBELLY
DUMPLINGS • BOOZE • BOWLS
ORDER NOW
DUMPLINGS!
VIEW OUR MENU

KUNG FU
HOSPITALITY
KIM-CREATIVITY IN THE HOUSE!
MASTER CHEF
CHEF BILL KIM
Award-winning Chef Bill Kim honed his culinary skills at world-renowned establishments Charlie Trotter's and Le Lan. Kim's story is a quintessentially American one that dives into the melting pot of cultures and experiences to create an identity that is uniquely his own. He started urbanbelly in 2008 to bring together his wide-ranging passions. Asian + American. Fine-dining techniques + neighborhood comfort. Classic dishes + joyous creativity.

MENU
LOCATIONS & HOURS
CHEF BILL KIM'S
URBANBELLY
DUMPLINGS · BOOZE · BOWLS
ORDER NOW
MENU
WE DELIVER!
ORDER NOW
WICKER PARK MENU ▾
WEST LOOP MENU PDF
Gluten Free | Vegetarian
DUMPLINGS
1. PORK & CILANTRO - $1.50
URBAN BOWLS

さんぴん
NEW HERO
LOCATIONS
WEST LOOP
1400 W. Randolph St. (map)
773-583-0500
Open today: 11:30AM - 10PM
WICKER PARK
1542 N. Damen Ave. (map)
773-904-8606
Open today: 11:30AM - 10PM
LOCATIONS & HOURS

DUMPLINGS, BOOZE, AND BOWLS
MENU
Take a tour of the world through Chef Bill Kim's creations. Honoring authenticity and confronting convention, urbanbelly presents the radically delicious and curiously familiar. These dumplings, booze, and bowls will make you happy for here or to-go.
VIEW MENU

Micropolis

Official Site

Design Agency
Trama Studio

Design
Sebastián Águila

Development
José Soler

Client
Micropolis

URL
micropolis.cl

This project is the website and branding design done for Micropolis, a collective group that studies the history of public transportation in Chile. They have released three studies so far focusing on Santiago, Valparaiso and the last one regarding the ETCE (Empresa de Transportes Colectivos del Estado), a national company that took care of different transportation solutions between 1940-1980. The main objective of the website is to showcase the three main studies of the collective and its historic photo archive. Also as part of the design process, Trama Studio developed a custom design font and various vehicle illustrations.

MICROPOLIS
1
1857
1992
ARCHIVO VISUAL
TRANSPORTE PÚBLICO DE SANTIAGO
VER RELATO

AÁBCDEÉFGHIÍJKL
MNOÓPQRSTUÚV
WXYZ
CARROS DE SANGRE
SANTIAGO
TRANVÍAS ELÉCTRICOS
VALPARAÍSO

TRANVÍAS BELGAS
1923- 1952
CAPACIDAD 70 PASAJEROS
TROLES ETCE
1953-HOY EN DÍA
CAPACIDAD 80 PASAJEROS

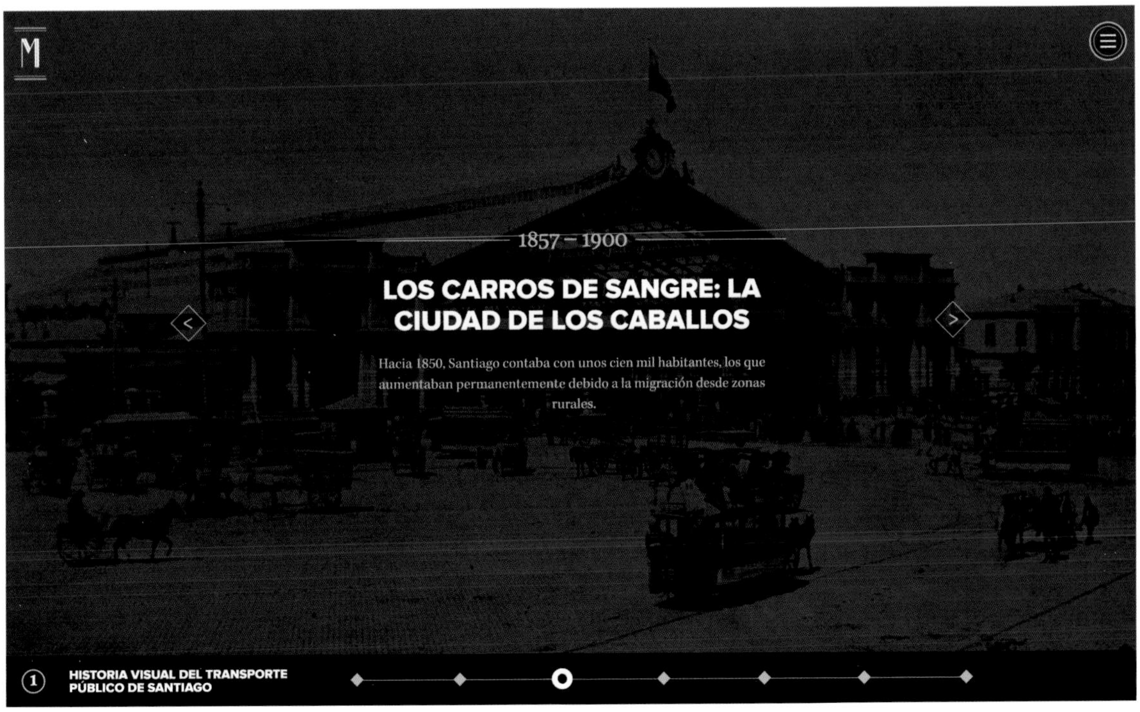
M
1857 – 1900
LOS CARROS DE SANGRE: LA CIUDAD DE LOS CABALLOS
Hacia 1850, Santiago contaba con unos cien mil habitantes, los que aumentaban permanentemente debido a la migración desde zonas rurales.
1
HISTORIA VISUAL DEL TRANSPORTE PÚBLICO DE SANTIAGO

M
6/19
111
1
HISTORIA VISUAL DEL TRANSPORTE
PÚBLICO DE SANTIAGO

Click

M
5/16
CINZANO
125
1
HISTORIA VISUAL DEL TRANSPORTE
PÚBLICO DE SANTIAGO

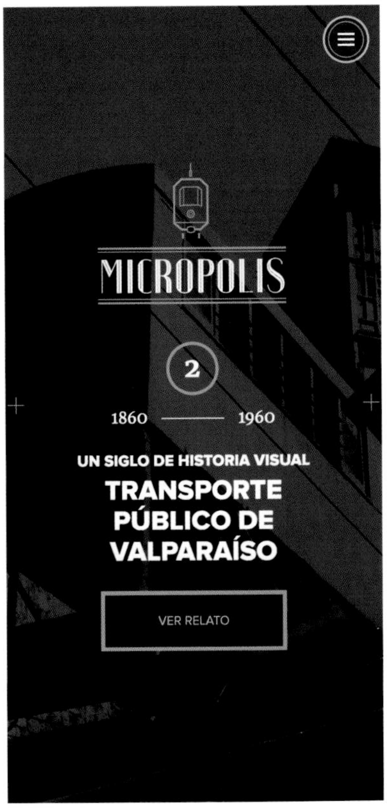
MICROPOLIS
2
1860 1960
UN SIGLO DE HISTORIA VISUAL
TRANSPORTE PÚBLICO DE VALPARAÍSO
VER RELATO

M
TRANVIAS BELGAS
1923-1952
capacidad 70 pasajeros aprox.

M
1863
TRANVÍAS DE TRACCIÓN ANIMAL
En 1863 se inauguró el servicio de tranvías de tracción animal, tercero de su tipo en toda América Latina. Estos vehículos eran carruajes de armazones metálicos instalados sobre rieles, lo que representó una innovación frente a las formas de movilización tradicionales de la época.

Tap

M
1/10

M
7/10

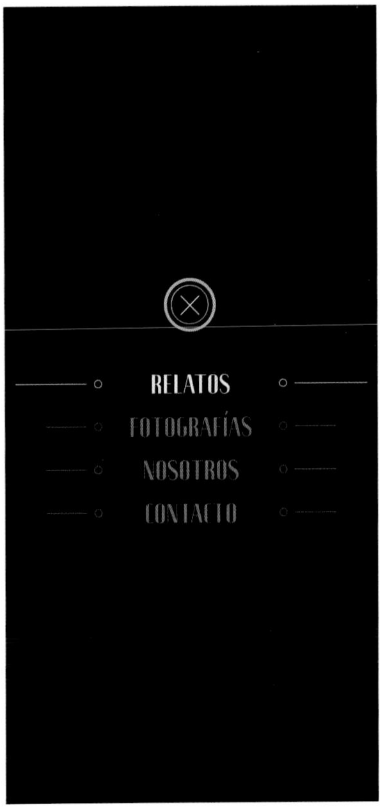
RELATOS
FOTOGRAFÍAS
NOSOTROS
CONTACTO

Vintage Web Production

Design and Development
Vintage

URL
vintage.agency

Official Site

Vintage is an award-winning web production company in Ukraine. For the agency's website, the designers wish to use cutting-edge technologies to show to the world that they are the trend-setters in the web space.

The Vintage's website was created with a pinch of glitch, interactive scroll, and piece of love in every detail. The logo on the home page is a pulsating form consists of polygonal glass particles. The designers have used minimalistic black-white corporate style and combined it with eye-catching elements, like pink triangles, or different fonts. For the portfolio section, they have surprised the visitors with a VR portfolio that visitors could experience the agency's work in an immersive way.

BLOG MENU
RU
EN
WEB PRODUCTION
CREATORS OF WORLD-CLASS WEBSITES
VINTAGE
WEB
PRODUCTION
PORTFOLIO

Scroll

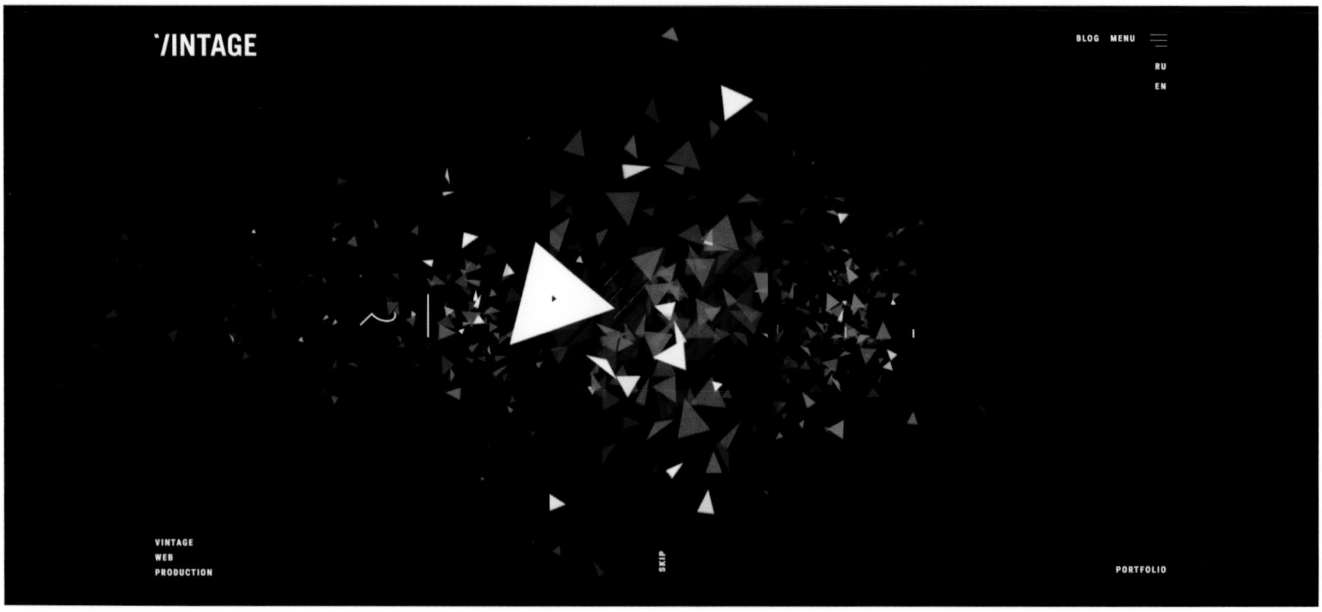
BLOG MENU
RU
EN
VINTAGE
WEB
PRODUCTION
SKIP
PORTFOLIO

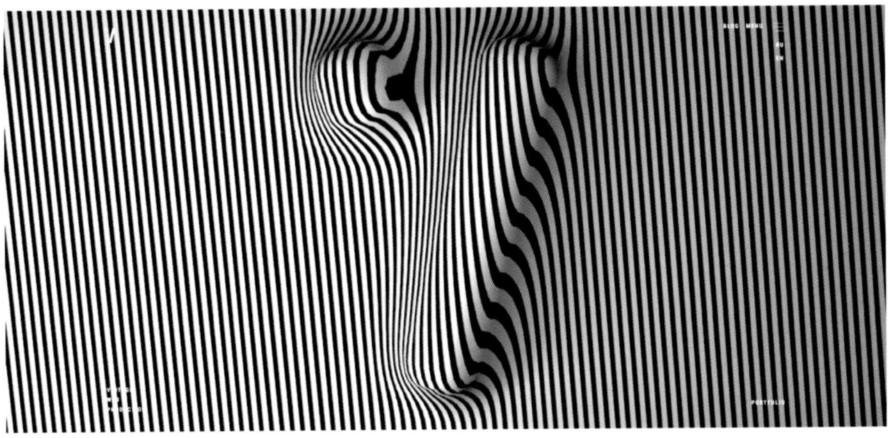

/INTAGE
GO BACK
SERGEYMAKHNO
RGEY MAKHNO
VINTAGE
WEB
PRODUCTION

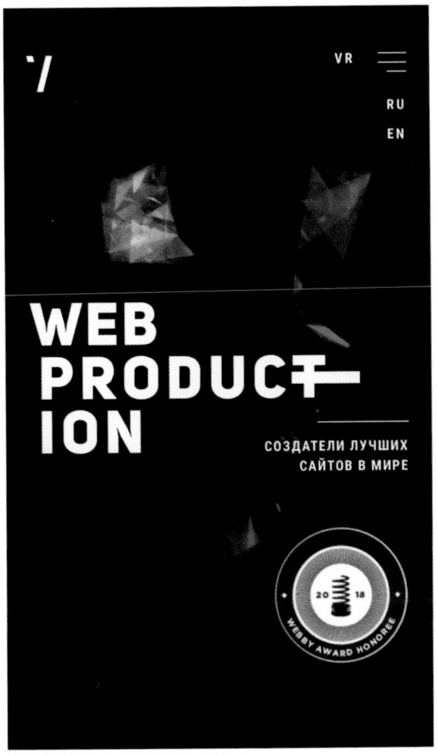
VR
RU
EN
WEB
PRODUCTION
СОЗДАТЕЛИ ЛУЧШИХ
САЙТОВ В МИРЕ
WEBBY AWARD HONOREE

VR
CREATIV
TY
ПОСМОТРЕТЬ КЕЙС
KHNO

VR
AIIA
OBERIG JEWELRY

MoMu

Design Agency
Base Design

Client
MoMu

URL
www.momu.be

Official Site

Antwerp's fashion museum MoMu closed its doors in 2018 for renovation and will reopen in 2020. Although the museum building is not open to public during the renovation, it is still organizing activities and setting up exhibitions elsewhere.

In order to convey the above message, Base Design worked with the museum team to design a brand new informative website. At the same time, they grabbed the momentum to push MoMu's digital visual identity to a new level, in order to better reflect the museum's new and inspiring vision of its future.

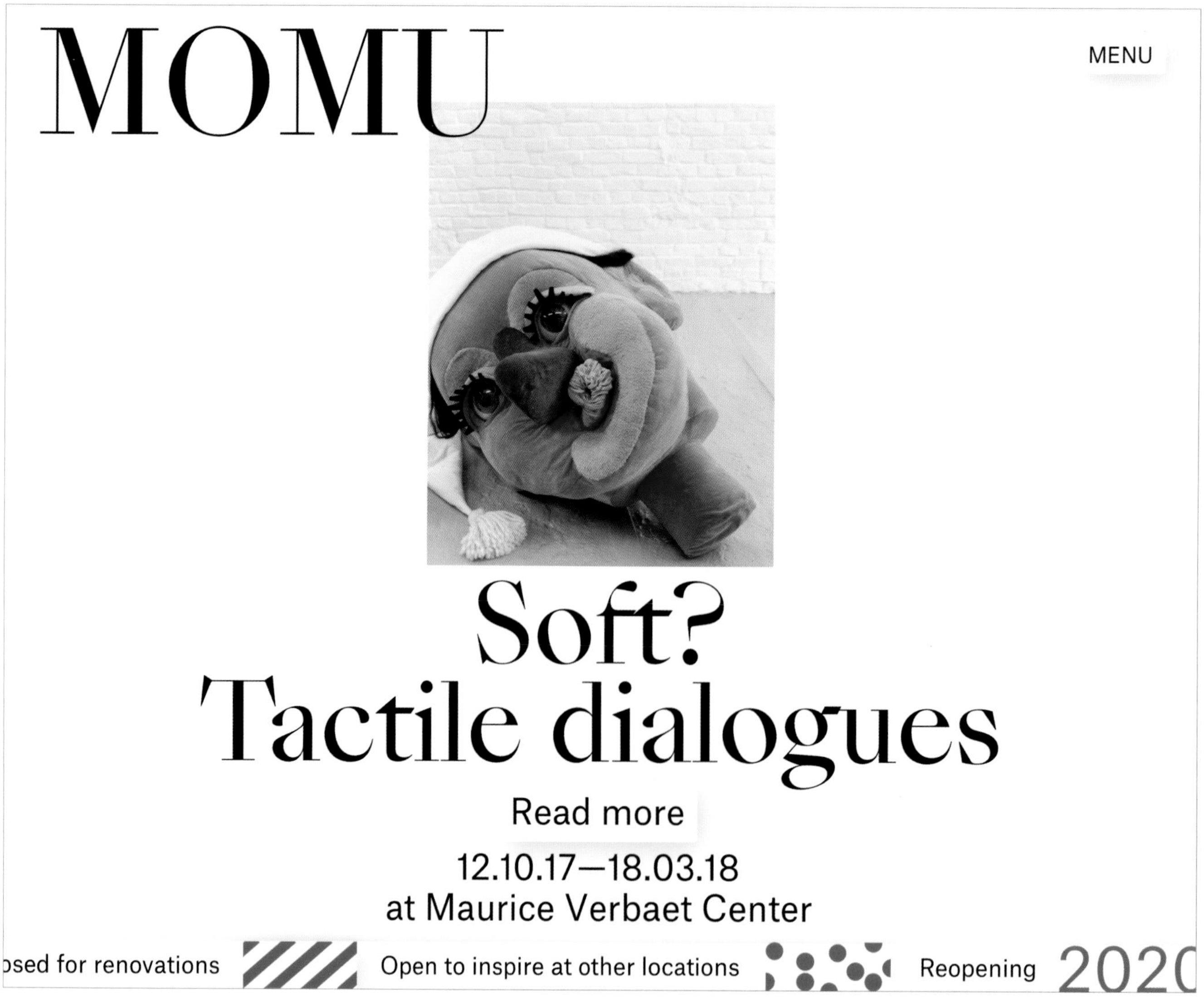
MOMU
MENU
Soft?
Tactile dialogues
Read more
12.10.17—18.03.18
at Maurice Verbaet Center
osed for renovations
Open to inspire at other locations
Reopening 2020

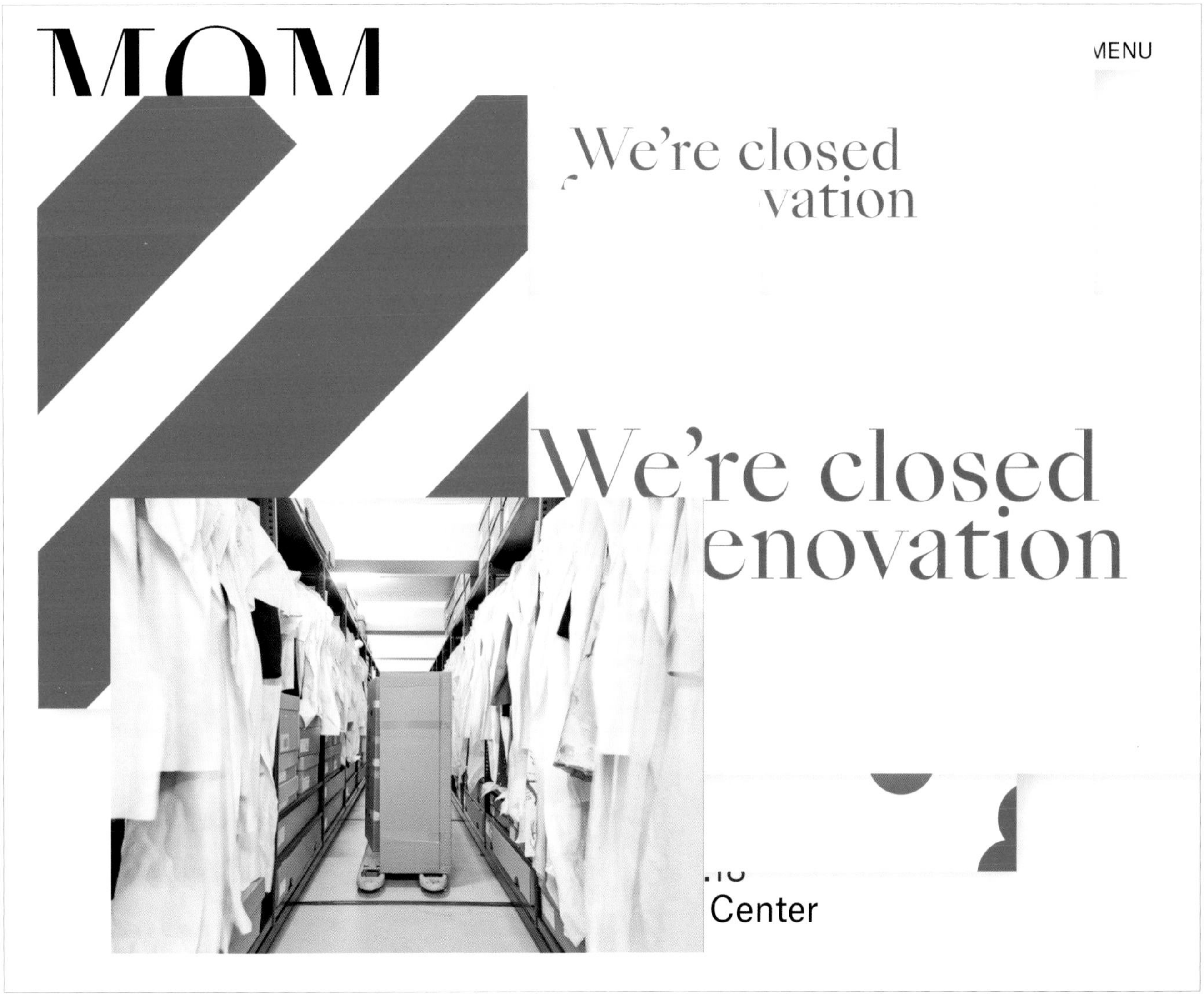
We’re closed
We’re closed
Center

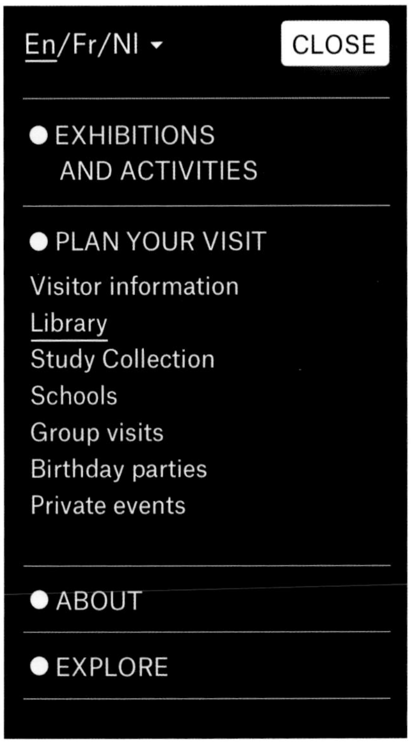
En/Fr/Nl
CLOSE
EXHIBITIONS AND ACTIVITIES
PLAN YOUR VISIT
Visitor information
Library
Study Collection
Schools
Group visits
Birthday parties
Private events
ABOUT
EXPLORE

MOMU
MENU
Olivier Theyskens, She walks in beauty
More info
12.10.17 — 18.03.18
At Maurice Verbaet Center

EXHIBITION ARCHIVE
2017 ↓
2016 ↓
2015 ↓
2014 ↓
2013 ↓
A
Vlaanderen
verbeelding werkt
De Museumstichting
Press
Open Fashion
Privacy statement

Festival Papillons de Nuit 17th Edition

Website

Art Direction and Development
Murmure

URL
archives.murmure.me/papillonsdenuit2017

The Papillons de Nuit Festival is a music festival held in France. In 2017, it has renewed its trust in Murmure to design its visual identity and website. A special request was made this year: to pay tribute to the Monterey Pop Festival "Music, Love and Flowers".

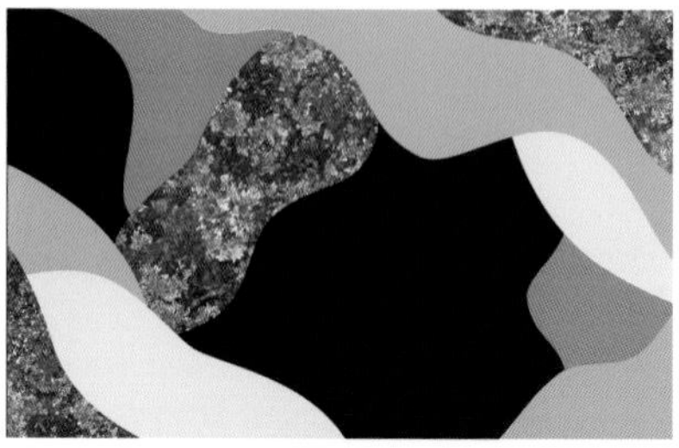

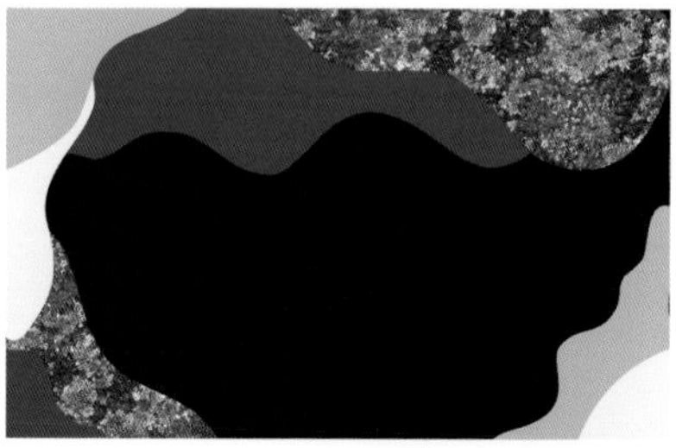

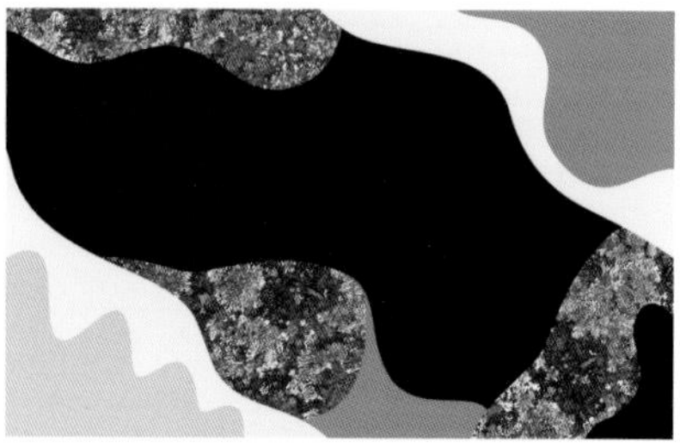

FESTIVAL
PAPILLONS
DE NUIT
2.3.4 JUIN 2017
Normandie

FESTIVAL
PAPILLONS
DE NUIT
2.3.4 JUIN 2017
Normandie

FESTIVAL
PAPILLONS
DE NUIT
2.3.4 JUIN 2017
Normandie

FESTIVAL
PAPILLONS
DE NUIT
2.3.4 JUIN 2017
Normandie
PROGRAMME • BILLETTERIE • PAY&PLAY • PRATIQUE • L'ASSOCIATION • BLOG • CLUB P2N
Actualités P2N
12.07.2017
P2N Summer #3 : le concours de l'été revient !
Tentez de gagner des cadeaux : 3 forfaits 3 jours pour Papillons de Nuit 2018 à gagner pour les 3 meilleures photos sélectionnées par la team P2N ou des abonnements 3 mois gratuits à Spotify Premium pour les 20 meilleures photos suivantes.
Lire la suite
24.06.2017
Les nouveautés de P2N Pay&Play
Depuis 2015, le paiement des consommations sur le site du festival se fait grâce à P2N Pay&Play, notre dispositif de paiement dématérialisé. A l'aide de la puce sur votre bracelet, vos règlements sont instantanés et sécurisés. Découvrez les nouvelles options cette année ! Afin d'améliorer toujours plus le dispositif, des nouvelles options sont disponibles.
Lire la suite
ACHETEZ VOS BILLETS
INFORMATIONS PRATIQUES

FESTIVAL
PAPILLONS DE NUIT
2.3.4 JUIN 2017
PROGRAMME
BILLETTERIE
PAY&PLAY
PRATIQUE
L'ASSOCIATION
BLOG
CLUB P2N
Programme
GRAMATIK
JAIN
MARTIN SOLVEIG
THE KILLS
ADOPTEZ
L'ESPRIT FESTIVAL
REVIVEZ LE FESTIVAL

P2N
JAIN
LIVE
Artiste précédent
Artiste suivant
ELECTRO / POP - FRANCE
Samedi 3 Juin
23h15 - 00h30
Scène Vulcain

P2N
LIVE
FESTIVAL
PAPILLONS DE NUIT
2.3.4 JUIN 2017
Normandie
Pratique
SUR PLACE
P2N, c'est bien plus que des concerts ! Retrouvez tous les services proposés sur le site du festival et le camping.
CAMPING & HÉBERGEMENT
L'expérience P2N continue aussi sur le camping du festival ! D'autres solutions d'hébergement sont également à votre disposition.

Murmure has played with those graphic shapes that were typical in the 1980s and explored a new material, one that is botanical and unexpected: Lichen. Naturally graphic, this organic matter used in black and white adds depth and highlights curved shapes. Used flat, these shapes form a contemporary graphic pattern.

For 3 years, Murmure has developed, alongside the Papillons de Nuit Festival team, a custom website based on the WordPress CMS. They improve it every year by adding features that specifically meet the festival's needs. They pay great attention to optimising code quality so that navigation may be optimal on mobile devices.

Xavier Cussó's Portfolio

Design
Xavier Cussó

Development
Christian MacMillan

URL
xaviercusso.com

Official Site

This is the portfolio for visual designer and art director Xavier Cussó. The site features a variety of selected projects designed by Xavier during his time working at several design studios, advertising and digital production agencies around the world. The main objective was to give visibility to what Xavier is capable of now that he is available as a full-time freelancer.

XAVIER CUSSÓ
BARCELONA
ART DIRECTOR & VISUAL DESIGNER

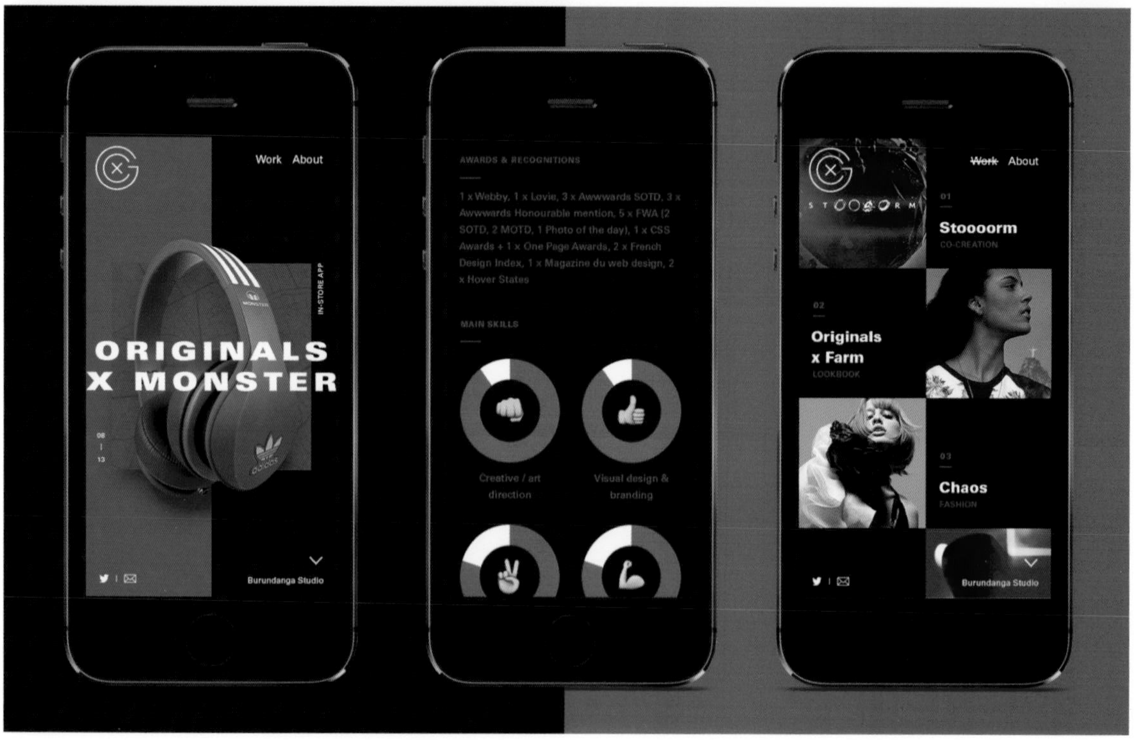
Work About
ORIGINALS X MONSTER
IN-STORE APP
Burundanga Studio
AWARDS & RECOGNITIONS
MAIN SKILLS
Creative / art direction
Visual design & branding
Work About
Stoooorm
CO-CREATION
Originals x Farm
LOOKBOOK
Chaos
FASHION
Burundanga Studio

Work About
EXPERIENCE
SCENT
HUNTER
FLORIENTAL
COMME des GARÇONS
06
12
Say hello
Burundanga Studio, 2018

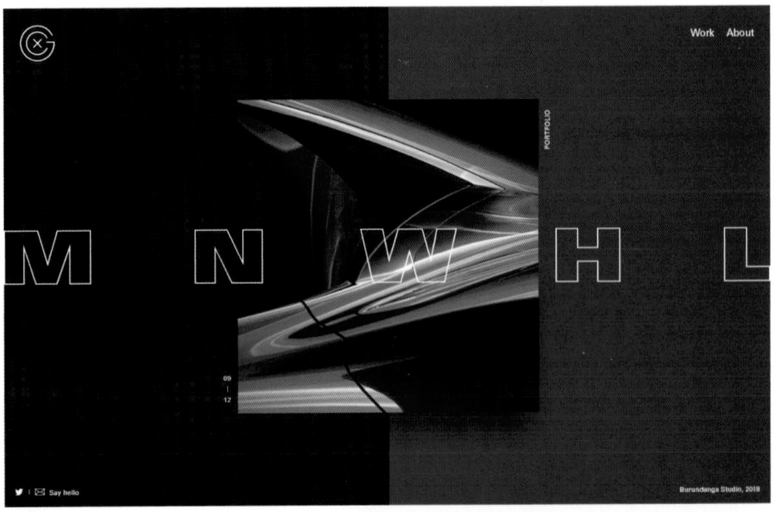
Work About
PORTFOLIO
M N W H L
09
12
Say hello
Burundanga Studio, 2018

S T O O O R M
02
Chaos
PORTFOLIO
04
Work About
Scent Hunter
EXPERIENCES
01
Stooooorm
CO-CREATION
03
H2O
ART GALLERY
05
FLORIENTAL
Say hello
Burundanga Studio, 2017

European Music Incubator

Art Direction and Development
Murmure

URL
music-incubator.eu

Official Site

European Music Incubator is a European project coordinated by the Trempolino team (in Nantes), who entrusted Murmure with designing its visual identity and website.

Through a strong highlighting of the project's graphic charter and identity, the Internet user is directly immersed within the brand's universe. A one-page website, entirely manageable, is recreational and dynamic, custom-designed in order to communicate on the project and present its timing, content and partners.

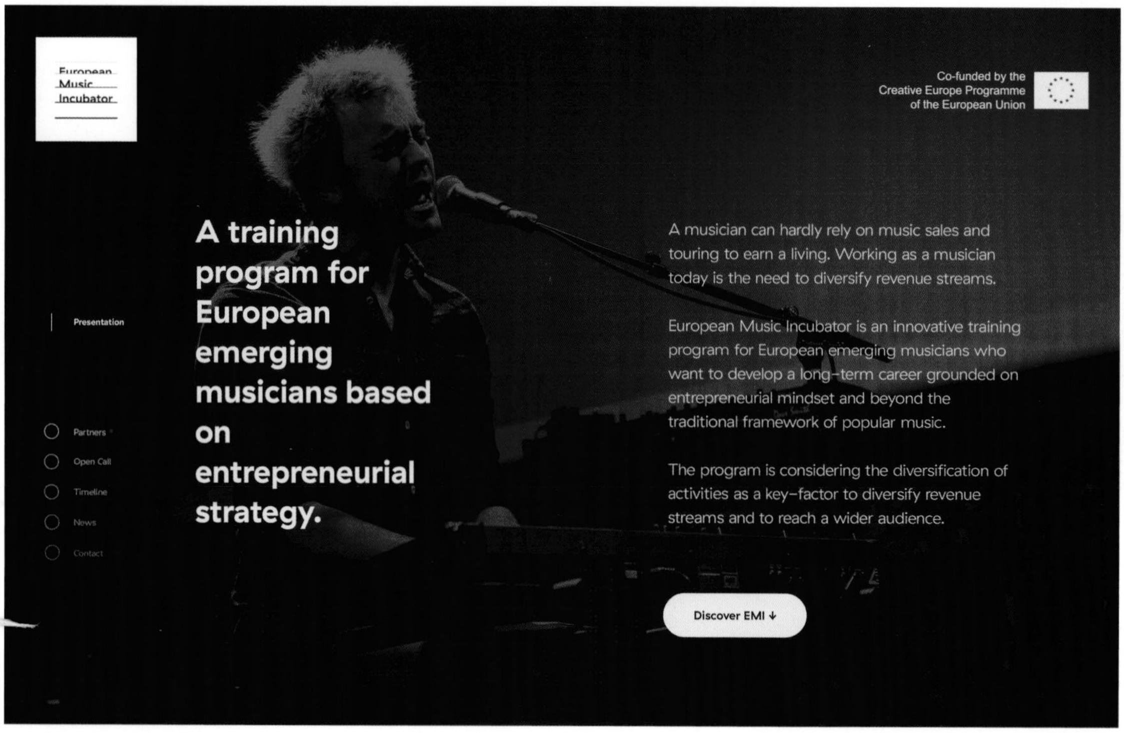
European Music Incubator
Co-funded by the Creative Europe Programme of the European Union
Presentation
Partners
Open Call
Timeline
News
Contact
A training program for European emerging musicians based on entrepreneurial strategy.
A musician can hardly rely on music sales and touring to earn a living. Working as a musician today is the need to diversify revenue streams.
European Music Incubator is an innovative training program for European emerging musicians who want to develop a long-term career grounded on entrepreneurial mindset and beyond the traditional framework of popular music.
The program is considering the diversification of activities as a key-factor to diversify revenue streams and to reach a wider audience.
Discover EMI ↓

Click

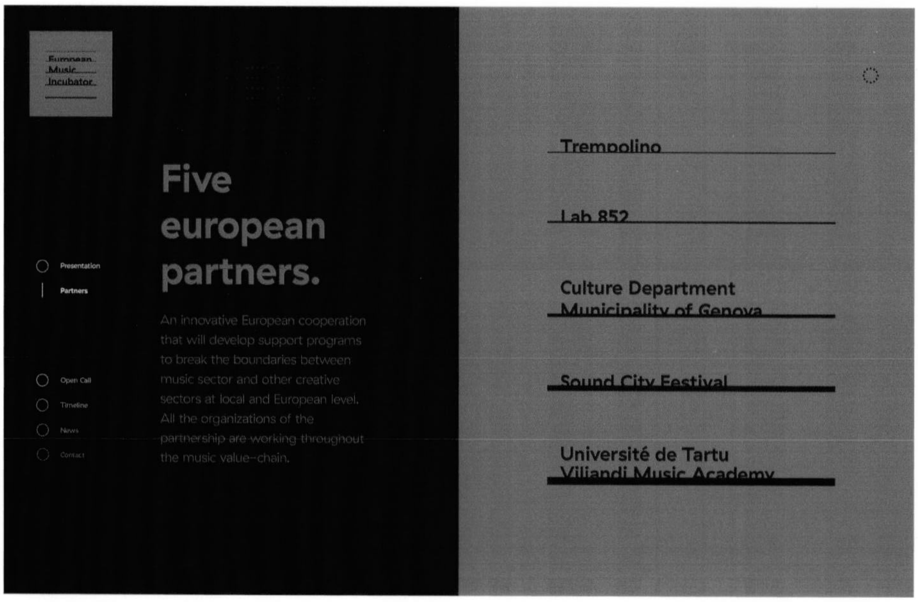
European Music Incubator
Presentation
Partners
Open Call
Timeline
News
Contact
Five european partners.
An innovative European cooperation that will develop support programs to break the boundaries between music sector and other creative sectors at local and European level. All the organizations of the partnership are working throughout the music value-chain.
Trempolino
Lab 852
Culture Department Municipality of Genova
Sound City Festival
Université de Tartu Viljandi Music Academy

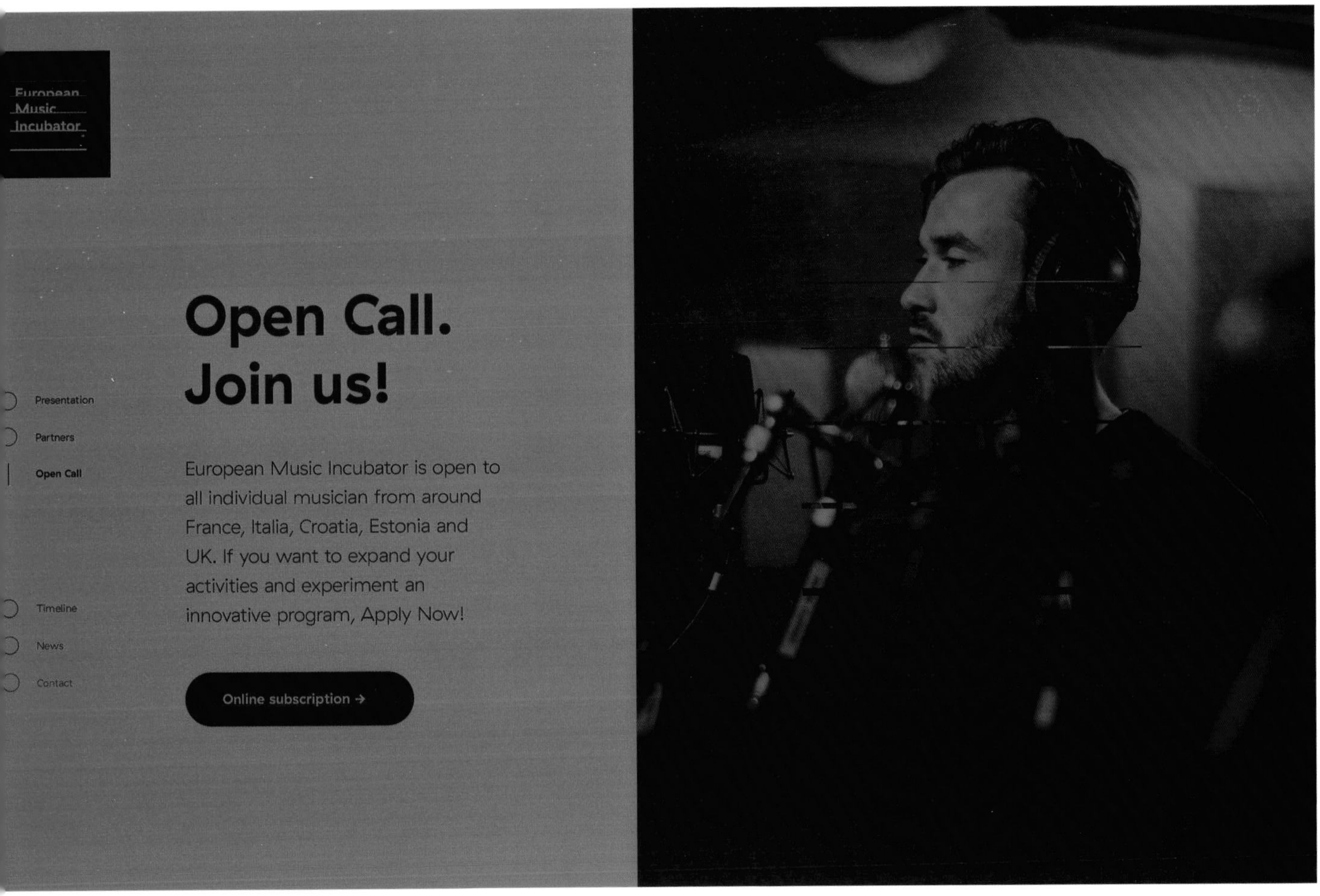
European Music Incubator
Presentation
Partners
Open Call
Timeline
News
Contact
Open Call.
Join us!
European Music Incubator is open to all individual musician from around France, Italia, Croatia, Estonia and UK. If you want to expand your activities and experiment an innovative program, Apply Now!
Online subscription →

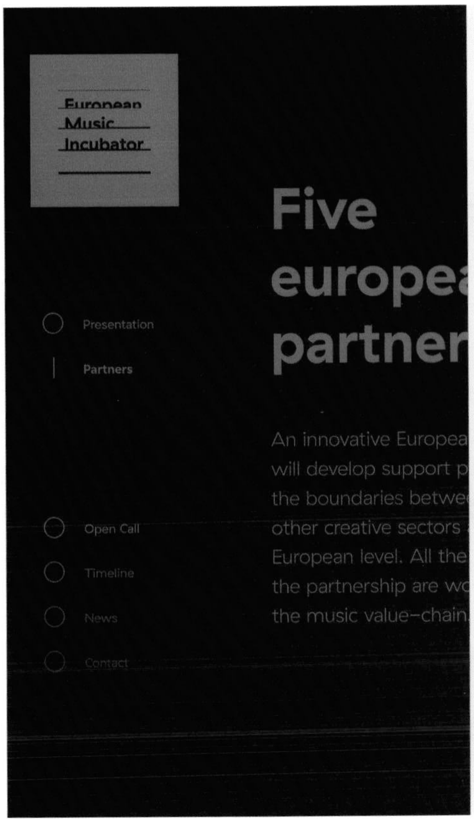
European Music Incubator
Five europea
partner
Presentation
Partners
An innovative Europea
will develop support p
the boundaries betwe
other creative sectors
European level. All the
the partnership are wo
the music value-chain
Open Call
Timeline
News
Contact

← Back
Music & brands.
Trempolino
Nantes (France)

Arche68

Design and Development
Bureau Cool

Project Management
Vertical Paris

URL
www.arche68.com

Official Site

Arche is a French fashion brand that specializes in shoes and leather goods. Celebrating their 50th anniversary, Arche Paris released a new collection called "Arche68". Design agency Bureau Cool was asked to develop a website that enables users to explore the collection and the campaign in a new and exciting way.

The first highlight is the entry of the site. Bureau Cool came up with a circular, 3D treatment for the main navigation. Each menu line rotates at its own speed when scrolling. To connect the different sections with the menu, the active menu line stays visible in the background, mixing its 3D-style with the flat content on top.

EN FR MENU
ZER
ORE
MUNITY
ARCHE68 – A
NTATION
TION
OMIZE

EN FR MENU
TRAVELLING STORE
ARCHE68 looks forward to seeing you here... And elsewhere: our travelling store has been designed specially for the occasion by Karim Rashid, who, like us, is dedicated to welcoming environments and settings that exude positive energy.
Paris 14.05 – 03.06.2018
New York SOON
Berlin SOON
Tokyo SOON

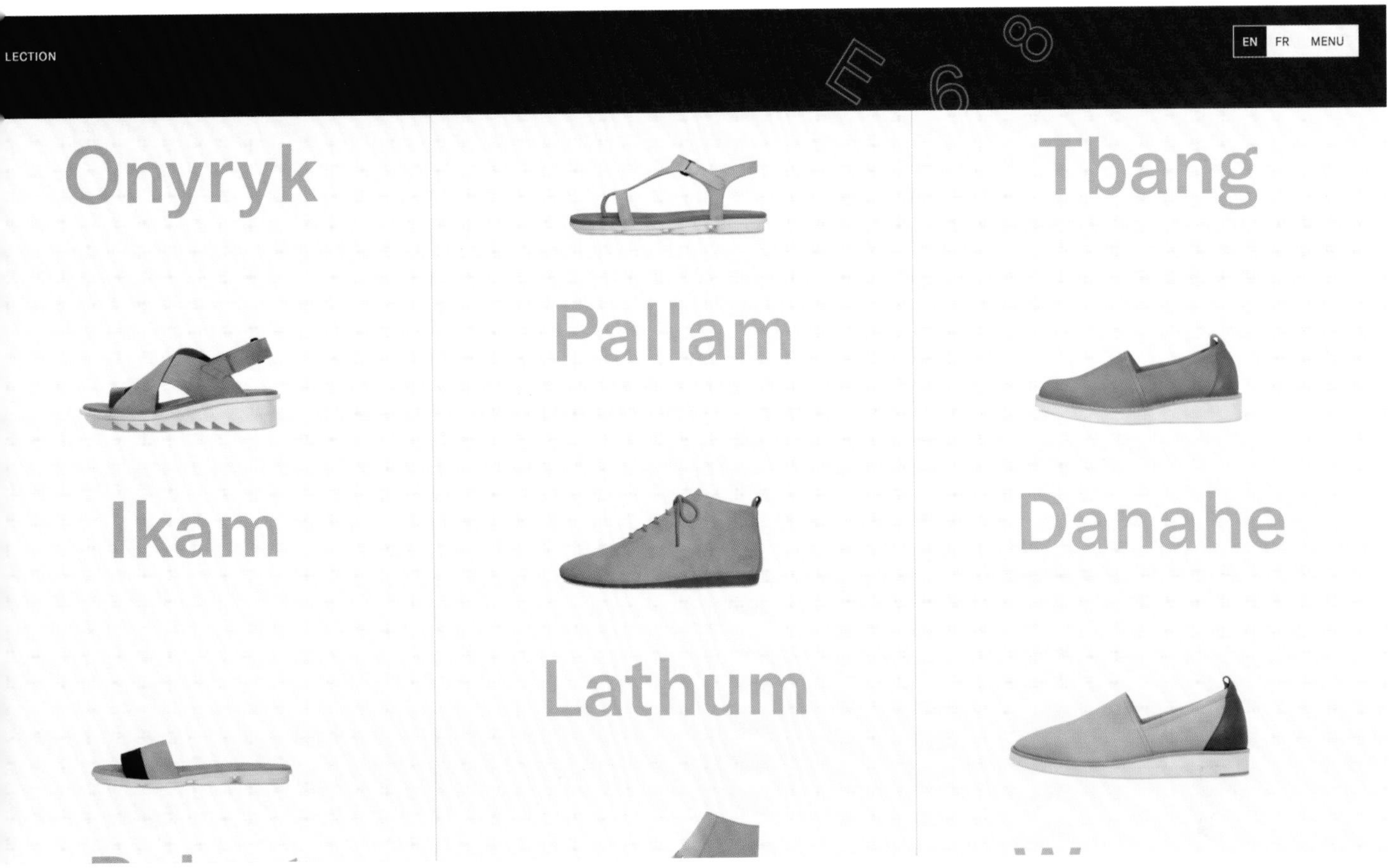
LECTION
EN FR MENU
Onyryk
Tbang
Pallam
Ikam
Danahe
Lathum

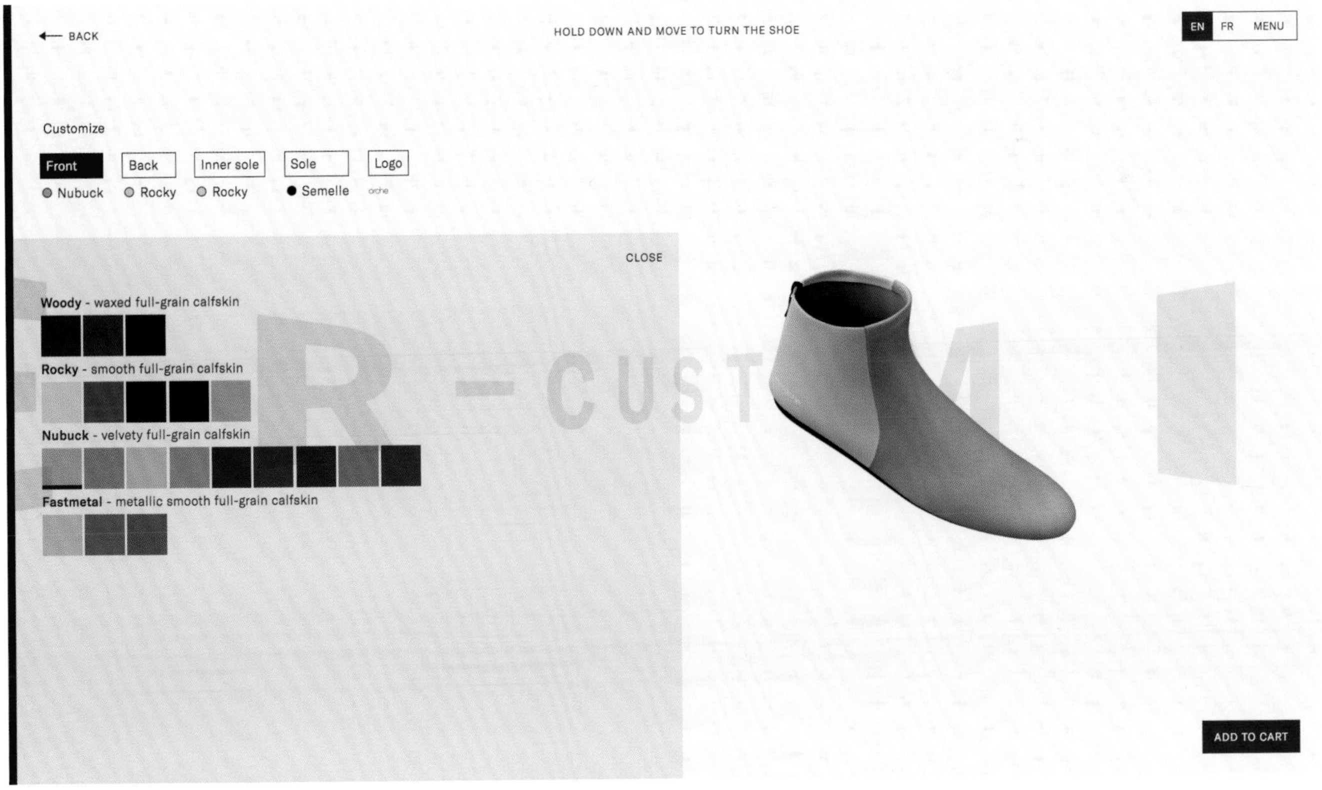
BACK
HOLD DOWN AND MOVE TO TURN THE SHOE
EN FR MENU
Customize
Front
Back
Inner sole
Sole
Logo
Nubuck
Rocky
Rocky
Semelle
CLOSE
Woody - waxed full-grain calfskin
Rocky - smooth full-grain calfskin
Nubuck - velvety full-grain calfskin
Fastmetal - metallic smooth full-grain calfskin
ADD TO CART

Another highlight of the site was the shoe customiser designed for newly-released models. Shoe models were used in realtime 3D to let the user view any angle, and have a feel of different materials and colours. The overall design was purposely kept clean, working with bold typography and vibrant colour of the campaign.

Fazeta Producciones

Design Agency
Twenty Two Degrees

Creative Direction
Rubén Sánchez, Vicente Lucendo

Art Direction
Rubén Sánchez

Creative Development
Vicente Lucendo

Client
Fazeta Producciones S.L.

URL
fazetaproducciones.com

Official Site

Fazeta Producciones is a project that serves as the portfolio of one of the main event management and production companies of Spain. The objective is to make an easy to browse website that serves as an online business card for the company, and in the meantime highlights the technological component.

The homepage illustrates the company's character in a conceptual and visual way, while also serves as a menu to direct to the other sections. The three main sections of the site are each identified by one bright colour. Design agency Twenty Two Degrees carefully chooses the colours based on how they transition from one to another.

For the graphic design part, they made a custom grid in which all the elements could be positioned and aligned. In the development phase, they used a custom made preload system to present the user all the images so there would not be in-between preloads and waiting time.

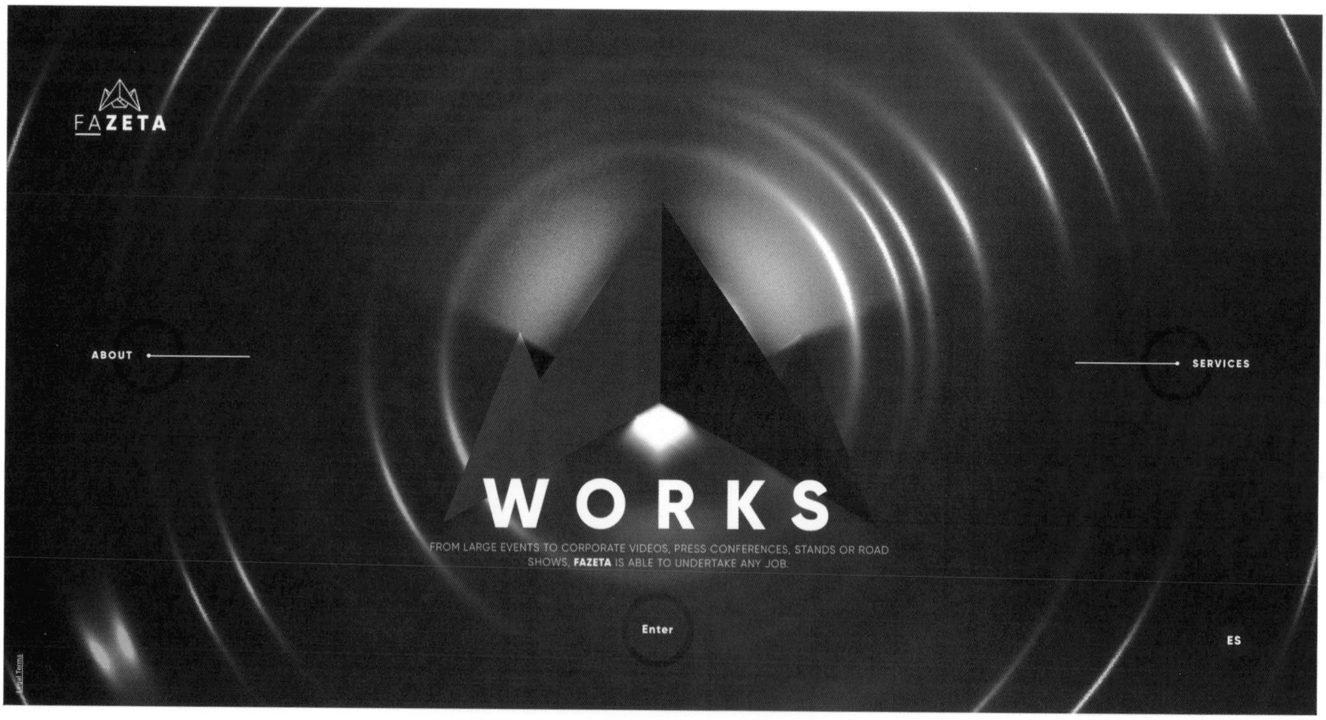
FAZETA
ABOUT
SERVICES
WORKS
FROM LARGE EVENTS TO CORPORATE VIDEOS, PRESS CONFERENCES, STANDS OR ROAD SHOWS, FAZETA IS ABLE TO UNDERTAKE ANY JOB.
Enter
ES

FAZETA
WORKS
ABOUT
SERVICES
Enter
ES

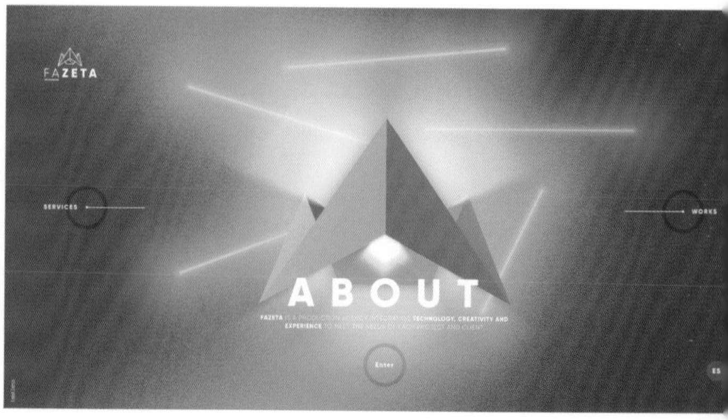
FAZETA
SERVICES
WORKS
ABOUT
Enter

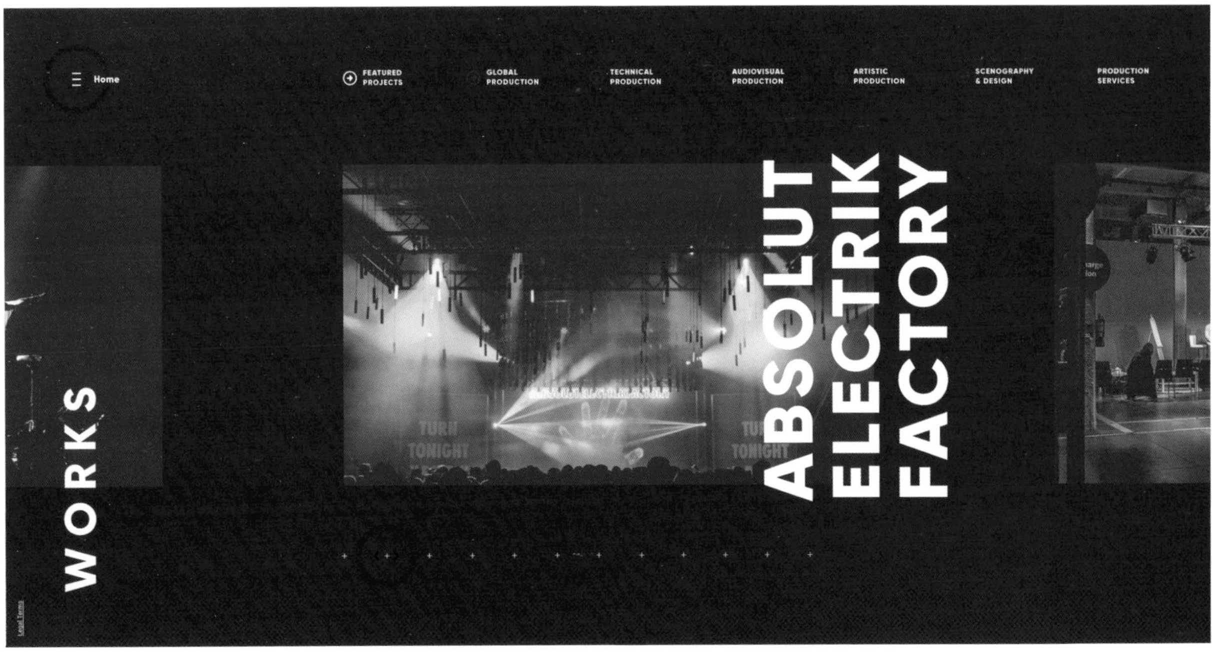
Home
FEATURED PROJECTS
GLOBAL PRODUCTION
TECHNICAL PRODUCTION
AUDIOVISUAL PRODUCTION
ARTISTIC PRODUCTION
SCENOGRAPHY & DESIGN
PRODUCTION SERVICES
ABSOLUT ELECTRIK FACTORY
WORKS

Click

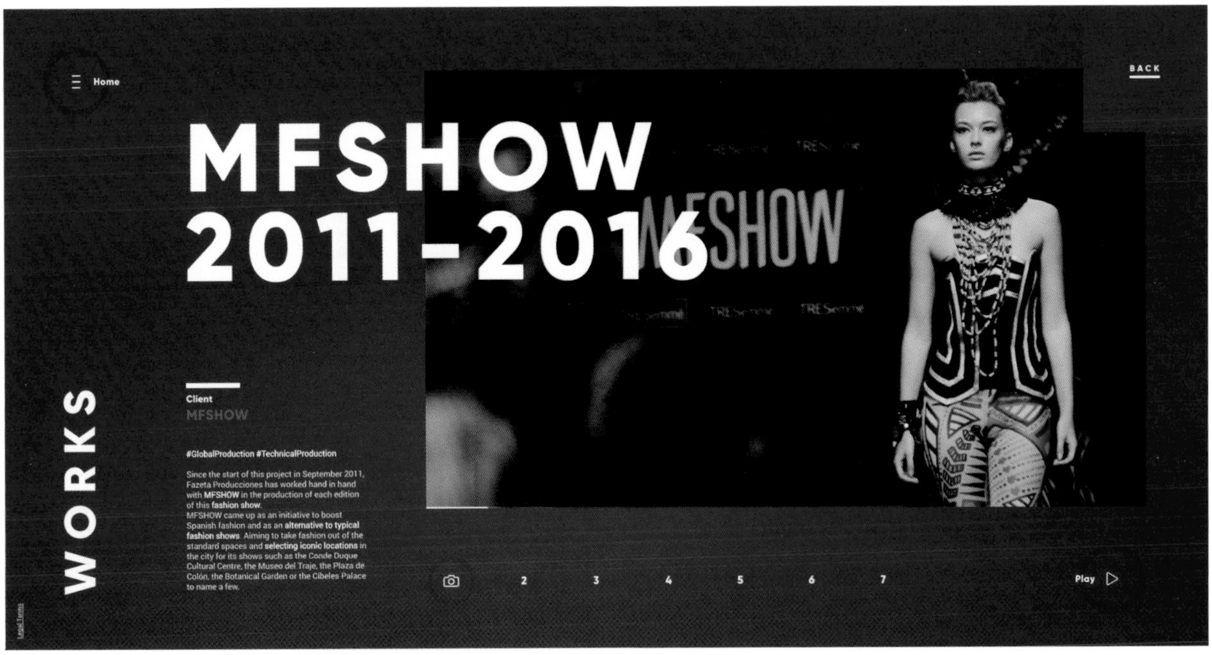
Home
BACK
MFSHOW 2011-2016
Client
MFSHOW
#GlobalProduction #TechnicalProduction
Since the start of this project in September 2011, Fazeta Producciones has worked hand in hand with MFSHOW in the production of each edition of this fashion show.
MFSHOW came up as an initiative to boost Spanish fashion and as an alternative to typical fashion shows. Aiming to take fashion out of the standard spaces and selecting iconic locations in the city for its shows such as the Conde Duque Cultural Centre, the Museo del Traje, the Plaza de Colón, the Botanical Garden or the Cibeles Palace to name a few.
2 3 4 5 6 7
Play
WORKS

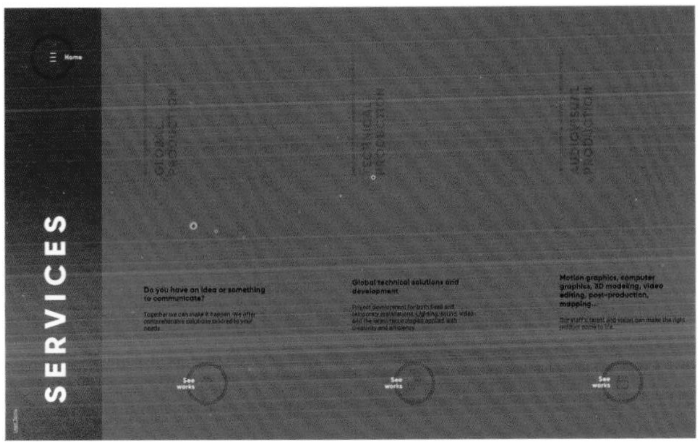
SERVICES

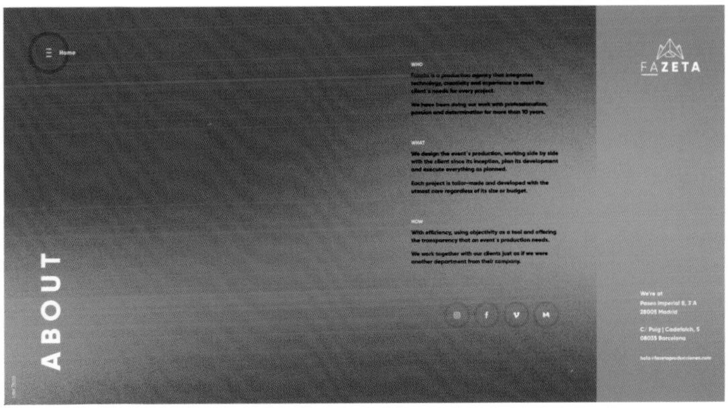
FAZETA
ABOUT

WTF is Data Science?

Design Agency
Gladeye

Client
Thinkful

URL
www.thinkful.com/blog/what-is-data-science

Official Site

Thinkful offers career education in a variety of technical disciplines, one of which is data science. They commissioned a long-form editorial story called simply: WTF is Data Science? The design challenge for Gladeye was to make potential students experience that story online, in a way that was both informative and inspiring.

Gladeye's solution was to overturn people's general impression of data science. They aimed for a design that was bold, confident, entertaining and interactive. This design inherited its form from function, taking inspiration from the key historical milestones in computation and data analysis, from the dawn of computers to the advent of artificial intelligence.

A critical design challenge was to visually represent the processes involved in machine learning. Their solution was the design of three animated visual metaphors that communicate these functions in a way that's both accurate and accessible to an audience without specific domain knowledge.

BLOG
WTF
is data science?
More and more, data science is finding a way deeper and deeper into our businesses, our communities, and in some cases, our lives.
But just what exactly is data science?

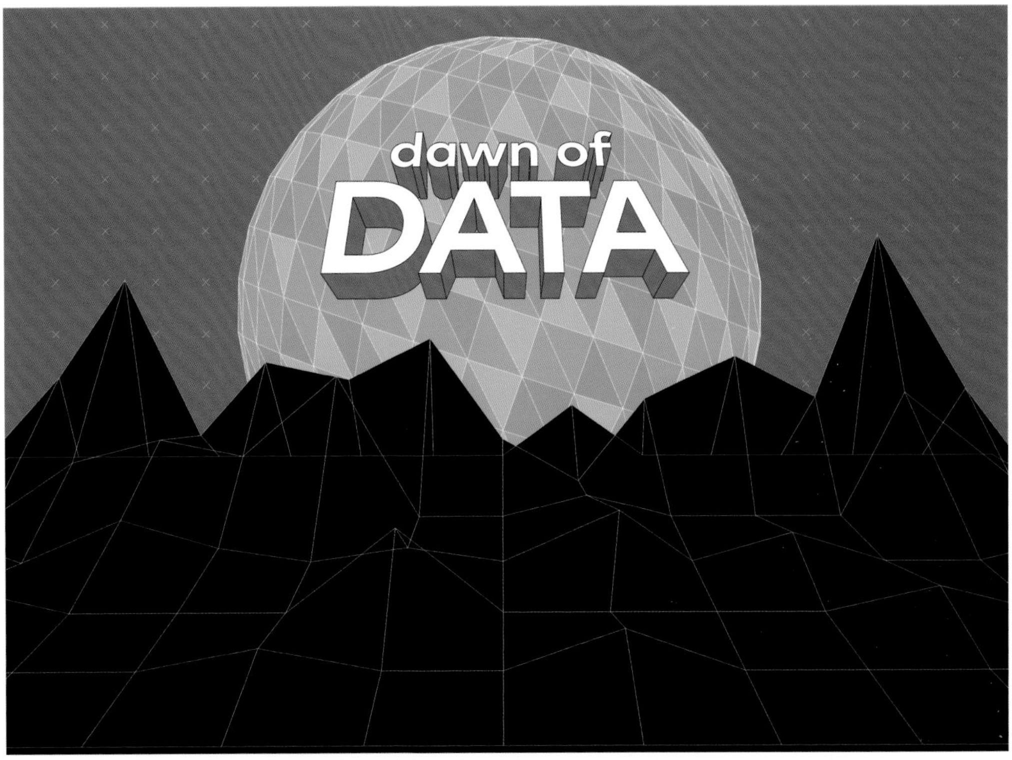
dawn of
DATA

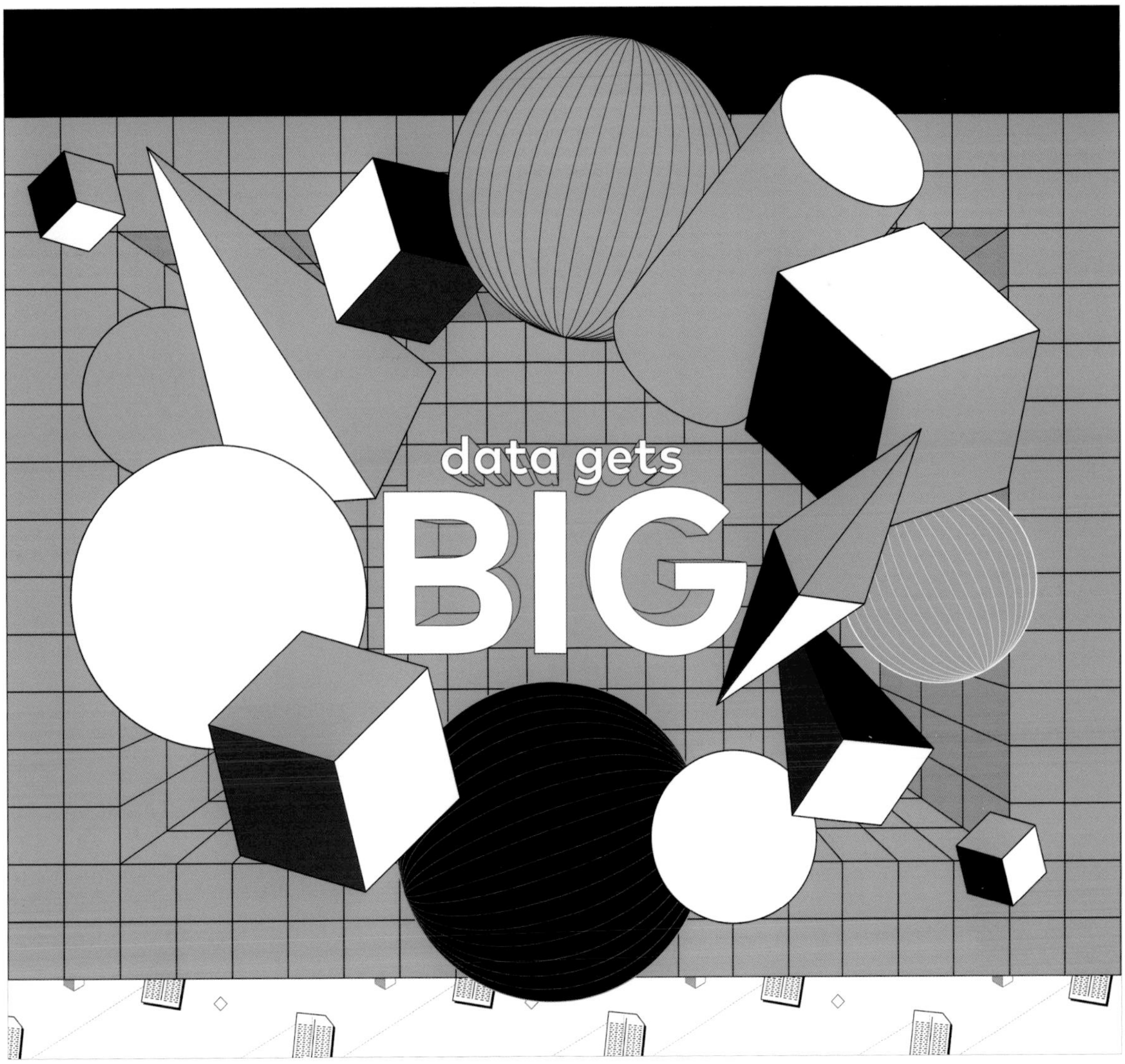
data gets
BIG

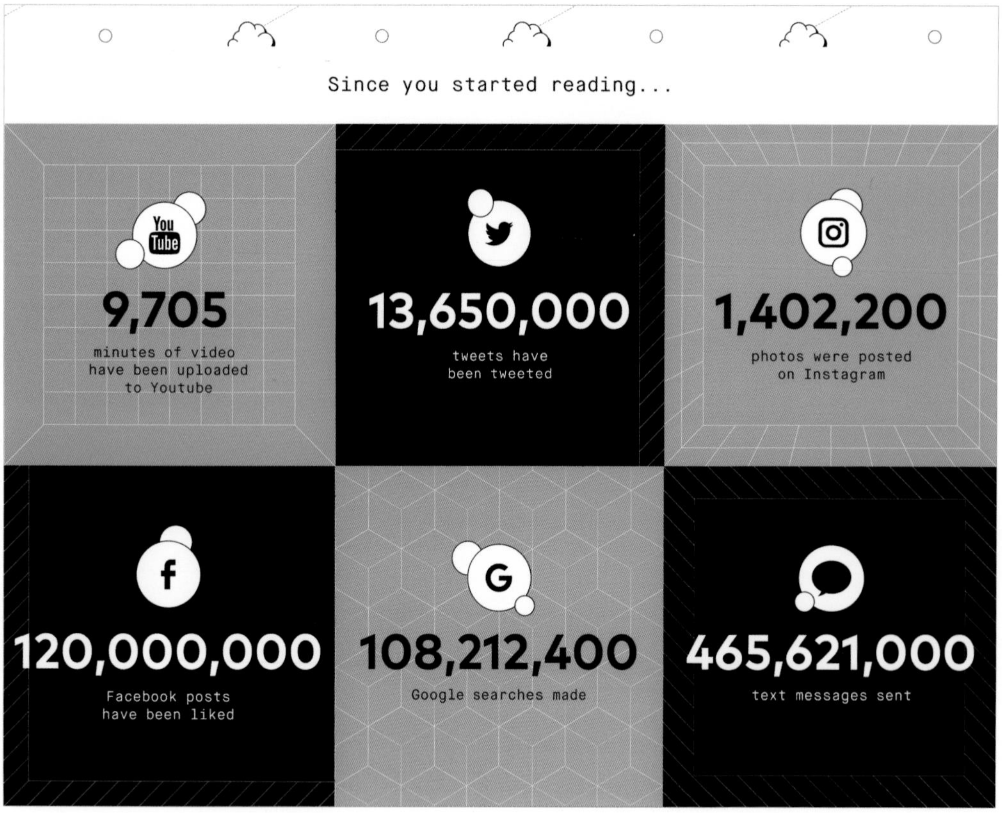
Since you started reading...
9,705
minutes of video have been uploaded to Youtube
13,650,000
tweets have been tweeted
1,402,200
photos were posted on Instagram
120,000,000
Facebook posts have been liked
108,212,400
Google searches made
465,621,000
text messages sent

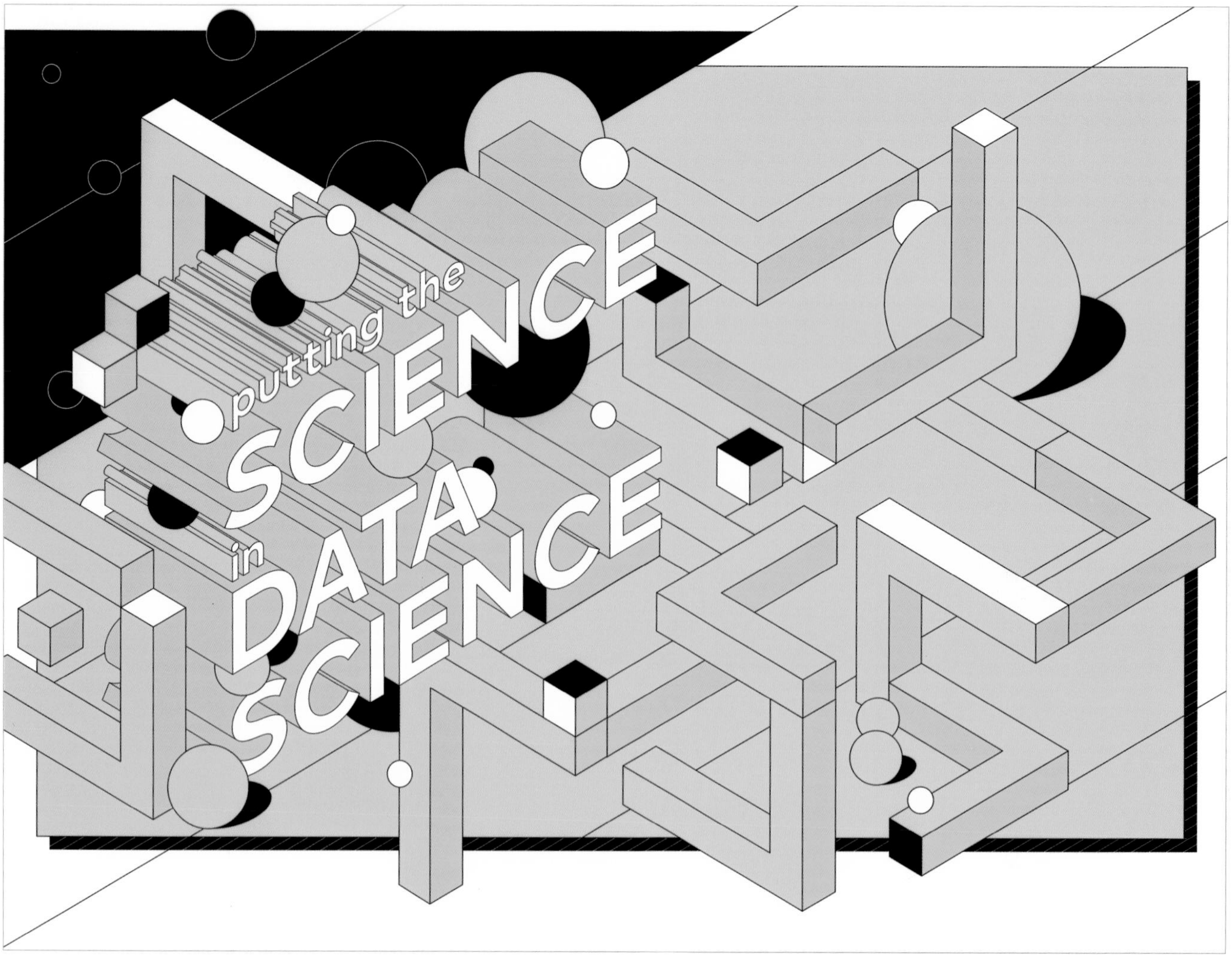
putting the
SCIENCE
in
DATA
SCIENCE

Supervised Learning

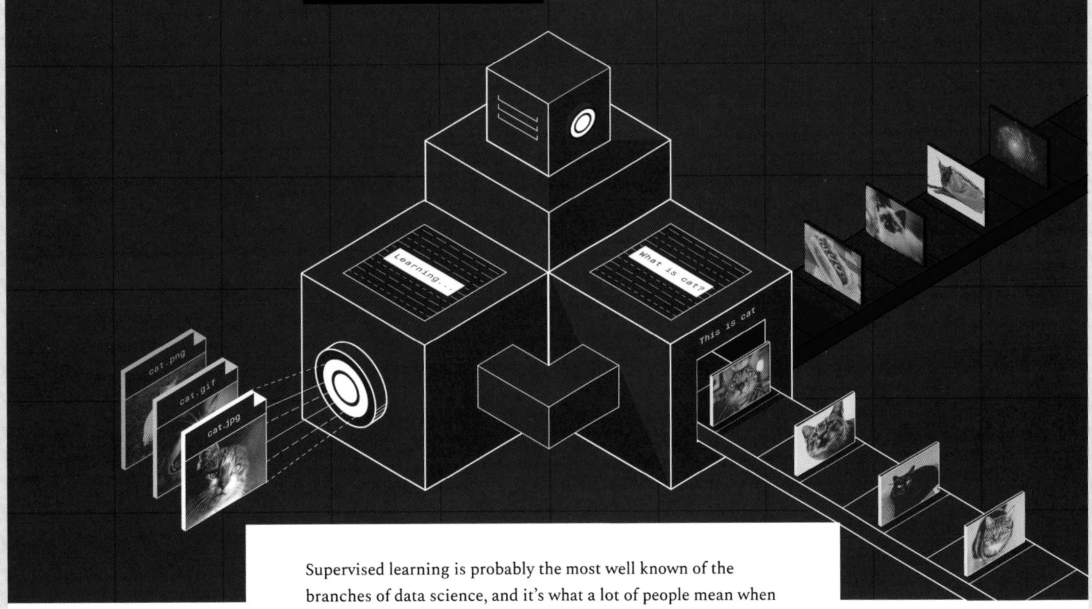
Learning...
What is cat?
This is cat
cat.png
cat.gif
cat.jpg

Supervised learning is probably the most well known of the branches of data science, and it's what a lot of people mean when they talk about ML. This is all about predicting something you've seen before. You try to analyze what the outcome of the process was in the past and build a system that tries to draw out what matters and build predictions for the next time it happens.

This can be a really useful thing to do, for everything. From predicting who is going to win the Oscars to what ad you're most likely to click on to whether or not you're going to vote in the next election, supervised learning can help answer all of these questions. It works because we've seen these things before. We've watched the Oscars and can find out what makes a film likely to win. We've seen ads and can figure out what makes someone likely to click. We've had elections and determine what makes someone likely to vote.

Before machine learning was developed, people may have tried to do some of these predictions manually, say looking at the number of Oscar nominations a film receives and picking the one with the most to win. What machine learning allows us to do is operate at a much larger scale and pick out much better predictors, or features, to build our model on. This leads to more accurate prediction, built on more subtle indicators for what is likely to happen.

Unsupervised Learning

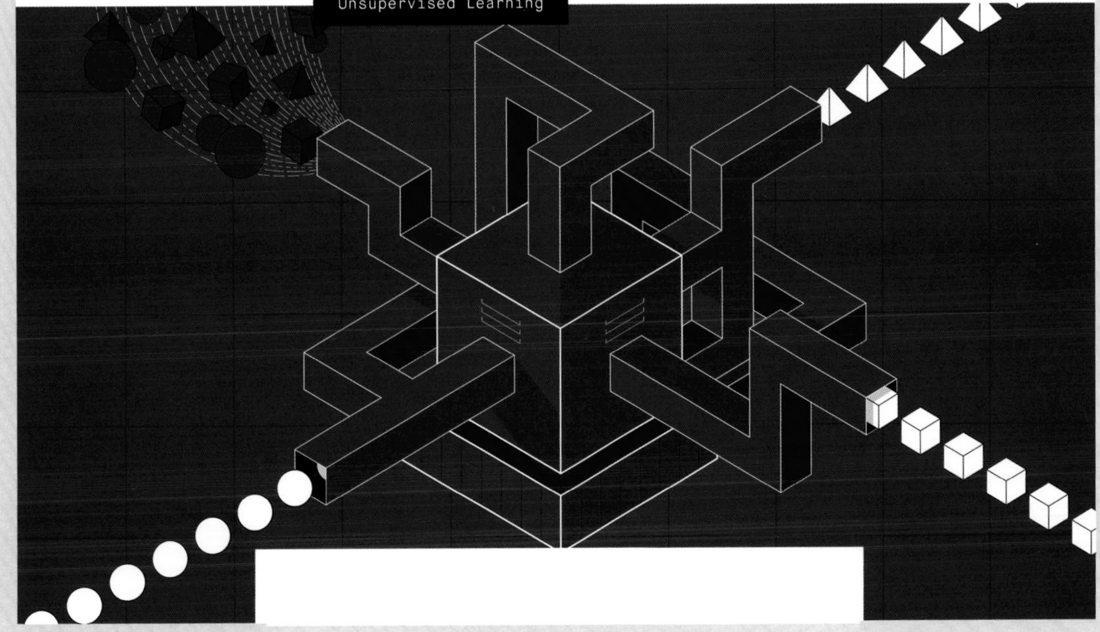

Marianopascual.me

Creative Direction
Achos

Development
Chanel Mepschen

Artwork
Mariano Pascual

URL
www.marianopascual.me

Official Site

Mariano Pascual is a digital artist based in Barcelona. He worked with Achos agency to renew his online portfolio. The idea to create an operating system came from their insight that there is nothing more personal than people's own computer. It allows the user to dive deep into Mariano's world, and enjoy the interactive experience at the same time.

Mariano designed all the features of this personal operating system with his own style, trying to have the functions found in a regular computer, but transferring everything to the artist's own language.

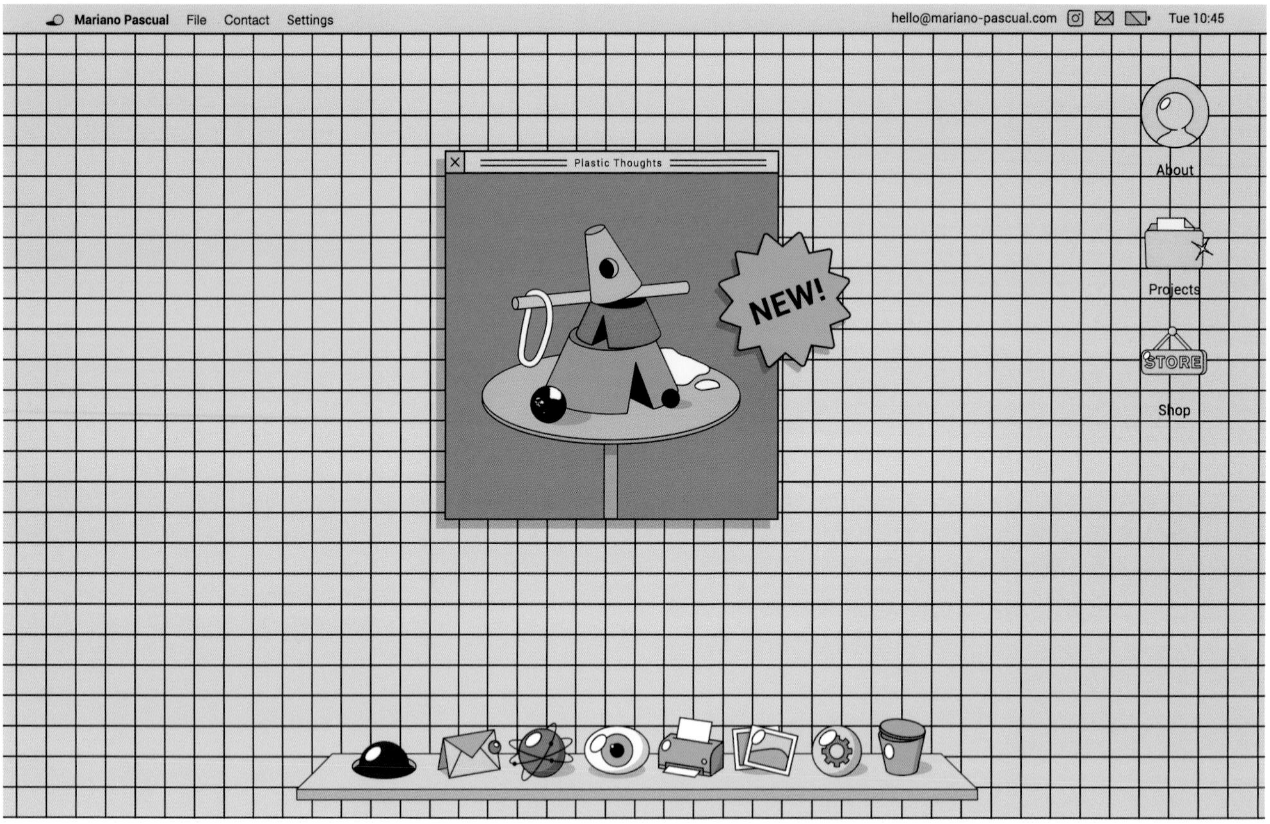

Mariano Pascual File Contact Settings
hello@mariano-pascual.com
Tue 10:45
Plastic Thoughts
NEW!
About
Projects
STORE
Shop

Click

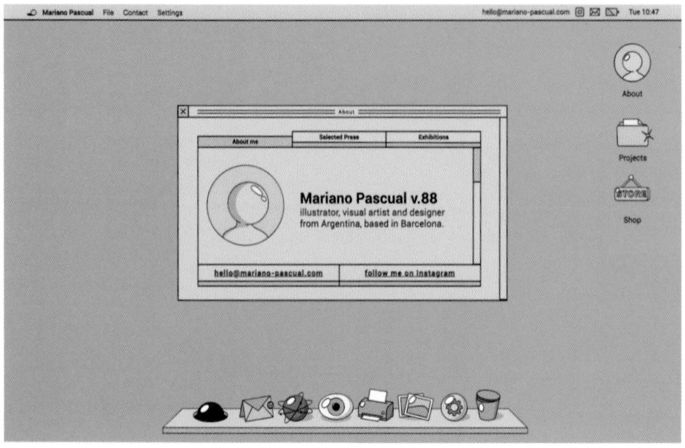

Mariano Pascual v.88
illustrator, visual artist and designer from Argentina, based in Barcelona.
hello@mariano-pascual.com
follow me on instagram

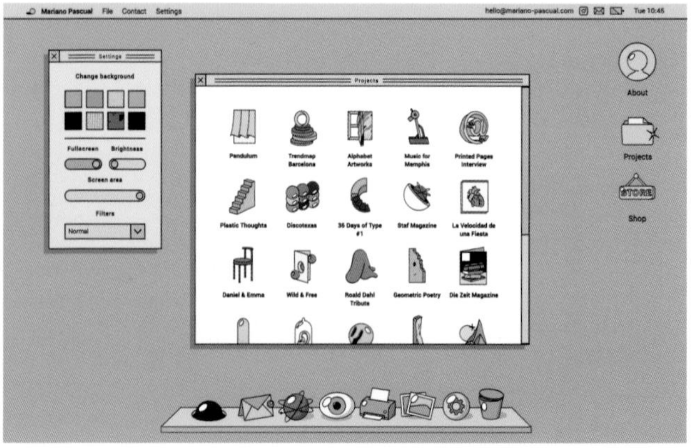

Mariano Pascual File Contact Settings
hello@mariano-pascual.com
Tue 10:47
IT IS NOT A JOKE
You are the 100,000th visitor of the day!
claim your prize!
Explorer
CLICK FOR LIVE WEBCAM CHAT
NO BOYFRIEND? NO PROBLEM!
ORDER NOW
CLICK HERE
INSTANT ACCESS
+18
JOIN NOW
SCAN NOW!
Search
About
STORE
Shop

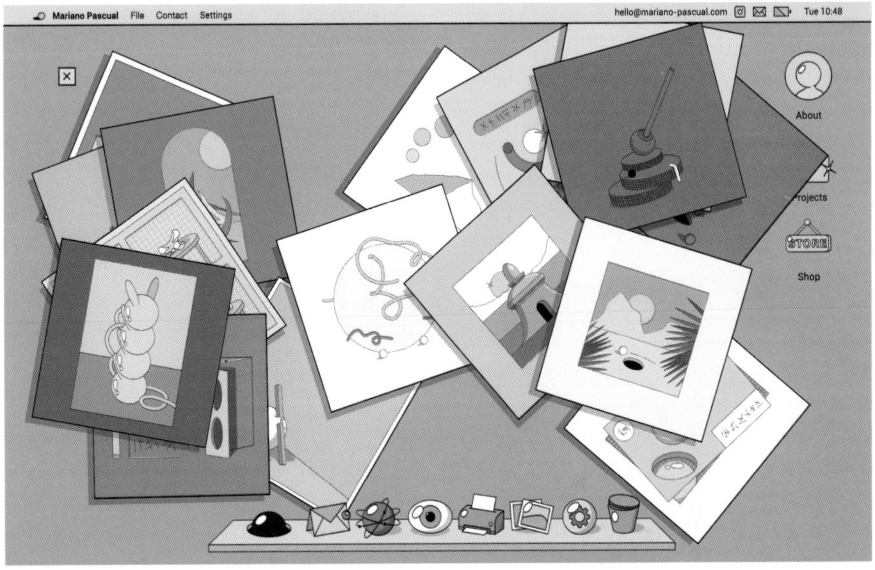
Mariano Pascual File Contact Settings
hello@mariano-pascual.com
Tue 10:48
About
STORE
Shop

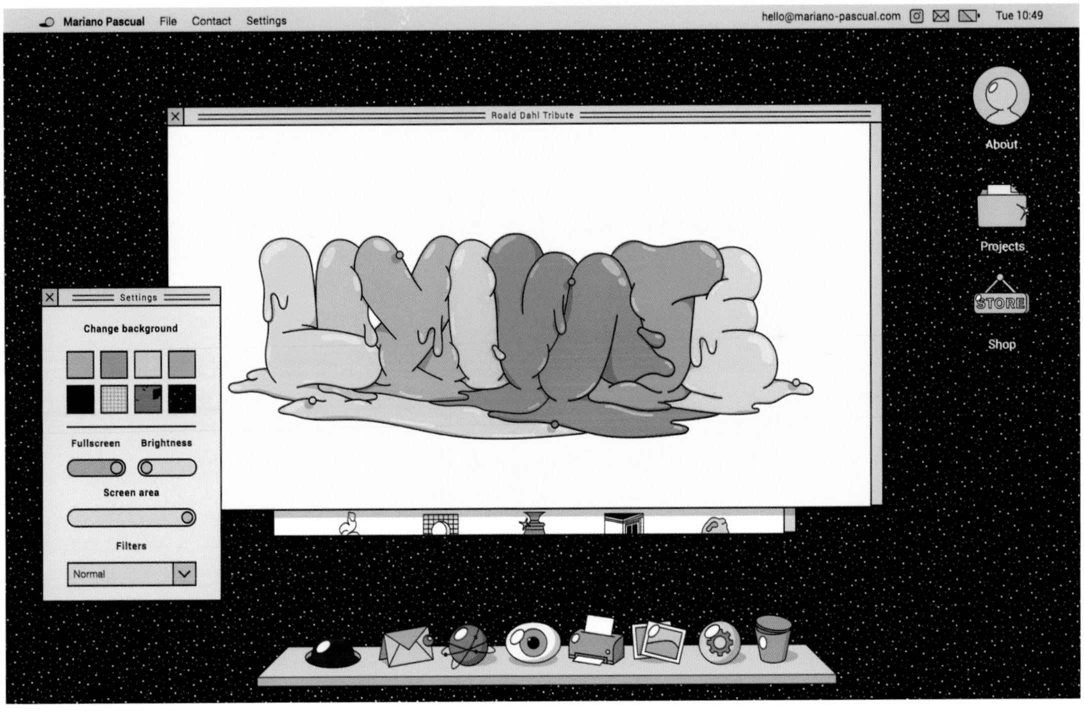
Mariano Pascual File Contact Settings
hello@mariano-pascual.com
Tue 10:49
Roald Dahl Tribute
Settings
Change background
Fullscreen
Brightness
Screen area
Filters
Normal
About
Projects
STORE
Shop

pill & pillow

Design and Development
pill & pillow

URL
www.pillandpillow.com

Official Site

This is the portfolio website of creative agency pill & pillow. Using a short, conversational style, the text-based layout shows information in chunks, letting viewers explore their 100+ works bit by bit.

Hi, we are pill & pillow, an independent digital studio. We work with clients big & small: ifc mall, T · PARK, Shadow Harp, PYE 2015, Cathay Pacific – Artmap, Very Hong Kong Very Hong Kong, NIKE HK – MvsW, Lane Crawford minisites, Tai Kwun, New World Development, Integral Conversation 2017, Milü, etc...
We're hiring.
We've won a few awards.
Want to know more? Let's talk.

Click

ifc mall
shopping
dining
movies
happenings
services
announcements
life is beautiful

PYE 2015
PYE
A new website showcasing PYE's shirt-making process

INDEX

51North

51North is an award winning digital design and development studio based in the Netherlands. They are a small but fast growing studio always striving to create top notch digital work. They work for some of the world's leading advertising agencies and brands, including Mercedes-Benz, KLM, Scotch & Soda, TomTom, Achtung! McGarryBowen, DDB & Tribal, TBWA, INDIE Amsterdam, JWT and BBDO.

www.51north.nl

P190–191

Achos

Achos is an interactive digital design and communications agency based in Barcelona and Bali which strives to create the best collaboration work with a vast network of artists and professionals.

www.achos.es

P230–231

Alan Cheetham

Alan is a graphic designer living in Nottingham, the UK. In his full-time design job, his design focus is largely based around brand and digital work. However, in his spare time, he is very interested in illustration and type and tries to have a dabble regularly. After staring so much at a screen all day like a robot, he finds it nice and therapeutic to revert back to pen and paper.

www.behance.net/booyah

P104–105

Alex Pluda

Alex Pluda is a self-taught digital product designer born in Milan, Italy, with a passion for disruptive technological ideas.

www.behance.net/alexpluda8447

P056–057

Amelia Rams

Amelia Rams is a UI/UX designer based in Krakow, Poland. She is interested in illustration and icon design. She likes simple and useful solutions, and believes good design can form an attitude and help people resolve many problems in a pleasant way.

www.behance.net/ameliar

P030–031

Annie Hall

Annie Hall is a freelance graphic designer and photographer based in Salt Lake City, Utah. Her work ranges within branding, packaging, interface, and commercial/lifestyle photography. She has created work for corporate and local clients ranging from: Starbucks, Reebok, Adobe, Superheroic, and more. Aside from when she's not photosynthesizing from the warm glow of her computer screen, you can catch her catching some rays in Utah's wilderness, watching too many extraterrestrial documentaries, and often finding any excuse to adopt a dog.

www.anniehall.co

P014–015

Anqi Pan

Anqi Pan is a graphic designer and design thinker. She focuses on motion graphics, UI/UX, branding, and typography. She received a BA in Art Education from Guangzhou Academy of Fine Arts and an MFA in Graphic Design from Maryland Institute College of Art.

www.behance.net/angel_pan

P074–075

Artur Konariev

Artur is the founder and product designer of Wadoo agency. He specializes in design-thinking, user-friendly interface development and creative approach. By providing significant, up-to-date design, he helps clients' business grow and expand.

www.wadoo.space

P042–043

Awesome Design (Awsmd)

Awsmd is a data-driven UX and UI design agency based in San Francisco. Powered by in-depth product and user research, they solve problems and meet their clients' goals through expertise in human-centred design.

www.awsmd.com

P132

Base Design

Base is an international network of studios led by creatives in Brussels, New York and Geneva. Base understands context, verbalizes strategy, defines concept, creates strong design, seeks clarity, and builds empathy. Base specializes in strategy, branding and digital.

basedesign.com

P214–215

Belén Fernández-Santos Ruiz

Belén is a Spanish UI designer based in Madrid since 2012, who started her career as a graphic designer. During her early design stage, she reflected the traditions, fashion and art of Andalusia's region in her editorial design projects. She discovered her interest in UI design in 2017 while studying a Master's Degree in Web Development and User Interface. The desire of improving on visual design and user experience took Belén to develop new concept projects.

www.behance.net/belenfdezsantos

P034–037

Bezantee Bao

Bezantee Bao is a senior UX designer at Minglabs.

www.behance.net/bezantee

P082–083

Build in Amsterdam

Build in Amsterdam is a branding agency specialized in e-commerce. They combine strategy, branding, and e-commerce to bridge the gap between digital and physical touch points. They see e-commerce platforms as digital flagship stores. So they intentionally develop platforms as brand experiences that inspire, engage, and convert in an infinite loop.

www.buildinamsterdam.com

P150–151, 198–199

Bureau Cool

Bureau Cool is a boutique design studio, bringing together aesthetics, animation and code to create mesmerising experiences.

bureau.cool

P222–223

Bureau for Visual Affairs

Bureau for Visual Affairs is a London-based digital agency, working with clients from the cultural and lifestyle sectors. Bureau is focused on delivering strategically-led content and utility-driven user experiences.

www.bureau-va.com

P172–173

Camille Frairrot, Victoire Douy

Camille and Victoire are young designers, specializing in interactive design. They both graduated from Gobelins in Paris.

vyctoire.com

www.steviaplease.me

P070–071

CLEVER°FRANKE

CLEVER°FRANKE is a design agency that uses data to create interactive products and experiences. They invent new solutions that exceed boundaries and help organizations in their data driven digital transformation. Founded by Thomas Clever and Gert Franke in 2008, CLEVER°FRANKE has grown to be an internationally recognized design agency. They combine strong analytical skills and strategic thinking with a holistic design and technological approach.

www.cleverfranke.com

P108–111

Clique Studios

Clique Studios, LLC is an award-winning digital design and technology firm based in Chicago and Denver. They specialize in creating elegant, compelling Content Experiences for great businesses and organizations, ranging from start-ups to Fortune 500 companies.

www.cliquestudios.com

P206–207

Cody Cano

Cody Cano is a multidisciplinary designer based in the greater Los Angeles area. He is currently obtaining his BFA from California State University, Long Beach.

www.behance.net/CodyCano

P136–137

Doeun Shin

Doeun Shin is a graphic and UI designer based in Seoul.

www.behance.net/ShinDoeun

P054–055

Effie Zoumpouli

Effie Zoumpouli is a graphic designer who creates brand identities, websites, packaging, retail concepts, illustrations and everything in-between. From an early age, she immersed herself in drawing, and love of illustration remains a hallmark of her work. With an educational background in architecture, museum studies and finally graphic design, she loves interdisciplinary environments, being engaged in experimental creative processes and cooperating with resourceful teams.

www.behance.net/effiezoumpouli

P096–097

Elena Saharova

Elena Saharova is an interactive designer and art director living and working in Moscow. For 10 years, Elena has been engaged in graphic and interface design. She prefers to work on complex tasks and large interfaces. Elena is concerned about working with fonts and space, in her opinion this is the basis of design aesthetics. At the moment Elena teaches Visual Design on the educational platform "Soft Culture," creates new products as a maker in cosmetics shop "The Chayka shop" and helps companies build websites and user experience for their customers.

eessoo.co

P114–115

Erik Bernacchi

Erik Bernacchi is a polymath mind whose areas of wizardry range from product design, UX, art direction, illustration, animation, 3D and programming. Wildly obsessed with good ideas, art and software, Erik has an innate attitude to stretch the boundaries and challenge the benchmarks. Originally born in Milan, he has dedicated his last 10 years between Italy and Australia crafting products and experiences for the world's biggest companies.

eeerik.com

P146–147

Fabián Vadillo

Fabián Vadillo is a multimedia and interaction designer, graduated from UADE (Universidad Argentina de la Empresa), Argentina. His passion is to discover design solutions in 360°, combining different areas.

www.behance.net/FabianVadillo

P126–127

For The People

For The People is a design and strategy agency focused on getting businesses closer to people through design, storytelling and technology. They work with startups to tackle big questions for which there aren't conventional answers, and also cooperate with established businesses to discover new vision for the digital age.

forthepeople.agency

P144–145

Gaeul Lee

Gaeul is a UX/UI designer based in Korea, with a background in fashion design. She draws inspirations from the textures and colours of various fabrics and exquisite curves of the human body. She designs engaging products, user-friendly interfaces and web applications for both desktop and mobile. She is passionate about showcasing well-branded digital products that enhance people's life quality.

gaeullee.com

P098–099

Gladeye

Gladeye is the creative agency for a connected world. They create value for forward-thinking brands through storytelling, experience design and digital product innovation. Their strength is the combination of strategic thinking with the capabilities of a world-class digital production studio and the accountability of a data-driven digital agency.

gladeye.com

P226–229

Griflan

Griflan is a creative agency based in Philadelphia and Atlanta. They innovate and set things in motion through design and creative problem solving.

www.griflan.com

P166–167, 202–203

Heco

Heco is the Chicago-based studio of JT Helms and Matt Cowen. With over two decades of experience in design, content, and creative direction, they make better user experiences and more interesting brands.

helloheco.com

P092–093, 156–157

Huy Phan

Just a kid cannot handle his own life but never stops being better.

www.behance.net/huyphan2602

P040–041

Hyemin Yoo

Hyemin Yoo is a UI designer based in Seoul, South Korea.

www.behance.net/hyeminyooo

P128–129

Inventos Digitais

Inventos Digitais is a creative agency based in Brazil. Since 2015, they have been giving life to ideas, helping startups create teams and develop their products or services. With a team that combines know-how and a willingness to innovate, they assist entrepreneurs to take their project forward. They approach their work with a good deal of inspiration and take into consideration high performance team tools and techniques for maximizing individual and collective productivity.

www.inventosdigitais.com.br

P162–165

Irene Molina

Irene Molina is a UI designer with a strong focus on digital design and UX. She has 10 years of experience designing digital products from concept and MVP definition to prototypes and high-fidelity pixel perfect interfaces and QA supervision. She has worked several years as a principal designer and creative director in studios and agencies. Irene enjoys team work, and she always thinks about solving usability problems through the interface or about how to get a better user experience by seeking a creative and simple way.

irenemolina.design

P044–045

Iris Chu

Iris Chu is an interaction designer specializing in UI/UX, digital product design, and visual system design. She is passionate about creating engaging, excellent and delightful digital experience for technical products. Before working as a designer, she worked as a software engineer at IBM. Iris codes and also enjoys the process of creating. Her background in both technology and design as well as her experience of building various digital products over the past few years allow her to always deliver the best visual and technical solutions for her clients.

irischu.com

P130–131

Isabel Sá, Liliana Ferreira

Isabel Sá and Liliana Ferreira are digital designers living in Porto, Portugal.

www.behance.net/isabelsa

www.behance.net/liferreira

P022–023

Ivan Kolle

Ivan was born in Moscow. Although he holds degrees of Bachelor of Commerce, Commercial Advertising and Brand Management, he considers himself a designer and creator in the soul and in the essence. He specializes in UI/UX design of highload B2B projects. In the past, he was the co-owner and creative chief of digital agency Three Zeta Studio. Currently he works on federal Internet of Things projects in MegaFon PJSC at lead UI/UX designer position.

www.behance.net/ivankolle

P116–117

Jakub Carda

Jakub Carda is a freelance graphic designer who helps brands grow and increase their visual value and prestige. Jakub enjoys merging aesthetics with functionality and designing user-friendly products. He specializes in UI, web design, logo design, branding and print design services to businesses of all sizes around the world. Jakub lives with his family in the inspirational city of Prague, Czech Republic.

www.jakubcarda.cz

P038–039

Jessica Elliott

Jessica Elliott is a graphic designer and typographer living in Seattle. She graduated from Savannah College of Art and Design in 2016 with a B.F.A in Graphic Design; since then she has produced work for a myriad of companies such as Esurance, Jif, Pillsbury, Microsoft and currently works as a UX designer at the Xbox Studio. When she is not doing interaction design, you can normally find her out on the water or in the mountains.

www.seejessdesign.com

P133

Jordan Richards

Growing up, Jordan Richards was fascinated with the joyful experiences he had when holding well-designed products. His curiosity for the process and people behind the designs led him to study design at Oklahoma State University. His main interests are interactive design, packaging design and iconography. Now he resides in Seattle and pursues visual design in the tech industry.

www.behance.net/jordanrichards

P102–103, 174–177

Julia Shkatova

Julia Shkatova is a product designer and interaction maker based in Berlin. She started her career as a graphic designer but then switched to interaction design. Julia's multimedia background helps her see the big picture and not be constrained by one medium. In every project, Julia tries to challenge the impossible, erase borders but never forget to ask and listen to the users. She is inspired by Russian avant-garde, classic movies, and millennial pop culture.

readymag.com/julyshk/portfolio/

P062–063

Julien Renvoye

Julien is a freelance designer and creative director based in Texas. Julien led the art direction at Mixpanel, a SaaS company, for 5 years and he's now leading the art direction at Digital Asset, a fintech company.

www.renvoye.com

P168–169

Kakao corp.

Kakao is an internet company which provides mobile lifestyle services that make everyday connections boundless and better.

www.kakaocorp.com/service/KakaoStory?lang=en

P080–081

Kevin Mikhail

Kevin Mikhail's graphic expertise goes from CGI to brand identity, as well as editorial design and type design. He defines himself as an art director in search of newness. His work approach is to make every project unique, which motivates him to constantly try out new type, software or printing techniques.

kevinmikhail.com

P186–189

Kevin Oehmichen

Kevin is a UI/UX designer based in Berlin, Germany. His passion is creating digital experiences, including app, web applications and digital interfaces. He has been working in the digital industry since 2011 and he still keeps the initial enthusiasm towards his job.

www.behance.net/kevinoehmi0b2a

P020–021

Kim Baschet

Kim Baschet is a French freelance designer. She graduated from Gobelins in 2018. She designs interfaces and motion designs in order to create great user experience.

kimb.dribbble.com

P072–073

Kirill Emelyanov

Kirill Emelyanov is a multidisciplinary designer and art director with a focus on apps and interactive design.

www.behance.net/EmelyanovK

P032–033

Kommigraphics

Kommigraphics is a print and digital communication agency, based in Athens, Greece. They aim to be at the forefront of all trends of communication techniques and technologies, by working with national as well as international brands and companies. They love challenges, and that's why their work for every project is different, with a perfect balance of creativity and results.

www.kommigraphics.com

P152–153, 170–171

KR8 bureau

KR8 bureau focuses on brand strategy, identity and design. Their highest influence is sociology and the observation of change in every aspect. They create brand strategies and design that not only look nice and advertise the brand, but also actively open dialogues with users in order to maintain a base of identification and interaction with their social environments.

www.kr8bureau.at

P106–107

lg2

lg2 is the story of two entrepreneurs: Sylvain Labarre (the "L") and Paul Gauthier (the "G"). The two of them, along with Gilles Chouinard, started to build a small agency with big ambitions. More than 25 years later, with over 250 talented employees and thousands of awards for some of the most innovative and well-known brands in the world, the founders' relentless focus on their people and their product remains just as strong. And their bold ways have since been successfully passed on to over 20 new entrepreneurs, who work just as tirelessly to preserve their independence and creatively driven business model.

www.lg2.com

P048–049

Like Digital

Like Digital is an award-winning agency based in London and Dubai. They deliver key, complex, creative digital projects for global brands, in luxury, fashion, entertainment and hospitality. They pride themselves on providing innovative User Experience Design, informed by insightful data and forward thinking strategy for the future of digital. Their Shoreditch studio has facilitated over $100,000,000 of e-commerce transactions, and everything they do is driven by customer growth: revenue, engagement and rich data.

like.digital

P182–185

LOOT

LOOT is a graphic design studio founded by Ana-Maria Grigoriu and Stelian Dobrescu in 2011. LOOT's expertise is in laying out a favourable environment for projects, whether they are new brands, apps, or websites. The studio looks into everything from market insights to company structure and brand guidelines to make solid design choices. They attempt to push the edges of design with each of their projects. They pay close attention to the clients' need and goals.

www.weareloot.com

P200–201

Luca Volino

Luca is a designer who specializes in UX/UI, currently living in Rome where he has been working as a freelancer for about 6 years. He works from the user experience to the visual details and then transforms these into working code. He considers himself a minimal designer and he really likes the simple and elegant style.

www.lucavolino.com

P088–089

Łukasz Peszek @ 7ninjas

Łukasz Peszek @ 7ninjas—one of the "dinosaurs" with 11 years of experience as a designer. His key to success is to stay fresh and open-minded which makes him a perfect match for a member of 7ninjas, a digital product agency. In 7ninjas, Łukasz creates clean and aesthetic designs for both desktop and mobile apps. The company itself was founded in 2015 in Poland and creates unique experience for companies from all stages of the business journey: starting with concept products for startups, through new product launches for SMB, all the way to product optimization for global corporations.

7ninjas.com

P094–095

Marco Almeida

Marco Almeida is a Brazilian digital designer focused on changing and simplifying people's lives through the design and technology. Over the last seven years of working with digital products, he has always brought that purpose to his projects.

aboutmarco.com

P066–067

Martina Hirschler

Martina Hirschler is an experience designer who studied graphic design and is obsessed with information architecture, communication and aesthetics. She works as a digital nomad by immersing in really different environments and searching for a better understanding of people.

www.behance.net/HeyMarts

P122–123

Maven Creative

10 years in business, Maven Creative is an award-winning creative advertising & branding agency in Central Florida. They focus on branding, messaging and design.

mavencreative.com

P148–149

mono.

mono. is a digital studio based in Italy. They are a fast-growing, open-minded, sometime-crazy group of perfectionists who love whitespaces and observe every detail. They believe that simplifying serves to eliminate the superfluous and make sure that the necessary can stand out as it deserves. They take advantage of their maniacal attention to detail to take care of strategy, design and development.

monodigital.studio

P012–013

Murmure

Divided into two offices located in Caen and in Paris, Murmure is a human-sized team, led by two art directors: Julien Alirol & Paul Ressencourt. Since 2010, Murmure has reconciled meaningfulness and creativity to enable their clients to communicate with strength, coherence and originality. Together, they design and develop elegant, singular and modern visual solutions in line with the client's image.

murmure.me

P216–217, 220–221

Olga Shevchenko

Olga has been interested in design since a young age. While her childhood friends liked to play different games, she liked to play with fonts. She loves her work, which constantly inspires her and helps her grow. Now she is a member of the jury at Awwwards, CSSDA, Webby and proud to be a creative director at Vintage, the most awarded web production in Ukraine.

vintage.agency

P212–213

Olha Uzhykova

Olha Uzhykova is a product designer with a solid experience in mobile and web design, including UX, UI, interaction design, building prototypes and proficiency using the latest design tools. She has been working with startups, medium and large businesses to create easy-to-use web and mobile applications. Having a strong balance of both visual design and user experience design, she engages with product owners to validate design solutions, and conducts usability tests, incorporates results into the design process and most importantly understands the user.

uzhik13.dribbble.com

P028–029

Oui Will

Oui Will creates award-winning brands and strategically designed experiences for a digitally driven world. Inspired by the European aesthetic and American can-do spirit, they are united by the same intention: to create remarkably beautiful things that make an impact, shape culture and connect people.

www.ouiwill.com

P178–179, 194–195

Paul DeCotiis

Paul DeCotiis is a graphic designer and art director living in Brooklyn, New York. Paul has over 10 years of experience designing, building and scaling digital products and solutions and creates novel forms of visual communication grounded in rational and functional design sensibilities.

www.pauldecotiis.com

P154–155

pill & pillow

pill & pillow is a digital studio based in Hong Kong. It is founded by designer and media artist Henry Chu in 2004. Since its founding, the studio has won more than 140 awards.

www.pillandpillow.com

P138–141, 196–197, 232

Qiner Wang

Qiner Wang is a current graduate student of visual communication design at Arizona State University. During her undergraduate years at ASU, she designed mobile theme icons for Android/ios and got millions of downloads. Currently she is also a part-time UI designer of Desicion Theater Network to help with visualizing solutions to complex problems. She enjoys designing and enjoys a life as a graphic designer.

www.qiner72.com

P076–077

Ray Yeunsu Shin

Ray Yeunsu Shin is a visual/interaction designer, who delights in making creative, imaginative and detail-oriented design that will positively impact the world and its people. As a designer, his long-term goal is to create accessible solutions to meet the problems of everyday lives. He wants to lead people to live their lives more enjoyably and efficiently, by using his cross-cultural awareness, detail-oriented aesthetics and direct communication.

www.heyraystudio.com

P112–113

Rhys Wallace

Rhys is a British UI and interaction designer specializing in designing digital products with effortless user experience. Having been passionate about human-centred design from a young age, he obtained a degree in visual communication in France. He enjoys crafting user-centred solutions to problems through sleek design to build intuitive and visually stunning products. Fueled by a burning curiosity and a persistent drive to create, Rhys is always learning and discovering new fields and techniques.

rhyswallace.co

P084–085

Shangning Wang

Shangning Wang is a New York based award winning graphic designer, illustrator and all around creative. He focuses on branding design, data visualization, commercial art, illustration, report design, and interactive design. He also sits on the jury for more than 15 international design competitions.

www.behance.net/Shangning

P078–079

Shirley Xuebing Han

Shirley graduated from Wuhan Polytechnic University in Industrial Design. She has been working as a UI/UX designer for more than five years.

www.behance.net/wuhanxi140d601

P124–125

Significa

Significa is a digital agency focused on user centric interfaces. They take on products from inception to launch, from business model to people's pocket, from wireframe to continuous deployment.

www.significa.pt

P086–087, 090–091

spiilka design büro

Spiilka design büro is co-founded by award-winning design directors Nastya Żerebecki and Vladimir Smirnov.

spiilka.com

P050–051

Stephen Tjoa

Stephen is a UI/UX designer and interaction designer who is interested in digital product design and simple illustration. He is now working in Sea Group (Garena), Singapore. His purpose is to design a digital product (website or mobile apps) which fulfills utility, usability, and brand experience aspects.

www.behance.net/StephenTjoa

P024–027

Studio Naam

Studio Naam is a full-service design agency based in Utrecht, The Netherlands. With a mix of strategy and smart design solutions, Naam creates visual products that shift brands forward.

www.studionaam.com

P158–161, 180–181

Supre Foundation

Supre Foundation funds programs that educate, support and empower girls globally. Their dream is to see this generation and future generations of girls having access to all they need to fulfil their potential. Since 2014, Supre Foundation has been raising funds through the sale of products at Supré stores globally, with 100% of proceeds going toward fostering a world where all girls can achieve their dreams. In Australia, they tackle the issue of bullying and in New Zealand they fund programs into schools that build confidence, resilience and self esteem in Kiwi youth.

www.supre.com.au

P204–205

Taehee Kim

Taehee Kim is a product designer based in Berlin, Germany.

www.behance.net/taeheekim-design

P018–019, 128–129

Tamerlan Aziev

Tamerlan Aziev is originally from small Russian republic Ingushetia. After several years of freelancing and studio work in Russia, he moved to Dubai and joined Tigerspike team as UI designer. There, Tamerlan worked on Emirates website redesign. Then he joined TenTwenty as senior UX/UI designer. There he created new website for TenTwenty and the team got Site of The Day on Awwwards. After few months Tamerlan became design jury on Awwwards.

www.behance.net/aziev

P192–193

Thomas Birch

Thomas is a graphic designer living and working in the UK, with a focus on creating concept-led brands that build meaning and connect with people.

www.behance.net/birchplease

P100–101

Tink

Tink is a Swedish fintech company, helping banks create better financial well-being for their customers.

tink.com

P064–065

Tofu Design

Tofu Design is a UI/UX and branding agency founded by Daniel and Daphnie – a pair of passionate creatives joining forces to create simple but meaningful design solutions for companies and brands.

www.tofudesign.co

P068–069

Trama Studio

Trama Studio is a group of creative professionals focused on combining great design ideas with the best user experience development. They love design and they love coding, so they integrate both disciplines into their creative process. This comprehensive ability enables them to pursue unique and beautiful results that will have a positive impact on the brand, project and website.

tramastudio.net

P208–211

Twenty Two Degrees

Twenty Two Degrees is a digital creative studio based in Madrid, Spain. They centre their efforts in the development of websites and experiences that impact users through design, creativity and innovation. For them, every project is a new opportunity to make something new and different, that's why they invest a big part of their resources into the experimentation of new ideas and concepts that help their clients meet the goals.

www.veintidosgrados.com

P224–225

Ueno

Ueno is a full-service creative agency that designs and builds beautiful brands, products, and marketing experiences. Founded in 2014, Ueno now has more than 60 full-time employees and four offices in Iceland, San Francisco, New York, and Los Angeles. Clients include Google, Verizon, Airbnb, Apple, Chubb, Cisco, Dropbox, Facebook, Fitbit, Lonely Planet, Medium, Red Bull, Progressive, Reuters, Samsung, Globo, Slack, Uber, and Visa.

ueno.co

P046–047

UIG Studio

UIG is a design and web development studio in Poland. They design and develop beautiful and cutting-edge apps and websites.

uigstudio.com

P058–059

Unbong Kang

Unbong Kang is an interaction designer with a passion for UX. He is interested in the fusion of design and development, and he enjoys developing simple, clean and slick websites that provide real value to the end user.

lain.kr

P060–061

Universal Favourite

Universal Favourite is a Sydney based design studio, creating strategic design, brand & digital solutions for startups & established businesses. Driven by purpose, made with love.

universalfavourite.com.au

P010–011

Vide Infra

Vide Infra is a Riga and Moscow based design and technology studio that produces high-class award-winning solutions for the web and beyond.

www.videinfra.com

P118–121

What The studio

What The is a multidisciplinary design studio with a focus on visual communication, founded by designers Sara Landeira and Ekhiñe Domínguez. With a thoughtful and research-based design process, they create bold concepts that are translated into distinctive visual languages, helping their clients stand out and connect with the audiences. Through their self-initiated projects, they create content and design around themes they find relevant for society, politics and culture.

www.what-the.studio

P142–143

Xavier Cussó

Xavier Cussó is an award-winning visual designer and art director with 10+ years of experience bringing to life on-brand interactive experiences and platforms for leading clients and advertising agencies worldwide. He is currently freelancing full-time.

xaviercusso.com

P218–219

Yana Syrevich

Yana Syrevich is a Belarus-based designer working with illustration and interaction design, focused on games and medical/fitness products. She holds a Bachelor's degree in Fine Arts in Belarusian state arts academy, and has more than 8 years' experience in digital arts and usability.

www.behance.net/ianpavetra

P016–017

Yejin Choi

Yejin Choi is a product designer based in Berlin, Germany.

www.behance.net/choooiyeji7e4d

P018–019

Yong Yang

Yong Yang is a UX/UI designer with a strong visual design background. He currently works as design lead at RICEPO and is ready for new challenges.

yycreate.com

P052–053

Yuree Kang

Yuree holds a Bachelor's degree in Industrial Design. Now she is a freelance GUI and web designer based in South Korea.

yureekang.com

P134

Acknowledgements

We would like to thank all of the contributors for granting us permission to publish their works. We are also very grateful to many other people whose names do not appear in the credits but who made specific contributions and provided support. Without these people, we would not have been able to share these beautiful and insightful design works with readers around the world.